Comparative Psychology
of Mental Development

Comparative Psychology
of
Mental Development

HEINZ WERNER

G. Stanley Hall, Professor of Genetic Psychology

Clark University

With a foreword by Gordon W. Allport, Ph.D., Professor
of Psychology, Harvard University

Revised Edition

INTERNATIONAL UNIVERSITIES PRESS, INC.

New York   New York

COMPARATIVE PSYCHOLOGY
OF MENTAL DEVELOPMENT

Third Printing, 1964

CONTENTS

Contents

BOOK III. THE WORLD AND PERSONALITY

FOREWORD

Broadly speaking, there are two contrasting approaches to the subject matter of psychological science. In this volume Dr. Werner labels these two approaches the *mechanistic* and the *organic* respectively. There are, to be sure, important distinctions of outlook among the schools of thought represented within each of these two groupings; yet between the two there is such a basic divergence of approach—one bent on the discovery of elementary detail, the other on the discovery of significant complex structures in mental life—that the separation is justified.

Now for various reasons the mechanistic approach is more familiar to American students than is the organic. The reasons need not concern us here; suffice it to say that they are bound with the pragmatic emphasis upon habits and capacities so characteristic of the American ethos. Until recently it has been necessary to go to pre-Nazi German psychology to find thoroughgoing scientific expressions of what Dr. Werner calls the organic approach. Around the central concept of *Struktur* there had grown up in Germany in the first quarter of the present century the movements known as *Gestalt* psychology, the psychology of the *Komplex-qualität*, the *Geisteswissenschaften*, and *Personalistik*. Although there were differences to mark these schools, all of them agreed on the basic tenet that the study of mental *patterns* should take precedence over the study of mental *elements*. The introduction of this general point of view into American psychology has been taking place gradually during the past two decades.

In spite of its cultural predilection for the reductionistic and mechanistic approach, American psychology has shown hospitality toward the new concept of structure. The impact of this concept (sometimes spoken of as the Gestalt revolution) will, no doubt, prove to be as significant in its effects on the psychology of the future as the impact of the behavioristic and psychoanalytic revolutions.

The rate of assimilation of the structural point of view into American psychology has been speeded up by recent political disasters in Germany. Outstanding psychologists have sought refuge in the United States, and important expressions of the structural line of thought have found their way into the English language. Among the significant translations of the past few years one would mention W. D. Ellis, *A Source Book of Gestalt Psychology;* K. Lewin, *Dynamic Theory of Personality;* W. Stern, *General Psychology from the Personalistic Standpoint;* K. Goldstein, *The Organism.* To this distinguished list Dr. Werner now adds his *Comparative Psychology of Mental Development,* extensively reworked for the American reader, and rewritten in clear and agreeable English. For some years the book has held a position of recognized merit in Europe. Its appeal will now spread rapidly in this country, particularly among teachers and students of social psychology, child psychology, and abnormal psychology. One can predict too that cultural anthropologists will read it with excitement and profit.

An outstanding feature of the book is the author's use of the comparative method. He finds the same structural principles of mental organization to hold in the mental life of children, of "primitive" men, and of certain psychotics. In all these groups he discovers essentially the same utilitarian concreteness of mental life, characterized by syncretism, synaesthesia, animism, conservatism, and magic. From the point of view of the civilized adult this type of mental life lacks the capacity for discriminating what is essential from what is non-essential. This judgment, of course, may reflect nothing more than a species of provincial prejudice to which civilized people, no less than savages, are liable. However that may be, the course of mental development from the primitive to the civilized is one of increasing differentiation, articulation, and organization according to abstract and hierarchical principles.

The book, then, deals with precisely the kind of mental life that scientists do not have, and, not having, tend to overlook. The author himself accomplishes the unusual feat of avoiding the customary ethnocentricism of the scientist and yet with the scientist's own language clearly depicting global, pre-scientific forms of thought. What civilized adults often dismiss as the imagination of children, the illogicality of primitives and of the masses, and the aberrations of the insane, is here presented as essentially natural mental operation, to be understood not as a departure from a civilized-scientific norm, but as ordinary modes of perception and reasoning employed by minds that have not developed to the plane of differentiation and abstraction.

It is only in the most highly developed individuals that one finds a sharpening of the polarity between subject and world. Between the primitive or the child and his environment there exists a raw, syncretic relation illustrated by fusions between dreams or imagery and perceptions of outer reality. What to our minds is a mere poetic metaphor represents to the undeveloped mind a convincing causal relation. Notions of space and time, highly abstract to us, are egocentric and utilitarian in the primitive and in the child. Whereas our abstract concepts evolve through the repeated analysis of critical features embedded within complex situations, the less developed mind clings to salient signs or properties that are tangible, near, and active. Preoccupation with global and salient structure prevents theoretical knowledge from accumulating. Where theoretical knowledge is lacking, magical practice takes its place.

We who think with such assurance of the attributes of human personality—to cite but one example from the author's imposing array of topics—are startled to learn that a vast portion of mankind makes no effective distinction between the physical body and objects that have previously been connected with it, or between a person and his name, or between an individual and his possessions, or between a man's motives and his deeds.

Although Dr. Werner does not expressly make a point of it,

his vivid accounts of syncretic perception and thought give the reader aid in understanding the ordinary mental operations of himself and his fellow men. No matter how confidently we pride ourselves on our logical acumen and capacity for scientific inference, our thought too turns out to be primitive much of the time. While tactfully confining himself to children, primitives, and psychotics, the author tells us in a sly way more than a little about our own mental lives.

GORDON W. ALLPORT

BOOK I

Introduction

Chapter I

THE FIELDS, THE PROBLEMS, AND THE METHODS OF DEVELOPMENTAL PSYCHOLOGY

THE FIELDS OF A COMPARATIVE DEVELOPMENTAL PSYCHOLOGY.
What is developmental psychology, and what are its problems? The concept "developmental psychology" is perfectly clear if this term is understood to mean a science concerned with the development of mental life, and determined by a specific method, i.e., the observation of psychological phenomena from the standpoint of development. On the other hand the concept is not so precisely defined if the question of subject matter is raised, of what are the specific fields of inquiry which can be approached from the point of view of development. There are certain investigators who, when they use the term "developmental psychology," refer solely to the problems of *ontogenesis*. The mental development of the individual is, however, but one theme in genetic psychology. Related to the developmental psychology of the individual is the developmental study of larger social unities, a field of interest intimately linked with anthropology and best known by the name of *ethnopsychology*. The question of the development of the human mentality, if not arbitrarily limited, must lead further to an investigation of the relation of man to animal and, in consequence, to an *animal psychology* oriented according to developmental theory.

For a long time the majority of psychologists have assumed that a developmental point of view is a necessary presupposition in the comparison of definite psychological entities—in the comparison of the child, the primitive man, and also the animal with one another and with mature man. Only

3

in comparatively recent times, however, has developmental psychology been directed to the study of those mental phenomena which, in the psychiatric sense, are abnormal, or which appear in the highly developed consciousness as transitory abnormalities, e.g., the dream, or any condition of intoxication. The question now arises whether the *pathological mentality* can be integrated within a theory of mental development. Can the "childishness" of many psychopaths, let us say, be related to normal childhood or to the primitiveness of so-called uncivilized peoples? And, still further, can that primitiveness of the normal adult as exhibited under certain conditions—in the dream or in intoxication, for instance—have any significance for a theory of development? We shall see that these questions are pertinent in a psychological analysis of mental levels.

Finally, it will be noted that the genetic approach is of essential importance even in the study of the mental life of the *adult normal man*, for the following reason. Even if such states of consciousness as the dream are disregarded, the normal man does not always function on the same level of mental activity. The same normal individual, depending on inner or outer circumstance, may be characterized by entirely different levels of development. His mentality, genetically considered, is not the same when he is utterly distracted as when he is in a state of perfectly organized concentration. It varies as he moves from some sober scientific or practical work to an emotional surrender to people or things. It may be said that mental life has different strata. At one time man behaves "primitively" and at another he becomes relatively "cultured" or "civilized." In general, then, developmental psychology attempts to demonstrate that primitive modes of behavior in the normal adult not only appear under certain extraordinary conditions, but are continually present as the basis of all mental being, and are of vital importance in supporting the highest forms of mentality.

And so the circle is closed. Each field of psychology—the

psychology of the individual and of the human race, animal and child psychology, psychopathology and the psychology of special states of consciousness—all these can be approached from the genetic standpoint. The final procedure of a comparative developmental psychology is to compare the results gained from work done in the specialized fields, and from this comparison to derive developmental laws generally applicable to mental life as a whole.

THE BASIC PROBLEMS OF DEVELOPMENTAL PSYCHOLOGY.

The specialized developmental psychologies are bound together by a main concept—the concept of development. An understanding of the fundamental problems of the whole field of developmental psychology is evidently dependent on the manner in which this concept of "development" is formulated. Formally considered, then, developmental psychology has two basic aims. One is to grasp the characteristic pattern of each genetic level, the structure peculiar to it. The other, and no less important one, is to establish the genetic relationship between these levels, the direction of development, and the formulation of any general tendency revealed in developmental relationship and direction. The discovery of the structural pattern of the isolated mental level, whether we are concerned with the development of the individual from childhood to maturity or with the development of the human race, etc., is one genetic problem. Complementary to it is the task of ordering the genetic relationships between particular levels.

In order to gain some idea of the complexity of these problems it will be illuminating to trace the historical change in the fundamental points of view in the particular fields of developmental psychology. Since the earliest beginnings of developmental psychology there has been a distinct modification of the basic scientific assumptions in the studies devoted to these problems. Originally the concept of development was assumed to be of a mechanistic order. Today it is oriented according to an organic point of view. This means that each level is conceived organically and that the relationship between levels is organic in nature.

A brief historical survey of the different developmental psychologies will reveal this fundamental conversion to an organic approach.

MECHANISTIC AND ORGANIC APPROACH IN ETHNOPSYCHOLOGY: THE CONCEPT OF CULTURAL PATTERNS AND CREATIVE CHANGE.

Ethnopsychology, in so far as it is a field of developmental psychology, must conceive the psychophysical entity of a people or a folk group as an organically developing totality. This organic conception should also apply to the idea of "culture" and all its forms of expression in language, religion, social organization, and custom. But this necessity has not always been recognized. The older psychologies especially are lacking in this concept of the organic totality of a people, and also in the concept of cultural level in an organic sense of the word.

In Germany, for example, what was known as "ethnopsychology" was sterile for a long time because its founders, Lazarus and Steinthal,[1] borrowed a great many of their basic notions from the dominant psychology of the day, that of Herbart. Herbart's completely mechanistic bias is opposed to an organic method of approach. What is the mentality of a people according to him? It is an aggregate of individual activities impinging on each other and repelling each other inhibitively.[2] On the basis of such a conception it is impossible

[1] Lazarus and Steinthal, 76.

[2] Even though Lazarus and Steinthal repeatedly refer to the ideal unity of a people as the "folk soul," their definition of this "folk soul" as "that which is common to the diversified activity of all the individual members" betrays the mechanistic prejudice. The concept reveals the mechanistic attitude of Herbart in so far as it proceeds out of an idea of individual units and an idea of abstraction, that is, the selective repudiation of all special cases in order to arrive at one common to all. The folk mind is not that which is common to all. It is that part of the individual which can be conceived only in its folk significance, in its social meaning.

to understand how an inner unity could ever come about a unity clearly expressed in the fact that a particular folk or a definite cultural level has a characteristic language and art and its own ethical and religious attitude. For this reason serious students of human culture ignored psychology despite the express efforts of Taine to unite the two (*la base de l'histoire doit être la psychologie scientifique*), and despite a similar attempt made by Lamprecht in his *Deutsche Geschichte*. The Herbartian psychology does not recognize a folk as a living whole, or a cultural level as an organic unity. There is here no concept of a folk mentality which might have furthered and supported the work of the specialist in cultural history.

In opposition to this trend, the folk psychology of Wundt, in trying to avoid a mechanistic theory, made an extraordinary advance toward an organic determination of generic unities.

Wundt attempted to base his psychology on certain specific principles by means of which it would be possible to distinguish theoretically between the physical and the mental. His system takes a middle position in the transition from the Herbartian psychology of elements to modern psychology. He tries to discover principles inherent in and proper to psychological phenomena alone, but he does not succeed in freeing himself completely from mechanistic preconceptions. In his theory the idea of mental phenomena as combinations of elementary forms of experience is still definitive. In the concept of "creative synthesis" he actually has a specific principle of mental activity.[3] According to this principle, there arises out of the synthesis of elements not merely a sum, but a completely new whole. Through the conjunction of several tones there appears a melody which is more than the sum of the tones. Through the union of individuals there is formed a mass, an ethnic group, a nation, which in its total form cannot be derived in any way from the component parts.

And yet the very advance made by the Wundtian system

[3] Wundt, 150, vol. 3, last chapter.

with respect to that of Herbart exhibits that immanent contradiction which of necessity led to an intrinsic and radical revision of basic psychological concepts. This attempt to formulate the basic concept of social science, that is, the concept of unities of a higher order built up from elements by synthesis, revealed the inadequacy of the approach to the problem more clearly than ever before. For it could be shown, in any case, that a totality could be created in many ways, that the so-called elements of which the totality consisted could change without modifying the character of the totality itself.

It will be seen (Fig. 1) that dots in themselves do not account for the fact that together they constitute a circle. Nor

FIG. 1.—Element and Configuration.

does the circle depend on any collocation of dots by synthesis. Elements of a certain kind can be used to construct many figures and, on the other hand, quite different elements can be used to build the same figure. As we see, the little crosses, instead of the dots, may make a circle with equal facility. The character of a totality cannot be defined by synthesis. The totality is not a superordinated unity built up of elements and something more than their sum. It has an entirely different origin; it is prior to any division into elements whatsoever.

A radical change was needed in the fundamental attack on the problem, and this change is actually mirrored in the more recent phases of ethnopsychology. If it is impossible to derive the totality from a synthesis of the elements, it follows that the only course left is to seek an explanation in the totality itself. The entire problem is now reversed. The elements are not precedent to the whole, but the whole, as a basic entity, is the precursor of its component parts. Psychology, including ethno-psychology, must proceed from larger living unities and arrive by analysis at unities of a lower order. It is not the concept of "creative synthesis" but that of "creative analysis" which leads to fruitful results. The component members of a mass are dependent parts of this mass, which represents the real, living unity. The single man as a member of a generic unity possesses characteristics which are his because of his integration within a totality, and are intelligible only in terms of this totality. The problem of generic unity can be solved only by conceiving this unity to be a non-derivative whole governed by special laws which affect the human bearers of this unity in their rôle of dependent members. Neither by sum-mation nor by the fusion, the synthesis of the mental traits of many individuals, is it possible to conceive the living folk mentality. Such various forms of expression in this generic individuality as language, religion, the law, customs can never be rooted in the isolated individual. Exactly the reverse is true. The individual thinks, speaks a certain language, and acts in a characteristic way because of his participation, his integration, in the whole; and his thinking, talking, and acting are primarily understandable only in so far as he is identified with this totality.

The same holds true for those patterns which, as diversified forms of "culture," represent the human mind in its objective form.

A purely quantitative approach in ethnology, wherein cul-ture is defined by "trait complexes," can be traced back to Tylor. In his article "On a Method of Investigating the De-velopment of Institutions" he attempted to introduce a statis-tical treatment of traits and their relations to one another. Traits like exogamy, tabu, residence of the husband in the wife's house, and so on, correlate beyond any mere con-tingency. Such a coincidence of traits is based on what Tylor calls "adhesion."[4] This term, "adhesion of traits," a thoroughly mechanistic concept, has been the guiding principle of all quantitative studies of trait distribution carried on by such men as Wissler, Kroeber, Elliot-Smith, Graebner, and Father Schmidt. An increasing opposition to this mechanistic approach is, however, gradually developing among psychologists and ethnologists. As early as 1915 Felix Krueger, in his systematic study "Über Entwicklungspsychologie," pointed out the opposition between the mechanistic and the organic methods of approach, while making a critical analysis of "culture patterns."[5] There is no doubt that the concept of cultural pattern, or "style" is of great value both to historical studies of culture and to ethnology. But this concept has been distorted by leading ethnologists—by Graebner, for example—in such a way that it cannot be reconciled with the organic nature of a cultural unity. Graebner uses this concept to demonstrate that a cultural unity is characterized by a complex of related cultural elements, each of which has a distinct form and geographically determinable distribution.[6] For instance, Graebner and Ankermann define a cultural pattern found both in Africa and in the islands of Oceania as "nigritic." This cultural pattern in Africa is known by huts shaped like beehives, throwing clubs, parrying sticks, shields supported by sticks, rude wooden drums, digging sticks, and the custom of scar-tattooing, knocking out the front teeth, boring holes through the lips and ears, and keeping a house dog.[7] This considerable number of qualities is arrayed as a collection which lacks an inner, significant continuity. A genuine continuity, an intrinsic significance, can be arrived at only by avoiding any definition of the cultural form as the sum of the cultural elements. There must be a uniform cultural gestalt from which the concrete objective expressions of the culture draw their meaning. The

[4] Tylor, 133.
[5] Krueger, 69, 171 ff.
[6] Graebner, 41, 99 ff.
[7] Graebner, 40; Ankermann, 3.

unity of any such generic, all-embracing pattern is intelligible only as a psychological unity. All these concrete symbols of a cultural level, whether they are customs, weapons, dances, or melodies, are characteristic for one particular pattern only because the human mind expresses itself within it and functions through it. The mentality of an ethnic group becomes audible in its folk songs, one might say, just as it becomes objectively visible in its arts and crafts. One of the best-informed students of primitive music, von Hornbostel, explains this idea very clearly when he says that the tonal movement which we call music is so intimately the symbol of the race that, if there were nothing more than their songs on the basis of which to trace back a uniform lineage and further distinguish among the innumerable tribes of Indians, from the Polar Eskimos to the Fuegians, there would still be little room for erroneous opinion. A blind man could separate the three tribes living in Ruanda—the Hamitic Watussi, the Bantu-speaking Bahutu, and the Batwa dwarf-men—as soon as he had heard them sing.[8]

Let us turn to another illustration. The "animal mimicry" found among so many primitive tribes might at first sight be considered as an element, a detached, self-subsistent phenomenon. But we recognize quickly enough, on closer inspection, that the meaning of this mimicry is linked with and controlled by the totality of the culture involved.[9] There are many kinds of animal mimicry with diverse meanings. There is the simple animal mimicry of the hunter which has the practical purpose of fooling the game in order to creep within striking distance of it. There is another kind of animal mimicry which, though partly rooted in practical need, is bound up with the magical aspects of some cultural pattern. Hunters in all parts of the world believe in the workings of magic. The efficacy of this magic depends on the belief that dances representing the lives and habits of animals will draw

[8] Hornbostel, 211.
[9] Werner, 141, 2 ff.

them nearer. But there is still another distinct form of animal mimicry with a special significance; this is the totemistic animal pantomime of the Australian aborigines and the animal-god ceremonies of certain tribes of American Indians. In these totemistic rituals a distinctly new aspect of the mentality of the cultural pattern is exposed. This is the honoring of the tribe and the tribal ancestors who, by virtue of their embodiment in the animal totem, become living, active participants in the ceremony. A comparison of these different types of animal mimicry shows that they cannot be "elements" in any rigid, atomistic sense. The meaning of each form is mutable, and varies as the totality of the mental pattern changes. At one time the mimicry is outside the sphere of magic. Another time it may become a magic ritual, and again it may be a part of the specifically totemistic pattern, etc. What some psychologists call a cultural element is not really an element at all. It does not determine the whole, but its sense and its content are derived from the whole.

This organic point of view in defining culture is also growing in recent times among ethnologists proper. "The meaning of an element of culture," says Radcliffe-Brown, "can only be defined when the culture is seen as a whole of interrelated parts."[10] Malinowski, from his "functional" standpoint, is also deeply convinced that a concept of culture "as a jumble of disconnected and unrelated traits robs the whole concept of life and significance."[11] Paul Radin criticizes the quantitative approach as a method borrowed from the physical sciences, and therefore as one wholly inadequate for the analysis of culture.[12] Ruth Benedict's work, which we shall discuss later, affords direct proof of the efficacy of the organic approach in the determination of diversified cultural patterns.

Apart from any general theoretical consideration much doubt has been cast upon the evidence offered by the "trait ethnol-

[10] Radcliffe-Brown, 110.
[11] Malinowski, 98.
[12] Radin, 113, chap. 5.

ogists." R. B. Dixon, another of the foremost opponents of any analysis of culture based upon the assumption of trait complexes, shows, for instance, that of nineteen specific traits which Father Schmidt believes to be characteristic of a primary culture in Oceania, only one—a certain house form—may be really typical.[13] Trait complexes indicative of certain cultures dispersed through the world are simply "an illusion," to use Dixon's own words.[14] He points very clearly toward what I should like to call the "constancy fallacy" of any trait theory. It is the fallacy that a trait may be self-subsistent and therefore unchangeable. Even if one admits a dispersion of a trait among several cultures, these dispersed "traits" will certainly change not only as to degree, but also as to kind. On the other hand, apparently identical traits may actually have different origins, different social meanings, and in consequence different relationships with respect to other traits. One of the most impressive examples of this situation is the "age-group" characteristic which conditions the social structure of certain primitive civilizations. The age group societies of such widely separated peoples as the Plains Indians of America, the Masai of East Africa, and the people of the Banks Islands of Melanesia are only superficially identical; they have different origins and different meanings.[15]

We may conclude that the "constancy fallacy" in any trait theory consists of two main factual errors. It neglects the fact that two seemingly identical traits, depending on the context of the two different cultures in which they are found, may have varying functional meanings. And further, two traits, although morphologically at variance, may function identically in two different cultures.

The second problem to undergo a fundamental reorientation in the course of time concerns the genetic relationship of one developmental pattern to another. Often it was assumed that

[13] Dixon, **19**, 236.
[14] *Ibid.*, 238.
[15] *Ibid.*, 210.

mental development exhibited an unbroken mathematical continuity, and that this development could be symbolized by an unbroken line. In many instances it was taken for granted that there is a gradual, purely quantitative increase in the logical capacities of man as he moves toward a norm of mentality represented by the western mind. This conception, beyond doubt, is dominated by a mechanistic bias rooted in the older biological theories of evolution. It is perhaps superficially justifiable to conceive of certain phases of anatomical development as representing a continuous growth. The brain exhibits an increasing number of convolutions, and its relative weight is continuously increasing. But even here a theory of unbroken continuity would hardly receive the full confirmation of the modern biologist. It is a misunderstanding that accounts for the fact that in some modern biological works there is the tacit or overt assumption of an imperceptible transition from one form to another. This misunderstanding contradicts the experimental results in the isolation of small but distinctly separated closed groups of forms (so-called "pure lines") which do not overlap.[16] If this unbroken continuity, which has been so excessively stressed in its quantitative aspect, cannot apply to anatomical development, it applies still less to mental growth. It is quite meaningless to say, for example, that tactual sensations gradually evolve into sensations of tone. Even if apparently transitional phenomena are demonstrable in such a developmental series—i.e., the so-called vibration sensations studied by Katz—it is still possible to assume that the tone sensations themselves, with respect both to tactual sensations and to vibrations, are newly created and self-subsistent, and not continuously derived from what has preceded them.[17] We can speak of a true continuity only in those measurable situations treated in mathematics and physics.

These considerations apply even more strongly to the development of higher mental activities. It has been all too readily

[16] Tschulok, 132, 129.
[17] Katz, 721.

taken for granted that there is only one kind of higher thinking, one that is either more or less logical in nature, depending on the intellectual advancement of the individual or the community. All the time it becomes more apparent that this view leads to fundamental errors and that we can explain nothing by it. It cannot account for the mental structure of the child, of the psychotic person, or of the animal, nor can it throw any light on the mentality of primitive man. More recent investigations tend toward the belief that development cannot be symbolized by a continuous, mathematically conceived line, but rather must be thought of in the form of typical mental patterns, with the relatively higher levels being understood as innovations emerging from the lower.

A few illustrations may serve to clarify this basic revision of attack. It is often said that primitive people do not think as logically as civilized people. How could it be otherwise when, for instance, Australian aborigines designate wood and fire by the same name? How else account for the fact that the Melanesians of the Bismarck Archipelago, when they speak of *ciki* (drops), may mean many other things besides drops of water falling from a tree? They may mean the spots of wet made by the drops after they strike the earth, or the pattering sound of the drops, or the regular intervals at which the drops fall, or the sudden, unexpected act of dropping itself. Does this plurivalence in concept or name reveal a logical weakness? It is obvious that the primitive man exhibits a different mode of thinking in his naming of things. But it is pointless merely to define it negatively, from our own standpoint, as representative of an inadequate, unadvanced logic. We can gain an insight into such thinking only when we resort to a positive approach, and actively try to understand its peculiar structure. It is one of the most important tasks of developmental psychology to show that the advanced form of thinking characteristic of western civilization is only one form among many, and that more primitive forms are not so much lacking in logic as based on logic of a different kind. The premise of Aristotelian logic that when a thing is *a* it cannot at the same time be *b* would not hold true for the primitive believer in magical and mythical association. Gods may change into animals, for example, and yet still remain gods, as in Polynesian myths.[18] In the old Vedic cult the number three is often the same as the number seven or nine.[19] For the Mexican Indian corn, deer, and the hikuli plant are, in a certain sense, one and the same.[20] Here we are dealing with a mode of thinking that is neither illogical nor "pre-logical." It is simply logical in another, self-contained sense.

A great many primitive people see no contradiction in believing that various forms of life, continuously changing, represent one identity. A Congo native says to a European: "During the day you drank palm-wine with a man, unaware that in him there was an evil spirit. In the evening you heard a crocodile devouring some poor fellow. A wildcat, during the night, ate up all your chickens. Now, the man with whom you drank, the crocodile who ate a man, and the wildcat are all one and the same creature."[21] The primitive man therefore holds that it is quite thinkable that one being, *a*, should also be another, *b*. And it cannot be said that herein lies a weakness and a lack of logic. It must be acknowledged that this kind of interpretation is rooted in an altogether different mental pattern, a differently constituted faculty of conception, from that exhibited by the scientifically thinking man. These primitive conceptions, however strange they may appear to our mind, may nevertheless be quite consistent with the variant mental pattern and representative of natural consequences within it. The thinking of primitive mental levels cannot be conceived simply as lower in any graduated quantitative scale, and the level of thought of the intellectual man of western civilization as higher. There is a qualitative difference between the

---

[18] Quatrefages, 263, 54.
[19] Bergaigne, 161, vol. 2, 147-156.
[20] Preuss, 261, vol. 1; Lumholtz, 231, 18.
[21] Lévy-Bruhl, 84, Fr. ed., 44.

two. The abstract modes of thought of civilized man—in its
highest form, scientific thinking—are by no means a product
arrived at by unbroken transition from the thinking of primitive levels.

At this point it might be advantageous to correct some of the
misinterpretations of the concepts and aims of developmental psychology. *Developmental psychology is not evolutionistic psychology.*
Not in any strict sense. The typical evolutionist (deriving his
mechanistic concepts from Darwin) is primarily interested in the
evolutionary history of mankind. He tries to express the data of
anthropology in terms of evolution. He believes that at some time
the forefathers of the European man must have had a culture similar
in structure to the cultures of certain living primitive people, such
as the Veddas or the Australian aborigines. He is interested in such
historico-evolutionary problems as the original structure of the
family and whether a matriarchate or a patriarchate should be considered the earlier form of organization.

Developmental psychology is not concerned with such problems,
for two reasons: (1) It does not deal with any actual or speculative
history of mankind; it deals with developmental levels. We ask,
e.g., not whether a pattern of functions is relatively early or late
in the historical scale, but whether it represents a low or a high
level of mentality. (2) Developmental psychology is concerned not
with such factual characteristics of culture as matriarchal or pa-
triarchal organization, but rather with the *formal* characteristics of
primitive or advanced *thinking*.

Another misinterpretation centers about the concept of *primitive
mentality*. Some anthropologists claim that there is no essential
difference beween civilized and primitive man. The difference, such
as it is, lies only in the cultural sets; the one people lives in an
advanced culture, the other in a primitive one, but the mental functions of the individual are fundamentally the same. Any argument
which tends to reduce differences in mentality to differences in culture certainly appears to move in a circle. It fails to recognize that
culture is not something that conditions the mentality of the group,
but is the objective aspect of this mentality. Actual mentality is the
product of an interdependence of outer and inner factors. Moreover,
the idea of "culture" as a maker of mentality is a reversion to an

atomistic psychology, as is also the idea of mentality as an innate entity preceding culture. Both ideas assume non-existent atoms, innate mentality, and external culture.

Dr. Klineberg, in his criticism of developmental psychology, argues that primitive man reasons in a primitive way only because he lacks the fund of knowledge accessible to members of a western culture.[22] From the standpoint of a non-atomistic psychology, this is a truism that simply obscures the problem of primitive mentality. Of course actual mentality changes if the cultural set with which it is bound up changes. But developmental psychology directs its efforts not toward the solution of the tricky problems of innate versus acquired function, but only toward the establishment and description of genetic types of mental activity.

With this we now come to the last point in our critique. The theory of a qualitative difference between primitive and advanced mentality has been rejected for the simple reason that enough evidence for primitive behavior can be found in our own culture. But developmental psychology does not deny that there is a good deal of primitive activity in western civilization; on the contrary, since it is so clearly demonstrable wthin our own sphere, this fact is one of our strongest proofs of the existence of qualitatively different levels of functions. However, the human organism as a whole functions more uniformly and homogeneously on a thoroughly primitive level than with genetically advanced groups where higher functions are interconnected with primitive ones.

In this respect it is interesting to inquire into the formal difference between functions on an altogether primitive level and primitive functions found in the highest types of human being. We may perhaps approach this problem from a biological angle. It is a well-known fact that, in a genetic series, those species which ultimately developed into higher forms were not specialized as early as those which do not rise beyond a lower level. We may safely say, then, that the lower branch of any genetic group is characterized by specialization on a more primitive level. The lower group remains low because it adjusts itself through a specialization of the means it already possesses, whereas the higher group develops new means. The term "development" may consequently assume two meanings: development in terms of creation and in terms of specialization. Al-

[22] Klineberg, 64, 332.

though in actual genesis specialization and creation are interlocked, true development itself rests in creation. In the great apes the creative development of the features of man's ancestors has been blocked by an early specialization, just as it was blocked in the Neanderthal man within the human family itself.[23] If we accept these considerations, we can understand why it is unlikely that the living primitives are actual copies of the ancestors of the more developed human beings. They must differ from the latter in so far as they represent specialized, "one-track" primitive types. At the same time, the ancestors of more advanced peoples should be conceived as representative of a much less specialized primitive mentality. "The aborigines of Australia and Tasmania," says Duckworth, "furnish the example of the greatest concentration of ape-like characters. But we must not conclude that the oborigines present us with a facsimile of a human ancestor, for these very aborigines are themselves remarkably specialized in adaptation to their surroundings."[24] From this it may be inferred that the "primitiveness" found among the more advanced groups is still different from the primitiveness existing in lower civilizations. Primitiveness in our sphere is the none too clearly defined background out of which and against which higher activity may arise. In lower cultures primitiveness is the highly specialized pattern of mental life itself. Radin and others are certainly justified in stressing the admirable adjustment of the aborigine to his surroundings; but this all too perfect adjustment is the sign of a lower form of behavior, rather than of an advanced. A primitive, highly balanced, "one-track" culture[25] lacks that friction between individual and environment, that flexibility and freedom in unceasing attempt to readjust, which is the very life and essence of higher, advanced cultures.

THE REMAINING DEVELOPMENTAL PSYCHOLOGIES.

In the remaining developmental psychologies we find the same reversal of approach in the basic understanding of the problems involved. The evolutionary series of the *animal* kingdom was originally conceived from a specifically human

[23] Elliot Smith, 119, 83.
[24] Duckworth, 20, 544.
[25] Wissler, 149, 355.

standpoint. At one time, for example, experiments on animals were conducted in order to discover how closely an animal's accomplishments could approximate man's, with the idea of measuring the gap separating the two. It is only at a comparatively recent date that the biologist and psychologist began to consider the individuality of the animal mind, and to study the animal in its own world. One of the pioneers in this method of analysis is undoubtedly von Uexküll.[26] The earlier studies of such Americans as Thorndike, and the investigations of such German psychologists as Koehler, Hans Volkelt, and others,[27] have proved especially fruitful, since they proceeded not according to a rigid conception of intelligence with man always as the criterion, but rather in terms of certain mental types admitting of arrangement by levels.

So far as the relation between different genetic types of animal mentality and that between animal and man are concerned, perhaps nowhere could there be found a clearer statement of the approach proposed in this book than that in Herrick's work on *Brains of Rats and Men*. He says: "Mankind has grown up; we have not merely enlarged and complicated the behavior patterns of rats and monkeys; we have . . . added new patterns not elsewhere known. . . . Evolution is creative in the sense that the elements of organization are recombined in original ways at every transition from type to type." And again, "Symbolic thinking is a new kind of function [in man], though the steps by which it was fashioned can probably be traced . . ."[28]

The case is the same in the history of the study devoted to the mental development of the *child*. In the earlier times the child mentality was characterized not organically, but according to mechanistic analogy as what might be called a bundle, an aggregate, of physical elements. It was commonly said, for instance, that the child's memory is primarily associative, and

[26] Uexküll, **695, 696.**
[27] Thorndike, **692**; Koehler, **664, 665**; Volkelt, **699.**
[28] Herrick, **652,** 348 ff.

his will ruled by transitory emotions. It was assumed that the child is incapable of logically ordered processes of inference in his thinking. All these characteristics, genuine or otherwise, were formulated without any attempt to comprehend the level of childhood as organically coherent. The current developmental psychology, however, deliberately seeks to feel out that individual pattern of mentality on the inclusive basis of which it is possible uniformly to understand children's modes of behavior in their varying aspects, just as in the case of primitive people of some particular cultural pattern. The phenomena of memory, the particular kind of willing, of feeling, of thinking and acting—all these are considered in the light of the characteristic mentality from which they spring.

To illustrate, as children learn how to draw they pass through a stage in which their drawings are schematic. Certain non-individual, schematic lines are used to represent "a man" or "an animal." Is it not possible to go still further and ask whether we are not observing an example of behavior generally characteristic of the perceptual and conceptual formations of childhood? Without forcing the issue it is possible to set up the relation between this schematic drawing and the "schematic" in child language. This means that in early childhood one word of apparently general significance can stand for remarkably diverse objects, in precisely the same way that a single schematic form in a primitive drawing may be used without modification to represent any one of the child's acquaintance, or even his animal pets. This striking similarity in widely separated functions of the child mentality justifies speculation as to the basic characteristics of this mentality seen as a whole. The phenomena of mental growth in the child are intelligible and can be formulated in terms of a genetically conceived structural totality, the mental pattern of some particular stage of childhood.[29]

This fairly recent change in the method of approach applies

[29] Cf. Bühler, **350**; E. Köhler, **429**. See further, Murphy, *et al.*, **102**, 298 ff.; Allport, **1**, chaps. 5, 10.

not only to the problem of the genetic level itself, but also to the genetic relation between these levels. The direction of development in childhood has usually been regarded in the sense of a physical movement forward, or as a gradual accumulation of characteristics, and not in the sense of its organic unity. According to the older view, the development from childhood to manhood was conceived to be the quantitative unfolding of potentialities, of qualities present latently. The child was thought of as a man in embryo. True, he did not think so logically or act so purposefully as the grown man, but the measure of his thinking and acting was fulfilled more and more completely in the adult sense the older he became. Or, from another angle, in the older point of view one had only to subtract certain capacities from the mentality of the adult in order to arrive at more primitive beings. The entire older conception of development is governed by this mechanistic idea of subtracting or adding qualities, a procedure in diametric opposition to an organic understanding of the problem at hand. In more recent methods of attacking the problem the notion is paramount that development is creative development. This means that each higher level represents a new entity with respect to the one preceding it, and is understandable in terms of itself. The more primitive level is not to be derived by the subtraction of single qualities from the higher level. Any level, however primitive it may be, represents a relatively closed, self-subsisting totality. Conversely, each higher level is fundamentally an innovation, and cannot be gained by merely adding certain characteristics to those determining the preceding level.

The fact that the principal phases of development in childhood and adolescence appear as crises should alone discredit any theory of unbroken continuity. Both developmental level and developmental direction, as befits any science of living things, must be conceived organically, not mechanistically as they generally were in the older point of view.

The basic attitude in a study of child mentality is naturally revealed most clearly and methodically in specialized experiments dealing with the subject. Suppose that the child's capacity for inference was to be tested. In that event it was formerly assumed that the child's powers of thinking were to be measured in terms of some logical and scientific category. Therefore, as illustrated in the instance of Schüssler, Aristotelian syllogistic forms were presented to the child, and his ability in mastering them was observed.[30] He might be given this problem:

The heathen worship many gods.

The heathen are men.

Therefore, ? . . . [There are men who worship many gods.]

In this case it has been presumed that certain forms schematizing processes of thought logically are calculated to solve the problem of the child's developing capacity to infer. No doubt there is value in this test, especially if one is interested in knowing to what extent a child is able to use artificial logical models. But such a test does not reveal anything about the child's state of mind so far as inference in its broad sense is concerned. Otherwise it would lead to the absurd conclusion that uneducated mature individuals are unable to make an inference. Instead, then, of investigating the structure of the actual living thought of the child, a thought which naturally unfolds only within the child's sphere of interest, there is merely a demonstration of how far the child can go in reconstructing the intellectual models of the logician.

We find a similar situation in genetically oriented *psychopathology*. A whole series of mental diseases are important to developmental psychology in that they represent the regression, the dissolution, of the higher mental processes, or inhibitions of the genetically advanced levels. Pathological regression was formerly mechanistically conceived. Investigations were carried out with the idea of discovering just which functions were relatively less intact. First was the norm of an educated adult established, and then various subtrac-

[30] Schüssler, 501, 480 ff.

tions were made from this norm. Currently, however, there is an increasing tendency to utilize the standpoint that takes into account qualitative differences in mentality. A distinct attempt is made not only to characterize the disease by circumscriptive defects, but also to "understand" the patient. This means, on the one hand, that the aberrations in reaction are approached in terms of a whole picture of the psychotic mentality and, on the other, that the investigation is directed toward understanding the change in the whole organism as a consequence of a circumscriptive defect. There can be no doubt that there are other ways of perceiving, feeling, and thinking than those of the mature normal man. And it is precisely because psychiatry has tried to understand pathological individuals in the light of the mentality peculiar to them that this science has greatly deepened its insight.[31]

THE COMPARATIVE POINT OF VIEW AND THE PROBLEM OF GENETIC PARALLELISM.

The basic problems of the various developmental psychologies are two in number: the establishment of developmental levels and of genetic relationships between these levels. At the same time it is necessary to consider the problem of a comparison of mental developments in different fields as a question of essential importance for a comparative developmental psychology. What value has child psychology for ethnopsychology and psychopathology? In what way can the study of ethnopsychology further the knowledge of child psychology?

Let us attempt to make a brief comparison of child psychology and ethnopsychology. It is well known that in biology Haeckel has strictly formulated a "law of recapitulation"— the development of the individual is a recapitulation of the development of the species. A corresponding law for the mental aspect of the organism has been proposed: The mental

[31] Cf. the work of Jaspers, **579**; Schilder, **599**; Kretschmer, **585**; Storch, **605**; Goldstein, **562**; and others.

development of the individual is a recapitulation of the development of the human mentality (Stanley Hall, and others). There are opponents to this hypothesis. Wundt denies its validity for the development of speech, of the capacity to draw, etc.;[32] and Meumann is in agreement with Wundt.[33] Only with great caution does W. Stern introduce the term "genetic parallels."[34]

Embryology throws much light upon the general problem of biogenetic parallelism. Here von Baer's formulations still seem to be valid. Von Baer set up certain laws of embryonic genesis as follows: "The general characteristics of any large class of animals to which the embryo belongs appear in development earlier than the special characteristics." (E.g., the chick is first a vertebrate, after which it becomes in succession a land-vertebrate, a bird, a land-bird, a gallinaceous bird, and finally *gallus domesticus.*) "The embryo of any given form, instead of passing through the stages exhibited by other definite forms, on the contrary separates itself from them." From this Baer concludes: It is because the adult forms of a lower, less differentiated level have advanced but relatively little beyond their own embryonic forms that a seeming similarity between them and the embryonic forms of a higher level appears, a similarity which, falsely construed, would lead to some notion of recapitulation.[35]

If these observations are applied to the problems of a comparative genetic psychology, the following two points may be inferred:

1. There exists certain similarities between developmental series. These similarities, for instance between the child's mentality and that of the primitive man, cannot be reduced to conform with any law of recapitulation (Haeckel, St. Hall). It is the very fact of development itself, in so far as it implies

[32] Wundt, 151, 296.
[33] Meumann, 453, 40.
[34] Stern, 511, 309.
[35] Cf. Russell, 688, 126 ff.

a change from generalized to more specialized forms, which gives the false impression of a recapitulation and occasions certain parallel phenomena in two related genetic series.

2. For all practical purposes one may speak of a principle of parallelism: development in mental life follows certain general and formal rules whether it concerns the individual or the species.[36] Such a principle implies that, apart from general and formal similarities, there do exist specific material differences in the comparable phenomena.

Returning to a consideration of the relation between *child psychology* and *ethnopsychology*, we find that it seems to be quite obvious, according to what has just been brought out, that any hypothesis of recapitulation has to be rejected. That is, although formal similarities must be admitted, it would be absurd to identify the child of our own cultural sphere with primitive man at any cultural level whatsoever. At present a true developmental psychology is interested primarily in genetic levels of mentality considered in their formal aspect, and must take into strict account essential differences between the child and the primitive man. The fundamental differences seem to be the following:

1. The child is a growing, labile organism. Primitive man's behavior is completely developed, fixed in tradition, and continues through long periods of time.

2. The child grows out of his child's world into an alien world of adults. His behavior is the result of an interaction between these two worlds. The primitive man, on the other hand, lives permanently in his own world.

Even if child development in primitive societies is compared with that in advanced cultures, these essential differences again seem to hold true. One might safely claim that there is greater *plasticity* in the individual development of the western child than in that of the primitive child. Plasticity implies two characteristics: a qualitative (dynamic) and a quantitative (temporal) plasticity. The development of the

[36] Stern, 511, 309.

western child exhibits a greater plasticity in a qualitative sense, i.e., there is a more intense interaction between the older and the younger generation. It is possible to explain this difference, perhaps, on the basis of the difference in the social meaning of adolescence in primitive and in more advanced societies. Adolescence in the primitive society means the period of preparation for entrance into an immutable social sphere. The young man, after initiation, becomes an actual part of the past of the tribe, since the life of the community consists in the preservation and continuance of its eternal patterns. Adolescence in the advanced cultural form, however, may mean all this, and something more. It may mean preparation for new patterns of life, for an ever-changing future, and for a projection of youthful ideals into an aging world. Therefore, in primitive societies there is an abrupt break between the two rigid social patterns of childhood and manhood, a break clearly defined by the initiation ceremonies. In advanced cultures there is a slow, long-lasting, plastic transformation from one stage of life into the other because of the intimate interdependence and interaction of the life patterns.

The development in our own sphere also shows more plasticity in a quantitative (temporal) sense. Development among primitive people is characterized on the one hand by precocity and, on the other, by a relatively early arrest of the process of intellectual growth.[37] Weule remarks that "at the same age when a child of the Caucasian race needs the close attention and care of his mother, the Negro offspring is left to his own devices."[38] Even children of the tender age of four are remarkably self-sufficient. At the age of seven or eight the Nyamwezi child breaks away from the authority of the mother and lives in a club house.[39] Kidd speaks of a bird snare constructed by three-year-old children which is skillfully made and of practical use. The ability of primitive children to draw

[37] Franke, 373; Kidd, 219.
[38] Weule, 322, 647 ff.
[39] Franke, 373.

and to knead clay into plastic objects has often reached the last stage of development at the fourth to seventh year. In any case, it can be demonstrated that the intellectual accomplishments of the primitive man advance little, if any, after puberty.[40] Children of primitive tribes who attend mission schools hold their own with the white children, even outstripping them in some ways, during an initial period. But after this period their development ceases, they fall behind the white children, and they may even exhibit a retrogression. This is true of African children as well as those of the South Seas and Australia.[41]

3. The social pattern of the child, especially that of the very young child, is but vaguely organized. The primitive man, however, is socially conditioned and governed to the highest degree. In great part his outlook and his life activity are intelligible only in so far as they spring out of a social structure.

Although the biogenetic principle of recapitulation is not applicable either to the mental or to the anatomical-physiological sphere, nevertheless it is still highly expedient to employ the principle of parallelism. If the peculiarly concrete thinking of the child is compared with certain forms of thinking typical of primitive people, if the drawings and the musical expression of early childhood are compared with the drawings of the Australian aborigines and with the songs of the Andaman Islanders and of the Vedda,[42] certain striking parallels will be found. These parallels must be taken as such, as merely indicating a similar mental structure in a general and purely *formal* sense. In a particular and *material* sense, there will be irreconcilable differences in the behavior of the child and of the primitive man.

Formally considered, a child may exhibit concrete thinking quite as much as the primitive man. Since the child's thought,

[40] Kidd, **219**, 148.

[41] Franke, 373. As previously stated, these differences should not be interpreted as differences in innate potentialities between primitive and civilized man.

[42] Cf. Levinstein, **435**; Werner, **532**.

however, is in constant conflict with the abstract thinking of the adult world, this concrete mentality will not express itself explicitly in any characteristic concrete language, as in the case of the primitive man, but will tend to translate the adult abstractions into words of concrete meaning. A child, for example, may ask actually to "look at" the springtime, or want "to take the winter cold in his hand."

Furthermore, because the child is but slightly conditioned and integrated socially, no more than fragmentary sociological parallels are possible. It is indeed true that we can find the beginnings of magic in the child's mentality, but only in very rudimentary forms. Magic achieves systematic expression only when it is a social, and not an individual, phenomenon.

The study of child psychology is nevertheless enriched when the ethnopsychological approach to the problem of mentality and its specialized results are brought to bear on it. This is also conversely true. When, for example, Jaensch[43] demonstrates that the imagery of the child is, to a considerable degree, eidetic—that is, in popular language, marked by hallucinatory characteristics—he is suggesting a similar problem in the psychology of primitive races. Specifically this problem is to discover whether the difference between the sphere of imagery and that of sensation among primitive people is not less sharply defined than in higher types.

All we have said up to the present applies again to the relation of the mental levels of child mentality to animal mentality. Here, too, with respect to an analogous formal structure, the typical difference between the two mentalities demands serious consideration. The level of animal mentality is relatively fixed or rigid, compared with that of the child mentality which is in a continual process of change.

The difference in plasticity of development comes clearly into view in a comparison of various ontogeneses in the animal and the human sphere. That is, the epoch of plasticity in any

[43] Jaensch, **416**; Kroh, **430**.

form of life appears—*ceteris paribus*—of longer duration and richer in content, the higher the species.

Excitability of the motor cortex appears earlier after birth in the lower mammals than in the higher species. Experiments by Marinesco, Kreindler, and Sager showed that in the guinea pig the cortex reacts to galvanic stimuli on the fifth day after birth, whereas in the cat motor reactions can be obtained only after 14 days.[44]

The accompanying table showing the genesis of motor functions in *Macaca rhesus* and in man, brings out the relative brevity of the period of development in apes as compared with man.[45]

Motor Functions as Moments of Development	Age of Appearance in Macaca	Age of Appearance in Man
Crying, sneezing, sucking at breast, winking	1 day	1 day
Response to sound (without adaptation)	2 days	. . . . . .
Head and eyes turn to follow objects	3 days	2–3 mos.
Grasping at seen object	5 days	5–6 mos.
Recognitive response to sound	11 days	. . . . . .
First attempt to walk	12 days	12 mos.
First solid food eaten	4 weeks	6–12 mos.
Scooping at object with palmar prehension	3 weeks	6 mos.
Opposing thumb and fingers	5 weeks	7–10 mos.
Sustaining weight by reflex clasping	0–3 days	0–3 weeks
Picking up pellet by opposing thumb and fingers	6 weeks	10 mos.
Attempt to draw mother into play	5 weeks	10–18 mos.
Head steadily erect and gazing about	5 days	3–4 mos.
Following moving hand with eyes	6 days	3–4 mos.
Attempt to crawl	12 days	9 mos.
Running	14 days	18–24 mos.
Attainment of virtually all adult vocalization	9 days	12–24 mos.

According to this table *Macaca rhesus* exhibits a rapidity of development in various abilities which is up to fifty times as great as the analogous development in man. On the other

[44] Dusser de Barenne, **638**, 888.
[45] Gesell, **377**, 345.

hand, the development of the anthropoid apes is much slower than that of other species. Wallace,[46] who had the opportunity of comparing a young orang-utang with a monkey (*m. cynomologus*) of the same age, remarks that the latter was relatively precocious, and that the orang-utang, in comparison, behaved like a baby and was utterly helpless.

Such differences notwithstanding, there must be a recognition that there are definite parallels between the concrete mental activities of higher animals and of children. These parallels have encouraged such child psychologists as Stern[47] to draw comparisons between important phases in the development of the child and certain aspects of animal mentality. Bühler [48] speaks of a "chimpanzee-stage" in the development of the child. On the other hand, some of the testing methods used in studying animal intelligence have been utilized by child psychologists.[49]

Similar considerations apply to the relation of developmental theory to *psychopathology*. One of the first neurologists who attempted to establish a parallelism between development in general and the findings of neuropathology was H. Jackson. He applied the doctrine of evolutionary levels to different pathological forms. According to his theory, pathological functioning is occasioned by a process of dissolution of the higher nerve centers. Such pathological symptoms as illusions, hallucinations, and delusions emerge from an "activity on the lower level of evolution remaining."[50] Later on Monakow, Kraepelin, Head, Goldstein, and others showed that neurophysiological and mental disturbances could be treated to advantage from a genetic point of view. These investigators consider that many of the pathological phenomena can be attributed to a breaking

[46] Gesell, 377, 350.
[47] Stern, 121, vol. 1, 299.
[48] Bühler, 351, Germ. ed., 77. On the entire problem, cf. Koffka, 427, Germ. ed., 30 ff.
[49] Kafka, 660; Szymansky, 518; Koehler, 664, 665; Lipmann and Bogen, 440; Révész, 494; Maier, 448.
[50] Jackson, 577.

down of the subordinating regulative centers, thereby admitting genetically lower systems into independent activity. Most of the positive symptoms of neurological disturbances, says Goldstein, are not entirely new products of the diseased organism. These symptoms are phenomena also discoverable in normal individuals; they become salient in pathological states because they are functionally isolated. The organism falls prey to the influence of primitive tendencies as soon as the lower functions are freed from the dominance of the higher activity destroyed by the pathological decline.

Psychotic, psychopathic, and neurotic behavior have been considered from the genetic standpoint by Gaupp, Kraepelin, Schilder, Kretschmer, Storch, and others. Gaupp and Kraepelin found that neurotic and hysterical behavior occurs predominantly in individuals with more or less under-developed personalities. Hysteric symptoms arise through the abnormal irradiation of affective activity into various biophysical and mental fields of function. According to Kretschmer, hysterical "hypobulic" reactions (hysteric spasms, paralysis, trembling, etc.) and "hyponoic" reactions (dream-like states of consciousness, hysterical trance) can be understood as phylogenetically archaic forms of reaction set free by lack of control.

The genetic principle has been applied even to such specific fields as the pathology of sensory function. According to Monakow, visual perception is built up of different genetically determined systems: the systems of subcortical reflexes; the systems of space form, and color perception; and the system of visual cognition. Poppelreuter, following Monakow's lead, analyzed various visual disturbances in parieto-occipital war cases. He confirmed Monakow's theory that the more primitive function patterns (e.g., space orientation) acquired at an earlier age are less easily disturbed than functions on a higher level (visual cognition). Poppelreuter distinguishes four stages of impairment and, consequently, four complementary stages of recovery. In the most severe injuries, where there is a loss of perception of color, size, form, and movement, the patient is thrown back to a primitive visual stage where only differences in brightness are registered. When the injury is less severe, or on partial recovery from the most primitive pathological stage, the patient can vaguely distinguish sizes and may be able roughly to localize light stimuli. A third stage is characterized by the development of a rudimentary form perception. At the normal, or approximately normal, level, various differentiated kinds of sizes and forms are recognizable.[51]

Pathological findings of this sort support the view that a certain parallelism exists in regard to development in general. It might be expected, therefore, that psychopathology will shed light on the genetic data of other developmental fields.

It is this genetic concept of neuropathology which apparently allows us to make a certain comparison between primitive activity in the normal child and an abnormally functioning nervous system. Irwin[52] describes the diffuse "mass activity" of the newborn child, explaining it as due to an immature neural organization of a subcortical, i.e., predominantly thalamic, type. He points out certain neuropathological parallels, using Jackson's principles and Head's interpretation of a diffuse over-activity as linked with thalamic organization in the event of a lack of control by higher centers. "Upward progress in the nervous system [due to maturation in the child, or to restitution in a disturbed adult nervous system] is shown in the replacement of diffuse mass reflexes . . . by a highly organized and specific response. On the other hand, the tendency to answer by a stereotyped and diffuse outburst of motor energy, to stimuli differing widely in place and kind, is a sign that lower mechanisms are set free from control."[53]

The results of psychopathology therefore become valuable in many ways for the general picture of the mental development, just as psychopathology is itself enriched and its methods facilitated and reinforced by the adoption of the genetic ap-

[51] Poppelreuter, 592.
[52] Irwin, 411.
[53] Head, *et al.*, 573, 507.

proach. But here, it must be noted, the theory of *recapitulation*, according to which mental illness is the "recapitulation of a special organic process in that form in which it [normally] appears on a lower level of organic nature,"[54] leads to an unjustified identification of psychopath or psychotic with primitive man, and this conclusion we must reject. We must speak of parallelisms whenever there seem to be corresponding phenomena in the various fields of developmental psychology. The developmental psychologist must therefore keep in mind that there are essential differences between a "primitive" behavior due to pathological processes in an adult of our cultural sphere and the primitive behavior of a member of a low civilization. A "pathological primitive" differs fundamentally from the "genuine primitive" in at least two ways:

1. The primitive man lives in a world to which he is admirably adjusted; the pathological individual tries to adjust himself by means of primitive behavior to a world for him inadequate and non-primitive.

2. Just as any developmental stage preserves vestiges of the earlier stages from which it has emerged, so will any degeneration bear signs of the higher level from which it retrogressed.

A concrete example will perhaps clarify these statements. There are cases of a pathological primitivation of language (discussed later in this book) known as aphasia which, so far as formal characteristics are concerned, bring the language very close to that concrete language found among primitives. But in spite of all formal similarities there is still a basic difference. The language of primitive man is concrete because it must be so in order to designate a world marked by an immensely rich variety of concrete things and events. It is quite possible that the primitive man does not use a general term for "knife" because he is primarily concerned with the specialized functions of the knife in cutting different objects, or with the functions of many specific knives used in performing varied

[54] Carus, 12.

operations. It is quite different with the aphasiac. He may, for instance, substitute the term "something to cut with" for the word "scissors" and accompany the phrase with appropriate gesture. Such an extremely concrete designation does not, however, arise because of any richness in highly specialized concepts or because of any need for them; it is merely an expression in a simplified vocabulary. A term in the vocabulary of the aphasiac does not completely lose certain traces of the abstract thinking from which it has degenerated. Such terms are frequently *non-specific*, concrete linguistic expressions *substituting* for the more abstract original.

The present book, because of the paucity of thorough analyses of the subject, cannot go far toward setting up the problem of a differential psychology of "primitive types." All that can be done currently is to stress the formal character of genetic parallelism and to point toward "primitive typology" as an important study for the future.[55]

THE RELATION OF GENERAL EXPERIMENTAL PSYCHOLOGY TO COMPARATIVE DEVELOPMENTAL PSYCHOLOGY.

It is at once paradoxical and revealing that the founder of the newer ethnopsychology, Wilhelm Wundt, should have drawn a sharp line of formal distinction between the two fields. He contended that it is the task of an ethnopsychology to investigate the objective phenomena of a culture—the language, the myths, and the customs—whereas experimental psychology must concern itself with studying by laboratory methods the more or less elementary processes of mental life. More recent methods of investigation have broken down this line of demarcation from both sides.

In the first place, this has come about in so far as ethnopsychology has adopted experimental methods. Experiments in the field of ethnopsychology have been initiated with most excellent results by Myers and Rivers,[56] the English psycholo-

---

[55] Cf. Gelb, 556, 428.
[56] Reports, 268, vol. 2; Rivers, 271.

gists, and by the German anthropologist, Thurnwald,[57] and others. It is true, of course, that the psychological experiments arranged for adult civilized people cannot be applied without modification in the study of primitive man. The observations and their evaluation must proceed with full consideration of the peculiarities of the cultural pattern involved. The investigation must be carried out so that the experimental situation is "biologically relevant" with respect to the milieu. This principle has not always been adhered to in some recent investigations of this type. Such an otherwise accurate authority on ethnopsychology as Neuhauss, who tested acuity of vision among the natives of the South Sea Islands by means of Cohn's tables (cards with letters of different sizes printed on them), falls into the error of employing a device completely without significance when applied to primitive man. His report that the natives see less acutely, on the average, than the European is simply bizarre.[58] Even such a basically peripheral function as visual acuity can be tested only under conditions that are psychologically and biologically relevant. Experiments might be carried on with freely moving objects in nature, or with some substitute for the natural moving object. In other words, to be significant for developmental psychology the experiment must of necessity be genetically oriented.

This basic principle applies, naturally, to all fields of developmental psychology. Siekmann, for example, has recently demonstrated that, in the case of patients suffering from brain injuries who have retrogressed to a more concrete level of mentality, tests on acuity of vision will have varying results depending on whether a concrete or an abstract situation is presented in the test.[59]

In the second place, the division created by Wundt between developmental psychology and the experimental psychology of the normal adult does not hold because the genetic point of

[57] Thurnwald, 128, 129, 140.
[58] Neuhauss, 254, vol. 1, 110.
[59] Siekmann, 601.

view has entered into experimental psychology itself. The genetic problems reach down into the experimental approach which deals particularly with the normal adult; indeed, it is just this genetic insight which accounts in ever-increasing measure for the significance of the laboratory experiment.

What, then, are the principles that developmental psychology must follow in setting up experiments of value for general experimental psychology? There are two types of "genetic experiment." The genetic experiment may seek to analyze the development of certain processes that have been either naturally or artificially created in the laboratory, or it may study "primitivation" appearing in the adult under certain controllable conditions.

Experiments on the Development of Normal Mental Processes.—Psychological events, on the one hand, are unfolding processes—no matter whether we are concerned with perceptual, conceptual, or volitional events—and as such are processes which go through stages of development. This development, as in the case of normal perception, can be consummated in a single second's duration, or even in a small part of a second. Or, as in intellectual events, it may continue throughout a considerable period of time, days and weeks, perhaps, under certain conditions. In suitable instances it is possible to follow this development.

Let us consider an example illustrating how, by the use of a "genetic experiment," it is possible to utilize the developmental approach in dealing with laboratory problems. The problem will be one of tone psychology: the investigation of the gradual development of the impression of and the differentiation between two tones of nearly the same pitch.[60] It will be found that, among several, two phases are characteristic: an earlier and a later phase. The first phase is characterized by a tonal movement understood as a relation of dullness and looseness (of the lower tone) to sharpness and

[60] Werner, 734, 735. These experiments have been continued in the Harvard psychological laboratory; the results will be published later.

clarity and density (of the higher tone). Now, in a subsequent phase, melodic qualities emerge out of this original movement from blurred to clear, a melody consisting of two qualitatively different tones. In this case we may assume that a genetic process has been revealed by the experiment in that the auditory gestalt of the first melodically indeterminate phase develops into a melody built up out of two fixed tonal qualities. The movement from blurred to clear evolves into a melodic relationship. The results of this type of experiment seem to throw light on the actual development of intervals in the history of music itself. A whole series of facts indicates that the tonal consciousness of man has developed in just this way, that the tonal relationship based on "brightness"[61] unfolds into a consciousness of melodic quality in the narrower sense of the word. Furthermore, with this idea in mind, a "micro-scale" consisting objectively of diminutive tonal intervals (about 1/12 of a normal whole tone) has been developed. Subjects have been able to perceive "micro-melodies," the genesis and structure of which follow essentially the same laws of construction that characterize the common "macro-scale."

Genetic Experiments on Primitivation.—The second type of experiment is based on the fact that the normal adult, even at our own cultural level, does not always act on the higher levels of behavior. His mental structure is marked by not one but many functional patterns, one lying above the other. Because of this the isolated individual, genetically considered, must occasionally exhibit in his varying behavior different phases of development.

The belief that normal adult mental life on our own cultural level occurs in but one mental sphere is closely bound up with a definite psychological prejudice. This point of view is found in the so-called element and association psychologies, which attempt to explain all mental events in terms of fixed elements. Out of these elements are built up all perceptions,

[61] For the definition of "tonal brightness," cf. Hornbostel, 49.

all willing, feeling, and reflective thinking. A strictly atomistic conception of the world is the precept and norm of such a mental structure. In accordance with this original hypothesis, a psychology arises which accepts the mechanistic idea as the measure and the touchstone of all mentality. The developmental method of approach, in direct opposition to this, shows that the European mentality is, genetically considered, highly variable; that man possesses more than one level of behavior; and that at different moments one and the same man may belong to different genetic levels. In this demonstrable fact that there is a plurality of mental levels lies the solution of the mystery of how the European mind can understand primitive types of mentality.

As we have indicated in a previous section, it is therefore quite misleading to define the difference between the man of lower and the one of higher civilization by contending that the one exhibits a primitive behavior and the other does not. The distinguishing mark of the advanced type is that an activity at a higher level is at his disposal which includes, rather than excludes, primitive activity.

If this is true, it is justifiable to contend that the psychology of the primitive man provides a valuable means of understanding the civilized man in his totality. Another means of furthering our understanding of civilized man is by the use of the "genetic experiment" dealing with primitivation, that is, an experimental situation which introduces certain objective or subjective conditions leading to the primitivation of the individual. In our Hamburg laboratory we carried out experiments on primitivation in the field of sensation and perception for a period of several years. We detected sensory genetic levels down to a point where the acoustic and optical qualities tend to merge into an undifferentiated, affective unity.[62] Similarly, we tried to reveal primary levels of language perception ("expressive" or "physiognomic" language), and studied the gen-

[62] Cf. the later discussion on synaesthesia and the unity of sense (p. 96 f.).

eral problem of primary (physiognomic) perception by the use of linear forms.[63]

Another approach to this genetic problem in the field of perception is the experimental analysis of the so-called lower senses. The gustatory and olfactory senses, for example, are distinguished by certain formal peculiarities which indicate their primitive nature.[64] The inseparability of subjective and objective content in the olfactory experience, the frequent lack of differentiation between smelling and tasting, etc., all indicate a primitive nature. An insight into such primitively organized fields of perception is undoubtedly of great value in understanding, for example, the sensory function in those lower organisms which exhibit a visual structure formally analogous to the so-called lower senses of higher organisms.[65]

Experiments in primitivation have also been made on the affective and intellectual processes. Dembo's work, for instance, has shown that the affective situation creating a high tension (anger, helplessness) may lead to a momentary primitivation (regression) of the motor and intellectual behavior.[66]

THE NATURE OF DEVELOPMENT.

It is no mere coincidence that Goethe, a man of powerful intuition who saw deep into the nature of all things, should be the first to express in clear language the idea of organic development. For him the very essence of the development of biological forms is symbolized by the differentiation of the organic parts and their subordination to the whole of the organism. In the introduction to his *Morphologie* Goethe says: "The more perfect the creature becomes, the less similar become the [morphological] parts to one another. On the one genetic pole the whole is more or less similar to the parts, and on the other the whole is dissimilar to the parts. The more nearly equal the

[63] Werner, 738; Krauss, 723.
[64] Henning, 716, 717.
[65] As to the neurophysiological characteristics of primitiveness of the lower senses, cf. Dusser de Barenne, 638, 892; Marquis, 679, 808.
[66] Dembo, 713; Lewin, 88.

parts, the less are they subordinated one to another. Subordination of the parts indicates a perfect creature."

Indeed it does appear that the development of biological forms is expressed in an *increasing differentiation* of parts and an *increasing subordination,* or *hierarchization.* Such a process of hierarchization means for any organic structure the organization of the differentiated parts for a closed totality, an ordering and grouping of parts in terms of the whole organism.

An example from biology will make this clear. If one considers the genetically ordered series of annelidans, millepedes, and insects, he will see that there is an increasing differentiation and centralization of the rings. In the first and most primitive organic form there is an equal disposition of segments, a

A   B

Fig. 2.—Types of Annulation: A. primitive; B. differentiated.

homogeneous structure, while in the higher forms there is a differentiation into annular groups. In the highest forms, the annular groups tend to be disposed at various centers—the head, the breast, and the posterior section—and in the groups themselves there is an increased annulation centralized about some nodal ring. Schematically this would be represented as in Fig. 2.

Since a living organism is a psychophysical unity, one has to expect a correspondence in mental development and in physico-biological genesis. We come to the conclusion that there is a parallelism from the mere observation of the anatomical-physiological basis of psychological phenomena, from an examination of the structure of the nervous system and its phylogenetic development.

There is perhaps no other organic system in the animal kingdom which displays such orderly progress as the nervous system.[67] Its first and most primitive form is a diffuse, undifferentiated, and uncentralized series of nerve cells with branching fibrils running indiscriminately throughout all or part of the body. As yet there is not the first sign of differentiation or centralization. The nervous system of the corals is of this type (Fig. 3). The next higher stage is already marked by incipient

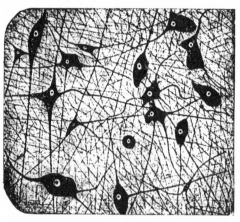

FIG. 3.—Ganglion Cells and Nerve Fibers of an actinia. (After Hertwig.)

differentiation and centralization. A nerve plexus balls together at certain points and becomes distinct from other parts of the system. This is the case in a nervous system in which a central cord stands in contrast to a peripheral plexus (Fig. 4). A more notable differentiation in the nervous tissue starts with the worms. The anterior pole of the body possesses a relatively high sensitivity, which decreases toward the posterior end. There is also a certain centralization; a cephalic ganglion appears at the anterior end, making possible specifically directed movements. This cephalization is increased in the higher worms. The excitation of receptor cells, concentrated mainly

[67] For general orientation, cf. Maier and Schneirla, 677.

at the anterior end, passes through the cephalic ganglion and is discharged throughout different parts of the body. An increase in centralization means a decrease in the independence of different parts of the system. For example, the cephalic ganglion of the marine annelid is more highly developed than that of the earthworm; the destruction of this ganglion impairs the sea worm's activity more than it does in the case of the earthworm.

Fig. 4.—Primitive "Central Nervous System" of Medusa (*Rhopalonema relatum*). *a.* Ring-like duct with nerve cord. (After Hertwig.)

In the mollusks there is again an increase in hierarchization and differentiation. There are various nervous centers (cephalic, pedal ganglion, etc.). Although these centers are partially independent, the anterior section, to a limited extent, is dominant. The cephalic ganglion, at least in the highest forms of this group, has already acquired a specific controlling function as an inhibitory center. Uexküll has found in the cephalopods that the destruction of these centers resulted in a strengthening of the locally controlled activities and an increased general excitability. In arthropods the nervous system is present as a more advanced "ladder" form, with a pair of ganglia in each body segment. Although each part is still marked by a considerable degree of independence, hierarchic integration is definitely present. If the cephalic "brain" is removed, a crab moves only when actual stimuli are applied locally. On the whole, however, even in the highest invertebrates, the local nervous organization assumes many functions which in the vertebrates are controlled by higher centers.

The appearance of the true cortex (neopallium) as the highest center of correlation marks a new stage in the hierarchical development (Fig. 5). Into this center, first appearing in reptilia, the subordinated sensory systems (which are not very strongly correlated in the fishes and the amphibia) discharge their energy, a necessary condition for any higher degree of plasticity in behavior.

The fundamental law of development—increase of differentiation and hierarchic integration—holds true in the central nervous system of the vertebrates. The work of Lashley and others opened the experimental attack on the problem of brain differentiation in the vertebrate scale. Lashley and his students have shown that for a certain higher type of mental activity, such as is exhibited in the learning of complex mazes, the brain of rats functions in a comparatively undifferentiated fashion.[68] Loss in learning ability was dependent not on lesions in any particular part of the cortex, but rather on the amount of brain tissue affected. The experiments of Norman Maier show a certain correspondence between the extent of lesions in the operated brain of rats and the degree of deterioration in reasoning behavior (that is, in the ability to organize in terms of past experience).[69] From this it must be inferred that various cortical areas within wide limits are functionally equivalent (equipotentiality, mass activity). On the other hand, experiments by C. F. Jacobsen indicate that undifferentiated mass activity of the whole brain is a rather primitive property of the brain structure. Superimposed upon mass activity there seems to be a higher differentiation of function among higher vertebrates. Working with apes, Jacobsen has shown that extirpation of the frontal areas of both hemispheres resulted in a total and permanent loss of the capacity for a "higher" activity—for example,

[68] Lashley, 668.
[69] Maier, 675, 676.

A. Shark.

B. Lizard.

C. Rabbit.

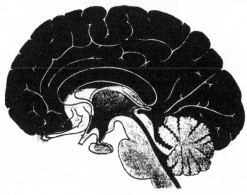

D. Man.

FIG. 5.—Development of Neopallium (new cortex; black) over Archi-
pallium (primitive cortex; gray). (After Edinger.)

delayed response. Extirpations in any other part of the brain, however, did not lead to such an impairment.[70] Recently F. T. Perkins studied the problem of increasing differentiation of the brain in vertebrates by the use of the action current technique.[71] By investigating the reactions of five genetically different types of brain (crayfish, frog, snake, pigeon, and rat), he was able to demonstrate a shift from homogeneity toward greater heterogeneity as one ascends the animal scale.

Perception and motor activity, accordingly, become more hierarchized the higher the species. In the evolutionary development from the fish to man a complete reorganization of the visual system has taken place. In the lower vertebrates the visual functions are carried out almost entirely by subcortical centers, whereas in man the cortex has taken over all the optic functions with the exception of the pupillary reflex to light.

In reptiles and birds there is a small optic projection to the forebrain, but these animals do not possess a true striate cortex. Within the mammalian series there is a progressive shifting of visual functions from the superior colliculus to the striate cortex.[72]

Experiments with operated animals confirm the genetic principle of increasing hierarchic integration. In fishes, the highest correlation center for vision can be disturbed without damaging the capacity for light response. Moreover, these fishes not only can learn new responses to varying degrees of brightness, but may retain responses learned before the loss of the optical cortex.[73] Rats, on the other hand, may be able, after operation on the optical cortex, to learn anew to discriminate between light and dark, but they lose discriminative responses established before the operation.[74] The effects of the removal of the visual cortex are similar in dogs. In these animals conditioned

[70] Jacobsen, **657.**
[71] Perkins, **681.**
[72] Marquis, **679, 812.**
[73] Sears, **690, 264.**
[74] Lashley, **672.**

responses to light established before the operation are not destroyed by the removal of the visual cortex. In monkeys destruction of the optical cortex demolishes the faculty to discriminate between differences of light. Conditioned responses to light, however, are not completely destroyed.[75] In man the bilateral destruction of the area striata results, so far as reliable evidence shows at present, in complete blindness.[76]

Experiments in pattern vision prove the same developmental law to hold true. Chickens whose cortex is entirely removed still retain the capacity for visual form perception.[77] Rodents, on the other hand, lose their pattern vision completely after the destruction of the visual cortex.[78]

Analogous facts are found in the consideration of motor activity. In the cat and dog relatively little motor impairment is present after extirpation of the sensori-motor cortex of one hemisphere. In the monkey a circumscribed lesion of the motor cortex is much more marked. In the higher apes the motor impairment after circumscribed lesions of the motor cortex is even more profound and longer lasting than in monkeys. In man the disturbances in motility caused by localized lesions of the precentral cortex are the most profound and of longest duration.

The decorticate dog can stand and walk within a short time after the total extirpation of the cerebral cortex. The decorticate monkey can sit upright to some extent but recovers no further; he needs support for his upper extremities.[79] The best-known examples of human beings without cortex are the children described by Edinger and Fischer, and Gamper. Neither posture nor locomotion was possible with these children. In the conclusion to the discussion of one case, Edinger and Fischer compare the behavior of the child with that of a

[75] Marquis, 679, 810.
[76] Dusser de Barenne, 638, 892.
[77] Layman, 674.
[78] Lashley, 670, 671.
[79] Dusser de Barenne, 638, 885; Rothmann, 687.

dog which also lived for over three years without the cerebrum. They report: "The dog soon learned to run again, and even to leap over a hurdle. The child lay contracted and almost motionless for three and three-quarter years. It made no attempt

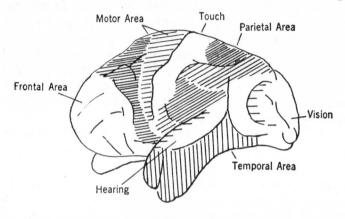

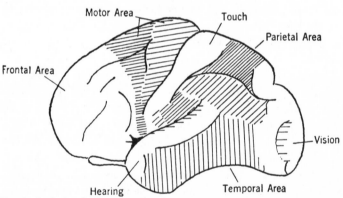

FIG. 6.—Left Cerebral Hemisphere of a Gorilla and of a Primitive Human Brain. (After Elliot Smith.)

to raise itself, to seize things with its hands, or even to hold things placed in them. The dog, which at first had to be fed like the child, later learned so much that it was merely necessary to place the dish before his nose to have him eat out of it. The child, on the other hand, had to be fed all the time."[80]

The transition from ape to *man* and the evolution within the *human family* itself show clearly the law of increasing differentiation and hierarchization. If the brain of man's nearest relative, the gorilla, is compared with the human brain, it will be found that the considerable increase in the cortical areas of the human brain chiefly affect three regions, the parietal, the frontal, and the temporal. These are the regions which are considered the areas of highest correlation (Fig. 6). As we

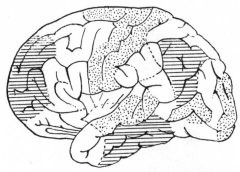

Fig. 7.—Myelogenesis of the Brain. (After Flechsig.)

know from the works of Flechsig, this development of the brain areas is paralleled in the ontogenetic development of man. Assuming that the time at which the connective fibers of the brain areas receive their sheath (myelinization) represents the beginning of the actual functioning of these areas, we may roughly distinguish three genetic zones in the brain: (1) primary zones which are connected about birth (Fig. 7, stippled areas); (2) intermediate zones (the blank areas) which do not begin to myelinate before the first month; and (3) terminal zones (the hatched lines·) which are the last to become connected. In other words, the areas myelinated last are

[80] Hempelmann, 651, 405.

the above-mentioned centers of highest correlation in the brain. Among these three zones, the frontal and pre-frontal parts seem to have a particular genetic significance (Fig. 8). According to Monakow, the younger parts of the central nervous system emerge out of the older ones by a development to-

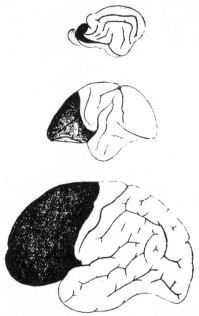

FIG. 8.—Frontal Area of the Brain of Cat, Monkey and Man. (After Edinger.)

ward the anterior top, the frontal pole.[81] Monakow's law of anatomical hierarchization becomes quite clear if one inspects the comparative measurements of these areas in the anthropoid ape, in Neanderthal man, and in modern man as compiled by Boule and Anthony.[82]

[81] Monakow, 101; Economo, 24, 25.
[82] Boule and Anthony, 9.

	Frontal	Occipital	Parietal	Temporal
Anthropoid ape	32.2%	10.4%	31.8%	25.5%
La Chapelle aux Saintes man	35.75%	12.0%	27.15%	25.05%
Recent man	43.3%	9.0%	25.4%	22.3%

Keith's measurements of the frontal area of the skull of the gorilla, Pithecanthropus, Homo Rhodesiensis, and the Neander-

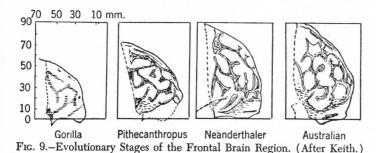

Gorilla　　　Pithecanthropus　　　Neanderthaler　　　Australian

FIG. 9.—Evolutionary Stages of the Frontal Brain Region. (After Keith.)

thal man present an instructive example of the law of hierarchic integration on these genetic levels.[83] The brain casts in Fig. 9

	Width	Height
Gorilla	83 mm.	55 mm.
Pithecanthropus	91 "	70 "
H. Rhodesiensis	103 "	83 "
H. Neanderthalis (Galilée)	105 "	88 "

made from the skulls of these species likewise show the development in the size and complexity of the frontal areas.

The fundamental law of development which, up to this point, has been demonstrated in the genesis of the nervous system may logically be applied to the *mental functions per se*. An increasing differentiation and refinement of mental phenomena and functions and a progressive hierarchization may be accepted as a basic principle.

In order to furnish an example of this law we shall present a situation which will be discussed at length in a later section

[83] Keith, 61, 476.

of the book. Among primitive peoples, and also children, there is found a kind of thinking which, with great justification, may be termed "concrete" thinking. Its distinctive characteristic lies in the fact that the conceptual activity operates in indivisible unity with motor-perceptual and imaginative processes. It is only gradually that a non-sensori-motor—that is, abstract— mode of thinking separates itself from this unity. But even then, it will be found, the differentiation never indicates a complete discontinuity of higher and lower function, a self-subsistent status in each. It is characteristic of higher mental organization that there should be an interrelationship of function and a subordination of the lower to the higher. Never is abstract thinking so self-sufficient that it can dispense with the material of sense. At the same time, thinking as a relating and comparative activity assumes the rôle of a central selective function commanding sensori-motor, perceptual, and imaginative data. It mediates among the confusing multiplicity of sensuous impressions by means of judgments and interpretations, and imposes order and measure upon this manifold.

This lack of differentiation between sensori-motor and intellectual functions *per se*, the absence of a general abstract mode of thought, is expressed, for instance, in the child's extremely rudimentary knowledge of causality. The child's world consists of pictures, a succession of images, which are more or less vaguely understood in their casual relation to one another. In his early years the child often does not know that it is the sun which brings the light of day, that it is the wind that shakes the bough, that water runs only downhill, and so on. The ordering of the world of phenomena in terms of general relation, of cause·and effect, of a genuinely abstract mode of thinking, has not yet occurred. This correlation and subordination of sensuous impressions by means of generalized thinking is reserved for the later and higher stages of development.

It is reasonable, therefore, to identify the development of the human mentality with an increasing centralization by means of superior ordering functions which give form and direction to the lower activities. A progressive knowledge of the world is arrived at by the formation of general and abstract modes of thinking arising from a sphere in which intellectual functions are embedded indiscriminately in perception, imagery, and motor activity.

A More Precise Definition of Some Important Concepts of Developmental Psychology.

We have found that the essence of organic development is the steadily increasing differentiation and centralization, or hierarchic integration, within the genetic totality. There now arises the question of framing this general developmental law in such concepts as will enable us more sharply to determine the nature of mentality and its genesis within the specific fields of developmental psychology.

The following pairs of concepts are especially useful in defining genetic levels of mentality: (1) syncretic–discrete; (2) diffuse–articulated; (3) indefinite–definite; (4) rigid–flexible; (5) labile–stable.

If several mental functions or phenomena, which would appear as distinct from each other in a mature state of consciousness, are merged without differentiation into one activity or into one phenomenon, we may speak of a *syncretic function* or a *syncretic phenomenon.* If, for example, a dream image is so constituted that it contains several meanings that would be at variance in the waking mind, yet in the dream have but a single fused significance, we may speak of this meaning as "syncretic." In the dream it is possible that the same person may at once be an uncle and a brother, and therefore can be classified as a syncretic phenomenon. Conversely, all those mental contents, acts, and meanings which represent something relatively specific, singular, and unambiguous may be termed *discrete.* A visual act, accordingly, since it is characterized by a higher degree of specificity with respect to some such syncretic act as smelling–tasting, is relatively discrete in comparison to the latter.

If the terms "syncretic" and "discrete" are understood to apply to the contents or functions of the mental sphere, to the acts and meanings discoverable within it, the conceptual pair *diffuse–articulated* must be understood to define the formal structure of the mental content. The term "articulated" denotes a formal construction of such a nature that distinguishable parts constitute the whole. In the advanced musical apprehension a melody is understood to be made up of single tonal motifs and tones which are distinct elements of the whole construction. A "diffuse" structure represents exactly the opposite. A structure of this kind is relatively uniform and homogeneous, one in which the parts have become more or less indistinct and are no longer characterized by a clear self-subsistence. A typical example of diffuse structure, one that represents the reverse of the differentiated melody, is a glissando:

, a sliding tonal movement. Here there is a "diffusion" of the tonal material without differentiation into distinct parts, i.e., single tones.

To sum up, the difference between the terms "syncretic" and "diffuse" is this: That which is undifferentiated is "syncretic" in a functional sense, and "diffuse" in a formal, structural sense. The genetic transformation of the syncretic into the discrete occurs as a singling out of function or content, whereas the transformation of the diffuse into the articulated occurs as a dividing up, a progressive disjunction, of the whole into related parts. We may say, therefore, that on the side of psychophysical functions and contents the conceptual pair "syncretic–discrete" will be definitive in fixing the developmental level, and the conceptual pair "diffuse–articulated" definitive in fixing the genetic level so far as its formal structure is concerned.

All these conceptual opposites: "syncretic–discrete," "diffuse–articulated," "definite–indefinite," and so on, imply a certain developmental direction, a movement which may be described as in the direction of increasing differentiation.

An increasing *hierarchization* and *subordination* are closely bound up with this development. This law of increasing subordination is exhibited on the side of mental content as well as on that of the formal structure of the mental content. We speak of an increasing hierarchic integration in the sphere of mental events and functions. The activities at the motor, sensory, or emotional level are subjected to the dominance of the higher functions of mentality. Again, we speak of an increasing centralization in the formal structure of phenomena. Through this centralization the perceptual gestalt is so articulated that certain central parts are salient and dominant with respect to others. One such instance is the construction of a rhythmic or melodic gestalt held together by focal points on which all the remaining constituent parts depend.

Intimately connected with these structural characteristics are certain dynamic properties. These dynamic qualities may be expressed by the two pairs of terms *flexible–rigid* and *labile–stable*. In general, the more differentiated and hierarchically organized the mental structure of an organism, the more flexible (or plastic) its behavior. Herrick, for example, points out that those activities of the rat which are cortically controlled are more plastic than purely subcortical activities.[84] This means that if an activity is highly hierarchized, the organism, within a considerable range, can vary the activity to comply with the demands of the varying situation. But the term flexible (or plastic) must not be confused with labile, or rigid with stable. If anything, they are rather at odds in their psychological connotation. In a later discussion it will be shown that the less differentiated and hierarchically patterned, the more rigid and yet less stable will the behavior be. The point is, briefly, that stability of behavior requires a flexibility of response in order to preserve the functional equilibrium of the organism in the face of mutable situations.

[84] Herrick, 652, 208.

APPLICATION OF THESE CONCEPTS TO THE PROBLEM OF
   LEVELS OF ORGANIZATION.

For those who are searching for genetic patterns, the analysis of mental organization at different developmental levels becomes a central task. In order to determine the changing nature of mental organization one must have a framework of genetic concepts.

Evidence is accumulating that, in accordance with these concepts of development, organization is less differentiated, more homogeneous at earlier levels than at more advanced stages. This seems to hold even for the most general relationships between mind and body.

To be sure, the wholesome organism is a well integrated entity. Many studies of the last decades were devoted to the problem of the relation of mental age to physical growth. Although this relationship may not hold from individual to individual,[85] it exists if extreme groups are taken into consideration.[86] As is well known, mentally superior children have been found physically superior, feeble-minded children physically inferior.[87] Olson's and Hugh's studies of the growth of the child as a whole and their conception of organismic age are outstanding recent contributions to this problem.[88]

On the other hand, psychophysical integration does not exclude the effectiveness of the law of increasing differentiation and specification. According to Lazarsfeld, the correlation between physical and mental growth is higher at lower levels (grades I to III) than later on.[89]

Many studies have been devoted specifically to the genetic analysis of mental organization. Garrett, Bryan, and Perl, examining 9- to 15-year-old children with a battery of ten mental tests, reported a decrease of correlation between abili-

[85] Dearborn and Rothney, **885.**
[86] Brooks, Cattell and alia, **874.**
[87] Hollingworth, **912**; Terman, **987.**
[88] Olson and Hughes, **961.**
[89] Locke, **937.**

ties tested with increasing age. The authors concluded that "in young children ability is amorphous to a greater degree than later. . . . The rôle of general ability is minimized in favor of special abilities as the child grows older."[90] In particular, functions such as verbal, number, spatial abilities and general memory, seem to be more closely related to each other in children than in adults. The trend toward specialization is again noticeable if correlations are computed between school achievements at various age levels. The decrease of correlation between arithmetic and vocabulary scores will be noted if one compares the coefficient of .52 obtained by Thorndike for elementary school ages, with Garrett's results indicating a coefficient of .21 at the college level.[91] Anderson, Monnin, Balinsky, a.o., also found changes of behavior from generalized to specialized forms of activity.[92] Asch's work suggests that intercorrelations between various performances in childhood, though higher than in infancy, decrease during adolescence.[93] His factor analysis indicates that a considerable portion of the reduction occurs with the factor of "general ability." The trend toward specialization arising from generalized intellectual behavior can also be inferred from studies that compare school achievement with the performance in a general mental test. The following table summarizes some of Cyril Burt's findings, which indicate a decrease of correlation between a reasoning test and school achievement.[94]

Age	10-11	11-12	12-13	13-14
r	78	81	64	59

Using Spearman's terms, the results mean that from the twelfth year on the influence of the general factor g on the individual's achievement decreases, the influence of factor s increases.

[90] Garrett, Bryan, and Perl, 898.
[91] Garrett, 897.
[92] Anderson, 857; Balinsky, 862; Monnin, 951.
[93] Asch, 861.
[94] Burt, 875.

Similar conclusions were reached by Marbe and Sell who correlated general school performance and chronological age.[95]

Another aspect of genetic changes of organization concerns the increase in hierarchic integration. The fact that the rates of growth of different functions are quite different is fairly well established.[96] It strongly suggests, as Asch points out, that functions most significant at earlier periods are displaced in subsequent periods by other functions.[97] The shift of significance seems to be caused by the emergence or strengthening of functions that possess a higher degree of subordinating power. Obviously such functions must have at least one of two characteristics:

(1) They must, by their very nature, be able to govern other heretofore independent functions. This development, known in neurophysiology as *encephalization,* reflects itself in the emergence of "higher" intellectual activities which are destined to control "lower" ones. Thus, emotions become intellectually controlled, abstract conceptualization of the environment replaces concrete perceptual organization, and so on. This aspect of mental genesis shall be discussed later more in detail with respect to various areas of behavior.

For the moment, it might suffice to mention a number of studies that illustrate the more general implications of this problem. Outstanding among these studies is the work by N. Bayley.[98] Mental growth was traced through the first three years: 61 infants were tested during this period with respect to sensory, sensory-motor functions, and adaptability to objective situations. Results suggest a shift of dominance of functions taking place during early development. The Sigma scores plotted separately for the sensory-motor and for the adaptive activities indicate: an increase of the former functions

[95] Marbe and Sell, 944.
[96] Jones, Bayley and alia, 926.
[97] Asch, 861.
[98] Bayley, 867.

up to the age of six months followed by a sharp decline; and a continuous, steady increase of the adaptive activities. In other words, a shift of dominance has occurred, after the first half year, from sensory-motor activity to functions of higher integrative power. Richards and Nelson, studying 80 infants, found a similar shift of dominance from a "general motor" toward a "mental" factor of intellectual alertness.[99]

(2) A function may gain a high degree of integrating power because of its changing relation to the total personality pattern of the growing organism. Depending on the need, or motivational, system of personality, certain functions may gradually acquire a central rôle. Shifts of dominance of this sort correspond with the process of individuation and therefore are part of the genetic psychology of individual differences as well as of personality in general.

An illustration may be presented that demonstrates clearly the emergence of integrating factors within the growing personality.

Razran, studying simple conditioned responses in children, found the susceptibility for conditioning increasing up to five years of age; from there on the susceptibility decreased. "The decrease in the speed of conditioning," concludes Razran, "is due to the emergence of a new factor . . . the child becomes more 'unwilling' to be conditioned." In the opinion of Razran, this new factor is a central attitudinal one: making its first appearance at the three-to-five age level, it is most probably connected with the child's growing capacity for conscious control.[100]

The final ambitious goal of experimental genetic research directed toward the analysis of organizational patterns, is a comprehensive theory of ontogenetic phases. The possible existence of such phases is unwittingly admitted even by those writers who—though insisting on continuity as an intrinsic

[99] Richards and Nelson, 971.
[100] Razran, 967.

property of development—are, at the same time, willing to accept a division into genetic periods such as early and late infancy, childhood, prepuberty, adolescence, and adulthood.

Some writers—such as the psychoanalysts, Piaget, Ch. Buehler, Spranger, a.o.—have attempted to outline ontogenetic epochs and to interpret their organismic meaning.

Freud's early stages of libidinal organization (oral, anal, genital) are well known. So are his genetic stages emerging from the dynamic interrelatiorship between the principle of pleasure and the principle of reality. (Infantile and early childhood: ruled mainly by the principle of pleasure; late childhood: repression, sexual latency and early sublimation of sex drives, early superego development; puberty: peak of libido sublimation; adolescence: integration of sublimated libido and reborn sex drives, maturation of superego).[101] Entirely different in scope is the genetic scheme offered by Ch. Buehler. Based mainly on the experimental findings at the Vienna laboratory, Ch. Buehler distinguishes five phases, each of them characterized by a change in the relation between the growing self and the growing reality. [2] Piaget's attempts are directed toward the distinction of stages with reference to specific rather than to general activity, such as causal reasoning or moral judgment. Some of his distinctions will be discussed later.

These various interpretations contain probably a greater amount of hypothetical elements than the available data warrant; but they function as valuable stimulants in an area in which the danger of an overflow of research that lacks principal ideas is, perhaps, greater than in any other field of psychology.

[101] Fenichel, 893.
[102] Bühler, 350.

BOOK II
Primitive Mental Activities

PART ONE

Sensori-motor, Perceptual, and Affective Organization

Chapter II

THE SYNCRETIC CHARACTER OF PRIMITIVE ORGANIZATION

THINGS-OF-ACTION.

General psychology distinguishes among different groups of mental events, such as those making up the processes of perception, feeling, motor activity, and so on. However expedient this classification may be in describing the highly differentiated mental life, it is quite inadequate for the analysis of primitive psychic events. For it is characteristic of primitive mental life that it reveals a relatively limited differentiation of object and subject, of perception and pure feeling, of idea and action, etc. The biologist Buytendijk says: "It appears that in the whole animal world the correlation of the animal and environment is almost as intimate as the unity of the body."[1] The perceptions of the animal exist, therefore, only in so far as they are part of a wider totality of action in which object and inner experience exist as a syncretic, indivisible unity.[2]

This leads us to the assumption that the perceived things of the primitive world are constructed differently from the things of advanced, civilized man. Things do not stand out there, discrete and fixed in meaning with respect to the cognitive subject. They are intrinsically formed by the psychophysical organization of which they constitute an integral part, by the whole vital motor-affective situation. Hence we may speak of "things-of-action," or of "signal-things" in such a primitive world.

[1] Buytendijk, **622.**
[2] Volkelt, **699.**

If the range of psychophysical motor behavior of an animal is deliberately constrained, as illustrated in Buytendijk's convincing experiments on the dog's capacity for recognizing forms, it appears that forms otherwise learned with facility become impossible, or at least far more difficult, to master.[3] The coordination of physical movement and sensory impression is basic for primary form perception. This notion of a total, or global, response fundamentally conditioned not only by sensory functions but also by motor activity is reaffirmed by the results of De Jong's experiments on dogs.[4] In these experiments the dog was placed in a cage and trained to open the door by treading on a small board placed horizontally. It became helpless, however, despite its training, as soon as the board was placed in a vertical position. Whereas man may regulate his behavior to accord with an insight into the purely perceptual properties of the object, the dog knows the object only in terms of its immediate reaction to it.

Because of this fact, it is of paramount importance in any animal experiment dealing with the faculty of discrimination that the conditions are so chosen that the objects or elements to be distinguished can be perceived as signals. Johnson, Williams, Szymansky, among others, were unsuccessful in their attempts to train the dog to discriminate forms.[5] Buytendijk, in certain experiments of crucial importance, demonstrated that a dog which, sitting at rest, was unable to discriminate between a circle and a triangle could perform the feat when allowed to run freely to and fro.[6] The simplest interpretation of this decrepancy in the dog's behavior would seem to be that in one case it was able to discriminate and act according to signal-qualities, whereas in the other case it could not do this.

[3] Buytendijk, 621.
[4] De Jong, 658.
[5] Maier and Schneirla, 677.
[6] Buytendijk, 623, 130.

One must bear in mind that even the most highly developed human beings, as in the case of primitive organisms, are constantly in contact with things-of-action. So far as our activity is confined to an entirely concrete, familiar situation, the objects seem to guide, to steer, our action by virtue of their signal-qualities. When we are tired, an empty chair "invites" us to sit down. In such a situation the chair exhibits a "sitting-tone," as Uexküll has it,[7] or a "demand character," or a "valence,"[8] which encourages us to sit down. Any stump in the woods may become a chair so far as its signal-quality (temporarily created by our need) is concerned. Of course, it is only to a limited extent that we live in a world-of-action. Usually we are able to revert with ease to a purely perceptual and conceptual activity. We can see and comment on the fact that the stump, although used as a chair, is part of a tree. It is precisely this latter ability which sets off more highly developed beings from those living altogether in a world-of-action.

One of the most promising experiments inquiring into a world built up of things-of-action and signal-qualities has been carried out by E. G. Sarris in Uexküll's "Umwelt Institut" in cooperation with our Hamburg Psychological Laboratory.[9] The problem at hand was to discover just what are the properties of certain objects of importance in the dog's world as controlled experimentally. What, for example, is a "chair" or a "basket" for the dog? The experiment was conducted in such a way that the animal learned to obey a command associated with the thing in mind. It was taught, for instance, to jump up on a common, everyday chair at the command of "Chair!" After successful training the next step was to find out just how much a chair could be altered in appearance and still have the dog react to the command "Chair!" In other words, what are the properties of an object necessary to occasion the right response? It was discovered that any ob-

[7] Uexküll, 696.
[8] Lewin, 87, 88; Tolman, 694.
[9] Sarris, 689.

ject, whatever it may be for human beings, has the significance of "chair" for the dog, if it can jump on to it, lie down on it, and look around. A "basket," on the other hand, is something "into which it may go and lie down, something which forms a protective wall about it." A "basket" may be a dog kennel, or a coal bucket lying on its side, or any hollowed-out object. The dog jumped into a wooden box open at the top upon hearing the command "Basket!" Conversely, when the

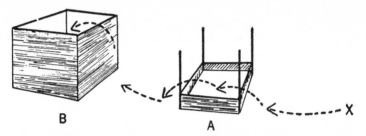

Fig. 10.—One of Sarris' Experimental Situations.

At the command, "Basket!" the dog, without hesitation, jumps over the upturned stool and goes directly to the open box, which has more "basket-like" qualities.

box was covered with a lid, the dog was prompted by the command "Chair!" and not by "Basket!" (See Fig. 10.)

The signal-properties of things-of-action are dependent on the biological "world" typical for the particular animal. For a robber-wasp, for example, any form that suggests a fly, even though it is only the head of a nail driven into the wall, will possess the signal-properties of an object of prey.[10] Bees can be trained to distinguish among certain forms, provided they are relevant to the bee's field of action. Not only can they learn to discriminate among certain figures of flower-like shape, they can distinguish in such figures those rich in contour and those relatively poor in contour. On the other hand they fail to recog-

[10] Demoll, **635**, 445.

nize any difference in simple geometrical forms, that is, forms which bear no resemblance to flowers.[11]

The following account shows how different from anything on an advanced level may be those signal-qualities that are effective in the world of biologically primitive animals. A sphecid wasp feeds her offspring mostly with grasshoppers; after she has stung and paralyzed them, she seizes them by the feelers and drops them into her nest. Fabre tells that he cut the feelers from a grasshopper paralyzed by a wasp, whereupon the wasp responded by grasping the prey by its palpae. But if these also were removed, the wasp was helpless. Contrary to what one might well expect, the grasshopper's legs did not exist as signal-qualities in the whole continuum of the event of seizing and dragging off the prey.[12]

However, the effectiveness of the signal-qualities may depend not only on certain biologically relevant objective characteristics, but also on the readiness for action, a motive which will bring to life an otherwise mute, inoperative signal-quality.

An excellent example of this occasional activation of signal-properties in a series of events is furnished by an observation made by Buytendijk.[13] A hungry toad was put into a small enclosed place littered with bits of matches and moss. The creature hopped about without reacting to the objects. When food was dropped in to the toad, it was immediately snapped up as soon as it was caught sight of. But the animal's behavior changed completely. Now when it came in contact with some hitherto indifferent "dead" object, the toad stopped, snapped it into its mouth, and spat it out on discovering its inedibility. After several of these unsuccessful reactions, the previous insignificance of the inedible objects was restored, and they lay untouched. The lifeless objects actually changed in meaning for the toad. If the real nourishment were a bit of worm, the

[11] Frisch, **643**; Hertz, **654**.
[12] Fabre, **639**.
[13] Buytendijk, **620**.

toad responded to the bits of match; if it were a spider, the strands of moss acquired a new valence.

The following observation reported by Demoll also shows the dependence of things-of-action and their signal-qualities on certain "mental sets" arising in the whole course of events.

"On the road from Sorrento to Amalfi I once observed some mason-bees which were using the chalk-dust of the road-bed in the construction of their apparently far-distant nests. In a very rapid, almost linearly direct flight they came across a valley in the hills and, without hesitation, settled down to their task of collecting the dust in a certain circumscribed area of the road. As I approached closer and closer, and stood nearby quietly watching, it appeared that the bees were greatly disturbed by my intrusion into their field of vision. Instead of settling down immediately on the road, they circled about the goal several times, and only after some hesitation did they continue with their work. They seemed to be particularly disconcerted when I waved my arm.

"But once they had finally alighted on the ground and had actually begun to collect the dust, I could even bend over them, put my hand near them, and cause light and shadow to play about them without their evincing the slightest discomposure.

"From this I conclude that changes in the visual field of the bees—by the appearance of an object in the optical field as well as by the movements of this object—are evaluated differently, according to whether the visual impressions are of greater importance, as in the orientation of a certain course of flight, or of lesser value, as in the fabrication of mortar while at rest on the earth."[14]

It is no mere coincidence, but a fact grounded in the very nature of the primitive habitus, that a relatively undifferentiated functioning leading to a predominance of things-of-action is characteristic of the earlier stages of *childhood*. Undifferentiated modes of behavior are particularly common in the neonatal period. Stern remarks: "All that we are fully justified in assuming for the mentality of the newborn child is a blurred state of consciousness in which sensorial and emotional phe-

[14] Demoll, 635.

nomena are inseparably fused."[15] This state of consciousness may be described as a mere state of feeling, a total sensation, in which object and subject are merged. Many of the young child's activities can be understood only through the assumption that the motor-emotional and sensory factors are blended into one another. If it is admitted that the things of the child's world are created as much by his motor-affective activity as by objective stimuli, it becomes intelligible, for instance, why a child can seriously consider a few wisps of straw to be a doll or a bit of wood to be a horse. And in this case there is little justification for the idea that the child must imaginatively supply the lacking objective qualities. His experience of a doll does not need to contain a head with two eyes, a nose, a mouth, and so on. On the contrary, it may be assumed that the perceptual experience of the doll is made up correlatively of both factual attributes and inner motor-affective needs and impulses. The affective and motor behavior of the child impresses itself on the world of things and fashions it. A thing has the significance of "doll" in so far as the child reacts to it mentally and physically as a doll.

The younger the child, the less purely objective and self-subsistent things become, and the more highly conditioned in their significance by emotional and motor reactions. Let us consider an example.

Miss Shinn speaks of her nephew, a child six months old, who was given a round rattle instead of the customary square-edged one. The child tried in vain to find and bite the "corners" of the round rattle.[16] This demonstrates that the infant's perception of the rattle was not determined by its qualities of angularity or roundness, that it was not an optically and tactually known form *per se*, but that it was rather a "thing-of-action," understood in so far as it was a signal for a specific motor-affective reaction. The rattle, for the infant, is not a thing standing out there in contrasting relation to the child

[15] Stern, **513**, Germ. ed., 46.
[16] Shinn, **505**, Germ. ed., 87.

as subject, a thing of distinct, fixed significance. The thing is there as "something to be bitten," and is accordingly determined by its motor-affective meaning.

The awareness of objects during early childhood depends essentially on the extent to which these objects can be responded to in motor-affective behavior. The investigations of Iwai and Volkelt dealing with the response of the child nine to twelve months old to diversely shaped objects show that those objects most easily gripped with the hands occasion a distinct preference.[17] They appeal to the child's "need to function," as K. Bühler expresses it.[18] Martha Muchow has also demonstrated that even for the younger school child the objects of the adult world exist mainly in so far as they exhibit a form which facilitates their use as instruments in motor activity.[19]

Later on it will be shown definitely[20] that the things constituting the world of the *primitive man* are primarily known as things-of-action, that is, pragmatically, and that their salient characteristics and totality are determined by their use, their rôle, in active situations. Malinowski, among others, has shown that any analysis of primitive culture would be futile if one lost sight of the pragmatic, or "functional," character things possess for the primitive mind.[21]

Similarly, in certain instances of *pathological regression*, when there is a reversion toward a more primitive reality, again it will be found that things-of-action predominate. In fact, things are often not known at all unless they are known motor-affectively, that is, according to their pragmatic value for the subject. One instructive case of "primitivation," probably due to some diffuse brain injury, was recently analyzed by E. Hanfmann and Rickers-Ovsiankina.[22] The patient was unable, for

[17] Iwai and Volkelt, 413.
[18] K. Bühler, 351, Germ. ed., 327, 456; Ch. Bühler, 350, chap. 1.
[19] Muchow, 460.
[20] Cf. pp. 402 ff.
[21] Malinowski, 97.
[22] Not yet published. Quotations used by the kind permission of the authors.

example, to recognize a key presented to him as an isolated object. Yet immediately upon seeing the key inserted and turned in a lock, he would shout, "Key, key, key!" The same thing appears to hold true even for the recognition of objects represented in pictures. This patient's recognition of bread seen in a painting obviously hinged on the motions he made simulating picking pieces of bread from the surface of the picture and carrying them to his mouth. It is plain that he successfully recognized an object only when he could utilize certain properties of the given object as signals for specific reactions.

PRIMITIVE PERCEPTION AS DYNAMIC: "PHYSIOGNOMIC PERCEP-
   TION."

The high degree of unity between subject and object mediated by the motor-affective reactivity of the organism results in a dynamic, rather than static, apprehension of things. Things as constituent elements of a dynamic event must necessarily be dynamic in nature. Animal psychologists and biologists have often described, from both the experimental and the theoretical standpoints, the importance of movement (the movement of the animal itself as well as of the object) in the construction and interpretation of the environment. There is no doubt that for Buytendijk's dog, which was able to discriminate forms only when free to move its body about, the qualities of things were dynamic. "Movement in response to an optical impression," says Uexküll, "is an integrating factor in the melody of the environment, by means of which the forms of objects are brought into inner realization." Large groups of animals, the amphibians for example, react primarily only to a moving optical stimulus. A frog will ignore an object of prey which does not move. But the same frog will snap up such small inedible objects (providing he is hungry, of course) as whortleberries, should they chance to be dropped within his visual range.[23] Hertz's beautiful experiments with bees make it appear proba-

[23] Hempelmann, 651, 353 ff.

ble that, for many insects flying over an object, a form is perceived by being transformed into a sort of rhythmic pattern of
successive elements, just as the spider's perceptual world is to a
great extent made up of various rhythmic-vibratory signals.[24]

Rubinow and Frankl carried out some instructive experiments dealing with the *child's* response to things. They traced
the development of the sucking response, and in this process
observed five genetic steps: The reaction occurs (1) when
there is a sudden movement of the object toward the child's
mouth, (2) when there is a similar movement of a pointed
object, or (3) of any object capped by a nipple or of any
other nipple-shaped form. (4) About the age of six to seven
months the sucking response becomes restricted to an object
(stationary or in motion) containing a white substance and
capped by a nipple-like form. (5) At the age of eight months
any object which contains a white liquid evokes the response.[25]
It can readily be seen that the child's reactions are at first directed primarily toward the dynamic properties of objects.
The older he grows, the more the static qualities—e.g., pure
form or characteristic color—condition the response.

Some recent experiments by Meili and Tobler have also
shown that the optical field of the child is dynamic to a far
greater degree than that of the adult. These two investigators
compared the ability of 38 children five to twelve years of age
to see apparent movement with the corresponding ability in 22
adults. It was demonstrated that the children could discern
movement in the kinematographically projected visual forms
at a lower rate of succession than could the adults. Children
between the ages of twelve and fourteen represented a mean
between the greater faculty in younger children and the lesser
in adults.[26]

This preference for interpretation in terms of dynamic rather

[24] Hertz, 655; Grünbaum, 648.
[25] Rubinow and Frankl, 498.
[26] Meili and Tobler, 450. Zietz and Werner, 750, have demonstrated
the general significance of dynamic factors for optical movement.

than static properties can be observed whenever the child is free actively to grasp the object in his own way. Gantschewa observed this fact in experiments in clay-modeling carried on with children of from three to six years of age. She says: "A dog, for the child, is not an objective structure possessing objective shape and parts. The dog is something that 'bites' or 'barks.' A 'woodpecker' is a bird that 'hangs on the side of a tree.' The children in the modeling experiments spontaneously called the mouse's nose 'the squeaker'; a bed, the 'lying-down-place'; a cube, 'the-cornered-thing'; a bird, 'the-greedy-thing'; a squirrel, 'the humpback.' "[27]

Such dynamization of things based on the fact that the objects are predominantly understood through the motor and affective attitude of the subject may lead to a particular type of perception. Things perceived in this way may appear "animate" and, even though actually lifeless, seem to express some inner form of life. All of us, at some time or other, have had this experience. A landscape, for instance, may be seen suddenly in immediacy as expressing a certain mood—it may be gay or melancholy or pensive. This mode of perception differs radically from the more everyday perception in which things are known according to their "geometrical-technical," matter-of-fact qualities, as it were. In our own sphere there is one field where objects are commonly perceived as directly expressing an inner life. This is in our perception of the faces and bodily movements of human beings and higher animals. Because the human physiognomy can be adequately perceived only in terms of its immediate expression, I have proposed the term *physiognomic perception* for this mode of cognition in general.[28] There is a good deal of evidence that physiognomic perception plays a greater rôle in the primitive world than in our own, in which the "geometrical-technical" type of perception is the rule.

There are two ways of inquiring into the nature of physiog-

[27] Gantschewa, 375.
[28] Werner, 739.

nomic perception in the adult sphere. One method is to question those who exhibit a natural tendency to perceive physiognomically rather than geometrically. The other is experimental in nature.

Several experiments on physiognomic perception have been conducted in the Hamburg Laboratory. The results of one of

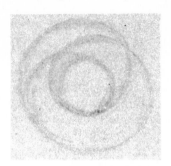

FIG. 11.—Drawing by One of Krauss' Subjects, Expressing "Gold."

them which dealt with the expressive character of lines have been published in a monograph by R. Krauss.[29] Fifty subjects were asked to draw lines to accord with a certain emotional content. Another group of subjects was given the task of choosing lines to match the emotional content of certain given words. Again, things rather than emotions, were verbally pre-

Iron   Silver   Gold

FIG. 12.—Expression Lines.

sented, and these had to be drawn or matched (Fig. 11). In a preliminary experiment, for instance, "gold," "silver," and "iron" were matched with the three lines in Fig. 12 with a unanimity of choice amounting to 80 per cent for the whole group.

[29] Krauss, 723.

In a more elaborate matching experiment eight lines were selected from the extemporaneous, linearly expressed ideas assigned to the fifty subjects (supposedly representing gayety, melancholy or sadness, rage, darkness, dawn, gold, iron, glass), and 242 subject choices agreed to an extent of 73.6 per cent of unanimity in the physiognomic meaning of the lines.

One of the important conclusions which Krauss draws from the experiments is that the geometrical properties of the lines are quite different from the physiognomic. Lines geometrically similar can express things quite contrary in nature, and vice versa.

Another approach to the problem of physiognomic perception is to collect information from those especially gifted in susceptibility to physiognomic experience. The self-descriptions of artists often reveal that it is normal for them to perceive things physiognomically.

Kandinsky is one of the great artists who sees the world physiognomically. He is also able to express this experience clearly in words. In his autobiography he repeatedly remarks about his physiognomic perceptions. He says, for example:

"On my palette sit high, round rain-drops, puckishly flirting with each other, swaying and trembling. Unexpectedly they unite and suddenly become thin, sly threads which disappear in amongst the colors, and roguishly skip about and creep up the sleeves of my coat. . . . It is not only the stars which show me faces. The stub of a cigarette lying in an ash-tray, a patient, staring white button lying amidst the litter of the street, a willing, pliable bit of bark— all these have physiognomies for me. . . . As a thirteen- or fourteen-year-old boy I bought a box of oil-colors with pennies slowly and painfully saved. To this very day I can still see these colors coming out of the tubes. One press of my fingers and jubilantly, festively, or grave and dreamy, or turned thoughtfully within themselves, the colors came forth. Or wild with sportiveness, with a deep sigh of liberation, with the deep tone of sorrow, with splendid strength and fortitude, with yielding softness and resignation, with stubborn self-mastery, with a delicate uncertainty of mood—out they came, these curious, lovely things that are called colors."[30]

Mabilleau, the biographer of Victor Hugo, points out the poet's fundamentally dynamic conception of the world. Forms, for him, were not so much forms as actions "expressing a living force contained within the limits [of the form]. . . . Victor Hugo does not see a viper glide; he sees a 'gliding.' . . ."[31]

It is characteristic of the child that the qualities of things should be much more physiognomic for him than for the adult. Child psychology has long been unaware of this radically different kind of experience which the adult has retained only for special situations. One speaks only too readily of the anthropomorphism of the child. But physiognomic perception is something more general, more deeply rooted, than anthropomorphism. The latter is itself a definite interpretation of the world. It must be borne in mind that anthropomorphism, in the strict sense, can be spoken of only when there is a consciousness of a polarity between the personal and the impersonal. During the physiognomic period of childhood, however, it is the very absence of polarity and the high degree of fusion between person and thing, subject and object, which are characteristic. The average adult generally has a physiognomic experience only in his perception of other human beings, their faces and bodies. The child, on the other hand, frequently sees physiognomic qualities in all objects, animate or inanimate. And this experience is by no means identical with the idea of anthropomorphizing objects, with the personification of the inanimate, with the reading of human qualities into lifeless things. Physiognomic experience is genetically precedent to anthropomorphism. When, for example, a child pronounces such a meaningless figure as this ⟁ to be "cruel,"[32] it does not mean that he has invested the figure with an actual face.

[30] Kandinsky, 57, 5, 6, 17.
[31] Mabilleau, 93, 132.
[32] Muchow. Unpublished experiments, Hamburg Laboratory.

It is the physiognomic quality of this sharp-cornered object to "behave cruelly," just as in the previously cited experiment certain lines were experienced as "gay" or "sad." When Preyer's son, two and one-quarter years old, cries out, "Poor zwieback," when the zwieback is broken into two pieces, how such a thoroughly utilitarian, impersonal object as bread could suffer pain would be virtually unintelligible on the basis of any anthropomorphism.[33] The case of the Scupins' two-year-old son is quite similar: "Upon seeing a cup lying on its side, he said: 'Poor, tired cup!' Apparently he sees a cup standing on its base as erect and strong, and a cup tipped over as lying down because it is fatigued."[34] Although this is a very telling observation, its interpretation exhibits the common error of over-rationalizing the child's point of view. There is the unjustified inference that in the child's mind there is an explicit anthropomorphic relation between the idea of fatigue and that of sitting or lying down. The "tiredness" of the cup is an immediate, concrete experience of a physiognomic kind, just as the "sadness" or "pathos" that the other child saw in the broken zwieback is directly known without the intervention of any anthropomorphic interpretation. That the cup is lying down is a causal interpretation gratuitously added by the observer to what is in actuality a completely naïve physiognomic perception.

The following instances reveal the same phenomenon: Neugebauer tells that his son at the age of two and one-half years called a towel-hook a "cruel" thing. When he was four and one-half years old he called the tripod of a camera a "proud" thing when it stood stiff and erect, and "sad" when it leaned at a precarious angle. At the age of three and one-half years he thought that one number 5 looked "mean" and another "cross." The number 4 appeared "soft" to him.[35]

Then there is the girl five and a half years old who went walking with her mother in the rain at the time of the day

[33] Preyer, **488**, 342.
[34] Scupin, **502**, vol. 1, 111.
[35] Neugebauer, **468**.

when the light was failing. "Mother," said the child, "I can't see a thing, it's so foggy. Everything is like whispering."

Gantschewa's experiments dealing with the behavior of children in modeling plastic forms from clay afford further interesting examples of physiognomic perception. In this situation younger children show a more lively behavioral response to their work than the older children. They exhibit a complete and enthusiastic surrender to the whole dynamic situation which results in the verbal expression of dynamic qualities. One child 3:7 years old while modeling a copy of a cactus in clay, exclaimed: "Sticks! So fresh! Stick-flower, knife-flower! You just wait and see . . . I'll make you out of clay with great big prickers!" Another child 4:8 yrs. old showed a more prosaic attitude. He said: "What's that? A flower? Does it hurt? Ah ha! Little thorns . . . flower-pot . . . earth . . . a round thing with little prickles. I can make that all right."[36]

Miss Muchow, in her experiments on the young child's perception of graphic objects, found similar facts. Children very often experience such objects physiognomically as conditioned by their affective and bodily response. A four-year-old girl, upon seeing some cards on which angular figures were drawn, cried out: "Ugh! What a lot of prickles and thorns!" And she hesitated to pick up the cards lest the thorns stick into her fingers.[37]

A further indication of the intimate relation between any such primitive drawing and the global psychophysical response is found in Volkelt's observation that the pointedness and angularity of actual objects are often strikingly represented as being physiognomic in character in children's copies of these objects.[38] The graphic representations of children are not merely optical phenomena, but are precipitates, so to speak, of a whole attitude which reaches expression in the physiognomy of the drawn object. The angularity and pointedness are experi-

[36] Gantschewa, 375, 18.
[37] Muchow, 458, 46.
[38] Volkelt, 528, 114.

enced psychophysically by the whole body, and this experience is projected on the drawing paper by the child. Miss Muchow, speaking of copies of non-realistic figures drawn by children, says: "Children often see pointed figures as shooting, flying, or aiming above, downward, or sidewise in some particular direction in accordance with the shape, and they copy them on the paper by setting down sweeping, tearing lines. I observed a little girl who, while drawing a large circle with a perpendicular line running through its center, involuntarily puffed out her cheeks. And, whereas previously she had as a rule diminished the size of the angular figure in her copying, this time the circle was inordinately large and expanded. One might say that she had packed everything into its rotundity!"[39] It is above all just such tactual and kinaesthetic qualities as pointedness to which the child responds with dramatically exaggerated and drastically expressed forms. A great number of the youngest subjects studied by Miss Muchow appeared to perceive sharply pointed figures as things that pricked. On this account, in copying down these figures the children often used the pencil as a sort of needle, and punched and ground heavy dots into the paper, often greatly in excess of the number of points actually on the figure itself.

An understanding of the nature of physiognomic perception deepens our insight into another peculiar phenomenon characteristic of child behavior—personification. There is no doubt that personification in a primitive interpretation of the world is derived from the physiognomic mode of expression and perception. Physiognomic perception must be considered as the primary phenomenon, and personification as a more advanced and specific form of childlike interpretation. It may be that the child apprehends persons physiognomically more readily than other objects in his surrounding world. This fact might give rise to the erroneous impression that the child first discovers physiognomic characteristics in human individuals and

[39] Muchow, **458**, 44.

then transfers them to non-human objects. The more direct assumption, however, and one which is in greater accordance with the facts, is that the child, grasping the world as he does through his motor-affective activity, will understand the world in terms of physiognomics before personifying. The relatively early understanding of human expressions and gestures is possible because of the early development of physiognomic perception.

Bearing this in mind it is necessary that one be extremely cautious in taking personification for granted in all cases where the child sees expressive features in inanimate objects. Two examples may drive home this point: Elsa Köhler's three-year-old Anna, while at the jewelry shop, pointed at a curiously made clock with two upright pendulums, and said: "Look there! It's making 'please . . . please!' "[40] When Stern's son, aged five and a half years, was busy playing with numbers, they often seemed to come to life for him, no matter whether they were printed or drawn by himself. "The '5' looks as if he were angry, and the '6' is walking along slowly."[41]

This does not mean that the clock or the numbers are perceived as a person. These examples simply prove that in a primitive world anything may behave physiognomically. Any movement may be easily seen as expression, as gesture. Gesture is something much more general and earlier in the process of genetic development than any conception of a specifically human behavior. To illustrate this point once more we might recall common experiences decidedly physiognomic in nature which adults may have upon looking at certain advertisements or posters. The letter in the illustration, Fig. 13, for instance, has an arm that "beckons." This means not that the curve of the letter has become a human arm, but simply that it is possessed of the physiognomy of an

Fig. 13.—A Letter with Physiognomic Characteristics.

[40] Köhler, 429, 92.
[41] Stern, 513, Germ. ed., 310.

arm. It would become an arm, in the adult and realistic sense, only after a quite dispensable naturalistic translation.

The following example again shows clearly that expressive phenomena are much more primordial than genuine realistic personifications. A five-year-old girl is asked by her mother during a thunderstorm: "What does the thunder look like?" The child replies: "He has a head, but no eyes and no nose or mouth." "Then how does he look?" "Oh, he looks like this . . ." and the child makes an angry face and draws her brows together.

Even in such instances when the child does perceive or represent human qualities, the general expressive character-

FIG. 14.—Drawing by a Seven-year-old Boy.

istics often dominate the specifically anthropomorphic. The drawing made by the seven-year-old child which is shown in Fig. 14 is conclusive evidence that walking is not always seen and represented as a certain anthropomorphic position of the limbs, but is rather frequently apprehended as a movement physiognomic and dynamic in character. There are physiognomic lines, it will be seen, which represent two different kinds of legs—"walking legs" and "running legs."

Physiognomic perception facilitates personification, so called, but it certainly is not identical with it. How, then, does personification arise? It is my opinion that, in the narrow sense, it appears when the child's need to handle objects in his everyday life as if they were persons comes into being. For instance, he wants something from the inanimate object, and as a result of this desire it inevitably comes to personal life. The child can become angry with it, or sympathize with it, or punish it. Personification is engendered principally by a specific attitude which the child must adopt in dealing with the objects of his world in a "social" fashion.

A person is a being of whom something may be asked and received, or through whom suffering comes. As the child learns that this mental attitude toward other beings is sometimes reasonable and pragmatically effective, and at other times not, he accordingly learns to differentiate between persons and things. Some examples will lend support to this interpretation, in that they demonstrate that the child personifies under the compulsion of an affective relation to the object. That is, things become persons as soon as something is desired of them.

Scupin, telling of the behavior of his small son, says: "Even such things as little boxes, rings, balls, and tassels seem to be alive for him. Today he wanted to get out a little box that had fallen into a deep pot. Pleading and crying as he looked down into the pot, he said: 'Please, please!' Another time he was dreaming and talking to himself, and he said: 'The canal came right up the steps and brought me a lot of little things, little stones, and the canal said, "Here you are, Bubi, a lot of little stones you can throw into me!"'"[42] Again, Scupin says: "As the child wanted to drink, but found the milk too hot, he struck out at the steam, and asked us to make the mean, old smoke go away."[43] "Today while Bubi was running around he caught his stocking on a woven cane chair. He explained it this way: 'The chair grabbed hold of my stocking.'"[44]

The emotion of sympathy creates strongly personified modes of expression. Queyrat tells us that Miss Ingelow remembered that, at the age of two or thereabouts, she experienced the

[42] Scupin, **502**, vol. 1, 74, 208.
[43] *Ibid.*, 186.
[44] *Ibid.*, vol. 2, 8.

whole world, even dead stones, as human. She thought how dreadfully boring it must be for the stones to lie forever in the same place in the road, and so moved some of them about, convinced that they would be grateful for a change in scenery.[45]

The statistical data obtainable on any decrease in the frequency of physiognomic behavior with the advance from infancy to childhood and beyond are as yet decidedly limited. C. Bühler has compiled a table listing the frequency and kind of physiognomic perception in the development of the Scupins' child.

This table shows a decrease in physiognomic perception and personification first with respect to physical objects, and later (at the age of three to six) with respect to natural events.

FREQUENCY OF ANTHROPOMORPHIC REMARKS MADE BY SCUPIN'S SON REFERRING TO NON-HUMAN FORMS [46]

Age	1 : 6–2 : 6	2 : 6–3	3–3 : 6	3 : 6–4	4–4 : 6	4 : 6–5	5–6
Physical objects	62%	42%	37%	31%	14%	....	....
Plants, animals	31%	16%	26%	31%	57%	67%	80%
Natural events	7%	42%	37%	38%	29%	33%	20%
Total	100%	100%	100%	100%	100%	100%	100%

Similar results may be read from the data obtained and formulated by Frances Markey, following observations of the characteristic types of imaginative behavior among children of pre-school age (two to four years). Averages were compiled on the basis of results gained during fifteen-minute periods of observation. (There were ten observation periods for each child.)

In this table it is especially noteworthy that "make-believe" or "fantastic" situations (e.g., shining shoes, pretending to eat or sleep, etc.) occur only half as frequently at the two-year level as games involving the physiognomic "transformation of

[45] Queyrat, 490, 11.
[46] Bühler, 350, 195.

IMAGINATIVE BEHAVIOR OF PRE-SCHOOL CHILDREN [47]

Age in Months	Con-struction	Conventional Games	Fantastic Transformation of Material	Make-believe Situations	Games Involving Personification	Dramatic
24–29	1.2[a]	0.5	3.6	1.7	1.6	0.4
30–35	1.0	0.7	4.9	2.5	2.1	1.2
36–41	3.5	0.7	4.8	4.7	0.6	3.5
42–47	3.9	0.8	4.0	5.5	1.1	3.9
48–50	5.6	0.4	4.1	7.7	0.4	6.2

[a] Average number of the fifteen-minute periods during which the child was observed to engage in the activity noted.

material" (pretending that a block is a train, etc.). At the three to four-year level, however, there is a decisive decrease in physiognomic perception, indicated by the fact that "make-believe" situations are observed almost twice as frequently as games involving the physiognomic transformation of material.

So far as *primitive man* is concerned it is hardly necessary to labor the commonly known facts of animism and anthropomorphism in primitive civilizations. It is my belief that the anthropomorphic concept of nature is only a secondary phenomenon based on a deep-seated dynamic and physiognomic perception. Nature when known physiognomically is alive throughout, not because the soul, the vitality, is invested in the inanimate object, but rather because everything is understood to behave dynamically, quite apart from and prior to the differentiation between object and subject.[48] Of course, it depends entirely upon the cultural level and the specific structure of the level whether the original physiognomic experience of nature develops into a purely magical, or an animistic daemonic, or a religious-theistic view of the world.

Under *pathological conditions*, in primitivation of mental activity, dynamization of the world may again become intensified. Although, as we have already indicated, there is an essen-

[47] Markey, 449, 67.
[48] Werner, 141, Chap. 2.

tial difference between the pathologically primitive types and all others, similarities exist so far as the formal aspect of primitivity is concerned. In certain pathological types one often finds a decline in the polarity of object and subject, by virtue of which objects are no longer evaluated in their pure objectivity, but absolutely interpreted in terms of the affective drives of the person. It is the schizophrenic world in particular which acquires a decided physiognomic character. Schilder, Storch, and others present a great number of pathological situations in which the visionary character of the schizophrenic world and the physiognomic quality of its objectivity are vividly illustrated.[49] For example, a paranoic schizophrenic says, looking fearfully at some doors that swing back and forth: "The door is devouring me!"[50] Affect, it will be seen, has once more become a factor in the configuration of the surrounding world as in the case of a genuinely primitive mind. And this occurs not in the sense that the world of things becomes invested with an especially strong overtone of emotion, but rather in the sense that affect actually forms the world itself. The doors and their movements in the case just cited are experienced directly according to physiognomy. The peculiar blurring, the gradually increasing "queerness" (*Verseltsamung*) of everything, the sense of abnormal focus and orientation of which the schizophrenic patient so often complains at the onset of the disease are partly grounded in the changed appearance of objects as the physiognomic and dynamic stand forth boldly. The properties of things cease to be entirely objective, geometric, and "out there." Actually they acquire and express a much greater "depth" and inner significance. It is the very roots of expression which are bared by the pathological retrogression and the gradual replacement of a higher by a more primitive psychological level.

Primitivation may also occur as the result of certain brain injuries and a consequent deterioration of the higher centers. In some of these cases it has frequently been observed that the

[49] Schilder, **596, 597, 598**; Storch, **603**.
[50] Storch, **603**, 13.

dynamic properties of objects are those least affected. In one instance of a diffuse brain injury which Hanfmann and Rickers-Ovsiankina investigated (the report is yet to be published), the patient could frequently understand the meaning of a situation represented pictorially according to gesture or the expression of the face, but was quite helpless when such dynamic factors were lacking.

It is also true that in certain states of intoxication (as when drugged by hashish or mescalin) in which the object-subject relation is less sharply articulated, the physiognomic and dynamic qualities of things stand out clearly. In a very real sense it appears that the optical field submits to a process of dynamization, and things continually change in form, size, and position. The whole world becomes physiognomically alive. One subject observed by Beringer says: "The crown of foliage on the laburnum which stands before my window seemed to me to be the image of something showering down, and that of the chestnut tree to be something striving upwards."[51] Baudelaire remarks that at times during a state of intoxication from hashish the "personality vanishes, and that objectivity sung of by the pantheistic poets becomes evident and indeed, abnormally, in that the perception of things in the outer world makes one forget one's own existence, and soon draws one into it. The eye fixes itself on a tree, harmoniously swayed by the wind; in a few seconds that which in the brain of the poet would be only a completely natural simile becomes a fact. In the tree one's passions, longing, or melancholy come to life; its sighs and tremblings become one's own, and soon one is the tree itself."[52]

UNDIFFERENTIATED PHENOMENA WITHIN THE SPHERE OF EMOTION.

In the preceding paragraphs we have found that the perceptual processes of the primitive sphere are syncretic to a high

[51] Beringer, 543, 41.
[52] Baudelaire, 540, Germ. ed., 45.

degree. Percepts are deeply conditioned by emotional and motor behavior. Syncretism is again characteristic of primitive emotion; that is, primitive emotional experience is much more intimately connected with somatic-motor activity than is the case on higher levels.

P. and F. Sarasin report that the very primitive Veddas when angry throw themselves on the ground and thrash about with their legs just like children. The whole body is possessed by a passionate movement. It is the same with other very primitive tribes, such as the Minkopi of the Andaman Islands and the Negritos of the Philippine Islands.[53] Pechuël-Loesche writes of the Loangos: "When any sort of news, or any event, catches them unawares, there is no restraining them. They become like a colony of ants stirred up with a stick. The men run about, grab their weapons, kick out wildly with their legs, and jabber in heated, broken language. . . . Troops of armed men dash about, dance, and roar. Vexation or fear paralyzes them, in the literal sense. After hearing of some misfortune, or as a result of chagrin or fright, or having suffered some injustice, the younger people are often gripped by a sort of rigidity. They cannot shake off the adversity that has befallen them. Hour after hour they remain standing or sitting without moving a muscle, until at last relatives or friends, seeing that the seizure is continuing too long, attempt to cheer them, or to lead them away."[54]

There are a great many verbal expressions among primitive peoples which point to a basic unity of feeling and physical experience. The Arandas of Australia say of a woman whose tribal symbol has been stolen: "Her bowels long for it." The Melanesians express the feeling of shame by saying: "My forehead is biting me." The Solomon Islanders in the South Seas speak of the heart burning within the body. The Boloki, a tribe in the Congo, use the expression, "His heart is hung fast to his ribs," to indicate that a man has courage. This physical em-

[53] Sarasin, 278; Man, 236; Blumentritt, 164.
[54] Pechuël-Loesche, 257, 23.

phasis on affect appears, again, in the lyric forms of primitive peoples. In one of the songs of the Moanu, inhabitants of the Admiralty Islands, a woman complains: "My jawbone was tired," to express her deep grief and disconsolateness.[55]

Among children it is common to hear syncretic expressions in which one can discern the influence of an affective excitement closely bound up with actual physical sensation.

A mother told me of her four-year-old daughter who, upon being given fresh clothes, said: "Oh, Mother, I'm so glad! The beautiful clothes. I'm happy right in the bottom of my stomach!" When she was somewhat older, the same child remarked: "Oh, you're so wide when you're happy!"

Little Hilde Stern, at the early age of 1:8 yrs., spoke of her own yawning and of that of others as *miede* (tired). At 1:9 yrs. she used the word spontaneously when she became tired from running about at play. At 1:10 yrs. she used the same term for describing other sensations which were unpleasant to her: being washed with cold water, for instance, or becoming bored with her games.[56] Here we recognize an excellent illustration of how an emotional expression is at first rooted in a limited physical event, the act of yawning. Then, later on, any feeling of apathy or antipathy represents a similar undifferentiated psychophysical state, and on this basis it becomes possible to transpose the word *miede* so that it can apply to many situations having the general characteristic of disinclination or unpleasantness.

At the age of 2:2 yrs. Lindner's son, when asked if his mother were good, snapped angrily: "No! she's sour!"[57] This is a clear example of the way in which a quality of sensation can be used to express emotional characteristics.

There is still another aspect of the undifferentiated character of primitive emotionality that will bear a brief discussion. The single emotional forms do not possess that distinctness

[55] Werner, 141, 11.
[56] Stern, 511, 36.
[57] In German, "sour" generally designates only a quality of taste.

and unequivocality typical of them in higher mental life. There seem to be primitive stages of emotionality in which certain states of affect such as hunger and love, or sadness and hate, which are sharply distinguished on higher levels, are but little differentiated. This is at least suggested by certain expressions from many parts of the primitive world, such expressions, for example, as those in which sexual gratification is represented by eating or biting. An Hawaiian woman sings: "I was torn apart by the great shark."[58] A song of the South Seas, which tells of a mother who gives up her daughter to prostitution, begins with the words: "Go, go, my daughter, and be eaten up."[59] A Klamath Indian woman exclaims: "The evil dog grabbed me, and was going to bite me."[60]

A consideration of the child's emotional experience results in the same conclusions. At the beginning of childhood, feeling is undifferentiated and linked with a whole, shifting affective situation. Gradually these ambiguous emotions develop and become marked by a relative purity and specificity. In his *Kindersprache* Stern says of the expression of unpleasantness: "Originally the expressions of discomfort are quite undifferentiated. Our child cried out a monotonous 'hey-ey-ey. . . .' This cry soon became differentiated, so that after a few weeks it was quite possible to distinguish the sound meaning hunger from the one meaning wet diapers."[61] I might draw another example of the process of differentiation from my own personal experience. At the age of two years a boy of my acquaintance designated everything pretty or pleasant by the expression "mimi," and he used this word especially to indicate that his food tasted good to him. Later, however, he narrowed the use of the term to refer only to what was pretty. When he was three years old, he was sitting on the floor walled round by a picture-book set on edge; he clapped his hands, and shouted

[58] Emerson, **187**, 220.
[59] Rienzi, **269**, vol. 1, 394.
[60] Gatschet, **194**, 184.
[61] Stern, **511**, 152.

"Mimi!" But at this time he used the ordinary word "good, good" when his food tasted pleasant.

Katherine Bridges, on the basis of her careful observation of the child of pre-school age, has set up the accompanying table for the development of emotions. In its principle and in the trends revealed, this table is in agreement with our own point of view. Emotions develop out of a general, undifferentiated affect which she calls "excitement." All parts of the autonomic system are probably involved in this generalized psychophysical state of "excitement." It is difficult to say, for instance, whether a very young baby is frightened, angry, or pleasantly excited.[62]

The splitting-off process in undifferentiated emotions which results in specific emotions is, however, still incomplete at the age when the child enters the elementary grades. The child's emotional values are often very confused with respect to one another: aesthetic, ethical, and utilitarian emotions are often interwoven into a close unity. Kroh remarks that "it is not unseldom that the younger child identifies the ethical with the aesthetic. 'Ugly' and 'unjust,' 'beautiful' and 'good' become identical concepts. This interpretation causes injustice to appear as a sort of dirtiness to children."[63]

LACK OF DIFFERENTIATION IN PRIMORDIAL PERCEPTION; SYNAESTHESIA AND THE PRIMORDIAL UNITY OF THE SENSES.

The sphere of the senses proper—of seeing, tasting, smelling, etc.—appears to exhibit a much closer intersensory relationship at the more primitive levels. In normal psychology we use the term "synaesthesia" to mean that one specific stimulus may arouse not only the specifically corresponding sensation, but a second sensation united with the first. A common instance is color-tone synaesthesia, as when the perceiving individual sees color while listening to tone. There is much evidence that synaesthesia plays a greater rôle among *primitive* and *archaic* peoples than it does at our own cultural level. In the cos-

[62] Bridges, 342.
[63] Kroh, 431, 248.

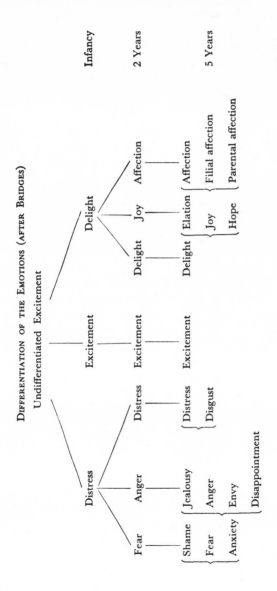

DIFFERENTIATION OF THE EMOTIONS (AFTER BRIDGES)

Infancy — Undifferentiated Excitement

2 Years

5 Years

mologies of the ancient peoples of Egypt, Babylonia, Mexico, China, etc., the universe is represented as a system of ideas divided into groups. In old China, for example, the cosmos is divided into the groups listed below, each one of which connects certain qualities of color, taste, and touch.[64] The underlying experience uniting these basic elements into a system is undoubtedly synaesthetic in nature.

White	Red	Black	Yellow	Green
Tiger	Bird	Warrior	Earth-master	Dragon
Dryness	Warmth	Cold	Dampness	Wind
Sharp	Bitter	Salty	Sweet	Sour

Each direction of the compass is given a particular color by the relatively primitive Zuñi Indians. Yellow belongs to the south, red to the east, white to the north, and black to the west.[65] A similar color system existed in old Mexico. Because of the universality of these correlations there is little doubt that we are dealing with a fundamental psychological phenomenon. The basis for this synaesthesia is an undifferentiated perceptual experience which permits the linking together of the separate realms of sense that is lacking or in abeyance in the highly differentiated and objectified forms of experience.

There are many indications that, generally speaking, this syncretic unity of the senses is characteristic of the *child* of our own culture. For example, the localization of smell and taste does not seem to be very clearly established in the infant. Preyer remarks that his little boy always opened his mouth when he smelled, and says that the unitary experience of smelling-tasting had not yet been differentiated into smell and taste.[66]

Instances of synaesthesia can be found in almost any carefully written diary of observations on child behavior. A few examples will suffice to illustrate this point.

[64] De Groot, 198, vol. 1, 317.
[65] Cushing, 179, 442.
[66] Preyer, 488, 236.

When Scupin's three-year-old son smelled a pelargonia leaf, he said: "The leaf smells green!" Smelling a purple pelargonia, he said: "That smells red." And as for lilac, "That smells awfully nice and yellow."[67]

Miss Stelzner, speaking reminiscently, says that synaesthesia was so dominant in her sensory experience from her third to her sixth years that she had to be corrected constantly in the use of verbal expressions. She spoke of the "light and dark-red whistling," the "gold and silver striking of the hour," etc.[68]

I do not believe that many of the so-called metaphors so common to children—that is, those in which a word denoting the one sensation is used to describe an unrelated sensation—are actual metaphors springing from any inadequacy of exact verbal expression. It is quite reasonable to assume that they are often rooted in an actual undifferentiated experience of sensation. We might note another instance recorded by Scupin. At the time of this observation his son was six years of age. "Today his mother lay on the sofa with her eyes closed. The boy began to tell her something, but broke off impatiently. 'Now,' he said, 'open up your eyes, or you won't hear what I'm saying.'" Scupin reports a further example: "Look, now! I've opened my eyes wide, and I've heard everything."[69]

Miss Shinn's niece also had synaesthetic experiences. This child, at the age of 1:8 yrs., wanted to see a tone and looked around the room for it. She did not realize that a tone is something to be heard only; she apparently believed it something to be seen with the eyes.[70]

Some surveys and experiments have been made that deal with a particular form of synaesthesia, one commonly known as "chromaesthesia." Chromaesthesia refers to color-hearing and to the synaesthetic experience of color in perceptions ordinarily devoid of it, as in the experience of numbers, letters, and so on.

[67] Scupin, **502**, vol. 1, 198; vol. 2, 3.
[68] Argelander, 331, 150.
[69] Scupin, **502**, vol. 2, 134, 166.
[70] Shinn, **505**, 132.

According to the majority of investigators this special field of sensory experience is quite frequent in children.

Révész, reviewing the earlier literature on synaesthesia, finds "color-hearing to be very common among children. Children often associate tones, words, noises, etc., with color of a certain value." He quotes Stanley Hall, who estimated that approximately 40 per cent of the pupils of a small school described the tones of various instruments in terms of color. Lemaître speaks of this as a widespread occurrence. Bleuler and Schumann discovered that many of their experimental subjects had been aware of their photism since early youth. Some could even tell fairly accurately just when they first noted it, most of them judging this to be somewhere between the ages of six and eight years. A more methodical investigation carried out by Révész in the Montessori School in Amsterdam tends to corroborate Hall's statement. Approximately half of the twenty children in the school definitely showed signs of chromatism. Révész was astonished to find that all the children readily answered the questions about color-numbers presented to them, regardless of whether in reality they were particularly gifted with the capacity for synoptic sensory experience.[71]

The question as to whether this chromatism tends to diminish in the course of individual development has never been satisfactorily answered. We do know, at least, that tonal color, in its common form is much more frequently ascribed to children than to adults. Bleuler and Lehmann found only 12.7 per cent of 596 adults to be gifted with chromatism; Calkins in a similar investigation set the ratio at 15.7 per cent. Chromatism as found in children and adults is in the proportion 50/14.2 according to these reports.[72] Argelander in her survey points out that photism is often known reminiscently by the adult subject; some adults declare that they noticed their photism during their youth but that it slipped out of their

[71] Révész, 493.
[72] *Ibid.*

mind. Révész compared the behavior of younger children with that of a group of school children who were all eleven years of age, and also with that of another group of ten children seventeen years old, in order to determine the relative frequency of chromatic experience; he came to the conclusion that there is a distinct regression of the faculty from the eleventh year onward. With eleven-year-olds the ratio of those having the gift of perceiving color-tone to those not so gifted ranges from 25-30 per cent.

Zietz's preliminary analyses on this subject which he carried out in the Hamburg Laboratory also indicate a more frequent occurrence of chromatism in childhood and, correspondingly, a regression with increase in age.

To all appearances the syncretic character of sensory experience as expressed in synaesthesia is frequently found among *psychotics*, especially in the *schizophrenic* types. Schizophrenics sometimes have peculiar systems of ideas, which to some extent remind one of similar constructions among primitive peoples, and which cannot be explained except in terms of synaesthesia. For example, one such patient set up the following "color-alphabet":[73]

1 a	— red — England	— beets
2 b	— bronze color	— metal
3 c	— red	— cochineal
4 d	— sunlight yellow	— color of street-dust
5 e	— orange color	— Germany
'		
'		
14 o	— day-white	— Austria-Hungary
'		
'		
17 r	— rose-red	— France

Etc.

Another patient had a similar system of color-number-letter which permitted interchanges. A statement made by one of

[73] Prinzhorn, **594,** 171.

Schilder's patients is especially revealing: "When I say red, that means a concept which can be expressed in color, music, feeling, thinking, and in nature. And when this idea is expressed in any one way, the other forms of the idea are felt to be there, too. Hence, man has not five senses, but only one."[74]

In view of such facts it must be assumed that synaesthesia as a primordial form of sensory experience may reappear as a consequence of a pathologically conditioned primitivation. An abnormal "primitivity" can also be experimentally induced. A state of intoxication caused by the taking of drugs represents an artificially created mental state analogous to psychotic primitivity. Mescalin, for example, one of the drugs used by Mexican Indians to engender religious ecstasy, has been used with normal subjects. In the experimental "psychoses" studied by Beringer and others there appears a primitivation of sensory function. The objective, rational world submits to a partial retrogression. The divisions within the general field of sense lose their quality of delimitation and tend to melt together indiscriminately. A subject under the influence of mescalin experiences color simultaneously with tone. High tones evoke vivid, garish colors, and deep tones engender duller colors. If there is a steady knocking on the wall, let us say, the subject will see optical images dancing before his eyes in a rhythm that synchronizes with the measured beat of the knocking. One subject described his sensations in this manner: "I think that I hear noises and see faces, and yet everything is one and the same. I cannot tell whether I am seeing or hearing. I feel, taste, and smell the sound. It's all one. I, myself, am the tone."[75]

If we have demonstrated that synaesthesia is a phenomenon common to all types of primitivity, there still remains the task of clarifying the deeper significance of this experience.

Synaesthesia must not be understood as a bizarre and merely aberrant way of perceiving. It is indissolubly bound up with

[74] Schilder, 597, 26.
[75] Beringer, 543. Cf. also, Baudelaire,. 540; Joël and Fraenkel, 580; Fraenkel and Joël 553, Klüver, 582, 583.

the very development of the faculty of perception. It was originally accepted as true by the psychology of elements that in certain isolated cases there was a close *associative* relation between tonal and color sensations. It can be shown, however, that often the synaesthetic person does not by any means experience a mere conjunction of color and tone. If a synaesthetic individual who asserts that a certain vowel is blue for him is asked where he sees this blueness, he does not say that he sees it near the vowel, hovering about it in some fashion or other, but that he sees the vowel itself as blue. And tone, for such a person, is just as much blue as it is characterized by a certain intensity or pitch. Synaesthesia gives much evidence that there are cases in which the otherwise specific qualities of perception are not sharply separated according to their modality, but on the contrary actually become intersensory in value. If it could be proved that this is not merely an exception to the rule and that such a sensory relation is potentially present in any mentality, we should have established firmly the primitive organic unity of the senses.

There happen to be a considerable number of experiments which apparently demonstrate that there exists latently an inner relationship binding together the seemingly discrete realms of sensation.

Zietz, Schiller, and I carried out experiments on normal subjects, and Goldstein and Börnstein on abnormal, which prove beyond any doubt that there is a reciprocal influence within the different fields of sense.[76] Three conditions[77] are necessary in order to demonstrate this interaction: (1) Results are initially dependent on the type of personality, the mental

[76] Werner, 736, 737, 740; Zietz and Werner, 750; Zietz, 751; Schiller, 729, 730; Goldstein and Rosenthal, 567; Goldstein, 562, Germ. ed., 167; Börnstein, 710.

[77] The success of the experiments will depend largely on the strict observance of these conditions. After the successful experiments carried out in the laboratories at Hamburg, Berlin, Leipzig, Frankfurt, Milan, etc., no longer is it an experimental problem of whether such an intersensory relationship exists; the problem concerns the conditions under which this phenomenon is demonstrable.

cast of the subject. Some persons are much more highly susceptible to the experimental inducement of such phenomena as chromatism than are others.[78] (2) The influential stimuli must be offered in such a way that the tones or colors are not so much objective and purely "factual" as subjectively framed. This will be explained later in greater detail. (3) The perceptions which it is the investigator's intention to influence should not be of the usual stable type. Rather, they should be markedly unstable phenomena, such as after-images, briefly exposed tones or colors, stroboscopically presented movements, or threshold sensations.

One of my students, Zietz, investigated for instance the influence of tone upon colors exposed for a 1/100th of a second.[79] He formulated his results in the accompanying table, in which are represented the changes in various colors under the influence of high and low tones.

INFLUENCE OF TONE ON COLOR

	Low Pitch	High Pitch
Red changes to	Dark red, bluish red	Yellowish red, orange
Orange changes to	Red, even bluish red	Yellow
Yellow changes to	Brown, reddish yellow, sometimes bluish red	Light yellow
Green changes to	Bluish green, blue	Light green, yellowish green, yellow
Blue changes to	Violet, dark blue	Clear, light blue, greenish blue

After-images furnish another group of labile optical phenomena. The previously mentioned conditions always being taken into consideration, it can be shown that tones may influence the perception of the after-image. Tonal vibrations may cause a vibrating movement in the optical after-image; high pitches sharpen the contours of the after-image, whereas low pitches blur them, and so on. In another set of experiments

---

[78] In our own experiments 20 per cent of the subjects did not yield to intermodal influence. Börnstein (710) found that with about 30 per cent of his subjects it was not possible to influence entoptical phenomena through other sensory phenomena.

[79] Zietz. 751.

a gradual change in pitch induced by a gradual change in brightness was observed, that is, the lowering of brightness conditioned a lowering of pitch. The optical stimulus in this case was a white surface offering a simple homogeneous image covering the whole optical field. If the brightness of the light in the field was very slowly varied and the single tone simultaneously presented was likewise varied, but in a contrary direction, despite this contrariety of direction the tone appeared to go up and down in pitch in direct correspondence with the change in the brightness of the light.[80]

We may consider another type of experiment dealing with flickering, or rhythmic, phenomena. As we all know, if two points lying in different parts of the optical field are presented in succession separated by a brief interval, a stroboscopic (kinematographic) movement of only one point is seen. If the two images are different in form—such as a point and an arrow (Fig. 15)—it will be discovered that most observers are

Fig. 15.—Patterns Used in an Experiment on Apparent Movement.

unable to see an apparent movement in the sense of a transition from point to arrow, or vice versa. However, if one keeps time with a rhythmic tapping that synchronizes with the change of image, often a sudden movement arises in the optical field. This shows, of course, that the acoustic phenomenon of tapping can influence the optical phenomenon of apparent movement.[81] Similarly, the rate of flickering can be demonstrated to increase or decrease according to the increase or decrease in the rate of beats produced simultaneously as acoustic stimuli.[82]

Up to this point we have shown that the phenomena susceptible to influence to some extent must be of a labile, flexible nature—after-images, briefly exposed colors, etc. There still

[80] Schiller, 729.
[81] Zietz and Werner, 750.
[82] Schiller, 730. See the recent study by Gilbert, 714.

remains the problem of describing the essential characteristics of these phenomena which have the power of influencing others. If a change is to be induced in a color image by means of tone, it will be found that the desired effect will certainly not appear if the tone is heard sharply and clearly in one definite place in the situation surrounding the subject. In order for the tone to be effective, it must be devoid of an objective character. It must have a "subjective" character. To illustrate, if a series of tones is played on a piano, several stages of awareness can be shown to exist, stages which differ as to the degree of subjectivity in the hearing of the tone. Commonly the listener perceives the tone as altogether outside himself, as coming from a specifically defined source of sound, as bound up with some particular object outside himself (e.g., a musical instrument). We may call such a tone an "instrument tone." In distinction to this, there is another type of tonal experience. Here the tone is no longer perceived as residing primarily in the object or instrument, but as filling the space around it, as occupying the whole room. This may be called a "spatial tone." Instrument tone and spatial tone both possess an objective character. And yet there is still another way of experiencing tone. In this last case the tone may be experienced as actually vibrating within the hearer. The listener himself actually becomes an instrument that resounds. One subject, describing this tonal experience, says: "I am filled with tone, as if I were a bell that had been struck."

Since an adequately descriptive term is lacking for this phenomenon, we may provisionally coin the phrase "vital sensation." Vital sensations are devoid of the objectivity which characterizes the instrument tone; they are psychophysically undifferentiated and involve pervasive bodily reactions to the stimuli. Such vital sensations, whether occasioned by optical, acoustic, or tactual stimuli, may or may not coexist with objectively experienced sensations.

The better to understand why intersensory influence is possible only when the conditioning phenomenon has the

character of a "vital sensation," we must examine this psychophysical experience more closely. Vital sensations occasioned
by stimuli directed to the different senses are clearly much
more closely related to each other than are the objective perceptions evoked by these stimuli. They are within the one
subjective body, as it were. There are, indeed, cases in which
the vital sensation of color or tone pervades the body so
searchingly that there is no longer any optical or tonal "matter" and the subject is at a loss to tell the modality of the
sensation. We are justified in designating this level of experience as a synaesthetic level. It is a "sensorium commune," a
generalized sensorium, an undifferentiated sense, the primitive basis for the development of the specific phenomena of
the several fields of sense.[83]

R. B. Cattell, a student of Spearman's, recently published results independently confirming our own experiments in the
Hamburg Laboratory through which we established the three
levels of sensory experience—objective, spatial, and vital.[84]
This investigator distinguishes among different degrees of subjectivity in perceptual phenomena according to a gradual loss
of localization and an increased fusion of sensation and feeling.
A complete subjectivity is characterized by the following data:
The sensation completely fills the consciousness, and sensation and self can no longer be separated. Sensation loses the
specificity which we usually ascribe to it; there is a loss of
modality. In brief, this level of highly increased subjectivity
has been demonstrated to be synaesthetic, as in our own experiments.

The stimulation of the body's psychophysical activity
through sensory channels (which obviously is the case in
vital sensations) becomes particularly clear when the centers
controlling and maintaining the physical equilibrium against
external influence are disturbed. In certain cases of a disturbance in the cerebellum, K. Goldstein and his students have ob-

[83] Werner, 736.
[84] Cattell, 712.

served that colors and tones have a decided effect on the posture of the body. A patient suffering from an injury to the cerebellum, when asked to keep his arms straight forward away from his body, quite involuntarily spread them wider on seeing red or yellow, and brought them together on seeing green or blue. These tonus reactions seem to suggest that the common phrase, "warm" or "cold" colors, is actually based on physical reactions.[85]

If one were inclined to speculate on the physical origin of the "vital" intersensory activity in the nervous system, he might possibly concentrate on such subcortical centers as the mid-brain and the thalamic region. These zones, on the one hand, are the focal centers of primitive sensory impulses (Parsons), and on the other are also intermediary agents in the centering of those impulses originating in the muscles, tendons, and joints. Sherrington, Magnus, and others have proved that the mid-brain contains those groups of subordinating centers connected with the acquisition and maintenance of posture.

The same problem of a differentiation of specific qualities from syncretic functions confronts us in the development within *each field of sense*. How account for the fact that the ability to discriminate among colors of different value develops with age? According to certain authors there is still a great deal of confusion in even the six-year-old child's perception of color. Preyer, for example, tells us that his three-year-old son confused blue and violet. And Garbini says that five-year-old children almost always mistake violet for blue. According to Engelsperger and Ziegler, orange is often perceived as red, and red as orange, by beginners in school and *nuances* of yellow or of blue cannot be separated. Blue and violet, violet and purple, rose and red are commonly indistinguishable.[86]

According to Peters, between the ages of six and fourteen years the increase in discriminative sensitivity with respect to

[85] Goldstein and Rosenthal, 567.
[86] Peters, 476, 151; Koffka, 427, Germ. ed., 192 ff.

brightness is 104 per cent, and the increase for chromatic sensation is 89 per cent. Other experiments raise this latter figure to 193 per cent.[87]

It is not unusual to find a confusion in the color sensations of primitive peoples, if the colors are not apprehended as the specific properties of some known objects (presented as colored paper, skeins, etc.). Rivers found that among the inhabitants of the Torres Straits rose was commonly mistaken for red, green for blue, and violet for blue.[88]

On the other hand, contrary to the above-mentioned results, there have been experiments which seem to demonstrate a rather early appearance of discriminatory ability, even during infancy. C. W. Valentine kept a record of the length of time that a three-months-old child looked at each of two colored skeins, both of which were held before his eyes at the same time for two-minute periods.[89] The colors chosen were black, white, red, yellow, green, blue, pink, violet, and brown. Various combinations were used. A compilation of the total time (in seconds) during which the child devoted his attention to one color in preference to any of the others presented in combination with it, resulted in the accompanying table.

	Time of Preference	Non-preference	Score in Per Cent
Yellow	525	137	79.3
White	680	246	73.4
Pink	476	186	72.2
Red	242	283	45.3
Brown	151	275	37.8
Black	149	263	35.7
Green	165	421	28.2
Blue	122	300	28.9
Violet	48	447	9.7

Whatever the shortcomings of this experiment, so far as the total behavior of the very young child is concerned there does seem to be some indication of a much earlier develop-

---

[87] Peters, 477.
[88] Reports, 268, vol. 1.
[89] Valentine, 523. A similar technique has been used by Staples, 508.

ment of the faculty of discrimination than the experiments of Garbini and others would lead one to expect. It is possible to reconcile these conflicting views if one bears in mind that the activity in terms of which Garbini observed differentiation and the corresponding activity in Valentine's experiments are totally variant in nature. It is quite probable that at a very early age a child may learn to discriminate among colors in so far as his perceptions are linked with physical and emotional reactions, and yet much later in the course of development fail completely when he is forced to order color on a purely perceptual basis. This interpretation can also be applied to the earlier experiments of Raehlmann and Krasnogorski on color discrimination in infants. These investigators trained infants to react to differently colored milk bottles, and found that children from six months on can learn to discriminate among all the primary colors.[90] If our argument is sound it follows that the early development of the color sense consists to a great extent of a gradually increasing domination of objective perceptual factors over a fused, syncretic activity in which colors are experienced as responses of the body in its totality.

If colors in their primary form are experienced as motor-affective reactions, it is to be expected that the child's original way of naming colors may not always coincide with that of the adult. Actually it often happens that the verbal response to color is at first an activity carried out on the basis of emotional reaction. Some children begin by grouping colors verbally into two kinds: vivid colors like red, and achromatic colors (Shinn, Stern, *et al.*). Stumpf's son discriminates verbally between colors which he calls *weich* (soft) and those he calls *ă* (black, expression of disgust).

Similarly, bodily reactions of an affective nature are at the bottom of discriminatory activity in other sensory fields. The sensations of extreme coldness and of great heat, because of the very similar quality of unpleasantness they occasion, may

[90] Peiper, 472, 19.

be expressed by the same word according to the child's point of view. No fewer than seven diaries devoted to observations on child behavior say that at the beginning of childhood the same word is used to indicate both hot and cold.[91]

To sum up the preceding paragraphs, it seems that the genetic problem of color discrimination can be answered satisfactorily only if the notion of discrimination as a unitary function is repudiated. Discrimination is rather an activity implying quite different functions or function patterns, as we move from one genetic level to another. It is misguided, therefore, to ask bluntly about the development of color discrimination without taking many qualifying factors into account. Color discrimination must be discussed in terms of the functions involved. We may find, for example, that color discrimination of the sensorimotor-affective type may, at a certain age level, be very highly developed, whereas a higher type—such as that operative in a color-matching situation—may be still comparatively unadvanced.

In the genesis of so-called sensory discrimination, at least three genetically distinct processes ("analogous processes") must be taken into consideration: discrimination on the motor-sensori-affective level, on the perceptual level, and on the conceptual level. Discrimination on the motor-sensori-affective level having been discussed, a few remarks on sensory discrimination at the level of perception proper will be in order. (For the problem of discrimination on the conceptual plane, cf. the paragraphs on primitive abstraction.) Let us take tonal discrimination as an example. According to Meissner's investigations, the ability to discriminate semitones (F-F sharp) amounted to 37.7 per cent for eight-year-olds, 44.3 per cent for nine-year-olds, 61 per cent for ten-year-olds, 73.3 per cent for eleven-year-olds, 75.7 per cent for twelve-year-olds, 81 per cent for thirteen-year-olds, 84.4 per cent for fourteen-year-olds, and so on.[92] If we now assume that the increasing sharpness

[91] Stern, 511, 240.
[92] Meissner, 451.

of judgment is based on an increasingly sharp impression of the perceptual relation of the two tones, on an ever-clearer impression of the specificity of each tone, the next question that arises is, how does this growing precision in tonal quality come about? So far as this problem of the differentiation of perceptual qualities is concerned, the "genetic experimental method" with adult subjects may be utilized to distinct advantage. Can such perceptual development be imitated under laboratory conditions?

We have carried out experiments on adult subjects in our Hamburg Laboratory which clearly revealed the nature of this developmental process leading from a lesser to a greater clarity of tonal discrimination. If, for example, two tones separated by only a few vibrations are presented in succession, at first neither of the tones is definitely distinguishable. Many of our experimental subjects say that both tones are completely ambiguous in their quality. Gradually, often only after repeated hearings, the "contour" of each tone becomes clearly defined and achieves a specific, fixed quality. The tones at first appear approximately on the same uncertain level, but after a time become perceptually separate. It is as if each tone were attempting to establish its self-subsistence and independence with respect to the other. The tonal interval actually *stretches out*, and the gap between the two tones widens. It may be safely proposed that in the ontogenetic development of tonal discrimination a process of subjective enlargement of the tonal distance must occur which is similar to that observed in our laboratory experiments.[93]

We have extended these experiments on tonal development to include tones in a musical system which, in its physical relationships, differs from our own. The experimentally conceived musical system was a series of tones separated by approximately equal intervals (tempered scale); the minimal step was about a sixth of the half-tone of our normal scale. As one gradually accommodates himself to the experience of a tonal

[93] Werner, 735.

system constructed out of miniature steps, clearly defined tones, musical intervals, and melodies finally appear from the blurred tonal ground, as if by a process of crystallization.[94] By means of this experiment on "micro-melodies" and musical "micro-scales" it becomes possible to understand the processes of rationalization which have taken place in the historical development of musical systems. With the experimental knowledge about development to guide us, we may also infer a similarity in the child's experience as he grows into our mature musical system.

[94] Werner, 734.

Chapter III

DIFFUSE FORMS OF SENSORI-MOTOR AND PERCEPTUAL ORGANIZATION

DIFFUSE ORGANIZATION IN LOWER ORGANISMS.

Up to this point we have considered mainly one characteristic of primitive organization: the fact that functions which, on higher levels, are discrete, are on the lower levels merged in one relatively undifferentiated and syncretic activity. Another primary quality of primitive organization is its relative diffuseness; that is, mental phenomena are less clearly articulated and more under the domination of qualities-of-the-whole.

The behavior of lower organisms furnishes excellent examples of this diffuse structure in the concrete field. H. Volkelt observed the habits of the domestic spider (*Tegeneria domestica*). This spider weaves a web which centrally becomes a crater-like structure narrowing into a funnel. In this tube the spider awaits her prey. Whenever a fly is caught in the outer meshes of the web, the spider rushes forth immediately, inserts her fangs in the victim, and paralyzes him. But if the smallest fly comes into the nest proper of the labyrinth, or if it is encountered anywhere except in the entanglement of the net, the spider will not touch it and may even flee from it.[1]

The least we can say regarding such behavior is that the organization of the concrete field must be quite different from that known by higher animals and man. A distinct object— i.e., "fly"—does not appear to exist in the world of the spider. The fly is not a detached, self-subsistent thing standing out there by itself in the situation. On the contrary, it is an intrinsic

[1] Volkelt, **699.**

part of the whole situation; it is, so to speak, a focal spot in the whole configuration of the sensory field.

Although (as Baltzer points out in his criticism of Volkelt's work) there are great differences in the behavior of various individuals of the same species, this author himself furnishes some fine examples demonstrating the importance of the global situation in the spider's response to the fly as an edible object. He says:

"Living house-flies were entangled in human hairs and brought into the web. Then, as the spider quickly rushed out to secure its prey, the free end of the hair was fastened to something. The spider made surprisingly vigorous attempts to transport its booty, now ripped loose from the web, into the nest. This, of course, was impossible since the prey was anchored to the hair. Immediately the spider tried to bite through the hair with its pincers, but almost always this effort was also in vain. The duration of these activities lasted from a few seconds to 1½ hours, a variation for the most part applying to different spiders, but occasionally to the same individual. Only after many fruitless trials did the spider adjust itself to the unusual situation, and begin to suck nourishment from the fly directly on the spot. These experiments contradict Rabaud's recently published opinion that the spider will eat its prey indiscriminately either at the place where it is caught, or in the nest at the center."[2]

The objects of the spider's world are therefore present not as delimited objects, but as dominant factors in a situation from which they ultimately draw their significance.

We see clearly the diffuse organization of the concrete, sensori-motor field of action when we consider the fact that the spider's reaction is rigidly dependent on stimuli which, in themselves, are resultants of the whole constellation.

It is likely that such "dominant signals," the most active properties of the situation, are much less optical than vibratory in character. According to Grünbaum, this dominance of certain stimuli is expressed "not only in circumstances in which the reaction to the stimulus can prove biologically advan-

[2] Baltzer, 615.

tageous, but also in such cases as when the reaction is meaningless and devoid of biological import. In this respect the following experiment is characteristic. The spider sits in the funnel and is occupied with an entangled fly. A vibrating wire (48 cycles) is put through the wall of the nest and through the mesh of the web, and then brought into contact with the abdomen of the spider in the region of the spinning wart. As soon as the wire thread touches the body of the spider, she drops her prey, dashes forth from the nest, and fastens onto the wire in the mesh of the web, shrouding it industriously with her spinnerets. Although the wire cannot possibly serve as food, the spider does not cease her attack so long as the wire continues to vibrate."[3]

In a second experiment the white mass within the abdomen of a fly was introduced into the web. The spider, which had been lurking in her nest, was attracted to the periphery of the web by a vibrating fork. In order to reach the tuning fork she was obliged to pass by the lump of white food. On reaching the piece of fly meat, and even after touching the highly edible food, she did not hesitate, but hastened feverishly to the source of vibration. But if the tuning fork was silenced and the spider began to make her way back to the nest, the lump of food now acted immediately as a stimulus. The spider came to a full stop and proceeded to devour the food. This experiment shows that a vibratory stimulus is dominant in the sense that all biological responses to other stimuli are negated in its presence.

One of Baltzer's experiments again demonstrates vibratory dominance. Three living flies impaled on needles were placed before a cross-spider. Despite the violent movements of the flies as they struggled to release themselves from the needles on which they were stuck fast, and although the flies were apparently well within the range of the spider's visual field, the spider remained motionless anywhere from fifteen to twenty minutes. But if the flies were moved close enough to the spider

[3] Grünbaum, **648.**

so that they touched one of her legs, they were seized upon immediately, often at the first contact, and almost without exception after repeated contacts.

On the basis of these interesting phenomena we can thoroughly understand the diffuse embedding of the spider's "things" in the whole functional situation. For the more a thing is subject to certain dominant signal characteristics, and the less it is constructed in terms of a differentiated manifold of clearly ordered properties, the sooner may this broad dominant quality be related to the whole situation—the sooner, in short, may it become totally representative of it. The quality of vibration through which the spider "recognizes" its prey is expressed in the vibration of the spider's web. Web and fly constitute a vibratory-optical field in which thing and its surrounding field are inseparably bound together.

The investigations of M. Hertz dealing with the bee's sense of form prove that any isolated self-subsistence in things and their properties is most likely absent from the world of insects. Bees distinguish forms on the basis of qualities-of-the-whole effective only in a biologically relevant situation. "Isolated figures with absolute characteristics do not seem to be present in the perceptual experience of the bee."[4]

The dominance of the functional situation over things irrevocably embedded within it, and the configuration of these things by means of dominant signal-qualities, also appear to hold true in the experience of many vertebrates. Buytendijk and Hage have shown that the optical perceptual activity of the dog in a new learning situation is first directed toward the apprehension of whole-qualities, and that only after this preliminary act of cognition do distinct parts of the whole acquire a definite meaning.[5] Buytendijk and Fischel have established the fact that the optical training field as seen by the rat is not constructed of isolated, discrete component parts,

[4] Hertz, **655**, 108.
[5] Buytendijk and Hage, **626**.

but presents an unbroken figural situation. They conclude that activities within this field are guided by qualities-of-the-whole which comprehend several spatial factors in an inseparable unity.[6]

INFLEXIBILITY (RIGIDITY) AND INCONSTANCY IN LOWER OR-GANIZATION.

A consequence of the slightly articulated diffuse organization is the inflexibility of the stimulus pattern calculated to evoke a specific response. Objects on a more highly developed plane can be modified considerably without losing their essential character. As a matter of fact, we can speak intelligibly of an "object" in a true sense only if it preserves its essential character despite variations introduced into the situation surrounding it. A necessary prerequisite for the constant object is an articulation of the concrete field to the end that constant elements making up the object will be experienced in sharp contradistinction to the variable elements. The lower the species, the more dominant is the factor of inflexibility of behavior dependent on a rigid, diffuse organization of the perceptual field. A frog conditioned to react to a certain motion which takes place before its eyes as a dominant stimulus might well starve to death if the fly before it remains motionless.[7] Porter analyzed the gradual mastery of the intricacies of a training box by sparrows. Two horizontal trip-strings were used, one placed slightly above the other. One bird mastered the problem by lighting on the string intended to trip open the box. But if the strings were moved farther apart the bird failed to solve the problem because it persisted in landing on the self-same spot and therefore missed the string entirely. The bird had obviously learned to react rigidly to an inflexible situation marked by a dominant signal-quality, i.e., a definite motor-spatial quality. The constant "object," the string, was in no way an

[6] Buytendijk and Fischel, **625**.
[7] Schaeffer; cf. Maier and Schneirla, **677**, 202.

articulated, precisely defined element of the situation.[8] The importance of the global situation to the dog in the process of learning has been proved by several psychologists (De Jong, Buytendijk, and others). Buytendijk, for instance, trained a dog to open one of eleven similar boxes (Yerkes' multiple-choice apparatus). When the whole apparatus was faced in exactly the opposite direction the dog was utterly lost. It is a well-known fact that a dog which has been trained in one particular terrain may lose the acquired habit if this terrain is radically altered.[9]

Things-of-action do not have any fixed "objective" structure. They are an indissoluble part of the external and internal event. Therefore, and paradoxically, a diffuse sensori-motor organization is likely to be not only rigid but also unstable. For Buytendijk's toad (see p. 63), certain ineffective objects may acquire the qualities of a thing-of-action if beside them are put edible objects similar in shape. Things-of-action also change their meaning and their signal-properties according to the spatial and temporal position in which they appear in the biological continuum. Things-of-action may have a decisive significance at one phase in the whole duration of the event, and become indifferent, neutral in their import, in a subsequent phase.

A small solitary-bee uses the house of a certain species of snail as a place to lay her eggs. After the eggs are laid in the snail's shell, the bee makes a hole 6-7 cm. deep in the earth, and places the shell in this hole. When Ferton removed such a shell from the hole into which the bee had just slipped it, the insect continued with its work, filling the hole, smoothing over the earth, and otherwise finishing the task exactly as if everything were normal.[10]

Finally, the signal-properties in a continuum of action may undergo change. In this event their successive effectiveness

---

[8] *Ibid.*, 262.
[9] Buytendijk, **623**, 118 ff.
[10] Hempelmann, **651**, 312.

becomes a rigidly determined function of the succession of partial events. Baltzer, in his experiments with cross-spiders, demonstrated that several stimuli are effective successively in dealing with the prey snared in the web. As we have seen, the stimulus of vibration is the initial condition needed to occasion the response of enshrouding the trapped prey in a ball spun by the spinnerets. But in order for the object to achieve the additional status of edibility, certain taste and olfactory stimuli must become active which, in this stage, are now alone equal to insuring the eating response.[11]

All this leads us to the problem of the development of *constancy* in the specialized properties of objects, such as

FIG. 16.—Forms Used in Bingham's Experiment with Chickens.

geometrical form, color, size, and so on. Bingham has found that a chicken trained to react positively to a triangle set over against a circle failed to respond when the triangle was inverted (Fig. 16). We must therefore conclude that the triangle possesses no constancy of form for the chicken. We may assume that it responds to a non-articulated (physiognomic) quality-of-the-whole which is destroyed by a change of geometric position.[12]

We may take an analogous case from our own sphere. Human faces are usually perceived in terms of their diffuse, total (physiognomic) qualities. One may recognize inverted geometric figures, but not a photographic reproduction of the human face turned upside down.

P. E. Fields has studied this problem, using rats as experimental subjects. He discovered that they too did not react

[11] Baltzer, 615.
[12] Bingham, 618.

to the triangle to which they had been trained to respond, once it had been inverted. But the rats would continue to react if the triangle was moved toward total inversion by degrees during successive experiments.[13] Again, Buytendijk demonstrated that his dog subject was not successful in recognizing the inverted triangle, but did respond to it spontaneously on the following day when smaller sizes were used. Once having learned the proper reaction to the smaller size, the dog later learned to respond to the larger size as well.[14] Chimpanzees, on the other hand, seem to react instantaneously to inverted geometrical figures.[15]

All these experiments, though not completely devoid of ambiguity, seem to indicate that a constancy of form develops within the phylogenetic scale.

It is true, of course, that form constancy may not only be dependent on the developmental level, but also be a function of the biological situation and of biological necessity. Coburn's experiments with crows make it appear very probable that birds which search for food while flying above the ground possess a much keener faculty for form constancy than do gallinaceous ground-birds such as the domestic hen.[16]

Constancy in the properties of objects is intimately related to the flexibility of apprehension. If the animal cannot recognize the object in its varying appearance, if it is bound to react specifically and rigidly to a specific unalterable stimulus pattern, a world of constant things cannot develop. The animal can never see the object *per se* if it cannot accommodate its reaction to the object as it varies from time to time.

DIFFUSE PERCEPTUAL ORGANIZATION IN THE CHILD.

The development from a diffuse perceptual organization characterized primarily by "qualities-of-the-whole" into an

[13] Fields, 640.
[14] Buytendijk, 621.
[15] Gellermann, 646.
[16] Coburn, 632.

organization in which the essential feature is a decisiveness of parts standing in clear relationship can be observed in the growth of the child's mentality.

The following report on the Scupin boy when four and a half years old may serve as an illustration of a diffuse perceptual formation: "Whereas the child was at first terrified by the living spiders themselves, he is now afraid of the spider web, and of floating bits of the web which catch on his clothes. Today he even found it terribly upsetting to discover a little hair stuck to his hand. When the hair was removed, he asked, very much concerned: 'Didn't the hair bite your finger?' "[17]

Here we have a typical diffuse pattern. The global quality of "biting" is related not merely to the spider proper, but to everything characteristic of the spider web. "Spider-like" is a property common to the entire situation and expressed in every part of it. The structure of the percept is homogeneous. It can be described by the familiar phrase, *pars pro toto*—any part has the quality-of-the-whole.

It has been frequently observed that small children may recognize a certain animal in a picture book without being able to point out the animal's separate characteristics. This parallels certain cases of pathological primitivation in which the patient is perfectly able to name the animal, but is at a total loss when asked to point out the head or tail. An interesting example of this kind of perception among children is the following: I once showed a little four-year-old girl a drawing made by another nine-year-old child which was intended to represent a duck sitting on a rock (Fig. 17). The little girl pointed to the place on the drawing marked by a cross, and said: "Duck!" I asked: "But where is the duck?" The child indicated the large circle. I repeated the question, saying: "Where is the duck's head?" The child pointed to the duck's breast. Finally I asked: "How big is the duck, then?" The child replied by framing the whole contour of the picture with her

[17] Scupin, 502, vol. 2, 42.

hands. It is clear that the entire picture is the "duck" so far as the child is concerned, although for us the representation of the duck is separated objectively and indeed sharply from the stone. The global quality of "duck-like" stretches out to cover the entire picture, and in consequence the single parts of the representation are but little differentiated with respect to each other.

Fig. 17.–"Duck." Drawn by a nine-year-old girl.

In this diffusely organized, homogeneous perception it is fundamental that each constituent part contain some of the quality-of-the-whole, and that these parts be instinct with the situative meaning, the broader meaning of the totality. Dix speaks of his two-month-old son who instantly stopped crying for food as soon as the bib to which he was accustomed was fastened about his neck. Two more cases of infant behavior almost identical with the one just quoted were reported to me. In one of them the mother emphasized the fact that her child did not cease to express his impatience at that stage of the feeding act when he had grown a bit older. These are instructive examples of a diffuse situation where a part (the bib) acquires the significance (i.e., of being fed) of the totality. A similar report on a three-month-old child is given by Baldwin: "A lighted match suffices to end his crying for food, although this is really only an external sign for the preparation of the child's meal. No other light would serve."[18]

This diffuse character of the child's experience of objective

[18] Dix, 362, vol. 2, 37; Baldwin, 4, 115.

situations explains partially, at least, the often remarked, excellent "mechanical memory" or "associative memory" of children. Pérez tells of a girl three and a half months old whose uncle picked her up in his arms. The uncle was wearing a rose in his lapel. Immediately the child began to show signs of wanting to take the breast. The nurse explained that some days before she had worn a little bunch of violets at her breast when out walking with the baby.[19] There is no doubt in this case that a total situation, in which the signs of being carried and of smelling flowers are parts colored by the quality-of-the-whole, released the impulse to suck at the breast. We must avoid being led into the error of adducing the principle of association by contiguity to account for this behavior. The common, global significance of a situation in which any part may represent the whole—in this case a situation which fulfilled the need to take the breast—acted again to occasion an identical reaction in a similar version. It is because of this that the child often tries to complete a situation on the basis of a fragmentary part which, for the adult, might not necessarily show any relation at all to the whole, but which, for the child, may be shot through with the same coloration as the previously experienced total situation.

The Scupins write of their 1:10-yr.-old child: "One time, and this was out of the ordinary, the boy was set down on a cushion and given some thimbles to play with. He placed them together, one inside the other, as if building a tower. Suddenly it occurred to him that something bright belonged in the hole of the topmost thimble. He cried: 'Please, please . . . light!' We gave him something sparkling to put in, and he was placated. Some three weeks later he was again put by mere chance on the same cushion. Scarcely had he been seated there when again he clamored: 'Please . . . finger . . . pretty . . . light!' and continued to do this until we had fetched what he wanted."[20]

[19] Pérez, 475.
[20] Scupin, 502, vol. 1, 86.

One of the few experimental investigations dealing with the problem of primitive organization in the perceptual field was made by E. Knoblauch in the Hamburg Laboratory.[21] She worked with mentally defective children (of varying degrees of feeble-mindedness), with normal children, and with adults. She trained her subjects to respond positively to a circle of solid black set against an angular figure. These geometrical figures were glued to the tops of boxes, the boxes identified by the solid black circles containing a toy. After successful training to the positive figure, a variety of two other geometrical figures was substituted for the original pairs of a solid black circle and an angular figure. The problem was to discover how often the subjects reacted positively to any of these forms when set against some other figure. That is: How great is the similarity between a solid circle and any other geometrical figure measured in percentages on the basis of the number of times a subject will accept that form as a substitute in lieu of the circle?

The pairs were made up of the following figures in 72 combinations: Three solid ellipses of varying breadth, a simple circle, a circular hole cut out of white cardboard, a low cylinder, a tall cylinder, a sphere, a cone, and four angular solid black figures, that is, a square, a triangle, an oblong, and a diamond-shaped figure.

If we compute the average range of similarity between the original solid black circle and the substituted figure on the basis of percentage frequency of choice, three typical series result (see page 116).

If a comparison is made of the three series representing reactions on three different planes of mentality, we must conclude that the development of optical percepts occurs through an increase of articulation. Children very low in the developmental scale may base their choice more often on the vague qualities of blackness, solidity, etc., rather than on real figural qualities. They may even choose angular forms in preference

[21] Knoblauch, **425.**

Low-grade Feeble-minded		Normal Children		Adults	
Tall cylinder	100%	Sphere	88%	Contour circle	100%
Cone	81	Cone	86	Circular hole	92
Sphere	76	Low cylinder	80	Low cylinder	83
Low cylinder	71	Tall cylinder	79	Wide ellipse	75
Square	66	Circular hole	74	Medium ellipse	66
Wide, large ellipse	64	Wide ellipse	64	Sphere	59
Diamond	51	Medium ellipse	46	Narrow ellipse	46
Oblong	44	Narrow ellipse	41	Cone	46
Triangle	34	Contour circle	40	Tall cylinder	33
Medium ellipse	30				
Narrow ellipse	27				
Circular hole	0				
Contour circle	0	Angular figures	0	Angular figures	0

to those that tend to circularity, though the normal children (of five to seven years of age) never respond in such a fashion. The children with an abnormally primitive mental development obviously do not respond to circularity in its specific sense; there is a negative reaction to the contour circle and to the circular hole. Normal children five to seven years of age may still tend to stress such "qualities-of-the-whole" as blackness and solidity, but they also react distinctly to circularity *per se*, that is, to the specific geometrical shape. Of course, the more advanced the optical organization becomes, the more the subject will react on the basis of a strictly optical form. Therefore, with the adult, whenever the outlined circle appears as a member of the pair, it will be chosen as the most adequate substitute for the solid black circle.

Heiss and Sander carried out some ingenious experiments proving that a young child has more difficulty than an older child in breaking up the totality of a pattern.[22] Patterns devised from variously shaped blocks (Fig. 18 A) were to be completed as quickly as possible by the selection of the missing block either from an amorphous group (B), or from a strongly configurated group (C).

A comparison of the time elapsing before a satisfactory re-

[22] Heiss and Sander, **400.**

sponse in these two experiments yields the graph shown in Fig. 19.

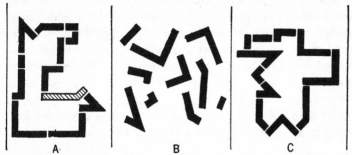

A   B   C

Fig. 18.—A Sample of Heiss and Sander's Completion Test.

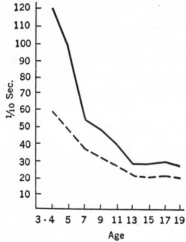

Fig. 19.—Relation Between Age and Speed of Performance in Heiss and Sander's Experiment. Solid line indicates selection of blocks from C; broken line, selection from B.

The younger the child, the more time was required for the selection of the missing block from the strongly configurated Group C, with respect to the time necessary for selection from

Group B. This indicates that the younger the child, the greater the influence of the totality of the organization in his percept.

In another type of experiment H. Volkelt and Dora Musold proved that the faculty of size discrimination in children is greatest when objects characterized by a clearly knit, comprehensive totality are involved, and least when relatively detached, abstract size qualities are dominant.[23] The accompanying table shows the development of the discrimination limen for three objects—sphere, solid disk, and line—in two groups of children, one of kindergarten age and the other of grade school age. The standard object has a diameter (or length) of 50 mm.

DIFFERENCE IN THE LIMEN OF DISCRIMINATION OF SIZES
(STANDARD SIZE, 50 MM.)

	Sphere	Disk	Line
Kindergarten children	0.95 mm.	2.1 mm.	2.7 mm.
Grade school children	0.9 mm.	1.1 mm.	1.7 mm.

It is noteworthy that there is an almost negligible difference in the limen of discrimination for the two age levels in the case of the sphere, whereas there is a considerable difference in the case of the more "abstract" figure.

DIFFUSE PERCEPTUAL-MOTOR ORGANIZATION IN THE CHILD.

An excellent method of approach to the problem of primitive organization is by inquiry into perceptual-motor activities in the child as revealed in drawings, melodies, rhythms, and so on. One of the leading methods is to have the child copy geometrical figures. As demonstrated in various experiments by many investigators, it will be found that the deviation from the adult method of representation will always tend toward a more diffuse type of organization.

Katz has shown that in children's drawings the cylindrical form is frequently represented something after the fashion shown in Fig. 20. The side view is affected by the cylinder's

[23] Volkelt, 528, 96.

"roundness" and the straight vertical lines are bulged out.[24]
A dominant quality-of-the-whole of roundness pervades the
figure, and is expressed in each part. The extraordinarily pervasive effect of these global qualities in children's drawings, as
expressed in homogeneous forms, is shown still more clearly in
experiments carried out by Muchow, Volkelt, and myself.[25]
The task given the child is, for example, that of drawing a

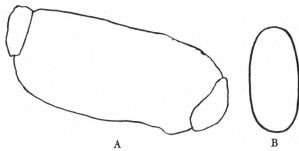

FIG. 20.—Childlike Copies of a Cylinder. A. Girl, six years old (after
Katz); B. Girl, five years old (after Volkelt.)

six-sided pyramid set on a cylinder. One child combines two
qualities-of-the-whole, one from each figure, that is, roundness
and angularity (see Fig. 21).

The physiognomic characteristic of "pointedness" or "angularity" is expressed very clearly in the drawings in Fig 22,
which represent copies of a geometrical pattern by children
four to five years old.[26]

The child masters his task by arranging the two global qualities of "closure" (roundness, squareness) and of "pointedness" into an organic, though primitive, form.

Fig. 23 furnishes an example of the development in visual-
motor organization in a single child from the fourth to the

[24] Katz, 419, 244.
[25] Muchow, 458; Volkelt, 527.
[26] Volkelt, 528, 114.

FIG. 21.—Six-sided Pyramid on a Cylinder Drawn by an Eight-year-old Girl. (Hamburg Psychological Laboratory.)

FIG. 22.—Copies of a Diamond-shaped Figure Drawn by Four- and Five-year-old Children. (After Volkelt.)

seventh year. There is present an increase in the factor of articulation. The homogeneous circular form is replaced by the more highly articulated square. The physiognomic quality of pointedness is finally replaced by the strictly optical-geometrical qualities of the three squares (the only sides visible to the child).

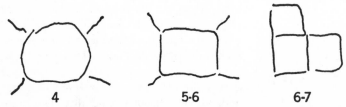

4   **5-6**   **6-7**

Fig. 23.—Development of Organization on a Primitive Level. One Child's Copies of a Cube during Her Fourth to Seventh Years.

To meet the objection that "homogeneity" or "globality" in children's drawings is due simply to an immaturity in motor coordination, Volkelt made some experiments which demonstrated that the child not only organizes forms primitively when copying them, where play-motor factors operate, but also exhibits a preference for such primitive forms in his simple perception.[27] He allowed children to choose between "primitive" copies of certain figures and more articulated forms. He found that in a great many instances the children showed a preference for the primitive as against the highly articulated copies. (In one instance children chose 50 per cent primitive forms, whereas adults chose none at all.)

One of many possible examples may serve to illustrate how strongly marked is the tendency to homogeneous forms in the drawings of early childhood. A three-year-old girl drew a man in the act of running, and represented him as having a great many legs. The pervasive whole-quality of "many-leggedness"

[27] *Ibid.*

in this running figure (Fig. 24) is expressed in the fact that the legs are drawn in a homogeneous, radiating fashion around the whole body.

FIG. 24.—"Many-legged Man." Drawing by a three-year-old girl.

The child's method of copying figures is extremely important in furthering an understanding of the general tendencies of a primitive perceptual-motor organization. The "errors" in the representation must be evaluated positively as well as negatively. Since the child is unable to reconstruct highly differentiated forms he will regress, not to dissociation or to disorganization, but to a more diffuse organization consistent with his own level of mentality. Disorganization, something quite different from primitively organized patterns, will usually occur only in case the mentality is itself in a state of dissociation. Among the high-grade morons of the Wayne County Training School (Michigan) we found disorganization in copied patterns displayed only by children with brain defects (see Fig. 25).[28]

We may summarize some of the fundamental changes that come about through the primitivation of the original pattern, using the material collected at the Hamburg Laboratory.[29] The observations were made on children of kindergarten age.

A tendency toward homogeneity and greater diffuseness may be revealed:

1. In the strong emphasis on qualities-of-the-whole:
   (a) Making a figure more uniform, indivisible: □ → ○
   (b) Closing an open figure: ⊃ → ⊙
2. In the homogeneization of directions and parts by:
   (a) Making parts alike: ⅃ → ⅃⅃
   (b) Simplifying directions: ✳ → ⚡
   (c) Using symmetry: ∫ → C

[28] Werner and Strauss, 538.
[29] Cf. Muchow, 458.

Besides this radically homogeneous *global* type of graphic representation, there is another which we may call the *chain*

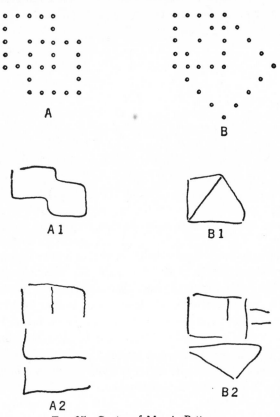

FIG. 25.—Copies of Mosaic Patterns.
A, B two patterns. A1, B1: global forms; copies by a generally retarded child. A2, B2: disorganized forms; copies by a child with a brain defect.

type. This latter is characterized by the concatenation of pieces of the whole, an arrangement in which the distinguishing marks of higher geometric forms—the subordination of single parts, the presence of centers, and so on—are lacking. The drawings of South Sea Islanders, in which a cube is represented by five squares, may be similar to some children's drawings based on mere concatenation (see Fig. 26).

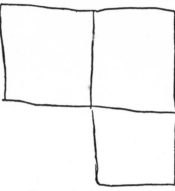

FIG. 26.—A "Chain Type" Drawing of a Cube by a Girl Six Years of Age.

Diffuseness and homogeneity in the childlike organization are expressed in this "chain" characteristic. The distinguishing sign of the chain type of drawing is the relative lack of definiteness in the relation of the parts. This is occasioned by the fact that these parts are experienced as global units, and are not conceived as figurally related and strictly centralized according to one comprehensive aspect.

The genesis of *melodic patterns* again points to a law of development from a diffuse, homogeneous type of organization to one in which definite, articulated parts stand in clear relation to one another. In melodies, as in the case of drawings, inquiries have been made into spontaneous and copied patterns. In my early experimental work on the spontaneous melodic creations of children between two and five years of age, I demonstrated by means of phonographic records that there is an early development of creative melodic patterns.[30] It is

[30] Werner, 532.

EARLY APPEARANCE OF MELODIC ELEMENTS IN CREATIVE SINGING (AFTER WERNER)

Age in Years	Direction of Melodic Movement	Gestalt	Ending	Ambitus (total range between low and high)	Number of Different Tones in the Motif
2-3	Descending: ∖ (rare form: monotone: —)	"Whole-Form" (The motif as a whole is repeated without repetition of parts: ∥ or ∧∧)	On the lowest tone	Minor third	Two tones
3¼	Ascending-Descending ∧	------	On the same tone as beginning	Major third	Three tones
3½	------		------	Fourth, fifth	More than three tones
3¾		Repetition of descending part: ∧∧		------	------
4		-----			
4¼		Repetition of ascending part ∧	On a middle tone between low and high		
4½		-------	On a tone toward which the low tone is leading upward		
4¾	Double-Form: ∧∧ x (tone x belongs to both parts)	Overlapping steps in ascending part: ∧	------		

likely that the genuine melodic germ is a diffuse descending glissando, out of which the so-called "ur-motif" (primary motif) may have developed as a descending two-toned pattern with the interval of a minor third. According to this investigation, the melodic forms in spontaneously creative singing show an early development in which new elements appear in the succession shown in the accompanying table, indicating the law of increase in articulation.

In our Hamburg Laboratory Brehmer carried on a comprehensive experiment in which he had children of all school ages *reproduce* piano melodies vocally.[31] He found that these melodies tended to be translated into more and more diffuse patterns, the younger the children became. On the other hand, the children showed less errors, the simpler the original melodic pattern. "Errors," therefore, indicate no more than a shift toward a more childlike organization. The intrinsic difficulty of the melody depends not simply on the number of different notes used in its construction, but on the relative organization of these notes.

Motif I shows only 35 per cent of error for children between the ages of six and nine years and no errors at the age level of ten to twelve years. Motif II, which is apparently no more complicated, results in 76 per cent error at the lower, and 50 per cent at the higher, level. The reason for the relative difficulty of Motif II is revealed by a tabulation of the types of error according to frequency. This shows that this motif is frequently rearranged to accord with one of these two melodic movements:

[31] Brehmer, 340.

The first beat of Motif I is made up of two pairs of notes, both of which descend in the scale, whereas one of the pairs in Motif II descends and the other remains on the same level. This complexity is one reason why Motif II presents more difficulty than Motif I. The child attempts to avoid the difficulty by making the two notes of both pairs either descend or remain on the same level. In brief, a homogeneization takes place which brings Motif II closer to a more primitive form such as that in Motif I.

As one examines the results of Brehmer's experiments, he will see easily enough that the general tendency toward a more primitive and less articulated organization almost parallels the tendency revealed in the experiments with the drawings of children. We may enumerate parallel trends in the tonal and graphic patterns:

1. Expression of the "quality-of-the-whole":
   (a) Continuity: The "glissando" characteristic in the singing of very young infants tends to disappear with older children, but a marked inclination to increase the continuity of the original pattern remains in the event of large tonal intervals ("leveling tendency").
   (b) Tonal closure: The tendency to a closure of the "open figures" in the drawings is translated here into a tendency to finish with a low note, as the note *par excellence*, rather than with the actual middle note.

2. Homogeneity of direction and parts:
   (a) Parts are made more alike (see as examples above the two copies of Motif II).
   (b) Simplification of direction: If the melodic movement is strongly articulated like this (♩♪ ♪♩) it will tend toward simplification into this: (♪♩♩♩)
   (c) "Symmetrization" of ascending and descending parts frequently occurs whenever the model is asymmetrical:

(𝅘𝅥 𝅘𝅥𝅮 𝅘𝅥) becomes (𝅘𝅥 𝅘𝅥𝅮 𝅘𝅥𝅮 𝅘𝅥)

(Aside from these deviations on a purely melodic basis obvious changes occur which follow a tendency to simplify the harmonic relationship.)

LABILITY AND RIGIDITY IN THE SENSORI-MOTOR AND PERCEPTUAL ORGANIZATION OF THE CHILD; THE DEVELOPMENT OF CONSTANCIES.

As we have already pointed out, any phenomenon known in terms of qualities-of-the-whole, rather than in terms of strictly articulated qualities, is apt to be perceived by the young child as undergoing a complete change, even if no more than minor details in the situation are altered. From this general diffuseness three characteristics of child behavior can be derived:

1. Sensitivity to change in the concrete situation.
2. Fluidity in the organization of material (such, for example, as that displayed in play situations).
3. Infantile conservatism.

1. One expression of a general lability is the extraordinary sensitivity of the young child to any change in the external circumstances in which a person or thing appears. It is a matter of indifference to the older child whether his mother appears before him in a green dress or in a black one. He recognizes her definitely with her hat either on or off, whether she is wearing her glasses or not. But this is not the case with the younger child. He may fail to recognize his father dressed in new black clothes, or his mother with her new hat or dress. Centralization according to discrete parts, the organization of the whole by the subordination of the less essential to the more essential—in brief, the hierarchical structure of our perception is what guarantees the "stability" of objects despite the mutable situations in which they appear.

A limited objective constancy with little articulation and centralization often occasions an identification (e.g., in experiments in discrimination) of different forms as a result of the dominance of certain qualities-of-the-whole. It is in this way that a child may identify the three figures shown in Fig. 27.[32]

FIG. 27.—Forms Used in Muchow's Discrimination Experiment.

Crudden performed an experiment in discrimination in the Ann Arbor Laboratory in which children had to respond positively to one of two linear forms quite dissimilar from an adult standpoint.[33] It was very instructive to observe that success in discrimination sometimes depended on the spatial position,

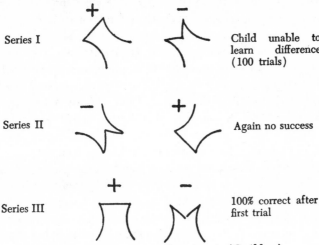

FIG. 28.—Form Discrimination Experiment. (Crudden.)

the orientation, of these figures. Fig. 28 shows the results with one pair of forms, the subject being a boy three years of age.

[32] Muchow, 458.
[33] Not yet published.

In this case these results may be safely interpreted, it would appear, by understanding the child's perception to be dominated by certain qualities-of-the-whole which vary with a change in spatial orientation. In the first two series the dominant qualities are apparently much the same in both figures, whereas in Series III the tops of the figures are dominant and therefore permit discrimination.

2. In all those cases in which the child is not compelled to organize his perception in the adult way because of strongly and clearly defined objective situations, he will handle material very loosely. This lability is certainly due in part to the child's ability to shape things much more according to his own needs than can an adult. And it can also be partially attributed to a primitive manner of grasping material in terms of non-articulated global qualities, whereby otherwise important details are quite neglected. Especially in the constructive activity of play, e.g., in drawing or in building with blocks, it is often found that the younger child is continuously changing the meaning of the object as the work progresses. According to an investigation by Hetzer, a child is between four and five years of age before he will expressly plan to draw a certain object and then actually fulfill his initial intention.[34] With the younger child, however, as the work goes on, the changing lines and contours suggest a changing content to his mentality.

3. There is an inner relation between the global manner in which the child experiences objective situations, and his well-known conservatism which causes him frequently to reject innovations. A global interpretation of a situation implies that the situation is the result of numerous unanalyzed elements. From the child's standpoint no one of these elements need be more essential than any other, since all of them contribute to the characteristic coloration, or tone, of the situational totality. Such a "whole-structure" tends to a rigid traditionalism, since any element that is changed or left out may completely trans-

[34] Hetzer, 402.

form the total situation to which the child is adjusted. It is because of this fact that, as Sully remarks, "children show an instinctive respect for what is customary and according to rule, such as a particular way of taking food, dressing, and definite time for doing this or that."[35]

The Scupins say of their 1:10-year-old child: "Custom is law for him, and he repudiates any inconsistencies."[36] Sully tells of a five-year-old child who conducted himself with the greatest precision and ritualistic order in all his activities.[37] His cup and spoon had to be placed in exactly the same place every day; the course of the day's events had to be carried out according to a strict order—lessons before the walk, walk before going to bed, and so on. "Any departure from the usual he regarded as a sort of irreverence or disrespect." This compulsion to act according to rule often leads to the peculiar ceremonial needs of the child which will be discussed later.

Because their impression of the whole is inflexible, children are often much more susceptible to changes in their physical environment than are adults. At the age of 2:8 years, the Scupins' child regularly noticed, long before his parent's attention had been attracted to the fact, the removal of some small object from one place to another, or any other minor alteration in the arrangement of the room. It often happens that children are painfully overcome when their customary routine is changed. "When his mother made bold to put his toy away in another place than the customary one, he sprang hastily from his chair, and said: 'You can't do that, Mama!' He then tore it from her hand, and returned it to exactly the same spot where it had been before."[38]

The problem of perceptual *constancies* and their development is intimately connected with lability in primitive organ-

[35] Sully, 517, 143.
[36] Scupin, 502, vol. 1, 85.
[37] Sully, 517, 144.
[38] Scupin, 502, vol. 1, 144.

ization.[39] Child psychologists in recent years have devoted considerable effort to investigating the ability to apprehend objects according to their constant qualities. Consider, for instance, brightness constancy. The brightness of objects may appear to remain approximately the same despite different intensities of illumination. Chalk seems to have about the same degree of whiteness, or coal of blackness, even though the physical intensity of the light reflected from the surface may vary considerably corresponding to a change in the source of illumination.[40] There is some perceptual mechanism at work which tends to keep the color properties of these objects nearly constant, as if the eye were making due allowance for a change in the optical frame of reference, that is, the illumination. The same is true of other properties of objects, e.g., size and shape. The size and shape of an object, within certain limits, may remain approximately constant even though there has been a definite change in the retinal image because of a variation in the distance of the object or in the visual angle.

Beyrl, in order to inquire into the development of size constancy, carried out an experiment dealing with children between the ages of two and ten years.[41] He used a standard disk 100 mm. in diameter with which other larger disks of varying size, placed 2 to 11 m. behind the standard disk, were to be compared. The task was to vary the size of the disk behind so that it appeared to be identical in size with the standard disk. It is obvious that the ability to keep the apparent size of the objects constant can be measured by the actual physical difference in size between the standard disk and the one that is varied. The larger the varied disk has to be with respect to the standard disk for an apparent identity of size to be main-

[39] In my work on "The Psychology of Intensity" (731), I have shown that the problem of constancy concerns not only optical perception (from which angle it has received frequent experimental treatment), but also all other sensory fields, especially the auditory and tactual.

[40] Katz, 722.

[41] Beyrl, 337.

tained, the less the capacity for constancy. Fig. 29 shows, for different ages, the average size of the variable disk which ap-

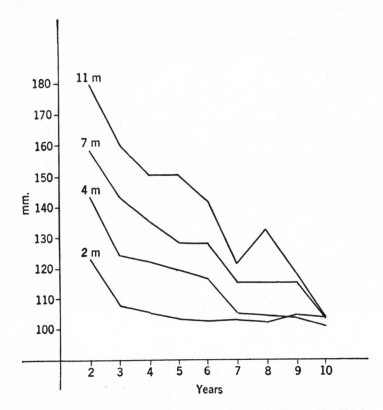

Fig. 29.—Development of Size Constancy from Ages Two to Ten Years. Age level indicated on the abscissa; on the ordinate, size of the variable distant disk apparently equal to the front disk of 100 mm. Four curves represent the results with four different distances between the disks (2, 4, 7, 11 m.). (After Beyrl.)

pears to be identical with the standard disk of 100 mm. It is apparent that the younger the child, the less the ability to exert a size constancy.

A similar development takes place in brightness constancy (Brunswik). Furthermore, as shown by Klimpfinger, there is

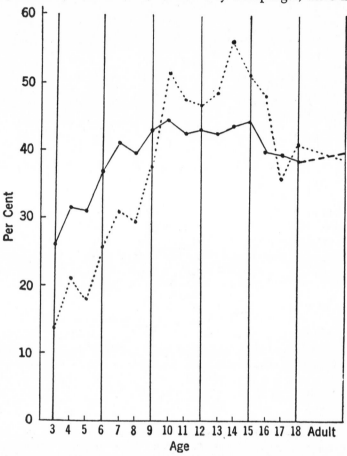

Fɪɢ. 30.—Development of Brightness Constancy (solid line) and Shape Constancy (dotted line). Ordinate represents percentage of "perfect constancy" (100%). (After Brunswik.)

also a development in form constancy, viz., in the ability to maintain the identity of a gestalt at varying visual angles. As

Fig. 30 shows, the curve for shape constancy ascends steadily up to the age of fourteen to fifteen years.[42]

The problem of constancy is actually somewhat more complicated than is presented here. As in the case of sensory discrimination (see p. 101), there may be a difference in the development of constancy according to the experimental situation and the contributing functions involved. Perceptual constancy seems to be highly developed even during the early period of childhood, providing that the situation is not abstract but concretely articulated, so that it may furnish many cues for the subject. If, for instance, Beyrl's set-up is changed in such a way that the varied disks are presented not singly, but simultaneously as a series of increasing sizes—o, o, o, O,— even two-year-old children may achieve adult constancy in the selection of one apparently identical with the standard.[43] These results prove two things: (1) It seems to be futile to search for any absolute genesis of constancy. We may speak correctly only of a mere growth of constancy. (2) Constancy is a function of the concreteness of the problem presented and the richness in clues of the field.

DIFFUSE PHENOMENA IN THE WORLD OF PRIMITIVE MAN.

In the visible world of the primitive man-of-action things have meaning in so far as they are integral parts of the context in which they function. It is hardly possible for him to conceive of a thing detached from the totality of the concrete situation in which it is embedded.

The embedding of things in the concrete situation demonstrates clearly what is meant by a relatively global, or diffuse, type of organization. This peculiarity in the primitive mode of experience is reflected in the verbal denotations of things or events. As Malinowski has very ably pointed out, in the highly developed Indo-European languages a sharp distinction can be drawn between the lexical meaning of words and the grammatical modifications of these words. This means, for instance, that we are able to take any event A expressed by a lexical

[42] Brunswik, **344, 345**; Klimpfinger, **424.**
[43] Akishige, **707**; Koffka, **67, 239.**

word, and follow it through the past, present, and future by a modification in the grammatical form of the word. We may do this without reference to the actual situations which arise during the course of the event, even though they may differ noticeably from each other. In native languages, however, the distinction between radical meaning and grammatical modification is by no means so clearly established; in fact, both functions are often most remarkably confused. Let us take an example from the Melanesian language. In the Trobriand branch of the Melanesian group of languages there is the word *ma*, which means "come" or "move toward." The Indo-Germanic languages can express the event of the moving of a canoe toward the shore in terms of temporality: we might say, "it will soon come (toward the shore)," "it comes," "it came," "it has come," etc. The Trobriander will use the term *boge lay-ma* to say, "it has been coming this way." But in order to say "the canoe is now coming to the shore" (in the sense of present arrival), he will substitute "paddle" for the word meaning "come," since the canoeist, on drawing close to the beach, furls his sails and takes to the paddle. And, again, in case the canoe has already come to the shore, i.e., it has already arrived, the native cannot use the root *ma*, but must speak of "anchoring" or "mooring." This example demonstrates that an event which we express verbally as remaining identical through temporally successive stages, in the eyes of the native is viewed as in intimate relation with the changing situation, and is thus to be expressed by different words.[44]

Another instance of global-diffuse organization is found in primitive drawing. In the free drawings of many primitive peoples we find that things are often represented according to dominant total-qualities which are either taken directly from the collective situation or affectively attached to it. The Brazilian Indian represents a fish by drawing a triangle since fish are caught in a three-cornered net. The Sakei of Malacca represent a deer by reproducing the three-cornered track left by

[44] Malinowski, 96.

his hoofs. Certain South American Indians indicate the multiplicity of the stars in the Milky Way by drawing one frog, though in their opinion the Milky Way consists of a vast multitude of frogs. In all these cases, in one way or another there is a definite tendency to represent things by a global quality, in a *pars-pro-toto* manner.[45]

Again, consider the ornamental designs of the South Sea Islanders in which, as is commonly known today, the figures are not conceived from the standpoint of pure ornament, but are intended to symbolize some dead or living object. In one ornament a triangle will represent a bird; a grate-like figure, rain.[46] This is possible because the primitive man has a genuine ability to grasp things in terms of simplified qualities, that is, qualities-of-the-whole, or physiognomic qualities.

Some interesting parallels to the child's visual-motor organization are revealed in reproductions of geometrical figures

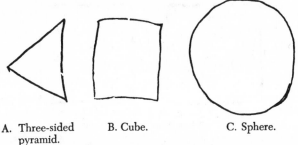

A. Three-sided   B. Cube.   C. Sphere.
   pyramid.

Fig. 31.—Drawings by Solomon Islanders. (After Thurnwald.)

drawn by South Sea Islanders.[47] The three-sided pyramid in Fig. 31 is drawn not as a figure bounded by four surfaces, but as a figure characterized by a certain "triangular" quality-of-the-whole. Similarly, the cube is not a body articulated in such a way that it has six definitely related sides; rather it is distinguished by the general property of "squareness." Corre-

[45] Werner, **143.**
[46] Stephan, **298,** 48 ff.
[47] Thurnwald, **129,** Table 5.

spondingly, the sphere is apprehended as something "round," and therefore represented by a mere circle. Whereas the intellectualized man would draw geometric figures built up of several articulated surfaces, the primitive man may content himself with uniform common qualities of a non-articulated, diffuse nature.

Furthermore, we may recall that in the case of children, besides drawings based on qualities-of-the-whole, there were

FIG. 32.—Drawing of a Cube by a Solomon Islander. Example of a primitive "chain type." (After Thurnwald.)

"chain type" drawings. This "chain type" of organization is often found in primitive drawings. The lack of a uniform centralization in the visual grasp of primitive drawings is the reason why representation according to the laws of visual perspective never occurs. A South Sea Islander draws a cube by setting down five successive squares standing side by side. (The sixth side, that is, the bottom surface, naturally cannot be seen; see Fig. 32.) In the mode of representation illustrated in this figure there is a distinct absence of centralization, in so far as the conception of the object as a whole proceeds not in terms of one visual orientation, but as if each surface were viewed separately and without intrinsic relation to the others actually bound up with it. The relation binding the parts together is reproduced primitively by a mere coupling, a close juxtaposition.

This "chain type" of drawing points to the fact that, in the primitive mentality, particulars often appear as self-subsistent things which do not necessarily become synthesized into larger entities. It is characteristic, for example, that "in the language of the Hereros there is no word describing their whole geographical territory, but only words for various parts. Their minds possess no generalized images of these localities, but only a multitude of spatial particularities."[48] Similarly, the natives of the Kilimandsharo region do not have a word for the whole mountain range which they inhabit, only words for its peaks. It is a significant fact that only the relatively advanced people on the coast have a term for the whole mountain area.[49] The same is reported of the aborigines of West Australia. Each twist and turn of a river has a name, but the language does not permit of a single inclusive name for the whole river. What appears as a self-subsistent, rigid unity to the mind of the primitive man submits to the domination of a larger inclusive whole only with extreme reluctance.

Because of this, where the advanced, intellectualized mentality would conceive the unity of a larger whole with the diverse attributes and parts subordinated, the primitive mentality may sometimes see a diffuse succession of parts or attributes. Boas,[50] one of the keenest students of the Indian mentality, insists that that class of ideas which we understand to be attributes is often known in the primitive mind as a manifold of independent objects. And Radin remarks: "When we try to discover what are the connotations of such simple things as a

[48] Hahn, 204, 48.
[49] Schwanhäusser, 286, 120.
[50] Boas, 7, Germ. ed., 200.

tree, a mountain, a lake . . . for the primitive man-of-action
. . . the first positive fact is that an object is not thought of as
the [integral] sum of all the sense data connected with it. A
mountain is not thought of as a unified whole. It is a continually changing entity. . . ."[51] The Winnebago Indians may consider the sun to be a number of discrete yet contiguous entities or similar attributes (disk, warmth, light, etc.), even
though advanced members of the tribe are perfectly able to
synthesize all the attributes into one unity of objective existence. Similarly, the average Indian of the Dakota tribe conceives as sixteen distinct gods what the more advanced tribal
"philosopher" will unify into one deity.

LABILITY AND RIGIDITY IN THE CONCRETE WORLD OF PRIMITIVE
MAN.

Since the meaning of the objects in primitive spheres largely
depends on the context, primitive man is conscious of a continuous fluctuation in the properties of objects according to the
change of situation. Radin, in his searching study, *Primitive
Man as Philosopher,* emphasizes the fact that the primitive
man ("the man-of-action") lives in a world that is "dynamic
and ever-changing. . . . Since he sees the same objects changing in their appearance from day to day, the primitive man
regards this phenomenon as definitely depriving them of im-
mutability and self-subsistence." The things of the world exhibit this or that property, depending on the changing frame
of activity in which they are bound fast. A Fiji Islander says
to an investigator: "A thing has strength—'mana'—when it
works; it has no 'mana' when it does not work."[52] The dependence of the meaning of the thing on the situation as
magically conceived, which will be described at some length
in a later section on reality in the sphere of magic, is common
to all primitive mentality. South Sea Islanders may know

[51] Radin, 111, 200.
[52] *Ibid.,* 244.

writhing lianas as a love medicine or as the symbol of mortal agony in death magic.[53]

As a result of this fluidity in the meaning of things and of the primitive man's comparatively high sensitivity to change, his reaction to alteration in his familiar world differs radically from that of intellectual man. For the primitive man a trivial variation in the appearance of some object of daily use or of cult significance in his house or in his local world is interpreted not as a mere transposition or transformation of an unessential detail, but as a revision of the whole, a revolutionary change in the impression of the totality. On account of this, the most indifferent alteration in custom and daily ritual, in milieu and in the things of this milieu, a change which would affect us not in the slightest, can work most disturbingly on the primitive man. We can see, accordingly, how this mode of perception must engender a tendency to resist, for self-preservative reasons, any change which might disrupt customary usage. The magic notion of the evil linked with any change in environment, a conception almost universal among primitive peoples, is rooted deeply in this prime necessity. We may observe a few instances of this instinctive dislike of change. If, for some reason, a hut is to be demolished by the Loangos, no more than roof and walls at the most will be torn down; the framework of the dwelling must be left intact. Similarly, if a stranger leaves the village he must take great care not to injure or destroy any plants or corn in the gardens.[54] In the same way primitive people hold tenaciously throughout hundreds of years to dances and songs that have become virtually unintelligible, preserving and handing them down in their totality unrevised even in the smallest detail. Carven images and tools are fashioned generation after generation exactly as they were by ancestors of long ago. The Indians of British Guiana exhibit considerable skill in making various objects of domestic use, but never do they attempt to improve on the traditional pat-

[53] Werner, 141, 48 ff.
[54] Pechuël-Loesche, 257, 212.

tern. Year in and year out they continue to make them exactly as their forefathers did.[55]

Even when the primitive man sees plainly that the white man has better customs and devices, better means of providing nourishment, etc., he is still reluctant to adopt new methods. We may observe a striking example of this phenomenon. In New Pomerania the outrigger of the canoe is always on the left side. When the outrigger is to the windward it acts satisfactorily and breaks the waves. It stands to reason that, if possible, the outrigger should be kept to the windward, and the canoe maneuvered in such a way as to break the thrust of the sea. But the natives make no attempt to do this. When Count Pfeil, the explorer, pointed out to them this simple advantage, they readily admitted its cogency, but said that they could not change their old practice. They continued their ancient custom even though if the waves happened to come from the right side, their canoes were filled to the gunwales.[56]

Barnett presented some striking evidence of the way members of an essentially concrete-ritualistic culture perceive changes that seem slight to the Western man. The Tsimshian Indians refused to accept the rowboat as a substitute for the indigenous canoe. Barnett points out that a main reason for the rejection was the rigid regimen of ritual procedure, taboos, etc., connected with the constructing of the canoe. "The rowboat was judged to be something entirely distinct from the canoe, because it was put together differently. My informants found the suggestion of transfer of the ritual associations to the rowboat rather ludicrous."[57]

[55] Bernau, 162, 46.
[56] Lévy-Bruhl, 84, Germ. ed., 295.

[57] Barnett, 753, 23. To the problem of "acculturation" and the dynamic laws of cultural change see Herskovitz, 767, 768; Hallowell, 766; and Linton, 782.

PART TWO
Primitive Imagery

Chapter IV

SYNCRETIC AND DIFFUSE ORGANIZATION IN IMAGERY

SYNCRETISM OF FUNCTION IN IMAGERY.

On the higher levels of mental organization the image is distinctly differentiated from the percept. Perceived objects have a "real" character, they are felt to be independent of the ego, and so on. Imagined objects are our own inner products, and are felt to be controlled by and dependent on the activity of the ego. On the other hand, there appear to exist in more primitive states of mind certain phenomena which stand between the objectively conditioned percept and a completely ingenerate image. Insight into a primitive syncretism in the field of imagery is afforded by E. R. Jaensch's work on eidetic imagery in children as based on the original findings of Urbantschitsch.[1]

According to the results of Jaensch's experiments, there are phenomena which possess certain characteristics of both percept and true image. There is, as it were, an intermediate stage between the perception of a thing and the pure memory image of a thing, a level which Jaensch calls that of the "eidetic image." "Hallucinatory" phenomena, eidetic images, are a relatively normal constituent of the child's mentality. Children may be given the task of reproducing from memory a picture they have seen but once, and then only briefly. Some of them will see their images as real projections on some surface in outer space involving no effort of will. These inner images appear to be possessed of a sensuous vivacity equal to that of

[1] Jaensch, 415, 416; Kroh, 430; Allport, 329.

the true percept. Often these children are able to see and describe with an inner eye certain details in the eidetic images that they certainly did not originally observe in the experimental objects to which the eidetic images refer.

Such an eidetic image is, however, not a mere sensory phenomenon, i.e., a (positive) after-image occasioned by the experimental object. In part, at least, it is subject to laws other than those governing the sensory phenomena. For example, it can be influenced by the will and can undergo a radical inner change, which is certainly not true of a sensory after-image. This susceptibility to imaginative influence, to creative fantasy, links the eidetic image to the free, genuine memory image. But the eidetic image is not a mere memory image either, the thing as seen altogether by an inner eye. Beyond being marked by the vividness and the immediate impact of the percept, the eidetic image is capable of actual fusion with a true percept. An experiment in the mixing of colors will illustrate this: To a child who has this eidetic faculty there is presented a blue square on a white screen. Once the child's eidetic image has been established, a yellow screen is substituted for the white one. It may then happen that the eidetic image of the blue square on the screen will become gray, in accordance with the laws of spectral color mixture, because of a fusion with the yellow background. This remarkable change is not pure fancy suggested by any reflective process on the part of the child. Indeed, he himself is often astonished and bewildered by what has occurred; for these colors, in the light of the instruction in mixing oil colors that he has received, should become not gray, but green. This experiment proves that the colors of eidetic images may become fused with the objective colors as if they were true percepts. Another instance of the interrelation of eidetic images and the perceptual background: If the image of a chair is seen on a wall, with the pronouncedly eidetic type of observer everything behind this projected image will vanish, exactly as if the image were "real" and three-dimensional.

It may be said, then, that eidetic images have properties

which are linked in part with percepts and in part with a memory image. The tendency to experience eidetic imagery is not confined to the optical field, but applies to all fields of sense. According to Jaensch it is a normal developmental characteristic of the child, one that decreases with age. From 10 to 60 per cent of all children exhibit this faculty.

Should the results gained by Jaensch and his colleagues be substantiated more fully we may then assume that a primordial functional unity exists in the sensory and imaginative fields, and that out of this undifferentiated function arise the true memory and fantasy image (the knowing of an inner world) in contradistinction to objective perception (the knowing of an outer world).

In view of Jaensch's findings the problem now arises as to whether this type of experience is found in primitive man. There is a possibility, on the basis of a genetic parallelism, of assuming that the perceptual and imaginative activities of the primitive man are more closely connected than is the case with intellectual man. Since it is only recently that the subject has been broached in Jaensch's experiments with children, it is to be expected that as yet the questions involved have received no satisfactory answers.[2] Yet as a provisional insight which will serve until we are supplied with an adequate fund of observation on this aspect of the primitive mind, the idea of a gradual differentiation is extremely useful. It may be that the existence of this primitive imagery among peoples of low culture can never be demonstrated conclusively, for the reason that the aborigines of modern times have passed beyond the first stages of primitivity. Nevertheless, there is a series of facts which apparently indicate a much closer functional relation between percept and pure image even in the contemporary primitive mentality than in the mentality of the man of ad-

[2] L. Peck and A. B. Hodges (471) recently studied the eidetic imagery of 200 white, 50 American Negro, and 50 Mexican children. They found a distribution of 50.9 per cent for whites; 54 per cent for Mexicans; 84 per cent for Negroes.

vanced culture. Many of the forms of imagery among primitives, although not strictly eidetic, certainly approach the outer limits of the eidetic sphere.[3]

We might emphasize the fact that aborigines are much more subject to the compulsion of visions than western man, visions which arise spontaneously or are suggested by the shape of trees, the rocks in a cliff, and so on. It is plain that affect, as I have previously attempted to show, is of vital moment in this experience. But these visions would be impossible, so far as their concrete sensuous character is concerned, were they not supported by a lack of differentiation between the objective perceptual experience and the subjective representation. Everywhere in primitive society we find that visionary appearances not only are accorded an objective value, but are also invested with a superior significance, in that they may even supersede the common reality of life from day to day. One is proud of seeing things that others do not. A young Australian medicine man, speaking of his initiation into tribal mysteries, says vainly: "After this test I saw things that my mother could not see." He added that he had asked: "Mother, what is that thing over there which looks like a man walking?" and she had answered him with apparent awe, saying: "There is nothing there, my child."[4]

Further evidence of the close functional relation between percept and ideational image is the amazing sensuous memory of the primitive man who, in this respect, shows a striking likeness to eidetic children. It has been reported of Indians, as well as of Australian aborigines and members of African tribes, that their memory of natural forms and localities borders on the incredible. Grey tells of an intelligent native who, without the slightest hesitation, identified the three thieves who had stolen some potatoes, merely by glancing at the footprints of the culprits; he immediately named two women and a small

[3] Cf. Kroh, 430.
[4] Lévy-Bruhl, 85, Germ. ed., 44.

boy.[5] Galton remarks on the almost fabulous geographical memory of an Eskimo whose feats were directly observed by a Captain Hall.[6] With no aid except his memory, this Eskimo drew a map of a territory whose shores he had explored but once in his kayak. The strip of country was 1100 miles long as the crow flies, but the coast line was at least six times this distance. A comparison of the Eskimo's rude map with an Admiralty chart printed in 1870 revealed a most unexpected agreement. Galton never saw any map drawn by a white man from memory which could compare in accuracy with the Eskimo's.

It is furthermore probable that the so-called naturalistic art of primitive hunters (Eskimos, Bushmen, etc.) is based on eidetic images which are actually seen as projected on the surface of the material on which the picture is to be drawn or painted. If this interpretation is correct, then the drawings are indeed naturalistic, in so far as they are a tracing out and reproduction of a realistic image projected, so to speak, on the surface of the drawing. (I found that the silhouettes cut out with scissors by an artist of my acquaintance were made by following the lineaments of the eidetic image as seen on the paper.)

One report, albeit an isolated one, describing the manner in which a Bushman set about the business of drawing a figure, supports this interpretation. "He always began by putting down a number of isolated dots on the paper or board which showed no relationship or any trace of contour of any kind to the looker-on, but appeared like a picture of the stars. When he had convinced himself, after considerable deliberation, of the sufficiency of this group of dots, he began to draw free, bold lines from one part of the field to another. As he did this [connected the points] there developed spontaneously the form of an animal—horse, buffalo, elephant, or antelope. This was all done in freehand, and with such unerring precision of line, that not one stroke stood in need of erasure or improvement. The young man told me that this was the plan always

[5] Grey, 197, vol. 2, 247.
[6] Galton, 38, 72.

followed by other artists of the tribe when they produced their highly skilled drawings and paintings."[7]

Similar verification of the nature of this vivid imagery is found in the extraordinary acoustic memory of primitive people as noted by travelers in all parts of the world. W. E. Roth says that the aborigines of N. W. Central Queensland were able to sing from memory a series of songs with a text utterly unintelligible to them, even though five nights were required to complete the memorizing.[8] Thilenius told me personally about the South Sea Islander's ability to produce in a similar fashion an endless series of songs and imitations without aid of any kind.

In brief, there are many facts which suggest that, with primitive man, images and percepts are more nearly related and are less differentiated with respect to one another than is the case with the man of advanced culture.

There is further evidence for the assertion that primitive imaginative processes are syncretic to a comparatively high degree. This evidence is summed up in the fact that in the primitive sphere there is a very close connection between *emotion* and memory image. Reality, in retrospect, is shaped strongly by the affective need. The boastful revision of accounts of martial exploits found everywhere among primitive and naïve people are evidence of a mnemonic reality formed through affective influence. Pechuël-Loesche reports that the Loangos incline to the most extravagant forms of exaggeration even when referring to events to which they have been eyewitnesses. Anyone struck by a bullet or anyone on whom blood is running is reported as killed, and anyone who suffers a slash from a weapon is reported as dead after being horribly cut to ribbons.[9] We find this phenomenon again in the exaggeration of affectively conditioned drawings from memory. If

[7] Mann; cf. Kroh, **430**, 134.
[8] Roth, **275**, No. 19, 199.
[9] Pechuël-Loesche, **257**, 23.

the Brazilian Indian draws a picture of a battle between a jaguar and a tapir, the jaguar—as the more powerful member of the situation—will be represented in a size out of all proportion (Fig. 33).[10] The drawings of Bushmen in which they represent themselves as giants and their enemies as dwarfs are well known. The objective representation is determined to a large degree by an affective evaluation. We might speak here of "emotional perspective,"[11] a common feature, as we shall see, of children's drawings.

FIG. 33.—Jaguar Attacking a Tapir, Drawn by a Brazilian Indian. (After Koch-Grünberg.)

It is a generally recognized fact that the *child's* memory is often radically transformed under the influence of affect.[12] This is true, for example, of the memory of size. Such a metamorphosis can be followed most clearly in representations of the eidetic type. In eidetic children, transformation according to affective compulsion may even reach out into the immediate perceptual reality. For example, one of Jaensch's subjects, a schoolboy, sees certain scenes from a play which impress him so deeply that the actors grow to enormous proportions before his eyes.[13] Kroh tells of an interesting case of an eidetic youth who always saw the cigars which chanced to suit his taste as much larger than all the rest in the cigar-store window.[14]

In the Hamburg Laboratory some occasional experiments

[10] Koch-Grünberg, **220**, 36.
[11] Cf. Werner, **143**.
[12] Stern, **512**.
[13] Jaensch, **415**, 345.
[14] Kroh, **430**, 126.

were carried out with eidetic children as subjects. Five children, all about five years of age, were asked to show the size of their Easter eggs by spreading their hands. All the children without exception indicated an exaggerated size (in the case of two little girls, twice the real size). The Sterns tell of a similar case. Their small daughter received a toy rabbit as a present; the mother put it away for safe-keeping. A day later the child was again given this toy. But she maintained stubbornly that it was not her rabbit at all; hers was much larger, and she would have no other.[15]

An example from the diary of the Scupins' child when he was 6:4 years old illustrates the increase in size with the passage of time. One day he reported that his kite flew to the height of a five-story house. Some time later he said that the kite had flown as high as the rooftops of some taller buildings in the town. Two and one half weeks after this he declared that the kite had been just a tiny dot far, far up in the sky.[16]

This emotional perspective is found in the drawings of children as well as in those of primitive people. The most important factor, that which is most significant to the subject, is drawn as very large, and the elements which have no affective emphasis are diminished or neglected entirely. It is because of this emotional bias that the first human figures drawn by children are mostly all face and very diminutive of torso, and that at one time the arms may be drawn extraordinarily long and dangling, while again they may be barely sketched in. Everything depends on the child's momentary interest. In his zeal to express what interests him most, the child may give the face several eyes or the body several legs, etc. In a book by Rouma there are a great many illustrations of the emotional perspective of children's drawings. For example, a 4:6-year-old child set himself the task of drawing three boys grinding coffee in a coffee mill. The coffee mill, the most interesting object

[15] Stern, 512, 61.
[16] Scupin, 502, vol. 3, 16.

in the drawing, was represented as being far larger than the boys themselves.[17]

A primitive syncretism of image is also found as a characteristic feature in such *pathologically regressive* types as the hysteric or the schizophrenic. The visions and hallucinations so common among these patients are, so to speak, a kind of eidetic imagery, an undifferentiated group of phenomena standing between perception and the true image. Moreover, the visions of the schizophrenic or the hysteric are often nothing more than the products of emotional anxiety and wishfulness. In this they again reveal their syncretic character. "A face without a body appears above the box—a woman who wears a blood-red shirt on her head—the beloved one comes through the door in the form of a shaggy, unkempt monster—in the air, there is a horrible, ugly, grimacing face sun-shaped, out of the rays of which grow thin, reaching arms."[18] In brief, things appear as they commonly do in dreams stemming from anxiety. With these psychotics, affect as a productive, organizing factor in imagery is of extremely potent moment, one much more commonly found and more strongly expressed than in the experience of children or of primitive people. The memory images, as well as the hallucinatory images, of psychotics are also formed under the pressure of wishfulness or anxiety. Memories of daily events may undergo a metamorphosis that becomes fused with magically beneficent or daemonically evil visions.

If we inquire into the reasons for the progressive decline in the frequency of eidetic images during adolescence, it appears that we can best explain it less on the basis of a circumscript physiological change than on the basis of a psychophysical change in the whole personality. This view is supported by the fact that the strength and frequency of eidetic phenomena are dependent on the pedagogic milieu, that the eidetic faculty may endure latently and be

[17] Rouma, **497**, 78.
[18] Kretschmer, **585**, Germ. ed., 73.

used in those situations where it is genuinely significant (cf. the eidetic faculty of the artist, etc.).

The image, so we may suppose, originally rooted in the sensuous sphere of feeling and of fantasy, is gradually changed in functional character. It becomes essentially subject to the exigencies of abstract thought. Once the image changes in function and becomes an instrument in reflective thought, its structure will also change. It is only through such structural change that the image can serve as an instrument of expression in abstract mental activity. This is why, of necessity, the sensuousness, fullness of detail, the color and vivacity of the image must fade. Faintness of sensuous attribute and a fragmentary character, which from the standpoint of concrete experience represent an inadequacy, are actually positive rather than negative signs of the new structure of imagery dictated by utility in abstract schemata.

In the pathological sphere we find some convincing evidence for this hypothesis of developmental change in the structure of the image from a purely sensory phenomenon to an abstract schema in reflective thought. In his famous analysis of aphasiacs, Head shows that patients suffering from a regression away from the sphere of abstract intellectualized behavior in an objective world simultaneously lose the ability to create images of a schematic character, that is, images which serve to illustrate ideas in the linguistic thinking process. The common ability to imagine, to create images, is not disturbed. On the contrary, the purely "sensuous" images of the aphasiac may be extremely lively, even to the extent of disturbing his free flow of speech. In spite of this, or perhaps because of it, there is nevertheless a loss of the ability to express schematic images derived from the realm of abstraction.[19]

SYNCRETISM OF MEANING IN PRIMITIVE IMAGERY.

The prototype of syncretic content in images is found in the dream. Here one person, X, can also be another person, Y. One thing can have several meanings, meanings which would naturally appear contradictory if referred to a real object in waking consciousness. The Freudian school performed a great service in drawing attention to the multiple meanings of dream

[19] Head, **572**, vol. 1, 373.

images, which they named "condensations." In the sphere of syncretic imagery the Aristotelian proposition that something cannot be both A and not-A does not hold. In the dream there is such a thing as "wooden iron."

The primitive mentality is unusually rich in "condensations." Fantasy images, which appear in their purest form in the primitive lyric, often have a syncretic content which would be virtually impossible to express in the poetry of western culture. Some examples will illustrate. A Melanesian maiden's love song is as follows:

"You would always like to spit on my fringed skirt,
  The torrent has carried it off!
  When he swam away with it, she [the fringed skirt] set the war-
    clubs in motion,
  Notched by the warriors.
  Oh, may the torrent make the clubs move,
  While chieftains battle over the fringed skirt."[20]

The wish expressed in this girl's love song is that she be fought over and thus be avenged for her lover's neglect. But at the same time the sexual motif, the desire to be satisfied by a man, is woven into the poem. The torrent as a battle motif, as part of the coarse sexual metaphor of the carrying away of the skirt and as a symbol of the transports of coitus, the phallic significance of the moving club—all this is both martial and sexual in meaning.

The following is an example from the Solomon Islanders, recorded by Thurnwald. It is a song of derogation.

"Your body [i.e., your shame] it is, in the realm beyond, the tree of fate; it is the tree's protector, who kills the shadow-spirits."

Here the female body—a metaphor of local significance being used—is likened contemptuously to the sycamore. A pure similarity of image is the basis for the first comparison. Syncretically included, however, is the sycamore as the home of the death-bird which draws souls to it and never allows them to

[20] Thurnwald, 309, Text 117.

return to the joyous world again. The whole metaphor may be interpreted in this manner: "Your whole body looks as ragged as a sycamore, and you are just as dangerous." The symbols of ugliness and danger are united in the one image.

This peculiarity of primitive imagery, out of which undifferentiated double meanings and condensed meanings arise, may also be the source of the primitive man's delight in play on words. The *double-entendre*, as I have attempted to demonstrate in my work on the origins of the metaphor, has become a socially important means of expression, that leaves out of consideration any playful aesthetic meaning it may contain.[21] A Melanesian woman who comes from the "West Country" says, in order cautiously to express the fact that she does not like to take another man in place of her dead husband: "He is with the people in Araukaria!" Now, this is the section in the western part of the Islands which leads to the underworld. The sentence has two meanings: (1) "My husband is in the West Country, that is, in the underworld." (2) "He is also in my homeland, in my birthplace, that is, he is with me." The double meaning of the word "West Country" therefore leads to the implication: "My man is in the underworld, but he is also with me, and I am still true to him."[22]

A syncretism of meaning is a common feature of the imagery of *children*. Children's drawings, narratives, plays, etc., indicate that a condensation of meaning is frequently characteristic of the childlike fantasy. This suggests that the imagery of the young child is more closely related to the dream than is adult imagery, an assumption which is supported by some interesting experiments on pronouncedly eidetic children. It appears that the eidetic image, like the dream image, tends to combine in one optical form the properties of several forms which would be known separately in the waking consciousness. A syncretic tendency was revealed experimentally by Freiling and Jaensch in their investigations of eidetic

[21] Werner, 141.
[22] Thurnwald, 309.

images.[23] If a child first observes two wires placed side by side, one wire being linear in form and the other of a zigzag shape, and then projects the images of the wires eidetically, the linear form will frequently tend to assume a zigzag form, or vice versa. The following experiment may illustrate still more clearly the character of condensation in the eidetic image. Two threads, one blue and the other red, and placed 2-3 cm. apart, are presented to an eidetic child. After their removal the child may see the eidetic image of the two threads as a single thread. This single thread combines the qualities of the two threads in so far as it appears to be made of intertwined red and blue colors.

The child's non-eidetic imagery often possesses this same characteristic. H. Neugebauer, speaking of the syncretic images of a 2:8-months-old child, remarks: "Snakes, bears, elephants, and so on are imagined by this child as having many legs. Cows and horses lay eggs, frogs have legs on their heads, etc."[24] This syncretic characteristic of child imagery is particularly obvious in play activities: A horse may stop for gas, or a train responds to such commands as "Whoa!" or "Giddap!"[25] The drawings of children, as mirroring fantasy and memory images, are rich in syncretic forms. While at an exhibition, Stern's five-year-old child first saw a picture representing figures of Indians. Later he saw a diver, fully equipped in his diving-suit, standing in a great basin of water. The next day he drew from memory the figure of a diver suspended by a rope held by an Indian. This fantasy image combined two otherwise discrete forms, bound together by the emotional needs of the child.[26] Another common experience of undifferentiated syncretic form appears in the drawings of animals as human beings, or in the well-known "mixed profile," in which both front and side are presented in one figure. In Fig.

[23] Freiling, 374, 129.
[24] Neugebauer, 468.
[25] Markey, 449, 79.
[26] Stern, 510, 13.

34 we see a fish drawn by a girl in such a way that it has both mammalian and fish-like characteristics.[27]

FIG. 34.—Fish with a Mammalian Neck, Drawn by a Thirteen-year-old Girl. (After Levinstein.)

Related to this condensation in imagery is a lability, an inconstancy, of meaning. Just as in the dream image there is a blurred, shimmering, indeterminate quality because of its multiple meaning, so too does the child's image tend to fade and blur from one meaning and form into the other. A toy may change in meaning in exactly this dreamlike fashion. The same piece of wood may be, in rapid succession, a doll, a cart, or a hat. A drawing in process of accomplishment varies in significance with every stroke; it is first an animal and then a man, or first a house and then a train. The dreamlike lability of the memory image may again be recognized in the young child's manner of telling a story, where there is but little consistency in the meaning of situations and objects. Groos relates of his three-year-old daughter: "When I was in the city a little while ago," said the child, telling a story, "there were such beautiful stores and flowers there. Anna (the doll) wanted to pick a flower, and just then a bear came in. Now my six children were frightened, and I hid them in the bath-oven and shut the door and turned the key. But the bear opened the door, and I was so frightened. . . !"[28] This is a clear example of lability in the flow of narration. In place of the doll Anna six children appear. The situation suddenly changes from the city back to the house where the bath-oven is located.

[27] Levinstein, 435, Table 12.
[28] Groos, 389, 162.

Psychotic imagery provides abundant examples of all kinds of syncretic condensed forms. "Primitive" psychotics, such as hysterics or schizophrenics, tell of their lovers who appear to them as animals, or of inanimate objects with human feet, of men with the bodies of animals, etc.

Here it becomes clear that we must distinguish between two factors in the so-called condensation of imagery: (1) the multiple meaning of a single object; (2) the condensation, into a composite gestalt, of various figural characteristics de-

Fig. 35.—"Water Spirits." Schizophrenic drawing. (After Prinzhorn.)

rived from different objects. It must be assumed that the tendency to condense several meanings into one conditions the further visual realization of this syncretism in a compound gestalt. When a psychotic combines father and lover in one person, this person will have a mixture of the physical characteristics and the external attributes (clothing, cane, etc.) of both. We get a particularly clear idea of the characteristics of hallucinatory images from the drawings in which psychotics depict their visions. The drawing in Fig. 35 was made by a schizophrenic day-laborer.[29] He describes the genesis of the hallucination represented in the picture as follows: "I was

[29] Prinzhorn, 594, 103.

sitting in bed, and suddenly there came out of the water such—how shall I say it!— . . . brutes! My mother was with them. They were half men and half animal. I saw that clearly. There was black magic there. I thought my mother wanted to pull me into the water and that I was going to die that way. When I lie still, everything comes back again and again. I see it all in the air, and best when it is twilight."

An hysterical patient drew a picture of her hallucination (see Fig. 36) while in a state of trance.[30] She explains the

FIG. 36.—"Hallucination." Drawing by a hysteric patient. (After Kretschmer.)

meaning of her drawing in this manner: "The animal is a goat, a satyr, and represents the disposition of man, of which it is a part. It has two heads, one a 'preacher's' head and the other a 'not-preacher's' head." Here there are two of the patient's lovers whom she knew in her youth growing out of the one goat-like torso (symbol of masculinity) and combined in a syncretic unity.

A comprehensive multiple meaning is expressed in the

[30] Kretschmer, 585, 74.

schizophrenic drawing in Fig. 37 (published by Prinzhorn).[31] The large circle surrounded by rays is a monstrance (a symbolic object in the Catholic Church). At the same time the circle is the "world-clock," the sun, the Lamb of God, Christ, and also the artist himself.

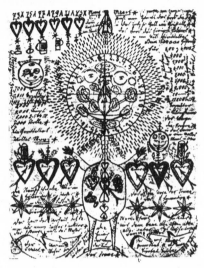

FIG. 37.—"Lamb of God." Schizophrenic drawing. (After Prinzhorn.)

DIFFUSE ORGANIZATION IN PRIMITIVE IMAGERY.

It is characteristic of primitive memory—and fantasy—images that the meaning content is not only syncretic, but diffuse. Primitive images, like primitive perceptions, are much more undifferentiated than their intellectualized counterparts, and in consequence are much less hierarchically organized and ordered in terms of essential and non-essential moments. This is evident in the temporal succession of the verbalized images as revealed in primitive narrations.

Narration among primitives, as Pechuël-Loesche has observed with the Loangos, often exhibits this peculiarity: the

[31] Prinzhorn, 594, 222.

series of events must be recounted in exactly the order in which they were experienced. "Otherwise the thread of the tale is irrevocably lost, and the whole story has to be told over again from the very beginning." In many primitive stories there is little distinction between what is essential in the situation and what is not. The recitation of tribal myths so typical of the South Sea Islanders, for instance, must proceed in a uniform fashion, in the manner of singing and declaiming long established by a dim line of ancestors. This primitive type of narration may be conceived as a concatenated organization in which all the parts appear to have an approximately equal importance ("chain type"). Its structure may be likened to the homogeneous, relatively uncentralized structure of the sensori-motor, or perceptual, phenomena described earlier in this book.

Again, in the sphere of primitive fantasy we encounter a diffuse, less articulated form of imagery. A highly differentiated imaginative pattern consists of salient parts remaining relatively self-subsistent within the whole. Not so the primitive analogue. Diffuse imagery has a global character which colors each individual part, a pervasive quality in which all the constituent parts are embedded. On the basis of this diffuse structure there arise poetical similes so strange that the man of western culture follows them only with the greatest difficulty. We shall present some examples of primitive poetical imagery. The first one is from a poem of vilification sung by a Solomon Islander about a woman: "Your body is a bat which I look at with fear, and which flies through the giant fig-trees and breaks branches."[32]

This bit of satire may be translated as follows: "You are as odious to me as the bats swooping through the trees. You are as repulsive to me as the sticky giant-fig, which drips resin." But as a matter of fact there is no genuine duality in this metaphor, no division in the image. The "poet" likens the woman's body to a global situation. The negative quality-of-

[32] Thurnwald, 309, Text 134.

the-whole, of revulsion, of offensiveness, is shot through the whole image. It is present in the bats, in the broken branches, in the gummy exudation, and so on. A quality-of-the-whole colors the imagined situation, and is its primary element.

Still more curious is another Solomon Islander's satire directed toward a woman:

> "Your shame, it is the missionary's phonograph:
> When recently the carpenter wound it up,
> And it began to sing loudly,
> The Kugumaru people were alarmed."[33]

This is a very remarkable metaphor. The comparison of the woman (or the woman *qua* vagina) to a phonograph is based, first of all, on the open horn of the machine. But at the same time the sexual factor is symbolized by another aspect of the collective situation: the winding up of the phonograph with the inserted handle. Finally the sound issuing forth (which represents yet another aspect in the comparison) is supposed to cause terror and consternation like the sensation aroused by the spectacle of the woman herself. Here we are confronted by an imaginative situation intelligible only in terms of primitive imagery, an imagery in which there is no sharp separation or opposition of parts. There is no isolated relation between handle and horn, or between these and the sound issuing from the horn, or between this latter event and its effect on the listeners. In short, there is a unity comprised of many elements not easily reconciled from the standpoint of logic. Only when we assume that the situation lacks a primary center, a dominant aspect, only when we recognize that any part, or function, of the phonograph is of equal importance in the image as a whole, does the song become understandable. Every part of the unity is homogeneously colored. Only because of this is the elasticity of the image possible, an apparent illogicality which allows the comparison of woman and phonograph to be constructed first in terms of one aspect of the

[33] *Ibid.*, Text 23.

global situation and immediately afterward in terms of still another aspect quite unrelated to its predecessor.

Another phenomenon characteristic of primitive imagery,
and also common to the child's mentality and the dream world,
is so-called "displacement." This, too, can be explained on
the ground of diffusion in the structure of the image. A native
tribe in New Zealand has a war cry: "The Waikato's paddles
are twisted."[34] This is an allusion to the treacherous, "twisted"
character of the Waikato themselves, who are an enemy tribe.
Without going too deeply into the matter, we might say that
a certain quality of the enemy, namely, their treachery, has
been "displaced," i.e., transposed to the paddle. Another example: In an Hawaiian love song there is the line, "Dripping
with rain on the place where you are lying." Here the displacement is clear. The wetness of a woman's body excited by
erotic passion is carried over into the landscape.[35]

The frequency of these displacements encourages us to assume that we are dealing with a basic structure in primitive
imagery. This notion becomes all the more tenable when we
consider similar displacements in other primitive fields, as in
the normal dream. Kraepelin has afforded us some very instructive descriptions of displacement in dream language. I
mention one of his examples because incidentally it tends to
coincide with the just-cited war cry of the New Zealand natives.
The dreamer says and actually visualizes in his dream: "The
straight director, the bent writer." This is reputed to mean:
"He writes differently from what one might expect."[36] The
quality of a dishonest way of writing is transposed symbolically
to the crookedness of the person's body.

All these transpositions are evidence of the diffuse structure
of the primitive image. The symbol of "twistedness" in the New
Zealander's war cry is not something applying to men alone,
men as seen in contradistinction to something else in abstract

[34] Taylor, 307, 146.
[35] Emerson, 187, 69.
[36] Kraepelin, 584, 45.

analogy. It is a quality-of-the-whole seeping through the whole structure of a global situation and affecting every part of it. "Twistedness" is a property that colors the whole image of "men paddling canoes." When the quality is thus stressed it may well appear in any element of the situation and occasion an apparent displacement. And the same is true of the instance taken from the dream world. The twistedness, the "bentness," of the director's body is a symbol-of-the-whole which, since it is a quality shot through the entire image, permits displacement. It is therefore, in actual fact, somewhat inadequate to speak of a "displacement," although it is exactly this from the logical standpoint of an outside observer. In a psychological sense the phenomenon is an expression of a homogeneous, global quality attached to every part of a fused situation.[37]

O. Pötzl has directed attention to the diffuse and labile character of the imagery of psychotics. He has also pointed out the relation between hallucinations and normal dream images, and has stressed the connection between this type of experience and the visual experience of the peripheral optical field, or the tachistoscopic vision of normal people. The optical field and, indeed, the whole mental field of certain abnormal individuals is characterized, so to speak, by an absence of division according to essential and non-essential parts, to central and peripheral elements. In conformity with this homogeneity, this globality of imagination, "it is the fundamental characteristic of the paranoic that he allows to enter into his inner world that which normally would remain in the periphery of consciousness. Impressions received while passing someone on the street, scraps of overheard conversation, glances, gestures—all become invested with a portentous meaning."[38]

Structural diffuseness and a lack of hierarchization in imagery and image relations are also characteristic of the *child's mentality*. The tendency to think in terms of homogeneous, concatenated units, each unit having an equal value, may account for the well-known fact that small children strenuously

[37] Cf. Werner, 141, 180 ff.
[38] Pötzl, 593, 337.

object to any change, however trivial, in their favorite stories. Sully found that "children noted with displeasure the slightest variation in their favorite tales."[39] One woman tells of having made the hero sit on a chair, rather than on the cupboard top, in the familiar story of Puss-in-Boots. A barrage of protest followed this error. Another time while recounting a fairy tale she came to the part where the heavy sigh of an animal "made the glasses on the table shake." At this point she was supposed to add ". . . and nearly blew out the candles." This she neglected to do; thereupon the group of children, with a concerted shout of reproach, remedied the omission with great clamor.

Gantschewa affords us another example of the child's compulsion to supply the whole continuum of the event, even though he has been asked only to recount some isolated detail.[40] A four-year-old child, says Gantschewa, returned home after his modeling lesson and excitedly told about everything that had happened there. When his mother asked him again: "Did you make a mouse?" he immediately repeated his story from start to finish—"I had a plate . . . and pears . . . a mouse . . . and a bird . . . etc."

A series of experiences recorded by Cramaussel show the close dependence of the small child's memory image on the global situation. Cramaussel mentions the case of a 3:3-year-old child who, after a period of separation, failed to recognize a girl of whom she had previously been very fond. But the next morning, when this same girl tied the child's hair ribbon, she was immediately recognized. A 1:7-year-old girl did not know her father when he returned home after a considerable period of absence, and even began to cry because of his strangeness. But in a short time, when the father had caressed the child in his usual fashion, his daughter's attitude was the same as before.[41]

[39] Sully, 516, Germ. ed., 53.
[40] Gantschewa, 375, 11.
[41] Cramaussel, 357, 71.

So long as objects are not centered according to essential and non-essential signs, but are determined by global qualities, it will be found that it is these qualities-of-the-whole, this fused, inclusive dominance, in terms of which the child fixes and knows a familiar situation. Under such circumstances there is a subsequent recognition of the familiar only provided that the customary dominant center appears. For example, a 2:5-year-old child returned home after a two months' vacation without apparently recognizing anybody or anything in the house. But as soon as the child entered his own room, he shouted happily: *"Li-lit à moi!"* (My bed!), and pointed at it without hesitation. The next morning, with his own room as a focal starting point, his recognition of his surroundings was complete.[42]

LEVELS OF ORGANIZATION IN MEMORY

As one would expect, the capacity for retention during childhood has been found to increase with age. According to Starr, to the Terman-Merrill revision of the Stanford-Binet test, a.o., the normal memory span increases steadily from two to six digits between two and one-half and ten years of age.[43] Also quite obvious are the general findings that the memory span varies with the material presented. What is the cause of this increase? We know at least one of the principal causal factors: viz., the growing capacity of the child to organize material to be retained. The younger child tends to apprehend and to reproduce the material in continuous, chain-like wholes, while the older child does it in patterns in which parts are related to one another and to the whole. One of our experiments with children two to ten years of age seems to illustrate well the effect of organization on span of attention. If presented with a number of digits greatly exceeding their capacity for retention, the younger children performed far below their normal

[42] *Ibid.*, 72.

[43] Munn, **955**, 339.

memory span; older children and adults were able to retain a number of digits closer to their individual capacity. The younger children broke down, obviously, because they were unable to build a continuous whole under these circumstances, whereas older people were capable of gathering discrete items for retention.

Factors of organization seem to be related also to the delay of responses. Memory traces are more stable the better they are organized (Koehler, Katona); therefore, they are less easily disturbed by interfering stimuli:[44] Hunter, Miles, Skalet, and Buehler showed that maximum delay increases in organisms, phylogenetically as well as ontogenetically.[45]

One of the most important though little noticed developmental problems of memory deals with the genetic shift in memory function due to the emergence of hierarchically higher activity ("cerebration"). Brunswik, Goldscheider, and Pilek performed a comprehensive investigation of the qualitative changes of memory that occur during mental growth.[46] They examined experimentally the growth curves of the following forms of memory:

(a) Memory for concrete, digit-like material: One series consisted of nine unrelated movements, such as hand clapping, lifting arms, making a bow; another series contained nine colors; a third, nine simple geometrical forms. The score consisted of the number of correctly reproduced items.

(b) Memory for concrete relationship: Here, the same material as in (a) was used; but the score pertained to the correctness of sequence of items.

(c) Memory for logically apprehended material: For instance, stories presented in twelve pictures had to be verbally reproduced.

The growth curves for the three forms of memory have been

[44] Katona, 774.
[45] Hunter, 406; Miles, 949; Skalet, 983; Bühler, 349.
[46] Brunswik, 346.

found to differ significantly, indicating genetic shifts of memory function during development. The curves for discrete, concrete digits increase up to ten to twelve years, declining somewhat after that age. Curves for concrete relations show a considerable rise up to fourteen years; after that the increase is steady but slow. Curves for logically apprehended material rise slowly till twelve to fourteen years and rapidly during adolescence.

Earlier work by Winch and McGeoch also seems to be related to the problem of memory levels. In Winch's experiment children were presented with a simple picture, the score consisting in the number of items recalled. Winch reported a peak of the growth curves for these concrete items at about seven to eight years of age.[47] McGeoch used three types of material on children nine to fourteen years of age: (a) cards picturing simple objects; (b) a picture entitled "The disputed case"; (c) a carefully rehearsed event. Memory for single concrete objects (a) improved up to twelve years; the recall scores for the picture and for the event (b, c) were found to rise steadily. The scores for the report on the event showed a definite spurt between twelve and fourteen years of age.[48]

The various experimental results, though not conclusive, indicate a shift during development in terms of the replacement of a lower memory function by a higher one.

A functional shift toward higher levels of memorization is revealed also in experiments on delayed reaction. A significant study about the relation between delay and body orientation was performed by Emerson.[49] Children 2:3 to 4:11 years old watched the experimenter place a small ring on one of 42 pegs that were distributed regularly over the surface of an easel. They were then asked to copy the experimenter's performance; since the easel had been rotated in the meanwhile, the task

[47] Winch, 999.
[48] McGeoch, 942.
[49] Emerson, 892.

required bodily turns of various degrees. The bodily disorientation during delay caused a decrease in accuracy. The decrease was less noticeable with older than with younger subjects. The experiment indicates that bodily cues are of primary importance with young children; these cues become slowly subordinated to more stable perceptual relationships as a child grows older. We repeated these experiments with children six to ten years of age and found that the peg position was accurately determined by many subjects through numerical-verbal means. Thus, with increasing age, delayed response patterns seemed to become reorganized in terms of functions of a genetically higher order. We are probably justified in distinguishing at least three genetic levels: At the primary level, the delayed response appears mainly based on bodily (sensory-motor) cues; at a higher level, concrete perceptual relationships gain increasingly in importance; finally, verbal-conceptual activity may become a significant factor in the delayed response pattern.

PART THREE

Primitive Notions of Space and Time

Chapter V

PRIMITIVE NOTIONS OF SPACE

Spatial Ideas of Primitive Man.

So far as the primitive man carries out technical activities in space, so far as he measures distances, steers his canoe, hurls his spear at a cerain target, and so on, his space as a field of action, as a pragmatic space, does not differ in its structure from our own. But when primitive man makes this space a subject of representation and of reflective thought, there arises a specifically primordial idea differing radically from any intellectualized version. The idea of space for primitive man, even when systematized, is syncretically bound up with the subject. It is a notion much more affective and concrete than the abstract space of the man of advanced culture. This space is indissolubly linked with the individual personality and the tribal life and culture. It is not so much objective, measurable, and abstract in character. It exhibits egocentric or anthropomorphic characteristics, and is physiognomic-dynamic, rooted in the concrete and substantial.

The study of primitive languages is of great help in demonstrating the development of space concepts and space relations. Of course, one can scarcely presume to state exactly to what extent the linguistic terms coincide with the actual spatial experience of the aborigine. We must be content to suppose that the primitive linguistic terms would not be what they are, had they not at some previous time emerged from a vivid, extremely concrete spatial experience. Primitive terms for spatial relations suggest that the body itself with its "personal dimensions"[1] of above-below, before-behind, and right-left is the source of a psychophysical system of coordinates. Therefore it may be inferred that objective space has gradually evolved from this primitive orientation. Ernst Cassirer says: "Where the more highly developed languages, in order to designate spatial relations, normally use prepositions, particles, and post-positions, there are nominative expressions in the aboriginal languages, which either stand for, or refer directly to, parts of the body."[2] The Mande (African) group of languages expresses "behind" by an anthropomorphic substantive, "the back." The word "before" becomes "eye"; "on," "neck"; "in," "stomach," etc.

Sometimes it is possible to reconstruct the actual situation in which anthropomorphic spatial relations, as linguistically expressed, must be rooted. Baldus tells us that "if the Tumerehá Indian sees an object he speaks of the side nearest to him as 'behind,' for the reason that this side is facing in the same direction as his own back. The reverse side he speaks of as 'forward,' because it corresponds to his own frontal aspect."[3] It is natural for him to orient himself in a space with which he is identified corporeally and dynamically, which exhibits the spatial directions of his own body, and not in a space that stands out there, over against him as subject.

The comparative study of primitive tongues suggests, furthermore, the concrete character of primitive space, its being embedded in a broader, concrete, global situation. Space, spatial relations and directions, on the one hand, remain highly material and devoid of abstract interpretation; and, on the other, they are dynamic and conditioned by the influence of events.

In any archaic or primitive language we find place-names which are by no means specific, abstract designations, but rather expressions for material elements of a thoroughly con-

[1] Stern, 122.
[2] Cassirer, 15, vol. 1, 157.
[3] Baldus, 156, 114.

crete space. Substantive forms such as "upper part of the body," "lower part of the body," "track," "outskirts,"' and so on, become the primitive equivalents for "over," "under," "behind," and "about" in some Ural-Altaic languages. Similarly, in some Sudanese tongues "over" becomes a word analogous to "air," "under" is expressed by "ground" or "earth," etc.[4] It is above all characteristic of primitive languages that spatial relations are fused in the concrete situation of which they are a part. To take one of countless examples, when the Yahgans of Tierra del Fuego use pronouns, the spatial orientation of the person involved is always simultaneously expressed. The Yahgan terms for "he" and "she" differ entirely, depending on whether they refer to someone sitting at the upper, outside end of the wigwam, or at the entrance of the wigwam, to the right or left side of the wigwam, or directly on the threshold.[5] Only gradually do such spatial relations become self-subsistent and stripped of the concrete fabric in which they are interwoven as a dominant, accented component, one that will ultimately develop into abstract purity.

Primitive systematizations of space and spatial relations can be observed outside linguistic expression, especially in the sphere of the myth. Here the fundamental discrepancy between our geometrized concepts and the primitive spatial ideas becomes startlingly clear. Mythical space and spatial relations are again not abstract forms serving to measure the world, to order phenomena quantitatively, but are qualitative in character and fused to a considerable degree in the very concrete substance and emotion of the whole tribal existence. A few examples may establish this fact.

In the totemistic culture of certain Australian tribes, space is systematized not according to geometrical or geophysical aspects, but so to speak as "totemistic space." Space as a whole is divided into as many distinctly separated regions as there

[4] Cassirer, 15, vol. 1, 157.
[5] Bridges, 168.

are clans in the tribe. A Wotjobaluk explained to A. W. Howitt[6] the particular organization of such a space by arranging a number of sticks as shown in Fig. 38. This orientation shows a division into northern and southern halves, one of which is

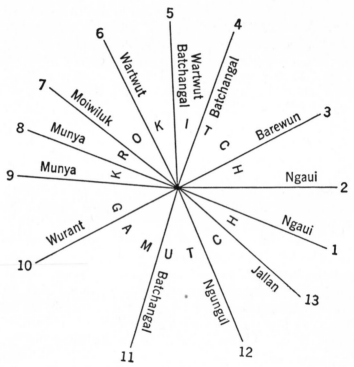

FIG. 38.—Diagram Representing the "Totemistic Space" of an Australian Tribe. (After Howitt.)

identified with the main group, "Krokitch," and the other with the "Gamutch." Each tribal subgroup occupies a particular area with the two main divisions, and each suborientation is definitely related to the whole and to the other constituent

[6] Howitt, 213, 62.

sections. This is not simply a geographical diagram of local significance. It represents a spatial division of the whole world with all its concrete and mythical content as the Wotjobaluk sees it.[7]

This mythical systematization of space is encountered on a much higher cultural level in the religious ideology of the Zuñi. In accordance with a tribal partition into seven clans, universal space is also divided into seven sections. This mythical space is visibly represented in the typical partition of the Zuñi village into seven sections. In terms of this basic mythical form, the whole political, social, and religious life of the tribe is minutely ordered.[8]

Mythical space, however highly organized it may be, is essentially different from our geometrized, physical, abstract space. It still retains some of the salient properties of primitive space, particularly its concreteness and dynamism. This qualitative dynamism may come to view in such physiognomic or expressive terms as "holy" or "unholy," qualities on which a mythical space may be based. In its highest and most elaborate form this qualitative dynamism appears in the astrological-cosmic space concepts of our own early cultures.

In a certain Babylonian text we find: "When the star Marduk (Jupiter) is in ascendancy (that is, when it appears low on the horizon), it is then Nebo (the Babylonian Mercury). When it has risen (here the actual figure is omitted) so many double hours, it is Marduk. When it stands in the middle of the heavens ('culminates'), it is Nibiru (that is, fulfillment, the god of midday, the highest one, the omnipotent god). Each planet becomes this at its zenith."

This Babylonian text, according to Winckler, expresses the notion basic to all astrology that stars, and especially the planets, receive their daemonic strength from their spatial position. What the text really means is this: The planet Jupiter, at a low point in its path when just over the horizon, becomes the planet Mercury. That is, the planet has the mythical attributes of Mercury when occupying

[7] Cassirer, 14, 21.
[8] Cushing, 179; Stevenson, 300. Cf. Cassirer, 14, 22.

this particular position in heavenly space. When it arrives at its zenith the planet is then Jupiter, in correspondence with the mythical omnipotence of the god. Every planet (including the sun and moon) has the powers and effects of various other planets by virtue of a coincidence of position in this daemonically organized space.[9]

It would appear, therefore, that the totemistic, or the sociomythical, or the astrological idea of space must be characterized as a rationalization of a still much more primitive experience. This general kind of space is thought of as being fused with the whole shifting complex of human activity and emotion. It is the concrete ground of life visualized in spatial relations. There must be a complete revolution in the history of the human mind in order to uproot the idea of space from its primitive, anthropomorphic, qualitative-dynamic ground and thereby elevate it to the free sphere of physical-geometric abstraction.

THE CHILD'S NOTION OF SPACE.

The ontogenetic development of the spatial idea may be understood in terms of a gradual widening of the gap between the ego and the external world, an increasing objectivation. Space is originally one aspect of the child's consciousness of his body. Space literally ends at the periphery of the physical being; it is enclosed, so to speak, within the skin of the child. Coghill and Carmichael point out that, in the fetus, the limb is able to respond with promptness and accuracy to any stimulus arising within the body as the result of a particular posture, but does not respond to a stimulus arising externally.[10] For the infant, surrounding space and private, corporeally centered space are one, and together constitute an *Ur-raum*, i.e., a "primordial space" (W. Stern). The mouth is the primitive means of knowing objects, that is, in a literal sense, through the grasping of the objects. The spatial knowledge of an object results from a sucking in of the thing through the mouth, and

[9] Winckler, 148, 48.
[10] Coghill, 633, 21; Carmichael, 628, 114.

a consequent tactual discovery and incorporation. Out of this "primordial space" there gradually arises, in the course of a few weeks, a space-of-nearness, of propinquity, in which the space surrounding the body becomes differentiated from the body proper. Objects are now known and oriented by reaching and touching, particularly with the hands. That which can be touched bounds the space of the very young infant. During the course of the second quarter of the first year this objectivation proceeds rapidly. Space continually expands into more and more distant regions, particularly because of an increase in the power and discriminatory ability of the optical function. But in spite of this, the space of the child remains closely bound up with the ego for a comparatively long period.

We may follow the course of development in spatial relations by using as a main example the progressive variation in the child's notion of "left" and "right." In this process of objectivation the following steps may be roughly outlined:

1. In this first stage there are a space-of-action and spatial qualities-of-action. Although left and right may not be experienced as specific objective qualities attached to spatial forms, they are actually known, however, as qualities-of-action. The Scupins report of their three-year-old boy: "While visiting the bear-cages in the Zoological Gardens we went up one flight of stairs leading to the place and left by another. Today, when we approached the same place by the stairs by which we had left the day before, the child held back, saying angrily: 'These are the wrong steps; these are the going-down steps . . . the others are the going-up steps.'"[11] Space is given to the young child primarily as a personal space-of-action. Places are oriented and receive their dimensions through action. Stern gives an example of the childlike space-of-action inherent even in familiar situations. When the 3:8-year-old child was asked by his parents: "Do you know where your bed-room in Breslau is?" he replied, "When you're in the loggia you first go through the play-room, and then the steps go down, and

[11] Scupin, 502, vol. 2, 77.

then you're there. And then you go all the way to the dining-room. Don't you know that whenever someone comes to stay at the house there's always something nice to eat!"[12]

An amusing instance from the diary of the Scupins' child when he was six years old illustrates how spatial relations like "behind" and "before" or "in front of" may still retain their character as part of a dynamic situation. "When asked where he went during the school recess, he said: 'Wherever Herr G.'s [the teacher's] back is.' "[13]

2. According to Binet, Terman, and others, an average child is able to demonstrate the positions of right and left on his own body when he is six or seven years old. Although at this time the normal child certainly has developed these spatial notions, they are still present egocentrically; that is, he cannot distinguish right and left on bodies outside his own.

3. At the third stage, which comes a little later (according to Piaget, at approximately eight years), the child acquires the ability to distinguish between the left and right sides of other persons. According to Gordon, the nine-year-old child will correctly imitate the movements of the left and right hands of someone facing him. The two positions are now seen from the standpoint of the person opposite.[14]

4. In the fourth stage right and left are understood as special properties of even inanimate objects (the eleven-year level, according to Piaget).

These age levels must not, of course, be taken as absolute in value, since the child's reactions depend to a great extent on the complexity of the particular situation involved. What we are interested in, however, is the succession of steps which reveal a steady development of spatial ideas characterized by an increasing separation of ego and object. Piaget devised a test scale which is useful in the analysis of this development.[15]

[12] Stern, 512, 105.
[13] Scupin, 502, vol. 3, 22.
[14] Piaget, 481, 107; Head, 572, vol. 1, 169.
[15] Piaget, 481, 107 ff.

The average child of seven years can solve the following test. A coin is placed on the table to the left of a pencil. The child is now asked to tell whether the pencil is "to the left or to the right." Again, if three objects are placed side by side, their spatial relations to one another cannot be analyzed until the eleven-year age level has been reached. (Here a key is placed to the right of the coin and the pencil, and the child is asked whether the pencil is to the left or right of the key, etc.) This amazing difference in the difficulty of the two tests is obviously due to the fact that in the first test the child can answer egocentrically by referring directly to the left and right parts of his own body, whereas in the second test he is successful only providing he understands spatial relations in a truly objective sense as applying to the objects *per se*.

Recently we made a study on the genesis of the perception of spatial relationship in mentally retarded children at the Wayne County Training School. The procedure used in these experiments resembles that of the Knox Cube test. There are two series. In the first experiment—which we shall call the "tap test"—the experimenter taps 4 square holes of a screen in a given order, e.g., 1-3-2-4 or 1-4-2-3. The child is asked to repeat the tapping. In a second experiment—the "flash test"— the (12) combinations are the same but are presented not by tapping but by successively lighting up the square holes.

Whereas the lower mental age groups (six through eight years) are superior on the tap test with respect to the flash test, the higher mental age groups perform better on the flash test than on the tap series. The psychological differences of perception of space relationship in the two series are as follows: (1) spatial relationship as perceived through the experimenter's tapping is rather concrete and personal; spatial relationship grasped through successive flashes is more abstract and impersonal. (2) In the tap series, visual movements are outstanding characteristics of the stimuli, whereas flashes are more static in nature. The growing superiority of the perform-ance on the flash test over the achievement on the tap test indicates, therefore, a shift from a dynamic, concrete, and personal perception of space relationship to one which is more static, abstract, and impersonal.[16]

Related to the primitive experience of a concrete, egocentric space are the frequently observed diffuseness and instability in the orientation of more complex spatial units. Since for the child the complex spatial pattern is syncretically bound up with duration, and since space is conceived as a succession of movements, he finds it difficult to attain a stable objective in the spatial situation. A child may be able to orient himself perfectly well so long as he can carry out a familiar sequence of movement, but be quite lost if he has to start from some new point of departure. A good illustration of this experience is found in the previously quoted incident (p. 165) reported by Cramaussel. The two-year-old child returning from a long trip orients himself in his home only after he has entered his own room. This room is the focus of all his movements within the confines of his home. In other words, primitive space-of-action retains the property of a temporal succession, that is, irreversibility.

Another example of diffuseness and instability in the spatial situation is seen in the following account of the behavior of the Scupins' 7:1-year-old child. "Today Bubi was taken through the woods by the forester. Without following any path, over brooks, mounds and through clearings he went to the tree-nursery where the men were digging. On the way back, at a spot some five-minutes' walk from the forester's lodge, the man showed the boy a strawberry patch. In the afternoon the child's mother, armed with a pail, thought she would let him lead her to the strawberries. Unable to reconstruct the return route in a reversed direction, the boy led her all the way through the woods, over the brooks and through cleared spots to the place where the men were at work at the nursery, and thus found his circuitous way to the strawberry patch. To her amused astonishment, Bubi's mother found that it had taken

[16] Werner, 536.

her three-quarters of an hour of trail-making to arrive at a place not five minutes' distance from the forester's house where they had started. A whole chain of associations and memories had guided him. He spoke in a long monologue, saying: 'Here at the threshold the forester said, Watch out! Here's a step up! Here the forester said, Sit down and slide. Here—wait a minute—how do you go from here? Oh, yes . . . the grass is trampled . . . we're right. There's Gold Brook already! The forester jumped across first and reached over his stick to us. . . . Look! there are the men working!' "[17]

The concrete space-of-action can be clearly observed in feeble-minded people. Goddard reports on a subject (actual age twenty-five years, mental age five years) who cannot trace out direct routes on the Porteus maze patterns unless he transforms this abstract problem into one that is highly concrete: "Oh, I see, it's a train. S . . . that stands for station, don't it? . . . I'll take Ethel home to Washington. (Finds opening at finish.) Here it is. Write Washington there, please. Here we go . . . too-oo-t . . . ps-e-e-e . . . choo-choo . . . choo-choo-oo! Here we are. Ethel got home without getting hurt. Washington! All change cars!"[18]

PATHOLOGICAL PRIMITIVATION OF THE IDEA OF SPACE.

A great variety of mental disturbances of the regressive type lead to a primitive notion of space. In such cases, generally speaking, space becomes less objective and abstract than egocentric, affectively conditioned, physiognomic-dynamic, a structure embedded in the concrete event.

A great number of pathological cases, all of which, despite a difference in clinical causes, are marked by certain primitive characteristics (the aphasiacs and agnosiacs of Head, Gelb-Goldstein, Woerkom, and Grünbaum, among others) exhibit a relapse to a conception of space intimately linked with the ego and the body, and therefore with physical activity and movement.

[17] Scupin, 502, vol. 3, 22.
[18] Goddard, 560.

For such persons left and right are often not objective dimensions, but qualities determined by the system of coordinates represented by the body. If, for instance, the examiner touches his own left eye with his left hand and tells the patient opposite him to do likewise, the movement will often be imitated in a mirror-like fashion, that is, the patient will raise his right hand to his right eye.[19] Siekmann also found that with his patients spatial directions were somatically determined and concrete, and almost never of an abstract, objective significance.[20] When such a patient lay down horizontally, closing his eyes, "up" was still at the anterior region of his body, and "down" somewhere near his feet.

The surrounding space for such individuals has primarily the character of a field-of-action whose center is the patient's own body. The patient will orient himself with ease in such a space-of-action, but only in so far as spatial points and directions are signals for certain movements and activities. One of Head's patients distinguishes between left and right by identifying these spatial directions with somatically focused activities. Right is that side which carries out the movement of writing; left (on the street) is that direction in which the traffic goes.[21] If a subject has only a space-of-action, the things about him are spatially oriented only in so far as they constitute elements of some physical action. They are spatially without significance if they are not thus physically related to the subject's body. Head's patients could often point to things without being able to explain the spatial order of these things in relation to each other. Siekmann's patient could throw a ball first into a hat and then toss another ball into a cap lying beyond the hat. But unless he measured the distance by pacing it off, etc., he was unable to say which of the two objects was farther from him. He was also unable, by merely looking at the models, to put

[19] Head, **572**, vol. 1, 169.
[20] Siekmann, **601**.
[21] Head, **572**, vol. 1, 188.

down matches in the forms shown in Fig. 39. Nevertheless he was able to accomplish this without difficulty once he had imitated with postures of his own body the spatial relations of the matches. On the other hand, he was equal to the task of copying a little house of matches without preliminary posturing—a problem more complex for the normal person than the first—because in this case the abstract spatial relations

Fɪɢ. 39.—Arrangement of Matches. Forms Used in Siekmann's Test on Spatial Relations.

were securely embedded in a material structure familiar to him.[22]

These individuals, who conceive space only as a concrete field-of-action, have lost a great deal of their ability to represent space and its relationships as removed from the subject, that is, space which is not connected with the subject's motor activities. This function of spatial representation can be disturbed in varying degrees. Many aphasiacs can orient themselves in space by means of some action, but cannot construct an image of any kind, verbal or drawn, that involves spatial relations. Some are able to make a sort of naturalistic drawing of a space—of their own room, for example—but they are still powerless to reconstruct the abstract relations of parts in an objective schema. And, again, others can draw a plan of their room on paper, but only when their usual sitting place has been marked down so they will thus have an egocentrically determined point in the schema on which to base their reconstruction.

Space known in this way must of necessity exhibit signs of a relatively *diffuse* structure. If space is essentially the egocentric space-of-action of the previously mentioned examples,

[22] Similar cases are reported by Woerkom, 613.

it follows that the differentiation of spatial parts into an objective relationship will remain undeveloped. Spatial points will show a relationship only to the extent to which they are conditioned by the whole continuum of the event to which they are bound.

Storch, using mazes, has tested experimentally the faculty of orientation in debile patients.[23] At times he found a remarkable power of orientation, but one which was, at the same time, strictly dependent on a certain continuum of motor behavior, on a rigidly defined succession of movements fixing the elements of the physical situation and investing them with a locally significant spatial and temporal character. The diffuse nature of this spatial orientation, its dependence on the continuum as a fixed whole, is revealed in the fact that the successful accomplishment of the task at hand was bound up with the preservation of the smallest details of the activity, and that the slightest variation in the physical conditions of the maze completely disrupted what had been previously learned. Besides this "global" type, in which spatial-temporal orientation must proceed in terms of an inseparable and irreversible continuum of action, Storch defined a second type. This type, as pathologically known—one particularly associated with patients suffering from Korsakow's disease—is marked not so much by a lack of differentiation as a lack of centralization. The spatial-temporal whole is broken into discrete bits, so to speak, in such a way that in imitating any action the order, the proper mode of sequence, of the original is lost.

The diffuse character of pathological space and spatial relations can furthermore be clearly observed in drawings. One of Head's patients, for example, did not know where she was supposed to place the tusks of an elephant she was drawing.

This syncretic and diffuse cast in the pathological notion of space is the cause of a relative absence of objective stability. The transposition of spatial point and direction, any slight change in the spatial pattern, completely disorients the patho-

23 Storch, 607.

logical subject. Many of Head's patients were unable to find their way about the city unless their goal was approached from some specific direction; otherwise they were utterly lost.[24] Siekmann's patient was likewise unable to cope with any sort of new orientation. There is only one way ("his way") from home to the center of the city. In consequence, for such people, personal everyday objects must have their precise place. Any alteration in this pedantic organization, and the rigid spatial structure which the patient has painfully constructed will tumble in ruins.

[24] Head, 572, vol. 1, 418.

Chapter VI

PRIMITIVE NOTIONS OF TIME

TEMPORAL NOTIONS OF PRIMITIVE MAN.

Temporal relations as expressed in the languages and myths, and in the profane and religious practices of primitive peoples afford us a mass of data indicating that time, in the primitive sphere, is not so much an abstract measure of order as a moment embedded in the whole concrete activity and social life of the tribe.

The words used by primitive people to express time represent really no more than certain salient events within a continuum of action.[1] Uganda tribesmen who raise cattle have a complicated system of dividing up the day, but it is by no means a generally applicable, abstract schema. The temporal divisions are implicit in the series of events constituting the day's work; e.g., six o'clock is "milking-time"; three o'clock in the afternoon is "watering-time"; five o'clock, "home-coming time for the cattle," and so on.

Similarly, the Aranda of Western Australia have twenty-five different divisions of the day, e.g., *lentara,* when the first streaks of light are seen in the east; *artyelboniwia,* when the streaks of light begin to widen; *altábatara,* twilight; *ingúntingúnta,* when the birds begin to twitter, etc.[2]

Among the Bigamul of Australia the seasons of the year are defined in terms of the trees which bloom during this or that period. There is a time of "yerra blossoming"; of "yerrabinda" (in September); of "nigabinda" (the time when apple-trees bloom about Christmas). The midsummer season is called

[1] Nilsson, 104, chap. 1; Cassirer, 15, vol. 1, 166 ff.
[2] Strehlow, 304, vol. 2, 44.

tinnakogealba, that is, the time of year "when the ground burns the soles of the feet."[3]

The primitive systematization of time frequently is intimately connected with the particular activity pattern of the tribe. Just as one might speak of the "cattle-raising-time" of the Uganda peoples, he might speak of a "fish-catching-time" among the Eskimos of Greenland. The ebb and flow of the tide mark the divisions of the Eskimo's day, but with no reference to the motion of the sun or moon.[4] The Trobriand Islanders (of Melanesia), as Malinowski has demonstrated, have developed an extremely elaborate system of "gardening-time."[5]

The cultivation of gardens by the Trobrianders is in accordance with the full rhythm and measure of seasonal change throughout the year. Even the name of the year is *taytu*, a small species of yam. The past year is literally the "time of the past *taytu*." Again, the year is divided into the season when gardens have yet to bear fruit and the season when they are in maturity. The native who wishes to define an event temporally will always refer to the concurrent agricultural activity. He will say: "This happened *o takaywa*, that is, during the cutting of the scrub." Or he may use the expression *wa sopu*, "in the planting time," etc. Gardening activities are also correlated with a sequence of lunar phases. There are, in all, thirteen moons which coincide, approximately, with some agronomic activity; but the lunar divisions of time are themselves of ancillary importance as a chronological measure. Even the sequence of the years is determined by the agricultural reference. The natives have a name for each field, and the past years are identified with the time that such and such a strip of land was put under cultivation. By adding together different combinations of fields they are able to count the years back through several decades.

Concrete time-of-action, embedded in a continuum of activity, naturally exhibits an altogether different structure from the quantitatively continuous ordering schema of the intellectual man. Time may be thought of as filled with certain emo-

[3] Howitt, 214, 432.
[4] Cope, 177.
[5] Malinowski, 235, 52 f.

tional qualities. Among African tribes time is divided into lucky and unlucky periods. On the basis of this affective (physiognomic) aspect, a temporal daemonism can develop in the mythical sphere (holy and unholy periods, etc.).[6]

Furthermore, because of the action-character of the temporal, certain logical peculiarities in the temporal structure may appear. Present and future may become congruous, for example, since the simultaneity of events is defined not so much by their objective synchronism as by their coincidence in effect. The evil thought, in the conception of the Loangos, is temporally identical with the evil deed.[7] Omens, dreams, and magic ritual are to a certain degree simultaneous with the event that occasions them, or which they occasion. Mythical happenings long past can be vital and effective in the immediate present.

This concrete time-of-action hinders a perfect temporal systematization (centralization). Temporal divisions (such as the year) are arranged in terms of dominant events. Often these temporal divisions are thought of not as growing out of each other or as following each other progressively in a continuum, but as standing side by side in isolation. In this situation temporal gaps can actually be left unaccounted for. Or there may be a partial overlapping of certain temporal periods because of the lack of an abstract frame of temporal reference. The Tumerehá Indians say that the year has ten months and two more during which the year is dead, that is, the two months when the algarrobo is ground. During the algarrobo harvest time there are feasts and drinking "for there is no year."[8] The Malecites Indians have a concrete qualitative sequence of lunar periods marked by frequent gaps. The moon is born and commences to grow (5th-6th day); is nearly full (11th-12th day); has passed its fullness (16th-18th day); begins to die (22d-23d day); etc. The Cree Indians of the

[6] Cf. Werner, 143.
[7] Pechuël-Loesche, 257.
[8] Baldus, 156, 141.

Plains apparently disregard those days on which the moon is invisible.[9]

Since in the simpler types of temporal system among the American Indians there may even be intra-tribal differences, differences in the selection of natural phenomena and objects in the construction of a temporal frame, a curious lack of consistency may appear in these primitive calendar forms. Sapir reports that not all Nootka Indian families use the same temporal divisions. In consequence there are frequent quarrels about the selection of a date for tribal ceremonies, since different families are sometimes as much as one or two months at variance in their definition of a certain time.[10]

These and similar facts from all corners of the primitive world indicate that the primitive temporal concept generally lacks that central focus, that continuity and consistency in counting which mark a fully abstract, quantitatively determined temporal system.

THE CHILD'S NOTIONS OF TIME.

With small children the temporal idea is marked by a concrete and affective character-of-action. The very language of the young child mirrors this peculiarity. For example, the temporal values of the child are primarily expressed in terms of affective and motor activities which contain an implicit temporal reference.[11] A two-year-old child says, for instance, "Bath, bath!" and by these words expresses a desire in which the time element of the near future is involved by implication. The adverb of the future ("tomorrow," "soon," etc.) is often identified with an immediate wish, just as the adverb of the past ("all done," etc.) is linked with satisfaction for some sort of completed activity. The embedding of the temporal in the actual current event or series of events, a continuum in which time and space exist undifferentiated, may result in

[9] Cope, 177, 127.
[10] *Ibid.*, 131.
[11] Decroly and Degand, 359.

the phenomenon of temporal ideas possessing spatial characteristics. The duration of year and day is understood by many children to be an entity materially extended in space, a dynamic entity. The Scupins' 6:8-year-old son "looked up at the sky and said, pointing with his finger: 'That's where the day comes out, and there, farther along, is the night, and right up at the top is Christmas day.' "[12]

E. C. Oakden and Mary Sturt, in their careful investigation of the development of temporal knowledge, remark: "The season to children seems to be much less a mark of time than a description of concrete, material things that enter directly into their experience. Winter really means snow for them; spring, flowers. On a very warm day in March a child may say: 'It's summer . . . it's so hot today!' "[13]

Many children believe that the calendar "makes" time, and that tearing off the calendar sheets actually brings about an advance in time. Katz emphasizes the fact that the calendar has a deep significance for his children as a realization of time. "Sunday is the day when the number on the calendar is red; a week-day is any day when the number is black."[14]

For the child, systematization of time does not begin with the construction of a continuous, quantitative schema, but rather with the conception of time as a sort of substance brought together as discontinuous pieces and determined by concrete and affective qualities. Time is often thought of as objectively discontinuous. When the Scupins' 6:8-year-old son learned that it is night in America when it is daytime in Germany, he inquired: "Where is the line on the earth where day begins and night ends?"[15] In the child's experience temporal events are fulfilled in a series of sudden transitions varying qualitatively. Up to the time when they have reached school age, many children believe that they really become

[12] Scupin, **502**, vol. 2, 199.
[13] Oakden and Sturt, **469**, 315.
[14] Katz, **421**, 109.
[15] Scupin, **502**, vol. 3, 21.

older, a different person, by having a birthday, or that the change of months occasions a fundamental, substantial change in the world. While tearing the sheet marked "June 30" from the calendar on the first day of July, the Scupin boy, at the age of eight years, said: "Look! no more June bugs!"[16]

The child slowly masters time as he masters space. From a personal, egocentric concept he slowly advances toward a time which encompasses that "which is farther away," the event that is not yet seen or presaged, the abstract, objective, and general event. Katz says: "The child long before he refers the course of events to some periodicity, to some temporal scale, splits up these events into affectively salient, isolated happenings. As a result there appears a qualitative arrangement very irregular in structure. Each day, for example, is divided off into breakfast, midday nap, supper, and so on; each year into birthday, Easter, Christmas."[17]

As Grigsby points out, even children in the early school years may still use ego-related concrete situations to designate time.[18] Grigsby, examining a group of six-year-old children, found that, when they were asked what time they got up, 82 per cent of their answers were of this sort: "When my mother comes in and calls me." The development from an egocentric, "personal" time to a "universal" time is well illustrated in some of Oakden's and Sturt's results.[19] The accompanying table lists the percentage of correct answers to the following simple questions: 1. "What time is it for your mother at home now?" 2. "What time of day is it in X [another neighboring town]?"

Age	4	5	6	7	8	9	10
Question 1 (% correct)	50	75	60	84	84	92	100
Question 2 (% correct)	14	58	60	54	64	84	86

[16] *Ibid.*, 37.
[17] Katz, **421**, 243.
[18] Grigsby, **387**.
[19] Oakden and Sturt, **469**.

A child eight years of age who knew that it was Saturday in Cambridge said: "It would be Sunday in London, because that's a different city, and there are even towns where it could be Monday!"

From these and other results we may draw the conclusion that the child's concept of time is based on an egocentric and concrete mode of experience, and that it tends to develop steadily toward a universal schema. A child may already be able to conceive time in a general sense so far as his family or visible surroundings are concerned, and yet be unable to do so for distant towns and scenes.

PATHOLOGICAL PRIMITIVATION OF THE NOTION OF TIME.

However different in clinical cause and appearance the pathologically degenerated ideas of temporality may be, all the regressive changes exhibited have certain formal characteristics in common. The basic factor behind these structural changes is a de-differentiation of the acting subject and the objective world against him. Through this shrinking of the gap between object and subject, the individual is plunged into a swift stream of events; he more or less loses the ability to en-mesh this flux of activity within a temporal schema, and thus fix and order it.

In case of a serious degeneration of the distance between object and subject, the individual is actually thrust into a stream of events bereft of any device by means of which he can articulate his present existence in relation to his past and future. Pinned down as he is to the momentary situation, he may be said to be a "situative cross-sectional being."[20] Hochheimer paints a vivid picture of the behavior of such a person, one who has been torn loose from a world in which ego and outer existence are discrete, and thus forced into this type of cross-sectional existence.[21] According to one of his patients' own description, only "that which is momentary" exists for

[20] Cf. Storch, 607.
[21] Hochheimer, 574.

him. He says of the past: "Something new is always coming along. What has gone can never be recaptured"; and of the future, "There may be something of that sort for others, but I cannot know that."

There are a great many reports on the most diverse types of pathologically disturbed time, and all of them exhibit a much greater egocentricity and concreteness in the temporal experience than is common to the normal person. The regression of the temporal may occur in such a way that the adjustment of personal time to world time, which is characteristic of the normal adult, no longer is carried through completely. The result is an ego-morphic, vital-affective notion which no longer corresponds to world time. Bouman and Grünbaum describe the case of a patient with post-encephalitis in whom was observed a shrinkage of time.[22] The patient's idea of the duration of his personal existence fell into two parts. One period, which actually coincided with objective time, was that preceding his sickness. The other, which he conceived to be of three years' duration but which was actually twenty-nine years, was the period following the acute stage of his sickness. Into this shrunken schema were packed all the events, both recent and long since past, of the entire second period, now diminished to miniature proportions. The patient was evidently defective in his ability to arrange the personally experienced flow of time in terms of an objective schema.

Again, in various psychoses—as in schizophrenia—when the fundamental polarity of ego and external world is disturbed, the ego time with its affective content becomes independent and dominant with respect to world time. The objectively temporal order may collapse completely. Time, says one schizophrenic, falls together like a pack of cards. Another schizophrenic's experience of time during his quiet phase differed from his temporal experience during the phase of terrible anxiety. In the calm phase time moved on with great rapidity; ten months were as one. In the anxious phase, on the contrary,

[22] Bouman and Grünbaum, 548.

events hung motionless in a temporal vacuum.[23] Shrinkage of time is characteristic of many cases of paranoid schizophrenia.[24]

Finally, there may be a materialization of time. This may result in a sort of daemonism. A certain schizophrenic shot at the clock which he said was "his worst enemy."[25] "The past engulfs me," another says. "Time can overcome me" is a common expression with such psychotics, and their experience brings to mind the mythical temporal idea of the aborigine, with its daemonic realization of the past in the present.[26]

The degeneration of the objective temporal sense is of course often less acute than in the cases just described. There are many instances where the eventual succession can be grasped by some substitute concrete expedient after the abstract scale has been disturbed. Head describes aphasiacs who, following a loss of the abstract schema, employed a concrete time-of-action. Although such a patient could not tell time by the clock, he was nevertheless able to order his day punctually. He had a concrete-qualitative time scale made up of dominant moments in the succession of daily events: "Then, when you eat." "Then, when we arrive there," etc. These and similar expressions constituted the temporal divisions used by this individual.[27] For these aphasiacs the temporal is fused with the concrete flow and thrust of events, as are spatial directions and orientation. Woerkom tells of one of his patients who could not imitate or follow by tapping even the simplest temporal intervals and rhythms. On the other hand, this same person mastered such problems without undue difficulty by the circuitous method of clothing these rhythms in some melodic relationship.[28]

[23] Merlos, 587.
[24] Israeli, 576, 59.
[25] Minkowski, 588.
[26] Fischer, 552.
[27] Head, 572, vol. 1, 187.
[28] Woerkom, 613.

PART FOUR

Primitive Action

Chapter VII

THE NATURE OF SYNCRETIC ACTION; ACTION AS BOUND TO THE CONCRETE SITUATION

Higher types of action are formally characterized by an interaction of personality with an outer discrete world, both polar elements being relatively self-subsistent. In more primitive types of action, however, there is a lesser degree of differentiation between object and subject. This is tantamount to saying that the primitively acting organism is intimately bound up with the concrete situation. Development from a lower to a higher type of action—in terms of differentiation—is marked by the appearance of circuitous approaches, that is, means of action, instruments of mediation. On the level of the most primitive action, object (stimulus) and subject (response) are not separated by the devices of mediation; that is, the interaction is *immediate*. Development in the mode of action is further determined by a growing specificity of the personal and subjective as against the objective aspect of the action involved. The growth and differentiation of the personal factor in action are demonstrated in the emergence of a specifically personal *motivation*. The growing recognition of a self-dependent objectivity is reflected in the development of *planful behavior*. In brief, the striking characteristics of primitive concrete action are *immediacy, limited motivation,* and *lack of planning*.

IMMEDIACY.

The most primitive forms of concrete human action are

seen in the movements of the newborn child. These movements reveal a complete subordination of the infant to the
vital global situation, utter helplessness and no knowledge
whatsoever of instrumentality, a mere floundering about with
happy or unhappy results. The first glimpse of a polarity between object and subject appears when the child begins to
use parts of his own body to master the situation. The employment of instruments—even if they are simply his own legs
and arms—indicates a certain release from the domination of
the concrete field, a partial differentiation of the happening in
which object and subject are fused virtually into one. Here
there is "circuitous action" in a very primitive form.

A circuitous action, however primitive it may be, represents some degree of polarization between object and subject.
In a beautiful cinematic study Kurt Lewin shows how difficult it can be for the three-year-old child to accomplish such
a simple circuitous action as seating himself on a stone. The
child must first turn his back to the object in order to establish a physical contact. Gottschaldt has shown that the behavior
of both the very young child and of considerably older, but
feeble-minded, children is guided by a relatively immediate
contact with the global visual situation. A feeble-minded
child standing inside a gate may be able to use a stick to
reach for an object outside. The success of his action will
depend on whether both stick and object lie before him in
the same direction. If they are at opposite sides of his body
so that he loses sight of the object when turning to secure the
stick, or vice versa, more than likely he will fail to carry out
the action.[1] The circuitousness of the situation makes too great
a demand on the child's ability. Köhler, Yerkes, and Meyerson
and Guillaume, among others, have conducted a great variety
of animal experiments which serve to establish the difference
in the level of intelligence or behavior by revealing the relative facility in utilizing circuitous action in solving a problem
situation. If a rake (Fig. 40) is leaned within reach against the

[1] Gottschaldt, 382, 128.

bars of an ape's cage and a piece of fruit is placed between the base of the cage and the rake (although still out of reach), the ape readily grasps the rake-handle in order to draw the fruit to him. On the other hand, if the fruit is placed beyond the prongs of the rake, the animal is at first at a loss as to what to do. He must now carry out a circuitous action, that is, extend the prongs of the rake until they are beyond the fruit, and thus bring it within grasping distance.[2] Meyerson and Guillaume came to the conclusion that it is the circuitousness of the action which occasions the principal difficulties for the animal in most of the problems presented to him.[3]

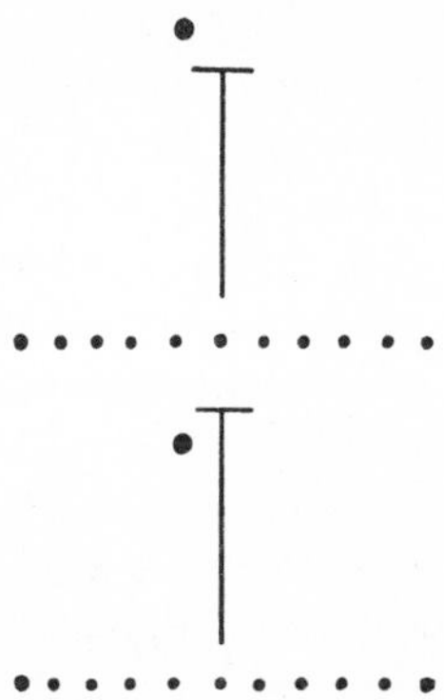

FIG. 40.—Problem Situations of Differing Difficulty for the Monkey.

There is much evidence from data on pathological mental conditions which illustrates how difficulties in completing circuitous action may arise when there is a primitivation of behavior. Head tells us of patients who, although at one time excellent billiard players, have lost their faculty for play because they are no longer capable of accomplishing indirect shots using the banks, that is, literal circuitous actions.[4]

In brief, the more primitive the mentality, the greater the difficulties presented by a situation demanding the use of mediating devices.

Development in the sense of increasing instrumentality implies willful organization, or rearrangement, of the situation in terms of mediating devices. These instrumentalities are first

[2] Fischel, 641, 322.
[3] Meyerson and Guillaume, 649.
[4] Head, 572, vol. 2, 122, 171. I. Krechevsky (666) recently demonstrated that these findings in human pathology apply for mammals as low in the vertebrate scale as rats. Rats with injured brains show a loss of plastic behavior as compared with normal animals.

wholly concrete, and gradually become abstract with the increasing intellectualization of mental tasks and actions.

Another mark of the release of the subject from the domination of the concrete field is the extension of the action beyond the visibly given field. The action of the small child is usually governed by the actual visible constellation. When Stern's 1:3-year-old child throws his napkin ring behind a piece of furniture and retrieves the object now hidden from view, he exhibits a certain minor degree of freedom from the dictates of the concrete situation.[5] According to Bühler it is at the nine months' age level that the child's capacity for action is sufficiently advanced to enable him to take an object from the experimenter's pocket and to find it again after it has been hidden before his eyes. The data from animal psychology show that transcendence of the immediate concrete situation is a fundamental indication of development in action. Révész found that chickens no longer bother to scratch for grain if it has been buried beyond their immediate reach or covered with a carton.[6] M. Hertz observed similar facts with the sea gull. On the other hand, crows and jackdaws behave more like the higher vertebrates, who always seek hidden food.[7] Apes in particular are astonished or enraged when they are fooled by the experimenter and do not find the food they have anticipated.[8]

MOTIVATION.

The development of action occurs, again, in terms of a differentiation of specifically subjective factors as against specifically objective factors. The increasing specificity of the subjective factor is revealed in the growing intension and complexity of purely personal motives. There are no genuinely personal motives in the primitive mode of behavior. Primitive action is set in motion by vital drives on the one hand, and by the concrete signals of the milieu on the other.

[5] Stern, 513, Germ. ed., 402.
[6] Révész, 684.
[7] Hertz, 653, 654.
[8] Tinklepaugh, 693.

The significance of vital needs and affect in animal behavior has been solidly established. Animals often learn some relatively difficult form of action only when activated by an appropriate vital compulsion (hunger, nesting instinct, maternal instinct, sexual instinct, etc.).[9] Szymansky found, for instance, that rats learned to negotiate mazes only under the pressure of hunger.

Such vital drives are also important as motivating factors in infant behavior. The true "mental" or "intellectual" aspect of the personality does not play any part in the motivations of the very young child. The infant does not experience a desire to solve some particular task confronting him. He moves, not because he is experiencing any form of aspiration, but rather because vital needs force him to move. Katz and Révész have demonstrated experimentally the dominant role of the vital drive in the behavior of young children. If the 2:6-year-old child is given the task of removing every second object from a series, he will hardly be able to accomplish this unless some such affectively positive objects as pieces of chocolate are used. Affectively neutral objects such as pasteboard coins bring about little response.[10] According to experiments carried out by Charlotte Bühler, children three to five years of age satisfactorily accomplished the task of fetching a promised piece of candy hidden in a certain place 45 per cent more times than when the task was fetching a key. In the case of children five to six years old, the more vitally important task elicited but a 25 per cent superiority of response.[11]

The development of personal motivation is clearly revealed in the genesis of action involving choice. On the primitive level, choice is guided by the signal-values of the concrete situation. This is concrete choice in terms of affective needs. The preference is governed by the relatively higher affective valence of some one of the objects. A genuine act of choice

[9] Kafka, 660, 114 ff.; Szymansky, 691; Maier and Schneirla, 677, 412.

[10] Révész, 494.

[11] Bühler, 350, 187.

appears much later. This subsequent act is not entirely concrete; it will be consummated not in a visible field of objects having diverse signal-values, but in the person. It is a choice among motives. It is a fundamental step in the development of character in the normal child from four to six years of age that a choice of motive should supplant choice based on the demand-character of the affective situation. Gottschaldt shows that the behavior of children of retarded mentality (actual age, four to eight years), when contrasted with that of the normal child, is marked by a fragmentary, poorly developed motivation, and that a conflict between two strong motives, such as is common in the experience of the normal child of comparable age, is little known.[12]

PLANNING.

Development in action refers not only to the factor of "person," but also to the factor of "world." In this respect the development is a movement toward a stronger recognition of objectivity, and in consequence it is also a movement toward an adequate mastery of the increasingly difficult situation. The steadily growing adequacy of physical movements can be seen even in earliest childhood, perhaps in the infant's effort to brush away a cloth laid over his face by the investigator. In the earliest stages of infancy, as Charlotte Bühler has shown in experiments dealing with this subject, movements are altogether lacking in specificity and direction. At the age of a month and a half, at least a quarter of the infants who try to get rid of the cloth over their faces show purposeful movements. At four and one-half months only half of the physical movements are without direction, and at the age of seven months successful manipulations begin to dominate the unsuccessful.[13]

Experiments on the infant's handling of objects plainly show this development from an egocentric to a planful action which takes into account the objective characteristics of things and

[12] Gottschaldt, 382, 60 ff.
[13] Bühler, 350, 421.

situations. Up to the age of five months, according to Kautsky, the child's own body is preferred to any toy. Beyond this age objects are preferred which permit such physical activities as touching, pressing, crushing, and so on. The experiments of Iwai and Volkelt also show that at the earliest period there is a decided preference for such objects as have a pronounced "graspability" (a ring or a bowl, for instance, as contrasted to a less easily held wooden block).[14] At this stage we may speak of a "lack of specificity in handling the material" so far as the material proper and the particular demands characterizing it are concerned. This stage is succeeded by a growing tendency to achieve an adequate handling of the material at hand, as may be readily observed in the creative efforts of older children. Blocks, for instance, now become recognized as building elements, instead of being squeezed or used as noise-making instruments.

The increasing recognition of the material character of the surrounding world is expressed not only in an increasing adequacy in the handling of the material, but also in the appearance of planning which accords with the specific material at hand in anticipation of the end effect in the course of action. In this respect it is interesting to note the age at which the child begins to name the object or the situation which he is trying to represent in a drawing. During the earlier years it is simply a case of pure functioning with paper and pencil, the scribbling stage. Gradually the level of planning is reached, and there is an intentional presupposition of some particular object to be drawn.[15]

The active behavior of abnormally primitive individuals, whether mentally retarded or neuropathological, is characterized by a relative lack of exactitude in planning and in the understanding of goals. As Gottschaldt has shown, when faced with a task they are unable to master, feeble-minded children of a low mental age often completely lose sight of the goal and substitute an indeterminate action. The normal child

[14] Iwai and Volkelt, 413.
[15] Hetzer, 402, 73, Table 7; Bühler, 350, 170.

EARLY AGE LEVELS AT WHICH OBJECTS ARE NAMED IN DRAWING
(After Hetzer)

(Figures refer to percentage of cases.)

Age, Yrs.	Not Named	Named Afterwards	Named While Being Drawn	Named Prior to Being Drawn	Total
3	90%	10%	0%	0%	100%
4	18%	9%	37%	36%	100%
5	0%	0%	20%	80%	100%
6	0%	0%	0%	100%	100%

of a corresponding actual age who discovers that an activity is too difficult to master (e.g., building a tower with blocks) chooses as a substitute one as similar as possible to that originally intended (building a tower less complicated in structure, one not so high, etc.). Gottschaldt's feeble-minded subjects, on the contrary, often chose a substitute goal that was utterly remote from the original. Instead of building a tower they counted the blocks or put them together in rows, etc.[16]

Head has described as the "symbol-blind" aphasiac a pathological type who, as a result of his defect, is forced back into a more primitive, concrete life space and mode of action. The more serious the mental disturbance, the more thorough the lapse into the confines of the immediate event, and the more limited the ability to behave in terms of an anticipatory scheme of action. Head emphasizes the fact that any action requiring some sort of prevision becomes increasingly disrupted as the regression becomes more pronounced. At the same time a concretely expedient means of action is substituted for what requires prearrangement. Many such patients can move from one place to another by feeling their way along, but they are totally unable to plan these movements. They are bound fast to the eventual situation as it is experienced and are bereft of the capacity to execute an action according to a preconceived schema.[17]

[16] Gottschaldt, 381, 382.
[17] Head, 572, vol. 1, 209, 415.

Chapter VIII

THE DIFFUSE CHARACTER OF PRIMITIVE ACTION

MASS ACTIVITY AND UNCOORDINATION AS TWO TYPICAL CHARACTERISTICS OF PRIMITIVE MOVEMENT.

After observing the development of behavior in amblystoma (the salamander in its aquatic stage), Coghill came to the conclusion that "behavior develops from the beginning through the progressive expansion of a perfectly integrated *total pattern* and the *individuation within it of partial patterns.*" The development of specific, individualized reactions out of a primitive totality diffusely comprehending large parts of the body ("mass activity") is confirmed by various studies devoted to the embryonic stages of the rat, (Angulo y Gonsález, Raney, Carmichael, etc.), of the cat (Coronios), and even of man (Minkowski).[1] Diffuse activity is the rule during the earliest stages of development in the human organism, although at three months the fetus is capable of some directed movement. "Each skin area may serve as a reflexo-genic zone for various reactions, which have a tendency to irradiate over the entire organism. With older fetuses movements are often less generalized."[2] There is considerable unanimity of opinion that much of the behavior of the newborn infant takes the form of "mass activity." "Most of the responses," writes Pratt, "tend to involve most of the major segments of the body, and the participation of smaller parts is likewise conspicuous."[3]

Two types of primitive diffuse movement may be distinguished. The first type, the "global," is a wholly integrated mass

[1] Carmichael, **628**; Coronios, **634**; Raney and Carmichael, **683**; Angulo y Gonsález, **614**.
[2] Minkowski, **455**, 923.
[3] Pratt, **487**.

activity. The second, although involving large areas of the body, is marked by a lack of hierarchic integration, of co-ordination, among the different parts of the total movement. According to this division, there would be two directions in development. The first direction would lead to individuation of generalized response; the second to the hierarchic integration of uncoordinated partial response.

Development starting from the global type of mass behavior is seen in the sucking response. Originally this reaction brings into play a great many of the facial muscles (cheek muscles, etc.), but gradually it narrows down to an activity in the region of the lips.[4] The smiling response (R. W. Washburn) and the act of grasping provide further examples of this type of growth.[5] Prior to the second half of the first year, legs, hands, mouth, and feet are all used in the movements of grasping. The legs come to have their specific function during the last quarter of the first year.[6]

Development emerging from an uncoordinated type of motor activity seems to be best illustrated by the growth of the infant's defense reactions (stimulus: pressure applied to the face). Sherman and Flory have demonstrated that there is a considerable increase in coordination in the newborn infant from day to day, probably due to a development in the function of the cortex as the seat of hierarchic coordination.[7]

DIFFUSENESS AND RIGIDITY (ALL-OR-NONE REACTION) IN PRIMITIVE ACTION.

Diffuse global action, which as defined here means an action reeled off as a total response, is commonly characteristic of the invertebrates, although it is found to a lesser degree among the vertebrates. The more frequent this global action, the lower the animal in the biological scale.

[4] Pratt, 486.
[5] Irwin, 53.
[6] Bühler, 349, 53.
[7] Sherman and Flory, 504.

The behavior of the sand-wasp is typical. The entomologist Fabre carried out the following experiment: "The sand-wasp makes herself a hole out of which she flies after her prey. She paralyzes the prey with her stinger, and then transports it to the entrance of the hole. Before dragging her booty into the lair, she first goes in as if to see whether everything is in order. While the sand-wasp was in the hole Fabre removed the prey some distance from the place where it had been temporarily abandoned. When the sand-wasp emerged she soon recovered the prey, and again dragged it to the entrance of the hole. Upon doing this the instinct took effect once more, and again she 'reconnoitered' within. This she continued to do as long as Fabre removed the prey, and in this given case the process was repeated 40 times."[8]

The behavior of the sand-wasp must mean that it is the action as a totality which alone is significant for this insect. A small variation can disturb the whole of the event so thoroughly that the entire course of action has to be commenced anew. The whole of the activity is rigid, inseparable into relatively self-subsistent parts, and not susceptible to a division into members forming a series. The partial goals, the one following the other in a succession, which are characteristic of our volitional acts, do not exist here. There is a single goal which can be realized only in the totality of the course of action. One part of the whole event follows its predecessor as a matter of necessity, for none of the parts has in itself any kind of independence. We are confronted with a global reaction which must either run its particular course as an unbroken whole or, even if slightly disturbed, suffer abortive failure. Such a continuum of motor activity may be designated as an "all-or-nothing reaction."

From a formal standpoint the diffuseness of the gestalt of this activity is recognizable not only in the dominance of the totality and its striking inseparability, but also in the lack of centralization, in the equal value accorded to all the parts, and

[8] Volkelt, 699, 29.

in the absence of any subordination of the non-essential to the essential moments. The gestalt is, so to speak, a series without profile, without any hierarchization of the important with respect to the unimportant parts. In this sense primitive action is "homogeneous."

The spider affords us another example of rigid global activity. For the cross-spider capturing and devouring food are activities consisting of several successive acts: enshrouding the prey; glueing it down; moving around the web away from the prey and returning to it; sucking the trapped insect dry, etc. If a fly impaled on a needle is offered to the cross-spider on some support outside the web, it will be found that the spider moves away from and back to the fly exactly as if it had been captured within the web. "She runs on the support some 4 cm. away from her booty, all the time spinning a thread behind her, as is characteristic of all web-spinning spiders when temporarily abandoning their prey. Before returning she fastens this thread to the support, and only then does she make her way back to the prey. The spider's orientation is apparently facilitated by the self-spun Ariadne thread. It is obvious that this side-excursion which, under normal circumstances, would take place in the nest at the center of the web, and result in a reversal of the head, after dragging in the food, in order to achieve the proper sucking position, has no significance in this situation. But since it is carried out despite this lack of significance, it may be understood to be an instance of rigid behavior, and prove that the roundabout excursion is an indispensable factor in the normal feeding-activity."[9]

[9] Baltzer, 615. It is apparent that the spider's behavior is plastic only in so far as this plasticity is biologically relevant. A spider will not enshroud a fly if the experimenter offers a fly already enshrouded by another spider. We may understand this plasticity from the fact that spiders leave their enshrouded prey to one side if there is opportunity to suck nourishment from another object of prey lying nearby. The spider can always return to the prey, once enshrouded, and eat it at leisure. Here the very biological situation admits of such plasticity, i.e., a relative independence of a partial activity. This, of course, is not true of all situations. The behavior of the animal in natural situations must therefore be borne in mind in evaluating experiments on plasticity of action.

This form of global behavior is also found among birds. One part of the hen's activity in seeking food is a preliminary scratching of the ground. The hen will always scratch for its food, even though the action may be purposeless. If the bird is placed on a plate strewn with corn it will persist in scratching, even to its own detriment.[10]

There are certain rigid activities which, on biological grounds, can occur only once in the history of an organism (e.g., a bird). In this case the animal will not be able to repeat such a globalized activity, since it is impossible to execute it again in all its details. For instance, the thermometer-bird lays its eggs on mounds of tufted, dried grasses and sand. The young bird breaks through the shell and, by beating its wings, raises itself up through the loose sand about it. However, if the young bird is again buried in the sand from which it has just emerged successfully, it will be unable to repeat the action of beating its wings, and thus perish.[11] Obviously, since the bird cannot return to the egg, the temporal succession cannot be reproduced.

A cat which has once learned the trick of freeing itself from a training box by operating certain mechanisms will continue to maneuver this awkward escape even if the cover of the box is left open and it is free to jump out at will.[12]

A comparatively diffuse form of behavior is again demonstrable on the *human* level, especially in the normally primitive types of mentality (children, primitive man), and also in the pathological mentality or, in consequence of some form of primitivation, even in the normal adult.

The manner in which *primitive* peoples recite their songs affords us one example of the "all-or-nothing reaction." Many aborigines are unable to begin their songs at any point in the text, but always have to commence anew at the very beginning or fail completely. The Papuans, for instance, cannot start

[10] Hempelmann, **651**, 383.
[11] *Ibid.*, 382.
[12] *Ibid.*, 416.

a new song until they have danced and sung the very last verse of the one traditionally preceding it. Different strophes in a song cannot be interchanged. Similarly, no figure in the dances of these people may be omitted, or the whole intention of the dance is disrupted.[13]

Rigidly global forms of behavior are encountered among those suffering from regressive *pathological* disturbances. According to Head, certain aphasiacs are able to carry an activity to its conclusion only if it proceeds in an habitual fashion. One such patient, an army officer, could write his name only when, in keeping with his long-established custom, he was allowed to inscribe rank and regiment before it. This same patient was unequal to the task of completing many other simple activities unless they were reproduced in every slight detail.[14]

The diffuse global type of activity is particularly noticeable in younger *children*. We all recall the way in which children recite poems and sing songs. It is his experience of a global, interdependent series which usually forces the child to begin again from the first line once he has faltered. The small child's tendency to carry out certain activities according to a painfully exact routine is common knowledge.

The Scupins often observed this penchant for action according to a rigid routine in their child. "Bubi (4:4 years) has the habit of pulling the corner of the quilt up to his chin just before going to sleep. This morning when his mother took him in bed with her and cautioned him to go back to sleep, he took hold of the quilt on her bed, handed it to her, and said: 'Here, you have to take this.' He evidently accepted this ceremonial act as an inevitable preliminary in the business of going to sleep. Also, he apparently expects that others have his own habits because, on one previous occasion, since he believed that he could go to sleep only when sucking his thumb, he grasped his mother's thumb, and tried to put it in her mouth for her so that she, too, could go to sleep. . . . Bubi's behavior

[13] Werner, **142**, 195.
[14] Head, **572**, vol. 1, 99.

with respect to one of the four corners of his blanket is most extraordinary. When he has been covered up for the night he reaches for the nearest corner, looks at it fixedly, feels it carefully, and usually thrusts it away from him with the words: 'That's the wrong one!' Quickly he reaches for another corner, inspects it, and persists until he has found the right one. His preference seemingly depends on some slight defect in the material which is present at only one special corner."[15]

From the foregoing it is clear that every detail of a global activity is important and indispensable in the fulfillment of an "all-or-nothing reaction."

Rüssel mentions an instructive case: "Tr. [a two-year-old child] was playing near the cupboard. I chanced to be standing nearby, and gave her a piece of chocolate. This pleased her, and she ran about happily. Then she turned around, laid her chocolate on a chair-bottom, brought out a stool from under the table, and pushed it across the floor to the place where I was standing. A chair that blocked the way was thrust to one side. After doing this she fetched her chocolate, climbed on the stool, twisted about so that she faced the room, and began to eat. As she ate she kicked her feet and laughed. Then she climbed down, and returned the stool to its former position, shoving it under the table in a certain way. Shortly afterwards I again put myself in the same position, and gave Tr. a second piece of chocolate. Once more she was overjoyed, and started to lay the chocolate on a chest, but finally decided on a cushion. Again she fetched the stool, stopped, and smiled at her mother. She placed the stool where it had previously stood, climbed up, arranged herself, and commenced to eat. Hardly had she swallowed the last bite when she jumped down and returned the stool.

"At first I could not understand the child's peculiar behavior. Some time later it dawned on me that the child sits at my right side during meal-times, and her actions referred to this

[15] Scupin, **502**, vol. 2, 10, 25.

habitual procedure. 'Eating' means sitting by her father's side."[16]

Gottschaldt, Lewin and his students, and others have experimentally demonstrated the rigid, inseparable total-character of primitive child action.[17] If, for example, a four-year-old child of retarded mentality has learned how to use a round stick to pull objects toward him through a grating, he will at first be unable to use an edged stick for the same purpose. Gottschaldt reports a subnormal child two and one-half years of age who learned to use a stick to draw objects toward him when they lay on the other side of a fenced-in area. If the whole arrangement is moved to another corner, the child continues to run to the position to which he has become accustomed, and tries in vain from this now disadvantageous point to reach the object outside.

Stereotypy, or rigidity of behavior, is especially common in feeble-minded children of the lower grades.[18] Once having learned to do an activity in one particular way, the child of low mentality cannot modify his behavior to accord with changed conditions. He is able to solve a problem only if he has been previously trained to cope with exactly the same type of situation.

There is the case of a feeble-minded girl whose mental age was 10 years, who was helpless to do anything in a kitchen if the customary arrangement of objects had been changed. This same girl could make her own bed, yet she was thrown into hopeless confusion by anyone interrupting her activity in order to help her.[19]

The synthesis of two activities learned singly is extremely difficult for an organism whose behavior consists principally of rigid totalities. If, to illustrate, a child of feeble intelligence has learned to employ either of two devices in order to secure

[16] Rüssel, **499**.
[17] Lewin, **88**; Gottschaldt, **382**.
[18] Gottschaldt, **382**, 124 ff.
[19] Goddard, **560**, 102 ff.

some desired object—let us say climbing up on a box, or reaching with a stick—it is quite likely that he will be at a loss should he have to use both means at the same time. In a synthesis there must be a reorganization of the two activities that have been learned separately, and this capacity for reorganization is the sign of a relatively plastic behavior.[20]

The diffuse global structure of the child's behavior, the "all-or-nothing reaction," appears, as we have already shown, in the ceremoniousness with which the child carries out certain habitual actions. Already during the suckling stage, children begin to insist on eating in a certain way or being dressed according to a set routine, etc. An habitual succession of acts must be fulfilled in the one special fashion because of the tendency to act in terms of a whole which cannot be separated into the essential and the non-essential. Bearing in mind the need for a uniform, uninterrupted course of action, we are able to understand B. Zeigarnik's experimental results pointing to the fact that "uncompleted actions remain more deeply implanted in the child's memory than successful ones." This statement also applies to some extent to adults, but not nearly so much as to children. Zeigarnik, in her analysis of this phenomenon, comes to the conclusion that, as a result of the importance of the unbroken totality by means of which the child characteristically attempts to fill his needs, the disruption of an activity is a much more vivid experience among children than among adults.[21]

Childlike actions exhibit relatively little articulation, not only because of their global character, but also because they are more or less lacking in hierarchic organization. Whereas for the older child an action is divided into parts which are more essential or less essential with respect to the goal, the structure in a more primitive stage is relatively homogeneous. Therefore, besides the "global type" of action described in the preceding paragraphs, there is another primitive form, the

[20] Cf. Maier, **448.**
[21] Zeigarnik, **749.**

"chain type" of action. We recognize it in its simplest form in the monotonously repetitive movements of children at play. Preyer tells how his son, at the age of 1:1 years, took off and put on the cover of a tin no less than 72 times. The Scupins' 2:11-year-old child spent an hour and a quarter mixing meal, salt, and water together, and in pouring this mass back and forth from one container to another. Such a primitive form of action is therefore lacking in the centralizing factor of a goal and in a structure made up of diversely accentuated parts. It is an open structure, a "paratactic" form, which in later development will be supplanted by a "syntactic" mode of action. This uncentralized structure may be plainly discerned in any of the child's productive activities. E. Hanfmann observed that the block-building of the very young child proceeds chain-like, step by step. The child always concentrates his attention on the next single move, on the placing of the one next block. Only at a much later stage of development does the work move along in terms of larger units of activity to which the smaller steps are subordinated.[22]

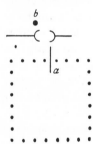

Fig. 41.—Problem Situation Used by Gottschaldt with Children.

Gottschaldt, in his fine experiments on the structure of child action, has subjected this paratactic form to a searching analysis.[23] For example, children standing within a railed space (Fig. 41) were given the task of retrieving through the bars, by means of a short stick, the longer of two sticks with spoon-shaped ends in order ultimately to secure an object which lay still farther beyond. In the case of very small children, the single parts of the whole action involved in this task are in such poorly established syntactic relation that a part of the action may become severed from the whole as a self-dependent goal in itself, and in consequence the undertaking is often bungled.

[22] Hanfmann, 396.
[23] Gottschaldt, 382, 126 f.

As likely as not, the children busy themselves with the problem of retrieving through the bars not only the longer but the shorter of the two sticks as well, an activity quite extraneous to the final solution of the task at hand. Only from the age of six years on is this action conceived in terms of a syntactic, well-articulated, and properly subordinated relationship.

A diffuse form of action has not yet advanced toward the stage at which each part of the continuum of action has a functional and temporal significance depending on its proximity to the end at hand. According to Gottschaldt, feeble-minded children of a low mental age exhibit a different behavior from that of normal children when engaged in the task of building a tower of blocks, in that they lack a feeling for the distance of the goal, a feeling that normally changes with every step as the action approaches closer and closer to fulfillment. This temporal perspective is of fundamental importance in any activity directed toward a set goal. This perspective is freed from the limitations of a chain-like homogeneous activity, in which the various successive steps exhibit no difference in value with respect to one another as the goal draws closer and closer. To the child of low mentality each step in the tower-building activity seems to be merely a repetition of the one preceding it. The steps in such a continuum of action stand as parts with a homogeneous, interchangeable value, since they are not at all subordinated to the final goal. For the normal older child, on the other hand, even "trying again" is not, strictly speaking, mere repetition. Because of the desire to "do it better the next time," it is rather one self-contained step in a larger activity that moves steadily toward the goal of greater perfection. It is a matter of indifference to the child at a low mental level at which point in the homogeneous whole he begins to work on the tower. He does not care whether he starts at the beginning of the task, or continues and finishes some structure already half complete. Any one part is equal to any other so far as the character of the action is concerned. Indeed, a single part may, *pars pro toto,* represent the whole. A healthy older child will not stop building his tower of blocks until he has completed the action in some fashion or other. The feeble-minded child, on the other hand, may come to a stop when he is halfway through and believe that he has done his work, since in his case the partial action may stand for the continuum of effort.

We may sum up the previous paragraphs on the development of action in terms of *plasticity of behavior.* This concept of plasticity serves to relate important qualities of the external form of primitive action to its inner factors, that is, motivation and adjustment to goals.

Higher activity has a plasticity of outer form and inner content. Primitive behavior is comparatively lacking in plasticity so far as *outer form* is concerned. The limited plasticity exhibited by the external structure of primitive action is illustrated with special clarity in the instinctive behavior of the lower animals on the one hand, and, on the other, the rigid global activity of the young child.

The plasticity of the *inner content* of action may be subdivided into a plasticity of the acting subject (*plasticity of motive*) and a plasticity in the object acted upon (*plasticity of goal*). Both plasticity of motive and of goal are comparatively limited in primitive behavior.

Any conflict among motives, a dynamics of motivation deriving from the various layers of the personality, and adjustment in motivation on the basis of the possibilities arising during action or the successive difficulties presented by the task at hand, are all only rudimentarily represented in the primitive mentality. Gottschaldt's analysis of the child's tower-building with blocks reveals how, in the case of the normal older child, a personal play of strength and will unfolds within the activity when specific difficulties arise (e.g., increased effort because of aroused ambition). Any such plasticity is more or less absent in the feeble-minded child's behavior.

A limited plasticity of motive corresponds to a lack of plasticity in the ends at hand. While for the normal older child the goal changes plastically as difficulties arise, so that there is a setting up of partial temporary goals or a lowering of the "level of aspiration" (Lewin), for the subnormal child there is an immutable rigidity of the end involved. When confronted by failure this child does not lower his level of aspiration, but in some circumstances may raise it still higher.

In the last analysis—and here we must refer again to the propositions stated at the beginning of Chapter VII—this rigidity and lack of plasticity in motive and goal are grounded in a comparative lack of polarity between the subject and the world. It is only after a certain advance in mental development that this polarity becomes clearly defined. This polarization may be described as follows: An ego that measures its ends and its powers ultimately stands opposed to an objectivity which enforces an adequately organized activity, that is, an activity fitted to cope with objective properties and potentialities.

PART FIVE
Primitive Thought Processes

Chapter IX

CONCEPTION

The Nature of Syncretic Thought; "Analogous Processes" in the Development of Thought.

We have tried to show that in different types of primitive mentality psychological functions are more intimately fused, that is, more syncretic, than in the advanced mentality. We may recall that the term "syncretic" does not imply a summation of functions. Syncretic function must be understood as a specific phenomenon differing in kind from any of the functions which may emerge from it as the result of a process of differentiation.

In advanced forms of mental activity we observe thought processes which are quite detached from the concrete sensori-motor perceptual and affective sphere. In the primitive mentality, however, thought processes always appear as more or less perfectly fused with functions of a sensori-motor and affective type. It is this absence of a strict separation of thought proper from perception, emotion, and motor action which determines the significance of so-called concrete and affective thinking. Concrete and affective thinking are therefore characteristic examples of syncretic activity.

The fact that a certain kind of activity called thinking may appear in genetically different forms involving different functions brings to mind the general biological phenomenon of "analogous processes." It has long been an established fact in biology that there need not be any identity of organ and the functions performed by that organ. It is to Owen that we must give credit for the first clear distinction between "homologous" and "analogous" organs.[1] In comparative anatomy the term "analogous process" refers to a biological type of activity which may be performed by organs distinctly different in physical structure. The respiration of vertebrates, as a simple illustration, is carried on by gills in fishes and by lungs in mammals. Analogous mental processes, which we may define as processes at different genetic levels directed toward the same achievement but involving different function patterns, can easily be demonstrated to exist in almost any field of mental activity.

A good example is afforded by the ability to apprehend objects on the basis of their constant properties, which we have alluded to at some length in an earlier discussion. The brightness of objects may appear approximately the same to us in different intensities of illumination. Chalk appears to have about the same degree of whiteness and coal of blackness, even though the physical intensity of the light reflected from their surfaces varies considerably because of a change in illumination.[2] A mechanism is here at work tending to keep the color properties of the objects comparatively constant. It is as if the eye were making allowances for a change in the optical frame of reference, that is, the illumination.

This tendency of the organism to stabilize the color properties of objects is evident in mental processes on three different levels. The most primitive level of adjustment to varying illumination is the physiological adaptation in the retina to light and dark. Again, there is the tendency just mentioned to perceive the brightness of objects as more or less constant despite varying illumination. This is a higher level of function, a level of perceptual interpretation on which illumination is perceptually related to the object. Physiological adaptation is probably fully developed in early childhood, while perceptual constancy in color and brightness develops more slowly, reaching its peak

[1] Owen, **680**, 374-379; Russell, **688**, 108.
[2] Katz, **722**.

at about age fifteen. The perceptual interpretation of brightness and color is in turn superseded by a mental activity on a higher level. This is a process by means of which the properties of things are determined conceptually. It is "known," for example, that chalk is white and coal black. We can readily see that these three different processes achieve their end with increasing efficiency. The least effective of the three is, of course, retinal adaptation, and the most effective—and one also found only in man—is the conceptual relating of characteristic color properties to things.

The curves for perceptual constancy of brightness (and also of shape and size) decline after ages fourteen to fifteen. This decline is probably due to the growth of the conceptual function which now replaces, at least partially, the function on the lower, perceptual, level.[3]

As we have previously shown, discrimination may also be considered as a field of activity in which "analogous processes" are operative. Certain experiments suggest that mammals comparatively low in the biological scale distinguish different pitches on the basis of "conditioned reflexes" and not by means of any true perceptual organization. For example, the same guinea pig that fails to react to different pitches in the "discrimination box" will react readily when the conditioned response technique is employed.[4] Again, genetically related analogous processes of discrimination can be observed in the growing child. As we have pointed out in an earlier paragraph, a very young infant may exhibit a differential bodily reaction to a great variety of color stimuli. But this same child will not be able for some years to carry out without mistake a matching experiment requiring color discrimination stemming from a higher perceptual level.

To sum up, the following assumptions with respect to the genetic development of thought appear to be justifiable:

1. It is more or less futile to inquire into the absolute genetic

[3] Cf. Brunswik, 345.
[4] Upton, 698; cf. Maier and Schneirla, 677, chap. 13, 14.

origin of any mental activity. It would seem to be more constructive to analyze mental development in terms of genetically related, analogous processes. We must not frame the question to ask: "At what age level does concept formation first come into existence?" Rather, we must ask: "What are the different function patterns underlying the concept formation which appears at different age levels?"

2. Analogous processes of a lower order stand in genetic precedence to the processes of a higher order.

3. As a rule the lower level is not lost. In many instances it develops as an integral part of a more complex organization in which the higher process dominates the lower.[5]

PRIMITIVE FORMS OF RELATIONSHIP.

Some well-known experiments performed by Koehler, Jaensch, and others reveal that the apprehension of relation-

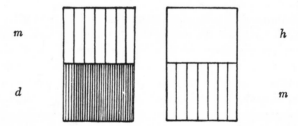

FIG. 42.—Experiment with Chickens on Brightness Relationship.

ships is firmly established in the lower vertebrates.[6] A typical experiment on these primitive forms of relationship in the chicken proceeds as follows (Fig. 42): Chickens are trained to pick grain from a gray background *m*, and to leave the grain on the darker field *d* untouched. (The corn on the darker field is glued to the ground, and that on the lighter ground is left freely scattered.) If, after the completion of the training period, corn is scattered freely over a pair of fields which are

[5] Werner, 535.
[6] Koehler, 664; Jaensch, 54.

so arranged that the area of brightness m is retained but is adjoined to an area of increased brightness h, it will be found that the chicken no longer picks corn from the field m—that is, from the one to which it was trained to respond—but rather from the new field h. In short, the chicken transfers its response to the relatively brighter area. Naturally it does not make any sort of human judgment. It reacts in a specific way to one part of a total area of varying brightness, as against another part. This configuration constituted by the two brightnesses is transposable, like an interval of tone. The brighter part is the signal for eating, the area where nourishment is to be found; the darker area is of neutral value.

Here we are obviously dealing with a primitive type in the apprehension of relationships. This apprehension of relations on a sensori-motor level seems to represent an "analogous process" with respect to an abstract grasp of relationship, such, for instance, as that underlying the verbal judgment of the comparison "part 1 is brighter than part 2."

Such a primitive, concrete grasp of relations may be defined by the differential response of an organism to one part of a configuration as against another part of the same configuration. When two areas of gray are united in a brightness configuration and acquire different functional values ($+$ and $-$) with respect to the food-seeking activity, we may safely assume that the animal has constructed a relationship on a sensori-motor level. This phenomenon will become still clearer, perhaps, if we consider an example of concrete relationship from Koehler's experiments with anthropoid apes.[7]

In order to draw objects to him which are beyond his reach, a chimpanzee is given two bamboo rods, one of which may be stuck in the end of the other as in a fishing rod. This extension by joining the two rods is possible, of course, only when the diameter of one rod is less than that of the other. The animal always takes the heavier rod in his left hand and, holding it still, he thrusts into it the lighter rod, which he has grasped

[7] Koehler, **664**, 56.

in his right hand. One rod, as it were, is passive during the operation, and the other is active. For a correct operation, therefore, it is necessary to apprehend accurately the relation ship between the two diameters. Evidence for the accurate concrete conception of such a relation is given by the following experiment: The chimpanzee is first given a pair of rods suitably varied in diameters (1 and 2 in Fig. 43). The smaller of this pair is then taken from him and he is given another one to replace it, this one larger in diameter than the one he has been allowed to retain. Obviously, if there are three rods with

1   2   3   4

FIG. 43.—Cross Sections of Sticks Used in Koehler's Experiments with Chimpanzees.

increasing diameters—1, 2, 3—then in the relationship 1-2 rod 2 will be the *passive* element, whereas in the relationship 2-3 the same rod 2 should be the *active* element. The chimpanzee understands these relationships immediately after a direct optical examination of the diameters; it is not a question of trial and error with him. This means that his perception is directed not toward absolute sizes but toward the relationship between sizes. The relation between the two diameters is grasped perceptually and manifests itself in the differential functional value of each rod in the course of the action involved.

This primitive function of relationship on a sensori-motor level seems to appear very early in *childhood*. A child eleven months old is able to comprehend the size relation between two hollow blocks which fit into each other. Like the chimpanzee in Koehler's experiments, the child of one year is successful in an attempt to fit two hollow rods together.[8]

Rüssel experimentally investigated the apprehension of re-

[8] Bühler, 349.

lationship in children from 1:7 to 5 years old.[9] Once these children had learned that by touching one of two figures which exhibited contrast in form or size a bell would ring, they were able to adjust their choice to a variation in these figures (providing that the figural relationship itself remained the same). Having grasped the fact that it was the larger with respect to the smaller, or the round with respect to the angular, or the symmetrical with respect to the asymmetrical, which was the "ringing figure," they made a correct choice even when presented with variations of these contrasting pairs. The child understands and is able to transpose diverse opposites: outline vs. solid, symmetrical vs. asymmetrical, thick vs. thin, small vs. large, round vs. angular, etc. As was true of the animal, at a very early age the child already exhibits a concrete grasp of relation. Two parts are so embedded in a continuum of action that in their togetherness one part has a positive and the other a negative optical-acoustic-affective value as a signal.

It is reasonable to assume that relationship exists as "analogous processes" on different genetic levels. At least three such levels may be distinguished: relationship on a sensori-motor level such as that just described; relationship on a predominantly perceptual level; and relationship on the level of abstraction. Relation on the predominantly *perceptual* level appears, for example, in W. Line's card-sorting experiment.[10] The child is given two cards which he must use as standards of comparison in setting up two series from a number of mixed cards, all bearing figures related to one or the other of the two standards. One of the standard cards may exhibit a concrete relationship of difference, that is, contain two squares of gray differing in tone. The other may exhibit a concrete relationship of likeness, and show two identical squares of gray. All the other cards, then, are to be sorted on the basis of whether they reveal a relation of concrete difference or of concrete sameness.

[9] Rüssel, **499**.
[10] Line, **439**.

These experiments show that there is a progression from relatively simple to more complex relations. And there is also a clearly defined development from relationship on a purely perceptual level to that involving the use of abstraction. For instance, four lines of given proportions are shown on one card; the child's task is to select other cards having four lines of the same figural proportions as the standard. If the lines are presented as a definite, complete figuration (Fig. 44, A), the task can be performed at an earlier age than when presented as separate units (Fig. 44, B).

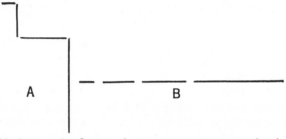

Fɪɢ. 44.—Patterns Used in Line's Experiment on Perceptual Relations.

These results may be explained by the fact that when the lines are presented separately, as in B, matching can be achieved only with the aid of some comparatively advanced (abstract) mental operation, usually by the use of language.

This leads us to the problem of how concrete perceptual relationships and those that are *abstract* in character are genetically linked. An analysis of the actual processes used in the making of a comparison may throw some light on the subject.

To illustrate, we may use the psychophysical problem of comparing two lengths presented in succession. The process of comparison often is not immediately carried into the abstract sphere. At first the subject attempts to arrive at a perceptual relationship between the two lines. It often seems, for instance, as if the two lengths are visually related in terms of apparent

movement: ── ─────. In perceiving b after a many sub-
      a b
jects see the line b as growing larger. On the other hand, if b
is smaller than a and is seen after it, they experience a shrinkage in b.[11] Or the observer may perceptually grasp the two
lengths $a < b$ as the two bases of a trapezoid which tapers toward the bottom, etc. In short, the establishment of a relation
of size between two lengths proceeds initially out of the perceptual togetherness, out of a preliminary figuration. The perception of an extension, or shrinkage, movement in line b implicitly contains the subsequent verbalized judgment: the
second length b is the greater (or the smaller) of the two lines.
The stage preceding the abstract judgment proper may therefore be thought of as the concrete relating of two elements by
means of figuration. In this perceptual operation there is implicitly expressed that which emerges into explicit expression
in the abstract relationship. The abstract judgment can be directly inferred from this primary relation because it is already
latent within it, embedded concretely, syncretically. In a similar fashion concrete relations are present in the abstract comparison of acoustic phenomena. Two tones that are to be
judged as to which is higher and which lower are frequently
brought together in a musical figure, a melodic interval, for
instance: ♩♪. The relation is present implicitly. The motif is
one that ascends, therefore the second tone is higher. The
judgmental and, in consequence, the abstract conception can
be derived directly from the very figuration of the melodic
interval, and in the act of derivation the primitive process of
relating is superseded by a higher one.

In brief, two separate phases are often observable in the
thought processes of comparison. The first is the formation of a
perceptual relationship—the relation between two parts is
grasped in a certain configuration. The second is the deriva-

[11] Jaensch, **54.**

tive abstract form of the relationship as expressed in a verbally constituted judgment.

These and other facts support the hypothesis that the actual formation of an abstract relationship is in itself a developmental process *in nuce*, in which the primary genetic stage of configurational relationship is still effective.

CONCRETE GROUPING AS AN ANALOGOUS PROCESS OF CONCEPT FORMATION AND CLASSIFICATION.

There is an intimate connection between the perceptual formation of relationship just discussed, and concrete perceptual grouping. We may consider the activity of grouping in the perceptual field as an analogous process of conceptual classification; that is, the conceptual activity of arranging and ordering things according to identical characteristics is present here on the perceptual level. We may illustrate this with a simple phenomenon, one easily verifiable in experiment. Suppose the vowel *a* is sung, in company with the rest of the vowels, at one definite pitch: *a-e-i-o-u.* Next the vowel *a* is sung alone to the tune of some melody. It is most interesting to note

a - a - a - a - a - a - a - a - a, etc.

that in the first instance the vowel character of each single sound is expressed with singular clarity, while the tonal experience is decidely subordinate. In the second case exactly the reverse is true. The vowel is scarcely heard, whereas the tonal experience becomes vivid. In other words, the "same" *a* is experienced at one time as tone and at another as vowel. What does the experiment indicate? It indicates that the grouping or figuration is of primary importance in conceiving of the single thing. Whether I "conceive" a thing as tone or as vowel depends on the figuration in which it stands. If the configuration is a structure of melodically related entities, of melodic equals, then there is melody and the single part is "conceived" as tone. If the configuration is a structure with a vowel character, the single part is grasped as a "vowel." A configurational grouping is the most concrete arrangement in which diverse material is grasped in uniformity. The configurational grouping of a manifold of material may be thought of as a process analogous in the perceptual sphere to conceptual grouping and ordering.

This perceptual grouping is dependent on a basic tendency in perceptual organization to bring elements together which exhibit any kind of perceptual similarities. For example, our desk is in great disorder. Papers lie scattered round, strewn amid books, inkwell, pencils, pens and knife. Observe how, when we cast a critical eye over the surface of the desk, the white papers unite in a sort of group. Other objects also tend to come together. Hard objects such as the penwiper, ash tray, and inkwell seem to attract each other. Long objects such as pencils, penholder, knife and scissors group themselves together. And so, of a sudden, a harmonious organization arises out of disorder. It is characteristic of this grouping that it may be completed in the purely perceptual sphere with hardly any conceptual-abstract support. It operates according to the laws of configuration.

Max Wertheimer was the first to point out that within each figuration a "law of equality" is effective. When dealing with "ambiguous" figures, other conditions remaining equal, that figuration will be established which contains a maximum equality of parts.[12]

In the upper portion of the illustration (Fig. 45), the gestalt will be vertical, whereas in the lower it will be horizontal. It is apparent that the bare laws of configuration anticipate the grouping procedure of concrete thought. Naturally we must distinguish between the mere configuration as such, which depends on an ordering function inherent in any sensory

[12] Wertheimer, 745.

organization, and a grouping process which utilizes the implicit logic of this primary configuration.

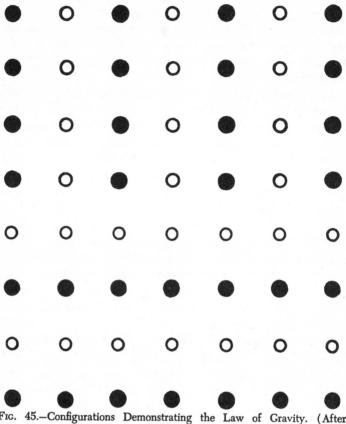

FIG. 45.—Configurations Demonstrating the Law of Gravity. (After Wertheimer.)

Here the question arises as to which is antecedent—the knowledge that the constituent parts are equal in value, or the experience of unity. In other words, does the grouping proceed on the basis of recognized similarity or equality, or do the constituent parts appear equal after the primary group formation has been established? Usually we are inclined to assume, taking our cue from familiar mental operations, that the equality or similarity is self-evidently first recognized, and that the grouping follows. But in primitive situations this does not necessarily hold. It can easily be demonstrated by introspection that objects may have a remarkable dynamic relation, a cognate relation, which precedes the experience of an equality in parts. Certain things belong together, fit together; and it is in this cognation that a concrete equality of parts is implicit, to be revealed explicitly as the grouping process continues.

To sum up: A perceptual grouping is an operation analogous to the conceptual classification of the abstract sphere. The grouping of perceptual material represents a sort of supervising or directing of the innate tendencies of organization, an operation through which the essentially similar is more or less immediately arranged into unity.

This brief theoretical analysis of the perceptual grouping process will perhaps be of some help in understanding primordial methods of classification in the primitive man, in the child, and in the pathological individual.

It appears that grouping on the basis of perceptual configuration is reflected in the classificatory phenomena of *primitive languages*. One peculiarity of these languages is that the verbal classification of several single objects by means of one name common to all is not always dependent on any actual common likeness. Often it is based on a naturalistic grouping. This means that here the primitive grouping is determined by a togetherness in the real optical configuration. With the expression *tu ku éng* the Bakaïrí Indians of Brazil designate the following colors: emerald green, cinnabar red, and ultramarine. This surprising conjunction of colors so decidedly different in quality is explained by the fact that *tu ku éng* is the name of a parrot which bears all of them.[13] Here the concrete togetherness is determined not by an actual similarity, but rather by a realistic configuration. The Melanesians of Buin also express diverse colors by the one name.[14] *Tonúbarou* stands for light

[13] Steinen, 297, 81.
[14] Thurnwald, 129, 90 ff.

green and a reddish brown. The word is derived from *tonuba*, a tree with leaves of these colors. *Tanai* means sulphur yellow, bronze, light green, and a dark moss green. This term comes from *tana*, a yellow taro plant, and designates the various colors of its leaves as well as of its root. Among the Australian aborigines we discover similar naturalistic groupings as the most primitive form of ordering. These natives often use the same word for fire and wood—*buree*, for example, in the Bumbarra language. Good and sweet, food and eating, thirst and water also have the same names.[15] In all these cases the grouping depends not on objectively similar characteristics, but on the membership of parts of the group in some naturalistic situation.

This primitive type of classification based on a togetherness of different things in a realistic situation can be clearly observed in the early ontogenetic stages of *child language*. Lombroso reports one child who designated both duck and water by "qua-qua." Another used "afta" to mean drinking-glass, pane of glass, window, and also what was drunk out of the glass.[16] In such cases the collective meaning is based on the uniform concrete situation in which all these objects belong. Darwin tells of his grandchild who used the word "quack" to mean not only duck but water and all other liquid substances. Sully relates the interesting case of a child who called his nurse "mambro." This term came to include the sewing machine at which the nurse occasionally worked, then a hand organ which vaguely resembled the sewing machine, then still later—in connection with the hand organ—a monkey, and finally a toy rubber monkey.[17] Similarly, Egger's son used the word "papa" not only for his father, but for all objects belonging to the father; and when he used the word "hand" he meant not only the hand proper, but the glove worn on it.[18]

Such childlike ways of connecting different types of things

[15] Curr, 178, vol. 2, 5.
[16] Lombroso, 441, 37.
[17] Sully, 516, Germ. ed., 152.
[18] Egger, 363.

by the same name have sometimes been explained on the grounds of association. But this interpretation does not go beyond the superficial aspect of the primitive thought process. The inner relationship expressed in the child's collective naming of things is fully intelligible only when referred to the fundamental principle that primitive classification is rooted in the concrete naturalistic situation. Water and thirst are designated by the same name in the language of the Australian aborigines because they are both elements in a common situation, because they both exist in the same continuum of experience. Similarly, when the child uses the same word for water and glass this is not because of an association in the sense of contiguity, but rather because the grouping operation is derivative from a realistic concrete unity. Water and glass actually do belong together, in so far as they both share the same quality-of-the-whole through which the experience of a unity is known and named.

In conclusion we may mention some of the grouping experiments with children, experiments which demonstrate the young child's tendency to conceive of a group as a naturalistic situation in which the single elements are embedded and from which they get their meaning. Martha Muchow's experiments, which she carried out in the Hamburg Laboratory, afford illustrations of this phenomenon.[19] When children from four to five years of age are given the task of ordering circles according to size, they often arrange them in concrete situations. Sometimes the collection of circles is thought of as a "family." The largest may be the mother, the second largest the aunt, and the smaller ones the children down to the very smallest who cannot walk. Ordering and grouping in this case proceed in terms of a naturalistically conceived collective situation (a family), in which each part of the whole is given a characteristic value. The circles are ordered not according to size alone, but rather according to "size" within the family.

E. Weigl carried out ordering experiments with children of

[19] Muchow, 457.

pre-school age using concrete objects. He also came to the conclusion that in the case of young children grouping occurs not in terms of abstract signs, but rather according to participation in a concrete collective situation.[20]

From a great number of objects one seven-year-old boy selected the following to group together: a hammer, bench, candle, match box, bread, pipe, and a small toy dachshund. All these things he saw as members of an imaginary work-situation.

Hammer-bench ("you can make one with a hammer"); candle ("you use it for light when you hammer"); match box ("you stick the candle on it"); bread ("you eat it when you get hungry from working"); pipe (". . . and afterwards you smoke your pipe"); dachshund ("the little dog has to watch the shop for the man when he goes away").

It is especially instructive to observe how the concrete naturalistic grouping appears in the *pathologically* regressed mentality. A catatonic woman created a language that exhibits a most extraordinary method of word construction. She compiled a whole dictionary of normal terms translated into her private language. Instead of the word "thistle," for example, she used "le stone" (with the French article). A childhood memory accounts for this particular word. When the patient used to walk through the fields with her mother as a child, she often rested during the heat of the day on a large stone near which a thistle grew. The verbal identification of "thistle" and "stone" depends on the fact that they both belong to the same (affectively conditioned) collective situation and are therefore interchangeable. This interpretation holds true again for this woman's usage of the word "fess" for a whole group of objects without logical connection: road, tree, kiss, horse, etc.[21]

Grouping experiments carried out by Gelb and Goldstein on individuals suffering from brain injuries reveal to what great extremes of realistic concreteness a group formation may

[20] Weigl, 531.
[21] Tuczek, 609, 293 f.

regress.[22] One of their patients, when told to arrange in order
a number of objects on the table before him, grouped together
an opened beer bottle, a glass, and a beer bottle cap. He left
out the bottle opener because, as he pointed out, the bottle
was already open.

Of course, there are other forms of grouping besides those
depending on a naturalistic, collective situation, that is, grouping based on concrete similarities. It is possible immediately
to conceive objects as a concrete group because, as we have
stressed in an earlier passage, a basic law of perceptual organization is operative, that is, the law of equality. The quality
common to all objects appears as the basic property of the
totality.

A concrete classification in the verbal expression of primitive tongues becomes clearly intelligible in the light of this
coalescence of objects based on the configurational law of
equality. In the Melanesian and American Indian languages,
for example, diverse objects are verbally grouped according
to thoroughly concrete characteristics. By means of certain prefixed syllables, the language of the Klamath Indians classifies
a whole manifold of objects which have a round, or approximately round, form. There are other prefixes for flat thin
forms, and for long tall forms. The prefix *shl* classifies objects
that are thin and pliable, and those which can be rolled up
in a bundle or wound together in a ball. Clothes, blankets,
hats, etc., fall into this group. *Shla-ish* is mat; *shla-psh* is bud,
and so on.[23] This method of classification naturally brings together objects which we ordinarily never think of as possessing
any common likeness, since our method of classification depends far less on concrete than on abstract qualities. The Haida
language (North American Indian) separates nouns into different groups on the basis of characteristic physical forms.
Various linguistic devices divide objects into groups of "long"

[22] Gelb and Goldstein, 566.
[23] Gatschet, 194, 282 f.

things, "thin" things, "flat," "angular," and "thread-like" things.[24] South Sea Island languages, especially those in the Melanesian group, classify by using prefixes referring to such concrete qualities as roundness or angularity. Ernst Cassirer emphasizes the fact that this grouping is quite different from anything known to the European type of language. Expressions for the sun and moon are classified together with those for the human ear, for fish of a certain shape, for canoes, etc. On the other hand, the nose and tongue as long objects may be brought under the same heading.[25]

Observation and experimental evidence point to the conclusion that the formation of concrete groups based on a realistic similarity develops early in *childhood*. Katz, in his reports of experiments in which children grouped simple geometric figures according to color or form, discusses a striking peculiarity of this concrete classification. "The qualities of objects," he says, "are not effective in isolation; they are effective through a dynamic affinity. Certain figures attract each other visually on the basis of a common content (i.e., either of form or color)."[26]

A mother writes of her child, three and one-half years old: "She has the gift for seeing at a glance what belongs together. In clearing the table she always stacks plates of the same size together. Even when merely looking at objects she groups them correctly. One evening recently we saw five lanterns at the lower end of our street which, in the distance, formed a sort of half-circle. 'Look at the pretty circle of bright lights,' she said."

Since the child has an original language only in a very limited sense, one cannot expect to find this primitive grouping tendency expressed verbally with such clarity as is the case with primitive man. Nevertheless, there are some instances which show how concrete similarities lead to a concrete form of verbal classification.

[24] Swanson, in Boas, **167**, vol. 1, 216, 227.
[25] Cassirer, **15**, vol. 1, 265.
[26] Katz, **420**, 64 f.

When Günther Stern, at the age of eighteen months, was shown a picture book, he could point out many animals if their names were first spoken aloud, and he could do this without further prompting. Nevertheless, without exception he grouped almost all the animals together under the common name of "bebau."[27] This whole concrete group of animals in the picture book was brought under the term "bebau" as a concrete "class." Later he used the word "psee" (probably originally a sneezing reaction) as a common term for leaves, trees, flowers, and fruit. The child's basic experience would seem to be a recognition of a multitude of things of the same character found together in a certain situation, e.g., a garden. Stern reports the following instructive example in the same category: Günther ran from one chair to another in the room, pointing to each one, and always asking whether that was a "chair."[28] Now, it might easily be assumed that the process of grouping begins with a collection of physically contiguous chairs—chairs standing together in a room. The group is grasped as a kind of general equality and with adult help is given a name. The process might be thought of as the recognition of contiguity in the members of a group, and the subsequent naming of this contiguity.

Grouping according to the configuration law of equality may be clearly observed in cases of *pathological* regression. It is interesting to note how such a mentality responds when confronted by the task of grouping a series of objects. A certain patient of whom Gelb and Goldstein made an exhaustive study brought the following things together: a large iron stamping tool, a metal ash tray, a metal stethoscope, a knife, a pair of scissors, a pair of pincers, and a metal punch. In another collection he placed a wooden yardstick, a wooden cigarette case, a wooden spade, and a penholder made of wood. It is notable that he did not group things according to a common logical-functional significance—i.e., cigarette and ash tray—but rather

[27] Stern, 511, 88.
[28] *Ibid.*, 179.

collected things according to the material of which they were made. In this primitive organization objects are brought together without logical-functional connection; everything wooden on the one hand, and everything metal on the other appeared to be the best ordering schema for this patient.[29]

Vigotsky, Hanfmann and Kasanin, and Goldstein demonstrated that schizophrenics behaved similarly to organically disturbed patients when confronted by the task of sorting objects.[30] In the sorting test the normal individual may not seem to differ from the schizophrenic as long as it is possible to perform a task successfully in a concrete way. But the normal individual is also able to sort in another more abstract way, whereas the schizophrenic behaves concretely on all sorting tests.[31]

The treatment of this subject would be incomplete if we failed to point out that groups concretely bound together are given this coherence not only by perceptual moments but by *affect* as well. The more the things of the surrounding world are experienced in terms of physiognomic and affective content, the stronger the role of emotion in the grouping process. A shrill tone within a melody stands out not only because of its special quality of shrillness, but also because it engenders a *nuance* of feeling which sets it in opposition to the rest of the tones. It is probable that affect is also operative where concreteness alone ostensibly accounts for the primitive grouping. In primitive languages, for instance, when certain nouns are united into a class by the use of suitable prefixes—one prefix indicating largeness, another smallness, etc.—it will be found that often this process is determined not by the moment of relative size alone, but also by an emotional evaluation. Things of equal affective value tend to come together. The "smallness" and "largeness" of objects or persons are not merely concrete,

[29] Gelb and Goldstein, 566.

[30] Vigotsky, 612; Hanfmann and Kasanin, 571; Bolles and Goldstein, 546.

[31] Bolles and Goldstein, 546, 24.

factual qualifications; they also represent affective evaluations. In the Bantu language there is a class of persons and also a class of things. But all persons who are in any way contemptible or unworthy are relegated to the class of things. The blind, the deaf, the crippled, and the idiot all belong to this thing-like class.[32] The language of the Algonquin Indians often puts small animals into the class of inanimate objects, whereas large plants are often placed in the class of animate things.[33] In the Gola language of Liberia the prefix *o* denoting the human or animal class is substituted for the customary classificatory prefix when the object is to be emphasized as one that is especially large, valuable, or important. For instance, *ka-sie*, which means "oil palm," becomes "o-sie."[34] This clearly shows the importance of the affective factor in concrete classification.

Again, in the case of *children* we must assume that any kind of concrete grouping not only proceeds on the basis of concrete perceptual characteristics, but is also determined by the collectivity in its affective significance. In her Hamburg Laboratory experiments dealing with the child's grouping activity, mentioned above, Martha Muchow found that the grouping of figures is accomplished not only according to concrete content, but also according to the quality of expressiveness in the figures, to their felt physiognomy. Thus one series of geometric figures was united because they were "prickly," another because they were "mean" or "nice," etc.

There is one case on record, reported by Gabelentz, of a child whose private language had names in which the vowels changed in accordance with the size of the object.[35] A chair, for example, was called "lakeil," whereas a doll's chair became "likill" and a grandfather's chair "lukul." When his father stood before him drawn up to his full height, the child ceased

[32] Meinhof, **244**, 13.
[33] Boas, **167**, vol. 1, 36.
[34] Westermann, **320**, 27.
[35] Gabelentz, **37**.

to call him by the customary name of "papa," and used the term "pupu." This child used a flowing "mmm" sound to indicate rounded objects. Here, too, the vowels changed in keeping with the size of the object; he called the moon "mem," a large round plate "mom," and the stars "mim mim." All this demonstrates an implicit classification of sizes on an emotional and expressive basis, symbolized linguistically through the vowels. It calls to mind somewhat similar phenomena in primitive languages. In the Ewe tongue many names are spoken in a deep tone when they represent an important thing, and in a high tone when the object is of little importance.

Primitive Abstraction; Analogous Processes of Abstraction.

Abstraction may be defined as a mental activity by means of which parts of a unit are detached from the whole, and separate qualities—color, form, etc.—are experienced in isolation. Such a definition usually implies that abstraction is a unitary function which comes into being at a certain stage of mental development and increases gradually with age. If we hold, however, that the term "abstraction" does not mean a unitary function, but rather a process that may be effected by different functions on quite different levels, then any such question as determining the age at which the faculty of abstraction appears becomes meaningless.

It is more fruitful to look for "analogous processes" of abstraction emerging at different genetic levels. As in any other mental activity, we may find a primitive type of abstraction on a purely sensori-motor, or sensory, level. A typical experiment dealing with abstraction in children is the one performed first by D. Katz and A. Descœudres, and later by Countess Kuenburg, C. R. Brian and F. Goodenough, and others. In one of Katz's original experiments the children (three to five years of age) were asked to select from a number of red triangles and green circles those figures which were the "same" as a standard form presented separately. This latter figure was either a green triangle or a red circle (Fig. 46). Curiously enough, the younger children never hesitated in their solution of the problem, and always failed to see any ambiguity in their choice. Their selection in the matching process was based predominantly on color, rather than on form.[36] A. Descœudres, using the same ambiguous problem of

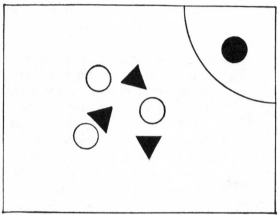

Fig. 46.—Katz' Experiment on Color-form Abstraction.

identifying non-realistic geometrical colored forms (Lotto I) found that younger children matched most often on the basis of color, and that with increase in age a choice on the basis of form became more frequent. If realistic pictures (Lotto II) were used as matching material, there was a general dominance of pure form in the reaction at every level as against color, and this dominance of form over color also increased with age.[37] Descœudres found, too, that all the younger children made their choice with comparatively no hesitation, whereas the older ones were embarrassed by the ambiguity of the task.

An analysis of this primitive type of abstraction will show

[36] Katz, 421.
[37] Descœudres, 360.

DESCŒUDRES' RESULTS ON THE LOTTO TEST

| | Lotto I | | Lotto II | |
	Color	Form	Color	Form
3– 6 yrs.	67.5%	32.5%	40%	60%
7– 8 "	43	57	20	80
10–13 "	35	65	17	83
15–18 "	32	68	10	90

it to be based on a primary law of perceptual organization, the aforementioned "law of equality." An examination of Fig. 47 shows that the number "2" is formed because of the tendency of certain elements of the optical field which have equal qualities to attract each other. In this particular configuration, organization is based on an equality of certain elements of form (dots). In the well-known test cards used in studying color-blindness it is the quality of color which binds the elements of the figure together, to the consequent neglect of form. This quasi-automatic attraction of equal elements seems to be operative in what we have called "primitive abstraction." Things with equal qualities tend to come to the foreground and arrange themselves in a unit. It may even happen that, as experiments using both children and adults as subjects have shown, if objects of the same color are scattered over a surface, these objects may be seen as a group before the color common to all of them has been clearly discerned. In brief, it is justifiable to assume that there is a primitive abstraction which goes hand in hand with the basic sensory organization. Such an interpretation explains why the young child is not disturbed by the ambiguity of the matching task in Katz' or Descœudres' experiments. In matching elements on the basis of either color or form the child sees the ele-

FIG. 47.–The Number 2 as Seen According to the Law of Equality.

ments as color-gestalt or as form-gestalt, and selects the one
quality, completely neglecting the other.

The choice of color or form depends on the relevance of the quality. This may change with the age level, with the kind of objects
used, and with the experimental situation as a whole. According
to Brian and Goodenough's experiments children below the age of
three seem to abstract non-realistic figures more frequently on the
basis of form than of color.[38] It is probable that this early dominance of form has a specific psychological meaning which distinguishes it from the dominant form reaction of older children. It
may be that for younger children objects are "things-of-action"
(e.g., "graspable objects"), and therefore their most impressive dynamic properties—that is, the forms—are stressed rather than the
colors. And it may also be that at a somewhat later age colors come
to the fore because at a stage at which things are not so rigidly
defined by motor behavior, they have a greater emotional appeal
than form, whereas at a still more advanced, realistic level form
again supplants color as a superior distinguishing quality of things.

But no matter what the correct hypothesis may be, there is no
doubt that either color or form can be relevant and definitive in a
concrete matching task. Countess Kuenburg set up a matching experiment using variously shaped boxes of diverse colors, the problem
being to select the proper cover for each box. She found that children were much more indifferent to color than to form; they often
put a green cover on a red box, and so on. In other words, they
tended to abstract form at the expense of color.[39] According to her
interpretation it would follow that the concept of form is more
deeply rooted than that of color. But actually it is nearer the truth
to say that under the particular experimental conditions form happens to be of greater relevance than color.

In summary we may say that "primitive abstraction" is a
mental process closely allied to sensory organization. Such an
organization brings forth qualities which do not stand out in
isolation, but suffuse and dominate the totality.

This sort of primitive abstraction is continually effective in

[38] Brian and Goodenough, **341.**
[39] Kuenburg, **432.**

the daily experience of the young child. A three-year-old child sees a painted landscape with a boat in it, and says: "It's summer now!" even though it is really a winter scene that is represented.[40] The boat is an individual moment in the childlike experience, and immediately determines the meaning of the entire picture. This form of abstraction may with justice be called concrete, because it does not stand apart from and superior to the perceptual configuration. The landscape is centered in such a way that the boat (as the characteristic of summer time) becomes the point of departure for the process of apprehension.

Again, concrete abstraction accounts for many verbal expressions for the qualities of objects the adult names for which the child has yet to learn. He may designate colors by naming familiar objects which characteristically exhibit these colors. For example, a boy four and a half years old is sorting color cards. He knows only the names "red," "blue," "white," and "black." When asked for the name of the yellow card he says, beaming with triumph: "The mail box!" (Austrian mail boxes are yellow.) According to Descœudres' report there are small children who designate "brown" by "chocolate," "white" by "chalk," and "blue" by "pen-box." This is concrete abstraction. The imagined objects and the colored test cards together build up a configuration in which color is the dominant quality-of-the-whole.[41]

Results from other types of experiments may further our inquiry into the ontogenesis of abstraction. Children are given geometrical figures of divers form and color, and are told to order them into groups. Different experimenters have found that up to approximately the age of four, grouping is usually carried out on the basis of only one selected category ("one-track abstraction"; Step I in the accompanying table). This category may be either color or form, but never both. Moreover, there is little or no freedom of choice in the grouping.

[40] Lombroso, **441**, 44.
[41] Descœudres, **361**, 132.

It appears that the conspicuous properties of objects themselves (color or form) quasi-automatically force similar things into groups. Blue objects "come together," and the same is true of red ones and of green ones. As a result of this seeming coercion, the younger child is unable to change his grasp of the situation in order to arrange objects still further into subgroups. For example, blue objects having once been grouped together, cannot be subdivided in a succeeding step on the basis of a variation in shape.

THE DEVELOPMENT OF ABSTRACTION IN A GROUPING EXPERIMENT
(after Usnadze)

	3 Yrs.	4 Yrs.	5 Yrs.	6 Yrs.	7 Yrs.
Step I (in %)	78	33	8	17	0
Step II	22	25	34	30	36
Step III	0	42	42	53	45
Step IV	0	0	16[a]	0	19[a]
Total	100	100	100	100	100

[a] Step reached with the aid of the examiner.

A somewhat higher level is reached (Step II) when the child is able to learn from the example set by the experimenter, who causes a division to be made which creates subgroups by bringing the remaining quality (shape, for instance) into play. Once having exhausted the possibilities of grouping according to color, an older child, usually one who has reached the age of six years, will continue unaided to make subgroups on the basis of form. After this he may continue to group according to size (Step III). In the highest type of performance, the one characteristic of the average normal adult, there is a prevision of the task which allows more than one category to be taken into account at a time (Step IV).[42]

This development does more than simply indicate the gradual growth of a unitary intellectual function which we call abstraction. It apparently involves specific changes in the

[42] Usnadze, 521.

process of abstraction itself. One who can shift his point of view in a purposeful grouping activity is no longer subject to the forces of sensory stimulation. He is able consciously to perceive that objects have different qualities, any one of which may be taken as the point of departure for an ordering process. In other words, this development indicates an immensely important step away from an abstraction closely allied to sensory organization and toward an abstraction guided by deliberately selected categories such as color, shape, number, size, etc. The behavior involved in this higher form of abstraction has been called *categorial behavior* (discussed later in the text). In Usnadze's experiments, not one child between the ages of three and eight years was able to reach unaided the level of categorial abstraction in the strict sense of the adult performance. According to certain other experiments using the same type of material in the Hamburg Psychological Laboratory, children usually reached the level of this categorial abstraction at the age of eleven to twelve.[43]

There is a good deal of evidence that primitive abstraction, as allied to sensory organization, is characteristic of the mentality of *animals* at a comparatively low level. A form of primitive abstraction accounts for the choice of one of two materials offered the animal in the typical discrimination experiment. Hertz's experiments on form discrimination in the bee show that the insect reacts not to an absolutely characterized single figure, but rather to one standing in relation to another diverse form.[44] The figure is grasped not by the isolation of a distinguishing form, but rather by such a construction of the optical field that certain properties of two objects standing in relation are revealed. The dominance of these properties de-

[43] It must be kept in mind, however, that all experimental results are dependent to a large extent on the particular experimental set-up. So far as the relative age is concerned, the steps in the growth of abstraction may vary more or less with the conditions of the experiment. The sequence of steps, nevertheless, will follow the general scheme shown in the table.

[44] Hertz, 655.

pends on the relationship of the two forms. We may say that the function of abstraction is expressed here in a selection, a focusing, of qualities linked with a situative, concrete relation. Given such a relation, certain qualities stand forth of themselves.

On the other hand, abstraction at the level of sensory organization seems to have significant limitations. As K. S. Lashley has recently pointed out, a mammal such as the rat may be able to transpose a learned response so that it can be made to apply to the selection of one of two sizes or one of two degrees of brightness, but the animal's learned response fails if—to go one step further—he has been trained to select the middle member of a set of three, and this set of three is transposed up or down a linear scale. The more complicated situation, as Lashley remarks, requires something beyond "one-track abstraction." It presents *two* directional tendencies simultaneously. The intermediate is not only larger than one other member, but also smaller with respect to yet a third member.[45]

Primitive abstraction among *primitive peoples* will be dealt with more extensively in the section on concepts. At this point it must suffice to say that in primitive languages such qualities of objects as color are frequently conceived according to the laws of primitive abstraction. Colors do not stand alone self-subsistently, but are fused with the object they qualify. Thus the natives of New Pomerania use the expression *kott-kott* (black crow) for black; *gab* (blood) for red, etc. These primitive terms for color result from a configuration of the object in such fashion that it is dominated by color as a quality-of-the-whole; color has not as yet been fully released into self-subsistence.

Certain *pathological* examples are especially instructive for understanding the problem of primitive abstraction. One of the patients studied by Gelb and Goldstein, whom we have mentioned previously, exhibited primitive abstraction during the course of certain experiments in color selection in which

[45] Lashley, **673.**

he was a subject. Although he was quite unable to name the colors of objects, he could match the color of an imaginary object with the color selected from a large variety of colored skeins. He could in this manner match the color of a ripe strawberry or of a mail box. Seemingly the patient behaved exactly like the children in the so-called abstraction experiments. Here there is no abstractive isolation of color, but a configuration of the object so that color becomes the dominant quality. It is not the red or blue, but the "strawberry-like" or "mail-box-like" color quality which must agree in the matching of two colors. When the patient identifies a skein of wool with a certain object, he does this not on the basis of any abstract color *category*, but rather on the basis of a concrete color experience resulting from an organization of the object according to a quality-of-the-whole that is the particular color in question.[46]

Head had already found similar facts to be true of his aphasic patients, facts pointing to a defect in categorial behavior. He frequently observed that these aphasiacs could match concrete objects lying on the table before them, but were unable to point to the object after the experimenter had named it for them. But even when a patient is able to select according to verbal command, the experimenter must often first transform the word into a picture-like designation.[47]

Again in Goldstein's grouping experiments, the behavior of his patient was highly significant. If given the task of ordering varicolored skeins of wool, he exhibited a marked loss of capacity to organize according to normal methods. He was guided not by any conceptual schema in which things are divided into groups, but rather by the "concrete coherence" of sensory qualities. He showed a loss of spontaneity and intentionality comparable to that characteristic of the younger children in Usnadze's experiments. At one time he might group colors that are perfectly equal in hue; at another, the bright-

[46] Gelb and Goldstein, 566.
[47] Head, 572, vol. 1, 309.

ness of the colors, or their emotional-aesthetic value, might determine the ordering process, all depending on a change in the coherence of the sensory objects.

This pathological evidence again leads us to the conclusion that there are different levels of abstraction. We must assume once more that primitive abstraction as allied with perceptual organization is superseded during development by higher processes operating on the level of categorial activity.

THE DEVELOPMENT OF GENERALIZATION IN CONCEPTUAL THINKING.

The difference between a grouping based upon "concrete abstraction" and a generalization at the purely conceptual level is essentially this: Concrete grouping reveals a certain quality through the configuration of the elements possessing that quality, whereas in a true generalization the quality (e.g., a color) common to all the elements involved is deliberately detached—mentally isolated, as it were—and the elements themselves appear only as visible exemplifications of the common quality. The generic concept "leaf" is formed when a multiplicity of leaves is ordered in a group or class. There is always an awareness of a variability of appearance with regard to the concept, when this manifold is understood as a generalization. In the purely conceptual act the elements of a group are thought of as concrete variations of an ideal the invariant properties of which constitute the abstract concept. "Leaf" becomes the general idea to which all leaves as discrete elements are now subordinated, the idea within whose confines leaves are visible and diverse materializations.

Little is known of the actual process of transition from concrete abstraction to generalization in its true sense. Nevertheless, in the world of the *primitive mentality* the process of developmental change is recognizable. It appears, for example, that a preliminary step toward generalization occurs whenever the primitive man is faced with the task of naming an unknown object in terms of objects already known. In this case the subsumption characteristic of conceptual formation is presaged by an activity which I should like to call "concrete transposition." To illustrate, the Boloki, a tribe of African Negroes, call an umbrella a "bat." This is not a real subsumption. It is a mere transposition, the carrying over of a certain name to a new and hitherto unnamed object. This transposition is not to be interpreted as if the Boloki think of the new thing as subsumptive to the category of "bat," as if it were a true exemplar of this class. The action of spreading open the umbrella, its color, etc., correspond to the flapping wing spread of the bat in flight, to the color of the bat, and so on. Both umbrella and bat (by virtue of concrete abstraction) become, in a particular sense, concretely united. At the same time there must evidently be an awareness of a variability in the general term, of the difference in umbrella with respect to bat. It must be known, for example, that in one case the object is inanimate and in the other animate, even though this variability is not expressed verbally by the Boloki.

Such "metaphorical concepts" are also typical of the languages of the South Sea Islanders. The word *bani* means both the flickering of a flame and confusion. *Uru* means the chips of wood made when a log is cut up for a fire and it also means the pus running from a wound. *Ura* is both an image in a mirror and a shadow.[48] In all these instances it can be seen that a manifold of objects is comprehended in one name which somehow preserves the variability and the individual difference of the single objects. In this same category belong those expressions which arise from the need for a mutually understood means of communication between Europeans and primitive peoples, such as pidgin English. Analogous forms of expression result from a similar need in children, who must make themselves intelligible to adults while restricted to the use of a very limited vocabulary. In any such situation it is natural for the meaning of a word to become greatly extended by "concrete transposition." In the pidgin English used by the

[48] Thurnwald, 129, 900 ff.

South Sea Islanders the word *die* stands for all kinds of extinc-
tion. When one of two lamps is to be extinguished the
Melanesian cabin-boy says: "Me make him one fellow die."[49]
Similar concrete concepts resembling the metaphor are used by
the Ewe Negroes. A shoe is described as a "foot-shield."[50]
Here again there is a transposition rather than a subsumption, for the metaphor, so-called, is conceived on the basis of
a known, concrete name, that is, shield, and the shoe is understood as a special variety of this concrete object.

To sum up: It is characteristic of all these forms that they
should derive from a concrete name which, by primitive abstraction, is felt to be suitable for the new object. We must
be careful not to interpret this process as true subsumption.
It is actually no more than a transposition, in so far as one
object is used as the touchstone in discovering similarities in
another and in consciously ordering it within a group. In this
process there is not a general concept "bat" under which
"umbrella" falls as a special member of the class. The snuffing
out of the candle is not a particular form of dying. We are
dealing not with subsumption, but with coordinated membership in a concrete group.

There are other peculiar conceptual forms which are the
concrete forerunners of subsumptive class concepts. I should
like to call them "quasi class concepts." They are concrete
modes of generalization such as are frequently used even by
people on an advanced mental level when non-scientific
thought is to be communicated. Verbally they are expressed
by the common suffix "-like" or "-ish," or by the expression
"something like . . ." When we speak of pot-like hats, we do
not mean that these hats belong to the class of pots, but that
the impression made by such hats is approximately equivalent
to that made by a pot.

All these forms of a vulgar, non-scientific language are un-

[49] *Ibid.*
[50] Werner, 142, 45.

doubtedly precursors of scientific classification and generalization. In them is inherent the experience of ordering not only according to propinquity in a group, but also according to subordination. The conceptual tendency develops vertically as well as laterally, so to speak. A norm is chosen in relation to which whatever is to be described stands as a subvariety. Several of the more highly developed primitive languages are potentially capable, from the purely grammatical standpoint, of forming such "quasi class concepts." In the language of the Ewe Negroes, for example, there is a suffix *é* which expresses the fact that an object corresponds in some way to the *ur*-type:

ad*o*	squirrel (of the plains)
ad*oé*	squirrel (of the forest—literally, "a kind of squirrel")

similarly:

tsi	water
tsì (from tsié)	soup[51]

Among *children* certain primitive forms of generalization appear at an early age. A primary stage of generalization seems to be characterized by what William Stern called the "plural concept," which he considered genetically precedent to the true universal concept. "The child already knows," says Stern, "that 'horse' is not only an entity which he sees immediately before him, but something which he may encounter in many different exemplars. . . . He now orders each new exemplar so that it stands in conjunction with others previously known, but he does not subordinate all exemplars to a common term." In other words, "plural concepts" are built up by a process of "transposition" from one concrete concept to another in the manner earlier described. We may speak of "pluralization" in the case of Stern's 3:6-year-old daughter who, every time she saw a different bird in her book of animals,

[51] Westermann, **318**, 121.

asked: "Does this bird lay eggs?" and "Does this bird lay eggs, too?" The stage of pluralization appears to precede that step in the course of conceptual development which I should like to call the stage of "omnalization" (omne = all). A boy, 3:6 years old, sitting with his parents at breakfast, remarks: "I am sitting, Father is sitting, Mother is sitting . . . we are all sitting!" Upon seeing a brown horse with a white spot on his forehead, the same child, at the age of 3:8 years, asks: "Do all horses have white spots?" Such an omnal-concept is still not a true general concept because the "all-ness" (although more advanced than in the case of a "plurality") here refers to a concrete totality, rather than to a universality.[52]

One of the few experiments dealing with the generalizations of children was carried out by V. Hazlitt. She presented to her child subject four small trays on each of which was placed a pair of wooden objects. In the first series these pairs consisted of:

> a dog and a bird
> a dog and a pig
> a dog and a cow
> a dog and a sheep

In the second series there was a match box on each of the four trays, and paired with it in turn were a little figure of a man, a goose, a miniature hunter, and a little round tin. The children were then asked to tell what was the common element in each of the two series. Few children below five years of age could isolate the common element in either of the series. The youngest child able to answer the problem involving the common element of "dog" was three years and two months old. No child under four years correctly solved the problem of the second series with the match box. Yet none of the children had any difficulty in pluralization, i.e., in observing that "in this tray there is a dog," "in that tray there is a dog," and so

[52] Stern, 511, 236; 513, Germ. ed., 361.

on. The difficulty lay in the operation of "omnalization," that is, in grasping the fact that "all the trays have dogs."[53]

The mental process of subsumption inherent in the construction of a true generalization develops very slowly. During the first five school years the relation of the part to the whole is to a great extent a substitute for subordination. Even in the higher grades children will use the concept "sheep" when asked for the term subordinating "wool." J. Vogel analyzed the development of subsumption, and found that, in definitions, the following scale of proportion exists between the use of part-to-whole relationships and true subsumption:[54]

Age	Proportion
6 yrs.	20 : 1
7 yrs., 5 mos.	5 : 1
8 yrs.	3 : 2
9 yrs., 5 mos.	4 : 3
14 yrs.	7 : 10

An instructive example may serve to show to what extent generalization may be occasioned by a play situation.[55] Two boys, four and six years old respectively, are busy with their building blocks. One of the children does the actual building, and the other has charge of the "building supply." In order to communicate intelligibly with each other they create the terminology in Fig. 48 for the different sizes of blocks.

PRIMITIVE REPRESENTATION.

The mental function which enables us to represent an object by mediation (e.g., by a word or picture) is constitutive in the development of an intellectual world. Even though this "symbolic function" reaches its fullest expression on an advanced mental level, we must recognize that representation

[53] Hazlitt, 398.
[54] Vogel, 526.
[55] Observation furnished by the parents.

is already effective in the primitive sphere. The fundamental difference is that in the latter case we are dealing no longer with a representation that is relatively pure and abstract, but with one bound syncretically to a concrete series of events.

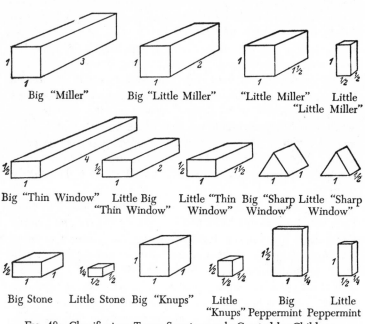

Fig. 48.—Classificatory Terms Spontaneously Created by Children.

Syncretic and implicit modes of representation may even be found in the mental processes of the higher vertebrates. If, for example, an ape is led to believe that he is about to get a certain food of which he is fond, and is then surreptitiously given something else, he will be taken aback on discovering the change. In short, he "expected" something else, and is consequently "disappointed."[56] But the ape's representation of the anticipated fruit must not be thought of as an explicit idea. Rather, as is often the case among human beings, the

[56] Tinklepaugh, **693**.

prospective thing is anticipated implicitly in terms of a certain psychophysical state of tension, of a specific affective attitude. This is syncretic representation; the object is represented not explicitly, but implicitly by means of motor-affective behavior.

In the case of *children* representation again passes through a primary stage of syncretism. At first it is an implicitly operative function fused within the affective totality. During the early stages of genetic development representation is included in the general motor behavior. This fact makes it possible to understand why symbolic functions of a higher order do not develop normally when sensori-motor activity is balked in some way. Sherman points out that the child who walks at the age of eighteen months develops an intelligence superior to that of children who learn to walk at two years, and even more markedly superior to that of children who first walk at three years.[57]

The function of representation in the strict sense (K. Bühler), which expresses itself in the capacity for communicating a cognition by symbolic formulation (gesture, sound, writing, drawing), moves through a course of development from a syncretic (implicit) symbolism to one that is pure and detached. The child gradually learns that names and pictures represent objects. The ability to grasp the representative character varies with the different kinds of symbolism involved. Whereas the child is undoubtedly conscious of the symbolic values of language between the first and second years, the representative character of the drawn figure, according to Hetzer, is not understood until before the third year.[58] The reason for this apparent paradox may lie in the fact that language permits a far greater use of syncretic representation (i.e., representation embedded in concrete motor-affective activity) than does drawing. It is true that during the earlier stages of childhood drawing is not mere visual representation. It is an integrated

[57] Sherman, 504.
[58] Hetzer, 402, 15.

part of a comprehensive physical activity. But language is much nearer to being a genuine instrument of activity at the earlier stages, since with but little exception it is action through words.

The fundamental dependence of the function of representation on concrete activity also holds true in the case of *primitive man*. The drawn images made by him are constitutive parts of his concrete life,[59] and language is an instrument of action. In primitive societies, according to Malinowski, the main function of language is not to express the thought or to duplicate mental processes, but rather to play an active, pragmatic part in human behavior. Words are linked with gesture, action, motion. Divorced from the context of action and affective situation, words are essentially devoid of any meaning.[60] It is apparent that language freed of its realistic context and conceived in its purely representative character often surpasses the power of conception, or at least the interests, of the primitive mind. Difficulties of understanding arise frequently when natives are requested by explorers to handle language in a purely representative manner, that is, apart from any relation to a realistic context. An Indian was asked to translate the following sentence: "The white man shot six bears today." He was unable to do this, and explained that a white man could not possibly shoot six bears in one day.[61]

Syncretic methods of representation can be observed nowhere to better advantage than in certain *psychopathological* conditions in which the symbolic function has regressed along with a general regression toward primitive behavior. Head, Woerkom, and Goldstein and Gelb in particular have devoted their efforts to the study of such disturbances. With some types of patients a disturbance in language is the symptom of a general disturbance in the symbolic function. The patient is frustrated whenever an idea is to be expressed, whether it be by

[59] Werner, 143.
[60] Malinowski, 235, vol. 2, 7 f.
[61] Cf. Radin, 111, 62 ff.

word, gesture, or a drawn figure. Such patients have not forgotten words as such, but they are quite unable to use them in so far as they possess an isolated, symbolic character (a "dictionary meaning"). With these aphasiacs the function of representation through drawing is likewise often disturbed. It is the intellectual ability to symbolize graphically, and not the motor activity of drawing proper which suffers injury. Patients who may have formerly been excellent draftsmen lose their power to draw when they suffer a disruption of speech.[62]

Whenever there is a decline in the power of the symbol the genesis of representation is bared, although of course in a reversed order.

1. The function of representation is in essence more primitive—which means the less easily frustrated under pathological conditions—the nearer it approaches complete syncretism, that is to say, the more the process of representation tends to be part of a concrete, natural situation. There are aphasiacs who, in situations where words are an integral part of the concrete activity, are able to use language with comparative facility. These same patients, on the other hand, are unable to cope with language when asked to give words or sentences *per se*, apart from their use in actual, immediate situations. An aphasiac studied by Head could not, on request, say "No" but, instead, protested in this paradoxical fashion: "No! I don't know how to do it!"[63] Conversely, when the verbal faculties of the aphasiac are in process of restoration the first sentences used are those related to the affective situation. Similarly, aphasiacs are able to gesture in a suitable concrete situation, even though any activity entailing the use of an isolated symbolism is beyond their powers. They may be capable of knocking at a door before entering the room, but be unable, as a pure fiction, to demonstrate the act of knocking. When coerced by circumstance they are able to exhibit a threatening de-

[62] Head, 572, vol. 1, 360.
[63] *Ibid.*, 322.

meanor, but they cannot illustrate this gesture when simply asked to do so. Furthermore, certain patients if asked and encouraged to communicate their experience by drawing are actually able to do so, although drawing for its own sake is beyond their powers.[64]

2. The function of representation is that much more primitive, the less intentionally planned and volitionally determined it is. Many aphasiacs are unable to speak correctly of their own free will, but are able to copy spoken sentences or to carry out spoken commands.[65] They cannot make a start in drawing the plan of a room, but they can finish the plan once it has been outlined for them.

3. Again, the function of representation is that much more primitively constituted and that much less affected by pathological influence the closer it is to immediate bodily action; that is, the more thoroughly the representation is fused with some motor activity. The ability to represent and to render intelligible by means of motor activity is often retained when the power of verbal symbolism, or symbolism within a purely optical field, has been lost. One of Head's patients, for example, was unable to express the hour of the day in words, but could do this by making suitable gestures with his hands. A patient of Gelb and Goldstein's could not recognize printed forms and other objects by optical activity alone, but finally solved the problem with the help of imitative movements of the eyes or head.[66]

4. The function of representation is that much more primitive, the more concrete the content of the idea to be represented.[67] The more abstract the language necessary for communication, the more frustrated is the aphasiac. From another angle, this fact indicates that the more completely detached from the concrete course of events, the higher the

[64] *Ibid.*, 389.
[65] *Ibid.*, 212.
[66] Gelb and Goldstein, 565.
[67] Head, 572, vol. 1, 213, 397.

genetic level with which the mode of representation is identified.

PRIMITIVE STAGES OF NAMING; "PHYSIOGNOMIC LANGUAGE."

The most important form of representation is language. It is by means of representation through language and through the naming process that the human mentality reaches the level of the abstract concept. But here again, in the field of language, development to the level of abstraction must apparently originate at a stage where language itself is identified with concrete action and where names are fused with objects they denote. The general belief among primitive peoples that the name is the property of the thing like any other quality, is clearly illustrated by this myth of the Solomon Islanders: Two brothers killed and burned their mother. On the spot where they buried their mother's bones there grew a palm tree which bore nuts. The older brother asked the *waran* the name of these nuts. The *waran* was of the Alu people, and could use only the word *riunu* in the Alu language for the name. This the brother did not understand. Then the dog-man came and said the name of the nuts: *muo, kukutú* (nuts three-quarters ripe); *kaba* (clot of mashed nut pulp); *kuru* (nut oil); and *taga* (ripe nuts). Now the man knew the names and could consider the palm his property.[68]

We see from this story that in the primitive sphere a name is in no sense regarded as something imposed willfully, or as something fortuitous, a mere sign. A thing cannot be grasped until its name is known. The name not only stands in intimate relation to the thing; it is part of the object itself.

The identification of name and thing is illustrated by a report made by Karl von den Steinen on the Bakaïri Indians of Brazil.[69]

"Their need to penetrate into the nature of the new things exhausted itself in questions as to whether I had made them

[68] Thurnwald, **309,** 399.
[69] Steinen, **297,** 77.

and what were their names. 'Eseti? . . . Eseti?' (What is it called?) the whole tribe called in unison, and all of them took great pains to repeat the Portuguese words. As the conversation continued one or the other would whisper the words all by himself. They were unable to pronounce two consonants in succession. When someone occasionally succeeded fairly well in pronouncing a word his joy was great, and I had the feeling that already the object appeared more familiar to him. The name for my notebook was *papera*, from the Portuguese *papel* (paper). The name once given to them, they quickly lost interest in the object which had previously fascinated them. From then on it was simply *papera*."

This belief that names are essential properties of things is the basis of all word magic; it will be discussed later. When a word is applied to a thing, this thing actually receives the quality expressed by the name. The Trobrianders firmly believe, to give one brief instance, that the pronouncement of the word "spider" induces a web-like structure in the taytu vine.[70]

Children experience names both as things in themselves and as fused in the object they denote.

This thing-like quality holds for the child's experience of any kind of sound form. The Scupins' two-year-old boy had just sung a song very well; on finishing, he asked: "What was that, Mama?" "Why, a pretty song." "Do you want the song?" "Oh yes, I'd like to have it." "Well, here it is . . ." With these words the boy reached in his mouth, pinched his tongue, and pretended to hand to his mother something which he held pressed between forefinger and thumb. Then he hopped about, much pleased, and shouted: "I just gave Mama a pretty song!"[71] Some children materialize tones or other invisible tonal things such as the howling wind, in their drawings.

Some investigators, Piaget in particular, have demonstrated the vital concrete connection between the name of a thing

[70] Malinowski, **235**, vol. 2, 230.
[71] Scupin, **502**, vol. 1, 178.

and the thing itself during the earlier stages of childhood. At an initial stage—up to five or six years, according to Piaget—the child believes that the name is inside or attached to the thing. In consequence he believes that he can recognize the name of an object simply by looking at it. When he is asked the question: "How do we know that the sun has to be called 'sun'?" his answer is: "Because it's hot," or "Because it shines" or something of the sort. If the child is asked still further: "Could we call the sun the moon?" his answer is likely to be: "No, because we can't make the sun smaller," or "No, because the sun is brighter." The further query: "Where is the name of the sun?" will elicit such responses as: "Inside! Inside the sun!" or "Right in the sun itself," or "High up in the sky!" etc. And if the small child is asked where his own name is, he may point to his chest and say: "Right here . . . in here!"

At a later stage (possibly eight to nine years of age) the child often believes that things are named by God or by some person. And now, even though the name is still conceived materially, it may no longer be thought of as residing within things, but as floating about in space, in the air, etc. It is only at a subsequent stage that the child realizes that a name is not something external and concrete. Gradually it ceases to be an immutable property of things and comes to have a conventional, traditional character.[72]

These facts introduce the problem of discovering why at a primitive level names can be conceived as material parts of things, or even as things in themselves. We may reconsider some general peculiarities of primitive behavior as a preliminary to the examination of these phenomena. It has been repeatedly emphasized that on the primitive level the objective world is experienced for the most part in terms of its dynamic properties. Things-of-action reveal expressive, physiognomic qualities. A wooden object "behaves" differently from a stone object. We look at these objects in a different way, we handle them in a characteristically different way. And yet we do not

[72] Piaget, 482, 61.

have to handle them physically in order to experience their dynamic qualities. We can see the heaviness, clumsiness, and durability of stone things, and the lightness, pliability, and splintery qualities of wood. In other words, behavioral, expressive physiognomic qualities are not limited to a certain field; they are not specifically kinaesthetic, optical, tactual, etc., in nature. In fact, they are intersensory qualities.

We may therefore speak in a very real sense not only of the softness of velvet, but also of the softness of a color or a voice. Expressive physiognomic qualities that are intersensory in character may exist in the sounds articulated by the human voice. That is, language itself has a physiognomic character. As a matter of fact, language is the most flexible and refined instrument for expressing the dynamic-motor aspect of the objective world.

It would be quite misleading to identify the physiognomic aspect of language with imitation (onomatopoeia). The theory that language is imitative—onomatopoeic—in origin springs from a mechanistic psychology, and contradicts the creative character inherent in all language. In language, by the selection and representation of certain aspects of a thing through the medium of sound, an act of creation—the creation of a mental concept of a thing—is involved. In this respect the function of language is no different from that of any other creative activity, particularly artistic creative activity.

Physiognomic language is not a hypothesis; it is an established fact. In an earlier work[73] I have demonstrated not only that physiognomic language plays an important role in poetry, but also that a certain type of mentality, particularly that of the artist, has a very clear conception of its importance,[74] and,

[73] Werner, 738.
[74] Balzac, e.g., in his novel *Louis Lambert*, admirably sums up the problem of a physiognomic language: "The modern languages," says Balzac, "have divided up amongst themselves the remainder of the primitive folk-words—those majestic and splendid words whose radiance and majesty diminish to the degree that society ages; . . . whose echo becomes forever weaker with the advance of civilization. . . . Is there not in the word 'vrai' (true) a fantastic strength of honesty? Does one

furthermore, that almost any subject can be trained to experience it.

It is fairly apparent that primitive language is much more physiognomic in character than language at an advanced level where it has become more and more a medium used predominantly for the communication of mere facts. Westermann, the well-known student of African anthropology, has given us some uncommonly instructive examples of the expressive character of primitive language as observed in the process of the actual creation of physiognomic words.[75] In the West African languages there is a group of words which are extraneous to all the real roots of the various dialects. These words are the so-called "sound-images" (*Lautbilder*). "By 'sound-image' I mean a complex of sound which, so far as the primitive man feels it, represents an immediate linguistic reaction to a sensuous impression. In other words, it is a spontaneous and complete expression for an inner feeling. Even though I am able to report only isolated cases from my own personal experience, I am nevertheless convinced that these sound-images are created each time anew to meet current need, and that we are dealing with an unlimited field of word-creation. While journeying with these natives one can see how they have an expression ready at hand for a far-distant movement that is seen but not heard, for a sudden, powerful odor, etc. The word for the smell may be recognized as intelligible by all those present by an appreciative wrinkling of the nose, or by

---

not find in the short sound which it commands a vague image of modest nakedness, of the inherence of the truth in everything? This syllable breathes forth an indefinable freshness. I have taken the form of an abstract thought as an example since I did not wish to clarify the problem by using a word too easily intelligible, such as the word 'flight,' where everything speaks to the senses. And is it not so with all words? All bear the stamp of a living force invested in them by the soul which they give back through the mystery of wonderful action and reaction between word and thought. . . . Through their physiognomy alone words animate the ideas in our brain, the ideas which they clothe. . . ."

[75] Westermann, 321, 319. Cf. Hornbostel, 50.

its repetition in chorus. The inner activity awakened by the external impression has freed itself in a suitable linguistic expression. And even though they do not belong to the language, these undomesticated words, as one might call them, exhibit a relation between sound and sense that is understood by the listener quite as well as by him who speaks them."

In any of the more primitive tongues, and aside from such extemporaneously created sound pictures, there are innumerable sound patterns which express things and events in such fine *nuances* that their exact value can scarcely be described even by the circumlocutions of the western languages. According to Westermann, the following factors are determinants in the sound patterns of the West African languages: rhythm (duplication), vowel pitch, vowel quantity, consonantal quality, muscle tension, etc.[76] In considering the formation of a physiognomic language we must always bear in mind, first of all, that here there is no one-track relationship between sound and meaning. Each speech element has many different aspects, one or another of which is dominant in accordance with the whole pattern of which it is a part. For example, Westermann has demonstrated how a *high pitch*,[77] may express:

1. Something fine, tender, small: *kàkrá*—little (as opposed to *kàkrà*—big, in the Tschi language). In the Yoruba language: *gbóró*—small (as opposed to *gbòrò*—broad, etc.).
2. Something narrow, sharp: *bí*—narrow; *fídé, kégé, bíduí*—pointed.
3. Something silent, secret: *wó*—silent (as opposed to *wò*—loud).
4. Something quick, agile: *gégégé*—tripping; *dógódógó*—swift.
5. Something energetic, fresh, alert: *míamíamía*—cool, fresh.
6. Something that is intense, or
7. Something that is loud of color, or
8. Something that is sour, sharp of taste.

[76] Westermann, 321.
[77] ′ = high pitch; ‵ = low pitch.

On the other hand, a *low pitch* may indicate:

1. Something big (cf. above, 1).
2. Something plump, awkward, slow: *kàlò, klànà*—slow; *gìligìlì*—awkward.
3. Something blunt: *gbùgblù, dògò*, etc.
4. Something loose, not dense: *fòflòkòdzò*—loose, the lungs.
5. Something confused, disordered: *kplòhò*, etc.
6. Something muggy, dim, dark: *fùlì*—not clear; *gèligèli*—smoky.
7. Something dull, silly, stupid: *gòlògòlò, lùsù*, etc.
8. Something swollen, sick: *kpòbò̀*, etc.
9. Something weak, frail, powerless: *dò̀, gbò̀*, etc.
10. Something colorless, tasteless: *yà̀, vō*, etc.
11. Something flat-sounding, hoarse: *bìdìbìdì*—drum.

Another group of examples shows the physiognomic significance of the consonant in the word pattern:

b—signifies something soft, decayed, rotten: e.g., *bayā*—soft; *abòbò̌*—snail; *botō*—soaked.

k or *kp* signifies something hard, strong, stiff: *katsakatsa*—hard; *kpam*—with force.

f signifies something thin, breakable, brittle; *flà̀*. Fricative sounds express roughness: *lochō, klitsā*.

Of course, even in primitive languages we are dealing with words which have a long history behind them, and which therefore have been subjected to many changes of meaning that obscure the original relation of sound and content. In the Ewe language *dè* means something quiet or silent, and should therefore have a high rather than its actual low pitch. But the fundamental meaning of this word is "slow," which would make it accord to the general rule for pitch.

Many reports on the linguistic sense and the linguistic forms of *children* point to the conclusion that the names of things are conceived much more physiognomically at this early level than in the adult sphere.

Ruskin tells how in his childhood the word "crocodile" **with** its long series of letters had for him something of the

sinuous, jointed appearance of the real animal. For him the
name of a Dr. Grant was always associated with a brown,
gritty, bitter powder (rhubarb). This powder was "gr-i-ish"
and "granty" for him. Isolde Kurz, telling of her early childhood, says: "At that time words were not purely immaterial
things. Clinging to them was that exquisite materiality which
they described." She refused to eat anything when its name
aroused her dislike. For example, the hitherto unfamiliar term
"bonbon" (candy) displeased her greatly; in the nasal "on"
and in the repeated syllable she discerned something lascivious
and disgraceful. Friedrich Huch writes in his autobiographical
novel *Mao*: "Thomas had a curious feeling that bound him
to the sound of words, and many he would not allow to cross
his lips. He could not be moved to repeat a little saying that
he had learned about 'Mister' Zeboath,[78] and lied, saying that
he had forgotten to learn it. Because of this he murmured each
word to himself secretly, but even then it could not escape
his lips. A strange, elegant man in his middle years, a man
dressed in a light cloak with the thick odor of raw venison
about him—such was 'Mister' Zeboath for him. . . . And then
he heard again the single-voiced violin melody that he had sung
to, a spiritual song in which there was something of 'Huld'
('clemency'), a word that sounded for him like pomade
smelled."

Many children's neologisms show a physiognomic origin.
A girl three and one-half years old was reported as saying:
"Mother, we're going over 'nubbles' (a sidewalk made of small,
uniformly cut stones half buried in the ground)." Again:
"Mother, you 'rohst' so! Why do you do that! ('rohst' referring
to the scraping sound made by shoes on gravel)." Another
time: "The moth is 'splilting' (way of flying)." On one occasion the mother was pouring water out of a pot, and the
child noticed a thread floating within and asked: "Mother,
why does that 'wengle' so?" "Mother, did the ice-man just

[78] Hebrew word for God.

come?" "Yes, how did you know?" "He made 'kolbs' on the floor when he put the ice in the box."

Stumpf's son called a peculiarly shaped stone "marage" and later explained that the stone looked just as the word sounded.

The physiognomic aspect of naming is revealed with particular clarity in those neologisms which change in meaning when a change is made in the content. In a language contrived by two English children the word "bal" meant "place." The larger the place, the longer the intonation of the vowel, so that in three variations the same word could mean "village," "town," and "city." Their word for "going" was "dudu," and the greater the speed, the more quickly was the word spoken. "Du-u-du-u," for example, meant to go slow.[79]

A four-year-old girl says: "Father talks just like Santa Claus . . . boom, boom, boom! As dark as night . . . ! But we talk light, like the daytime . . . bim, bim, bim!"

It was reported of Frau Neugebauer's 1:4-year-old boy: "In order to indicate large stones he spoke the word 't-tein' (Stein-stone) very loudly, making it deep and long drawn out, with his eyes rounded and his lips pursed in such a way that one clearly recognized a look of pleasant astonishment at so much size. Upon seeing some young trees he said 'tree' very shortly and in a high voice with his eyes squeezed tight, his nostrils pinched together, and his mouth screwed up, in order to express his pleasure at the smallness and daintiness of the trees."[80] Stern's 2:1-year-old grandson let a doll "smell" some flowers, each time saying "ha-psi." The first syllable "ha" was spoken in a normal middle tone, but the second syllable "psi" was pronounced in a very high squeak. While carrying out the same pantomime before a tall gum tree the child changed the tonal value of the expression. Instead of making a clear peeping sound he tried to speak gruffly, deepening his voice.[81]

[79] Jespersen, 55, Germ. ed., 393.
[80] Neugebauer, 466.
[81] Stern, 511, 184.

There is a great deal of evidence pointing to the further conclusion that the child has a physiognomic conception not only of the spoken language, but of the written and printed language as well. At an early stage of childhood, writing is often thought of as a sort of drawing, since the curves and strokes forming the letters are understood physiognomically, in accordance with the child's needs. Katz reports one instance: "Are you writing a picture?" the child asks his mother. "Will you read it to me tomorrow?" The mother (pointing to a written word) remarks: "This says 'eyes.'" The boy indicates a line drawn under the word "eyes," and says: "That's a hand, Mother . . . write my hand for me!"[82]

Martha Muchow and I carried on some experiments with a number of children ranging in age from seven to ten years in order to observe their capacity for copying down words physiognomically. We asked them to write down certain words with a definite affective value in such a way that we could "see what they were." Two examples (Fig. 49) may serve to show that for many children this task seemed a perfectly natural one. Note the cramped, narrow representation of ängstlich (scared), in comparison with the swinging, rounded width of froh (glad).

We may say that an insight into the physiognomic aspect of language enables us to understand primitive "word realism" and "word materialism."[83] It becomes quite intelligible that children (Piaget) should say it is the verb "to box" itself which strikes out at them. We now see why primitive people and certain pathological types experience names as belonging to things. In the physiognomic world the name is not a mere instrument of sound behind which there is a meaning. The word, by virtue of its concrete physiognomy, is directly related to the object itself. Or it may even go beyond this because the word, in so far as it shares the physiognomy of the object, is an integral part of this object.

[82] Katz, 421, 55.
[83] Piaget, 482, chap. 2.

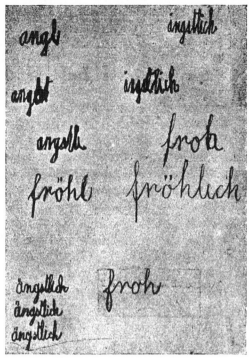

FIG. 49.—Physiognomic Word Forms Written by Two Nine-year-old Girls.

As the development of the naming process advances, names are no longer thought of as concrete and physiognomic in nature, as constituent parts of objects proper; they gradually achieve the status of symbols substituting for the objects themselves. At the same time the physiognomic quality of words may still remain as the sensuous ground from which the abstract meaning draws its vitality. For example, even though the word "ball" has an ideal, abstract meaning, in that it refers solely to the pure idea of ball and is detached from the actual appearance of this object, yet in the sound of the word or in its actual physical appearance there are many who experience a softness, a roundness, or a rolling quality which, to some degree or other, affords a concrete frame for the conceptual content. In this case the physiognomic stratum of the word will of course be subordinated to the higher symbolic stratum, but it is nevertheless still actively present.

The assumption that physiognomic language appears at a relatively early developmental stage receives some support from recent *puthological* observations. G. Engerth reports three cases of aphasia which at a certain stage of regeneration showed a very definite use of physiognomic language.[84] One patient, shown a picture of St. Stephan's Church in Vienna and requested to tell the name of this building, says: " 'Bitter' . . . no, not so . . . 'schatt' . . . its high, t is high, i is pointed, belongs to it. But down there it's also broad, o is broad: ot–ti, 'Gotisch' (gothic). I have it, it's a church, St. Stephan's Church, that's what it iṣ!"

The patient's naming response to the picture of an auger (German: *Bohrer*) is as follows: "o it must be! o makes a hole . . . lo, lor . . . yes . . . 'loch' (= hole) and err, this scratches, no . . . it makes a hole in a Brett (= board) . . . Brrrett . . . 'Bohrer' it's called!"

The recognition of printed letters occurs according to their dynamic physiognomic properties. Presented with the printed letter *t*, the patient said: "It goes upwards, it gets sharp quite yellowish, yes, sharp like yellow color. Yes, it's a t."

This physiognomic aspect refers also to writing. The patient writes the German word *heiter* (merry) as follows:

He explains: "Here is a wrinkle, there is a wrinkle, the teeth in the middle it makes you laugh to look at it."

The reports on these patients have a striking similarity to those on the subjects engaged in our own experiments on

[84] Engerth, 551.

physiognomic language. One of the patients, trying to name the color of black wool, says: "You have to jump over it . . . mountain and shad(ow) . . . schw . . . 'schwarz' (= black)."

Compare this with the report on one of our normal subjects who experiences the word *schwarz* as something towering, sinister: "One has to cross (phonetic) obstacles (schw) in order to arrive at the somber end."[85]

To sum up, we must conceive of the development of the naming function as proceeding somewhat in this manner: Initially the name is the physiognomic aspect of the thing, or of a part of the thing. Gradually it becomes a picture of the thing (the word "ball," so to speak, can "roll" without being the ball itself). Later still this physiognomy of the word appears as a mere "diagram" or "schema" by means of which the abstract idea is made visible and audible and thus represented. It is somewhat the same process as that involved when the idea of "dog" is made visible and communicable by a drawing of a dog. This sensuous character of a representation can also be ultimately lost, so that nothing remains but the name as a sort of algebraic sign no longer felt but simply "known" as the symbol of the object.

It is a debatable question whether there actually is a language in which words function as pure algebraic symbols. I am inclined to believe that even in the most thorough dematerialization of words there will still remain a certain remote dynamic character, useful as schematic representation of the word meaning.

A hypothetical scheme for the development of the naming process would be as follows:

1. The name as a material *property* of the thing.
2. The name as a concrete, physiognomic *picture* of the thing.
3. The name as a physiognomic *diagram* of the (abstract) concept.
4. The name as an *algebraic symbol* of the concept.

[85] Werner, 738, 156.

THE CONTENT OF NAMES AND THEIR DEVELOPMENT.

Syncretism; Concreteness of Primitive Concepts.—In primitive societies language is an integral part of the concrete daily life. In consequence it is inevitable that names themselves are predominantly concrete. This raises the difficult problem of the nature of abstract terms in the primitive mentality. So far as simple facts are concerned, there is obviously an abundance of evidence pointing to the existence of an excess of concrete and specific designations and a corresponding paucity of generalizations. This is characteristic of any sphere of syncretic thought. Conceptual terms are themselves concrete; concept and percept are fused in one indistinguishable entity in so far as the functions of concrete apprehension and conception proceed as one. The primitive concept therefore possesses certain of the properties of a picture-like image. Primitive people have an inexhaustible number of these "conceptual images," which may be thought of as a description and a concrete representation of the thing, as well as a conception of it. Conception and description, two distinctly separated functions at the level of logical thought, are fused in the primitive mentality.

The more primitive the society the less interest there is in the generic name. Names are above all individual names. The Bakaïrí of Brazil have a whole group of expressions for different species of parrots, but the generic name "parrot" is lacking in their language.[86] Among the Australian aborigines there are no such class names as bird, tree, or fish; but on the other hand there are special terms for particular species of birds, trees, and fishes.[87] The same is true in primitive African tongues, and in the languages of the South Sea Islanders.[88] Certain American Indian languages have many names for cloud formations; the Lapps have twenty names for different kinds of ice and forty-one words for the various kinds of

[86] Steinen, 297, 81.
[87] Smith, 292, vol. 2, 27.
[88] Kohl, 223, 229.

snow.[89] Yet in both cases the language has no corresponding generic terms. The Tamo of British New Guinea has no word for "to go," but he has words for "going north, south, east, or west."[90] Even among the more advanced primitive peoples, such as the Bantu or the Polynesians, there is still an extraordinary specialization in names.[91] In Kinyamwesi, a Bantu language—as in the case of the Papuan tongue just mentioned— there are names for several kinds of "going," but none for the inclusive form "to go." "To go walking" is *jumba*; "to walk along slowly and carefully with a convalescent man" is *zembela*; "to hop across earth seared by great heat" is *ganyaganya*.[92] The old Maoris of New Zealand gave names to each separate thing—their houses, their boats, their weapons, and even their clothing.[93]

In short, everywhere among primitive peoples it is apparent that the naming process has a different direction and emphasis from that of advanced cultures. The most important function of language among primitives is to describe, to copy reality, whereas in advanced cultures it is to serve as an instrument of judgment, to express a causal explanation of reality. Because of this it is quite as essential that the primitive man preserve the most highly specialized shades of meaning in names, as it is for us to express the general and the lawful. A Ponka Indian narrating an act of killing, does not express it in general terms. He does not say, e.g., "the man killed the rabbit." He says: "The man, he, one, having a soul, standing, deliberately killed, having shot an arrow, the rabbit . . . him, the one, having a soul, sitting down." One cannot just kill. One must kill a living thing, an animal or a man; one must kill with intent or by accident an object that is standing, sitting, or lying down; and he must do this with an arrow or some other missile. For all these possibilities in the

[89] Keane, 217, 235.
[90] Hagen, 203, 208.
[91] Andrews, 155, Introd.
[92] Dahl, 181, 462.
[93] Taylor, 307, 328.

form of killing the verb varies to a greater or lesser degree.[94]
Similarly, in the language of the Hurons, the word for "eat"
varies with each change of food. To see a man standing up
and to see one sitting down are two separate situations requiring the use of different verbs.[95]

The manner in which new names arise by compounding
throws some light on the character of the primitive concept as
a form which, at the bottom, is a concrete picture of the object itself. These compounds are often no more than descriptions. The Bokotudos, for example, use for the word "island":

nak	munia	pompö	nep
land	water	middle	here is

Again, their word for "cow" is:

po	kokri	zapu
foot	split	mother[96]

In the pidgin English of the South Sea Islanders the name
for piano is: "A box (that) cries (when) you hit him!"

Three points must be stressed in a résumé of this discussion
of the problem of general terms:

1. It is self-evident that one of the salient characteristics of
primitive languages is a scarcity of general terms and a multiplicity of particular terms. But we must avoid the common
error of drawing any gratuitous conclusion that the primitive
mentality is incapable of general concepts. We must keep in
mind that the so-called "primitive peoples," as they exist today,
represent various stages of development. The more primitive
they are psychologically, the more conspicuous is the lack of
general terms in their language, and vice versa. Furthermore,
whether or not peoples of a really primitive mentality have
the potential ability to think in terms of abstract language can

94 Powell, 107, 16.
95 Charlevoix, 174, vol. 3, 196.
96 Ehrenreich, 186.

be decided only by experience and experiment. Developmental psychology is currently concerned only with the actual characteristics of the primitive mentality.

2. Another moot question is whether the primitive man actually experiences general ideas even though they may not be explicitly expressed in his own language. It can be demonstrated that this really is often the case. General ideas, even though not present explicitly in the language, may nevertheless exist implicitly in "analogous forms" at the motor-affective level, i.e., exist as general states of feeling underlying certain activities. "Although among the Trobrianders," writes Malinowski, "nothing is so important as gardening, there are no expressions for 'agriculture,' 'crops,' or 'gardens.' They have no word for 'work,' 'effort,' or 'skill,' although they are certainly aware of the importance of skill, etc. The concept of magical force pervades their whole life but one does not find a concept equivalent to 'mana.' Are we then justified in assuming that these natives have no concept of magical force? Certainly not. . . . The concept of magical force exists in the very way they handle their magic. Therefore the Trobrianders have the meaning of magical force without the exact verbal concept. . . . The concept of magical force is embodied in native behavior and in their approach to magic."[97]

Generalizations may also exist implicitly in the organization of the language itself. We have already pointed out (p. 229) the fact that many languages scattered all over the world have a sort of grammatical classification without expressing explicitly the abstract terms underlying the group of objects. Although certain languages of the South Sea Islanders have no single general names to denote "long," "round," "flat," etc., there is a scheme whereby classificatory particles are used in connection with words in order to designate these very qualities.[98]

3. The third point to be kept in mind revolves around the

[97] Malinowski, **235**, vol. 2, 66 ff.
[98] Malinowski, **233**.

question of whether a great number of particular terms existing in conjunction with a remarkable infrequency of generalizations is a situation peculiar to the primitive mentality, or
whether it is found on more advanced levels as well. A great
deal of useless controversy is obviated when this problem is
evaluated from the standpoint of developmental psychology.
There can be no doubt that in certain spheres of activity on
advanced levels there is a plethora of concrete names and a
dearth of abstraction. There are fields of dominantly concrete
activity in every advanced civilization which demand a "language-of-action" that is bound to have characteristics paralleling those of genuinely primitive tongues. The farmer, the
steel worker, and the craftsman live—so far as their labor is
concerned—in a world-of-action, and they need a language to
meet the demands of this circumstance.

What is true of the individual mental structure constituted
of various genetic levels likewise holds true for the structure
of the different social organisms. The difference between lower
and more advanced societies does not consist of the fact that
primitive forms of behavior are absent in the latter, but rather
that the more primitive the society the greater the homogeneity
and the consequent dominance of primitive behavior. As the
society advances the stratifications of mental form stand out
with increasing clarity.

The original form of the "conceptual image" is as plainly
evident in the course of *ontogenetic development* as in that of
the phylogenetic. The child's concepts always have a concrete
content. Image and concept are an indivisible unity. The conceiving and the describing of a thing are not distinctly separated activities. As is true of primitive man, the child's need
of adjustment to adult language creates conceptual forms
which arise out of concrete perception, which are indeed both
perception and conception, which appear to be metaphors and
yet really are not. To this category belong such conceptual
pictures as those made up by Stumpf's son, who, when between
three and four years old, used the word "wausch-kap" (Fleisch

—kaputt = meat—torn up) for knife (*Messer*), and for the word "pencil" (*Bleistift*) the expression "pip-sch-sch" (Spitz-ma-schine—"point-machine".[99] A five-year-old American child calls a sunbonnet an "apron-hat" and a towel a "wipe-it-dry.[100]

In such examples we also see frequently the concrete-physiognomically known object transformed into physiognomic expressions involving the whole body. At the age of two and one-half, Frau Neugebauer's son created a whole series of these physiognomic-concrete terms.[101] "Keuchelein" (little coughs) meant small objects in his mother's sewing basket. "Big, thick 'Gebuhne'" was something he held out in a clenched and quite empty hand. Opening his hand flat, he would inspect this "Gebuhne" and watch it as it "flew up to the ceiling." He would reach for the "Gebuhne" to get it before it escaped him, and say "Snap!" as he snatched it out of the air.

The picture-like character of the child's concepts is revealed in such experiments as those made by Binet, who tested the child's capacity for defining names, and those by Pohlmann, who supplemented Binet's work.[102] Binet, for example, asked a five-year-old child to tell him what a wagon was. The child gave the following answers: "Men get into it. They give the horse a crack with the whip, and then the horse runs." It is obvious that here the name is conceived as a picture. Description and conception are not separated. According to some of Pohlmann's results, five children from five to six years of age defined a bottle in the following ways: 1. "There's lemonade in it." 2. "Where you put water." 3. "When a little boy drinks milk out of it." 4. "Where you pour something out of." 5. "The bottle has beer."

To conceive and define things in terms of concrete activity is in complete accordance with the world-of-action characteristic of the child. This initial method of defining names, it has

[99] Stumpf, 515.
[100] Bean, 334.
[101] Neugebauer, 468.
[102] Pohlmann, 485.

been repeatedly demonstrated, falls into gradual desuetude with increasing age. A tabulation of the results of Barnes' investigations may serve to illustrate this fact:[103]

	Age in Years									
	6	7	8	9	10	11	12	13	14	15
Definition in terms of concrete action	82%	71%	73%	68%	62%	48%	47%	37%	41%	33%

On the other hand, as might be expected, in experimental situations where the child's task is to describe pictures the average use of abstract words increases with age:[104]

	Age in Years							
	6	7	8	9	10	11	12	13
Percentage of abstract terms	0	1.1	1.2	2.1	2.7	5.5	5.5	5.7

Little has been done in tracing the development of the use of general terms as they appear during the early stages of childhood. Merely to compile a vocabulary of the first words used by the child does not suffice. It is necessary to inquire into the actual meaning with which the child invests the words, and into the change of meaning during mental growth. One of the few analyses of this sort has been made by P. Guillaume.[105] He noticed that seemingly abstract general terms used by the younger child actually have a highly individualistic, egocentric meaning. For instance, to a child eighteen months old the word *lever* (*se lever*, to rise) means: "I want to get out of my bed."

[103] Barnes, 333.
[104] Beckmann, 335.
[105] Guillaume, 392.

Ouvrir (to open) means: "Please open the door." In time these words will become more generalized. A few months later *ouvrir* will be used not only for opening a door, but for opening a box, a book, etc.

The conceptual activity of the individual who has regressed to a *pathological* form of behavior is also concretely determined. The decline of the concept from the abstract to the concrete is a specific pathological symptom.

According to Hughlings Jackson's genetic principle, it is the higher levels of intellectual activity which are the first to be impaired. In amnestic aphasia, for example, certain words may still be understood, but in an individualized, concrete sense. A barrel, for one patient, is "something that holds beer." He does not understand the word "manager" used as a generalization, but can use it correctly in designating the man he once worked for.[106] Aphasiacs often substitute concrete circumlocutions for general concepts. A kitten, for instance, may be spoken of as a "little fur-child," the scissors are "something to cut with," etc. As in the case of primitive man colors are designated by concrete adjectives. Black may become "dead" or "what one does for the dead."[107]

There is an interesting case of a schizophrenic who declared that he was able to paint any abstract concept so that others could recognize it. With a red and blue pencil he drew "spring," "equality," "difference," and "love."[108] Prinzhorn mentions another schizophrenic who was able to picture abstract concepts such as the idea of power and of violence.[109]

This calls to mind the manner in which abstract concepts are materialized by primitive man. Among the Maoris a peculiarly shaped stick represents the incarnation of life, health, and welfare. Another stick represents evil, misfortune, wrongdoing, and death.[110]

[106] Pick, 591, 41.
[107] Head, 572, vol. 1, 397, 526.
[108] See plate in Schilder, 597.
[109] Prinzhorn, 594, 253.
[110] Best, 163, 138.

Diffuseness of the Primitive Concept.—The conceptual names of primitive people (and also of children and pathological individuals) are concrete not only in the sense that they are cast in an individualized, picture-like mold, but also in the sense that they refer much more directly to some diffusely constituted, collective situation. This conceptual diffuseness may be clearly observed in languages of gesture, or sign languages, which to a high degree exhibit a "holophrastic" form.[111] By a "holophrastic" form we mean that kind of language in which the sign not only stands for a single, limited thing, but also connotes, suggests, a whole related idea. Let us consider, for example, the sign language of Northwest Queensland. The sign for boomerang does not so much express the single object as suggest a continuum of thought—the idea of hitting something with the boomerang and thereby killing it, or of selling the boomerang, or of finishing its manufacture, or even of stealing it.[112]

In its primary stage, name formation is not a function by means of which single, objectively concrete things are denoted. It is rather one which serves to denote these things as part of broad associations. Names may stand for both subjective and objective relationships. In its subjective aspect the name may be surrounded by an atmosphere of feeling unintelligible to the uninitiated, especially to the European who is used to thinking of names as applying to more or less strictly delimited objects. Thurnwald remarks how, among the South Sea Islanders, names are enveloped in an aura of feeling, and shimmer with overtones which suggest related ideas extending far beyond anything common to the European languages.[113] Hornbostel, telling of the recitation of tribal songs by the Wanyamwesi, says: "In many cases the words are so richly laden with associated ideas and feelings that a mere interjection may serve to bring to life a whole complex of inner image

[111] Cf. Witte, 747.
[112] Roth, 275, vol. 2, 72.
[113] Thurnwald, 129, 89 f.

as well or even better than could be accomplished by any lengthy description."[114]

A brief illustration may suffice to bring home this point. A crew of Trobrianders, sighting land after a long cruise off-shore, shout *"Pwaypwaya!"* (i.e., soil on which we tread and labor). Instead of using such a strictly limited and abstract term as "land" they naturally employ a word with broad emotional associations, since "they wish to convey not a fine, abstract shade of meaning, but merely the fact of a fortunate, joyful familiarity."[115] Such an example once again demonstrates plainly why primitive societies have so little use for general terms, since they are too circumscribed in feeling to express the kind of thoughts peculiar to the mentality.

A single name may express an objective association, a broad situation. We might recall the previously cited example of the Nyamwesi word *zembela* which means to hop across earth seared by great heat. In accordance with its very nature the verbs of a primitive language usually denote a diffuse, collective activity. Where we would use one verb there are many in the primitive tongue because here the verb has a holophrastic meaning. We have mentioned before that the Huron word for "eat" varies with the kind of food eaten.[116] In the language of the Abipone Indians the number of words with apparently the same meaning is amazingly large. They use different verbs to say "wound with human teeth," "wound with the teeth of an animal," "wound with a knife," "wound with a dagger," etc.[117]

A diffuse conceptual formation can be most clearly observed in the case of the *child*. At an early age the child's naming activity is directed not so much to the denotation of single, discrete objects as to the expression of a diffuse holophrasis.

When Preyer's two-year-old son says "tul" (*Stuhl*, chair) he

---

[114] Hornbostel, **210**.
[115] Malinowski, **235**, vol. 2, 71.
[116] Charlevoix, **174**, 196.
[117] Dobrizhoffer, **184**, 186 ff.

is expressing a holophrastic thought, rather than designating the single object "chair." He wishes to communicate such ideas as: "I should like to be lifted on to the chair" or "My chair isn't here" or "I want the chair to be brought up to the table" or "This chair isn't placed properly."[118]

Another characteristic example of the holophrastic quality of the child's words is found in this incident reported of the 1:5-year-old Scupin boy: "He circles by the stove and says anxiously: 'Hot . . . hot!' He also says this when standing before objects that he has been forbidden to touch. Apparently the child includes in the concept 'hot' not only the sensation of having burnt his fingers, but also the idea of not touching anything since that may result in unpleasantness or pain!"[119]

The child's own activity is often the dominant element in a collective situation to which he has given an inclusive, conceptual name. In one such instance "hat" was used to indicate anything that the child could place on top of his head, even the hairbrush.[120] Scupin tells that his son used the word "nininini" to express the idea of "snuggling and wriggling about in bed or on a fur rug."[121] This distinctly recalls the manner in which primitive people use a single word to express a whole situation or action (e.g., the Nyamwesi word *zembela*).

Personal names, remarkably enough, are not always limited to the strict designation of the single person. They may contain the emotional or concrete meaning which this person has for the child. In view of this fact it is quite inadequate to classify early linguistic forms in terms of adult grammatical categories. Individual names such as "Papa," "Mama," "Mary," etc.—as Guillaume justly remarks—are not so much nouns as imperatives, linguistic participants in concrete action.[122]

Scupin says of his son: "He associates definite ideas with

[118] Preyer, **488**, 338.
[119] Scupin, **502**, vol. 1, 170.
[120] Sully, **516**, Germ. ed., 151.
[121] Scupin, **502**, vol. 1, 81.
[122] Guillaume, **392**.

certain persons. When anyone speaks of his grandmother he says: 'O—Mama . . . oranges!' He is greatly impressed by the fact that he gets chocolate and oranges from her, and that she takes him walking. When his grandfather is mentioned he says: 'O—Papa! Tired! . . . 'rch . . . 'rch!'—because once, as a jest, his grandfather laid his head on his hand feigning sleep, and pretended to snore. If he hears the word 'aunt' he always says: 'Aunt! Cookies!' or 'Aunt! Bow-wow!'—because she often brings her dog with her."[123]

The names of the child's new acquaintances are often not the names of persons as such, but of persons in some characteristic situation. When the Scupins' two-year-old son visited the doctor he called him "Write-uncle" because the man wrote out prescriptions for the parents.

Because of its holophrastic character the child's speech continues for a long time to be elliptical and fragmentary. Even at a comparatively late age the child tends to employ inner relations of an affective-motor, concrete order in the naming process and, in consequence, his conversation seems to be rather subjective and logically incomplete from the adult standpoint.

Conceptual terms, even among older children, are concrete and diffuse to a far greater degree than is the case with the average adult. An example from my own experience will serve to show how careful one must be in judging the results of intelligence tests from an adult standpoint. Children aged nine to ten were given completion tests; from appended lists of words they had to select fitting terms to fill omissions in the text of a logically related narrative. For each gap there was a group of possible terms, one of which was correct. In this little story there was the sentence: "The farmer took the donkey by the neck." The word "neck" was left out here. In the group of possible choices was the word "voice," and in many classes almost 30 per cent of the children wrote: "The farmer took the donkey by the voice." At first this was construed as a gross error, but on further analysis it became evident that the children

123 Scupin, 502, vol. 1, 81, 175.

really meant "throat" when they used "voice." This is a striking example of childish thinking; voice, throat, neck, etc., constitute a diffusely uniform idea, just as foot and leg, or arm and hand, are considered to be a single unit.[124]

The so-called "contaminations" of child speech are added evidence for the syncretic and, at the same time, diffuse character of the child's naming process. "Trommel-pete" (drum and trumpet = trumpet); "Lampe-terne" (lamp and lantern = lantern); "Marme-ssokolade" (marmalade and chocolate = marmalade), etc., are all expressions commonly used by the Scupins' 2:5-year-old son. Similarly, Schleicher's son speaks of a sun that "blänzt" (*glänzt* and *blendet*) which might be brought over into English as "blares" (blinds and glares). And he uses the word "Nütze" (*Netz* and *Mütze*), which is perhaps equivalent to "nep" (net and cap).[125]

This diffuse conceptual process often expresses itself in such a way that a thing is described in terms of the whole situation in which it is found. According to Sully, for instance, a four-year-old girl describes her parasol, which is being blown about by the wind, as a "windy" parasol.[126] The "windy" global situation subordinates the element of parasol to the global quality.

Another similar case: A five-year-old girl is in great need of relieving her bowels, and lifts up her dress, saying, "I'm so potty," that is, "I feel I must use the chamber-pot as quickly as possible." The child describes her physical state in terms of a concrete, diffuse situation. All this is possible only when the naming process is related to a diffuse situation having qualities-of-the-whole which, for one reason or another, are emphasized.

Neither the word nor the sentence exists in the strict grammatical sense at the ontogenetic beginning of language. Language starts as holophrasis, a linguistic form in which word and sentence are not

[124] Werner, **533**.
[125] Egger, **363**, 53.
[126] Sully, **517**, 154.

yet differentiated. Neither one develops out of the other; rather they both develop simultaneously and separately out of the holophrastic basic form. An example may make this development more clear. Guillaume observed the primitive beginnings of the sentence form in the case of a child two years of age.[127] The child said: "brosse-maman," "brosse-papa," "brosse-Marie," etc. (*brosse*-brush). And yet the child did not understand the sentence: "*Brosse le chapeau.*" since *chapeau* is in itself a holophrastic expression meaning "put your hat on your head." From the child's standpoint it was therefore impossible to integrate this latter word syntactically with such an expression as "brush." On the other hand, such personal names as "maman," "papa," and "Marie" have already reached the status of words, and can therefore be related to the other term to form a true "sentence."

In like manner the verbal concepts of the *pathologically* regressive mentality are not only concrete, as we have previously demonstrated, but diffuse as well. One catatonic patient, whose particular language has been described by Tuczek, formed words by reference to the global situation in a manner similar to that of the children mentioned in a previous paragraph. Instead of naming the object proper, she stressed a dominant feature of the whole situation of which the object was but a constituent part. She designated "bird" by "song" and "cellar" by "spider web." The doctors she called the "dance" because during their visits they were "dancing around the professor."[128]

It is significant again that with the schizophrenic, as with primitive man and the child, the diffuse concept is often expressed holophrastically. The catatonic patient just spoken of used for the word "zero" the expression "name early le le." When questioned as to the reason for this she remarked: "In the morning a mother (i.e., herself) must ask her boy whether he has been to the bathroom. 'Zero' is a testicle, which looks like a zero." "Zero" is understood as a whole sentence: "Early

127 Guillaume, 392.
128 Tuczek, 609.

in the morning the mother asks her boy whether he has urinated."[129]

The most comprehensive analysis of schizophrenic thought is undoubtedly Schilder's monograph *Seele und Leben*. This author shows convincingly that schizophrenic concepts are formed through associations much more diffuse and numerous than anything characteristic of the normal conceptual process. "The normal concept-formation is directed towards single, definite objects; a schizophrenic concept includes a whole world of past experience."

Aphasia reveals another type of pathological primitivation in the conceptual process. Here the content of words definitely focused conceptually on the normal level has often degenerated into a "diffuse sphere of meaning." Within this vague sphere any one constituent element may be used to designate any other element. An aphasiac, when asked to show his tongue, may point to his teeth. To illustrate the word "hair" he may point to his mustache, and to his trousers for the word "socks."[130]

In the language of the hysterical, ecstatic "trance" (*Zungenreden*), the holophrastic form again appears as the expression of a syncretic and diffuse process of name construction. The "Seer of Prevorst," who was described at length by Justinus Kerner, had a peculiar type of ecstatic language.[131] The names of persons and things were so fashioned that they "contained both the value and the property of the thing, which is not true of ordinary words." For example, the name "Emelachan" means: "Your spirit is peaceful and quiet, your soul is delicate, your flesh and blood are strong. Steadily both (flesh and blood) roar like the waves of the sea, and then the tenderness in you speaks and says: 'Come and calm yourself.'" This woman also had a holophrastic script in which the signs often stood not only for single words, but for whole sentences. This

[129] Tuczek, **609.**
[130] Pick, **591.**
[131] Kerner, **581,** 149.

is quite in accordance with the general character of holo-phrastic name construction. We find analogies for this in American Indian civilizations, where the picture of a single object or word may stand for a whole cult song.[132]

In this respect interesting parallels may be found in dream language. Isolde Kurz remarks that in one of her dreams the word "sök" seemed to express for her a long series of aesthetic-philosophical ideas.[133]

Finally we might raise the question of the role of the diffuse concept on the *advanced*, civilized level of mentality. This problem may be summed up briefly: (1) In activity which is of a type approximating the primitive man's sphere of behavior we may expect to find similar properties in the process of conceptualization. Language as part of an emotional social intercourse, rather than as a tool for intellectual argument and exposition, is shot through with slang terms and other forms of expression holophrastic in character. (2) Experiments have shown that diffuseness has its place in any kind of creative conceptualization. In one of the experiments performed by Willwoll the subjects were requested to name a term which, as a superordinated concept, would be common to two given concepts: sun-glasses, lamp-shade: glare-protector, etc. The subjects succeeded best when they "dissolved" the two given words into diffuse spheres of broad association, and then discovered another still more diffuse sphere comprehending both of the former. In a further step in rationalization, this larger, inclusive conceptual sphere was "condensed" into the definite term.[134] These and similar results from genetic experimental psychology are but another demonstration of the principle that the primitive function is a necessary element in the mentality of any well-balanced person of higher activity. The difference between this diffuse conceptualization and that characteristic of a true primitive behavior is only that the pri-

[132] Schoolcraft, **284**, vol. 1, 374.
[133] Kurz, **586**, 14.
[134] Willwoll, **746**.

mary, diffuse conceptual formation is subordinated to suit the needs of a higher intellectual activity.

Lability; Apparent Inconsistency in the Primitive Concept.— Another essential characteristic of the primitive concept, and one of equal importance, is its relatively greater lability. In the primitive concept we find exactly the same characteristic as we noted in primitive perception. Because social interaction in primitive societies is never so thoroughly "lingualized" as in our own type of civilization, the meaning of a word depends largely upon the actual happening with which it is connected. This does not mean, of course, that there is any vagueness in the meaning of primitive speech or in the effect it produces. It means simply that single words do not need to have any high degree of precision, but may derive a species of exactitude from the context surrounding them. It is more fitting for a language-of-action to have words which have a relatively mutable content capable of eliciting broad associations. Because of this diffuseness the name refers to a collective unity in which this or that element may be stressed, thus bringing different qualities-of-the-whole to the fore. As an example there is the previously cited Melanesian term for "drop," *ciki.* At one time the word may indicate the thing itself; again it may refer to the act of a regular dropping; in a third case it may mean the impressions made on the earth by falling drops of water. Even though the diffuse total relation remains identical, it is variously centered, and therefore appears to be inconstant. This example brings to mind such Bakaïri words as *yélo,* which stands for both thunder and lightning. When this name is attached to an object the intention may be to convey either the "thunder-like" or the "lightning-like" quality of the object. Accordingly, when the Bakaïri use the word *yélo* to designate the ceremonial bull-roarer,[135] the concept is centered according to the thunder-like aspect of the word's content.[136]

[135] A slat of wood tied to the end of a thong, which makes a roaring noise when whirled about.
[136] Steinen. 297, 81.

In the following examples of the names of colors in the languages of the Brazilian Indians reported by Steinen we see even more clearly the lability attendant upon a diffuse conceptual construction. The Kamayurá call "blue" and "green" by the same name: *i-tsovü-maé*, parrakeet color. Parrakeet feathers are both grass-green and indigo blue. "No matter whether I showed the Indian a blue or a green spot, a string of blue stones, or a green leaf, he always responded with the same answer—'parrakeet-color.' "[137] In this instance it is clear how, through a shift of focus, through the selection of this or that part of a diffuse totality in accordance with the context, the content of the name itself undergoes apparent change.

The structure of such concepts might be symbolized by a web (Fig. 50A), the radial parts of which are focused in

A. Labile   B. Stable

Fɪɢ. 50.—Diagram Representing Two Types of Concepts.

shifting centers corresponding to a shift in meaning. The more detached the concept becomes from the concrete situation, and the more it moves toward the logical sphere, the more it will tend to be characterized by certain constant essential properties. These properties are those which give it stability and consistency (Fig. 50B). There are, of course, degrees of stability; essential and variable elements usually exist in conjunction with these rigid properties. The scientific concepts of our own cultural sphere represent the greatest advance toward a complete stabilization. These concepts are fixed in their essential outline so that despite the variability in the real objects the conceptual name remains stable and unambiguous.

At the beginning of *ontogenetic development* the concept is

[137] *Ibid.*, 420.

diffuse and, as a result, highly labile. We recognize the initially diffuse-indeterminate character of the child concept when the history of the development of certain names is traced. The following is one example from among many: At the age of 251 days Idelberger's son called a small porcelain figurine, of which he was very fond, "wau-wau." At 307 days he used the same expression to mean a dog barking in the yard, his grandparents' picture, a toy horse, and the clock on the wall. At 331 days he used this word for a fur neckpiece with an animal's head, and also one without the head; the glass eyes pleased him particularly. At 334 days he used it to mean a little rubber man that squeaked; at 396 days, for the black buttons on his father's shirt-front; and at 433 days, to mean the pearl buttons on a dress and also to designate a bath thermometer.[138] This simple exclamation stood for a whole number of things which might be ordered as follows: (1) Small, stretched-out, doll-like objects: fur neckpiece, rubber dolls, bath thermometer, etc. (2) Buttons and similar bright pearly objects.

We see from this case that the inconstancy of the name is occasioned by the fact that first one particular property of a diffuse, concrete-affective unity is brought to the fore, and then another quite distinct from its predecessor. Either the long form, or the shiny, eye-shaped character of extremely diverse objects may be expressed by the child's term. The child does not differentiate on the basis of essential and non-essential characteristics in his construction of the concept, but rather experiences the object diffusely and, in consequence, permits it to have a labile content.

What is salient and characteristic for a conceptual name at one time may not hold true at another. According to Piaget, a child may say that the sun, moon, and wind are alive because they move, yet the clouds and sea are not since it is the wind that moves them. At another time the same child may say that the clouds are alive because "they make it rain" and that the sea is alive because it ebbs and flows. The concepts of cloud

[138] Idelberger, 410, 18 f.

and sea are understood according to varying characteristics. The concept of cloud, when marked by the fact that the cloud is blown about by the wind, is centered differently than when thought of as a thing which lets rain fall. Similarly, the sea is one thing conceptually when moved by the wind, and another when it exhibits the property of ebbing and flowing.[139] In these child concepts there is an absence of "constitutive" signs which endure constantly, and which would serve to delimit the object as either "living" or "not-living." The diffuse structure allows the object to be determined by successive properties standing in logical contradiction.

The absence of subordinating foci, of constantly essential distinguishing characteristics, is very evident in the child's definition of a word. Piaget demonstrates that "strength," for example, may be defined by qualities of movement, rigidity, weight, etc., listed one after the other without any regard for reconciliation or centralization through any value common to all. For one child an object is strong because it is heavy, or weak because it is light.[140] When the same child was asked how it is that a ship floats on water and a stone sinks to the bottom he answered: "Because the stone is light," that is, because it is lacking in "strength." The ship, on the other hand, floats because of its "heaviness." In this case the concepts of "light" and "heavy" have a complementary meaning of weak and strong which an adult would never attribute to them. As a result of this fused complementary meaning, which now advances to a dominant position and now retreats into passiveness in the meaning-content of the name, there is an essential inconstancy in the sense of the word. For example, in the concept of "heavy" with respect to "light" the inconstancy appears when the child shifts the accent of his interest from strength to weight. One child (according to Piaget) says that small boats float because they are light, and big boats because

[139] Piaget, **479,** 85 f.
[140] According to a Hamburg Laboratory study; unpublished.

they are heavy.[141] In other words, "heavy" is centered otherwise than the concept "light," for the essential mark of heaviness is understood as strength, and of lightness as absence of
weight, in the adult manner.

The syncretic and diffuse concepts of the *pathological* mentality are often strongly marked by inconsistency. In contradistinction to those of normal people they are not organized
and stabilized in terms of essential features, but vacillate considerably in meaning with changes in the complex of experience in which they are involved. For one female schizophrenic,
to illustrate, the Virgin Mary is first an ally who punishes her
mother by transforming her into a snake. Later on the Madonna is thought of as the sun in the sky, from the sight of
which the mother is banned. Again the Virgin Mary is conceived as cast from her throne, thus making way for the
patient who mounts there in her place. In this diseased mentality "Madonna" is by no means an unequivocal, fixed concept,
but one which stands for a person who changes in meaning—
first the patient's protector and patron, then her rival, then
her protegée—all according to the flow of affect and the consequent domination of this or that symbolic factor.[142]

PRIMARY DEVELOPMENT OF THE NUMBER IDEA AS AN ILLUSTRA-
TION OF PRIMITIVE CONCEPT FORMATION.

The Number Concepts of Primitive Peoples: QUALITATIVE
CONFIGURATIONS IN TIME AND SPACE SUBSTITUTING FOR NUM-
BERS.—Counting is a process whereby a manifold of objects is
comprehended with precision. But not every manifold needs
to be conceived by this process of counting. A motor-rhythmic
configuration of two or three elements may be accomplished
without the use of a true number concept, even by apes.[143]
Again, an optical manifold, provided it is a unit composed of
characteristically different units—such as the family—may be

141 Piaget, **479**, 85 f.
142 Schilder, **598**, 56 f.
143 Bierens de Haan, **617**.

grasped without employing a true number concept. A peasant woman I met in the Bavarian Alps had to bethink herself before she could tell me how many children she had. The primitive American Abipone Indians can tell without counting whether one of their dogs is missing from the pack when they leave for the hunt; it is simply not necessary for them to count because they experience the individuality of all domestic animals in a characteristically concrete manner. Even when a group of totally unknown objects or persons is under consideration, the primitive man often tries to conceive it as a manifold of characteristically divergent individuals. Thurnwald reports of the Solomon Islanders: If five newly arrived persons are to be designated, one does not say that five persons have just come, not even if their names are not known. One may say: "A man with a large nose, an old man, a child, a man with a skin disease, and a little fellow are waiting outside."[144]

CONCRETE NUMBER CONFIGURATIONS AS "ANALOGOUS FORMS" WITH RESPECT TO THE TRUE NUMBER CONCEPT.—Frequently we find that abstract counting is supplanted by an optical, or even motor, configuration and ordering of groups among primitive peoples and, indeed, among the naïve of our own culture.[145] In other words, groups may be counted figurally. It is possible, for example, to order four mussels in a square or five stones in a pentagram. Each of these configurations contains implicitly a certain group number which is necessarily bound up with the optical appearance of the figure. Of course, in the configuration as such there does not have to be latent a group experience, any relation to the counting process. For instance, the configuration can be experienced aesthetically, as ornamental. Only when the cognitive interest is primarily numerical is it possible to express the counting experience in an optical configuration. This often occurs under practical conditions with the primitive man. If taro bulbs are being sold or

[144] Thurnwald, 131, 273.
[145] Wertheimer, 144.

divided up it is natural that the numerical group experience should come to light. According to Thurnwald, if the native lays these bulbs before the buyer in such a way that there are always three bulbs on a lower line and two in a line above, a configuration will appear which is no longer a mere gestalt in an ornamental sense, but is one in the sense of being a numerical organization. A number configuration which conforms to the demands of concrete thinking has been conceived.[146] It is therefore important to distinguish between a pure figure and a figurally organized group; only in the group figure is the counting function active. We may qualify this counting function as syncretic. This means that the number as a conceptual entity has not yet freed itself from the (optical) percept. In other words, we are dealing with a conceptual form *analogous* to the number concepts of abstract counting and operative within a more primitive—i.e., syncretic—stratum of mentality.

Formations of quantity linked with the individual-concrete, that is, with the qualitative, are revealed in the "number class names" denoting number groups of a certain class of objects. In the language of Kiriwina, "whenever the number of one group of objects is denoted the nature (class) of these objects must be included in the number-word."[147] The Tshimshien Indians (Northwest Canada) have a different type of number name for each of seven classes of objects: indefinite, amorphous objects; round, flat, or long objects; human beings; boats; measures. Other North American Indians have similar number classes.[148] Among the Indians of Florida *nakua* means ten eggs and *nabanara* means ten food baskets. In the Fidshi language an aggregate of ten boats is called *bola*, whereas ten coconuts are called *koro*.[149] We see that the name of the number is not yet free enough to resist change when the con-

[146] Thurnwald, **131**, 274.
[147] Malinowski, **233**.
[148] Boas, **166**, 655 ff.
[149] Codrington, **175**, 241.

crete material to which it refers undergoes change.[150] A number term of this sort may originally be limited to the designation of a group of certain particular objects, but gradually this same term may undergo a transposition that allows its application to diverse objects. On the Gazelle Peninsula, for example, "five" is *lima*, that is, the "hand." Originally a number class name, the term has become extended through transposition to apply to other objects. In New Guinea the number "ten" is the "crocodile" (that is, the ten toe tracks of the crocodile in the sand).[151]

CONCRETE (BODY) NUMBER SCHEMES.—A much more abstract form of the counting process results from systematization, from the construction of counting systems. Whereas the very primitive number concepts are bound down to the objective structure which is more or less qualitative in nature, a counting system represents an order which functions in a higher dimension than the purely thing-like, that is, in the dimension of gradations, of quantity.

But here, too, it will be found that the release from the concrete groundwork is only gradually achieved. This is evidenced on the one hand by the fact that the counting systems of the most primitive people have only a very limited structure. Many of these systems do not go beyond the numbers 3 or 5, anything beyond this being comprehended in the vague term "many." On the other hand the difficulty of achieving the status of pure number is indicated by the fact that a concrete foundation is initially visible as an integral part of a counting system. But now the relation between the concrete number gestalt and the counting function appears to be reversed. Whereas formerly a concrete configuration was found to be useful for the numerical task at hand, that is, known figures were used in such a way that they incidentally served to de-

[150] For that matter, such number class names are still extant at our level in everyday life. They are represented by those terms by which a concrete aggregate is designated by an individual expression rather than by a purely abstract number, such as "gross," "ream," "score," etc.

[151] Thurnwald, 131, 274.

note certain numbers, in this case a particular form is constructed which is to be used as a special means of numerical
thinking. The concrete number-construct becomes a *counting
schema*. The schema is a means of imposing mathematical
order on concrete phenomena. Nevertheless, although it is the
product of the ordering mentality, it does not entirely lose its
concrete character.

Most significant in the development of the number concept
is the primitive use of the body as a natural number schema.
With this most primitive of all counting methods, one which
is found all over the world, things can be defined numerically
by means of the articulations of the body. In the Murray
Islands of the Torres Straits group, the natives are able to
count verbally, that is, conceptually, only up to 2: 1 = *netat*;
2 = *neis*. Beyond this point the body serves as a counting
schema. With its help the natives can count up to 30. They
begin with the little finger of the left hand, proceed across
the other fingers of the same hand, then to the wrist, the elbow,
the armpits, the shoulder, the hollows at the collarbone, to
the chest, etc., and subsequently in reverse order down the
right arm to the little finger of the right hand.[152]

Here the body itself has become a numerical gestalt into
which the concrete fullness of objects fits as into a frame and
is thereby measured. At the beginning no schema is an abstract form purely mathematical in significance; it is a material vessel into which the concrete fullness of objects is poured,
as it were, in order to be measured.

This fact can often be observed directly. When a Borneo
native counts objects he always places a certain finger on a
certain object, one after the other.[153] And, similarly, among
the Brazilian Indians:

"How did they count things when the total number did not ex-
ceed 6? If I put down a grain of corn, the Bakaïri immediately answered 'tokále.' Usually he touched the corn and, at the same time,

[152] Lévy-Bruhl, **85**, Germ. ed., 159.
[153] Brooke, **169**.

using his right hand, seized the little finger of the left hand. All this happened so quickly and mechanically that the motion might seemingly have been dispensed with. When I put 2 grains before him he seldom neglected to employ the fingers of both hands. Especially when I plàced the grains some distance apart did he shove them closer together, and thereupon grasped the little finger and the ring-finger of the left hand before he began to count aloud. If I put down 3 grains and asked for the total number, not once did anyone of them count without first separating the grains into a pair and a single grain. The pair was first touched and examined by separating the two grains somewhat, after which the fifth and fourth fingers of the left hand were taken hold of by the right hand, and the word 'ahagé' spoken. The single grain was then touched and the third finger of the left hand closed against the fourth and fifth fingers and the word 'tokále' spoken. Finally came 'ahagé tokále.' I tested them out up to the number 6. Always little groups of 2 were first formed, then touched, and the fingers separated and counted.

"The right hand touched, the left hand reckoned. Without using the fingers of the right hand, that is, merely by looking at the grains and then counting on the fingers of the left hand, I found that it was impossible for them to reckon as soon as the number 3 was reached. The little heaps of 2 had first of all to be brought into order with the hand. I put 3, 4, 5, 6 grains before Rumayaua, and had him build the piles while holding his left hand. In such case very seldom was he able to count a group of three grains, or more exactly to hit upon the right number. If, however, more than three grains were presented, he could only say 'ahagé ahagé . . .' for any such aggregate. Both hands were indispensable when 3 things had to be counted. If necessary the reckoning could proceed without the use of the left hand, but never without the right one."[154]

Here we see plainly that any schema is primarily a concrete measure, a measuring vessel rather than an instrument for converting groups of objects into abstract series of numerical relations. This numerical schema is something of a material measuring device, somewhat like a liter measure into which

[154] Steinen, 297, 408.

concrete aggregates are poured. Measuring and counting are undifferentiated in this ordering method.

Primary Development of the Number Concept with the Child.—The spontaneous development of the number concept in the case of children may be obscured by their early acceptance of an adult system of numbering. Nevertheless certain characteristic preliminary steps can still be noted.

With the child, as with primitive man, there can be observed a stage precedent to the genuine counting activity when a manifold of objects is conceived as being so characteristically individualistic that purely numerical counting becomes unnecessary. Some observers assume all too readily that whenever, for example, the child remarks upon the absence of an object in a manifold, it is the pure counting experience which is dominating his numerical awareness. On the other hand, in the case of the child the numerical function undoubtedly originates in the concrete configuration itself, whether it is a configuration in the sense of being a real geometrical figure or a mere aggregate. The pair and the triad were such characteristic figural relations in the quasi-numerical understanding of the child twenty-six months old described by Decroly and Degand that the child immediately noted the absence of any element which was removed by the investigator. At the same time it was evident that this experience of a manifold was still so closely determined by the concrete gestalt that, for instance, an arrangement of building blocks such as this ||| could be easily copied, but not one of the form ⊔ . At the age of four and three-quarters, a child could designate a normal group of four by the expression "four"; but if two pairs of cherries each linked by a common stem were hung over each of his ears and he was then asked to tell how many cherries there were, he could answer in no other way except by saying that there was one pair here and another there.[155]

There is a close concrete relation between the experience of

[155] Decroly and Degand, 358.

a manifold and the thing-like structure. Binet carried out experiments on judgments of comparison with different sets of objects, using his own daughters aged two and one half and four years as subjects.[156] Two sets of identical objects were compared so accurately in number that even in a comparison of an aggregate of 17 with one of 18 the children, on request, correctly pointed to the larger set. When, on the other hand, groups of objects dissimilar in size were used, it became evident that the experience of an aggregate was dependent not on the actual number of single things, but on the concrete size of the area covered, since a few large objects were taken as equivalent to many small ones.

This same phenomenon is found in the pathological individual whose numerical powers have been inhibited or impaired by regression to a more primitive level. Smaller groups, for example, are often conceived numerically only when ordered according to some particular configuration. A larger aggregate is counted by breaking it up into smaller number configurations.[157]

The formation of a *number system* in its proper sense is bound up with two developmental facts: First, with the increasing abstraction; the number concept becomes more and more released from the concrete configuration and the qualities of the objects. Second, with the development of a schema for the number order in particular.

At first the systematization of the counting process in children is, as in the case of primitive man, closely bound down to the concrete givenness of things. Only gradually does a schema strip itself of its individualistic character and become generalized, i.e., adequate as an instrument for transforming a set of any kind of objects into a numerical series. These are facts supported by much experimental data. We are told of children who can count nothing but apples.[158] When asked

[156] Bühler, 351, Germ. ed., 199.
[157] Sittig, 602, 46 ff.
[158] Lindner, 438, 88.

how many fingers he had, a child four and three-quarters years old answered: "I don't know. I can only count my fingers."[159]

The development away from the concrete toward more abstract methods of counting repeats itself at the start of each new level. Oehl, for example, observed that school beginners who had already learned to count certain specific objects by higher units (by 3's, let us say, instead of by 1's) could not transfer this counting method and have it apply to unfamiliar objects. When confronted by the unfamiliar they returned to the earlier method of counting by 1's, and had to learn the more advanced system anew. Only by such a repetitive procedure was it possible gradually to apply the later method to any set regardless of the type of object involved.[160]

It is well known that low-grade feeble-minded individuals can do simple work with concrete numbers, but fail when more general numerical ideas must come into play. Goddard reports on an adult person with a mental age of seven years who was able to add 2 loads of coal to 3, but was balked when loaves of bread were substituted for the coal in the problem. The subject's success in the first case depended on his actual experience at shoveling coal.[161]

As is true of primitive man, the child's fundamental counting schemes are rooted in the *body* itself. A small boy begins of his own accord to use his fingers as a counting device, even though he can count verbally only as far as 2. For example, he has 3 stones before him. Holding out his three fingers he says: "That's more than two. . . . It's like this!" He will handle 4, 5, 6, 7 stones in the same fashion, even bringing the fingers of the other hand into use.[162] Thus he behaves exactly like the Bakaïri who can count immediately up to 2 or 3, but from there on no longer uses specific numbers, but places his fingers as so many measures one after the other on the aggregate of objects.

[159] Stern, 511, 283.
[160] Oehl, 470.
[161] Goddard, 560, 284.
[162] Descœudres, 361, 248.

Recently we have demonstrated—at least in the case of generally retarded children—that there is a definite relationship between the ability to articulate the fingers and the early development of the number concept.[163] Two groups of children from the Wayne County Training School in Michigan—one group showing a high ability and the other a disability in number work—were subjected to a "finger schema" test. This test was as follows: Each child was asked to point, with his eyes closed, to that one (or two) of his fingers touched by the examiner; or he was asked to indicate on the examiner's hand, or on a simple picture of a hand, which one (or two) of his own fingers had been touched. The results of this finger-schema test show (see the accompanying table) that the group with the higher arithmetical ability made almost no errors, whereas the group with the disability erred considerably.

RELATION BETWEEN FINGER SCHEMA AND NUMBER CONCEPT

	Errors										
	0	10	20	30	40	50	60	70	80	90	100
Ability group (14)	11	3									
Disability group (14)	1	1	1	3	2	1	1	2	1	0	1

Certain data from adult psychopathology support this evidence of a relationship between number concept and finger or body schema. Gerstmann detected in some of his patients an inability to respond to the request to name or pick out this or that finger on their own hands. He called this deficiency "finger agnosia."[164] It is significant that in many cases of "finger agnosia" there is a certain relation between the defect in the finger schema and a degeneration in the operation of numbers (so-called aculculia).

[163] Strauss and Werner, 514; Werner and Strauss, 537.
[164] Gerstmann, 558, 559.

All these facts support the assumption that the hand area represents a natural "number space." Any higher development of a number schema, however, will necessarily bring into play the optical field. In order to become dominantly optical in nature, "number space," as the modern educator will agree, must be largely stripped of the somatically oriented and motor-rhythmic elements included in the more primitive activity of finger counting. Little is known of the manner in which this transition occurs. Oehl has found that school beginners who are generally retarded mentally cannot count without motor accompaniment. Children will frequently pick up the objects they are counting and still later only point to them; finally only a glance is necessary.[165]

Concrete optical number space (number forms, number scales, etc.) seems to be the next step to which the child must accommodate himself before he can advance to abstract number operations. As we have recently demonstrated by experiment, an inability to grasp optical configurations built up of discrete elements such as dots is closely correlated with a deficiency in the development of the number concept.[166] Brownell stresses the fact that only those pupils who have already developed more advanced methods for dealing with optical numerical forms[167] are able to deal with abstract number concepts.

There is an organic transition from the level of concrete optical number groups to that of purely abstract number. The concrete number groups become stripped of their picture-like properties. This does not mean, however, that the earlier activity of perceptual configuration is completely lost in abstract number operations. With many adults, if not in all cases, the level of perceptual organization is still actively present in the form of a rather remote inner "number schema" underlying the abstract arithmetical operation.

[165] Oehl, 470.
[166] Werner and Strauss, 538.
[167] Brownell, 343.

The primary development of the number concept may be tentatively represented as follows:

I. Level of qualitative configurations, substituting for number:
   Motor-rhythmical, . . . optical (among others) configuration (herd, family).

II. Level of concrete number-configurations:
   Rhythmic configuration (counting).
   Thing-like (optical) number forms (:·:).

III. Level of concrete schematic numbers:
   Body number schemes (fingers, etc.).
   Optical schemata (tallies in a row, such as 1 2 3 4 5 6, etc.).   · · · · · ·

IV. Level of abstract number concepts.

Chapter X

THE PRIMARY STRUCTURE OF THOUGHT

STRUCTURE OF THOUGHT IN PRIMITIVE MAN.

Concreteness.—The reasoning of primitive man, so far as it participates and is embedded in the activity of concrete daily life, exhibits scarcely any difference from that of the man of western culture. It is only in the realm of theoretical reflection, in the seeking for an explanation of natural events in terms of cause and effect, etc., that essential differences appear. The thought of primitive man differs from the higher and above all from the scientific thought of western man in that it has a concrete and in consequence, syncretic character. Naïve, concrete thought is very close to the perceptual-imaginative level; primitive reflection always means concrete configuration. Typical European reflection is universal in nature, abstract; it functions more or less independently of the immediate, concrete reality, and is governed by an awareness of general laws. The thought of primitive man is pinned down to the reality of the thing-like world, and is therefore pragmatic, concrete, individual. Anyone who attempts to learn primitive languages is always confronted by the difficulty of adjusting himself to the concrete linguistic sense of the aborigine while normally equipped with a different manner of thinking in a language whose every expression and usage tends toward the universal. "The white man inquires after the general concept," says Stephan in his highly informative work on New Mecklenburg, "whereas the native indicates the fact."[1] If one wishes to learn the names for the different parts of the body and so directly points at or touches the physical part,

[1] Stephan and Gräbner, 299, 139.

the native will promptly supply the term for "my ear" or "my leg" (instead of simply "ear" or "leg").

The processes of *explanation* and of *inference* according to causality are thoroughly concrete in character. This means a much more syncretic and diffuse structure of thought than is the case on our own level. The civilized man's methods of explanations are representative of a universal, lawful mode of thought; particulars are brought under the general and the non-phenomenal. The sun appears in the morning in the east and sinks in the west on the basis of the law of gravitation. This is a universal principle to which certain phenomena are subordinated in the form of particulars. These phenomena are understood as concrete modes of realization, visible exemplifications of the universal law. Primitive thought functions quite differently from this. That which we call explanation or interpretation means to the primitive man the transformation of physical circumstance into picture-like configurations. It is not in keeping with concrete and, as a result, syncretic modes of thought that the particular be subsumed to the general. The tendency is to configurate the particulars individualistically, in a picture-like fashion. The sun is a personified being who comes out of his cave in the morning, to return there at night after a long journey throughout the day. Such is concrete thought; the explanation for natural phenomena is contained implicitly in the uncritically accepted particular event. It is a description and delineation of individual happenings. The primitive conception of astronomical phenomena is characteristic of this whole mode of thinking. Primitive celestial geography often consists of real star pictures, of celestial drawings. The stars have their predetermined, fixed position in relation to one another, since they are part of the gestalt of a concretely visible entity. South Sea Islanders think of the Baidam constellation as a fish (Fig. 51).[2]

The Brazilian Indians believe that Orion is a huge platform on which mandioca is dried. The large stars are the tops of

[2] Reports, **268**, vol. 4, 221.

the supporting posts, and Sirius is the end of a long diagonal beam which props up the stand from one side.[3] More often than not, this mode of thought remains dependent on the concreteness of phenomena. The change in position, and therefore in appearance, of a celestial body may give rise to the inference of non-identity. For the South African Dama the

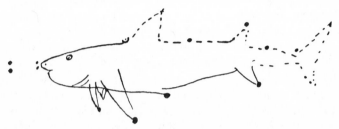

FIG. 51.—Baidam Constellation. A configuration of stars as perceived by islanders of the Torres Straits. (After Haddon, *Reports.*)

sinking sun is an entity distinct from the rising sun.[4] And, similarly, for many primitive peoples the moon is a different entity in each lunar phase.

It is also in conformity with this concrete thinking that the externally mutable, but identical in "substance," is not always conceived as identical by the very primitive man; it is quite possible that he may conceive of one and the same thing as being different objects belonging together. For the Papuans of New Guinea the moon is a woman—Bimbaio—whose head is the full moon, whose boat is the half moon, and whose dog is the evening star.[5] Thurnwald was laughed at when he said that caterpillar and butterfly were the same creature. "For these people the metamorphosis is linked with as great a discrepancy as that which for us exists between the food which a man eats and the body of a man built out of this food."[6]

[3] Steinen, **297**, 359.
[4] Andersson, **154**, vol. 1, 242.
[5] Moszkowsky, **251**, 951.
[6] Thurnwald, **129**, 106.

Within this field of thought we find tendencies to identify things seemingly much at odds, tendencies which apparently run counter to those revealed by the examples just given, and which lead us on to another distinguishing characteristic of syncretic thinking. Among the South Sea Islanders mentioned above, a man can be identical with a snake, a kangaroo, and a frigate bird. For the Cora Indians flowers and stars are the same, not because of any similarity in their brightness, but rather because they are both experienced as life-creating, as beings forever renewing themselves.[7] Star and flower, man and animal are identified not because they are conceived as exhibiting any material likeness, but because they are *felt* as identical. Identities established on the basis of affect, as the above instances show, are of a quite different nature from anything in purely objective thought. In brief, primitive thinking is not only concrete but affective as well. The structure of primitive thought is concretely determined in so far as it has a tendency to configurate pictorially, and it is emotionally determined in so far as it unites that which is affectively related.

Concrete and affective thinking does not comprehend the category of abstract, universal *necessity*. The primitive man is fully aware that certain events occur repetitively and that they must be explained and predicted according to this repetitive consummation; but that such a state of affairs exists because of lawful necessity is beyond his conception. Primitive thought does not extract the universal content of an event, because in it each event always remains an individual picture. The primitive man's judgments of the event consist of a declaration that it "is so and so," rather than that it "must be so and so." When Steinen spoke the following sentence to a Bakaïri Indian: "Every man must die," the native was silent for a long time. "This long pause which I had to overcome each time occurred whenever I presented to him any abstraction which, however commonplace to me, was alien to his manner of thinking. Through this I learned for the first time that the

[7] Preuss, 109, 12.

Bakaïri knows no 'must.' He has not yet reached the point where he can discern the necessity in a series of uniformly recurring events. And most peculiarly he does not know that all men must die. The idea impressed on us in the lowest class in the gymnasium 'Nemo mortem effugere potest' lies far from his thoughts. . . . Antonio's translation, which avoided the word 'must,' but which showed that he had understood my intention, after a quarter hour of reflection ran somewhat quaintly: 'I die only (and) we (die).' The interpreter shook his head in dissatisfaction, expressing the same sort of doubt we should feel if someone had told us that all men get killed by murderous assault . . . !"[8]

It must be emphasized, however, that at a somewhat higher level of primitive civilization a sort of necessity is inherent within what is understood to be an ever-recurring continuum of natural, concrete events. Death, for instance, is frequently conceived not as the end of a life subject to biological laws, but as a concrete state of existence coordinated with that which has preceded and, in some cases, even with a still more subsequent state to follow. The Solomon Islanders believe that the individual changes his form of life in definite steps throughout his whole existence; one ceremony changes him from the state of being a child into manhood, another ceremony makes him *mate* (dead), and even after having become dead he may still further alter the form of his existence. Since one can become *mate* by virtue of a ceremony, sick men or old men who are still biologically alive may enter the class of dead people.[9] It is quite clear that the necessity of death is utterly different from our biological conception of it. It is an "historical necessity," and not a logical-universal necessity, that is operative here, a definite sequence of stages in the social history of the individual.

More advanced primitive civilizations have acquired a particular concept of necessity which even to this day has not

[8] Steinen, **297**, 348.
[9] Rivers, **115**, 40 ff.

died out completely in European-Asiatic cultures. This is the mythical concept of "destiny," of a "fateful necessity," as it were. This concept is generated by a type of thought which we shall describe as "thinking in terms of fate." It will be discussed later at some length.

These concepts of necessity, no matter whether they are more or less advanced, all have the common property of concreteness. Necessity in its exact meaning as pertaining to abstract and universal laws can be conceived of only when thinking begins to function *per se*, free from any interdependence with respect to perception, emotion, and imagination.

The traditional *explanations* of primitive peoples are most often descriptive and narrative in form. The properties of natural objects are not derived from principles of a universal necessity, they are not conceived in any lawful sense; rather they stem from an individual history, a myth telling "how it came to pass." In place of a common causal background conditioning the properties and events of nature, "historical" grounds are adduced. For example, if the Brazilian Indian natives wish to explain why it is that the Jabutí-turtle has a flat split shell, they will not present zoological-systematic or biological grounds for this phenomenon, but will seek the explanation in a story which tells "how it happened."

"In one of the great swamps along the Amazon the Urubú-hawk made a bet with the Jabutí-turtle as to which one would get quicker to heaven, in which place a feast was being celebrated. The turtle smuggled himself into the hawk's lunch-basket, arrived safely and received the hawk, as he returned from a walk amidst the heavenly revels, with the announcement that he had already been there for some time and, in fact, had been waiting for him. The bet still being undecided, it was agreed again that they should race on the homeward journey to earth. Down the hawk flew, but the turtle let himself fall, and thus won. In falling he flattened himself and split his shell . . . as can be seen to this very day."[10]

[10] Steinen, 297, 357.

Of course, even in this kind of explanation there are tendencies which permit the theory of causality to develop in so far as this is possible within the inherent limitations of concrete thinking. This inclination to evolve a *concrete causality* expresses itself in advanced mythical thought in the conception of an epoch removed from any historical duration. The mythical period is conceived as creative, as containing the forces of genesis governing the appearance of this world.

"Once upon a time" (the ever-repeated *paá* of Tupi legend) is one characteristic mark of Indian tales. The greater number of these legends are intended to explain the origin of something or other; and since this can be accomplished only by demonstrating that once an extraordinary event occurred, the hypothesis must be accepted that there was once a time during which the mysterious and exceptional was the rule.

This *creative epoch*, this period of primordial events, when the rules of nature and society were laid down, at least points to the ultimate recognition of a causal principle, the recognition that appearance has an origin not directly identifiable with the concrete conditions of the everyday, empirical world of events. The archaic epoch is a lawgiving period containing the lawfulness of the world as it is known today. To this limited degree, then, concrete thought is able to conceive the principle of causality and lawfulness. But this causality is concrete. Causality is not, as in western scientific thought, *behind* or *beyond* empirical phenomena. It is here in the *same temporal dimension*, so to speak, as that of whose appearance it is a condition; yet it is separated from appearance by a gap, an historical chasm.

Diffuseness.—The structure of primitive thought exhibits not only a syncretic but a relatively diffuse character as well; i.e., the form of thought is global, but slightly articulated, and there is only little subordination of the less essential to dominant elements of thought.

Humboldt, in his great work on the Kawi language, set forth a hypothesis which was later accepted by many linguists, the hypothesis that words arise by a process of gradual separation or precipitation from the (holophrastic) totality of the discourse. No language of any of the lower forms of civilization in existence ideally demonstrates either the "holophrastic" (global) or the "paratactic" (chain-like) type from which higher forms of linguistic articulation may have emerged, that is, phrases and sentences consisting of different words integrated in a "syntactic" unit. Though the languages of living aborigines have retained one or the other primary characteristic—the incorporative languages of the American Indians tending to the holophrastic type, and the Australian languages to the paratactic—all of them have behind them a long history which must be taken into account. Nevertheless we find in the primitive sphere holophrastic expressions much more fluidly comprehensive than anything of a similar type (e.g., slang) in western tongues. For example, the Fuegian expression *mamich-lapinatapai* means approximately: "looking at each other, hoping that each will offer to do something which both want but are reluctant to undertake."[11]

This holophrastic type of verbal expression occurs all over the world with special frequency in the realm of magic. The single expression often stands for ". . . its own cycle of ideas, for a sentence, or even for a whole story." In a magic ritual of the Trobrianders the word *papapa* is equivalent to the phrase: "Let the canoe speed so fast that the leaves of the pandanus flutter."[12]

The character of diffuse thinking, i.e., thinking in terms of undivided totalities, can be perhaps best exemplified by the primitive concept of causality. Western scientific thought divides the phenomena of nature into two series: the causal conditions and the results of these conditions. Primitive man in his world-of-action tends to think of causes not as necessary conditions, but as inseparable parts of a continuum of action. The aborigine is interested not in "why" there is such

[11] Crawley, 17, 33.
[12] Malinowski, 234, 434.

a thing as light, but in "how" this light comes into existence. Since the event in its totality is the essential object of his thinking, he will seek causes in so far as the event appears incomplete to him. In the belief of the Huitsholi, night falls when the sinking sun blows clouds of smoke from his pipe. This is "causality-of-action," the most primitive form of a genuine causality. It conforms inevitably to that thinking in terms of totalities which is characteristic of primitive thought, a thought which does not inquire into causes as separate conditions, but one which is primarily interested in rounding out the continuum of action. A special form in which causality-of-action appears is the causality of magic. It might be erroneously supposed that here at last we are dealing with cause as the polar agent of effect. When the medicine-man or witch doctor carries out some magic ritual he builds up, as it were, the conditions that will eventuate in a desired result. But we know today that this supposition represents a far too highly intellectualized interpretation of the process, if taken literally. It is true that this might hold for magically advanced cultures, but originally it would stand in contradiction to the very nature of magic. At the beginning there is in no sense a mere connection and a strict mode of succession binding magic activity and the magical result. At first what might be wrongly construed as magical cause and magical effect are fused in a complete unity. It is a global activity. When an Australian burns his enemy's hair in order to bring about his death, this is not a form of symbolism, nor is there any temporally conceived distinction between the act of magic and the actual event of dying. It is the very deed itself, this burning of a hair. The desired event of any enemy's death is not causally "conditioned" by the preceding magic. Once the ritual has been fulfilled, the enemy, within this sphere of primitive thought, is actually killed as surely as if his head had been split with a boomerang. Fundamentally the ritual of magic is rooted in the primitive conception of a causality-of-action.

The concept of causality in its most systematized form within the sphere of diffuse and concrete thought has developed into a *causality-of-fate*. The nature of this causality-of-fate and the differences which separate it radically from the scientific causality of our own understanding of the world are well illustrated in the following example. Indians often interpret the strange and unexpected in natural phenomena as omens of war, sickness, or death. But the portent does not always precede the event of which it is a prescience; it may even come after it. When the Algonquins saw the eclipse of the moon that occurred in the year 1642 they said that they were no longer surprised at the massacre of their people during the past winter by the Iroquois. Now they saw the warning and the omen for this event, but it came a little too late to enable them to prepare for it.[13]

This instance illustrates what we might call the *fate-structure* of primitive thought. The eclipse of the moon is not the cause of the massacre, but stands as a symbol for a period of time dominated by the imminent global quality of disaster. The unity of this temporal period with a pervasive quality-of-fate is expressed in the fact that any event whatsoever in the period is determined by the sense of fatality dominating the whole. Evil times breed evil events. This sense of fatality, the assumption that there are periods with "signs" revealing the good or evil nature immanent in the period, is discernible anywhere in the naïve thought of our own cultural sphere. It underlies the principle that evil never comes unattended: "It never rains, but it pours!" In place of a connection between material cause and effect we find a concretely seen and felt eventual continuum in which each single event possesses the fateful quality-of-the-whole.

The diffuse type of causal thought has created pictures of the world which still persist on certain levels of our own culture. The Oriental and antique astrological concepts of the world have extended space and time into a cosmic space-of-fate and a time-of-

[13] Lévy-Bruhl, **85**, Germ. ed., 254.

fate. The fatalistic properties of the hour, the month, and the year are shot through the universe in its totality, and comprehend everything great and small, the most catastrophic of natural events and the most trivial situations of merely individual importance.[14]

Inconsistency and Consistency in Concrete Thought.—A further 'peculiarity of the primitive methods of explanation which results from their proceeding out of a concrete-diffuse type of thought is the relative inconsistency of the grounds adduced to account for natural events. Advanced thought tends to *centralize.* It seeks to overcome the contradictions and equivocalities of the world of appearance by the device of a general, abstract meaning uniting what is discrepant. The primitive man thinks quite differently. Since for him description substitutes for the most part for causal explanation in our sense of the term, he will seek for diverse reasons to account for the diversity of appearance, whereas we tend to group under one comprehensive idea and invest with one lawfulness. Indeed, he may even judge what we consider the same natural phenomenon on the basis of two irreconcilable modes of understanding. Eclipses of the sun and moon are given different explanations by the Brazilian Indians. According to their legend a medicine man once changed himself into an anu, a bird with blue-black plumage, and covered the sun with his wings. On the other hand these same Indians explain an eclipse of the moon by saying that an armadillo has covered the moon with its body; furthermore, they say that this action incidentally accounts for the various phases of the moon.[15]

"The primitive Brazilian Indian can accept without thought of contradiction anything whatsoever that is told him. Anything may stand side by side with anything else as the truth," says Baldus. "When his father tells him that the moon is a man, when another elder tells him that it is a woman, and a

[14] Cf. Cassirer, **14**, 28 ff.
[15] Steinen, **297**, 358.

wise man that it is an evil spirit . . . he will listen and believe all of them without evincing any surprise."[16]

It is intrinsic to the nature of individualistic description, as substituting for abstract causal explanation, that there can be but a limited degree of centralization. Centralization of meaning can emerge only when the multiplicity of concrete appearance is comprehended within the unity of abstract laws.

It would be false to assume, however, that there is no tendency to understand the world in terms of a uniform lawfulness, especially among the more advanced of the primitive cultures. But this centralization cannot proceed beyond the limitations common to the inherent concreteness of the mode of thought. The most primitive form of unification is found in the mythical legend. It is the unity of an imaginative pattern, not of an abstract law. Mythical explanations of the world have an inner consistency in so far as the narrative elements are linked together coherently. Steinen heard the following legend purporting to explain the origin of the five stars in Perseus.[17]

The giant armadillo met the hero, Keri. The armadillo carried a basket of piki fruit, gave some of these to Keri, and then went on. But Keri ran after the giant armadillo, held him, and the animal gave him more fruit, saying: "I shall give you no more." Thereupon Keri shook the armadillo, the fruit rolled to the ground, and the animal burrowed into the ground. Keri made himself claws of quartz and dug him out. This happened five times, and the five holes are the five stars.

"Here we have an encounter between Keri and the armadillo (which often appears in Brazilian legend)," says Steinen. "We know, still further, that stars are conceived as holes. What is more natural than that the armadillo, an animal remarkable for the speed with which he burrows into the earth, should make a group of star-holes in getting away from his assailant? All that was needed was a conflict to account for the pursuit and the flight, a quarrel over some typical 'fruit of discord.'

[16] Baldus, 156, 76.
[17] Steinen, 297, 356.

For this 'fruit of discord' the most highly prized fruit was chosen, one which is round, with flesh as yellow as butter, although any one might really have served quite as well. In short, the story arose out of the need to discover some means of linking together the qualities of an animal of mythical significance acting as he would in his natural habitat with the peculiar structure of a starry constellation."

Comprehensive, uniform methods of explanation appear among the more highly developed primitive civilizations in the form of systematized cosmic ideas. Let us consider as an example the "mytho-sociological" world concept of the Zuñi Indians.[18] World space is divided into seven parts: north, south, east, west, nadir, zenith, and center. This corresponds to an identical division of sociological space: The village consists of seven parts: each clan within the tribe, and indeed every single thing and event belong to one of these divisions. Each "space" is the source of a particular element, of a definite season of the year: the north is the place of light and of winter; the south of summer and of fire; the east of autumn and of earth; the west of spring and of water, etc. The division of social function follows this same principle: war is identified with the north and its clans; the hunt with the west; agriculture with the south; magic and religion with the east, etc. By means of this partition the whole political, social, and religious life of the tribe is systematized. "To such an extent is carried this tendency to classify according to the number of the six regions with its seventh synthesis of them all [the latter sometimes apparent, sometimes latent] that even each clan is again divided according to such a sixfold arrangement."

Such a "mytho-sociological" world concept, in its strict systematization extending to the smallest detail, approaches the systematization of our own scientific (physical) world ideas. At the same time this example exhibits the particularization and the limits of any systematization conceived by concrete thinking. Here the world is conceived as the concrete exten-

[18] Cushing, 179, 367 ff.

sion of the life space of the tribe in its literal meaning. The world is seen as a visible whole whose parts are of a material, thing-like nature. It is interpreted as a unity, but this unity is that of a concretely represented, mytho-sociological organism. The unity of the scientifically understood world, on the contrary, is based on the universality of abstract laws.

THE STRUCTURE OF CHILD THOUGHT: CONCEPTUAL RELATIONS.
The structure of child thought in the specific sense, the grasping and establishment of conceptual relationships, the methods of explanation of things and events, the judgments and methods of inference—in all these are to be seen certain parallels to various phases of the primitive mentality. Such parallels exist in spite of fundamental differences, and are rooted in the formal characteristics of syncretism and diffuseness common to both types of mentality. Let us proceed to examine some of the basic forms of child thought.

The conceptual relations created by the highly advanced mentality are intended to be objective, impersonal, abstract, and generally applicable. It is these characteristics which are not childlike. They are alien to the very nature of syncretic thought, in which relations are fashioned to accord with an egocentric standpoint and all its interests and thus pinned down to the level of concrete perception and action.

"Right" and "wrong," for example, which with us apply to objective relations, are for the most part conceived by the child in a highly concrete and ego-centered, personal sense. Piaget tells of a child who was informed that someone had added two and three to make six, and was then asked if this was right. The child said, "No, that's not right!" and when asked why it was wrong explained ". . . because the boy reckoned wrong!" This illustrates a type of thinking directed not toward the general mathematical truth, but rather toward a concrete situation, that is, to the fact that the boy had not worked out the problem correctly.

Like the primitive man,[19] a child does not think in terms of impersonal, abstract statements; he cannot grasp the purely hypothetical, or perhaps fictitious, elements of any assumption conceived instrumentally for the sake of its application to a theoretical problem, particularly when something contrary to his private experience is involved. My six-year-old nephew objected to answering the question: "If your brother is a year older than you, how old is he then?" since, as he protested, he had no brother. Mentally retarded individuals frequently demonstrate their incapacity to reason in terms of fictitious, impersonal facts. For example, a dialogue between an examiner trying to test proficiency in handling numbers and his adult subject whose mental age was seven years runs as follows: "Suppose you give your horse six ears of corn . . ." "We don't give him six ears of corn!" "Well, let's imagine that you do." "No, I can't . . . because we don't give him six ears . . ."[20]

When children are tested on their knowledge of family relationships it will be found that these relationships are not conceived impersonally and objectively, but are thought of as egocentric and concrete. Up to the age of ten years three-quarters of all the children examined by Piaget were unable to tell just how many brothers and sisters each brother and sister in his own family had. A typical answer is as follows: Previously the child has said, for instance, that there are two brothers in his family, which is correct. He is now asked: "And how many brothers have you got?" "One . . . Paul." "And has Paul got a brother?" "No." "But you are his brother, aren't you?" "Yes." "Then does he have a brother?" "No!"[21]

The relationships characteristic of child mentality are as diffuse as they are concrete, that is, they always refer to a concrete situation in which they are firmly, if not clearly, embedded. This diffuseness is demonstrated in a whole series of

[19] Cf. the example of the Indian on p. 251.
[20] Goddard, **560**, 284.
[21] Piaget, **481**, Fr. ed., 286.

reasoning tests that have been carried out through a period of years at the Institute in Hamburg.[22] The problem in one such test (an "analogy test") is to pick out the correct term from a group of possible terms to complete a relationship by analogy, e.g., day—sun; night—? In completing these analogies the child reveals most clearly all the properties of the diffuse mode of thinking. The relationships are that much more concrete and diffuse, the younger the child. And the higher the age level, the more marked the increase of frequency of relations that are differentiated, unequivocal, and centered according to essential, as against non-essential, elements. The child's thought is diffuse in so far as he does not conceive an exact relation between the words presented to him, but thinks of them as being attached to a global situation. An eight-year-old boy creates the following analogy: wash—face; sweep—*broom*. This he explains by saying: "You have to wash your face, and sweep with the broom." The relationship is not conceived with any exactitude. Obviously he thinks of the first two words as designating a collective situation, i.e., washing the face. The analogy is apparently completed according to this reasoning: "I wash my face (with my face cloth); I sweep (the floor) with a broom." It is characteristic of this diffuse total relationship that many elements are fused into it, elements which mature reasoning would ignore. Even the words themselves do not have single, highly differentiated meanings, certainly not the word-pairs and the word-relations. A similar instance is presented by the analogy completed by a nine-year-old child: "*Tischler—Holz; Schmied—schmiedet.*" (Joiner—wood; smith—"smiths," i.e., makes things of iron by heating and hammering). The viva-voce explanation, which can alone afford any insight into the child's reasoning, is in substance as follows: the blacksmith "smiths," that is, he works hard, furiously, noisily, whereas the cabinetmaker works smoothly and quietly with wood. Once more we see clearly that this solution is based on a diffuse mode of relating. The

[22] Muchow, 458, 53 ff.

meanings of the words are "holophrastic," the relation is embedded in a concrete total relationship. The child thinks of the comparatively easy, light work which the cabinetmaker does on the wood. "Wood" is representative of an activity accomplished with a soft material, whereas "smiths" stands for a laborious activity involving a hard material. The same is true of the following child analogy: lance—prod; gun—bullet. Such a diffuse mode of relating is possible because the single words already carry within themselves a holophrastic meaning, because for the child "bullet" is not merely a strictly delimited object, but one which also stands for the act of shooting.

The diffuse global character of such relationships becomes much more intelligible when we recall the general results of various analyses of child speech.

Preyer, Ament, Meumann, and, in particular, William Stern have labored to show that the sentence as the expression of a complete thought first appears as a linguistically global unit, i.e., as a "word."[23] For example, when a two-year-old child uses the expression "mid" (*mit* = with), it stands for a complete wishful thought, namely, *"Ich will mit dir gehen"* (I'd like to go with you). And just as he expresses whole sentences in the form of words so, too, on the other hand, he will understand the divisively conceived, differentiated sentences of the adult as single words. A two-year-old child says: "daissi" for *"Das ist sie"* (that is she).[24] A French child at the same age says "apu" for *"Il n'y a plus,"*[25] etc.

If the completely articulated sentence is taken as a criterion, the primitive sentence appears defective and truncated. Mary Fisher, who has investigated the development of sentence completeness, found that between the 18 to 24 months level and the 36 to 42 months level there is a sudden drop in incompleteness from 60 per cent to 15 per cent.[26] If we understand this incompleteness to refer not to the formal grammatical structure, but

[23] Stern, 511, 170 ff.
[24] Ament, 330, 164.
[25] Bloch, 338.
[26] Fisher, 369.

to the verbally expressed meaning, it would appear that Pohlmann[27] is correct in contending that even during the school years the child expresses himself in incomplete sentences. For example, when a seven-year-old child is asked to explain the phrase "edible fruits" and says "pears," he is actually referring not to the particular, isolated object "pear," but to a whole material content which is individualized and concrete in nature. "Yesterday we ate pears, and I was thinking about that, so I couldn't say very much," the child tells us. Here Pohlmann explains that an extensive sentence content was intended, one which would conform in effect to the content of a verbally correct and complete sentence form, except that it is represented in the form of a word rather than in the conventional adult manner.

Diffuse conceptual relationships are moreover characterized by a so-called *one-sidedness* (one-track relationship). Since a primitive concept is usually not cast in the form of a synthesis of many properties, but as a unitary form in which there is one salient sign of totality (or few such), the child does not think comprehensively of the many possibilities of relationship between concepts, but chooses perhaps one out of many on which to concentrate, to the neglect of all others. His relationships are therefore frequently indeterminate from the logical standpoint. In the analogy: Industry–laziness; bravery–?, only about 10 per cent of nine-year-old children hit upon the correct answer. Such possibilities as "ingratitude" or "stupidity," or their simpler alternatives, were often applied. In the specific relation between industry and laziness only one clue is grasped—the vague one which hinges on the opposition of good to bad. The indeterminateness of this relationship is in keeping with the diffuseness of the concepts.

The child's inability to grasp in simultaneity different aspects of a relationship, or a double relationship, is at the bottom of the difficulties encountered by children in dealing with some of Piaget's tests. One of the typical questions asked in these

[27] Pohlmann, 485, 310.

tests is the following:[28] "Edith is lighter than Suzanne; Edith is darker than Lily. Which is the darkest—Edith, Suzanne, or Lily?" These are typical answers: Fo (9:4), "You can't tell because it says that Edith is the lightest and the darkest." Gu (13:9), "Once Suzanne is the darkest and once Edith is, so Suzanne is the same as Edith, and Lily is the lightest." The difficulty of solution rests mainly in the fact that it depends on an understanding of the twofold relationship in which Edith stands. This further problem presents similar difficulties:[29] "If the animal has long ears, it is a mule, or a donkey; if it has a thick tail, it is a mule, or a horse. Well, this animal has long ears and a thick tail. What is the animal?" This answer given by a boy nine years and two months old is typical: "The animal can be a donkey because you say that if it has long ears it is either a donkey or a mule. But it can be a mule, for you say that if the animal has a thick tail it is either a mule or a horse." The solution cannot be realized because it demands a simultaneous understanding of a two-way relationship. This is alien to the child's tendency to build up a one-track relationship on the basis of a salient characteristic.

The diffuse, concrete mode of thought occasions a *lack of consistency* and a consequent *lability* in the relationship. This means that the salient characteristics which are stressed at one time in the construction of the relationship may be replaced by others at another time as, for example, in the tests involving the completion of analogies. On different days the same child will put down quite different answers to the same question. The lability of the single word meanings occasions a similar lability in the concept of relationship.

Some examples illustrate strikingly the inconstancy of the child's verbally expressed relationships. Piaget's tests to analyze logical coordination yield extremely interesting results. A list of proverbs is given in conjunction with a series of general sentences; each proverb corresponds in meaning to one

[28] Piaget, 481, 87.
[29] *Ibid.*, 222.

of the sentences. Let us examine three attempts to relate in this way.

One boy 8:8 years old links the proverb "When the cat's away, the mice will play" with the sentence "Some people get very excited, but never get anything done." The boy explains his choice by saying: "People run around, but afterwards they never get anything done because they are tired. That's like the cat who runs after chickens. He rests in the shade and goes to sleep. There are many people who run around, but afterwards they can't go any more, and have to rest."

A second boy, age nine years, connected "You can't get white dust out of a bag of coal" with "Those who waste their time neglect their affairs." According to his reasoning both sentences mean the same thing because, as he explains: "Coal is black and you can't make it white. Those who waste their time don't take care of their children, and then they get so black you can't clean them."

A third child, age ten years, linked "The cowl does not make the monk" with "Many people get very excited, but never get anything done." His explanation was: "Because people who run around excitedly do not do anything; because the cowl does not make the monk . . . and people who get excited don't do anything about it!"[30]

The child, it is apparent, connects sentences which to the adult are completely unrelated. With increasing age it can be seen how this lability in sentence meaning gradually becomes less and less marked. In the few instances quoted here an increased stabilization is visible in the verbal meaning.

Let us consider the first child's analogy. The cat runs around (first after the chickens, and later to find a place to rest). Because of this she can catch no mice. Here what would be a universal content to the adult is conceived as thoroughly concrete; it is this concrete conception that causes a sentence of general import with a clearly determined content to become

[30] Piaget, **479,** 71 f; **478,** 293 f.

vague, labile, and subject to any arbitrary, individualized interpretation.

In the third example we find an understanding of relationship which has progressed considerably toward the objective, stable, and impersonal. A general content is actually expressed in both sentences, namely, the idea of an outer appearance which is at variance with the inner nature to which it is attached (cowl—monk; rushing about—accomplishment). This idea is made the basis of the analogy. Of course, this conception, as we see it exemplified in the third case, is a completely arbitrary attempt at reconciliation. On the other hand, the error in coordinating the two sentences does not lie, as in the two previous cases, in a purely fantastic interpretation but rather in an over-emphasis of an incidental element in the whole relationship.

These examples illustrate how thoroughly inherent are lability and inconstancy in concrete thinking. The vagueness of such analogies diminishes as the child becomes more and more able to grasp the universal and objective content of such sentences.

THE CHILD'S CAUSAL REASONING AND ITS DEVELOPMENT.

The causal reasoning of the child generally exhibits all the formal characteristics of primitive thought as previously defined. This thinking is *subjective*; it is egomorphic, anthropomorphic, etc. Outer world and inner experience constitute an undivided unity, of such a kind that the events of the surrounding world appear to be intimately linked with the ego and its needs. This thinking is *concrete*; perceptual configuration and concept stand together undifferentiated. Finally, this thinking is *diffuse*, lacking in strict logical articulation.

Subjective Character of the Child's Causal Reasoning.—The development of the child's causal thinking, so far as its general aspect is concerned, may be defined as an increasing adaptation of thought to objective fact. Such a "de-personalization" may be conceived as proceeding in three successive fundamental steps.

The first represents a stage in which physical events receive egomorphic, anthropomorphic explanations. A boy five years of age was asked why it always gets dark in the evening. He said: "It's because the people get tired and want to sleep. First the children in the main house and then aunt Tita and uncle Otto and then you!" "It rains," says the same boy, "because the angels sweep the heaven clean with their brooms and lots of water." "What makes the lightning?" he was asked. "Oh, it's because God gets awfully angry. Then his face gets very very dark. But the lightning doesn't come to the houses . . . he shoots so, the lightning, that he doesn't hit the people!"[31]

During a second stage, one not altogether distinguishable in its beginnings from the first stage, events are somewhat more realistically defined. The conception of natural events typical of this step may be called a "naïve dynamism." The "causality of being made" predominates. Things and events are the products of man's activity (Piaget's "artificialism"). "Animistic" explanations of nature are not infrequent, explanations based on the dynamistic principle that things behave as they do because of some force inherent in them. A typical instance of the childlike "causality of being made" is this: While at the beach a boy five and a half years old was asked about the origin of the dunes. "Oh, I know," he said, "I think it was this way. At first everything was smooth (he shows how smooth with his hands), and then 'they' just shoveled up all the sand."

The third stage is marked by a realistic attitude toward the world. Piaget sets the arrival of this stage at approximately seven to eight years of age.[32]

[31] From an unpublished study at the Hamburg Psychological Laboratory.
[32] Piaget, **482**; cf. Hall, **395**, 32.

Naturally these stages, which are here defined as (1) ego-morphism and anthropomorphism, (2) naïve dynamism, and (3) realism, do not so much refer to definite age levels as represent a general trend in the development of causal thinking. In objection to the belief of many child psychologists that genetic stages of reasoning can be defined in terms of definite age levels we might point out that the experimental response, so far as causal reasoning is concerned, depends to a large degree on the subject matter, on the child's previous experience with whatever objects are brought to his notice, etc. We found in our experiments in the Hamburg Laboratory that, with respect to the origin of such natural phenomena as clouds, lightning, and rain, the average child remained much longer on the primary level of ego- and anthropomorphic thought than he did in the case of the physical-technical events of the immediate world.

Concrete Character of the Child's Causal Reasoning.—The law of development is here one of increasing abstraction and generalization. The younger child does not understand explanations on the basis of general, necessary determinants in the sense that these appear in a mature concept of causality. Rather, he contents himself with certain historic concrete presentations of the event, with the causal grounds for it given implicitly in the imaginative configuration, yet not abstracted in any specific form. The logical relation of cause and effect remains often undifferentiated, "syncretically" comprehended in the form of a narrative exposition. We could demonstrate this years ago by the typical failures to solve so-called ordering tests. Some of these tests present the task of ordering a series of mixed words according to causality. Among ten-year-olds approximately 20 per cent of the children arrange one series in some such manner as this: "Fall-doctor-broken·leg-bandage-getting better-healed." The reason for the reversal of the logical position of the second and third words, it is revealed upon direct inquiry, is due simply to the child's concrete manner of thinking. He conceives of the series of words as a narrative, or as a visually remembered experience; the doctor comes after the fall and announces that a leg has been broken.[33]

A series of experiments by Piaget, Raspe, Muchow, Zeininger, Huang, and others, with children of different ages, gives us some insight into the development of causal reasoning. The experiments are all of the same type. Some simple physical object or event is brought to the child's attention, and it is his task to find an explanation for it. The first stage is charac-

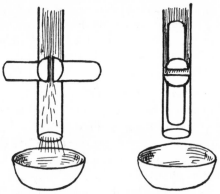

Fig. 52.—Object Situation, Used in Piaget's Experiment on Causality.

terized by explanations of a purely descriptive nature. For example, Piaget shows the children the illustration in Fig. 52.[34] The event represented here should be ideally described in some such manner as this: Water flows through a glass tube provided that the stopcock is in a horizontal position, and that the hole tapped through the cock is in a vertical position; otherwise water cannot flow through. In place of this causal explanation the younger children usually respond with the following type of description: There is a stopcock, and then you turn it, and then water comes which runs through the tube, and then so it can get out runs through the little tube, etc.

[33] Werner, 533.
[34] Piaget, 480, Fr. ed., 111 ff.

Huang showed children five to nine years old a small open cardboard box.[35] At the four corners of the box pieces of string were attached and knotted together in the middle. A penny was then put into the box and the question was asked: "What will happen to the penny if the box is turned upside down?" All the children answered this question correctly. Afterward, holding the box by the joined strings, he whirled it around fast enough so that the penny did not fall out. The children were then asked to explain why this occurred. It was found that the younger children usually responded simply by stressing descriptively some concrete part of the event. The penny did not fall out "because it's in a corner," "because it gets in the corner like that and sticks there."

On a higher level the child was able to grasp the more or less specific, concrete conditions of the event, even though the general causal background might still escape him. This type of causal reasoning has been called "if . . . then" thinking.[36] Whether these concretely interpreted causal factors are relevant or irrelevant depends on the child's age, the difficulty of the problem, etc. Even adults of a naïve mentality often do not get beyond this stage of causal reasoning. An example may serve to define more accurately this "if . . . then" form of causality. The majority of the older children in this particular experiment explained the phenomenon of the penny in the box by saying that "the box is going too fast." Very few children, and always the oldest ones, reached beyond this extremely concrete explanation and hit upon some more specific explanation such as "the box turns so fast that the penny doesn't have time to fall out."

The highest stage of causal reasoning is reached when the explanation proceeds in terms of universal, abstract, *necessary* causes. As a rule the child (and often the naïve adult) remains on the concrete level of "it's this way." Only very slowly

[35] Huang, 405.
[36] Zeininger, 539.

does he achieve the knowledge that "it must be this way because . . ."

The concept of *necessity* and the correlated concept of *chance* remain alien to the child for a long period. The inherent necessity of death, says Isolde Kurz, is generally strange to the small child,[37] just as strange as it is to the primitive Bakaïri whom we have discussed in earlier paragraphs.

In a beautiful experiment Loosli-Usteri shows how children, even those of school age, are often unable to grasp the concept of chance. The making of figures by the ink-blot method (a heavy blot of ink is made on one side of a creased paper and the paper then folded over to repeat the blot on the other side of the crease) is regarded by children not as being the result of mere chance, but as something predetermined. Even twelve-year-old children think they can "make" a dog's head this way.[38]

Diffuseness and Inconsistency in the Child's Causal Reasoning.—The child sees and thinks in terms of individual, concrete, and non-divisive relationships where the adult would analyze the concrete event by means of applying abstract causal reasoning. This is why children often explain diverse events by diverse causes when the adult would unify the diversity by some process of abstraction. A boy seven and a half years old, for example, explains the fact that the water in a jug rises when a stone is put into the water by saying that the stone is heavy. When the same effect is produced by a block of wood he explains the phenomenon this time on the basis of the lightness of the wood.[39] Since the event—namely, the rising of the water—is embedded in diverse total relationships, it is connected each time with a different element of the whole. The explanatory process in this case does not proceed in such a fashion that the child seeks for a universal

[37] Kurz, 433.
[38] Loosli-Usteri, 442.
[39] Piaget, 479, 75.

ground for a universal phenomenon. The indivisible, concrete relationship is understood as an individual unity.

This lability and inconsistency in the reasoning process expresses itself again in the fact that the conceptual connections between diverse contents are not enduring but mutable in accordance with the child's transitory state of apprehension.

"Rivers have strength," says an 8:6-year-old boy, "because they flow." A moment later the same child says: "Rivers have no strength because they can't carry anything." "Water isn't alive," says an eight-year-old boy. "It has no hands, it can't run on the grass. Fire is alive because it burns. Plants are alive because they grow."[40] Maria Hüpeden demonstrates in certain religious-psychological experiments that many of the younger school child's explanatory conceptions are variably centered.[41] In one and the same written composition Heaven is thought of as the place of the blessed and as an arch of clouds. Sun, moon, and stars are around God and are later described as moving across Heaven. The upholstered chair is first the seat of God, then later of Jesus and Abraham.

The structure and development of causal thinking can be revealed most instructively in statistical verbal analyses such as those worked out by Piaget. The conjunctions of motivation or causality ("because," "since," etc.) are seldom used by young children. Until the age of from seven to eight years narrative conjunctions such as "and" are used almost altogether as substitutes.[42] But even when the causal conjunctions are used, their meaning progresses through a characteristic course of development, one which may be divided into these three features:

1. The causal conjunctions grow more common in the child's language with increasing age.

2. The "because" function is at first the expression of an

[40] Piaget, **481**, Fr. ed., 200, 205.
[41] Hüpeden, **407**.
[42] Piaget, **480**, Fr. ed., 133.

anthropomorphic causality which only gradually evolves into a physical and relatively logically grounded form. When, for example, children were given this sentence to complete: "Paul says that he has a little cat that swallowed a big dog: his friend says that this is impossible because . . . ? . . . ? . . ." Piaget found that in the early school years some such answer as this would be given: "That's impossible, because it isn't true" or "because he's a liar."

According to the results of this test, the percentage of the logical "because" conjunctions increases in the following manner:[43]

| | | Age | |
	7	8	9
Boys	36%	50%	88%
Girls	38%	54%	61%

3. The sense of causality and logical justification is at first implicit, between the lines; it only slowly evolves into the explicit. When a child is given this sentence to complete: "Half of 9 is not 4 because . . . ? . . ." and he completes it in this fashion, "because there's one left over," the causality is not altogether explicit. The fact that there is a division of the number 9 into 2 equal parts is tacitly taken for granted. The implicit, incomplete character of the child's logical justifications in these experiments again points to a diffuse mode of thought in which the part actually expressed stands for the latent comprehensive explanation.

COMPLETE VS. INCOMPLETE JUSTIFICATION IN TWO TESTS [44]

| | | Age | |
	7	8	9
Boys	22 : 22	40 : 27	57 : 18
Girls	22 : 30	34 : 25	39 : 21

[43] Piaget, **481**, 35.
[44] *Ibid.*

THE DEVELOPMENT OF THE CHILD'S LOGICAL INFERENCE.

The child's methods of inference bear all the marks of primitive thinking; they are syncretic, concrete, diffuse-global, and poorly centralized according to focal elements. K. Bühler's assumption that the six-months-old child cannot reason, that it is unable to make inferences, has been repudiated with much cogency by Hazlitt,[45] who argues, "We find a small child trying to fill his mouth with his thumb and the nipple both at once, and only learning by experience that he must take the thumb out in order to put the nipple in." A primitive form of inference, then, is actually present in the physical actions of the child; his physical behavior represents an "intelligence of the body" as an analogue of thought on the verbal plane.

The verbalized inference itself appears at first as a concrete form of thought. William Stern correctly holds that the early form of inference can be neither induction nor deduction, since such processes involve general judgments. The primitive form of the inference is "transduction," that is, the leading over, the transition, from one concrete, isolated judgment to another coordinate, single judgment.[46] Here Stern distinguishes three subforms: the inference of equality, of difference, and of similarity or analogy. The basic premise in carrying out such a mode of inference is not that there shall be an abstraction by universal judgments, but that the child remain in the sphere of imaginative-individualized association.

A transductive inference of equality is of this sort: The 3:2-year-old Hilde asks: "What's hanging up there? Something to pin clothes on?" (Someone has strung a piece of rope across the iron railing of the balcony.) This is no logical deduction, but a form of reasoning which is closely interwoven with the concrete configuration. For such inferences are devoid of objective necessity; they are constructed on a basic principle of imaginative processes, a principle which in normal psychology (Selz) has been termed the "tendency of completion

[45] Hazlitt, 399.
[46] Stern, 513, Germ. ed., 272.

of (incomplete) configurations." If the piece of rope has been previously known according to particular associations—in this case in the global situation of supporting the family wash—then the present conception of the rope demands a completion of the whole situation in case it alone is seen as a part of a totality.

The experience of a totality that is in nature concrete and individualistic, the tendency to fill in the gaps of the totality, apparently constitutes, again, the basis on which rests the so-called "transductive inference of difference." The logical function of inference is here embedded in and inseparable from the whole concrete perceptual situation, even though these inferences do represent a more advanced type. Hilde's father, for example, eats very little of the vegetables served at lunch, and explains in answer to Hilde's question that he has breakfasted too heavily. Turning to her mother, who has more vegetables on her plate, she asks: "You didn't eat very much breakfast, then?" In this case, too, the inference of difference is grounded on an *ad hoc* imagined, concrete-personalized association (much breakfast—few vegetables; little breakfast—many vegetables). Again objective necessity is supplanted by an imaginative "togetherness."

"Transductive inferences of analogy" made by children also often appear on a perceptual, individualized level characterized by an absence of insight into general relationships. For instance, the Scupin boy, 5:1 years of age, asks: "Is the cloud made of gas so that it can fly?" This inference, too, proceeds not in terms of general relationships in which objective necessity is inherent, but on the basis of a familiar and isolated objective fact exhibiting an individual-concrete relationship (gas—balloon—flying), one that is assumed to be applicable in a quite different, isolated case. The following inquiry made by the Sterns' child, Hilde, then 5:2 years of age, again reveals the same tendency:[47] her grandmother has a wrist-watch. One day her father says to her mother: "You ought to have a

[47] *Ibid.*

wrist-watch, too." Upon hearing this Hilde asks, surprised: "Do people who aren't grandmothers also have wrist-watches?" In spite of the apparently mature form of the question, the inferential process is still grounded in a mode of reasoning dominated by individualized, concrete associations (grandmother—wrist-watch). It would be erroneous to think that this togetherness has any logical universality and necessity. It would be making the same mistake as drawing a parallel between the seemingly "general" concepts of the very small child and the real, universal concepts of the adult. For just as the true concept can develop only out of the opposition of particular to universal, so here, also, it is possible for a true inference to develop only out of the contrast between the fortuitous and the necessary, an idea which is foreign to a child's reasoning.

Many of the child's inferences are possible only on the basis of that characteristic of primitive thought which we have called *diffuseness*. At the bottom of the previously mentioned "tendency to configurational completion" is a diffuseness in the thinking process, a reasoning in terms of undivided totalities. Whereas the real, logical inference is built up on a logically necessary division of cause and effect, the child's inference is a diffuse, indivisible association of concrete parts. The inseparability of the elements in accordance with the diffuseness of the reasoning process is a primitive substitute for necessity.

Sully tells of a ten-year-old boy who, it happened, had once had both a tall and very kind teacher and another who was short of stature and cross. This child said to his new teacher, who struck him as short, "I am afraid you will make a cross teacher."[48] This is not only an example of concrete "transduction." In the completion of what the child has once experienced as a global association—small and therefore strict —and which, once experienced, has been established as an idea holding good in all cases, we see how logical necessity is sup-

[48] Sully, 517, 44.

planted by the inseparability of the elements of one concrete experience.

PATHOLOGICALLY PRIMITIVE FORMS OF THOUGHT.

In all those cases where there is a regression to a more primitive form of behavior as a result of some mental disturbance, it will be found that the reasoning process itself becomes undifferentiated, more concrete and diffuse. The often-cited pathological individuals studied by Head, Gelb and Goldstein, and others, exhibit a mode of reasoning which works only in a more or less concrete situation. If, for instance, one of these patients is given a text in which there are lacunae to be filled in, he appears to be quite incapable of doing the task.[49] Yet he can handle a completion test successfully if the problem is presented as part of a concrete situation familiar to him. For example, if when making a draft of a letter which the patient wishes to send to his wife, the nurse intentionally leaves out certain words, the patient can fill in the gaps with considerable facility when he makes his copy in turn. In every case where a task can be performed by tangible means, through concrete action, this patient successfully accomplishes what is demanded of him. Any transcursion of the concrete givenness that delivers him into the sphere of the "possible," of the "theoretical," causes complete failure. He is as little capable of solving an ordinary intelligence test as he is of reckoning without the use of concrete objects; he can understand neither fictitious narratives nor metaphorical meanings. Similarly, Benary's patient,[50] who was psychically blind, was balked as soon as he was confronted by abstract rather than concrete reasoning. This particular patient was unable to solve a problem in which a fourth concept had to be supplied in order to complete a set of three concepts presented in the form of a proportion. It was even impossible to make the idea of proportion intelligible to him. Such a sentence as "The lamp is the same for light

49 Siekmann, 601.
50 Benary, 541.

as the stove is for warmth" had no meaning at all for him. He understood clearly the single elements of the sentence, that the lamp gave light and the stove warmth, but the logical equality of the related propositions was not in his power to grasp. If he were asked whether it was correct to say such things, he consistently answered in the negative. The sentence "Fur is to cat what feathers are to bird" was repudiated because, as he said, "You can pluck out the feathers one at a time." Such answers as this show how fundamentally concrete and individualized are the meanings of each of the two parts of the sentence. The patient is simply not equal to the rather abstract problem of constructing a schema comprehending both sections of it.

Again in states of intoxication dominated by a primitive form of behavior we find that the reasoning processes are syncretic, concrete. Instructive reports made by Beringer's subjects, who submitted to intoxication by mescalin, illustrate this fact. One subject says: "Seeing comes to the fore, so that I value 'seeing' and 'thinking' equally. . . . The operations of reason are identical with the sequence of visual perceptions." The subject sees the thoughts of the experimenter as "parabolic curves moving through a sort of fluidity."[51] Similarly, another subject remarks: "I saw a thought coming out of me in the shape of a lattice."

Among schizophrenics we find once again highly syncretic, concrete, and affective reasoning processes in accordance with the concepts characteristic of this pathological level of mentality. Gruhle, in his work on schizophrenic thoughts, contends that, in general, all intellectual operations so far as they are related to the practical tasks of concrete life remain intact. It is only at the level of abstract problems that the deficiency, in form of a regression toward the concrete, becomes obvious.[52] Some of the patients are well aware of this change. "The single ideas are much more picture-like than before," says one

[51] Beringer, 543, 87, 203.
[52] Gruhle, 568.

patient. "Sometimes these pictures fill up the space completely." Another patient says: "It is no more thinking, it is somehow more like seeing many things one after the other." This concrete manner of thinking is brought out quite clearly in experimental test situations. A patient who is requested to interpret the proverb: "A new broom sweeps well," explains: "When a housewife has a new broom it works well. But she can also use old ones for a long time and may save a new broom. There may be old things which could be used. Why should it be always new things?" etc.

When one of Bleuler's patients says that such and such a one is too vulgar for her and she herself too good for him, she simultaneously raises herself on her toes.[53] The commonplace figurative-abstract expression "low," used in the sense of "a low fellow," here acquires a literal, concrete meaning. At times this meaning becomes so comprehensive that in one sentence is syncretically condensed the whole psychic life of the patient. As an example of such a syncretic condensation in schizophrenic thought I might cite the statement of one patient analyzed by Schilder in his book, *Seele und Leben*. This woman declared that in her fancy she "found release and happiness through sexual union with her father." "Because of this," says Schilder, "her mother had to be suppressed and driven away. A blurred sexual excitement, heightened by the memory of an attempted rape experienced at the age of fourteen, led to the belief that her mother wished to couple her with a man. In an acute attack of catatonia she developed the idea that God (her father) tore out her womb, thus giving her expiation. This removal of the uterus has the following significance: In her belief she has become pregnant during the rape. And the expiatory act also has a sexual connotation, since the patient says that it is God's intention to sleep a night with her. At the same time the form of God fuses together with that of the doctor in attendance. The connection between the two has been occasioned by the injection given

[53] Storch, **604**, 324.

the patient by the doctor, which ministration she thinks of as a sexual act." Accordingly, when the patient says that "*she has overcome her womb,*" to some considerable degree the whole complex of meaning generated by the psychosis is contained in the words. Behind this sentence stand the patient's experience of rape, and the suppression of a sensation in the genital region caused by the rape. The suppression has a special significance for her. She believes that by it she has prevented the maturation of the seed within her. The uterus itself appears as sensuousness concretely materialized, and at the same time as the mother herself. Now the thought arises that her mother refuses to take her to the doctor so that he can remove her womb and, further, that her mother wants to mate her with someone. By sleeping with her for a night God himself removes her womb.

In this same sentence is expressed the idea that the patient has united sexually with her father, is purified by God, and also that he has taken away her mother (her womb) as a symbol of uncleanness. (It must be noted that in German "mother" is *Mutter* and "womb" is *Gebärmutter.*) And, finally, the sentence contains the fantastic idea that the whole world has been saved by this self-sacrificial act.[54]

This example demonstrates the syncretism in the thought of the schizophrenic as well as its diffuseness. Schizophrenic thought lacks a unity occasioned by central objective ideas. Each individual partial content represents an unlimited plethora of subjective experience, and there is absent that organization by means of which the experience of an objectively functioning mind is centralized and brought under rigid control.

The lack of subordination in the various elements of thought to leading objective ideas is mirrored in the formal grammatical structure of schizophrenic language. As Schilder demonstrates in several cases, the language of the schizophrenic is lacking in formal grammatical differentiation and centraliza-

[54] Schilder, **598**, 60 f.

tion. The psychotic discussed in the preceding paragraphs furnishes an apt illustration. "All the raw sentence material is only provisionally configurated, piece by piece, without ever arriving at the stage of grammatical integration. The patient cannot formulate her single emotions by the exercise of a unifying will. There is juxtaposition rather than subordinative articulation."[55]

Schilder's characterization of schizophrenic thoughts is in accord with the contention of Berze, Beringer, and Gruhle that the fundamental peculiarity of schizophrenic mental operations is the lack of subordinative intentional activity. This lack in subordinating several mental elements to a unifying idea is sometimes well recognized by the patients themselves: "I do not have the course of thought under control—aside from the main thought there are running along with it other thoughts confusing my reasoning; my thoughts do not reach their logical end." Another patient compares the structure of her thinking with mosaic stones which do not form a whole.[56]

We may, finally, consider some typical schizophrenic attempts at *causal explanation*. According to such an individual's concrete manner of thinking, the phenomena of the world are to be explained in *concrete* and highly imaginative configurations. A cognitive theoretical complex of meaning can be expressed in a "picture," in the literal meaning of the word. Because of this, the graphic reproductions, or the hallucinations, of the psychotic are often condensed representations of his concept of the world.

One of Schilder's patients, for instance, had a vision which he represented in the form of a drawing.[57] "First there came a head with an elephant's tusk. The black dots were energy-points, fists. Underneath was the sexual motif, drawn lightly. In the eyes were black dots. Above there was something that

[55] *Ibid.*, 62.
[56] Beringer, 542.
[57] Schilder, 598, 26.

was dead material that had once belonged to him. It was like white of a cooked egg, something without vitality. This spot above grew increasingly darker, and he had the feeling that it was dead, but that the material could be brought to life if one wanted to do this. When he felt this red dots appeared. The memory-image of the incandescent bulb (after-image) remained above. Suddenly everything was crossed by flame, and the tulip-motif arose, which he experienced as love. The red color swept everything away, and down below he saw how man came from the earth. Everything melted and flowed together. He was terribly upset when this happened. He saw everything in music."

This picture is the delineation of this man's concept of the (sexually interpreted) genesis of the world. In general abstruse explanation of his vision the psychotic says that it represents the "union of energy and body as equal to the united action of material and ether as equal to the physical-monistic theory of Maxwell on the basis of logically pure mathematical partial differentiations."

We again encounter the *diffuseness* of the schizophrenic thought process in the psychotic conception of causality. As in the case of primitive man, differentiation according to cause and effect, according to condition and consequence, is supplanted by what we have previously called *thinking in terms of fate*. Certain compulsive ideas are the pathological parallels of the thinking in terms of fatality characteristic of the primitive mentality.

The schizophrenic conceives the happenings of the world as signs of destiny, as omens of important events of larger meaning. Strindberg's world is full of "signs." One of Bychowski's patients believed that a minister was forcing him to get married and, consequently, he was troubled by many evil forebodings which drove him to distraction. One day a ram broke into his sheep-pen and killed one of the sheep. The patient interpreted this event as a premonition of death; and, in fact, shortly thereafter—according to his story—his cousin's son died.[58]

Thinking in terms of fatality precludes any self-contained single things and events within a causal complex. In fatalistic thought each event is accommodated to a superordinated temporal association shot through with the global quality-of-fate, which may be either good or evil. An isolated event is relevant only in so far as it is characterized by this quality-of-the-whole. It has significance only as *pars pro toto* and, on this account, may stand as the symbol of some catastrophic occurrence.

Encephalitis is one of the pathological conditions in which reasoning in terms of fate plays a more or less dominant role. In certain individuals described by Bürger and Mayer-Gross this mode of thought appears in conjunction with an excess of impulsive tendencies beyond the control of the intellect (compulsive ideas and actions). The patient feels that in him the daemonic powers of the world have been released. Herein lies a certain parallel to familiar phenomena of the primitive mentality. In the encephalitic, also, as in the case of the schizophrenic, objects and external events may assume the character of premonitory signs. If you don't knock off the head of the thistle as you pass by, something terrible will happen to you. You mustn't put on the right shoe first, or you'll meet disaster.[59] By thinking in terms of fate, by letting himself be guided by signs and omens, the psychotic has chosen one way of adjusting himself to a pathologically regressive world governed by daemonic powers.

[58] Bychowski, 550, 29.
[59] Bürger and Mayer-Gross, 549, 659.

Chapter XI

THE FUNDAMENTAL IDEAS OF MAGIC AS AN EXPRESSION OF PRIMITIVE CONCEPTUALIZATION

Syncretism in Primitive Magic.

We have repeatedly emphasized the syncretic character of primitive perception. This means, in brief, that motor and affective elements are intimately merged in the perception of things. Because of this the objects of perception are not passive and neutral, but represent the foci of dynamic powers. Without any sort of interpretation of perceptual data in terms of true magics there are already magic-like characteristics in the very nature of primitive perception. A world "physiognomic" in its essence is on this sole account already daemonic in the larger sense of the term, even though this daemonism need not develop into any practice which would justify its being called a magic cult.

Things and persons in the sphere of magic are daemonical entities, the definition of which depends on how the emotions participate in the figuration of the milieu. The world becomes constituted of magic entities that are the reflections of the interplay of human fears and desires. Therefore, in any primitive society it is usually those activities that exhibit a dominance of emotion which evolve into magic practices. It is possible that magic may never encroach into other fields of activity, such as the making of fire, of baskets, and of stone implements. And in certain other activities, magic may come into use only under emotional tension. Malinowski contends that in a maritime community magic is not connected with fishing by poison, etc., so long as the ordinary activity functions satisfactorily. But the capture of fish by some means that entails danger to life will be surrounded by ritualistic practices. This is true of hunting and of other activities as well.[1]

The realm of magic is distinguished by the fact that all events and phenomena are linked together by magical interpretation. To a certain degree it is exactly as if reality had been given the index "magic." For us at a more advanced level, the contour or the gestalt of things, for example, is a thoroughly formal, objective quality. For the Zuñi, and for many other peoples of a primitive culture, the form of either an animate or an inanimate object represents in perception visible, figurated, mystic strength. Cushing, who has lived among the Zuñi for many years, says: "Everything made—whether building, utensil, or weapon—is conceived as living a still sort of life, but as potent and capable of functioning as actively and powerfully in occult ways either for good or evil. As for living beings, they observe every animal is formed and acts or functions according to its form—the bird because of its feathered form, the finny fish swimming—so, too, the things made or born in their special forms by the hands of man also have life and function variously according to their various forms. The forms of these things not only give the power but also restrict their power, so that if properly made and shaped as other things of their kind have been made and shaped, they will perform only such safe uses as their prototypes have been found to serve. It is therefore of the utmost importance that they shall be faithfully reproduced so that one may not have the fear of unknown 'powers' which a new form might possess."[2]

In the world of magic we do not find any line of demarcation separating dynamic from objective-concrete properties, a separation which is taken for granted in the scientific concept of the world. Here each objective, visible quality is at the same time some magic force.

Primitive man is certain that there is no fundamental dif-

[1] Malinowski, **97.**
[2] Cushing, **179, 361** ff.

ference between the sphere of subjective phenomena and that of (intersubjective) objective phenomena. This belief continues to hold true for the realm of magic. It is, in fact, out of this very fusion that magical and magical religious modes of thought are evolved.

We recall, for example, that in primordial thinking the dream and illusion are often evaluated as real. In the realm of magic this belief becomes an active conviction that dream and vision are magically effective realities. It is because of this similarity between the inner world of man—that is, his ideas and his personal striving—and the world of outer events, that in the magic sphere the wishes, intentions, and thoughts of man are self-realized, that these wishes and thoughts are even reality itself. "The evil intention," says Pechuël-Loesche of the Loango people, "is quite as effective as the evil deed. It works and is effective as the rays of the sun warm, as the wind cools, as flowers smell sweet and as fleshly decay smells bad, it works like the poisons of plant and animal. Evil thoughts can be successfully consummated, and can condition an evil conscience. . . ."[3] Countless examples from all parts of the world support this fact. Among the relatively advanced Cora Indians this mode of thought is found in a very clearly defined and deeply religious form. The thought or the reflection is the principal element of the magical activity of these people. And it is a matter of indifference whether the thoughts refer to gods or to men. If the thoughts have the correct form, the consummation in actuality is incidental or even unnecessary to attain the objective. The songs of these Indians tell of the god of the Morning-Star, who rises in the east and who, having killed the water snake in the west, will now retrieve his death-dealing arrow:

> "Our older brother knows how to care for himself.
> Does he not get his arrow by the strength of his thought?
> He has it while he is there, on the other side of the world
> (in the east)."[4]

[3] Pechuël-Loesche, 257, 335.
[4] Preuss, 261, vol. 1, xcvi.

Besides the peculiar syncretism of psychic function in primitive experience—the fusion of feeling and perception, of the affective-dynamic and the perceptual-concrete, of perception and imagery—there is also syncretism in the very meaning content of primitive conceptualization. In the magic sphere there is a rich development of this syncretism of meaning so common to the primitive mentality in general. This particular aspect of a lack of differentiation is revealed in the condensation and ambiguity of magic content. Syncretism may appear as the condensation of meaning in magically effective things and persons.

For example, daemons are often invested with several, and indeed with opposed, meanings. Even among the primitive Veddas we find this condensation of daemonic meaning. It occurs when these people appeal for help and call upon an attribute of a certain daemon which would normally belong to a quite different god.[5] In magic ceremonies ideas associated with human well-being, the hunt, and plant fertility are often intermingled.[6] The magic "bundles" of the Blackfeet Indians, which are instruments of central importance in the ceremonies of these tribes, represent an expression of the syncretically operating mind. In these bundles are accumulated many diverse objects. The "beaver bundle," for instance, contains such different objects as beaver skins, a pipe, two buffalo ribs, and skins of the muskrat, weasel, white gopher, badger, prairie dog, antelope, deer, mountain goat, and of many different birds. The ritual associated with this particular bundle and its manifold contents is a composite of many "quite different creations of the Blackfoot mind."[7] In the Vedda dances there is a condensation of hunting, plant, and honey magic.[8] This comes to light in the ceremonial objects employed in the drama: yam-stalks are used in the boar-hunt ceremonies, and arrows

[5] Seligmann and Brenda, **287**, 263.
[6] Cf., e.g., Matthews, **238**; **239**.
[7] Wissler, **327**, 168 ff.
[8] Seligmann and Brenda, **287**, 263.

in the ritual of honey magic represent honeycombs. Another form of condensation is exhibited in other Vedda ceremonies. Two arrows decorated with the leaves of the betel nut and overlaid with a chain of pearls represent propitiatory offerings to daemons, but at the same time they are tools indispensable to the literal physical consummation of the ceremony. One of the arrows is used in its ordinary capacity as a missile, and the other serves in smoking out the honeycombs. In the sago ritual of the Melanesians of Tumleo the sago is crushed and then spat upon from below upward to show that it must grow upward. Here growth appears as symbolized by the movement from below upward, but at the same time the act of spitting represents rain.[9]

We may assume, then, that a magical condensation of diverse ideas is made possible by a peculiar general characteristic of all primitive thinking whatsoever. In the magical sphere this condensation is subject to a specific condition; not all ideas are run together, but only those which are magically related or identical. The idea of the hunt and of agricultural fertility, for example, may be magically related, and in consequence are condensed into one magical idea. Under certain circumstances the sexual activity of man and the increase of plants or animals are seen as identical. This is the reason why, in so many parts of the world, ceremonies intended to augment by magic the fertility of the crops include sexual acts. The anomalous power, the omnipotence of such magic ceremonies, lies in primitive man's ability to encompass in terms of condensations natural activity in both a general and a particular sense.

The primitive root of the magic meaning content is exhibited not only in the condensation proper, but also in the fluidity, in the lability of the meaning which any event or thing may assume for magical ends. The quality of lability is important for the development and formulation of magical procedure, for this procedure reveals in its magic formulae

[9] Erdweg, 188, 344.

and cults, in conformity with the varying magic purpose, the most diversely interpreted meanings. In New Guinea entwined vines can be used as love magic and, at another time, be known as an image of the death throes when thought of in terms of death magic. The momentary attitude, the "magic apperception," as I should like to call it, is a factor which frequently determines what shall be the sense of the magical object. The Hawaiians, for instance, have no hard and fast rules in their interpretations of dreams. The dream is interpreted to accord with the current undertaking which occupies their attention.[10]

A few more typical examples of primitive behavior may show to what a remarkable degree the perception of things is governed by such a "magic apperception" or "magic focusing." "In Nauru (Micronesia) in order that there may be an easy delivery of the child, nothing may be shut tight, and no objects may be bound together. Everything is opened, and nothing may hang, but must be laid on the floor. Baskets and boxes are opened. And, at the moment when the child is coming into the world, all the people standing near the door remove their loin cloths."[11] In German New Guinea, also, the man removes his loin cloth in order to ease the delivery as his wife lies in labor.[12] In the Malayan culture, too, magic focusing is exhibited in the ritualistic procedure pertaining to childbirth. According to the Malayan belief the delivery of the child is facilitated if everything in the house—doors, windows, etc.—usually kept closed is thrown wide open. Amulets and ornamental objects are removed so that their power will not influence or hinder the birth.[13] We find exactly the same kind of magical behavior among the mountain Dama people of South Africa. If the parturition is not proceeding successfully the man must remove, throw open, or loosen everything he wears—his apron-

[10] Bastian, **157**, 60.
[11] Hambruch, **206**, vol. 1, 246.
[12] Neuhauss, **254**, vol. 1, 151.
[13] Maass, **232**, vol. 1, 447.

like girdle, his sandals, laces, shirt, etc. If he happens to be wearing suspenders he slips them from his shoulders so that they dangle loosely about his thighs. If he is a hunter he will loosen the string of his bow.[14]

In these instances we see to what extraordinary degree the "magic focusing" may participate in the apprehension of the surrounding world. We see how the idea of childbirth seeks to invade the entire world wherever it can be admitted, and how everything susceptible to this idea suffers a transformation. This magic apperception occasions a reorientation of the milieu in terms of a symbolization of the act of childbirth.

This principle of magic apperception is at the bottom of a great number of magic practices, even though they may not be such dramatic exemplifications of it as those just mentioned. I recall, for example, the great suspicion and apprehension with which the children's food is regarded by many tribes-people, who fear that it may cause harm when eaten if it exhibits certain characteristics of magic import. For instance, children may not eat long, narrow (spear-shaped) fish be-cause some day they might be killed by a spear thrust, etc.

Fixed attitudes also govern the magical thinking of more highly developed primitive cultures, notably that of the American Indian. These attitudes appear particularly in the form of tabu (negative magic). The great ceremonies of the Navajos—the object of which is to guard against death and prolong life—are carried out according to an exclusive magical interpretation of objects as symbols and bearers of life. Only living birds may be used in these rites, and the ceremonial stone knife must not be marred by cracks. The last breath of the sacrificial deer is stopped off with pollen so that a certain vital element may remain within the animal's body, etc.[15]

We see, therefore, how the fluidity and lability of perception are conditions which make possible the subjection of the things to the dictates of the magic attitude, the magic apperception.

[14] Vedder, 312, 42.
[15] Matthews, 239, 7 f.

DIFFUSENESS IN PRIMITIVE MAGIC.

Diffuseness is an essential characteristic of primitive phenomena. In such phenomena the totality overrules the differentiation into elements; we find the subordination of the non-essential to the essential rather poorly developed. When the transition from general primitive behavior to a specifically magic behavior has occurred, the properties of this primitive behavior, to a certain extent, are retained, but undergo a specific development.

Magic events come to be understood as relatively diffuse and homogeneous; ritualistic activities are known as indissoluble totalities, unitary acts which either fulfill themselves according to an all-or-nothing reaction, or are completely abortive. This is commonly exhibited in the fact that any temporally consummated act of configuration—whether it is some working activity, saying, or a song that serves magic ends must run its full course as a unified totality. Any disruption of the form, any failure in the performance—a stumbling, a stuttering, or even a pause—often occasions a magical inadequacy and inefficacy, since the very magical significance of the whole event is vital only within an unbroken totality. Hence here and there the curious fact is reported that in the incantation of magic verses only one breath must be used in uttering a group of words that constitute a single, cultistic meaning. Like the ancient Aryan prayers, which were marked by this same unity of rhythmic exhalation of breath,[16] there are old Hawaiian cult songs, each period of which must be recited in a single exhalation, after which a new breath is drawn in and released in the next period.[17]

This diffuseness is apparent not only in the magic quality-of-the-whole, but also in the lack of centralization, in the relatively negligible subordination of non-essential parts to the essential in the magic situation. The comparative equality of importance of all that is united in a cultistic association is one

[16] Werner, **142**, 205.
[17] Emerson, **187**, 139.

of the fundamental principles of magic. Again and again we see how every little detail, one we might consider of the most incidental value, is invested with a ritualistic importance and meaning quite equal to that of any other seemingly far more consequential part. Because of this it is impossible to make changes or omissions in a magical rite. Everything must occur in a prescribed cultistic order, an order in which is expressed both the global structure of magic forms and a lack of subordination.

Magical *things* as well as magical events and actions are effective and potent through mystic strength only so far as they are "whole." Only the global totality, the indissolubility, the faultlessness of the ritualistic objects insure the magical effect. Ritualistic implements may not be constructed or arranged while in use in any way that might represent a departure from tradition, nor may they have a faulty or fragmentary construction. Any kind of magical object is effective in its totality alone, and a change in the smallest part of it brings about a change in the whole. We are told of Indian tribes in British Guiana—to mention one among hundreds of examples—that ritualistic objects, in common with magic songs and texts, must not be altered in the slightest when they are being used or copied.[18] Only an exact imitation can succeed in insuring the presence of the magic power within the totality of the form.

Even in the most highly advanced magic cults the law of magical totality continues to be expressed in the inviolability and sanctity of the traditional magic order. As a fateful, daemonic source of effect through which each person, each thing or event, is given a particular place in the world, the inflexible magic order represents the culmination of a belief in the primordial strength of the global totality. In such highly organized forms of society as the ancient Chinese, the principle of an unchangeable order is the basic premise for a felicitous course of events. "When anyone suddenly falls sick

[18] Bernau, **162.**

or dies," says De Groot, "his family is instantly ready to foist the responsibility for this calamitous event on anyone who has brought about a change in the traditional order of things, or who has increased his holdings of land."[19] The traditional order in time and space is here the magical fundament and the venerable symbol of the completeness of human existence. In consequence any tampering with this order, with this fixed totality, must bring ill on the world.

THE NATURE OF MAGIC "THINGS."

The syncretism and diffuseness of magical objectivity are expressed particularly in those situations where there is a magic-practical intercourse with the things of the surrounding world. The practice of magic can occur only because of a special conception of the nature of "things." We shall now enter into a brief analysis of the structure of these things as magically known.

What is a "thing"? In the strict psychological and conceptually advanced sense of the word, a "thing" is a fixed substratum supporting essential (constitutive) and non-essential properties.

In the magic concept of a thing, however, the characteristic of having a constant, immutable substratum to which are attached essential properties as distinguished from the non-essential and variable properties is more or less absent. A "thing-category" in the scientific sense is simply non-existent, nor is it needed in the practice of magic. Nor is the essence of the thing constant, as shown in the mutability of both things and person, any more than the properties of the thing are stable, as shown in their susceptibility to transposition.

There are no essential and non-essential properties *per se*, for according to the magical standpoint the most insignificant detail may be of prime importance, and indeed the separative relation between the thing itself and its attributes is not clearly defined. In short, in comparison to the concept of thing as it is

[19] De Groot, 198, vol. 1, 1041.

known in advanced and non-magical thought, the structure of the specifically magical thing is far more diffuse and homogeneous.

Many facts point to a homogeneity of structure in the thing as magically known. For example, our things are endowed with properties which are strictly localized in these specific things. The roughness of an object resides in its surface. The wickedness of a man does not reside in his hair. All this is radically different according to the magical way of thought. Properties pervade things homogeneously. If the antelope possesses the most acute powers of sight, this quality does not center in the eyes alone, but also extends to the skin, hair, bones, and blood. The animal has the magic property of swiftness of movement not only in its sinews but throughout the whole body, in each smallest part, in the saliva as well as in its name. The attribute as a magically effective moment invades the entire object homogeneously and diffusedly. In addition, it is often endowed with a temporal duration; a property once exhibited may continue to endure through time, even though this be contradictory to the very nature of the thing involved. For example, the leopard's attribute of experiencing a powerful and sudden extrusion of the teeth while in the cub stage is believed by certain primitive peoples to continue in the animal's maturity as a magical attribute.[20] Again we recognize the general primitive conception of a thing, whereby the part is seen as the representative of the whole, and the whole consists of a diffuse union of global properties.

The *syncretic* character of magical things comes plainly to light in the fact that neither the thing itself nor its attributes are magically stable and unambiguous. We know that primitive things may acquire the properties of other entities, that the connection between persons and things, or between things and other things can be so intimate and syncretized that the properties become transferable. It is self-evident that, from

[20] Karutz-Lübeck, **59**, 584.

the standpoint of magic as rooted in a generally primitive mentality, things can exist and behave more syncretically and with far less stability than is the case with the advanced mentality. It is characteristic of the magical attribute that it need not be affixed, as a quality, to one individual bearer, but may be shared by several bearers. Hence it can be said that the magical attribute is "transposable." And yet fundamentally it is not the question of a susceptibility to transposition with respect to the attribute that is of prime interest. The concept of transposability of attribute is really too intellectual, at least for the beginnings of magic, too much colored by the European manner of thinking. It would be far better merely to accept this phenomenon as a syncretic union of attribute, such as we recognize in other primitive spheres (in the dream, for example), that is, as "condensation." Instead of speaking of the magical transposition of a thing's attributes to another thing, it would perhaps be more accurate to speak of a magical "confluence," a flowing together.

What we must understand by this term "magic confluence" becomes clearly defined in those magic practices that are known as the "magic of contiguity." According to the general idea on which this magic is based, the properties of one thing pervade another thing when the two are brought into contact. The Papuans, to illustrate, rub their backs and legs against the rocks in order to partake of their strength and durability. The total-quality of the rock, its pervasive hardness, is transposed by touch to the individual, or, better, this global attribute enters into the very body of the man and is borne by both him and the rock. In this same way Papuans draw power and resistance from strong trees which they embrace with their arms and legs. Leg-bands made of bast endow the sinews with the toughness of that material, and pieces of tropical trees which have very hard wood endow their bearer with a similar fortitude. The African Galla warrior stands on turtles and the Cherokee Indian brave binds them to his legs so that the soles of the feet and the leg muscles, respectively, may become as tough and hard as the shell of the reptile. Contact with the sinews of an antelope gives swiftness.[21] In all these cases we see how the attribute can be borne severally, a phenomenon in complete accordance with a syncretic mode of thought. In the custom of scalping the enemy we again discover the belief in a confluence of attribute. By possessing himself of the enemy's scalp, the Indian intends to make his own whatever attributes of courage and cunning the enemy may have had during his lifetime.

Just as the transposition of qualities in the practice of magic proceeds on the basis of a diffuse and syncretic structure in the thing whereby the single attribute both represents the diffuse totality and may also be common to several objects, so too is the magical acquisition of new qualities made possible by this same diffuse and syncretic structure. It is not necessary that an attribute be transposed from one object to the whole of another object, since in a diffuse structure the part may represent the whole. The transposition of qualities may proceed in such a way that the smallest part of the object or person receives them. The properties of good or evil can be invested in any part, and this may happen even when the part does not belong directly to the object. Hence it is quite as possible to work magic as efficaciously on the nails, the hair, and the spittle of some individual, or on the leavings of his meal, as on the whole person himself. In this category belongs that universally found magic which works on the name of the person. Furthermore, the transposition of new qualities rests not only on the possibility of endowing these qualities at will on different bearers, but also on the very inconstancy of the bearers themselves. The magic sacrifice changes the essential being of the persons involved. A man may become brave when he is cowardly, or handsome when ugly, etc.

On the peculiar concept of syncretic things and attributes rests another widespread form of magic, one usually called

[21] *Ibid.*, 582.

"magic by analogy" or "imitative magic." From the European standpoint the essence of magic by imitation may be simply formulated in this manner: the primitive man makes an image of some sort which, in one way or another, creates some desired magical effect. But from the standpoint of the primitive man himself such an explanation would hardly be adequate. When an aborigine hopes to bring about a successful hunting trip by means of some magical presentation, this presentation is not fundamentally an image, a symbol, a re-presentation in our sense, but a complete form of reality which, more often than not, very nearly approximates identity with the reality of the practical life which it is its object to influence. For just as the attribute, in some manner incomprehensible to us, can reside in all parts of the object (as, for example, the swiftness of the antelope not only exists in the legs but throughout the whole body), so, too, under certain conditions, it is possible that the attribute may reside quite as vitally in the image formed with magical intent as in the "real" object to which it refers via the image. Hence, the attribute may belong to a whole series of real things. These things are both the object within practical reality itself and the image formed by the sorcerer. When form is given to an image, reality itself is given form and direction. The new attribute, in accordance with the syncretism of this mode of thought, spontaneously becomes the attribute of the real object. In a deeper sense the magical procedure creates not alone an image from out of which the attribute is taken and intermediately transposed; but in creating the attribute in an image, the procedure likewise creates it simultaneously in the things showing identity with this image. This desired quality, therefore, belongs not to the image alone, but equally to the objects of everyday life involved in the whole procedure.

For this reason, instead of calling it magic by analogy or imitative magic, which would imply an altogether intermediary role that does not fit the facts when closely analyzed, it should be termed *creative magic* or *formative magic*, in so far as the desired attribute or event is not imitated or copied, but is actually brought into immediate being and formed objectively through the magical activity.

Some examples will serve to give concrete illustration of this peculiar property of creative magic. If a South Sea Islander wishes to attract a multitude of fish into his nets, he will represent fish in his mask dances.[22] The American Indian does this with buffalo or wolves when he wishes to have a successful hunting trip.[23] The buffalo hunt and its successful consummation are actually brought to life by the magical mask dance. The Indians, who wear buffalo masks, reveal the reality of the dance in that, according to their own report, they do not so much represent the buffalo as "become" the buffalo in actuality. The hunters who shoot down the buffalo in the dance are magically identical with the real hunters who will later carry out the actual hunt. Again, in New Caledonia the natives bury stones of the approximate size of ripe taros in the newly planted hills in order to insure an abundant crop. Here, too, the magic does not merely stop with the image, with the analogy; the stones have attributes which share a common identity with the tubers themselves.

This type of creative magic is carried out by means of various media: gesture, real objects, or even words. In New Mecklenburg, for instance, the following magical incantation is used to make certain the fruitfulness of the taro bulbs:

> "Moon . . . round!
> Child . . . round!
> Taro . . . round!"[24]

So far as a verbal reality is created magically by naming some objects, a reality which in its attribute is identical with the taro bulbs, the same attribute is endowed on the taros themselves.

The peculiar attitude which is at the bottom of all magic has

[22] Read, **266**, 218.
[23] Catlin, **173**, vol. 1, 144; Goddard, **196**, 21.
[24] Peekel, **258**, 91.

been termed "mystic." Lévy-Bruhl in particular has used this term in his monumental investigation of the nature of primitive thought. But in my opinion this term is inadequate and misleading. According to our usage, the word "mystic" means something pertaining to the mysterious, to the transcendental. As such, it is not relevant as here applied. Quite overlooking the fact that in the realm of magic no complete differentiation is made between magic events and natural events, the very state of mind commonly ascribed to the mystic is absent. The basic tendencies of magic behavior proceed out of a kind of thinking which, although deviating from the western man's point of view, is quite intelligible and in no sense is of mysterious import to the native himself. It is a type of thinking calculated to deal with syncretic and diffuse objects, a kind of thinking in which it is natural that the part should represent the whole and that the same attribute should be identified with more than one object.[25] It is natural that things should be mutable in essence and that several things should share a common identity. Only in higher civilizations, where natural and supernatural events are completely separated and where magic does not pervade the whole culture, is it possible for the specifically mystic experience to develop.

CONCEPTUALIZATION IN MAGIC.

The mental phenomena expressed in magic relationships and associations, the formation of concepts and abstractions in magic, the judgments and inferences of the magically dominated mind—all these show an origin in a syncretic and diffuse mode of thought. Concrete syncretic thinking is that in which the abstractive function has as yet not achieved release from the motor action and imaginative-perceptual activities. This thinking, so to speak, is implicit, limited to and enclosed within concrete, picture-like forms. It may be said that the ideas of the primitive man are materialized in his activities

[25] "Participation," to use Lévy-Bruhl's expression, is a natural and not a "mystic" attribute of the primitive mental life.

and in the things of his world with their properties. Little
distance separates such thinking from the sphere of mythical
and magical thinking. Magic thinking, too, is concrete, affective, and motor. For example, any magic "power" in nature
is somehow visible. It is from this principle of "magic concreteness" that the previously discussed creative magic ("magic
by analogy") is mainly derived. An Australian witch doctor
puts a bone, by means of which he would strike and destroy
his enemy, in a red-ant hill. The angry ants bite furiously at
the end of the bone and make it poisonous. Just as the ants
now run raging over the bone, so will the poison emanating
from it as bewitched run through the flesh of him whom it
strikes, and thus consume it.[26] The magic event is predominantly determined by the outer appearance. The identity between the image of creative magic and the subsequent real
event is made possible by the concreteness of magic thinking,
according to which the nature of an event or thing is determined by external form. The principle of the magic identity
of concretely similar things has an intimate bearing on the
genesis and growth of anthropomorphism. In its primordial
form—contrary to what it later becomes—anthropomorphism
is a magically conditioned "naturalization" of the personality.
In order to overcome nature, man, as it were, to some degree
transforms himself into nature. He *becomes* nature by virtue
of a unity of inner being and outer attitude.[27] An example
may clarify this point. In New Mecklenburg, during magic
ceremonies intended to bring rain, the medicine man scratches
the bark of a tree with a mussel shell, and this phrase is
chanted:

> "Rain, scratch wood! Come clouds, speak quickly,
>   Stand, call forth in breaking out in wind!"[28]

As the last words are spoken the sound of thunder is imitated

[26] Strehlow, **304**, vol. 2, 33.
[27] Werner, **141**, 23 f.
[28] Stephan and Gräbner, **299**, 121.

by a powerful vibration of the lips, and lightning is simulated by swinging the red lightning-fruit, as it is called, at arm's length. We can see here how the need for the magic control of natural events may lead to an anthropomorphic presentation of nature or, better, how man himself stands for nature, actually becomes it.

The highly concrete understanding of nature in anthropomorphism is, furthermore, present in any mythical attitude. Creative magic leads the primitive man to conceive and configurate natural phenomenà concretely. A concrete similarity of form between an image and the natural object frequently occasions a relationship of magic power and essence. When the Cora Indians represent clouds with cotton balls and clouds of smoke from their pipes during their fertility ceremonies,[29] it is plain that the magical identity of the natural object and its image is determined by a visible similarity.

But identifications are not always based on perceptual properties of objects, e.g., form. They are quite as much dependent on motor and emotional characteristics. And now another problem confronts us.

Earlier in this work we analyzed so-called "primitive abstraction." There is a "magically primitive abstraction" which corresponds to the concrete abstraction of primitive thought in general. By primitive abstraction we came to understand the determination of appearance in its global totality by means of conspicuous signs. Under certain conditions, therefore, it is possible that the chosen salient characteristics marking diverse forms may show identity.

Primitive abstraction, as previously demonstrated, may identify two objects magically on the basis of a similarity of form. But two such objects could also be thought of as identical on the grounds of an equality in the emotional-magical content. To the Cora Indians both flowers and stars are vital, eternally enduring, self-renewing entities and on this account—that is, because they show agreement in a certain emotional aspect

[29] Preuss, 261, vol. 1, xxiv, xxvii, lxxxviii.

stressed in the practice of magic—they are thought of as being identical. The magical goal of most of these ceremonies is to bring about a state of happiness. This emotional-magic idea expresses itself in the ceremonial identification of those objects which insure health, longevity, and the fertility of human beings, animals, and plants.[30] The Mexican Huitsholi consider the deer and the stars to be identical; in the magic ceremonies of this people the stars are hunted and slain like deer. On the other hand, they also identify the peyote, a variety of cactus, with the deer.[31] The peyote, too—from the standpoint of magic—is the sign of supernatural strength. A drink made from it affords a powerful and gratifying stimulation. The first peyote found on a long journey in October is shot down (ceremoniously) with arrows.

This magical-primitive abstraction which identifies through the emphasis, unintelligible to our way of thinking, of magically potent signs in things and persons, is therefore the source of a particular mode of conceptualization. The conceptual function fulfills itself—"exemplifies" itself in the precise sense of the word—whenever a series of objects is known as a class. In primitive thinking such an organization is concretely built up. This is true in so far as, in contradistinction to our scientific, purely abstract modes of conceptualization, there is an absence of detached, independent signs which serve as the guides and basis of the concept and, in cor.sequence, ultimately as the determinants of the class. It is the concrete and emotional relations between things which furnish the binding elements creating the conceptual unity of a class.

A classification grounded on a concrete emotional content continues to be effective in the realm of magic with the sole difference that the signs guiding the process of unification are magic-concrete and magic-emotional in nature. This means that whereas in the primitive sphere in general, classification proceeds in terms of outer, concrete signs, in classification ac-

[30] Preuss, **109**, 11 f.
[31] Lumholtz, **231**, 18 f.

cording to magic the external similarity is interpreted as a magical identity. When the Cora Indians think of clouds and feathers as being identical, when they consider fire, sun, and the blue-red tail feathers of the arara bird as constituting one class, there is indeed present a kind of similarity which might make this identification intelligible to the civilized man. And yet this Indian does not rely on any external equality to bind these objects together. To him they are as one because of an inner, magical equivalence externally expressed in the visible similarity of the objects.

This magical concreteness, uniting objects through an abstraction based on likeness in form, effect, or purpose, is ultimately capable of systematizing the whole of nature.[32] Proceeding out of the fundamental social-mythical division into two exogamous groups—"land beings" and "water beings"— the single clans and subclans of the Australian aborigines derive not only their totems, but a totemistic classification of all things and events in nature. Ernst Cassirer has brilliantly demonstrated that the magical-totemistic organization of nature is governed not by any kind of zoological, geographical, or mathematical principles, but rather by the specific aspect of totemism, by "totemistic abstraction," so to speak. The clan totemism of the Marind-anim of Dutch New Guinea, for instance, is a totemism that includes everything that exists. Everything in nature and all artifacts belong to one of the clans (*boan*). As Wirz asserts, the totemistic system is a universal classification which determines everything on the basis of a concretely visible or an emotionally felt relation to one of the totemistic elements. This universal principle even goes so far as to make it impossible to enumerate all the objects belonging to one class. Any new objects coming to the knowledge of the Marind will be readily comprehended by this totemistic "apperception." An ornamental tree with red blossoms imported from the outside instantly became integrated in the totemistic system. This tree entered the "fire-*boan*" because, as the Marind says, its

[32] Cf. Durkheim, **22**, Fr. ed., 50, 623; Cassirer, **14**, 25 ff.

blossoms are like fire. Such a systematization, or that of the Zuñi earlier described, is not an abstract analysis committed to some general, detached lawfulness. It is a system founded on the concreteness of magical and affective signs.[33]

And yet it would be erroneous to assume that this magical concreteness represents no more than a gradual intensification of a purely primordial concreteness. It is really more in essence. And with this we arrive, in conclusion, at the point where we must speak of the significance of this magical attitude for the development of thought.

A clearly defined meaning must be assigned to magical and mythical concreteness in the development of human thought. As a whole this magic concreteness is characterized by a peculiar antinomy which places it between a primordial concreteness and the abstract modes of thinking of an advanced mentality.

The intermediate genetic position of the sphere of magic is based on the fact that the concrete and emotional fullness of primitive thought is preserved, while at the same time, by the magical metamorphosis of thing and attribute, meanings arise from another source besides primitive concreteness, that is, as created by a centralizing "magic apperception." The genetic significance of magical-mythical apperception lies above all in its power to systematize. Long before the development of scientific abstract concepts of the world, creative magic (magical apperception) had formed relatively closed, universal systems.

CHILD MAGIC.

When we speak of the ontogenetic development of various forms of magic we must take into strict account the difference between a fully developed magic as it appears among primitive people and the magical tendencies of the child. The magic of primitive man is a phenomenon that is oriented in terms of his cultural pattern, a rounded, organized way of life. The magic of the child and the youth can occupy only an isolated position

[33] Wirz, 325.

within a cultural sphere radically at variance with its intrinsic tendencies.[34]

We must distinguish between an early and a later form of magic. The early form is but little different from any other primitive form of thinking and activity. In consequence it is difficult to determine whether it is a purely primitive organization, or one already oriented magically. The later form, in any case, may be thought of as "genuine superstition."[35] In the exposition which follows we shall enter into an analysis, necessarily brief, of the form of magic which appears at an early stage in the ontogenetic scale.

The small child lives as if in a shell, in an extremely conservative and intimate world marked by a concrete, unbreakable organization which occasions and demands rigidity of behavior. This fact is demonstrated by the frequency of the all-or-nothing reaction in the complex of events filling the child's life. We have seen that one specific exemplification of the law of an all-or-nothing reaction is the fact that in some forms of child behavior the sequence of events must proceed according to a most painfully prescribed order, and the habitual succession of acts must be fulfilled on the basis of a totality, instead of being divided into essential and non-essential parts.

We all know that during infancy children want to eat and be dressed in some particular, habitual fashion. In agreement with this attitude are those ceremonial rules and ritualistic practices of the child which endure long into adolescence, and may even continue throughout his entire life. These rituals may be so set that any neglect or alteration is felt to be a symbol of dis-

[34] The examples which are given are for the most part from an extensive collection made by the author in collaboration with Muchow, working with questionnaires.

[35] In the most extreme cases this later form appears to rise from an incipient inner need, from an inchoate anxiety in the face of the world, from the fear of injury to the person by oppressively felt daemonic powers as conditioned by the developmental transformations of the personality during adolescence.

ruption, of a state of affairs in which "something is wrong," and, still later, as an injury to the ego proper. We are unable to state definitely, however, just how and when the primitive all-or-nothing reaction evolves into the formal ceremonial, that is, when it becomes real magical behavior. A mother writes to Sully about her 2:7-year-old boy: "After I have kissed him and given him my hand I must also kiss his doll, which he calls his 'boy,' and which sleeps with him. Then I have to shake the doll's hands, and do the same to the four hoofs of a toy horse which lies at the foot of his bed. When all this has been done he rises in bed and begs, 'Kiss me again and say goodnight just once more.' "[36]

It would appear on the face of such evidence as this that cultistic ceremonies are already formulated at an early age. To me it seems extremely significant for the transition of the primitive form to one that has a symbolic meaning—i.e., magic formula and ceremony—that an overwhelmingly large part of the phenomena of childhood which have some bearing on this general matter should be linked with the manner of going to sleep. I suspect that the expectation of sleep, of the dream, and the mystery of the dark night encourage the formulation of rites which—originally simple rules to be strictly adhered to— come to have a symbolic meaning for the welfare of the child during his sleeping hours. In support of this hypothesis are some of the answers to the questionnaire Muchow and I used. One child clutched the corner of a pillow in his hand while going to sleep. A four-year-old girl held on to a corner of a certain piece of clothing. A boy between the age of three and five slept with a handkerchief under his cheek. A three-year-old girl had to have her handkerchief hanging over the edge of the bed. "When I was five years old," a nurse reports, "every night my mother had to give me a bright ribbon to hold in my hand, and it always had to be a brilliant color, or otherwise I could not get to sleep." Another woman writes: "I know that it was impossible for me to go to sleep unless my mother or

[36] Sully, 516, Germ. ed., 262.

father came in during the evening to tuck me in." Another nurse reports the following: "Three-year-old Ilse never went to sleep before she had pulled out her hair-ribbon at least three or four times. She kept right on crying until somebody came and tied it up again. And it always had to be the same red ribbon. . . . Ursula was never satisfied until she had balled her handkerchief in her little fist, and if she lost it during the night she set up a terrific howl."

Besides this formalized behavior there are many instances of verbal formulae serving similar ends that we might mention. One woman says that, when she was between five and eight years old she had to have the goodnight spoken in the form of a dialogue. It was "Goodnight, goodnight; adieu, adieu!"—this repeated three times. Another woman claims she remembers that during childhood the ceremony of saying goodnight had to be gone through three successive times. Since the age of three, a four-year-old girl said, every evening without exception, "Goodnight, sleep well, sweet dreams, about a sour pickle again. Mother, you must buy me another sour pickle!" A six-year-old child said a little verse every night: "I have my hanky and my Pucky [a little bear] and so now all's right; all the girls are in their rooms, so now goodnight, goodnight!" This curious custom continued until well into her tenth year. The goodnight formula as a dialogue is typical. For years on end two little girls used a verbal ceremony they made up themselves. The concluding word was "bogosho," which meant "goodnight." After this final word nothing more was said, or else the ceremony had to be wholly repeated. When a child, one woman had to perform a very involved and exhausting ceremony before going to sleep. She turned her pillow over one hundred times; she carried out the painful ritual even during the heat of the summer, although at the end she might be bathed in sweat. The characteristic child prayer easily becomes accommodated to this cultistic behavior. One child always felt compelled to say her prayers standing up in bed as straight and stiff as a ramrod; although, because of the lack of heat in the room, this was at times àn unpleasant procedure, nevertheless it had to be followed.

The child's desire to be protected by rules from the dangers of uncertainty at least partially explains his attitude toward the commands of adults, which are often endowed with an absolute significance. Sully remarks with complete justice that children have a tremendous belief in the commands of adults, in the sacredness of rules.[37] "I'm allowed to do this, but not that" is not merely the sign of superficial good conduct, but expresses the child's very need for order and rule.

One of the most fundamental preliminary conditions for any magic form of behavior is a highly integrated (syncretic) unity of world and ego. The world is separated only slightly from the ego; it is predominantly configurated in terms of the emotional needs of the self (egomorphism). But, conversely, the ego, seen from the opposite angle, is highly susceptible to the emotional stimulation from the milieu. The egomorphic view of the milieu means a "personalization" of things, of such a kind that things cease to be rigid, inanimate objects and become living, vitally effective entities. A genuine daemonism can arise on the basis of such ego- and anthropomorphism as soon as the emotion of intense anxiety begins to formulate the sinister elements of any situation. The Scupins report of their 2:3-year-old child: "Today we found our boy in the twilight of the bedroom, sitting up in his bed, his eyes staring fixedly at the stove. 'Look, the stove is making bäh . . . he's sticking out his tongue!'"—Katz, in his *Gespräche mit Kindern*, tells of one of his son's experiences of the daemonic: "His father is sitting near Julius who, in a tender, affectionate mood, is stroking his father's hand. While doing this one of his fingers chances to crook itself and lightly scratch the back of his father's hand. This frightens Julius terribly, and he asks his father whether he is hurt, and then explains that it was really the air and not the hand that had scratched him. He says, 'Is the air really bad?' And, when his father replies, 'No, the air

[37] Sully, **517**, 146.

isn't bad,' he goes on to ask, 'But why did the air's hand scratch you then?' " Such experiences of the sinister, which may become condensed in visionary forms, naturally occur often during the darkness of the night. The following instance is typical:[38] "It happened that every night I had to get up to go to the toilet. My grandmother always used to leave all the doors open. I would go by five different doors all right, until I came to the door of the red room. The moon shone in, the gardenias stood mustered all in a row, and in the corner was a large palm tree in a pot. I saw the palm tree coming at me I was unable to advance another step, and I could not cry out. This happened twice in succession. For many days I was stricken mute with fear, until finally I became sick abed with this fancy. The palm tree had to be given away."

This daemonization of the surrounding world is only the crudest and most obvious expression of a primitive unity of subject and object which, in a higher form extending beyond the period of early childhood, may become a consciousness of a fateful relation between ego and external nature that leads to magic practices. A more or less oppressively felt connection of the ego with a potent milieu occasions the sensation of a dependence of the human personality on this enclosing world, a world which can be mastered not so much by the employment of the technique of normal behavior, as by magic devices.

We must not be led to imagine, of course, that these same children are not ready at all times to make use of natural technical behavior. But it often happens that, in keeping with his whole response to life, the child feels that such means do not suffice. For example, a little ten-year-old girl learned her lesson well before going to class. She knew perfectly well that a properly learned lesson was an absolute requirement in the matter of getting good marks. In spite of this she was convinced that she could write well on what she had learned only if she used a special pen point and lucky penholder. For this child, then—quite outside the natural course of accomplish-

[38] From an answer to our questionnaire. The girl was nine years old.

ment—there was a magical relationship between the successful carrying out of her task and the pen, a connection beyond the technical aspect of learning. Such instances as this run directly parallel to certain phenomena of primitive life. The native who thinks in terms of magic may know that the poison he gives to his enemy is biologically effective; and yet he may also be convinced, fundamentally, that this technical effect, as we may call it, will not suffice, and that it is necessary that some magic power—the death wish, let us say—be added to it.

If the magic customs of the child are to be *systematically formulated* it must be borne in mind that the intimate relation between ego and milieu occasions the following two general effects: first, the dependence of the ego on a fatefully interpreted world, a world which is not to be mastered by reason or technique alone; second, as a consequence of the first, the evolution of magical activities with respect to both animate and inanimate objects of the fateful milieu.

On the basis of such a syncretic ego-world connection two kinds of magic activity are possible. The first may be thought of as the propitiation and shaping of destiny. The second is the questioning of destiny through some oracular device.

The guidance of fate can be accomplished by both immediate and intermediate means, and can occur in a positive or negative sense.

Direct magical attempts to influence destiny may take the form of wish magic or prayer magic. We know that it is the very essence of the child's mentality to impose the egoistic desires on reality. In the child there develops a profound conviction of the almost magical power of his own wishes, a phenomenon that Freud has termed the omnipotence of thought. Even an adolescent may believe that the sun, merely by wishfulness and a concentration of the will, can be drawn from behind the rain clouds which threaten to spoil some long-anticipated outing. "In my youthful years when I have been out walking," Goethe tells us, "the sensation of longing for some desired girl has overfallen me, and I thought long enough about it until I really met her." A special kind of wish magic is the utterance of the wish in the form of a prayer. The ceremonial attitude, the necessity of a definite formula on which the successful fulfillment depends, indicates that the child's prayers are often more or less a magic form of urgent request. "Through prayer everyone can have anything he wants . . . anything!" we are told in a certain woman's account of her childhood. As early as the age of three to six years there may be a definite prayer ritual. One must go to sleep, for instance, with folded hands in order to prolong the strength of the prayer throughout the night; one must say three amens at its conclusion, etc. We hear of a six-year-old who thinks of prayer as a magical protection against the maleficence of spooks. This boy is afraid of a little man who, so he thinks, haunts the house. Before going into the cellar the child crosses himself three times, and sings a hymn. Children also use the magic of prayer to ward off the terrors of thunderstorms. "When I had made my stepmother angry (at the age of three to six years), I had to go up to the attic and say my prayers to make sure that she would be mollified by my later plea for forgiveness."

An indirect, negative method of influencing fate is shown in the process of "calling down" something.[39] One must wish just the opposite in order to bring about the desired event. When one child between four and five years of age wants something particularly good to eat, he always thinks about sour black soup, a dish that he cannot endure. A woman says: "One day while out walking my five-year-old granddaughter brought me a raspberry that she had picked, and said, 'It's wormy, all right!' And then she leaned close to me and whispered in my ear, 'Grandma, I'm just saying that so it won't be wormy!'"

With these last examples we are out of the sphere of wish magic and into that of intermediary magic, the sphere of the

[39] For illustrations of this magic custom among primitive peoples, cf. Werner, 141.

magic ceremony and spell. These latter ceremonies represent an attempt to influence fate by some formalized gesture.

There is, then, a genuine "creative magic" (magic by analogy) among children and adolescents which exhibits a remarkable similarity to the magic of primitive peoples. The fundamental principle is that by the creation of some definite magic analogy the desired object or event is simultaneously assured in reality. Basically, the image and the reality consequent upon it are magically identical. A characteristic example of "creative magic" is the following: "Before any sort of examination or conversation with some superior person I would imagine the test or the conference to go off in a way most advantageous to myself. I presented myself imaginatively in the most favorable light, and I had the other person say everything that was pleasant for me to hear." The commonest form of magic by analogy is "achievement magic," a form which shows a close connection with the "oracular" type to be discussed in later paragraphs. In achievement magic an imaginative course of events is successfully carried out, and this is supposed to have a beneficent influence on the real happening that is to follow. If the consummation of the magic event is faultless, then subsequent success in the real situation is assured. Such magical achievements are often closely coupled with the ritualistic behavior of early childhood.

This sort of ceremonial behavior is especially common during adolescence, and almost reaches the status of a compulsive action. Everyone recalls how he was not allowed to tread on the lines in the sidewalk, and how he had to run his fingers over the bars of every grating he passed. This formalized behavior becomes a true magical activity when a mistake or an omission in the ceremony is regarded as unlucky, and successful accomplishment as lucky. These ceremonies are innumerable. In order to be "lucky," one child, for example, must repeat the text of an advertisement three times without stopping, another must say a difficult word ten times in one breath, while a third has to keep his eyes closed for a certain length of time.

The second main group of magic practices found among children and adolescents (as well as primitive people) may be termed the "magic of contiguity." The ego, which is susceptible to influence when brought into contact with magically potent objects in either a temporal or a spatial sense, may thus acquire desired or undesired qualities.

As a consequence of this magical notion, the things of the milieu stand in the closest relation to one another, one thing in "confluence" with another. The Scupins' 2:2-year-old child combed himself with a black comb, and said: "When Bubi combs himself with a black comb he'll get nice black hair!" After he had combed his hair for a time, he added with assurance: "Now I've got black hair!"[40] Many children are convinced that bruises or cuts can be cured by stroking or blowing. Sully tells of a 3:6-year-old girl who asked her mother to lay a large stone on her head so that she would not die. It seems that in this way she hoped to prevent herself from growing and hence from becoming old. Such forms of the magic of contiguity include magically effective names, things, places, etc., and so-called talismans and amulets. The use of the latter is especially common during the school years. One girl will never write her school work except with a certain pen; another will take her doll with her when she has some particularly important task to do at school, whereas still another has a certain bracelet for this emergency. There are children who put on lucky clothes for examinations. Again, the written work will be successful only if the child takes along a new blotter, if he avoids certain streets which represent an unlucky route on the way to school, etc.

A special form of magic is found in attempts to propitiate fate by sacrifice. The forms which this sacrifice take are as diverse as the psychological motives behind it. It may be the personal renunciation of something either material or ideal,

[40] Scupin, **502**, vol. 1, 180.

it may be the carrying out of an unpleasant act, self-humilia-
tion, self-castigation, and so on. The following are some concrete instances of this type of magic: "In order that my wish
to make a trip to the Königssee be fulfilled at the age of ten I
renounced, despite an enormous appetite, all but one of my
breakfast rolls. If I had eaten one more everything would have
been spoiled. But my sacrifices were not always injurious to
my health. Sometimes I held myself back from too much
gastronomic pleasure, or in some other way tried to play the
good boy. How often have I said to myself: 'Now, if you only
straighten up your dresser, you might get a summer trip after
all!' "

Two other important groups of magic ritual are those centered about the oracle. The psychological condition of any
oracle is a closely felt relation between the individual and all
his activities, and the natural or fateful series of events. Only
when he feels more or less clearly that he is somehow identified
with cosmic happening does he begin to evaluate certain acts
as the signs and symptoms of destiny. The oracular experience
of the child and the adolescent can be divided into two particularly important types: the oracle through achievement and
the oracle through omens. Either a certain achievement is
under the critical consideration of the author of the oracle,
and hence its success or failure is taken as a lucky or unlucky
sign, or the form or kind of certain happenings provides a sort
of augury without any intervention or volition on the part of
the person involved.

Among children of pre-school age oracles are seldom found.
They presuppose general psychic and intellectual abilities not
present at these earlier ages. In his *Confessions* Rousseau
tells us of a characteristic oracle of achievement. He tried time
after time to hit a tree with a stone. A miss boded ill, and he
considered a well-aimed shot to be the negation of a bad sign.
It is typical of such oracular activity that the tree had to have
a definite thickness so that the stone would not hit it too rarely.

The oracle by means of omens is to be distinguished from

that of achievement in all the forms it assumes during its transition into a genuine magic by analogy. There are countless varieties of the oracle of omens. If the trolley car on which one is riding to school goes very fast, there will be luck; if it goes slowly, there will be bad luck. It may be considered of oracular importance whether one trolley catches up to another, or whether one trolley car stops at fewer places to let off passengers than does another, or whether the passenger who gets out is male or female. One girl, for instance, took pains to note in church whether the name "Jesus" and the word "holy" were spoken more than ten times.

THE MAGIC FORMS OF PATHOLOGICAL INDIVIDUALS.

We have tried to show that magical thinking and activity are rooted in a primordial state of mind which of necessity leads to magic behavior and to a magical interpretation of the individual experience. This view is reinforced and given factual support when we consider how magical tendencies develop in certain pathological individuals whose mental structure exhibits primitive characteristics.

If the human mentality is so fashioned that the ego and its objective and subjective experience are shaped according to "syncretic" patterns, then it is logically understandable that there may develop a magically conditioned relation between man and man, between man and milieu, and with this a magical mode of grasping the world for the sake of the preservation and extension of the personality.

For example, schizophrenia is characteristically grounded in a partial transformation of the normal personality. There is a loss of the normal opposition of a closed, constant ego and a more or less stable and rigidly constructed objectivity.[41] The milieu invades the ego and, on the other hand, the inner experience spreads outward into the world of things. The milieu becomes daemonic and the ego susceptible to daemonism. This disturbance not only indicates the syncretic and

[41] Cf. Storch, **603**, 30.

diffuse character of the ego and the world of objects; it is also the condition of the specific forms of magic. Indeed, magic really becomes an almost unavoidable form of behavior, for the daemonism of the world occasions the need for some protection for the personality, which will take the form of defensive measures. This also accounts for the fact that the magic of the pathological individual seldom takes a positive form, but rather appears in the guise of a negative, defensive activity.

The magic of the psychotic exhibits a certain formal kinship to that of primitive man. Magic phenomena are relatively diffuse, but little centralized and differentiated, and much more syncretic in meaning.

The testimony of many schizophrenics shows that their conception of things and persons is much more diffuse in form than that of the normal person. For example, in the belief of some psychotics the magic strength emanating from a person is alive in every single part of this person, even in his hair or in his excrement; and on this account even the names of things may contain the magic energy of the real object. Here, too, in the psychotic sphere a typical word magic may develop in so far as the word possesses the magic potency of the thing itself. One patient, to illustrate, explains that he can make sausage by the use of the word "soup-soup."[42] Magic diffusion of this sort may proceed even further. Parts of single words can contain the magical essence of the whole word. Only on the basis of such an explanation does it become intelligible how the psychotic can take words apart and seek to express the magic nature of the whole by using one of its constituent elements. For one schizophrenic the English word "eye" in its full magic potency resides in the German word *Eiland*; that is, the single part diffuses its magic property throughout the whole.[43]

The objects of magic thought are diffuse not only in the sense that they are dominated by undifferentiated qualities-of-

[42] Schilder, 597, 68.
[43] *Ibid.*, 79.

the-whole, but also in that the strict delimitation and closure of the objects have degenerated. In our mode of thinking it is essential that things represent closed individualities and that they occupy a definite place in space. But this is by no means self-evident from the magical point of view. Here it is quite possible for a single object to occupy two places at once or, conversely, to shrink into nonentity. One mental patient declares that he has taken within himself all the heavenly bodies; they are hidden in his body, in his mouth and ears, and in his teeth. On questioning it appeared that nevertheless these same heavenly bodies were thought of as still existing in an outer world.[44] One of Storch's patients says, similarly, that he has the whole world within him.[45] "Even this room here, or the table?" "Yes!" "But that's outside you!" "Yes, that too." Schilder's patient can not only experience the same object at several places at the same time, but also cause an object (e.g., an apple) to vanish entirely.[46]

The magic meaning-contents of the primitive mentality also have their analogies in the magic experience of the psychotic. Meanings are syncretic. This syncretism is the basic sign of the magically experienced milieu. No longer is the surrounding world cold objectivity. The schizophrenic world becomes physiognomic and daemonic. The undifferentiated syncretic unity of objective and affective experience creates animate forms out of the things of the milieu, and in some way causes them to appear as vital and potent. The most indifferent things are invested with magical energies, and in the most radical sense the world is daemonized. The first stage ·in the schizophrenic decline is often characterized by a growing "queerness" in everything. Things come to have a hitherto unheard-of "deeper meaning"; they become sinister and alive with mystery, and any harmless object may be invested with signs and

44 *Ibid.*, 68.
45 Storch, 603, 80.
46 Schilder, 597, 68.

portents. For one patient, blackness on the door, for example, signifies death.[47]

The absence of any strict differentiation between the psychological and physical spheres causes both of them to be evaluated equally. Personal wishes and thoughts are accorded a value as absolute as the factual events of the outer world. Wish magic is often as clearly evident in the schizophrenic mental structure as in that of primitive man. It is characteristic of the schizophrenic that he should think not "in terms of reality, but in terms of his own desires."[48] One of Schilder's patients, for example, can have anything she wants merely by thinking of it. This woman constructs neologisms for her new mental activity. She says that she "presses down" and "shoots down" (*drücke ab* and *bumbse ab*). She explains that through thought she has "killed" the furniture, and that she can "kill" any object by mere thinking.[49] Another female patient believes that a magical instrument—a *Wünschelchen* (a little "wisher") —is necessary for the realization of her desires. This little wishing-rod is a span in length, and must be stroked as the wish is uttered in order to insure its fulfillment.[50]

The magical potency of thought, rooted in a syncretic diffuse unity of the egocentric and objective experiences, also leads to the practice of tabu. One schizophrenic will not "let out" her thoughts because she fears that by so doing she may injure others.[51] Thoughts, as this patient understands them, have lost their normal character; they are indeed phenomena produced by the ego, but nevertheless they have a separate, magically effective, thing-like existence in the objective world.

A salient characteristic of an undifferentiated syncretic mode of thought is its concreteness, which appears in this case in the specific form of magical concreteness. In the schizophrenic experience this concreteness is reached by a process of regression

[47] Storch, **603**, 85.
[48] Schilder, **597**, 53.
[49] *Ibid.*, 64.
[50] *Ibid.*, 60.
[51] Storch, **603**, 47.

from the higher level of the normal civilized man. Here the magical essence, the magical idea, appears as fused in an image, a concrete form; here thought is not abstract-conceptual, but concrete-magical. If, for example, a schizophrenic will free his fellow beings of "sin," he may proceed to do this by eating his own excrement. "To do the sinful for others" is not an abstract event for such a psychotic, nor does it entail the use of any sort of remote symbolism. It refers to a concrete reality. Kropophagy is something revolting and bestial, and therefore magically identical with all sinful activity.[52] Another patient, a catatonic, keeps the "wheel of the world" in motion by circular movements of his own body. This is a striking example of the concreteness of thought by means of which what for us is only a metaphor—"the wheel of the world"—becomes a real magical event, one stripped of the metaphorical.

The same is true of those magic-primitive states of intoxication which we have previously mentioned. When an experimental subject declares that crossing a street, setting foot on a new path, means the beginning of a new life, it would be false to interpret his words symbolically. "Movement, standing still, turning away, some disturbing act, a calling back of someone, a kiss—none of these stands for something symbolically, but possesses an immediate efficacy."[53]

In the magic of the schizophrenic, as in that of primitive people, the magical power exhibits itself as concrete, tangible or visible properties of the objects. One mental patient, for instance, has worked out a theory which discovers magic powers in colors. Colors are conceived as visible phenomena, but at the same time are thought of as magic energy. Colors make growth, and spend their power in thought. But this magical concreteness goes even beyond this. Certain specific powers correspond to specific colors and persons have definite colors according to their nature. Quarrelsome men are char-

[52] *Ibid.*, 51.
[53] Fraenkel and Joël, 553.

acterized by a dry color such as that of thin, sun-scorched grass, whereas jealous persons are marked by vivid colors.[54]

Visible qualities indicate magical beings and powers. Out of this basic condition of magical concreteness unfold not only positive magical activities, but also magical repudiations and acts of avoidance which correspond to the magical tabu of primitive peoples.

One schizophrenic, for instance, repudiates democracy because *Demokrat* (democrat) and *demütigen* (to abase) have a number of identical letters.[55] The similarity in the sound of the two words indicates a similar magical nature for the psychotic. This brings to mind analogous phenomena among primitive peoples. The homonyms and near-homonyms of tabu words must never be spoken, even though their meaning may, of course, be quite different from that of the originals. When a Melanesian uses the word "shed" instead of "house" because the word for house, *ima*, is a constituent part of the name of the tabu daughter-in-law, Tawur-Ima,[56] it is exactly the same as when a catatonic uses the word *ka-trauer* instead of *Kleid* (clothes) in order to avoid the verbal element *Leid* (suffering) that is a constituent part of *Kleid*.[57]

Magic by analogy, or creative magic, as we have termed it, rests in large part on that magical concreteness which identifies the magic essence with an external configuration. The transference of a tabu from a magically dangerous event to another event that exhibits a certain concrete similarity represents an instance of the workings of this magic. A schizophrenic refuses to take nourishment, saying that eating is "unholy." She must "think about evil circumstances in which anything might happen to her sexually."[58] Here we are dealing with a tabu emerging from a magical identification of the taking in of food and sexual conception. We also find this identification

[54] Storch, **603**, 42.
[55] Schilder, **597**, 66.
[56] Werner, **141**, 87.
[57] Storch, **603**, 84.
[58] *Ibid.*, 19.

of eating and sexuality in both the positive and the negative magic by analogy of primitive peoples.

Magic conceptualization as found in schizophrenics is concrete in a special pathologically primitive sense; that is, the abstract-analytical ideas of the normal civilized man become peculiarly remolded in magic imagery. A well-educated schizophrenic who came under Schilder's observation developed a theory of a "vis motrix" which animates all things as a primordial life force (see Fig. 53). The patient represents this "vis," this concept of magic power, by means of a wavy line, and then enumerates the particular forms in which this "vis" appears: life-ether-electricity-energy-will-judgment-

FIG. 53.—"Vis Motrix." Schizophrenic drawing. (After Schilder.)

understanding-instinct-geotropy-image-oscillation of ether.[59] The concreteness of this magical thinking is evident, in that the schizophrenic considers it a matter of course that such a concept as magic potency can actually be drawn objectively.

Up to this point we have concentrated our attention almost entirely on the syncretic form of mental *functions* within the magic sphere, on their fusion with respect to one another. Syncretism again becomes evident in the fact that the single *meaning contents* are not univocal, as in advanced thinking, but are frequently molded together. This fusion of several meanings in one uniform appearance often occurs in the magic attitude; the magic mode of conception works in such a way that a series of what would be diverse meanings at a higher level not only appear as magically identical, but may even be condensed in a single object. One female psychotic, for example, describes the disruption of her normal mental life first

[59] Schilder, 597, 31.

as the withering of a tree of life, then as the cutting into pieces of a snake, and then as the catastrophic fall of a starry constellation. In her fantasies she mingles fragments from one group of images with the group succeeding it.[60] It can be seen how the magic-dynamic identification of all these events creates the inner unity which permits condensation. Yet another magically condensed image is a catatonic's identification of himself with the "cow of Europa." In the mystic-religious image of the "cow of Europa" there are simultaneously fused many meanings related to the change of sex, to ideas of sexual generation and bestiality.[61] When a schizophrenic believes that many other words are latent within the one (magically effective) word, then the syncretic structure of magic phenomena has reached a verbal expression. For this particular patient the "good" word "lala"—that is, the magically effective word—holds within itself ninety thousand other words.[62]

It must be remarked, finally, that the multiplicity of meaning in magical objects and activities, their diffusiveness and interfusion, is related to an increased lability in form and content. In the magic sphere phenomena are labile, and this lability is extremely advantageous for the building up of the desired magical situation. Labile objects are much more easily reconciled to magical attitudes and wishfulness than are objective, constant things. However confused and broken the schizophrenic's notion of the world may be from the standpoint of the normal person, the meanings and objects, because of their lability, fit without any reluctance into the "systems" which he creates. As with the primitive man, the schizophrenic has "fixed magical apperceptions or foci," in terms of which the daemonic world is configurated into unity. One brief instance will show how a daemonic idea holds labile objects in conformity. A mentally disturbed philologist[63] suffers from a com-

[60] Storch, 603, 16.
[61] *Ibid.*, 17.
[62] Schilder, 597, 66.
[63] *Ibid.*, 78.

pulsion to self-destruction. The whole world commands him to carry out this challenge, and every object about him is twisted into conformity with the dominant idea. In the newspaper he sees an advertisement of the firm "Steigerwald und Kaiser." By a slight transformation of the sounds of these words he comes to *steig' er bald zum Kaiser* (may he soon ascend to the Emperor). The word *Kaiser* comes from the Latin *cadere* (to fall). Therefore the meaning of this phrase is: "to go up and throw yourself to the ground." As a result of his interpretation the patient tries to climb up and jump headlong from a ladder into the garden.

What a fundamental difference in the motives and meanings of primitive man's magic-mythical notion of the world and the daemonic concept of a psychotic! And yet, formally considered only, these mental phenomena are related. In both cases fixed magical ideas are present which order the world and its now labile, pliant objects into a cosmos shot through with fateful power.

BOOK III

The World and Personality

Chapter XII

PRIMITIVE WORLDS AND SPHERES OF REALITY

THE WORLDS OF ANIMALS.

It must be considered one of the fundamental errors of the older biological, psychological, and anthropological theories that the world was always thought of as identical for all forms of life. It was admitted that this identical world gradually became simpler, the lower the stage of development was, but nevertheless the same world still remained, that is, a so-called objective reality. Uexküll[1] was perhaps the first to attempt to demonstrate that each animal has its own qualitatively specific world, so designed that with it the animal forms a complete unity, an organism of a higher order. One of the most important tasks of modern biology is to determine the specific world pattern for each group of animals. Each animal species has its own world, which is the more qualitatively removed from the human world the lower the species in the developmental scale. The higher insects certainly live in a world in which optically perceived objects play an important role. But among the lower insects and the crustacea it becomes apparent that the contours of things slip more or less into the background. Bohn suggests by his experiments that *Carcinus maenas* lives in a world made up of lighter and darker spots, the contours of which are devoid of meaning. The further we descend on the phylogenetic scale, the more the optical world of colors and forms tends to disappear, and the more it tends to become transformed into a world of smells and mechanical resistances.

Since with the animals, at least, things are characterized by their functional valence, the different worlds and the

[1] Uexküll, **695, 696, 697.**

things in them should be defined in terms of functional value. In this respect one of the most promising experimental methods is that which Klüver has called the method of equivalent and non-equivalent stimuli.[2] For example, after a dog is trained to respond to the word "chair" by the act of jumping upon some particular chair, the problem is now to see how much the original object can be varied in size, form, etc., without changing the dog's original response. A great many objects are functionally equivalent to the chair, but others are not. Such a method of establishing equivalent and non-equivalent stimuli may solve a specific problem that can be formulated in this manner: "What is a chair in the dog's world?" and expanded to the general question: "What are the things of the dog's world in contradistinction to human things, and to the things of other animals?"[3]

A further problem deals with the different spheres of reality within one particular world. The "same" object may vary in meaning in different spheres. In the world of the hermit crab the cylindrical form of an actinia arouses quite different responses according to the changing needs of the situation. Uexküll describes three variations of the relation between the crab and the actinia. In the first, the crab has no actinia with which he can live symbiotically and which can protect him against the attacks of the octopus. In this event any actinia which the crab chances to encounter will have a "protection valence," and the crab will place the actinia on the snail shell in which he lives. In the second, if the experimenter removes this snail shell, the actinia acquires a "dwelling valence" and the crab tries to crawl within the animal, seeking shelter. In the third, when the crab is in a state of excessive hunger the actinia acquires a "food valence," and the crab begins to devour parts of it.[4] Howard gives many examples of reversals in a bird's behavior with respect to certain objects. These re-

[2] Klüver, **662, 65**.
[3] Sarris, **689**.
[4] Uexküll, **697**.

versals indicate that the world of a bird comprises different spheres defined by different sets of functions: a sphere of territory and movement within this territory, a sexual sphere, a nesting or brooding sphere, etc.[5]

The fact that a primitive world may be built up out of different spheres, each of which is a self-contained unity, is of special importance for developmental psychology. These diverse spheres are determined by different drive patterns among which there is little intercommunicability. One sphere succeeds the other like scenes on a revolving stage. Now the problem of the rigidity and constancy of objects appears in a different light. Since in poorly differentiated organisms the single spheres are more or less strictly closed off with respect to one another, and since an object is reacted to according to its attachment to a certain sphere, it is to be assumed that the meaning of the "same" object changes from sphere to sphere. Only when the spheres are not rigidly divided off from one another, but intercommunicate—where, in consequence, things can be grasped on the basis of different distinct aspects either simultaneously or as rapidly succeeding each other—is it possible to have an identity and constancy of things. Only in the human world, apparently, is there a full development of a relative constancy throughout changing spheres,[6] by means of centralizing intellectual functions.

A particular problem, and one that has been little investigated, is that of the pattern of "life space," or "home space." A stickleback's home space, for instance, may consist of a nest in which the young fish are raised. But beyond this nest, the "home" in the limited sense, there is also a "life space," a field about the nest which this fish will defend against other sticklebacks. Certain animals—the bees, for example—may have a "home" (i.e., the hive), but have no "home space" which they

[5] Klüver, 65.

[6] One might think, for example, of the relatively stable attitude of a man toward a woman with whom he shares different functional spheres (erotic, professional, social life).

defend against strangers. Magpies possess home fields which strange magpies are not permitted to enter.[7]

In conclusion, to illustrate the empirical method of determining the nature of an animal's life space we cite an experiment performed by Sarris and Uexküll in the Hamburg "Institut für Umweltforschung" (Institute for the Investigation of the Environment). This experiment deals with the dog's olfactory field.[8] During nineteen trips through a certain section of the Hamburg Zoo the spots where two males and two female dogs urinated were marked on a map. It was found that the male dogs were moved to urinate by certain optical signs. This was demonstrated by the use of a movable artificial "cornerstone." Urination, it was noted, might also be occasioned by olfactory signs alone (by the smell of the bitches' urine). The smell of the male dog's own urine tends to inhibit micturition, whereas that of a "rival" male intensifies the response. The mere presence of another male induces a remarkable increase in the flow of urine.

From this Sarris and Uexküll conclude that the male dog strives to act within a field of smell, and that he intends to dominate some particular area by the act of urination. The setting up of olfactory flags on optically prominent objects along the way gives notice to the canine world at large of the creation and extension of a (sexually emphasized) sphere of dominance. The coyotes, which are genetically closely related to the domestic dog, live on the plains where suitable optical signs are rare. Because of this, they make their own standards on which to imprint a private mark. Thus they will roll old tin cans to conspicuous spots and then vigorously urinate upon them.

The General Character of the Child's World.

The child's world is above all a *world of action,* a behavioral sphere in which everything is framed in terms of handiness

[7] Uexküll, 697.
[8] *Ibid.*

and unhandiness, of efficaciousness and inefficaciousness. Katz says that children approach nearly all objects with the questions, "What can I do with it?" "For what can I use it?" "Furniture which cannot be used for gymnastic exercises and houses in which no well-known acquaintances live hardly exist in the child's consciousness."[9] At the same time it is natural that this world of action, to whatever degree it may differ from the world of the adult, is continually changing at different age levels in accordance with a change in the basic attitude governing it. The Scupin boy at the age of eight no longer recognizes the sea which he knew at the age of four. At that time the sea was determined by different things-of-action. Such small objects as mussels and little stones, butterflies, and the wet sand ready to be molded into simple forms—these made up the world of the seashore for the four-year-old, whereas the eight-year-old conceives this same region as an arena for sports and swimming, and no doubt thinks of the tremendous flat surface of the water as an invitation to adventure.

The childlike world, moreover, is *ego-centered* and concrete; it is a world of *nearness at hand*. The younger the child the "nearer" it is, and the distance separating subject and object increases with age. As in the case of primitive people, the physiognomic character of the world is also an indication of its "nearness." Things are not fundamentally separated from the subject as substantial, external objects, but approach the subject in that they are characterized by possessing a kind of demeanor and active behavior which, under certain circumstances, may bring them to life. And the meaning content of this world is also egocentric, because it is so closely linked with the child's personal needs. If the child believes that the wind and rain come out walking to pay him a visit, or that the thunder roars in order to frighten him,[10] or that the happenings of a play are aimed at him personally—in all such instances the egocentrism and "nearness at hand" of all the

[9] Katz, 421, 226.
[10] Sully, 517, 61.

spheres of his reality are apparent. The first time that the Scupin boy went to a theater at the age of 5:8 years he saw a dramatization of a fairy tale, Grimm's "Snow White." "At first a little dwarf came on the stage and talked about good and bad children. As an example of the latter he mentioned children who sucked their fingers. Upon hearing this Bubi heaved a deep sigh, and asked in considerable anxiety: 'Why did the man talk about sucking fingers? He wasn't there when I was a little boy and sucked my finger.' He actually believed that the admonition was directed at him alone."[11]

The scale of values naturally changes not only to meet the demands of the current situation, but also with the age level. The nine-year-old Scupin boy, in raffling off his various possessions, valued a pocket mirror much less than his highly prized trick-toys; but as soon as he acquired a watch and chain and could observe himself, proudly decked out in his new acquisitions, in the mirror, this object immediately became very valuable, and he preferred it to all others. At an earlier age, girls often have preferences for certain pieces of clothing because of their "neatness" or "prettiness," whereas later on they will prefer other clothes that they consider "grown-up." The seven-year-old Scupin boy wants to look "tough," to have his pants as dirty and ragged as possible; at the age of eleven he wants well-pressed adult clothing so that others will think him a man. "Why do you always talk about looking 'nice'! I want to look like a young man!" he tells his mother.[12]

Events are not seen from the standpoint of things, or from that of other persons, but are interpreted according to their meaning for the child's own life. For the 7:11-year-old Scupin boy his mother's illness is a joyful occurrence because now he can sleep with his grandparents. Again at the age of 11:2 years, when talking about the recent recapture of Lemberg by the Austro-German army, he says plaintively: "Couldn't they have

[11] Scupin, 502, vol. 2, 35.
[12] *Ibid.*, vol. 3, 59.

captured Lemberg one day later?" so that the victory cele-
bration that followed would not have fallen on the same day
as his school holiday. The child's judgments of happenings
clearly reveal a scale of values that deviates radically from the
adult equivalent. If he receives a gift, it is not the gift's "objective" value, but its value in his private world that is the
important factor. The 8:7-year-old Scupin boy counts sixteen
things that were given him for Christmas, but leaves out the
new overcoat, gloves, and shoes. To his mother's protest he
replies: "Pah! those are just things you need. I'll just count
them as one, and then I'll have seventeen things." According
to his method of evaluation, the picture copy book which cost
twenty-five pfennigs is worth far more than these needed ar-
ticles which cost a hundred times as much. The adult's activities also have their place in this egocentric system of values.
At the age of 8:2 years this boy wanted to take home at least
twenty pounds of mussel shells and ten pounds of sand from
the seashore. "Why, you're taking mushrooms along, aren't
you?" he explained in the face of his mother's resistance.[13]

Perhaps the first attempt to analyze the child's world was
made by Martha Muchow in the Hamburg Laboratory.[14] The
first experiment aimed at defining the life space of children living in a certain section (Barmbeck) of the city of Hamburg.
These children (there were 100, from nine to fourteen years of
age) were asked to outline on a map of Hamburg those parts
of the city with which they were very well acquainted. They
were then asked to mark, with a pencil of a different color, the
sections with which they were superficially acquainted.

This experiment clearly demonstrates that life space is not
identical with geographic space. It is pragmatically defined by
function. Of course there will always be a partial congruence
of geographic and life space. For instance, the life space may
end at some such natural geographic limit as a canal. But

[13] *Ibid.*, 35, 47, 59, 102.
[14] Muchow, 461.

apart from any coincidence of this sort there are essential differences between the two categories.

As can be concluded from a number of the maps the parts indicating the life space are not bound together in a geographic continuum; there is a marked geographic discontinuity. The parts are bound together by the functional significance which they have for the life of the child. It is clear, further—and especially for younger children—that the center of the city space is determined not by any objectively salient feature, but rather by egocentric interest and need. The primary accent is usually given to the street where the child is "at home." This is "his street." It is the home section that the boy will defend against enemies from a "foreign street." It has been genetically demonstrated that the life of the younger child is almost entirely concentrated in and around his home street. The older he grows, the wider the extent of his life space; but the home street still remains the focal point. This life space is bounded according to a functional definition, and not geographically. Space ends where the child's activities end. For instance, one side of the street may be used for play, and the other not at all. The boundary of the life space may then lie along an imaginary line in the middle of the street. The other side may not exist, so to speak; it is "over there." A girl remarks in wonder: "The other side? But I could cross my heart that I was never over there in all my life!" "Near" and "far" are also defined functionally and not geographically. "Far" may be geographically very near at hand as, for example, the other side of the street in the case just mentioned. "Near" may be a playground at considerable physical distance from the home street, but in psychological perspective it is nevertheless close by.

Two further studies dealing with the structure of particular places have been made. The first is concerned with the structure of a certain place in Hamburg originally used for unloading canal boats. This place is sketched in Fig. 54.

For the adult the principal features of this place would be

the street, the path down, and the landing place. The child, particularly at an earlier school age, pays little attention to

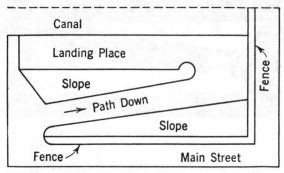

FIG. 54.—Sketch of a Hamburg Dock. (After Muchow.)

these elements. For him the main features are the wooden fence and the slopes. The fence which, for the adult, has the negative character of stopping movement, is for the child, exactly to the contrary, the very signal of movement. It invites the child to climb or jump up on it or over it. Similarly, the slopes, which would have an indifferent or negative value for the adult, represent a provocative field of action for the child. The two diagrams in Fig. 55 which show these different structures from the child's point of view and the adult's stand in a complementary relation to each other like positive and negative photographic plates.

It has also been observed that the functional meaning of the accentuated portions of this life space change during development. The child two to three years old frequently apprehends fence and slope as an area of independence, as a means affording a temporary, pleasurable separation from the mother standing on the other side of the rails. Children of kindergarten age use the fence as something on which to sit and balance themselves, whereas six- to eight-year-olds use it as a gymnastic device. For the three- to four-year-old the slope is something to

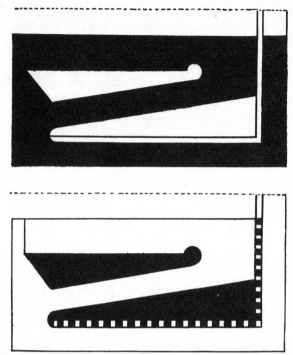

Fig. 55.—Structure of the Hamburg Dock from the Adult and the Childish Point of View. Black indicates the significant parts. (After Muchow.)

be apprehended in awe and curiosity as a field of danger. Somewhat older children try to master this danger zone by sliding down it on their seats. It is a "mountainous" region to children six to eight years old; they slide down standing on their feet, as if skiing, and then clamber up again to repeat the action.

A particular study was made of the functional meaning of a big department store for Hamburg children six to fourteen years old. This inquiry likewise tends to establish the fact that there is a fundamental difference between the child's own world and that of the adult. Moreover, it showed certain characteristic changes in the child's world at different age levels. Three age levels might be analyzed. For the younger child the department store is a huge field for action through which he can roam and where he can play games. Stairs, escalators, and elevators are of central interest, whereas little attention is paid to the goods themselves. For the nine- to thirteen-year-old the store represents a world of adventure filled with treasures. The child thinks of it as a kind of stage or fair. He begs continuously for this or that, collects all sorts of samples, rubber bands, advertising matter, and so on. Some children even jot down the prices of various goods and make a long list on a piece of paper. For the child between thirteen and fourteen years of age the department store is the "big world." One often sees a group of girls, for example, standing before a shop window dramatizing a discussion of what they would like to buy. Finally they enter the store. They are greatly pleased if the salesgirl treats them as potential customers, as full-grown ladies; and they walk circumstantially from counter to counter, pricing the goods, bargaining with much earnestness, and promising faithfully to come again. Within the anonymity of the crowd they can realize undisturbed their dream of an adult existence.

THE SPHERES OF THE CHILD'S REALITY.

The structure of reality as physiognomic and pragmatic, the "nearness" of this reality to the subject, involve a relative lack of differentiation so far as certain single spheres of reality are concerned. Considering this whole problem from the standpoint of psychological function, we find that two general spheres of reality appear to be rather clearly separated in the adult: the sphere of objectivity based predominantly on perceptual processes, and the sphere of fantasy based on imaginative processes. In the young child, however, there is a relatively close connection between perception and imagery. This is grounded, first of all, on the fact that the real percept possesses a great deal more of the character of an image than is the case with the adult. It exhibits that peculiar creative power which gives things "physiognomies" and molds the perceptual so that its form becomes related to that of the illusion. On the other hand, images are here much more perceptual in nature, much more "eidetic," than with the normal adult. Because of this, small children may consider an image not as something privy to them alone, but as an objective phenomenon. Miss Shinn's niece saw heat lightning for the first time at the age of two years. Later, when asked to tell what it had looked like, she shut her eyes, thrust out her arms, and cried: "It looks like that!"[15] Hence we see that the purely subjective character of imagery as standing in contradistinction to the intersubjective, generally communicable character of perception is originally not very clearly expressed.

For the child the reality of the dream and of the waking world are relatively undifferentiated. Children have to learn to distinguish between the dream and waking reality. At this stage waking reality often exhibits some of the characteristics peculiar to the dream; the events of the waking world, for example, are often immediately configurable through the emotions of fear or wishfulness. Some illuminating examples of this configurative power of the wish will demonstrate how much less well defined is the transition from the dream to the waking world of fantasy. A 4:2-year-old girl unintentionally throws her slate to the floor. I look at her angrily, and immediately she says in all seriousness: "The cat did it!" In this instance there was no jesting or playfulness. It may be said that the wish to put the blame on someone else realized itself spontaneously. (This is against all reason from the adult standpoint, because I had seen the whole occurrence clearly, and the child must have known this.)

The Scupins report a similar example with their son at the age of about four years. "Bubi's insistent demand to go downstairs with the maid was flatly refused. Apparently but little disappointed he trotted back to the kitchen, and we sur-

[15] Shinn, 505, Germ. ed., 12.

reptitiously followed him to see what would happen. We heard him say in triumph: 'Anna, Mother said that I could go!' When we admonished him severely for his lie, he looked greatly astonished, and suddenly cried out in tears: 'But you did say yes!' "

Another example shows the same attitude: "Bubi's mother, immersed in reading a book, told the boy to bring a message to the maid. She paid no attention as to whether he had carried out her order, but began to wonder when the girl did not appear. 'Yes, I told her,' Bubi replied to his mother's query. Again she told him to do the errand. To her surprise she saw that Bubi went only as far as the door, fumbled once or twice with the catch, murmured something to himself, and then suddenly turned around, ran to her, and said: 'I said it now!' 'But, Bubi, you didn't go there at all!' 'Yes, yes. I did!' he said, somewhat uncertainly."[16]

Apparently the realities of the child's waking consciousness are nearer to the *dream* in so far as their images are much more ego-centered and more often configured in terms of affect than is the case with the adult. It is because of this that we so often find instances of an unbroken transition from dream to reality.

Cramaussel tells of a 2:7-year-old child who complained on awakening that he had no "pan," or that his sister had taken away his vegetables for the soup; he cried as he awoke from sleep because he had lost his ball, or because he could no longer find his playmates. It was necessary to console him, and it always took quite some time to calm him.[17] Neugebauer's reports on her own son during the period between 1:11 and 2:10 years also demonstrate the realistic character of the dream.[18]

It is now interesting to trace the manner in which the dream gradually becomes a mere appearance in contradistinction to

[16] Scupin, 502, vol. 2, 10, 97.
[17] Cramaussel, 357, 62.
[18] Neugebauer, 467.

"real" reality. In time an intermediate reality is formed in which the dream image is indeed experienced as something thing-like, but yet as something clearly distinguished from waking reality. One small boy (according to Sully) asks not to be made to sleep in a certain room because there are so many dreams there. In this case it is apparent that the dream is experienced as something wholly real, but as a form of reality which differs from that of the rest of the child's world.

Piaget also finds this intermediate stage typical of the gradually developing sphere of consciousness: At the age of five to six years many children think of the dream as an illusory reality, one which is both a fiction and at the same time external to the dreamer himself, that is, in the room. Many children believe that the dream stays in the room. An eight-year-old boy knew that the dream was only imagined, but in spite of this he believed that it had a double existence—once in his bed, and again in the room. In bed: "C'étaient surtout mes yeux." But in the room it was the image which was "quelque chose." Another five-year-old boy says, "I, myself, am in the dream, the dream isn't in my head." A boy a year older says: "When you wake up the dream is in your head, but when you are asleep the dream goes out of your head."[19]

Carla Raspe has carried out experiments to determine what children think of the dream.[20] A ten-year-old girl says: "This is what I think of the dream. When people are good, God does not let out dreams, but when people are bad then he lets them come out." "I think that dreams are in a big prison during the day," another child reports. And yet another ten-year-old girl says: "When I dream I think it's just as if I were in the City Theatre, only I'm lying in bed." Hence the dream is indeed a reality, but a reality of another sort from that of waking consciousness.

In the course of the child's mental development there are,

[19] Piaget, 478.
[20] Raspe, 491.

accordingly, characteristic attempts to differentiate the sphere of the dream from that of everyday reality. These attempts are noteworthy in so far as the children admit that the dream has a different kind of reality, and is yet perceptual in nature. Only gradually does the child free himself from the thing-like character of the dream, and thus learn to recognize the dream world as an illusory, phantom realm.

Piaget[21] investigated the development of the child's understanding of the dream, and thereby established three different levels of interpretation between the ages of four and eight years. (1) The dream comes from without and is seen as external. It is not everyday reality, but it is nevertheless an objective phenomenon. And this objectivity can be of various kinds. Many children contend that other people can see their dreams, whereas others deny this. (2) The dream comes from within, but happens out there. For example, the child explains: "If you don't sleep the dream is in your head. While you're sleeping the dream comes out. When it's night, it's night, but when you sleep it isn't night any more." (3) Older children believe that the dream is "inside them," somewhere in their eyes, head, etc., and they also think that it stays in the body.

The young child distinguishes only vaguely, or not at all, between *aesthetic reality* and that of everyday experience. "While out on the promenade today Bubi (three years old) stared and stared at a marble statue. 'The poor man has lost his hand. The poor man is hurt!' . . . The boy (three years old) looked for a long time at a full-length photograph of his father, and then cried out: 'Why doesn't Papa come out of the picture?' . . . On the kitchen table lay a leg of venison. Bubi (4:9 years old) wanted very much to know what kind of animal the 'little leg' came from, and was told that it came from a deer, just such a one as the deer in his picture book. Right away he searched for his picture book among his other playthings, found the picture, and said somewhat reproach-

[21] Piaget, **482**, Fr. ed., 77 f.

fully: 'Why, look here. There's the deer, and the little leg is still on him.' "[22]

A four-year-old boy (according to Sully) saw a picture of some people going to church through the snow. The next day, pointing to the picture, he said: "Why, the people haven't been in church all this time, have they?"

An excellent example of the peculiar mingling of imagined space with real space is given by Katz: The boy says that a drawing of the summer home must be sent to the father in a letter. "Otherwise Papa won't know where we are," he explains. After he has drawn the house and the people in it he explains further: "Mother, you're small because we're so far away."[23]

In early childhood a similar confusion occurs over the images in a mirror. "When the mother asked Bubi [the Scupin child, 1:6 years old], who was sitting on her lap, 'Where is Mother?' he looked all about him, bewildered and at a loss. At last, catching sight of his mother's reflection in the mirror, he cried out joyfully: 'There she is!' "[24]

The sphere of a fictitious, *poetic* reality appears to be less differentiated from the reality of everyday life in the case of the child. At first the consciousness of fiction, of the artificially produced, is alien to his mentality. It is only slowly that an awareness of a created reality develops. In this event, too, as with the dream, an intermediate reality is built up, in so far as the fiction is thought of as being true, yet true in a different sense than everyday things and happenings.

We are told of the 6:6-year-old Scupin boy: "Although the concept of fairy tale has been repeatedly explained to him, he still believes that there is a far-off fairyland, where one can get to only after travelling many days and nights on the train. And now if something a little unusual is told him he asks doubtfully: 'Is that just in fairyland, or is it really where

[22] Scupin, 502, vol. 1, 140, 203; vol. 2, 69.
[23] Katz, 421, 138.
[24] Scupin, 502, vol. 1, 63.

we are?' The child is at a stage where he tries very hard to distinguish between the real and the fictitious."[25]

According to a survey of 150 Hamburg children made by Muchow and myself it is usually during the period between six and eight years of age that there arises a clear consciousness of the fictitious and artificial, of a purely phantom reality. This fits in with an observation made when the Scupin child was seven years old: "If he tells something that appears improbable to us, he breaks off short with a look of astonishment, and explains: 'That wasn't really so; I just made it up out of my head!' In other words, an increasingly strict distinction is arising between reality and fantasy, between the actually experienced and the imagined."[26]

But other than this there is another critical period during the development toward a separation of the fairy-tale reality from the "real" reality. This occurs at the time when children begin to reject the reality of the fairy tale, as something untrue or "silly," in favor of the adventure story, which satisfies imaginative needs without offending the sense of the real. The accompanying table, based on an examination of 300 Viennese school children, shows the curve of preference for stories of the Robinson Crusoe type according to years:[27]

	Age Level									
	9	10	11	12	13	14	15	16	17	18
Boys (%)	10	13	18	16	16	11	4	2	1	..
Girls (%)	..	4	12	12	10	6	4	1	..	..

The most extensive and intensive sphere within the child's world is that of *play*. This sphere is also relatively undifferentiated; it is a remarkable intermediate realm. We often conjecture as to whether the child is conscious of the illusory nature of his play, or whether he lives in this world as he does in everyday reality. This question is erroneously con-

[25] *Ibid.*, vol. 2, 184.
[26] *Ibid.*, 218.
[27] Bühler, 350, 219.

ceived; it is cast in terms of the experience of the normal adult. A full consciousness of "everyday reality" does not exist at all with the younger child, and therefore it cannot be set in opposition to the reality of play.

We can be sure of but one thing—the child lives completely in his peculiar world of play. The external world, which will not bend to suit the demands of the game, is either utterly ignored or felt as highly disturbing. It can be demonstrated, furthermore, that there are transitional stages between the reality of the fully awakened consciousness and that of the child's play. These intermediate stages appear in so far as serious natural needs find satisfaction in play. On the other hand, reality is often remodeled in terms of play to fit the needs of the child.

For example, my four-year-old nephew sees an illustrated paper which interests him greatly. Immediately he says: "You gave it to me, didn't you?" And without waiting for my answer he dances in joy around the room, shouting, "My uncle gave it to me . . . he gave it to me!" All smiling, he runs to each person in the room repeatedly crying out that I had given it to him. In this next example from the Scupin diary we again recognize the play-like, undifferentiated character of the child's everyday reality. "When the two-year-old boy got his breakfast roll without butter he took his knife and ran it over the roll exactly as if he were spreading butter on it. He then explained with satisfaction that the roll was now buttered, and eagerly ate the bread which a moment or two before he had professed to despise."[28]

We see, accordingly, how the everyday experience can be playfully refashioned through emotions of wishfulness. In this respect there is no fundamental difference between the reality of play and that of everyday life. And, on the other hand, play may be intimately related to ordinary reality in a similar manner.

A four-year-old girl and another who is a year and a half

[28] Scupin, **502**, vol. 1, 177.

older have a little friend whose name is Lili. Lili is sick at present, and they make believe that they miss her very, very much. After some time they begin to play a new game, "Lili is sick." They take turns in identifying themselves with Lili. The reason for this game, in part at least, is the desire to have their absent playmate with them, a wish that is spontaneously expressed in a dreamlike reality where such identification is possible. (The psychoanalytical school has rendered a great service in establishing the relation between identification and need. Freud tells of the case of a little girl who identified herself in play with her kitten after it had died.)

The intermediate character of play reality as it oscillates between fantasy and everyday life is clearly illustrated in the case of the 6:2-year-old Scupin boy.[29] He is playing in the sand with a little girl. The girl's governess is angry with the children because they are getting out of hand, and she takes her charge away. But once again the children draw close to each other. "Is she always like that?" asks the Scupin boy. Ingeborg nods. "Aw, if I only had my pistol here! I'd like to shoot her dead. Then we could play together." He has taken up a bit of stick, and aims it at the enemy's bench. "Wait . . . I'm shooting now. Bang! Now she's dead . . . there she is on the ground . . . come on . . . come on . . . let's bury her!" The piece of stick which has just served as a pistol now becomes the defunct governess, and a ceremonious burial ensues. And then the nurse says abruptly: "Ingeborg!! . . . just see how you look!" . . . and thereupon snatches the child away. The nice game is utterly spoiled. The boy's face, which has just been bright with triumph and joy, becomes amazingly transformed. In profile it looks like a nutcracker—the jaw thrust out and the teeth clenched. He stands there, rooted to the spot, and stares after both of them. He makes a rude gesture, as if he were going to throw a vengeful handful of sand after the governess. "You . . . you . . . ! You're supposed to be dead," he mutters.

[29] *Ibid.*, vol. 3, 13.

We must think of the spheres of play and reality as originally but little separated, since they both exhibit like characteristics; but the older the child grows the more he becomes aware of the fictitious character of his play fantasies. A sign of this development is the fluctuation of his attitude toward the creations of his own fancy.

"The constant fluctuation between fancy and reality [of the 6:7-year-old Scupin boy] is strange indeed. An example: The maid, while straightening up the room, let the beloved rubber parrot fall to the floor. Bubi squinted hard, trying to hold back the tears that have flooded his eyes. 'You oughtn't to throw my parrot on the floor all the time, you old Clara!' he says. 'That hurts him, and if you do it again I'll throw you on the floor, too . . . and then you'll see.' During the afternoon of the same day he asked his usual question: 'What shall I do now?' In order to encourage him to play we answered: 'The parrot will wonder why you don't play store-man any more.' To this Bubi replied at once, saying: 'The parrot isn't wondering at all, for he isn't alive.' "[30]

Let us return once more to the main problem. What is it, at the bottom, that occasions this slight differentiation of the spheres of reality? I have already remarked that the usual question as to whether the reality of play is taken "seriously" by the child is wrongly framed. If the child is immersed in this reality, lives in it, there is no sense in applying the concept of "seriousness." "Seriousness" has meaning, obviously, only as the diametric opposite of "playfulness." But it must be assumed that for the child play is originally neither "serious" nor "playful." At first he has no concept of either, and makes no such distinctions. Both are intermediate spheres which come into simultaneous being, and are gradually differentiated during the course of ontogenetic development. The grounds for a relative lack of differentiation among the spheres of reality are, I believe, the following: The mature spheres of reality are determined in two ways—by subjective behavior and ob-

[30] *Ibid.*, vol. 2, 188.

jective signs. Any object of art, for example, belongs to the "reality of images" because we behave aesthetically and not practically with respect to the artistic image, and because, on the other hand, the image exhibits certain objective signs (space is built up of colors and lines on the flat surface, the actor speaks in his typical dramatic intonation or in verses, etc.), that set it apart from anything in everyday reality.

The child's spheres of reality (and often enough those common to the naïve adult) are essentially emotional-reactive, less markedly characterized by an awareness of objective qualities, and in consequence of this less differentiated. When a child caresses her doll, she is not thinking whether the doll is alive or not. The intellectually intelligible objective signs are here more or less irrelevant. Because of this the child can give herself without restraint to maternal instincts. Adults also may react in this same way to their milieu. One often behaves toward small children, or toward animals, in such a way as if the infant or animal could talk back, as if the other being could understand every word of what is being said. But in this case, too, there is really no intellectual assumption that the small child or animal understands. One merely reacts emotionally as if he were dealing with an understanding mentality.

And now we begin to see exactly what the doll means to the young child. A piece of wood that can be a doll is not imaginatively completed in such a way that it acquires real eyes, a head, etc. These are all concrete signs which do not come into play in the specific child situation. The child reacts to the doll *qua* a living being, and it is on this account that the doll has the affective significance of a living person. The doll has become the child's own child.

The differentiation of a serious, everyday reality from the reality of play occasions a more or less rapid development. We must always bear in mind that this differentiation proceeds from the child's undifferentiated grasp of the forms of reality which confront him. More precisely, the process of differentiation does not occur first with respect to the concrete-objective, but rather with respect to the behavioral. In the world of play the child adopts another attitude almost unconsciously or instinctively, without, however, being actively aware of the objective distinction between reality and play. For example, in the play sphere he is more productive, and his gestures and actions are different from those of his everyday behavior. If the doll were actually alive, then it would have to be dealt with differently, and the child would behave differently.

In such a way, then, play and everyday reality become differentiated in the child's total behavior, even though the child need not be consciously aware of the difference. For his instincts and emotions which give to a piece of wood the value and meaning of a doll child are just as real and deep in themselves as are those other instincts and emotions which are related to natural objects. The child at play is completely integrated within the reality of play, and during the play activity knows nothing of any other sphere.

However, the older he grows, the more he becomes accustomed to paying attention to objective-factual signs, and in consequence to the disparity between objects in play and those of the real world. This results in a general awareness of the difference between the two realities, and more and more the world of play becomes the conscious sphere of pleasant, wishful illusion.

In the course of genesis the opposition between the fictitious behavior of play and the seriousness of reality is clearly defined. This behavioral opposition in time develops into a distinction within cognitive awareness. When the 6:7-year-old Scupin boy could not put his soldiers into his toy railroad carriage because the opening was too small, he was at first greatly taken aback, but soon got around the dilemma by saying: "You see, I'll just make believe the soldiers are really in the train; they really aren't there, but I'll make believe." Before this, his mother writes, he was immediately put out if anyone expressed the slightest doubt about his imaginings. In the verbal usage of the child this new fictive attitude becomes clearly expressed when, often quite unconsciously, he begins to use such phrases as "just like" and "as if." For example, the 7:1-year-old Scupin boy said, speaking of a thunderstorm, "It looks just as if God had a big piece of flint in his hand."[31]

The deliberate lies of children, the humorous, joking manner with which the older child grasps the physiognomic and anthropomorphic, and finally the contempt which he shows for the fantasies of the younger are all special mental attitudes through which the childlike physiognomic world is dissolved, and through which, again, the difference between illusion and reality becomes fixed. The Scupin boy, for instance, while at the early school age, still personified frequently, but for the most part only in humorous situations. At the age of 7:8 years he was asked whether he had had gymnastic exercises in school the day before. Instead of answering with a simple yes or no he acted out a whole comedy. "Exercises? . . . Let me see, I'll have to ask somebody. (He taps his head.) You, Mr. Head, do you know whether we had exercises yesterday or not? What! You've forgotten! Come on, now, think it over." And now he pauses for a time to give his head a chance to think it over. "No? We really didn't have any exercises? Thank you. Goodbye. (To his father.) You see, Papa, Mr. Head says that we didn't have any exercises!"[32]

As the spheres of reality become differentiated with respect to one another through the child's release from his uniform, diffuse reality, there is at the same time an internal differentiation within the regions of each sphere. With "serious" reality especially there appears a diversity of regions. And these intra-differentiations come predominantly into being through differential behavior, rather than in any intellectual way. The school world and the home world have their specific lawfulness, a lawfulness which the child does not think of so much concretely as a set of play rules given him to guide his behavior. He will respond differently to the same punishment, depending on the circumstances in which it is administered. A box on the ear in school means nothing at all to the 6:6-year-old Scupin boy, whereas at home he cannot endure the smallest reprimand without showing deep injury.[33]

[31] *Ibid.*, vol. 3, 20, 25.
[32] *Ibid.*, 32.
[33] *Ibid.*, 18.

It is in this manner that the plurality of milieus develops, above all because of a plurality of sets of behavior in which the specific lawfulness for each region of reality is present, more implicitly than explicitly, more emotionally and behaviorally than rationally.

THE PRIMITIVE MAN'S WORLDS AND SPHERES OF REALITY.

, *General Characteristics of Primitive Worlds.*—Primitive reality is above all a world of behavior, a world in which everything is seen as gesture, as it were—physiognomically—and where everything either personal or thing-like exists in action. It is not a world of knowledge, but one of deed; it is not static, but dynamic; not theoretical, but pragmatic.

Such a world of *dynamic powers* has been described very impressively by Radcliffe-Brown in a study of the primitive Andaman Islanders. Social life here is a process of complex interactions of powers present in the society itself, in each individual, in animal and plant, in the phenomena of nature, and in the world of spirits. On these powers the well-being of the society and its members depends. In any food which one may eat there is a power, a potential danger; during sickness, dancing, etc., one becomes exposed to various powers.[34] Radcliffe-Brown's description holds true for the higher Indonesian cultures. The Balinese feel themselves embedded in a natural power field, a "life space" penetrated throughout and structurally determined by various powers. Day and night, therefore, they must be aware of their proper orientation within this field of dynamic powers. There are three conventional postures that are permissible: standing erect, being seated, and lying down (asleep). If one should stumble while awake, and thus fall to the ground, he thereby becomes vulnerable to malevolent forces. Children never crawl, swing, or stand on their heads. Since north (*kadja*=mountain) is the sacred pole, and south (*kelod*=sea) the unholy one, every Balinese sleeps with his head either north or east, since any other direction

[34] Radcliffe-Brown, **265**, 307.

is incorrect and dangerous. To lose one's orientation means to be lost (*paling*) in the literal sense.[35]

Primitive reality is characterized by its extreme *pragmatism*. It is not that which is real which works, but rather that which works is real. Malinowski makes this pragmatism very clear in the following statement: "The outer world interests the primitive man in so far as it yields things useful. Utility here of course must be understood in its broadest sense, including not only what man can consume as food, use for shelter and implement, but all that stimulates his activities in play, ritual, war, or artistic production. . . . When moving with savages through any natural milieu . . . I was often impressed by their tendency to isolate the few objects important to them, and to treat the rest as mere background. In a forest a plant or tree would strike me, but on inquiring I would be informed, 'Oh, that is just bush.'. . . Everywhere there is the tendency to isolate that which stands in some connection, useful to man, and to bundle all the rest into one indiscriminate heap. But even within this tendency there is visibly a preference for isolated small, easily handled objects. . . . In the landscape, the small details are often named and treated in tradition, and they arouse their interest, while big stretches of land remain without name and individuality."[36] Radin above all others of late has subjected the pragmatic character of primitive reality to a searching analysis, and clarified it by a series of striking examples. One recalls the words of a Fiji god who, according to tradition, said to a fellow god: "When men no longer believe in us, we shall be dead!" This means, of course, that only through ceremonial activities, through ritual or belief, do the gods exist in reality.[37] Two other instances indicate this same thing. An Indian deliberately lied, saying that a god had given him the magic power to cure a sick relative. When this relative actually became well again

[35] Belo, 158.
[36] Malinowski, 96, 331.
[37] Radin, 111, 244.

some months later, the Indian said: "When I heard this I was astonished, and not sure whether after all I had not been blessed by the god." Again, in order to insure the success of a war party every Indian must be endowed with supernatural powers by his god. Without this warrant and blessing an Indian nevertheless managed to kill his enemy, and returned home a conqueror. Although this man's father knew that the god had not given his son permission to venture on the expedition, the fact of victory convinced the father against his better judgment that the authorization for a foray against the enemy had been granted.[38]

We can furthermore define this primitive world in terms of personal *nearness*. The world of the man of advanced mental development is marked by "distance." The subject is fundamentally separated from objects as things and from persons as "you"-entities. The road to knowledge of the world is endless. But the primitive man's world is near at hand. In many respects objects are of the same nature as people. They have a physiognomic character. The individual himself is to a great degree bound up with the other persons about him. There is a definite feeling of unity of life with plants and animals throughout the whole primitive world.[39] Even the sphere in which gods or ancestors are thought to exist is actually close to mundane existence. A real transcendental sphere is found nowhere in the primitive world; life after death, for example, has the same general characteristics as life before death.[40]

The order and the lawfulness of this world are also "near at hand." In the most primitive societies where there are no "learned" witch doctors, magicians, or priests, man learns these laws and discovers their meaning by the simple process of growing older, of becoming mature. The primitive man can grow up into a preformed world, whereas the man of advanced mentality—in the conflict of the generation—must for-

[38] *Ibid.*, 29 f.
[39] Gutmann, 201; Junod, 216, vol. 2, 521.
[40] Rivers, 115, 48.

ever seek anew and create his own forms. The world of the primitive man has a traditional, fixed character. In this world he lives like a snail in its shell, a shell which can scarcely be changed and which closely circumscribes the body within. So close is this world to him that he may, so to speak, feel out its structure and limits. This world is free from any sort of revolution. In its very essence it precludes any transformation of status. When the European revolts against existing custom he may run the risk of reprisal or of ridicule; but if the primitive man should do this he would cut off his own life. He must either fulfill himself in the society in which he lives, or die.[41]

Primitive Spheres of Reality.—A world in which all that is real is determined by the dynamically effective is necessarily more uniform in structure than our own world, that is, one in which the separate regions of reality—the region of practical, everyday life, of religion, of art, of science, and so on—are differentiated according to specific aspects. In such a world, where everything is "near at hand," these regions of reality are themselves characterized by greater propinquity with respect to one another. Primitive societies exhibit to only a slight degree the workings of the principle of differentiation of *social* function when compared to advanced civilizations.[42] The secret organizations of Melanesia afford an excellent example of societies in which many different sociological functions are bound into one. Such an association may have a religious significance as representing a ghost cult. At the same time it may have a political meaning. Wherever these organizations are found in Melanesia there is nothing which can be called chieftainship proper, the place of the chiefs being taken by men of high rank in the organization. The rank of chief is attained by successive steps of religious initiation. There is, moreover, an economical meaning in these organizations, arising mainly from the complex system of payments that accompany the initiations. Money has its chief function in con-

---

[41] Radin, 111, 42.
[42] Rivers, 114, 5.

nection with this type of secret society; often the society will control individual ownerships. Finally, they may also be said to have an educational function. In many cases the process of initiation is not only a period of education in the general knowledge of the community, but is also an education in special arts, the manufacture of domestic implements or weapons, for instance.[43] There are similar organizations in West Africa.

The *magic-cultistic* activity in such a pragmatically fashioned world is not essentially separate from profane affairs. Both are fundamentally coordinated by the pragmatic goal. "Thinking and acting," says Baldus of the Chaco Indians, "are not divided into sacred and profane categories. To swing a rattle for Eshetewuarha, the mother of daemons, is a business just as much taken for granted as cutting wood for the white people. The white man gives shirts, iron, and beans, whereas Eshetewuarha furnishes a tasty meal from the flesh of some wild animal."[44] Malinowski says essentially the same thing of the Trobriand Islanders of New Guinea. "The natives realize that on sandy or stony soil neither yams nor taro could ever grow. At the same time they attribute the supreme fertility of some districts to the superiority of one magical system over the other. The way of magic and the way of garden work are inseparable. The natives will not try to clean the soil by magic. Magic is based on myth, practical work on empirical knowledge. There are magical means of agriculture like miniature fences, certain horizontal sticks placed on the *kamkokola* (a large pole erected in the garden); there are practical means of agriculture like the ashes which fertilize the ground."[45]

The difference between *subjective* and *objective* reality is certainly not so clearly defined in the primitive as in the higher civilizations. One salient difference in the advanced world is the intersubjective character of the percept. But in

[43] *Ibid.*, 125 ff.
[44] Baldus, 156, 114.
[45] Malinowski, 235, vol. 1, 75.

primitive civilizations there is a widespread belief that an individual may be able to "see things," and therefore have a percept which is peculiarly his own and no one else's. The capacity for having "visions," for instance, is the basic characteristic of all the forms of magic and religion of the North American Indian.[46] Psychologically speaking, the reality of the vision has at once both subjective and objective properties. In its material vivacity the "vision" is like any other objectively conditioned percept, but it also has a distinct subjective character. "Recorded experiences from every part of North America all go to prove that a feeling of significance, a 'thrill' of greater or lesser intensity, is the distinguishing mark of the vision."

The *dream sphere* is similarly lacking in differentiation, and is situated midway between subjective and objective reality. Anywhere in the primitive world it will be found that the dream can assume an objective significance. Some examples, which could be supplemented at will, may illustrate this phenomenon.

A Dayak (Borneo) once dreamed of the unfaithfulness of his wife and, upon waking, punished her for her misdeed.[47] A whole village of Bororos (Central Brazil) wanted to flee because one member of the tribe had in a dream seen enemies slinking about.[48] And, similarly, among the Karagas (Brazil), when anyone dreams that one of his relations is dead he immediately gets into his boat and hurriedly paddles to the person's home to find out if his dream is true.[49] The dreamer can visit strange places in the dream. He can enter into the realm of the dead.[50] Among the North American Indians the dream is the source of the instruction in the supernatural given to the youth of the tribe. The dream is a means—as with the superstitious individual of our own culture—of informing men of

[46] Benedict, **159**, 43.
[47] Roth, **273**, vol. 1, 230.
[48] Steinen, **297**, 340.
[49] Krause, **225**, 332.
[50] Codrington, **176**, 277.

the will of supernatural powers. A naïve belief in the reality of the dream merges without a break into a belief in a magic reality. When we hear, for example, that among the Kai people of New Guinea a man who has had sexual intercourse with his neighbor's wife in a dream must make penance for this transgression,[51] we can readily see how naturally and inevitably a belief in the magical power of the dream must develop out of a belief in its reality. When a Cherokee Indian believes that he has been bitten by an animal in a dream he goes through the same healing ceremony as if this had actually occurred.[52] The Berens River Indians believe that cannibalistic monsters can be created "out of a dream" by a sorcerer and placed in the world to perform malignant deeds.[53] In the realm of magic the dream is intimately connected with reality. In this respect, according to the belief of many primitive peoples, it is possible to "realize" desired events merely by dreaming of them. When the Australian aborigine of Queensland wishes to kill an enemy it is sufficient, to his way of thinking, that he dream of the person's death.[54]

The dream not only may be inseparably fused with reality, but in spheres of advanced magic it may even become a superordinated magic reality, one which controls ordinary everyday events. Among the Blackfeet Indians, for instance, magic songs and magic drum rhythms which rule the world are discovered in the dream.[55] Among the Shoshones similar dreams unite men together in a secret religious alliance. The Arapahoes believe that during fasting and solitude snakes enter into the body of the dreamer to endow him with superhuman powers.[56] Again, the sick Dayak of Borneo is believed to be cured in the solitude of the mountains by daemons which ap-

[51] Neuhauss, **254**, vol. 3, 113.
[52] Mooney, **250**, 352.
[53] Hallowell, **205**.
[54] Roth, **276**, Bull. 5, 106.
[55] Wissler, **326**.
[56] Kroeber, **227**.

pear to him in his sleep.[57] When the Assiniboine Indians dream of an animal, it is sacrificed as a result and they can no longer eat its flesh.[58]

The *play reality* of the primitive man is not as detached from everyday life as it usually is with the man of advanced culture. It is a commonplace in all parts of the primitive world how quickly a joke can become a serious matter, even as it does with children of our own culture. This sudden seriousness may represent an unbroken transition from the sphere of illusion to that of everyday reality. We hear how, among aborigines all over the world, war games may lead to bloody conflict. It is reported, for instance, of one of the most primitive tribes that exist—the Veddas of Ceylon—that war games often lead to actual fighting.[59]

All this brings us to the problem of *aesthetic reality*. It is characteristic of the primitive world that there is no aesthetic sphere *per se*, that art is closely united with the social, political, and religious life of the tribe.[60] We can scarcely imagine how deeply a song, for example, may be embedded in the whole complex of the individual and tribal existence of a primitive society. Dorsey, speaking of the Pawnees, remarks that songs and legends may constitute a special part of the life of their owner. A young Pawnee explains: "I cannot recite all my songs for you, since I'm not ready to die." An old Pawnee says: "I no longer care about living, so there is no reason why I should not recite everything to you."[61] It is plain that giving up the legend is tantamount to relinquishing a part of the very personal existence.

Ancestors, daemons, and gods actually come to life in primitive sculpture. Among primitive peoples the sculptured representation of an ancestor is the deceased himself who continues to participate in the life of the community, is spoken to, has

[57] Roth, **273**, vol. 1, 185.
[58] Lowie, **229**, 47.
[59] Sarasin, **278**, 531, 537.
[60] Cf. Werner, **143**, 142.
[61] Dorsey, **185**, xxii.

food set before him, and is consulted for advice. Perhaps nothing throws more light on the real life of some tribal sculpture than the fact that it may be ceremonially initiated into the life of the community. In the Marquesas, as in some other parts of Polynesia, a song of creation is sung which introduces the "newly created" image into all that already exists. The same is true of the masks of the Congo Negroes, which are ritually born into the tribal life.[62]

It is almost needless to dwell on the fact that the primitive drama is fused with the whole tribal existence. Throughout all primitive civilization the reality in which the dramatis personae live and move never reaches a point where it becomes a self-contained aesthetic sphere. Nevertheless there can be observed various stages of development in the general direction of establishing a difference between everyday life and dramatic reality. This development may be illustrated by the dramatic performances of the Vedda tribes of Ceylon as linked with different, intra-tribal stages of culture.[63] A very simple dramatic ceremony is the arrow dance of the primitive mountain Veddas, in which an arrow is stuck in the ground somewhere in the forest. The Veddas dance around it (the Yaka spirit resides in it) in order to bring about a profitable hunt. The dramatic process is fulfilled in the natural arena of the hunting ground, and the dance itself is an integral part of the whole continuity of the current hunting activity. In contrast to this, among the more advanced coastal tribes this ceremony has developed into the mythological sphere. In the Bambura-Yaka ceremony, which is intended to occasion a successful boar hunt, a mythical scene is represented in which Bambura kills a boar. Here the dramatic action takes place no longer in a present time, but rather in a mythological time. The drama occurs no longer on the natural hunting ground, but on a "maesa," a ritualistic stage which merely represents the mythical hunting place. The primitive drama has been

[62] Vatter, 135, 107.
[63] Seligmann and Brenda, 287.

elevated into a historico-mythical reality. But this does not mean that the reality is completely severed from the actual tribal life. On the contrary, since all mythical persons and events exert their power upon the present tribal existence, the sphere of the mythical drama occupies a peculiar intermediate position between a naturalistic reality and the aloof aesthetic sphere of advanced societies.

Specific Patterns of Primitive Cultures.—Primitive worlds, like any other developmental series, may be analyzed as to their general genetic characteristics, or as to the particular patterns of existence in which the general forms realize themselves. Though in a strict sense the problem of specific culture patterns is only indirectly related to developmental psychology, it seems useful, nevertheless, to demonstrate how diversified and even opposed cultural configurations, all of them marked by primitivity, actually appear.

One of the best works in this field is Ruth Benedict's *Patterns of Culture.* Her study stands out among the few attempts to comprehend the particular mental designs which form the various cultural worlds of the primitive. She presents three impressive illustrations of her approach, and describes the life patterns of the Pueblos of New Mexico (the Zuñis in particular), of the Dubuans (island people, Southeast New Guinea), and of the Indians of the northwest coast of America.

The Zuñi way of life—to use the well-known Nietzschean epithet applied to Greek culture—is distinctly "Apollonian." The Apollonian man conceives life as a well-ordered cosmos. He lives tranquilly in accordance with the cosmic law, in contradistinction to the Dionysian man, whose main purpose in life is the heroic opposal of restrictive forces. Excess and conflict are, for the latter, the essence of nature and human existence.

The Zuñi places the greatest value on a ceremonious, inoffensive mode of living. One of the obligations of the priest participating in religious observances is not to feel anger. This state of mind binds the supernatural powers to hold to their share of the bargain. To suppress anger, therefore, has magical efficacy. Prayers are mild and ceremonious in form, and beseech an orderly, tranquilly happy life. In all their ceremonies, their evaluations of magical and mythical signs, one finds the Apollonian pattern quality; this is in sharp opposition to the Dionysian aspect of the cultures of most other American Indian tribes. Except for the Pueblos, the American Indian commonly carries out Dionysian practices in propitiating supernatural powers through visions or dreams; hideous tortures, fasting, drunkenness, and so on are widely used for this end. The Zuñi do not achieve supernatural aid by any such individualistic, disruptive experience as the vision. The supernatural is communicated with by means of strictly regulated ceremony, e.g., through membership in a cult. Vision as an extraordinary experience is not a sign of supernatural vitality, but a sign of death, and thus one to avoid. Fasting exists, but not as a Dionysian element. It is rather a requirement of cleanliness. The drinking of peyote is forbidden. The Zuñi dances do not have the ecstatic culmination common to most of the dances of the North American Indians. "The dance, like their ritual poetry, is a monotonous compulsion of natural forces by reiteration. The tireless pounding of their feet draws together the mist in the sky and heaps it into the piled rain-clouds. . . . There is nothing wild about these dances." Shamanism is alien to the Zuñi, who consider their priests as holy beings exalted beyond excess and violence, as superior persons who rule by peaceful and not militant measures. All the life crises—birth, puberty, marriage, death—are celebrated moderately by the Pueblos. The initiation rites of puberty are not the ordeals found among the Indians of the Plains. In Dionysian cultures death is frequently a dangerous situation; to meet it, violent forms of magic are employed, e.g., self-mutilation. In the Pueblo cultures death ceremonies attempt to symbolize the end of man's course, provide means of enduring the loss with the least disruption, and transform the calamity into a source of blessing.

In summary, then, Benedict demonstrates that the Pueblo cultural pattern is molded by a mental attitude strikingly different from that accounting for the cultural forms of other American tribes. It is some fundamental love of moderation, of "measure," which distinguishes this attitude, and which colors all phases of the tribal life.

Another instance of a distinctive cultural pattern is afforded by the Dobu Islanders. The Dobuans are generally considered by their neighbors as a lawless, treacherous people. However, they are not untrustworthy because they live in a state of anarchy, "but because the social forms which obtain in Dobu put a premium upon ill-will and treachery and make of them the recognized virtues of their society."

There is a natural hostility between the clan of the man and that of his wife. Since the man has to marry into the village of his wife, the hostility is carried into the very life of the family. The husband must endure the animosity of the *susu* (those belonging to the female line of descent). Faithfulness is not expected of either the man or the wife. Ownership is determined by the *susu,* and hence the gardens of man and wife are separated. Because magic plays an all-important role in the life of these people there is a fierce, though secret, competition for the possession of magic formulae. These formulae are owned according to *susu* inheritance, but even at that they are generally the property of only one of the sons. This method of inheritance occasions enmity even within the *susu* itself. Prosperity is believed to be due to the victory of one's own magical powers over those belonging to someone else. A good crop is thought of as something stolen, the richness of other gardens robbed by means of the exercise of magical powers. Whereas in all the surrounding islands the harvest is the occasion of a great ceremonial display of agricultural abundance, in Dobu, as a theft, it is kept a dark secret.

The most diversified charms are those pertaining to the spreading of disease of all kinds. Each man owns certain disease charms. This makes everyone responsible for the sickness and death of anyone else. The method of establishing a mark of ownership on goods or trees is to contaminate the property magically with their proprietary disease. The natives say, "That is Nada's tree," and mean that is the tree upon which Nada has put the curse of paralysis.

"Dobu cowers under a death as under a whipping," says Benedict. The death of a man may bring calamity on the owner of a certain disease charm but, above all, it brings it on the dead man's wife, who is usually considered the cause of her husband's demise. (This, of course, works both ways.) Wife and husband are in constant fear of each other. It is not unusual for the man or wife to attempt suicide, or to cut down his or her own trees, in order to arouse the clan against the hated spouse. "All existence," says Benedict in summing up her analysis, "appears to the Dobuan as a cut-throat struggle in which deadly antagonists are pitted against one another in a contest for the goods of life."

PATHOLOGICAL (SCHIZOPHRENIC) SPHERES OF REALITY.

It is Bleuler[64] who gave us the first deep insight into the nature of the schizophrenic world, into its egocentric, "autistic" character. Supplementing Bleuler's work, Storch[65] analyzed the spheres of schizophrenic reality, and showed how the schizophrenic experience oscillates vaguely between one sphere and another. But the various spheres of reality in the typical schizophrenic experience are different from those of the normal man. They are marked by a lack of differentiation between subjective and objective content. Out of this egocentrism, out of this autism and "nearness" of the ego to the external world, there is gradually constructed a kind of primitive world.

We may consider two different regions of the general schizophrenic reality: the perceived, visible world, and the world of fantasy and imagination. The typically schizophrenic

[64] Bleuler, 545.
[65] Storch, 604.

world of perception is characterized by a marked participation
of subjective factors in the process of configuration. Reality,
which represents a characteristically independent existence for
the normal person, is here known from a highly egocentric
standpoint; the outer world stands in a peculiarly intimate contact with the ego. A female patient describes this contiguity
very clearly.[66] She "transmits" her visual and auditory senses
to things, and in this way penetrates into them. Her eyes are
directed outward and touch things directly. Upon looking at
a landscape, for example, she carries away with her some of
the actual material of which it is constituted. This close relation between subject and object in the case of other patients
expresses itself in such a way that they influence the outer
world with their own bodies and their bodily movements. On
this egomorphic world relation rests one patient's mystic theory
that the harmony of the world depends on the movements of
his body. When he spreads out his arms and makes various
gymnastic movements, when he lies rigidly in bed, etc., these
exercises serve to restore the disturbed equilibrium of the
cosmos. Another patient believes that by movements of his
legs he brings the nations of the world into peaceful cooperation.[67]

Similarly, just as the visible world of objects exhibits
qualities which for the normal person would belong to the
subjective realm of fantasy so, too, on the other hand, the
schizophrenic world of fantasy possesses a certain objectivity.
When one of Schilder's patients was eating his meal he saw
daemonic human and animal forms in the meat. He needed
only to look at a book and the daemonic, evil aspect of some
configuration stood clearly before his eyes.[68] One of Storch's
patients sees the daemonic figures of his fantasy occupying the
same space as objective things; every time his watchfulness
relaxes, the daemons crowd into the room. It will be seen that

[66] *Ibid.*, 330 f.
[67] *Ibid.*, 334.
[68] Schilder, **597**, 101.

the reality of fantasy has the character of intermediacy for this patient, for he sees the forms objectively in space, though knowing all the while that they are a result of his own invention.[69] The reality of fantasy again reveals its intermediate character in that it oscillates between complete objectivity and complete illusion. One female patient, reporting on the objects of her fantasy, says that "the automobile was standing there waiting for me, and then Miss B. [her nurse, who was coming into the room at the time] took the words right out of my mouth, and everything became just another illusion." When one is carried away by one of these fantasies, another patient reports, one forgets oneself completely; upon awakening, it is as if one were waking from a dream . . . no more is there full reality.[70]

The schizophrenic world of fantasy, like the child's play reality, has the value of the real, not because things appear true to nature, but rather because strong emotions bring them to life. It may be noted that fusion of different levels of reality has been occasionally observed by Hanfmann in her experiments with schizophrenics. Schizophrenics, when confronted with the task of picture completion (Healy test), sometimes do not distinguish the pictured situation from the real. One patient, while trying to decide where to place a block with a picture of a boy, says: "Maybe I should leave the boy with his mother? If I put him here, he may be disturbed." Responses of this sort are often strongly colored by the patient's own wishes or fears. The patient said, for instance, about a certain picture: "This boy is losing his watch, but I did not do it. I did not hide anything on him."[71] The world is real because it is felt as real, because reality is grasped through affect. This phenomenon is illustrated very clearly in the case of a certain catatonic. When this man was asked why he was always spitting and smearing everything with his saliva, he replied

[69] Storch, **604**, 335.
[70] *Ibid.*, 336.
[71] Hanfmann, **570**, 254.

that this actually caused him mental hurt and was a severe test of his patience, but that he did it deliberately in order to take upon himself the responsibility for all the degradation and filth of the world. To further questioning as to whether he really believed that he could purify the world by his actions he answered: "My heart tells me yes." His opinion of the relation between his former normal life and his current existence was that he was now experiencing a "deepened" reality. Another schizophrenic also admitted that the character of the pathological reality somehow differed from that of a normal life in an objective world. And still "everything is reality now, but an outsider can never be shown this—it can only be believed."[72] A further example is that of a schizophrenic teacher, who stands in most intimate communication with God; he sees in the sun the wife of God and his own mother. He felt how the "will of the sun entered his body." Requested to tell about the reality of these experiences, this patient reports: "I said and sang this in a dream, but afterwards I said to myself—this can't be a dream; it's only that other people can't understand it . . . all that I am experiencing is only mental, but if one has only an atom of faith one can understand the most impossible things."[73] In this last statement we can discern with particular sharpness the nature of the schizophrenic spheres of reality. These realities reveal no concern for those signs of objectivity which have a common, intersubjective significance; they are devoid of a purely objective comprehensibility. The general schizophrenic reality is one that is personal, one that depends for its existence on "belief," that is, on the needs of the emotions, on the real as felt.

But however closely related the spheres of schizophrenic reality may be to other primitive types, they are still fundamentally apart from them in so far as they are pathological. The schizophrenic often experiences his daemonic images as

[72] Storch, **604**, 338.
[73] *Ibid.*, 340.

a disruptive intrusion, as the collapse of the stable, objective forms of a hitherto fixed, controlled world. Often he will try to master this dream world by practicing intellectual control. One schizophrenic says that at times it suffices for him to "purge" his visual field, and the "ghostly forms crumple up, become as dry as bone, and helpless."[74] It is especially true that in the incipient stages of schizophrenia the invasion of the subjective forms of activity into the objective world is felt not as an enrichment of the content of the personal life, as with normal primitive types, but as an impoverishment. A patient says: "Reality, as it was formerly, no longer exists. Real life has suffered a decline."[75] There is a specific sign, a sign not present in other primitive types, which is characteristic of schizophrenic reality, and that is its insubstantiality. Provided that the schizophrenic is not already completely wrapped in his own delusions, is not making himself at home in an entirely autistic reality, he will frequently feel this de-differentiation of objectivity as a loss of a stable, substantial, and secure world.

[74] *Ibid.*, 335.
[75] Storch, **606, 808.**

Chapter XIII

PRIMITIVE PERSONALITY

THE PRIMITIVE MAN'S IDEAS OF PERSONALITY.

The primitive man's awareness and formulations of his own personality and that of others reveal the same characteristics of diffuseness and syncretism previously discussed at some length. As it is known to primitive man, the structure of the personality exhibits a relative lack of articulation and hierarchization. To him personality appears as concretely presented, which means that it is apprehended as an externally effective entity in terms of palpable, visible characteristics. And because of its syncretic bond with the surrounding personalized world it is marked by a relatively low degree of individuation.

Diffuseness.—The diffuseness of the primitive personality has an internal and an external aspect. *Internally* considered (i.e., the personality as pure subject), the structure of the personality is more "homogeneous," more globally determined with respect to personality as known on higher levels. At the same time it is less articulated with respect to central as against peripheral characteristics.

Any one characteristic may suffice to define and represent the person in its totality. In the opinion of the Brazilian Bakairi the cannibalism of a neighboring tribe may be accounted for by the fact that these people are supposedly descended from jaguars. As a result of this ancestry, to a certain degree they still remain jaguars. The trait of cannibalism is enough to designate the personality as "jaguar."[1] Similarly, the Bakairi also believe that the Trumai are a certain kind of aquatic

[1] Steinen, 297, 353.

animal. This belief originates in the idea that these enemy people sleep on the river bed. "Whatever may have occasioned the Bakairi's notions of the Trumai, they are not to be shaken by any logical reasoning which might possibly lead to the conclusion that they are not fish after all. Since they sleep on the river, the Bakairi infer that these Trumai simply must be water animals. This one characteristic is enough to stamp them as animals, to bestow on them the character of a certain species."[2]

Another characteristic of diffuseness in the structure of the personality is a certain lack of discrimination between essential, and therefore constant, elements, and peripheral, transient elements. This makes for the belief in the transmutability of the personality so common in primitive spheres. It also crops out in the belief that in one person there can be a multiplicity of souls, or spirits, which are only partially integrated.[3] The most pronounced absence of centralization appears in the belief in a dual personality, in the existence of the one individual both as a human and as a non-human entity. Not only may one and the same being be transformed into the other, but this other being may exist simultaneously in an altogether different position in space. The primitive man finds nothing strange in this. In a Polynesian myth, a god from heaven becomes a pig on earth and still retains his supernal character. The transmutation is bound up with a "split" in the personality. The Bakairi believe that men have been created by blowing on arrows, and women by blowing on maize-pestles. But when the metamorphosis has been ritualistically accomplished, the newly created man still keeps his arrow, even though it is a magical instrument of creation, and the woman keeps her maize-pestle.[4] Despite the fact that the arrow has been transformed into a man, its existence in its own right continues. This "split" of the personality rests, at the

[2] *Ibid.*, 352.
[3] Rivers, 115, 104.
[4] Steinen, 297, 35.

bottom, on the characteristic law of diffusion, in so far as the arrow represents both the man's property and the whole of his personality.

Another instance of the belief in the transmutability of the personality is the primitive idea of a complete qualitative change in the individual at different stages in his life. The individual, in this conception, does not grow gradually from an embryonic state into infancy, from infancy into childhood, and then on into manhood. He changes from one state to another in a saltatory fashion, by the abrupt means of a ceremonial. The birth ceremony transforms the individual from a quasi-human, perhaps subhuman, being into an actual member of the group. A "second-birth" ceremony, or initiation ritual, changes the adolescent boy into a socially mature individual. Throughout many parts of the world these second-birth ceremonies simulate those of real birth. The adolescent boy may "die," come to life again, behave like a speechless infant, receive a new name, etc. "The difference between adults and minors which exists in Europe," says Bugeau, "is nothing compared to that between the circumcised and uncircumcised of Kikuyu. One might almost say that they are individuals of a different species."[5]

Again, in primitive experience the personality is diffuse in its *external* relations (that is, the personality considered in relation to the world in which it is embedded). The boundary line shutting off the personality from external spheres is far less definite than it is at the level of highly developed man. Its contour, so to speak, is blurred. This characteristic of "blurredness" in the contour of the primitive personality might also be defined in terms of the unusual extent of the "ego-halo." The ego-halo of primitive man is much more comprehensive than that of man at advanced levels. The primitive individuality resides in the whole body, in all that grows upon it, or comes from it as secretion or excretion. Hair, nails, tears, breath, voice, urine, excrement, seminal fluid, sweat, shadow,

[5] Bugeau, 170, 616.

footprints, etc., are participants in the individuality. Even personal possessions may be thought of as an essential part of the personality. Smith and Dale, reporting on the Ba-ila of Northern Rhodesia, say: "In the minds of the Ba-ila there is a very close connection amounting almost to identity between a person and his possessions, which leads to the peculiarity that these people use the same word to denote certain injuries to persons and offenses against the property of persons."[6] Kidd[7] tells us that a Kaffir child will often strike the blanket of a person with whom he has had a falling out, and likewise will cry when his clothing is beaten by someone inimical to him.

Magic ideas and practices in relation to the personality are based in many instances on the primordial conception of personal diffuseness. In magic, diffuseness means that the magic power is not focused compactly, but extends homogeneously throughout the whole ego-halo. Any part of the ego and its halo is of equal value to any other so far as magic power is concerned, and each part is at the same time representative of the whole. However remote may be the part of the ego-halo which is influenced, favored, or destroyed, the whole ego itself is similarly affected. On this phenomenon depends the casting of a spell over the person by magic brought to bear on pieces of clothing he has worn, on the remains of his meal, on his hair, nails, voice, name, on the bodily excreta, and so on. In Melanesia, for example, as in many other places, the voice is a concrete representative of the ego. When the person who is the object of the magic speaks, a noose of twine may be secretly drawn tight, and then hidden in a vine. Thereupon the person shrivels up and dies.[8] And what holds true for the voice also holds true for the name. The whole man can be magically transformed by influencing his name as a representative constituent part of the person. The Sulka, when on the warpath,

6 Lévy-Bruhl, **86**, 115 ff.
7 Kidd, **219**, 66.
8 Parkinson, **255**, 191.

call their enemies "rotten wooden branches," and believe that by so doing they can make the limbs of the feared opponents heavy and clumsy.[9] Since the name is often connected with the geographic circumstances of the birthplace, the ego through the name is often bound up with a certain locality in the religious-magical sphere.[10]

All this illustrates the effectiveness of the law of *pars pro toto*, namely, of the law that each part belongs in essence to the whole, and has a reciprocal effect on the totality. If any part of the ego-halo is injured, however insignificant it may appear to us, the ego itself is likewise injured. This law is also operative, of course, in relation to the milieu as part of the diffuse personality. In New Guinea, if a tree is uprooted by a gale of wind, its owner will fall sick.[11] Every part of the physical and spiritual ego and ego-halo to some degree or other represents the totality. On this belief that a person's possessions are a part of the individual himself rests the common primitive practice of burying the dead man's personal effects with him, or of destroying them. The Australian Aranda destroy the possessions of the deceased, the Australian Victoria tribes bury them with the corpse, and the Abipones of South America burn them.[12]

On this association of personality and milieu depends the belief in a continuance of the everyday surroundings in the beyond. Life after death is a copy of mundane life, for only in his proper environment may the person be preserved in his totality, even in preternatural zones. Hence, everywhere among advanced primitives is found the belief in a paradise that is a projection of earthly existence, in the *reinga* of the New Zealanders as in the Happy Hunting Ground of the American Indian.[13] This same belief is also found among people of

[9] *Ibid.*, 198.
[10] Werner, **317**, 103.
[11] Neuhauss, **254**, vol. 3, 133.
[12] Spencer and Gillen, **293**, 497; Smith, **292**, vol. 1, 104; Dobrizhoffer, **184**, vol. 2, 273.
[13] Taylor, **307**, 231.

the older cultures. *Aalu*, the dwelling place of the Egyptian dead, for example, is a land of many canals, where the deceased work on the soil and harvest crops, just as they once did on the banks of the Nile. In old China there was current the belief that the dead man retains the social position that he had during his lifetime; the dead have their armies, their battlegrounds, cemeteries, burial ceremonies, etc.[14] Similarly, among many primitive peoples the manner of burial corresponds to the occupation of the dead man during his life. In some South Sea Islands the custom is to bury the fisherman in the sea, and the bird-catcher among the trees.[15]

Syncretism.—For the primitive man the personality is much more syncretically perceived than for us. Generally speaking, syncretism appears in three aspects: (1) There is a lesser degree of differentiation between the inner (motivational) and outer (behavioral) characteristics of the personality. In other words, personality is less differentiated in the *dynamic* sense. (2) There is a lesser degree of differentiation between the physical and spiritual characteristics of the personality. The primitive personality is less differentiated, therefore, in the *psychophysical* sense. (These first two forms of undifferentiation constitute the *concreteness* of primitive personality.) (3) There is a lesser degree of differentiation between individual and individual, and also between individual and social entities. The primitive personality, consequently, is less differentiated in relation to *individuation.*

THE PRIMITIVE PERSONALITY AS DYNAMICALLY LESS DIFFERENTIATED WITH RESPECT TO PERSONALITY ON HIGHER LEVELS.— The primitive personality actually is that which it appears to be in action. In other words, it is present as a concrete personality-of-action, as one in which inner motive and behavioral expression are conceived and evaluated as non-differentiated. How completely the action may be judged as the essential property of the person, as part of his being, is well

[14] De Groot, **198**, vol. 1, 48, 924.
[15] Codrington, **176**, 258.

illustrated in the following incident reported by Kidd. A Kaffir, pointing to a wound on his arm, said, according to Kidd: "That's So and So," mentioning the person who had inflicted the wound. Kidd affirms that this identification was intended to be literal. "The Kaffir does not so much think as feel that actions are an intrinsic part of oneself."[16]

Miss Mead, speaking of the character traits of the growing Samoan child, in so far as these are evaluated by Samoan adults, brings out clearly the behavioral aspect of the primitive personality. "The whole preoccupation is with the individual as an actor, and the motivations peculiar to his personality are left an unplumbed mystery. . . . A good child will be said to listen 'easily,' or to act well. 'Easily' and 'with difficulty' are judgments of character. As we should say a person sings easily, the Samoan will say one obeys easily. . . . A chief, who was commenting on the poor behavior of his brother's daughter, remarked: 'But Tui's children always listen with difficulty'—as one might say, 'But John always did have poor eyesight.' "[17]

And, similarly, the Samoan code of virtue in children corresponding to the different age levels consists of an enumeration couched in terms of concrete qualities of conduct. Small children should keep quiet, wake up early in the morning, obey, work hard and cheerfully, play with children of the same sex, etc. Youths and girls should work skillfully, be retiring, marry with discretion, be loyal to their relatives, not carry tales, not be troublemakers, and so on. Adults should be wise, peaceful, serene, generous, anxious for the good name of the village, etc. "No prestige is given to the subtler facts of intelligence and temperament."[18]

Lowie[19] lists the following virtues as most highly regarded among primitive people: bravery, magic power (i.e., aptitude

[16] Kidd, 219, 73.
[17] Mead, 242, 127.
[18] *Ibid.*, 129.
[19] Lowie, 89, 343.

for religious experience and magic action), wealth (which actually means the ability to distribute goods with a lavish hand), dexterity and competence in the provision of food. All these traits pertain essentially to a personality-of-action.

From his varied experience with Indian tribes, Radin decides that ethical traits of personality are not thought of as living principles or potentialities inherent in the individual. He concludes that for a primitive people "ethics is based on behavior." "The Winnebago moralist would insist that we have no right to preach an ideal of love, or claim that we love, unless we have lived up to the practical implications of this sentiment."[20] It is not the motive, the hidden intent, but the action itself which determines the evil-doer. "Criminal intent," says Lowie, "does not play nearly the same role in primitive law as in our own jurisprudence." Goddard relates an incident occurring among the Hupas which might serve as a classic example. "A child was accidentally burned to death in a fire that some woman had built outdoors to heat water for washing. Although this woman was in no way reprehensible, the life of her own son was sought in recompense." Even if allowance is made for various exceptions to the rule, "it remains true that the ethical motive of an act is more frequently regarded as irrelevant in the ruder cultures than in our own courts of justice."[21]

Since the primitive man lives in a behavioral world where persons are conceived in terms of concrete qualities-of-action, it is no more than a logical consequence that commonly no essential differences are thought to exist between man and animal. Karl von den Steinen, in a discussion of the beliefs of the primitive Brazilian Indians, says: "We must quite disregard the boundaries between man and beast. Any animal can be cleverer or more stupid, stronger or weaker, than the Indian himself. He may have altogether different daily habits, but in the Indian's eyes the animal is as much a person as

[20] Radin, 111, 72.
[21] Lowie, 89, 400.

he is himself. Like human beings, animals are grouped into families and tribes, they have different languages like human tribes, etc. Human being, jaguar, deer, bird, fish—all are but persons with a diverse appearance and diverse characteristics. The deeper ground for this conception is that as yet there is no humanity in the ethical sense so far as the primitive Indian is concerned. Goodness and badness exist only in the rude sense that one can give another pleasure or displeasure, but a true moral perception and an ideal beyond the notion of reward or the fear of punishment are completely absent. In such case how could there be an impassable gap between man and animal? The external apprehension of daily custom to which the Indian limits himself can at the best accord man no more than the position of *primus inter pares*. Indeed the animal has no bow and arrow, or maize-pestle, but in the eyes of the Indian this constitutes a mere minor difference, in so far as the animal, like man himself, has other significant implements, that is, in the form of claws and teeth."[22]

PRIMITIVE PERSONALITY AS LESS DIFFERENTIATED IN THE PSYCHOPHYSICAL SENSE.—Concreteness is further exhibited in the primitive notion that the mental and corporeal characteristics of the personality are united undifferentially. The spiritual properties of man are not essentially different from the material. The custom of identifying a spiritual and moral purification with a physical purgation is explicable on the grounds of this personal concreteness. Among such Indian tribes as those in Mexico, in the Egyptian culture, indeed even among the South Sea Islanders, there is found a belief in the possibility of purifying oneself of evil qualities by washing the body, or by taking sweat baths.

The story is told that a Zulu king—with apparent success—rid his officials and military leaders of discord and a passion for squabbling by administering an emetic.[23] During pregnancy many primitive peoples not only are forbidden to eat

[22] Steinen, 297, 351.
[23] Flügel, 30, 46.

animals and plants of an ugly form,[24] because of the fear that this physical defect will be transmitted to the human embryo, but it is also tabu to eat the flesh of animals which have ugly traits of character such as cowardice. In Australia the fat of the kidneys imparts the courage of the sacrificial animal. The spiritual properties of the victim as present corporeally are transmitted simply by eating the flesh. Everywhere we come across the belief that the spiritual properties of the person are influenced by the diet, because physical and spiritual are thought of as an inseparable unity. Even among the Egyptians the spiritual and the corporeal were thought of as so closely connected that this identification becomes a basic factor in the magic death cult. Everything in the process of mummification was designed to the end of securing the use of the dead man's most vital organs in the world to come. Mouth and eyes were kept open so that he could speak and see.[25] A "soul" without the normal corporeal functions of mundane existence was quite unintelligible. Mummification as the preservation of both body and personality is found among many primitive peoples. In the South Sea Islands the body is often relieved of viscera and brain, and then painted after the bodily fluids have been drawn off.[26] Man thus continues on in his complete individuality so long as his body exists. It is for this reason that the Australian Dieri bind together the tips of the toes; this prevents the deceased from walking about and thereby running the risk of bringing injury on himself. In Queensland the knees of the dead are strapped together for like reasons.[27] On the Gazelle Peninsula the dead man's skull is a visible sign of the whole presence of the deceased, so much so, in fact, that a feast may be celebrated in his honor.[28] The corporeal-spiritual relation is thus considered so thoroughly intimate that

[24] Tessmann, **308**, vol. 2, 188; Parkinson, **255**, 398.
[25] Flinders Petrie, **191**; cf. Visscher, **139**, 142 ff.
[26] Gill, **195**, 212.
[27] Howitt, **214**, 449, 474.
[28] Parkinson, **255**, 23, 81.

even a single part of the body suffices to insure the presence of a person as a spiritual entity.

Primitive conceptions of the nature of magic powers and of the "soul," however different they may be in the complexity and subtlety of the thinking involved, are all based on an undifferentiation of psyche and physis.

In many parts of the world the spiritual element contains characteristics of psychophysical undifferentiation. Shadow, mirror image, light, heat, breath, body odor, etc., stand in an indeterminate position between substantiality and insubstantiality, a position which is particularly designed to serve in the representation of the spiritual aspect of the personality, that is, the "soul."

In the *mana* belief of the Melanesians the concept of a psychophysically undifferentiated spiritual (magic) power has developed in a markedly typical form. *Mana* is at once both power and substance, at once invisible and extended, both intangible and material.[29] In the monograph on the origins of the metaphor I have termed such a psychophysically undifferentiated spirituality "pneuma."[30] The idea of "pneuma" is universally disseminated in divers forms. In Polynesia it appears as *atua*,[31] in Borneo as *bali*,[32] in Sumatra as *tondi*.[33] The *wakanda*, *orenda*, and *manitou* of American Indian tribes are pneumatistic concepts.[34] The same is true of the *bukuru* of the Costa Rica Indians,[35] of the *gnama* of the African Bambaras,[36] of the *nikissi* of the Fiort,[37] and of the *ndjaka* of the Tonga (Bantu) tribes.[38]

One of the most illuminating instances of the complex of

[29] Codrington, **176**, 190 f.
[30] Werner, **141**, 37 ff.
[31] Shortland, **289**, 82.
[32] Hose, **212**, vol. 2, 29.
[33] Warneck, **315**, 8.
[34] Schoolcraft, **284**, vol. 1, 34.
[35] Gabb, **193**, 504.
[36] Henri, **207**, vol. 1, 2.
[37] Dennet, **183**, 45.
[38] Junod, **216**, vol. 1, 153.

ideas which may grow out of this general notion of a psycho-physically undifferentiated personality is found in Best's study of the elaborate Maori concepts.[39] The Maoris believe that several principles of personality coexist independently in each individual. The principles are sometimes dealt with as inter-changeable. The most important of them, which have emerged from the natives' mythical beliefs and magic practices, are the following: *Wairua* is the immortal shadow spirit, the astral body which leaves the physical body temporarily during dreams, and forever after death. *Mauri* is the general life principle, which is embedded in the body, and which is both material and immaterial. *Hau* is the vital strength, the *mana* of the personality, which is also both material and immaterial. *Ahua* is that material-immaterial principle which establishes the person's individuality. It can be readily seen that all these principles point to the conclusion that here the personality is conceived as concrete and psychophysically un-differentiated entities. Even the single personality traits are thought of as both concretely material and immaterial at the same time. A desirable quality as part of the *ahua* of a person may be taken away and kept for oneself in secret, for instance in the form of a lock of the slain enemy's hair.

Before proceeding any further it will be to our advantage to append a brief discussion of certain factors inherent in magical and mythical ideas that may have instigated a development of the conception of personality in the direction of hierarchic structure and psychophysical differentiation.

Above all we must take into account the gradually increasing differentiation of the personality under the influence of magic ideas and systems of evaluation. Whereas originally each individual corporeal part contained the whole nature of the personality, a distinct change takes place at a higher level of development in magical and mythical thought. Gradually there appears a differentiation between magically important and unimportant parts, a centralization and subordination in the sense that a kernel of personality is set

[39] Best, 163.

against the periphery of the personality. Such an evaluation of the spheres of the personality from the standpoint of magic has seemingly become established among the Dshagga Negroes of the Kilimandsharo.[40] These people distinguish between feelings of sensual lust and nobler feelings; the former arise in the belly, the latter in the chest. They fix this distinction and the reciprocal dependency of the parts by the designations "masculine" and "feminine." "The chest and belly are man and wife. . . . The chest has good words, love and anger, but the belly knows no good word, and is only full of heat." It is the belly which betrays men into thievery. "What the eye avoids, the belly will say 'bring to me.'" Hence, here we find a kind of centralization and differentiation based on a set of magical values. The centers of the personality are magically fixed in so far as there are organs of radiation as middle points from which the personality is externally effective. Such points of radiation are the throat as director of all excitation proceeding from the chest, the right hand, the right foot, and the sexual parts. In other words, man is corporeally-spiritually differentiated into higher and lower spheres. These spheres, in turn, have a focus of spiritual strength and a field of radiation around the focal point. The magic-ethical mode of evaluation is revealed above all in the fact that it is the higher mental powers which the individual seeks to hold through the agency of amulets as the most cherished qualities of the personality.

Here it can be seen how certain standards are formulated, how an equal evaluation of all parts of the personality is relinquished in favor of a selection (with ethical implications) of prized spiritual-corporeal organs, foci of the personality demanding magic protection, as against unimportant, or even unworthy and despised, parts that no longer merit preservation through magic. The differentiation and centralization of the personality into superior and inferior moments, into foci and surrounding fields of radiation, is in no sense based on either purely anatomical or psychological concepts. The basic principles of the personality evolve from the conception of magically valuable and valueless powers in the individual. These notions of personality are developed still further in the specifically ethical and magical-religious ideas of higher cultures, e.g., in the Egyptian.

[40] Gutmann, **200**, 7.

The gradual separation of the central, noble tendencies of the person, proceeding on the supposition of non-essential (animal) desires existing in opposition to these former qualities, finds its characteristic expression in the death cults of the Egyptians. Of these, Porphyrius says: "In solemn burial ceremonies, before proceeding to embalm, the intestines of the dead are placed in a special vessel, and in this are held aloft to the all-seeing sun-god. This while the priests intone in the name of the dead ——

> 'I have done nothing harmful . . .
> In life I have sinned, eating or drinking, which
>   was not right,
> But I have not sinned through myself, but through
>   these (the intestines) . . .'

"The priest thereupon throws the vessels into the river." Rosellini translates the last line of the hieroglyphs in this manner:

> "Righteousness to his spirit,
> His misdeeds to his belly."[41]

With this differentiation of the corporeal-spiritual personality into the higher, the ethical and essential, and the lower, the evil and magically meaningless, there comes another differentiation, namely, that of spiritual and corporeal essentialities. The tendency is to consign the lower, contemptuously evaluated functions to an animal body, and to fix the higher functions in some spiritual principle. In Melanesian Malanta, for example, the opinion is current that so long as a dead body continues to emit a stench, the spirit is weak. The spirit waxes strong when the material dissolution of the corpse has been completed.[42] In such magical conception is contained more or less implicitly the opposition between spiritual and bodily functions.

The gradual development of a specifically spiritual personality as against a specifically corporeal personality by virtue of a magico-religious differentiation can be readily observed in the Egyptian culture. In the death cult the corpse, originally equal to the whole personality in its living concrete entirety, retrogresses to a position of inferior importance. The central point of the death belief

[41] Bunsen, 171, Germ. ed., vol. 5, 545.
[42] Codrington, 176, 263.

now becomes the *ka*, that is, the immortal pneumatistic soul. The *ka*-belief of the Egyptians clearly shows that the spiritual principle is the godlike element, and therefore the immortal one. In this case, as in many other mystic-religious cults, the differentiation into a higher and lower personal being is closely bound up with the nascent concept of constancy and continued identity in the personality, a constancy which may become an eternal identity.

THE PERSONALITY OF THE PRIMITIVE AS LESS DIFFERENTIATED FROM THE STANDPOINT OF INDIVIDUATION.—The primitive personality is more syncretic than the personality on higher levels in that the primitive individual feels himself less separated from other living entities, whether these be man, animal, or the social world of which he is a part. This "condensation" of the structure of the personality is aptly illustrated by myths from all parts of the earth, legends telling of the identification of one man with another, of man with animal, etc. A Banks Island myth, for instance, tells of a man who is at the same time a shark. In recording the story, Rivers makes the following comment: "To say that the man changed into a shark (so appearing at certain times) almost assuredly involves the translation of the true Melanesian point of view into the language of our own fairy-tales. There is little doubt . . . that he is both man and shark, although to the eye he has the form of a shark at one time, and of a man at another. . . . The belief in identity between man and animal I suppose to be the psychological essence of Melanesian totemism."[43]

The feeling of a very intimate connection among relatives is especially strong everywhere in primitive societies. The idea that not only the sick person himself, but his relatives as well, should abstain from eating certain foods is common among the Indians of Guiana. "The piache's first prescription is to impose a general state of fasting on the patient and on all his kinsfolk."[44]

[43] Rivers, 272, vol. 2, 365.
[44] W. E. Roth, in Lévy-Bruhl, 86, 87.

The identification of the ego with other personalities is clearly expressed in some instructive examples from Thurnwald's studies of the Solomon Islanders. During the lizard dance it never occurs to either participants or spectators that lizards are merely being represented. The dancers actually are lizards to all intents and purposes. The following incident impressed on Thurnwald the completeness which this identification may achieve: "One day my houseman Ungi was hanging around the great wooden drum in the chiefs' hall, in a very upset state. When I asked him what was wrong he told me that he was sick. Inquiring further, I heard that 'he was sick together with everybody.' After a time he begged me for some medicine. As usual, when I could not make out any more exactly what was the matter, I gave him some aloë pills. In the afternoon he was still lying there. My houseboy now informed me that Ungi was sick because his wife was sick. Further questioning revealed that she had a bad wound, and I now gave Ungi bandages, and sent him home to his wife. Some days later he was cured, for his wife's health had improved."[45] Such an incident shows to what a remarkable degree of thoroughness an identification of personal sufferings with those of others may attain. A fusion of the ego and the alter-ego occurs here in a form so drastic as to be related to the condensation of personality known in the dream.

In the realm of myth and magic the natural feeling of closeness between parents and children has evolved some curious customs. A belief in the identity of father and child is particularly common. Certain tribal practices among the people of the Congo seem to imply that "before circumcision a male child is not regarded as possessing an individuality distinct from that of his father."[46] This identification is often expressed in the fact that during the wife's pregnancy the husband must follow certain rules of precaution as if, so to speak, he himself were bringing the child into the world (so-called couvade).

[45] Thurnwald, **128**, 163.
[46] Torday and Joice, **310**, 306.

With the Goalas of Bengal, the man must remain completely at rest at the time of birth.[47] In Amoy (China) during the wife's pregnancy the husband must be unusually careful in all his movements. If anyone makes the floor of the house vibrate, the embryo will be disturbed in its rest and its normal growth thus disrupted. It can happen that fathers who roll up their sleeping mats, if these mats have been stretched out flat for a long time, may have a child with curled-up ears. A child was born with a harelip because during pregnancy the mother, while mending her husband's clothes, carelessly cut into the cloth with a pair of scissors.[48]

Among the Abipones the man keeps to a certain diet throughout the period of his wife's pregnancy, and avoids all violent exertion.[49] During gestation the Bororo tribesmen in Brazil are forced to lead the lives of sick men. If the newborn child becomes ill, the father also takes the medicine prescribed by the apothecary.[50] All these cases illustrate not only an identification with the mother bearing the child, but the much more powerful magical identification of the father with the child itself. The West African Pangwe are governed by this same principle when they say that "the woman carries the man in her belly," that is, the embryo is really nothing else but the man who, with the woman as accessory, is formed anew.[51] According to Steinen, the Brazilian Indians also hold that the child is the "little father," and this regardless of whether the child is male or female.[52]

The syncretic ego-character found universally among primitive people is exhibited, again, in the belief in the ability to identify oneself with some chosen animal by wearing a mask. Here it must be assumed that the dancer who wears the mask, though he feels himself as actually being an animal, neverthe-

---

[47] Risley, **270**, vol. 1, 289.
[48] De Groot, **198**, vol. 1, 538.
[49] Dobrizhoffer, **184**, vol. 2, 231.
[50] Steinen, **297**, 289.
[51] Tessmann, **308**, vol. 2, 184.
[52] Steinen, **297**, 336 f.

less remains aware of his being the man he is in everyday life. As Steinen says, though an Indian can become a dove through the mere wearing of a mask, and in consequence may behave in voice and gesture like a dove, he still continues to be the tribesman who, bird that he is to all intents and purposes, can fetch a gourd vessel of pogu from the women of the village.

This strange equivocality of the primitive personality comes to light in the sphere of magic in a magico-mythical identification of the ego with that of others and with the non-ego. Totemism is based on the magical identification of the group member with a totemistic animal or plant, which is officially confirmed at periodically repeated festivals. Aborigines from all parts of the world insist that they do not represent animals, but actually are animals in the mimicry and dancing connected with such events. Steinen at the time was unable to conceal his incredulity when the Bororo people told him flatly that they literally were arara birds. It is not a name that they assume, he emphasizes, or any provisional relationship. They *are*, no more no less, arara birds. And the same literalness is true of the Mexican Indians, who do not represent the gods whose masks they wear, but become the gods themselves with all their attendant attributes as soon as they decorate their bodies for the ensuing dance.

The syncretic structure formed by the unity of personality and milieu may refer to a relation not only between individual and individual, but also between individual and *superordinated social unities*. In a higher form of society the relation of the individual to a superior social organism is that of a pronounced contradistinctive polarity. On a primitive level this polarity is hardly formulated at all. The individual is much more completely fused in the social group, just as, on the other hand, he is to a much greater degree the bearer of the totality. In all primitive societies his modes of relationship are governed to an extraordinary extent by the powers of the social group. "The force of social custom," says Rivers of the

members of the Melanesian culture, "is far stronger than individual feelings."[53] Radcliffe-Brown makes substantially the
same statement in relation to the Andaman Islanders, who are
one of the most primitive peoples known. The bonds holding
individuals to their social duties are determined much less by
personal inclination, or by the pressure of consanguinity, than
by purely social forces, e.g., the status of the individual within
the community.[54] It is said of the Ba-ila tribes of Northern
Rhodesia that a member belongs to the clan; he has no proper
self. If he is wronged, they (the clan) will right the wrong; if
he commits some culpable offense, the responsibility is shared
by the clan as a whole. Even the natural bonds between
parents and children are repudiated by this people in favor
of the peculiar custom of mutual adoption. "It is said that
only rarely is any child over six or seven years of age found
living with his parents, and this is so because it is considered a
compliment for a married man to ask to adopt one of his
host's children." It happens often that another friend will ask
the foster-father whether he may adopt one of the foster-
children, without even consulting the real parent.[55]

Again, with most primitive peoples, matrimony is "not an
individual, but a community affair."[56] "Matrimony," says Lowie,
"differs from modern arrangements in Caucasian civilization in
that the contract binds not individuals, but families."[57]

An interesting example of the strength of those bonds which
link members of a primitive group together is afforded by the
widespread custom of "levirate," that is, the inheritance of a
man's wife by a younger brother or by some other near kins-
man. So common is this institution in native life that "it is easier
to enumerate instances where it is absent, than instances where
it occurs."[58] The relationships in Australian tribes offer apt

[53] Rivers, 272, 138.
[54] Radcliffe-Brown, 265, 77.
[55] Smith and Dale, in Lévy-Bruhl, 86, 115 ff.
[56] Junod, 216, vol. 1, 121.
[57] Lowie, 89, 17.
[58] *Ibid.*, 32.

illustration of what one might call the "functional equivalence of brothers" in the social unit. Everywhere in Australia the father's brothers are also called "father," and in consequence the children of all the brothers are in turn called "brothers" and "sisters." The same is true of the mother's sister's children. This principle, says Radcliffe-Brown, is not simply a matter of nomenclature. It is a most important sociological principle running through the whole of Australian native life. It is the expression of a very strong, intimate, and permanent bond between brothers.[59] The principle of the functional equivalence of brothers is exhibited in the custom of the levirate, which makes the woman potentially the common wife of all the brothers. At times "potential" wives even become actual wives temporarily during certain ceremonies where sexual license is not only permitted but actually demanded of the brothers and their wives.[60] The principle of this equivalence is very primitive indeed, as is suggested by the fact that, in Australia, it is much more effective in simply organized tribes than in the more complex.

Another sign of the embedding of the individual within the social group is the manner of treating the ownership of property. In very primitive societies, such as those of the dwarf peoples of Africa, the Veddas of Ceylon, and the Andaman Islanders, the economic life approximates a peculiar form of communism. Other than the land, which is usually owned by the group, there is, to be sure, some individual property. But all these tribes have customs regulating the usage and disposal of private property so that actually there is a sort of communal ownership throughout. The Andaman Islanders,[61] as well as the pygmy tribes of Africa, have the social custom of constantly exchanging presents. In effect, then, everything possessed by the group is forever in circulation and changing hands.[62] With the Veddas, property not

[59] Radcliffe-Brown, **264**, 428.
[60] Warner, **316**, 212.
[61] Radcliffe-Brown, **265**.
[62] Immenroth, **215**, 97.

common to all cannot be transferred by the owner without the consent of the group.[63]

Reviewing all the facts mentioned up to this point, we must conclude that the primitive personality is identified much more closely with the higher social unit than is the case on more advanced levels. But this does not mean, as the French school of Durckheim[64] would have it, that the individual personality does not exist in its own right *per se*, and that the social totality is the actual personal entity out of which the single individuality has not as yet emerged. Developmental psychology holds to the view that the relation between individual and group is one that is marked by a reciprocity of effect. The process of differentiation applies to both factors of ego and surrounding world. At first, therefore, the individual is much more the bearer of the group character, and at the same time he is much more pervasively fused with the group. The individual personality and the social organization are both subject to contradistinctive processes of differentiation. In other words, in the case of the lower levels there is simply less polarity between individual and group than on more advanced levels. There is a lesser degree of specificity in the individual characteristics with respect to the group characteristics, and vice versa.

In general, the most primitive social group is a family-like organization concretely bound to the territory with which it makes up an indivisible unity.[65]

This primary form of social organization is as *personalized* as the individual member of the group is *socialized*. To a considerable extent the group neither recognizes the specific rights of the individual, nor does the individual member conceive the social totality as something existing *per se*, as independent of his own ego, as instinct with certain prerogatives of its own. His social spirit is egocentric to the degree that the society is

[63] Seligmann, **287**, 111.
[64] Durckheim, **22**.
[65] Lowie, **89**, 213; Radcliffe-Brown, **265**, 22; Immenroth, **215, 66**.

centered in the person himself. Since the main goal of the primitive social organism is the preservation of its equilibrium, the individual's social goals are primarily limited to the concrete, egotistic acquirement of prestige within the rigid limits of the community. The seeking of prestige, says Radin,[66] is possibly the most fundamental fact in primitive life anywhere in the world. Most authorities on the primitive personality will probably concur with Lowie's statement to the effect that "the primitive man is not a miser, nor a sage, nor a beast of prey, but, in Tarde's happy phrase, a peacock."[67]

These personal characteristics of vanity and hunger for prestige are not, as some authorities seem to believe,[68] a sign of a nascent marked individuation within the society. On the contrary, they are a token of egocentrism, i.e., of a low degree of differentiation between individual and society, between the private and specifically social goal. To repeat once more, the development of the individuality hinges on the relative polarity of person and society. Where there is a lack of non-personal, objective (or abstract) goals in a society, non-egocentric goals cannot develop in the individual. Where there is a rigid, immutable social pattern into which the individual is born and in which he must live without conflict or prospect of change, a true contradistinction between individual and social ends resulting in specific individuation is greatly hindered.[69]

THE CHILD'S PERSONALITY.

Primitive Characteristics of the Child's Personality.—The child's personality has a relatively diffuse and syncretic structure. The child's ego is more or less fused with its surrounding world, both the personal and the impersonal world. It is marked

---

[66] Radin, 111, 33.
[67] Lowie, 89, 357.
[68] Cf. Radin, 111.
[69] Cf. the statement of H. S. Maine, in his famous book, *Ancient Law*, p. 172: "The movement of the progressive societies can be characterized by the gradual dissolution of family dependency and the growth of individual obligation in its place."

by concreteness, by a lack of psychophysical differentiation, by its strongly behavioral character. All these facts have been more or less clearly observed and recorded by child psychologists.[70]

The young child's identification of himself with the mother, father, or other members of the family is one of the most common expressions of a *syncretism* in the structure of the personality. This relationship, especially between him and his mother, is often extraordinarily intimate. "The child does everything his mother wants him to do, and everything pleases him that makes her smile. If the mother is quiet, serious, calm, the child imitates her mood; and if she is irritable and nervous, so will be the child."[71] In a recent study of child personality L. B. Murphy makes the following observations: "The early dependence of the child on the mother, emphasized by clinical studies of childhood, appears in the child's readiness to react emotionally to any mishap to the mother. . . . But it is also apparent in our records that nurse, brothers, and sisters, or frequent visitors to the house, and playmates, share differing amounts of identification; that is, sympathetic response to their mishaps is far more intense than it is to the troubles of a total stranger. Mere chronic propinquity appears to be of immense importance to the little child in determining readiness for a sympathetic response."[72]

The earliest symptom of identification appears as some such empathic response as crying or smiling with the tears or smiles of another person. This early empathic response as a sign of the fusion of child personality and his surroundings is definitely distinguishable in Mrs. Murphy's records from later responses in which the ego is more or less clearly developed.[73]

This tendency to identification is developed particularly in play, e.g., the little child often identifies himself with his doll.

[70] For recent literature, cf. Jones and Burks, **418**; Allport, **1**, 131 ff.
[71] Hall, **393**, 325; Sully, **517**, 120.
[72] Murphy, **463**, 303.
[73] *Ibid.*, 303.

Laura Bridgeman, the blind girl, put a bandage like her own over the eyes of her doll. A six-year-old child who had measles painted red spots on her doll.[74] And so on. My four-year-old niece's behavior during play revealed this same inclination. She forbade her doll everything that she herself was not allowed to do; she endowed the doll with her own misbehavior, for example, a penchant for clambering up on chairs and sofas, whereas she herself played a mother who was, of course, permitted these breaches of conduct.

A strong similarity in essence is possible between the child's own self and every living being, because of the physiognomic aspect of the surrounding world which has such an important role in child perception. "A very high intelligence is often ascribed to animals," says Stanley Hall, "as if they understood our language and had their own, on which same ground there is occasion to fear them."[75] The 5:2-year-old Scupin boy simply would not believe that animals did not understand human language, and stubbornly defended the canary who, at least for one, understood everything that he said. "Just a little while ago I said to my dicky-bird, don't you want a piece of biscuit, and didn't you hear how he said to me just so you could hear his peeping, yes, Bubi, I want more cooky. I like biscuits so much, because they're my kind of cookies. . . ."[76]

Play also reveals clearly the syncretic character of the child personality as, for instance, in the case of a child playing horses who strikes his own legs with his whip, and thus becomes horse and rider at the same time.[77]

Another characteristic of the personality in childlike experience is its *concreteness*. The personality and its properties are taken as ultimately valid as they appear to be. As the child knows it, the personality is represented as a psychophysically undifferentiated unity. The child makes little or no distinction

[74] Sully, 516, Germ. ed., 420.
[75] Hall, 393, 403.
[76] Scupin, 502, vol. 2, 166.
[77] Neugebauer, 468.

between the "outer" and "inner" aspects, between the behavioral and motivational dynamics of personality.

A variety of observations may be adduced to prove a fusion of psychic and physical characteristics in the child's notion of personality. According to Piaget, children frequently believe that thoughts are material, that one can touch or see their thoughts.[78] They may even believe that their thoughts can be taken away from them. I once chanced to observe a six-year-old who wanted to tell the name of an "uncle" who had brought some chocolate with him. The little girl could not remember it, and inquired whether God had taken it (from her memory). A syncretism linking inner events and external behavior in the sense of fostering a personal "concreteness" aptly clarifies certain recorded expressions of the 4:9-year-old Hilde Stern. This child believed that animals thought with their mouths; later, at the age of 5:5 years, she considered goodness and laughter to be identical. "She is awfully good, for she laughed at me so," the child remarked.[79]

One of the factors having a bearing on the development of a differentiation between "inner" and "outer" sides of the personality is a decrease in the immediacy and overtness of the emotional response. In the very young child every emotion is immediately visible in the outward expression; the older the child becomes, the less is the "inner" life directly mirrored in overt signs. Jersild and Holmes, using as subjects 47 children ranging in age from 34-83 months, have conclusively observed the growth of this internality in the emotional life. During this interval of about four years, there is not only a decline in the frequency of a fearful response to certain concrete tangible objects, but also an increase in the fear of dangers imagined, and furthermore a consonant decline in the overt signs of fear.[80]

The findings of Clem and Smith afford excellent examples

[78] Piaget, **482**, 46.
[79] Stern, **511**, 237 f.
[80] Jersild and Holmes, **417**, 141.

of a development toward a differentiation of inner (motivational) from outer (behavioral) traits of character. In their study of the pupils of a six-year high school (seventh through the twelfth grades) they discovered that the attitude of children with respect to personal habits (swearing, drinking, gambling, etc.) becomes gradually more tolerant, whereas the attitude toward such expressions of inner traits of character as lying, conceit, selfishness, and so on, grows less tolerant.[81]

The child's notion of personality as cast in terms of concrete behavior and outer conduct, rather than of inner motivation, is beautifully illustrated by Piaget's experiments with the child's concept of responsibility.[82] In this experiment the children were told several pairs of stories. In each of the two stories a person, in substance, acts wrongly, and the child is asked to judge which of the two misdeeds is more reprehensible. Here, for example, are two such connected tales:

Story I—There was a little boy called Julian. His father had gone out, and Julian thought it would be fun to play with his father's ink pot. First he played with the pen, and then he made a little blot on the tablecloth.

Story II—A little boy called Auguste once noticed that his father's ink pot was empty. One day when his father was away he got the idea of filling up the ink pot to help his father, so that it would be ready for him when he came home. But while he was opening the ink bottle he made a big blot on the tablecloth.

In the conversation which followed the telling of the stories is revealed the attitude typical of the seven-year-old child: "A little boy," the child repeats, "sees that his father's ink pot is empty. He takes the bottles, but he is clumsy, and makes a big blot. There is another little boy who was always touching things. He took the ink and made a little blot." "Well, are they both equally naughty?" "No." "Which is worse?" "The one who made the big blot." "Why did he make the big blot?" "To help

81 Clem and Smith, 355.
82 Piaget, 484.

out." "And why did the other boy make the little blot?" "Because he was always touching things. He made a little blot." "Then which is naughtier?" "The one who made the big blot."

This example plainly demonstrates that the younger child's moral concept of the personality is framed not according to inner motivation, but according to objective conduct, to the physical effects of a person's actions. Once again we may recall the primitive man's ideas concerning the personality-of-action, as revealed in his customary evaluation of criminal action as a matter of objective rather than subjective import. Of course, the idea of moral default and responsibility as something to be judged in terms of physical action diminishes as the child grows older. Piaget was unable to find a single definite case of it in children after the age of ten years. The results of his tests seem to indicate that the nine-year level marks a turning point toward a definite preference for the idea of personal responsibility as evaluated in the light of motivation.

In analogy to the structure of the primitive personality the structure of the child personality is not only syncretic, but also *diffuse*; that is, it has a much more extended "ego-halo" than that of the adult. Clothes, for example, belong to the personality; a change in dress can change the person entirely. Sully tells of a child who exhibited decided unwillingness from the ages of seven months until two and a half years to submit to putting on any kind of new clothes. It is recorded of the Scupins' 2:10-year-old son: "When the boy happened to see, quite by exception, his father dressed in a completely black suit of clothes, he looked at him open-mouthed, and asked, 'What are you now, Papa? . . . Are you Grandpa?' "[83] Even at the age of 6:3 years this same child expressed a similarly curious notion with respect to the difference between boy and girl: "To Bubi's way of thinking the difference between boy and girl consists mainly in the difference between their clothing and between their given names. Accordingly, he seriously

[83] Scupin, **502**, vol. 1, 169.

asked us a short time ago to have Lottie put on pants, and for all of us to call her 'Bubi,' so that she could be a little boy."[84]

Names are often included in the ego-halo. "Now I am a clown," said Katz's son. "Mother, write down on the ticket that I'm called Karl now, for a clown can't be called Julius. Julius is a little boy's name, and when I go into the railroad station, the conductor will think that I'm a clown [if you change it]."[85]

Even the mere visual surroundings are often strongly ingrown with the child's ego. His visual world belongs to him and to a certain degree to him alone. The Scupin child at 5:3 years, "cried out tearfully that Lottie shouldn't see his mother; she belonged just to him."[86]

It is in keeping with this diffuseness that, as in the beliefs of primitives, the peculiar law of *pars pro toto* should be so often effective in the child's personality. Basically the name and pieces of clothing are representative of the whole for the child: "I must put something on the school table that looks like you," said Katz's son, "and then I'll think of you. I must put your glasses on the table, then I won't forget you."[87] And, again, for instance, the child's head may be considered as more or less identical with the whole person; when the head is hidden, so is the whole body.[88] "To him the head seems to be the most essential part of the body. He sticks his head under the sofa, and although his whole body is visible from the shoulders down, he cries: 'Look for Bubi, he's not here any more!' and so long as his head remains out of sight, he considers himself to be hidden from view."

The diffuse character of the child's personality sometimes results in a belief that appears to us as very abstruse indeed. This is, simply, that single parts of the body can themselves

[84] *Ibid.*, vol. 2, 170.
[85] Katz, **421**, 160.
[86] Scupin, **502**, vol. 1, 103.
[87] Katz, **421**, 323.
[88] Scupin, **502**, vol. 1, 187.

bear important properties of the whole, such as seeing, hearing, and thinking. The Scupin boy, at 4:10 years, asks:[89] "What is my tummy saying when I drink tea? . . . Does he think it's milk?" Immediately his flow of thought continued with: "Does my tummy have eyes and a mouth and a nose, too?" Another incident recorded of the same child, this occurring at 5:1 years, is the following: "Soon he went out on the balcony, and said 'Bare-legs want to see something!' " Similarly, two children, mentioned by Piaget believe that a little mouth is in their forehead through which they talk (think).[90] It is, then, a special variation of the *pars pro toto* structure which permits the single parts of the body to exhibit characteristics of the whole. We have called such a structure "homogeneous."

An added characteristic of the child's personality, one intimately linked with its syncretism and diffuseness, is its *lability*. This lability often reaches extremes that are virtually incredible to the adult. This quality appears when a changing significance is attributed to the ego, and in a transmutability expressed most strikingly in so-called "play." Again, lability is marked in the child's theories concerning the nature of the personality, of the soul, of God, etc.

According to an inquiry carried out by G. Stanley Hall,[91] the child pictures the soul as a dove, a butterfly, an eagle, a turtledove, a mouse, worm, caterpillar, snake, spider, cat, hawk, bird of paradise, maggot, lion, wolf, and so on, as soon as any verbal similarity directs the attention to any one of these possibilities. These forms, Hall concludes, are connected with the universally dominant idea among children that they can, or have at some time, become animals, and less frequently is linked with a tendency to imitate animals. In the course of play, a child can, without the slightest difficulty, represent a post, a street lamp, a mirror, a tree, etc. The 3:2-year-old

---

[89] *Ibid.*, vol. 2, 75, 90.
[90] Piaget, **482**, 50.
[91] Hall, **393**, 306.

Gunther Stern finds it perfectly natural to say to his mother: "Mama, will you be a net, so I can throw you into the water?"[92]

Katz has collected a most impressive series of examples of the child's belief in the mutability of the personality. Both of his children believe that their mother can change into a bear by the act of growling.[93] His younger son can turn himself into a wolf, in the eyes of the older brother, merely by announcing that this has happened.[94] Hall tells of a six-year-old boy who was terribly afraid that older children could turn their hands into claws and scratch him.[95]

Associated with this childish belief in the mutability of the personality is the frequently occurring assumption that at different periods of life there occur real saltations in the personality, changes in an abrupt and absolute sense. Julius Katz is convinced that when he grows up he will no longer be Julius or be named Julius, but that he will become Theodor (that is, his older brother).[96] This notion of saltatory change—in keeping with the child's psychophysical concreteness—also applies to the physical. Entering the third grade, the 8:10-year-old Scupin child began to fasten his own underwear, the kind that buttoned up the back. "Before my arms weren't long enough," he said.[97]

It is possible that a relatively enduring imaginary transformation of the personality may occur, a phenomenon frequently emphasized by child psychologists. At the age of 2:9 years, Stern's boy began occasionally to call himself "big sister" and to call his older sister "Mieze." After ten days or so the illusion became permanently established, and his mother writes: "Himself alone he calls 'big sister,' whereas Hilde is now 'Mieze,' I am 'Grandma,' and his father has become 'Grandpa.' " This fantasy continued for another week; the thoroughness of the

[92] Meyer, 454, 3.
[93] Katz, 421, 104.
[94] Ibid., 169.
[95] Hall, 393, 403.
[96] Katz, 421, 128.
[97] Scupin, 502, vol. 3, 55

transformation is demonstrated by the fact that he thought of himself as "big sister" not only while absorbed in play, but also in any quite factual situation that might be unpleasant or disturbing. One evening, for example, when the curtains had already been drawn to darken his bedroom, he remembered that he had lost his ball while out for a walk, and so cried out into the gloom: "Tomorrow Grandma's got to go with big sister to look for the ball."[98]

I was told of a similar case of a boy where there was an even more complete realization of the self-conceived role. When he was between seven and eight years of age, this boy played at being the owner of a factory for months on end. He would answer all objections to this fantasy with deep seriousness. Someone said to him, for instance, that while recently traveling in Czechoslovakia (where the boy's factory was located) he noticed that all the workers were out on strike. "Oh no," the boy replied, "the workers just didn't go to work that day, but I gave them permission not to. It was like this—a little while ago there was so much to do that the men worked really harder than was called for. So I gave them a day off. That must have been the day you were there."

The peculiar transformation of the ego, so often misleadingly referred to as a change of "role," really involves mutations of the personality of amazing stubbornness and duration. For instance, in the case just mentioned the play dream of being a factory owner had not spent itself even after the course of a year. It is precisely this perseverance which points to the fact that we are dealing not with mere play roles, but with serious needs in the child that are essentially satisfied only by the possibilities of an ego radically divergent in point of lability from that of the adult. Because of this pervasive lability of personality there are possible a multiplicity of transformations normally outside the range of the adult ego, with its sharp contours and consistency.

The child's objective world of personality, the continuum

[98] Stern, **513**, Germ. ed., 230.

of you-persons, is frequently endowed with much greater indeterminateness than is the case with the objective personal world
of adults. Adults respond to the persons in their everyday surroundings according to a more or less constant attitude (of
sympathy, antipathy, indifference, etc.). The objective persons
are conceived according to essential values which represent
emotionally fixed attitudes and intellectual judgments. This is
not true of the child. A person does not make an enduring impression of sympathy or antipathy on the child. The determination and significance or the objective personality depend much
more on the momentary constellation, on the mood, in other
words. Only isolated individuals—e.g., the mother or the
father—have that constancy of significance within the surrounding world of personality which is characteristic of the adult's
general response to personality.

In conclusion, a further important indication of a relative
lack of constancy in the ego-content, an absence of constancy
in the response to character, is the frequently encountered
"split personality" of children. Such splits of personality apparently often develop under a condition of conflict, as in the
experience of the contrast between a will to do the wrong thing
and a good intention. A twenty-months-old girl, having
squealed with unseemly vigor, would immediately whisper to
herself: "Be good now, Babba." One woman says she practiced
the subterfuge of telling her boy, whenever he misbehaved,
that he was not himself, but one of his playmates, whereupon
he would go out and come back a "good boy."[99]

The parents of the Scupin boy report the following in their
diary: "He distinguishes between a good, serious Bubi, and a
naughty, frivolous Bubi. If the frivolous Bubi begins to climb
all over the place, the good one warns him, 'Look out! You're
going to fall!' or 'Now, Bubi, whatever are you doing up there!'
When he does something previously forbidden him, he says,
'You, stop that, bad boy! Mama will spank you.' Nevertheless,
the irresponsible Bubi does what he wants, and the serious

[99] Sully, 516, Germ. ed., 268.

Bubi with all his admonitions does not take it so much to heart after all."[100]

Again: "When Bubi poured some tea he had made into a bottle, and was not quite sure just how we would take this action, he said apprehensively, 'Bubi gave me some ink!' He talked of himself, so to speak, simultaneously in the first and third person. Shortly afterward we found him sobbing bitterly, and to our outburst of questions as to what had happened, the wretch stammered, 'Bubi just pulled my hair,' and then gave drastic illustration by reaching up and yanking violently at a tuft of his own hair. In no other instance does it become so clearly evident that the child distinguishes between two persons in himself—a good, brave self and a naughty 'Bubi,' on whom are heaped all variety of dereliction and bad behavior, who persists in being bad, and who pesters and teases his better self."

Another example: "When the boy was forbidden to hit the wallpaper with a hammer, for a time he fell heavily silent, and then said of a sudden, 'I just told Bubi something.' 'What did you tell him?' 'Well, I told Bubi . . . if . . . if he bangs like that the hammer will break.' In this case it appears that the intelligent Bubi, as represented by the 'I,' brings to task the heedless self (as represented by 'Bubi') with the weighty argument that the hammer will fall to pieces if he keeps on striking the wall with it."

As a young girl George Sand[101] had a strange impression of the sound of her own name and voice. She imagined that somewhere about her was a second self that looked at her and answered her words. Hartley Coleridge[102] as a boy distinguished between a picture-Hartley and a shadow-Hartley.

The universally encountered phenomenon of the imaginary playmate is closely connected with a primitive "split" of personality. The imaginary companion, usually has a definite

[100] Scupin, 502, vol. 1, 115, 181, 190.
[101] Sully, 516, Germ. ed., 105.
[102] *Ibid.*

name and appearance, and his reality is never questioned. A recent survey of this subject,[103] in the course of which some 700 persons, both adults and children, were interrogated, revealed that 31 per cent of the women and 23 per cent of the men could remember having imaginary playmates during their childhood. It appears that this phenomenon generally begins to wane during the tenth year. Eighty-one per cent of the girls and 60 per cent of the boys believed in the reality of their imaginary playmate. It is also of interest to note that the majority of the children kept the existence of their playmate a secret. According to the results of an earlier inquiry,[104] with few exceptions the playmate is of the same sex and usually of the same age.

Developmental Stages in Individuation.—As we have already demonstrated in our discussion of the personality of primitive man, increasing individuation is the counterpart of increasing socialization. The basic process underlying individuation is the increase in distance between ego and world, the growing differentiation between person and society as interdependent, yet fundamentally discrete, organisms.

The initial person-world relation is highly egocentric. Before entering into any further discussion of this relationship, it is indispensable that we make a brief critical analysis of this term "egocentric." The word as used originally by both French and German writers on child psychology has now lost much of its definiteness, principally because of its erratic employment in recent literature, particularly in American literature. It should be used to mean merely a typical primitive *social* attitude. It does not refer at all to any strongly individualized response that characteristically overrides the demands of the personal surroundings. Such a response is anything but childlike. Egocentrism implies a social structure that has at least these two salient marks: (1) There is a relatively intimate bond between ego and the persons round about. (2) The ego is the vividly

103 Hurlock and Burstein, 408.
104 Harvey, 397.

dominant element standing out against a more or less blurred social background.

There are critical periods during which sudden transformations take place in the ego-world relation, that is, a rapid decline in the egocentric structure and a rapidly increasing consciousness of individual subjectivity as against social objectivity. There are at least three such "crises" in the development of the child's personality: (1) the period when the infant is weaned; (2) the resistance period of the young child; (3) the period of pubescence.

It is during the period of weaning that the very intimate bonds linking mother and infant are severed. The child's resistance to the demands of his social surroundings, a natural response to a world that is changing from one which yields readily to the magic will of its young master to another of irreconcilable solidity, reaches its peak approximately at two to three years.[105] The normal child, of course, learns quickly and easily to adapt himself to this shift, the adaptation customarily taking the form of blind obedience to authority. A relation between person and world dictated by pure authority still retains many of the marks of egocentrism. This is true in so far as blind obedience represents a form of behavior gauged to meet highly personal ends, that is, an avoidance of pain and a desire for the pleasant. Strict obedience is blind in the sense that it involves a refusal, or inability, to recognize objective social goals.

In an interesting experiment where he used a game of marbles as the play situation, Piaget has analyzed the development of a consciousness of social rules. The results clearly reveal the manner in which egocentric forms of social relationships diminish with the growth of individuation and socialization. Children between four and five years of age treat the rules of the game rather casually. Around six years the rules of the game are strongly emphasized. They have come to represent dicta which do not admit the slightest alteration; they

[105] Caille, 352; Reynolds, 495.

are now rigidly authoritative. "When the child imitates the rules followed by his older companions, he feels that he is submitting to an unalterable law stemming from the authority of his parents (or of older children)."[106] Cooperative behavior among equals, however, brings about a change in the child's practical attitude and reduces this almost sacred respect for authority. This leads to a subsequent phase which will be treated in later paragraphs.

A similar development in individuation can be observed in those situations where the child is free from all the restraint of rule and authority. Kroh has carried out an analysis of the development of a desire for superiority in competitive situations in children of the early school grades. He found that during the first year of school and the first half of the second year, the desire for superiority is satisfied by momentary triumphs. During the second half of the second year only one-third of the boys observed exhibited this altogether primitive, egocentric response to competition. Another advanced third clearly showed an entirely new type of self-consciousness. Some awareness of individual *capacities* as enduring characteristics of the personality begins to dominate. A reciprocal appraisal of one's own achievements with respect to those of some other child increasingly replaces a pure rivalry of action. One child may now speak of another's performance in school work as "not bad for him" or "he could do better," etc. This new attitude, indicative of an important step in individuation, also comprehends adult achievements that reach into the child's world. Those who are physically strong, who are rich, who can draw well and reckon quickly, and so on, become objects of admiration. Eventually an older person becomes the model, the ideal, which the child tries to emulate.[107]

And yet, even now, individuation in the adult sense is still far off. The child's world is still a behavioral world, and his personalistic discriminations are based solely on action. There

---

[106] Piaget, **484**, 53 ff.
[107] Kroh, **431**, 141.

is still a lack of insight into inner motivational traits and social goals. A good deal of that feeling of intimacy in the ego-world relation continues to be present, and permits the emergence of wishful feeling and action.

Egocentrism at this comparatively advanced stage of individuation comes to light in boasting and in the formation of the childlike ideals. According to Kroh's investigations, boasting is a noticeable trait in the beginner in school, and reaches its peak at the age of ten years or thereabouts. At first the content of the boasting refers irrelevantly to any type of transient achievement, but in time it becomes identified with the more enduring individual capacities.

The first conversation that Bubi Scupin carried on with his school teacher was as follows: "Have you ever been up on the Altvater [a mountain in Silesia]? No! . . . But *I* have. Ha, ha!"[108] Vorwahl tells of a ten-year-old German girl who pretended to be able to sing French songs. All her performance actually amounted to was the singing of so many meaningless syllables. A little boy who was listening to her showing off reacted promptly by saying: "Huh, that's nothing! I sing in all languages!"[109]

Investigations dealing with the reasons given by children for their preference with respect to other persons reveal a development from egocentric relationship to one based on an insight into inner values. The turning point in this process of development seems to be around twelve to fourteen years. According to Fischer, ten-year-old children, for example, mostly give egocentric reasons for their preference for some particular person. He observed that 50 per cent of the children explained their preference for their mother by saying: "She tells me I can do it," or "She brings something good home with her," or "She helps me," etc. Again, 30 per cent of the children like their uncles because "He brings something with him," or "He gives me money." The child's liking for the

[108] Scupin, **502**, vol. 3, 60.
[109] Vorwahl, **530**, 90.

father in 7 per cent of the cases was explained in such phrases as "He gives me things," or "I can give him something to keep for me."[110]

A further highly important step in this entire process of development occurs during the stages of immediate preadolescence and of adolescence proper. In this stage the interrelationship between individuation and socialization is clearly shown. In preadolescence and adolescence there is a development of objective social goals. There is a marked growth in the understanding of individual differentiation in a differentiated society, in the desire for self-determination with respect to the social role and the authority chosen.

As in the case of the child two to three years old, this period also begins with a "crisis," a negative phase succeeded by years of positive development. The crisis is expressed as overt or secret mutiny against old authorities, a severing of the intimate bonds linking the child with the family, a withdrawal into a personal, secret life.[111]

But the collapse of that social structure hitherto accepted as authoritative is more than a negative phenomenon. It is a preliminary for the establishment of a new relation between personality and society. When this sense of a personal freedom of choice exists, the individual acquires a new sense of responsibility, however limited, in relation to the society in which he lives and carries on his personal struggle. This expanding consciousness of personal responsibility signaling release from the egocentric structure of the child is the primary cause for the eternal conflict of generations within our own culture. In primitive society where the basic concept is adherence to rigid, indurated authority there is no awareness of the struggle of generations. Margaret Mead tells us explicitly, to illus-

[110] Fisher, 368.

[111] Vorwahl, in his excellent monograph on prepubescence, considers personal secrecy as one of the outstanding symptoms of the awakening self-awareness. He gives many examples of the emerging private world not existing before prepubescence.

trate, that Samoan adolescents do not experience the emotional conflicts of western youth.[112]

Piaget's work on the development of the child's moral judgments provides good examples of the relation between individuation and social differentiation. For instance, the investigation dealing with response to the rules of the game, previously discussed, brings out the fact that beyond the age of ten years the consciousness of authority undergoes a fundamental transformation. No longer do the rules of the game appear to the child as external laws, sacred precepts springing from the adult world. According to Piaget there are three symptoms which mark this arrival at a stage of free decision and earned respect: (1) The child will now submit to a change in the rules of the game provided that this change is unanimously agreed upon by all participants. (2) The child ceases to consider the rules to be external. (3) The rules are no longer thought of as representing an authority beyond the influence of the child's own decision. A rule is henceforth conceived as the free pronouncement of the actual individual minds themselves.[113]

Again, this development of interrelationship is discernible in the child's notion of justice. Children seven to twelve years old, when asked to give examples of what they considered unfairness, generally answered by naming the first three of these four types of unjust behavior:

1. Behavior opposing adult command—lying, breaking things, stealing, etc.
2. Behavior that is tantamount to an infraction of the rules of a game.
3. Behavior that outrages a consciousness of equality (e.g., unfairness in meting out punishment).
4. Less immediate injustices connected with the adult world (unfair economic or political behavior).

[112] Mead, 242.
[113] Piaget, 484, 57 f.

The percentage distribution of these answers at two age levels is shown in the accompanying table. This table indicates the

Age	Breaking Commands	Breaking Rules of Game	Inequality	Social Injustice
6–8	64%	9%	27%	..
9–12	7%	9%	73%	11%

developmental trend away from an idea of justice based on pure authority toward one in which the individuality rests on self-determination.

Piaget specifically defined these three main stages of development: an initial period (seven to eight years) throughout which justice is invested in the dictates of adult authority; a second period (eight to eleven years) marked by a progressive sense of equalitarianism; a third period (eleven to twelve years) where pure equalitarianism becomes tempered by a consideration of the inner and outer circumstance conditioning the individual.[114]

That the state of individuation is intimately related to the concomitant state of socialization may be demonstrated with simpler groups even within our own civilization. Sherman and Henry, who studied the social life in several mountain hollows in the Virginia country, found few individual differences in children below the age of five years, and in the two most primitive communities children even as old as twelve years showed but little differentiation in the pattern of the personality.[115]

The personality grows and becomes differentiated in reciprocity with respect to the differentiation of the social organism to which it belongs. It develops as it participates in the formation of objective values and as it bends itself to achieve ends established by the group.

[114] *Ibid.*, 312 f.
[115] Sherman and Henry, **288.**

THE PATHOLOGICALLY PRIMITIVE (SCHIZOPHRENIC) STRUCTURE
OF THE PERSONALITY.

There are pathological changes in the personality, paralleling the previously discussed changes of mental activity, which
produce states exhibiting a structure which approximates in
some respects a genuinely primitive personality. Although
there is no doubt that a fundamental difference exists between
the pathological personality and the primitive—with regard
both to dominant motives and to content itself—nevertheless
in a purely formal sense there are many striking parallels.
Developmental psychology cannot leave out of account the
primitive-pathological type.

It is precisely in those forms of psychosis which may be
characterized by a de-differentiation of the sensori-motor, affective, and reasoning activity that one finds a concomitant
de-differentiation in the structure of the personality. The work
done by Storch, Schilder, and others on the archaic-primitive
mentality of the schizophrenic clearly reveals the pathologically
primitive structure of the personality.

This pathologically primitive structure as found in various
schizophrenic types is marked by a relative diffuseness and
lack of centralization, as well as by a profound syncretism and
mutability in the personality.

That the psychotic personality is more *diffuse* and blurred
in structure than that of the normal person is shown, for example, in the fact that it has a magic ego-halo by virtue of
which the contours bounding off the person from the surrounding world are much less clearly defined. Just as in the
case of the true primitive, clothing, hair, voice, name, etc., as
well as the bodily excretions, belong to the personality itself.
In consequence, again paralleling the case of the real primitive,
the "magic of contiguity" can be practiced on the hair, voice,
or name, for all these are literal parts of the subject. It is for
this reason—that is, in order to preserve in the ego all its magic
powers and its wholeness—that some schizophrenics eat their
own excrement.[116]

[116] Storch, **603**, 30 ff.

This diffuse personality is, furthermore, not really divided into peripheral and central regions, but is built according to a *pars pro toto* structure. The whole personality is affected by any influence brought to bear on but one part of it, and under certain circumstances the very integrity of the personality may be thus endangered. For example, a magical transposition of thought may be accomplished in the case of one schizophrenic, through the hair; the hair-endings receive the magic fluid of other peoples' thought. Another fears that her thoughts are being actually taken away from her when the doctor writes down her statements.[117] A patient reported by Freud will not write her name, or show her handwriting at all, for fear that by so doing she might relinquish something of her personality.[118]

Corresponding to the diffuse extension of the personality into the world of objects, the person and the results of his handiwork can also acquire a new and much more substantial significance. One female patient believes that in all things created by man there is hidden a piece of the personality. The cabinetmaker who builds a table "has put a part of his ego into the piece of furniture, and has thereby given it strength and personality." Whereas we speak symbolically when we say that someone has put his heart or soul into his work, this patient actually experiences the process in which "the strength of the soul is drawn to some beloved object left behind."[119] A piece of clothing can contain a part of its wearer's personality. This same woman put her red frock on the floor and covered it with firewood. By this action she released the "maternal woman in her, in order not always to be remembering that she had never borne a child."[120]

The diffuse lapping over of the person into the surrounding world may be forcefully demonstrated again in those experimentally in-

[117] *Ibid.*, 38, 40.
[118] Freud, **34**, 77.
[119] Storch, **604**, 331.
[120] *Ibid.*

duced psychoses resulting from intoxication, whereby the tension and distance between ego and world are all but eliminated. "Just now I was an orange," says one person intoxicated with hashish.[121] Beringer's experimental subjects affirm that while intoxicated with mescalin this relaxation and fluidity were most startling. "I felt as if a part of my ego was standing out there in the trees as a branch. . . . The knocking outside in the yard arose from me." Upon hearing tones played softly on a mouth-organ, another said: "I am music, I am climbing in music."[122]

Ego and world, acordingly, constitute a diffuse togetherness. The objectivity of the world, the resistance offered by the thing-like, becomes relaxed and vanishes. "Objects give the impression that they are made of rubber; the walls, too, are soft, and rigid objects have a waxen malleability." And it may happen that the person's own body "floods over without limit into the surroundings."[123]

We have found that *psychophysical undifferentiation* is another characteristic of the primitive personality. The personality is experienced not as abstract—as psychic in nature—but rather as both "spiritual" and physically concrete, substantial. It is because of this that such personal qualities as "good" and "evil" can be expressed realistically and physically.

We recall the patient who would rise up on her toes when she pronounced such and such a person to be too common for her, and herself too good for the other.[124] This action illustrates that concreteness of the personality which is reflected in many varieties of schizophrenic ideas concerning the nature of the "ego" and of the "soul," and also in the magic practices constructed on the groundwork of these primitive notions. Psychotics often imagine psychic powers to exist in the form of a fine materiality. Through this materiality it is considered possible to exercise direct magic influence from person to person. Ideas of the soul as breath, as a bodily exhalation, etc., recall the "pneumatistic" concepts of the true primitive.

[121] Fraenkel and Joël, 553, 102.
[122] Beringer, 543, 79, 202.
[123] *Ibid.*, 55, 58.
[124] Bleuler, 545; Storch, 604, 324.

One of Schilder's patients[125] says that after his father had breathed on him he suffered injury from poisonous damps he had inhaled. In his older years Strindberg feared that his glance could be trapped, which would cause him to squander his ego. It is on account of such beliefs that schizophrenics often develop all sorts of magic practices calculated to assure the immunity of the ego from the effects of evil spiritual powers. Some psychotics tie towels about their heads or stop up the body orifices in order to escape this malign influence. Magic activities of this sort are analogous to the primordial forms centered about the magic of amulets. It will be remembered that the preservation and retention of one's own spiritual strength is achieved magically by primitive peoples also by wrapping skins around the body, or twining cords about single parts.

The syncretic unification of the ego with one or more persons—as known to normal people in the dream—is of frequent occurrence among schizophrenics. "What I was, and what you were, I often could not tell," one patient said. On another occasion this same person asked: "You and I . . . it's all the same, isn't it?"[126] Another characteristic statement made by one of Storch's patients is the following: "There was a flickering and twilight in the streets, and I felt myself drawn to the stars; at the same time the names of persons ran through my head, and I felt myself as one with these people."[127]

A female psychotic reports over and over that the people around her change in appearance. She believes her husband to be a "combination" of herself and of him. She greets the doctor entering the room as a woman, because he has taken into himself the "woman in her" in order that he may grow younger.[128]

[125] Schilder, 597, 96.
[126] Storch, 603, 26.
[127] Ibid., 73.
[128] This incorporation of a part of her personality in the doctor was in accordance with her own wishes. "I wanted to force myself in him altogether, so that if he had any will of mine in himself, he would send me

Yet another schizophrenic woman maintains that parts of different persons have become incorporated in her, that she feels the voice, the senses, and the physical parts of others in herself.[129] Another patient describes with grotesque exactness the manner in which strange beings become incorporated in her: "When one of them has a bent foot, then I feel my own foot become crooked. In the morning I often take a girl into me, and then my neck grows thick. If one of them is a strong man, then I have hard work to hold myself up straight, and it is not easy to walk."[130]

The inception of friends or members of the family into the ego is particularly significant. This syncretism, found among primitives in the peculiar custom of couvade, also has its typical expression in schizophrenics. In this respect we might take Strindberg's ideas as characteristic: "For me the family has become an organism, like a plant, a whole of which I am a vital part. I could not exist alone, or alone with the children without the mother. It is a system of blood vessels interlinked. If a single one is cut off my life would ooze forth with this blood, and the sand would soak it up." (*Confessions of a Fool*, Part III.) The manner in which magic practices can develop inevitably out of such a syncretism of personality is illustrated in Strindberg's avowal that with his thoughts and love he is able to surround the now departed wife in such a way that she is unattainable for others. His sorrow becomes a sign on her forehead, and she is marked so that no one will approach her any more. (*Second Blue Book.*)[131]

This syncretic relationship with members of the family is also clearly illustrated by one of the cases described by

---

home out of the hospital." Here we see affective-dynamic motives for a condensation of personality, analogous to what is familiar in dream analysis. This dynamics in condensation is probably similar to that found so commonly in the magic-daemonic beliefs and practices of primitive peoples. (Storch, **604**, 331.)

[129] Storch, **603**, 39.

[130] *Ibid.*, 39.

[131] *Ibid.*, 45.

Schilder.[132] In this instance a female patient identifies herself with her sister. Her brother-in-law's sexual intercourse with her sister is a source of pleasure to her. But still further, she feels that she experiences sympathetically any such sexual act in the whole world. Her personality has therefore expanded to include all mankind. This community of personality is again revealed by the fact that she must begin to sing as soon as she hears anyone else singing.

The syncretic inception within the ego need not be limited to a single human being.[133] One patient says, for example: "Everything from the largest to the smallest is contained in me!" "How many persons are there in you, then?" he was asked. "Oh, many thousands." "Can there really be so many persons in you?" "Oh, it really doesn't matter. I stay just one person, even though I contain them all."

The syncretic personality can become so comprehensively extended that it can finally contain the whole cosmos. A psychotic woman has the experience of being united with the sun and stars. Apparently she is describing some sort of natural catastrophe, and yet as a matter of fact it is really only her multiple-formed and extended ego of which she speaks: "Many stars have fallen down and a part of the planetary system has been disrupted because my life is so terribly torn apart." Hence, we see in this case how an inner connection between the cosmic event and the personality may result from a syncretic structure. The rupture in this patient's life and the disturbance in the heavens are identical events, and are the necessary expression of an immeasurably extended, syncretically and diffusely constructed, cosmic personality. In this megalomaniac idea are hidden roots which in a healthy form spring forth as astral cults and the astral mythology and astrology of the older cultures.

The shimmering, diffuse personality, furthermore, often exhibits an extraordinarily increased capacity for metamorphosis,

[132] Schilder, **598**, 74.
[133] Storch, **603**, 73, 80.

a marked inconstancy, and a tendency to split. For example, one patient tells that she considered herself to be St. Teresa. A picture of this saint, for whom she was named, hung over her bed, and for this obscure reason she supposed herself to be the saint. Such an ability to metamorphose the self seems perfectly natural to the schizophrenic. One of Schilder's patients[134] says that he is able to creep into the furnace mouth in the form of a mouse. Another schizophrenic believes that by magic means he has become a woman and a child. As in other cases, this transformation is not merely a spiritual one, but one that is literally corporeal and sensuous: "I am much more delicate than a man should be—now I can have a man's sexual organs, now organs like a boy's, and I can even feel a woman's organs." In opposition to this magic diminution there can be a transformation in the form of a gross enlargement, a veritable apotheosis, of the ego. A schizophrenic woman experiences union with God in that she simultaneously feels herself united with the nurse in attendance on her. She believes that she and the nurse are both one, that the nurse is God, and she, the patient, is like the nurse: "I have my nature and her being; she has her own being and my nature."[135]

This last example brings us to the phenomenon of *bi-presence* and the *split* of the pathologically primitive personality—a condition paralleling certain phenomena found with true primitives. In keeping with the de-differentiation of the personal structure (in the sense of a greatly increased diffuseness and syncretism) there develops a personality that may not necessarily be fixed to one place in space at the same moment; it can occupy several places at the same time. Storch's conversation with a schizophrenic of this type is quite illuminating: "I feel that I went out through the walls." "Do you go through the wall often?" "Yes, I sit over there, but just the same I went through." "If I sat there, how could I possibly be going

134 Schilder, **597**, 94.
135 Storch, **603**, 57.

through the wall at the same time?" "Oh, not you—you couldn't! But I can."[136]

The decentralization of the personality is also evident in experimentally induced psychoses (intoxication through the use of hashish, mescalin, etc.). In such intoxication there is often a profound release of the central ego with all the consequent phenomena of the split personality. One report reads: "One of the most impressive experiences of my life now began. For an hour I stood confronting my own character, and with it carried on a dialogue."[137]

The degeneration of the hierarchically constructed personality, that is, the release of the constant focal center of the ego, causes the feeling of personal integrity, of oneness, more or less to approach the vanishing point. The polarity between person and world is either reduced or disappears. The schizophrenic oscillates between a loss of the ego-pole and a loss of the world-pole as between Scylla and Charybdis.

Many of the magic-mystical ideas and practices of the schizophrenic are expedients adopted by the ego to protect itself from the destructive daemonic powers of the world round about. To this category belong such corporeal acts as kropophagy, or the swallowing of the male semen. With some psychotics these acts express the idea of not wishing to lose the psychic power inherent in all bodily excreta. And to this same category belong the ideas of rebirth, which are designed to overcompensate an ego-insufficiency.[138]

Ordinarily there are two ways of escape, two "methods" open to an individual whose personality is in danger of being inundated by the flooding press of the world. He can either shut himself off from the world, or identify himself with all its daemonic powers. Schizophrenics use both these "methods" of pathological adjustment. One female patient experiences every uprush of thought, every relation to another person, as a giving up of a part of her personality. "Gradually I

[136] *Ibid.*, 80.
[137] Beringer, **543**, 217.
[138] Cf. Storch, **603**.

can no longer distinguish how much of myself is in me, and how much is already in others. I am a conglomeration, a monstrosity, modelled anew each day." She experiences the "immolation" of her individuality thus: "It is only snow, only a poetical image of myself." Finally she arrives at an autistic negation of the world: "My daily life was just a game for others. Happily I now live a life designed for me alone, and strange for the rest of the world."[139]

Another means of preserving the personality before the onrush of malignant, ego-disruptive forces in the surrounding world is typified in a series of cases described by Storch.[140] Fears pertaining to the overpowering of the personality—in female patients usually ideas with a sexual drift—are here overcompensated by a device which takes the form of a mystic conception of union with the cosmic powers, with God.

All these facts have significance for developmental psychology in so far as they represent evidence for the intensity of that urge to restore the lost constancy and centralization of the personality present even in the pathological human organism.

Otherwise this press toward reconstruction differs fundamentally—as a pathological process necessarily must—from the normal genesis of personality as known to child and ethnopsychology. In the schizophrenic the mental activity designed to restore the central focus of the personality is concerned solely with the ego. The normal growth of personality is not an autistic, self-dependent process, but part of that whole development culminating in a balanced polarity of ego and world. Personality normally grows and becomes differentiated as against the growth and differentiation of the social world.

[139] Storch, 604, 341.
[140] Storch, 603, 66 f.

Addenda

N11. The study on the Nuer by Evans-Pritchard illustrates well the structural approach to cultural anthropology. "Most of the social activities of the Nuer," this author writes, "concerns cattle; 'cherchez la vache' is the best advice that can be given to those who desire to understand Nuer behavior. . . . The Nuer tend to define all social processes and relationships in terms of cattle. Their social idiom is a bovine idiom." We learn from Evans-Pritchard's analysis how cattle determine local and kinship structures, influence thought, play an essential rôle in the economic structure, in social gatherings, and in individual relationships.[103]

N12. The functional anthropological school stems primarily from England: Malinowski and Radcliffe-Brown had many followers, such as Warner, Powdermaker, Fortune, Hogbin, Firth, a.o.[104] In their dynamic approach, they are opposed to the agenetic historical school. Thus, Leslie White, an American protagonist of dynamic anthropology, sharply criticises the agenetic school in these words: "The anti-evolutionists, led in America by Franz Boas, have rejected the theory of evolution in cultural anthropology—and have given us instead a philosophy of planless hodge-podge-ism."[105]

N14. The Flexners and Straus clearly demonstrated the existence of spurts during fetal development of the brain.

---

[103] Evans-Pritchard, 823.
[104] Firth, 824-826; Fortune, 828; Hogbin, 835; Powdermaker, 844.
[105] White, 811.

They observed two periods of spurt, the first about halfway, and the second about four-fifths of the way through gestation. Both were characterized by rapid increase of the nerve cells of the cerebral cortex, and by abrupt changes of their form and of the quantity of pattern of the Nissl substance in the cytoplasm.

In its broadest aspects, the problem of integrative levels of development has been lately reformulated by Novikoff, Schneirla, a.o. Novikoff's concept of integrative levels attempts to define the progress of evolution of the inanimate, animate, and social world. It stresses the qualitative uniqueness of each level. Schneirla emphasizes the qualitative differences between biopsychological levels of organization: similar biological factors underlie the unity of groups, from insect societies to societies of higher animals; since these factors, however, are embedded in essentially different wholes, their significance varies from level to level.[106]

N22. The inspection of physical growth curves, of gradually increasing test scores, and of steadily rising learning curves lead psychologists to the conclusion that continuity is a basic property of development. In their zest to quantify mental life by analogy to physical events, they became quite oblivious of the fact that discontinuity—even more than continuity—is a basic characteristic of biological, and even physical, activity. "All our experience," says Lecomte Du Nouÿ in his remarkable book on *Biological Time*, "leads to the admission that continuity exists nowhere, and that one of the roles of consciousness is to manufacture continuity from discontinuity."[107] The principal facts of physiology support this view: the existence of a threshold of nerve excitation, absolute and relative; the propagation along the nerve in terms of electrochemical explosions; the all-or-none law of nerve stimulation; and various

[106] Novikoff, 795; Schneirla, 801.
[107] Du Nouÿ, 758.

other equally well-known facts. All point to abruptness and selectiveness as basic signs of life processes.

Continuity as a property of development has been "manufactured" by handling the data in a twofold manner: (a) by not only measuring, but also interpreting development solely in terms of overt achievement; (b) by averaging individual, abrupt scores, thus obtaining a composite curve that pictures continuous growth.

The number of child psychologists who are not entirely satisfied with this method of approach and with the results obtained by it, is increasing. They see the lack of proportion between the elaborate measurements of a great many data and the often trite conclusions derived from them. Only little is added to our understanding of development by finding that the number of words, the length of sentences, the span of attention, the ability to reason, etc., rise steadily with age. These psychologists are also certain that the leaps and bounds of individual curves, often blotted out by the emphasis on achievement and on group scores, are significant symptoms of processual changes underlying overt performances. The modern genetic analysis is beginning to take cognizance of the emergence of novel functions, of the creative reorganization of mental elements that takes place during growth.

Even within the area of physical development—which many psychologists look upon as the prototype of gradual growth—the change of emphasis is clearly noticeable. Developmental anatomists, like Wingate Todd, advocate a shift away from purely quantitative measurements of isolated somatic elements toward examination of changing textures and configurational patterns. Though it might not be possible to subject these patterns to perfect quantifications, they can be profitably ordered in sequences of maturation.[108] If individual curves of physical growth are combined, not in regard to average ages

[108] Frank, 894.

but according to their shape, that is to their crests and troughs, changes of growth rate become clearly visible.[109]

Studying mental growth longitudinally, by individual curves, investigators such as Honzik, Freeman, Flory, a.o., found rates of growth consistent only over short periods.[110]

The disagreement that still exists between those who find evidence only for gradualness and those who argue for saltatory changes seems to be less based on differences of techniques used, than on the general methodological approaches that direct the formulation of the experimental problems and procedures. McGraw, for instance, contended that infantile motor development is an entirely gradual and continuous process: this conclusion she drew after having observed two infants five days every week for many months.[111] On the other hand, M. Shirley found considerable evidence that many new behavior items emerge, full-fledged, by fits and starts.[112] Her inference was based on examinations of 25 infants so closely spaced as to make observation virtually continuous, and on daily records kept by the mothers. The difference between the results does not seem to be caused, as it has been argued, by the wider spacing of Shirley's observational periods as compared with McGraw's; it springs from the two experimenters' different aspects of observation. Results derived from an analysis of elementary functions and results coming from observations of patterns cannot easily be reconciled.

N34. The fallacy of identifying "regression" with recapitulation of developmental stages in reverse is nicely demonstrated by Barcroft's studies on biological frustration of sheep embryos. A sheep embryo of fifty days conveys specific, orderly, and co-ordinated patterns of movement: they are respiratory movements of the upper part of the body. If deprived of oxygen,

[109] Meredith, 946, 947; Shuttleworth, 982.
[110] Honzik, 913; Freeman and Flory, 895.
[111] McGraw, 943.
[112] Shirley, 979, 980.

the embryo "regresses" to an earlier stage of mass activity. But the "regressed" activity contains these marks of the previously attained higher level: (1) the mass movements are less crude than those of a younger, normally developing embryo; (2) sporadic respiratory movements are present.[113]

N35. Some psychopathologists, such as Cameron, Weisenburg, and McBride, caution us on the use of the regression concept in the analysis of aphasia, schizophrenia, etc. Cameron, for instance, writes: "If we are to make use of the terms 'regression' and 'deterioration' to characterize schizophrenia generally, it will have to be with the clear realization that we are taking serious liberties with these concepts in the interest of convenience and brevity. The schizophrenic thinking we have found in our studies can be described neither as childish nor as that of ordinary organic deterioration."[114]

N50. De Crinis has recently demonstrated successive development of cortical areas in man by using cell prolification as a criterion of maturation. In accordance with Flechsig, he found that sensory and motor areas are the earliest developed in infants. Latest in development are the areas of highest integrating power, such as the frontal-lobe regions. Only after three years do the pre-frontal regions reach the stage of maturity that the motor regions have already attained at eleven months.[114a] Tilney's most recent studies on brain development have been aptly summarized by McGraw.[115]

N51. The general laws of development transcend the distinction between maturation and learning. Any true learning consists essentially in the reorganization of behavior in terms of increased differentiation and integration. Many neurophysiologists of today hold that, physiologically, the processes

[113] Barcroft, **752.**
[114] Cameron, **1005.**
[114a] De Crinis, **757.**
[115] McGraw, **788**; Tilney, **807**; Tilney and Kubie, **808.**

of maturation and learning are of the same nature. "The conception," remarks Coghill, "that a neurone grows during a period of maturation, and then ceases to grow and becomes simply a conduction in a fixed mechanism, is erroneous and wholly inadequate to account for the function of the nervous system as a mechanism of learning."[116]

Inner growth, like learning, is an organismic response to stimulation.[117] Maturational changes are responses predominantly to "internal field" conditions.[118] In learning, the external field conditions are of great significance; the effect upon the organism varies, however, depending on the maturational state.*

* As to the controversy on the concepts of maturation and learning see McGraw, **788**, 337 ff.

CHAPTER II

N60. The same interpretation holds for the results gained from experiments with children. Instead of asking: "at what age do children discriminate colors, forms, etc.?" one should rather inquire into the stages of form- or color-discrimination in terms of bodily responses, or in terms of perceptual relationships, etc. (See the discussions on pp. 101-3 and 215.)

N65. The technique used by Uexküll and Sarris with dogs is basically identical with the "method of equivalent stimuli" that Klüver and others so successfully have applied to problems of discrimination in animals.[95] If two animals are trained to respond positively to a trapezoid, the one may transfer its response to a square but not to a triangle; the other animal may respond to a triangle but not to a square. On the basis of these differences in type or range of equivalence, animal

[116] Coghill, **633**, 83.
[117] Marquis, **785a.**
[118] Child, **631.**
[95] Klüver, **65**; Sarris, **689.**

I may be said to have reacted originally to the triangle-like aspects, animal II to the square-like characteristics of the trapezoid. It is surprising that this beautiful method has hardly ever been applied systematically to problems of child psychology. The experiment by Knoblauch described on pp. 115-16 uses a technique closely related to the method of equivalent stimuli. Stern and other investigators of child language have inadvertently employed this method in defining the range of meaning of certain words. To illustrate: Stern's daughter[96] designated by the word "puppe" (doll): (1) all sorts of dolls; (2) a toy rabbit, a toy cat, and other toy animals. However, she never called a toy bell by this name, but named it "deedeléedelee." One might assume that all the objects called "puppe" were functionally equivalent; that is, for the child, they were little objects that could be handled as animate things, hugged, and moved around in a certain fashion, etc.

N66. Two objects, though strikingly different for us, may be perceived by the primitive man as similar, if "functionally equivalent."

The Tsimshian Indians, for instance, consider thimbles similar to deerhoofs because both are used as jingles, tied to the ends of the dance apron fringes. Another example is the use by these Indians of pearl buttons substituting for abalone spangles as blanket decorations. "In these and similar cases," writes Barnett, "the testimony of informants is to the effect that such substitutes looked, felt, smelled, or sounded the same. . . . Thimble and hoof are formal variants; they operate on the same principle (agitation of a cluster or of resonant forms) and serve the same function (dance percussion accompaniment)."[97] Of course, things-of-action are perceived by the naive Western man in quite similar ways: he may use,

[96] Stern, 511.
[97] Barnett, 753, 28.

for instance, souvenirs of war, such as an empty shell, for various decorative or domestic purposes.

N77. In his book on "The Nature of Creative Activity," V. Loewenfeld has illustrated the expressive ability of children by many drawing examples. For instance, he asked children to draw a man searching for a pencil that he had lost in the grass. Loewenfeld found that the younger the children, the more expressively—and the less realistically—did they picture that scene.[98]

N79. A similar sequence concerning the decrease of animism repeats itself in later years on the verbal-conceptual level. Piaget[99] in particular has made several significant investigations on the meaning of the words "life," "feeling," etc., as attributes of objects and organisms. He was able to demonstrate a genetic sequence of stages leading from an animistic to a realistic understanding of the objective world.

One should be careful, however, not to confuse the anthropological term, pertaining to the belief of primitive people in mystic forces or souls that reside in objects, with the term animism as used in the analysis of child-like concepts. Here, it merely means a failure to distinguish living, biological forms from inorganic objects.

Piaget concluded from his studies that four developmental stages of animism can be distinguished: at the first stage, life is characterized by activity in general; at the second (6-8 years), life is indicated by movement; at the third (8-10 years), life is denoted by spontaneous movement; at the fourth (10-12 years), life is restricted to animals and plants. Using a standardized testing procedure, Russell and Dennis confirmed, on the whole, Piaget's results. In order to evaluate these studies, one should be aware of the tremendous individual

[98] Loewenfeld, 938.
[99] Piaget, 482.

variations at any given age level. The nature of the child's responses probably does not depend only on his chronological or mental age, as Piaget seems to believe; it depends partly upon the familiarity with the objects at hand. We found in our own studies that remote phenomena, such as lightning or celestial bodies, are apt to elicit more animistic responses than common technical events. The factor of psychological environment and training has also to be taken into account. Therefore, the simple averaging of performances at successive age levels can hardly be considered a valid approach. Longitudinal studies might reveal that, though the rate of this development may vary greatly with each child, the genetic sequence, as presented by Piaget, is on the whole correct.

The effect of personal experience upon this development has been indirectly demonstrated by Werner and Carrison[100] in a study of animistic thinking in brain-injured children. Using a standardized procedure similar to that employed by Russell and Dennis, the authors found that brain-injured children conveyed a higher degree of animistic conception than did non-brain-injured controls. They also found that the brain-injured group, compared with the control group, was not retarded in the definition of words in general. Hence it had to be assumed that the higher degree of animism was due to response patterns peculiar to an abnormal development. It is known that brain-injured individuals are influenced to an inordinate degree by extraneous stimuli. In such an organism, greatly steered by outside stimulation, the essential difference between the person who acts upon the world and the objects must necessarily be felt less than in a normal individual. Furthermore, the brain-injured organism often displays a lack of spontaneity (inability to shift, perseveration, lack of emotional control, etc.). Thus, again, one may assume that an individual who is lacking in willful, self-directed behavior is less aware than a normal individual of the difference exist-

[100] Werner and Carrison, **994.**

ing between the spontaneous activity as a characteristic of a person and the behavior of a thing.

N81. Hanfmann and Kasanin analyzed the grouping performance of schizophrenics on the Vigotzky test. Not infrequently, schizophrenics grouped together blocks varying in size, color, and shape, on the basis of physiognomic impressions rather than geometric qualities: "Objects appear not as large or small, having this or that color and shape, but as powerful, weak, harmonious, threatening, etc."[101]

Similarly, K. Goldstein found schizophrenic responses to Rorschach's Ink Blots to abound in physiognomic interpretations.

N86. In recent years experimental studies have brought forward much evidence for genetic changes in emotional behavior in accordance with the developmental laws discussed in the preceding paragraphs.

First, a genetic change from "syncretic" (bodily motor-affective) and massive behavior to specifically emotional reactions was observed. One of the signs of this trend is the decrease of overtness ("internalization") of the emotional response. Bayley, Blatz, Lippmann, a.o., studied the diminishing rate of crying during early infancy.[102] A comparison of Goodenough's records on the behavior of young children with that of older subjects demonstrates the decrease with age of the frequency of public display of anger.[103] H. E. Jones, using the galvanometric method with infants and preschool children, found a genetic trend toward the inhibition of overt (somatic) expression concomitant with an intensification of visceral responses.[104]

[101] Hanfmann and Kasanin, 1008.
[102] Bayley, 868; Blatz and Millichamp, 871; Laycock, 934.
[103] Goodenough, 901.
[104] Jones, H. E., 925.

Closely connected with this development is the increasing differentiation of the emotional content. Techniques more refined than those employed by K. Bridges—such as the use of the oscillograph by Klein, Gray, and Jeffress—made it possible to distinguish the crying pattern of hunger, fear, and rage at an age level at which earlier work, employing cruder methods of observation, had failed to show evidence of differences in emotional expression.[105]

Another important genetic trend is the increase in hierarchic integration of emotional behavior. Intellectualization, that is domination of emotions by higher functions, advances with the growing child. Primitive emotions are un-co-ordinated, blind, momentary outbursts. Emotions of growing children are short-lived and ever-shifting events. According to Jersild, after-effects of anger were almost twice as frequent and prolonged in children over four years of age, than in those two years old.[106] Goodenough, Blatz, a.o., have analyzed the increasing ability of the child to react adaptively in annoyance-producing situations.[107] Emotional patterns of lower degree of adaptability are replaced by those controlled by higher functions; this genetic order is excellently illustrated by Blatz's and Millichamp's study on infants.[108] In the beginning, massive unadapted outbursts are found to be the rule. As the infants advance in age, their effort directed toward the removal of unpleasant situations expresses itself in increasingly higher forms of integrated behavior. First, adaptation occurs entirely through locomotor activity (turning or running away, etc.); later on, at about two years of age, symbolic forms of expression (hiding face, verbalization) are added to the means of adjustment. Here, as in other areas, the development repeats itself at higher levels: for instance, in situations of social

[105] Jones, Mary and Burks, **418.**
[106] Jersild, **919.**
[107] Goodenough, **901**; Blatz, **870.**
[108] Blatz and Millichamp, **871.**

conflict among school children, crying and shouting—as expressions of helplessness—decrease and are more and more replaced by the use of adaptive language.

Another aspect of this development pertains to the causes of emotions. The first causes are immediate and concrete. Fear, as Jersild has shown, is created in the young infant by disturbing events, such as loud noises, which act in an immediate and direct manner upon the child. As the child grows older, factors of a non-immediate, imaginative, anticipatory nature become more prominent. In Jersild's subjects between the ages of 1:11 and 5:11, fears caused mainly by immediate and concrete experiences—such as loud noises, pain, loss of support—decreased, while those induced by imaginary creatures, darkness, and dreams, increased.[109] The growing effectiveness of potential danger has been studied by M. C. Jones. Jones's two-year-old subjects showed no fear if a snake was suddenly exposed before their eyes; two- to four-year-olds demonstrated increasingly more and more cautious apprehension; children over four years of age exhibited definite fear at the sight of the snake.[110] The positive correlation between these anticipatory forms of fear and I.Q. is a further indication of the mounting intellectual control.[111]

N100a. A technique similar to Valentine's, but with better control, was used by Staples.[112] She employed subjects ranging from six to twenty-four months of age. Her results indicate a clear differentiation of the four primary colors at the twelve-to-fifteen-month level. Up to that age the "warm" colors, particularly red, are preferred over the "cold" colors. Such duality, in color preference is in keeping with our assumption of primordial reactions to color in terms of bodily responses.

[109] Jersild and Holmes, 921.
[110] Jones, M. C., 928.
[111] Jersild, 920.
[112] Staples, 508.

N100b. Though very young infants seem to be able to discriminate the primary colors on the basis of bodily reactions, the matching of these same colors, demanding the capacity for perceptual relationship, advances more slowly. According to Cook, two-year-olds were able to match the four colors with an accuracy of only forty-five per cent. At the six-year level the accuracy increased to almost one hundred per cent.[113]

Again, color naming, which demands a still higher function (verbal conceptualization), is more slowly advancing than matching. At six years of age accuracy in color naming increased to only sixty-two per cent.

The same problem of functional levels of discrimination pertains to visual form perception. Munn and Stiening[114] had tremendous difficulties in training a fifteen-month-old child to discriminate between a cross and a square. Their method consisted in rewarding the child whenever he opened the lid of one of two boxes on which the figures were pasted. The child succeeded only after about four hundred trials. Recently, Miss Ling[115] was able to train much younger children (six- to twelve-month-olds) to differentiate between various forms in relatively few trials. The discrepancy in the results of the two experiments is most likely due to the difference of technique; the two experimental situations obviously brought different functions into play. In Munn's and Stiening's experiment perceptual and associative relationship between a specially marked box and food reward was requested. In Miss Ling's situation a much more direct approach toward the figure existed: the positive figure, previously immersed into a tasty solution, was simply the "sweet" figure for the child. Thus, the child reacted positively toward a figure which was "lickable." In other words, discrimination was in terms of things-of-action, whereas in Munn-Stiening's experiment perceptual

[113] Cook, **880.**
[114] Munn, **955.**
[115] Ling, **935a.**

relationship rather than direct bodily reaction was primarily involved.

N101. Various experiments suggest that sensory discrimination on a non-verbal level develops early and, after having reached a peak in childhood, may possibly even decrease. Peckham, using a non-verbal form of Snellen's test, concluded that children only 1:11 to 5:2 years old possess a visual acuity similar in range to that of adults.[116] According to Peters, brightness sensitivity reaches its peak at about fourteen years of age.[117] The peak for the tactile sensitivity seems to be attained much earlier; Friedmann found even a decline of the tactile threshold after six to eight years of age.[118]

The emergence, or increasing prevalence of higher forms of activity during development seems indicated in another group of findings: viz., a shift of dominance, for certain situations around eight years, from tactile-kinesthetic (contact-receptive) to visual (distance-receptive) factors. We inferred from our results with the marble-board test, that the performance of younger children was guided by predominantly tactual-kinesthetic factors; with older children visual form factors became increasingly dominant. This shift of dominance occurred around the eight- to nine-year level.[119] A similar shift was found by us in an experiment in which the child had to tap four squares in a certain order. The order was indicated previously by the experimenter in two ways: by tapping in one series, and by light signals in the other.[120] It is probable that the more abstract the task, the later during development may the shift be expected to occur. Experiments performed by Renshaw obviously dealt with such an abstract situation. Children were requested to point, with open or closed eyes,

[116] Peckham, 964.
[117] Peters, 477.
[118] Friedmann, 896.
[119] Werner, 990.
[120] Werner, 536.

to an area on their skin that had been previously touched by the experimenter. He found a shift toward visual dominance occurring at about thirteen years of age.[121]

CHAPTER III

N118. Volkelt's results seem to be closely related to observations made some time ago by Furness on the discriminating ability of a chimpanzee. He noticed that the ape had greater difficulties on the form board with the abstract shapes (square, oblong, lozenge) than with complex forms, such as the five-point star or the equilateral cross.[58]

N128. Roettger studied the imitation of adult words by children eighteen to thirty-six months of age. The phonetic pattern changes reveal a basic trend toward more global and homogeneous structurization.[59]

CHAPTER IV

N145. The trend toward specialization is noticeable also with reference to material types of memory. Many psychologists of today probably agree that, at least in the adult, a general memory factor hardly exists. There are almost as many "memories" as there are areas of mental operations. However, if one descends the ontogenetic scale, one should expect a closer relationship between the various areas of memory. Some experimental evidence has been brought forward in support of such conclusion. Anastasi, for instance, found practically no correlation at the college level between immediate "memories" for various visual material, vocabulary, and number operations. On the other hand, Bryan reported a high correlation between these faculties at the preschool level.[50]

[121] Renshaw, Wherry, and Newlin, 970.
[58] Furness, 1020.
[59] Roettger, 975.
[50] Anastasi, 855; Asch, 861.

N150. J. S. Bruner[51] has presented excellent experimental evidence of the effect of "emotional perspective" in the perception and memory of children. The task was to adjust a variable circle to the apparent size of a penny, nickel, dime, quarter, and half dollar. Settings were made both with the coins present six inches from the variable circle, and from memory. Ten-year-old children overestimated the sizes of the coins in proportion to the value: pennies were seen as ten per cent larger than their actual size, half dollars thirty-five per cent larger. The tendency to overestimate perceived coins was significantly more marked among poor than among rich children. In another situation the coin was replaced by a candy in circular form. After having eaten the candy, the apparent size increased by five per cent. There was also evidence (according to personal communication by the author) that the amount of overestimation decreases with increasing age.

N151. Change of size through emphasis (emotional perspective) is present in the hallucinatory images produced by mescaline. One subject in Maclay's and Guttmann's experiments reported that everything he perceived in his hallucinations elongated itself in whatever direction he turned his attention. A man's arm grew longer and longer during his attempt to draw a picture of it.[52]

CHAPTER V

N169. In primitive societies—as in the less sophisticated areas of Western civilization—space is measured qualitatively and in terms of bodily action rather than systematized on a quantitative scale. The Salteaux, for instance, measure distance in units of activity. The distance between two villages may be

[51] Bruner and Goodman, 874a.
[52] Maclay and Guttmann, 1010.

measured by the number of "sleeps." The bodily yardsticks by which these Indians measure things vary with the material and the objects at hand: canoe ribs are constructed three fingers in width; birchbark canoes are measured by "stretches," that is by the length between the fingertips when both arms are stretched out; etc.[25]

N177. Ingenious experiments by Edith Meyer brought forth evidence supporting the interpretation of space development as outlined above.[26] One of her experiments with children two to five-and-a-half years of age may be briefly described: a board, six inches high and fourteen inches long, was mounted on a pivot. A horizontal crosspiece containing two platforms was fastened at each of the lower corners of this perpendicular board; thus, a chip could be placed on one of the platforms 1, 2, 3, or 4 (see figure with view from above):

The child watched the placement of the chip. Thereafter, the chip as well as the three other platforms were covered with a cardboard. After the board had been rotated at 180° the child was asked to get the chip. From trial to trial the chip was placed on a different platform; moreover, the position of the whole apparatus relative to the child was changed. After a series of tests the child was finally asked to make predictions: "Where do you think the chip will go when I turn?" Three distinct genetic stages were observed, indicating a development from an egocentric space-of-action toward objective space. At the first stage (up to two-and-a-half years), children did not understand that the movement of objects involved a shift from one location to another. During a second stage,

[25] Hallowell, 766.
[26] Meyer, 948.

the children perceived object motion as a shift in position; but the new position was only vaguely anticipated. During the third stage (around four years of age), the children apprehended the correct spatial relation between motion and displacement. Even at this age space was of such concrete and pragmatic nature that the child could determine the displacement only if the movement was carried through before his eyes: though able to secure the chip correctly after rotation, the child usually could not predict the exact future position before the known rotation was actually performed.

CHAPTER VI

N188. Louise Ames[29] studied the development of the time sense in children 1:6 to 8 years of age. Her results indicate the slow emergence of an objective socialized time concept from egocentric time-of-action. Good illustrations are the answers of children to questions on duration. These are typical responses of children of various ages to the question "how long do you stay in school?":
"We will take a nap and then our mother comes" (4-year-old).
"Until lunchtime" (4-year-old).
"Until twelve" (6-year-old).
"Four-and-a-half hours" (7-year-old).

CHAPTER VII

N192. Decrease of immediacy of action signals a development through which the organism gains greater freedom of movement. This genesis has been studied by experimental devices testing the degree of indirectness of behavior. Following the lead of Koehler's work with apes, Gottschaldt, Alpert, Lipmann and Bogen, a.o., have reported on the rising ability of the child to master the environment by indirect

[29] Ames, 854.

action; this involves the use of circuitous routes, instruments, and the ability to delay and to plan.[18]

N193. Growing spontaneity of action is another indication that the child is able to differentiate his organism from his objective environment. From a neurophysiological point of view, the great motor systems that are little subjected to voluntary control—the autonomic and the extrapyramidal systems—seem to precede genetically the voluntary system. The very young child is "stimulusbound" (Goldstein); he is passively subjected to the stimuli of his surroundings. During the first year, according to Buehler, spontaneous, that is, searching and exploratory movements, increase from 0 to 30% of all movements registered. Strong stimuli of sound and light at first cannot be mastered by the organism: hence, he reacts negatively to these stimuli by crying, turning away, etc. Later, at about six months, the predominantly negative responses change to predominantly positive reactions; this is an indication that the child organism has learned to "digest" intense stimulation.[19] We may add that many reflex-like responses undergo a similar change from object-negative to positive reactions. Thus, the Babinski reflex of the infant develops into the plantar reflex of the older child.[20]

Genetic characteristics of motor action can be observed also in experiments on primitivation. Dembo, Lewin, Barker, Patrick, a.o., have shown that a frustrating situation may cause a momentary regression of motor behavior.[21] Such "development in reverse" leads to stages of decreased differentiation and hierarchic organization. In their recent work, Barker, Dembo, and Lewin achieved frustration with children two-and-a-half to five years of age by placing a transparent screen between the playing child and a number of desirable objects. The

[18] Gottschaldt, 382; Alpert, 853; Lipman and Bogen, 440.
[19] Bühler, 349.
[20] Clarke, 878; Hooker, 914; Goldstein, 562.
[21] Barker, 863; Patrick, 963.

488   *Comparative Psychology of Mental Development*

effect of the frustration could be determined in terms of regression to a genetically lower stage of play measured in points of constructiveness.

CHAPTER VIII

N200. Hooker's work furnishes an excellent illustration of the process of individuation in the human fetus. The young fetus of eight weeks responds to facial stimulation with a neck and upper-trunk movement. Later on, the movement expands caudally. By fourteen weeks, the massive movements have become circumscribed and specified; the fetus responds now with a number of discrete and specific movements.[24]

The controversy between those who argue for original global patterns of activity and those who believe in local reflexes as primary motor elements still continues. Coghill, Hooker, Barcroft, a.o., who belong to the first group of investigators, are not unaware of the evidence pointing to early reflex-like responses in young fetuses. But they interpret these facts in a manner that differs strikingly from the hypotheses of the second group. Barcroft comments on the locally circumscribed movements that precede the appearance of mass activity, as follows: "The partial movements appeal to me as being the tuning of the individual instruments, but when that stage is over there comes a moment at which the orchestra as such breaks forward."[25] Windle and Orr[26] distinguish between solely mechanical stimulation and spontaneous activity. They admit that the chick's primary response to mechanical stimulation is in the nature of a local reflex; but, at the same time, spontaneous activity, such as swimming, conveys primary, well-integrated, total behavior patterns.

N205. Not all rigidity can be directly related to globality or lack of differentiation. In a critical evaluation of the con-

[24] Hooker, 914.
[25] Barcroft, 752, 19.
[26] Windle and Orr, 1031.

cept of rigidity, I suggested distinguishing a rigidity due to immaturity of reaction (de-differentiation) from an abnormal rigidity as a symptom of organic lesion.[27]

CHAPTER IX

N215. As is well known, perceptual size constancy, because of the lack of binocular cues, breaks down at greater distances: here, "conceptual constancy" replaces much of perceptual constancy. How little developed conceptual size constancy is in small children is illustrated in a report on Stern's daughter. The three-year-old child called soldiers seen at a considerable distance from the window "Kindersoldaten" (child-soldiers).[168]

N219. Rüssel studied also the degree to which these qualities aroused the perceptual attention of the child.[169] What relationships, one might ask, are most easily observed by the child and, therefore, are most readily abstracted from the objects of his daily surroundings? Rüssel collected pertinent data from so-called crossed series. For instance, the child had previously learned that the larger figure, relative to the smaller, was positive; in another series it was the round figure, against the angular one, that was positive. "Crossed" pairs were then presented: they consisted of figures with both negative and positive characteristics:

Preceding Series: large vs. small;   round vs. angular
                    +   −   +   −
Crossed Series: large and angular vs. small and round

In the various crossed series all possible combinations of figural characteristics were presented that had been used in the foregoing simple series. The relative frequency with which size relations were chosen against relations of shape, thick-

[27] Werner, 1017, 1018.
[168] Stern, 511.
[169] Rüssel, 499.

ness, symmetry, etc., was an indicator of the relative importance of that perceptual property for the child. Rüssel found
that the various relationships appealed to the child in the
following order of preference (per cent of choice):
Contour-solid: 73%; Thick-thin: 64%; Large-small: 49%;
Round-angular: 39%; Symmetrical-asymmetrical: 17%.

N228. Naturalistic groupings of geometrical objects have
been reported by Hanfmann and Kasanin.[170] One schizophrenic placed a large block next to the small thin blocks,
with the explanation that the policeman (viz., the large block)
was whipping the workers (viz., the small blocks).

N233. Similarly, schizophrenics may group objects together
in terms of affective-physiognomic qualities. One of Hanfmann's patients put first the small thin blocks and later the
yellow blocks together explaining, "Don't you think they look
sick?"[170]

N243. Goldstein and Scheerer[171] exhaustively treated the
problem of concrete behavior in brain-injured patients. They
summarized previous work and presented further analysis concerning lack of abstract behavior of the brain-injured organism
in various test situations.

N246. The Papago form "quasi-class concepts" of color by
prefixed modifiers. Light colors of a certain hue are designated
by the prefix *cah,* meaning "a little like" or "almost." They
also use a modifier for indicating blackish colors.[172]

N248. Ray investigated generalization in twelve-year-old
children with a method reminiscent of Rüssel's technique for

[170] Hanfmann and Kasanin, 1008, 25.
[171] Goldstein and Scheerer, 1007.
[172] O'Neale and Dolores, 796.

the abstraction of relationships.[173] Pairs of pictures were exposed, one pair at a time. In each series of pairs the "correct" members possessed common properties. For instance, the first series consisted of curved versus straight forms; the second of animate versus inanimate forms; the third of quadrupeds versus non-quadrupeds. There were two keys, one for each of the two pictures. By pressing the correct key a green light flashed on; a red light appeared if the key under the incorrect picture was pressed. The child's task was to get a sequence of green lights for each series as soon as possible. The child thus conveyed its ability to generalize by pressing the correct key, which was always connected with objects of identical property. The observations made by the experimenter suggest that perceptual-concrete generalization precedes generalization explicitly stated in terms of verbal concepts.

N250. Whether animals are capable of representative, or symbolic, behavior cannot be simply answered by yes or no. The answer will depend on the inclusion or the exclusion of syncretic or implicit forms. Yerkes [174] makes the statement that apes are capable of symbolic behavior. The fact that they can learn to handle tokens as substitutes for food[175] does not prove to him that they are capable of symbolic processes; on the other hand, he is convinced that the experiments by Nissen and Taylor, Riesen,[176] and others, on delayed reward in discrimination learning involves symbolization. Chimpanzees can learn to discriminate between two colors even when the reward is delayed a few seconds. Riesen interprets this accomplishment as follows: "Such learning is dependent upon intraorganic stimulus-response-stimulus sequences, which serve as representation of the critical stimuli until reward or no reward

[173] Ray, 966.
[174] Yerkes and Learned, 1035.
[175] Wolfe, 1033.
[176] Riesen, 1027.

occurs." In other words: color is here represented implicitly, by intraorganic behavior, thus denoting syncretic representation. Such behavior should not be confused with forms of explicit representation that is truly human.

N266. The significance of physiognomic forms in primordial speech cannot be decided, as some philologists seem to believe, by linguistic history.* Compared with prehistoric speech development, the epoch of historically traceable changes of language is infinitesimally small. Linguistics can hardly make any valid statements, even with respect to onomatopoetic (sound-imitating) forms in prehistoric language; the same science is even far less in a position to evaluate the factor of physiognomics, which so frequently is being confused with imitative language. Child behavior is probably the only area where reliable investigations could be performed and from which valid insight into the developmental process of language might eventually be gained. Few psychologists of today think of the early acquisition of names in terms of blindly conditioned associations between sounds and objective meaning. Psychological reasoning, as well as some evidence, favors an hypothesis suggesting primacy of natural symbolism. Such a theory implies that a linguistic epoch of intimate relationship between perceived properties of things and sound patterns must have existed before a stage of remote, and seemingly arbitrary, connections between them could be attained.

N274. An interesting study of the development of abstract concepts at early ages has been performed by L. Welch.[177] Children 1:9 to 6 years old were presented with a number of toy objects which they had to handle according to the experimenter's requests: for instance, "put all the people over there and give them all the vegetables." Thus the experimenter

* See for instance Sapir's remarks, 800, 6.
[177] Welch, 989.

was able to determine whether a child knew not only the name of an object (viz., potato), but also one or more hierarchically related concepts. If he knows the object as "potato" and as "vegetable" he possesses a "first-order" concept; he has acquired a "second-order" concept if, in addition, he knows this object also as "food." Up to 3:10 years of age very few children (20 per cent) were found to possess a second-order concept. Between 3:10 and 5:4 years of age the number of children who acquired one second-order concept rapidly increased (62 per cent).

N296. Werner and Carrison recently studied the development of the finger schema in retarded children of mental ages ranging from six to ten years. They used the "finger schema test" as described in the text. The accuracy in differentiating the fingers was found to increase on each item, as well as on the whole battery. The relation between the ability to differentiate between the fingers and to operate with numbers was again demonstrated: groups of children showing extremely high and extremely low scores on the finger schema test had, respectively, low and high arithmetic achievement scores.[178]

CHAPTER X

N302. Malinowski[60] has shown that, with the Trobrianders, the perception of similarity between relatives is strongly influenced by social-affective attitudes. Resemblance between child and father is regarded as natural and proper, and is therefore assumed always to be present. Resemblance between mother and child, as well as between brothers, is socially unacceptable and therefore denied to exist.

N324. Critics of the work of Piaget and others on the child's conception of causality have raised the question whether the

[178] Werner and Carrison, 993.
[60] Malinowski, 785, 88.

peculiarities of childlike explanations might not simply be due to a lack of experience and knowledge, rather than to a mode of thinking different from that of adults. M. J. Williams[61] conducted, under the direction of the author, a comprehensive experiment on the influence of experience upon the concepts of causal relations in children. The experimental group included over one hundred children six to ten years old. In the first part of the experiment the children were requested to explain simple physical phenomena that were shown to them by the experimenter. The second part was conducted a month later; this time the children were presented with various situations so designed as to afford them the opportunity for thoroughly familiarizing themselves with physical causes involved in the previously presented events. These demonstrations were immediately followed by the repetition of the first part of the experiment. A control group of almost one hundred children went through the same procedure with the exception of the experience situations, which were omitted.

One of the experiments dealt with expansion by heat. A flask containing a colored solution of tetrachloride, into which a test tube was immersed, was shown to the child. He had to hold the flask in his hand and was asked to explain the rise of the liquid in the test tube. The experience period was used for observations of related events, such as the rise of the level of colored alcohol in a test tube held over a flame; the rise and fall of the mercury with temperature; the increase of the temperature of a nail when held in the fist; etc.

Another experiment dealt with the speed of falling bodies depending on relative weight. A sheet of paper was cut into equal pieces before the eyes of the child; one piece was pressed into a ball, the other piece was left unfolded. The child had to explain the different speeds of the two objects when dropped to the ground. During the experience period the child was made to observe the gliding of a paper aeroplane (kite); the

[61] Williams, 997.

downing of a toy parachute, open and closed; the falling of a square piece of paper, first unfolded and then crumpled.

Another experiment involved the change of the water level through the immersion of a large wooden block and, later on, of a small pebble.

The explanatory concepts could easily be ranked in terms of superiority. For instance, answers to the question "why does the water rise higher with this object (wooden block) than with this (small pebble)?" were answered at three levels of accuracy: (1) "because it's wood;" (2) "because it's heavier;" (3) "because it's bigger." "Wood"—"heavier"—"bigger" represent explanations of an increasingly higher order. Similarly, if the child explained the rise of the tetrachloride in the test tube by saying "because I squeezed it," he employed a concept inferior to that of "heat."

In four of the six experiments, the experimental group, after having been exposed to the experiences, showed a significant shift toward explanatory concepts of a higher order. The effectiveness of the experience upon causal explanations was limited by two factors: One was the relative concreteness of the children's thinking—causal explanations did not go beyond the concrete and perceptual. Hardly ever would a child conceive of the non-tangible elements of a situation. Many children achieved an understanding of the relation between heat and the rise of tetrachloride, or of size and the change of the water level; but they did not arrive at explanations involving the concept of expansion, or that of volume. The second limiting factor was the stage of maturity: the experiments offered some evidence of a relationship between age and ability to profit from the opportunities provided by experience. To illustrate, the most superior explanation of the fall of paper objects utilized the concept "air" ("the open paper falls more slowly because the air catches it," etc.). The table shows the increase in the use of this concept from part one to part two of the experiment at two age levels:

496   *Comparative Psychology of Mental Development*

| Age Level | Experimental Group | | Control Group | |
	Exp. I	Exp. II	Exp. I	Exp. II
6/7	9.8%	35.4%	25.7%	19.9%
8/9	20.8%	68.9%	48.9%	46.8%

To sum up, Williams' study suggests that causal reasoning can be raised to a superior level by experiential opportunities. The results indicate also that such improvement is limited by the child's maturational status: older school children profit more than younger subjects by the opportunities afforded them; but even they do not rise above the level of concrete "if-then" explanations.

N330. Genetic studies on syllogistic reasoning have been performed by Muller[62] with subjects ranging in age from seven to seventeen years. Muller found that younger children tend to represent the premises by imagining concrete situations, a tendency that diminishes with increasing age. Moore, in his work on syllogistic thinking, presented evidence of a decrease of autistic (egocentric) reasoning during the school years.[63]

Strasheim's extremely ingenious experiments dealt with the application of previously learned problem solutions to new situations.[64] In the first part, children, four to ten years of age, were presented verbally with a problematic situation, and were given a way of solving it. They were then placed in a number of similar imaginary situations, to see how far they were able to transfer what they had learned before to the new problem. They first were told about two boys who wanted to toss for first pick in a ball game; as they had no money with which to toss, they had to find another way. One boy picked up two pieces of paper from the ground and made one piece shorter than the other. He then held the two pieces

[62] Muller, 954.
[63] Moore, 953.
[64] Strasheim, 986.

in his hand with only the tops sticking out and let his friend draw. The next nine situations also dealt with tossing. The testees had to find out what materials could be used for the draw, if, for instance, the two people of the story were swimming in water far away from the beach. As each succeeding situation became less and less similar to the original story, the difficulty of transfer through the abstraction of common elements increased from step to step. Strasheim observed that transfer was greatly limited in younger children. Their eduction of the common elements was on a perceptual, rather than on an abstract, level. This stage of thinking was succeeded by a higher level, at which the children became capable of conceiving the relations separately from the perceptual context.

Applying to new problems what one has learned previously often demands the ability to synthesize creatively two experiences. According to N. Maier the ability to unite into a novel experience two previously learned experiences is a function of age.[65] Maier's assertion that associative learning is the predominant intellectual activity of the young child is in accord with Strasheim's conclusion. This author claims that "bare retentivity or its special form, associative reproduction, plays by far the greatest part in the young child's mental life. . . . The fact that this is the more primitive stage explains to us why there is a constant tendency to relapse into it, even when the later stage has been attained."[65a]

The problem of qualitative stages of reasoning. At this point it might be advantageous to discuss some of the misconceptions about the problem of qualitative levels of reasoning that have arisen in recent experimental literature.

(1) As discussed before, if we restrict our efforts to the calculation of average age scores and developmental curves of achievement, the essential goal of genetic psychology, viz. the understanding of the processes of growth, can never be achieved. The concept of the child as an imperfect adult may

[65] Maier, 448.

be sufficient for practical applications, such as measuring the mental or educational status; it seems, however, wholly inadequate as a guiding concept in an integrated analysis. The problem of genetic levels is intimately linked with this argumentation: one cannot logically believe the child to be more than an imperfect adult and, at the same time, discard the concept of organizational levels.

(2) The genetic concept of qualitative differences has been criticized for the reason that adults often display a behavior similar to that found in children. This seems to be the belief of Abel, Deshaies, a.o.[66] However, the display of primitive behavior by adults has hardly ever been overlooked by those who advocate qualitative levels. On the contrary, it has given rise to important considerations like the following: (a) developmental sequences repeat themselves at various stages of maturity; (b) primitive levels do not completely disappear during development, but become merely subordinated to higher forms of activity. Only because of these facts is it possible to conduct experiments on primitivation in adults; these experiments were of great help in the study of qualitatively different levels of human behavior.

(3) Another misconception centers around the problem of gradual versus sudden development. The belief in gradual development and the belief in qualitatively different stages are not necessarily mutually exclusive. A stage may be characterized by the predominance and frequency of forms of behavior "critical" for that stage. One might, therefore, reasonably expect a good deal of overlapping of lower and higher forms of behavior. This is particularly true when calculations are derived from a great many subjects. Thus, with respect to frequency of dominant characteristics, the concept of gradual development may be applied to qualitative stages; but this does not mean that gradualness necessarily pertains to processual changes. There are some who still believe trial

[66] Abel, 852; Deshaies, 888.

and error to be the prototype of problem solving behavior. They are opposed by those who, like the Gestaltists, find the essence of reasoning in sudden, insightful reorganization. Experiments by Harter, Roberts, and Jones seem to suggest that trial and error behavior is the more frequent the more artificial the relationships are that have to be detected.[67] In truly meaningful situations, suddenness of part- or whole-solutions seems to be the rule rather than the exception (Alpert, Kreezer and Dallenbach, Hazlitt).[68]

(4) Much controversy stems from a confusion of the concept of qualitative differences with that of innate differences. It has been argued, for instance, that children reason in a primitive way only because they lack the fund of knowledge that education later on provides. This argument is irrelevant as to the problem of qualitative levels; it refers solely to the relation of maturation to training. With few exceptions, little effort has been put forward toward an analysis of this relationship. Williams' experiments, outlined before, indicate that certain experiences were capable of lifting the children's causal concepts to a higher level. But the results also show that there are limitations to this advancement corresponding with the child's state of intellectual maturity.

(5) Other arguments concern the relation between reasoning stages and chronological ages: Piaget's and other writers' insistence on a definite relationship between levels of reasoning and chronological age have brought about undue criticism of the concept of thinking stages *per se*. The criticism is justified in so far as the levels of reasoning cannot be considered to be a matter of chronological (or mental) age alone. They depend, to a large extent, on the nature of the task at hand, its difficulty and familiarity; they also depend on the child's psychological environment and on his training. We may, therefore, not be able to identify stages of reasoning simply

[67] Harter, 905; Roberts, 974; Jones, 924.
[68] Alpert, 853; Kreezer and Dallenbach, 933; Hazlitt, 399.

in terms of chronological ages. We may, however, quite reasonably direct our effort toward the analysis of developmental sequences of thought, which are less strictly related to chronological age. It has been generally found, for instance, that Piaget's subjects coming, as they do, from poor homes, were retarded in concept formation when compared with children employed by us and other investigators. We also found that, with respect to explanations of—psychologically—remote phenomena, such as clouds, lightning, rain, etc., children remained for a longer time on a primitive, egocentric, and anthropomorphic level than they did with respect to interpretations of common technical events. Norman Maier found that creative synthesis of two learned experiences—considered by him as the essence of reasoning—was not operating before five to six years of age. However, it must be conceded that the genetic appearance of reasoning most probably depends on the type of the task involved. A good illustration is afforded by K. Buehler, Alpert, Richardson, a.o.[69] For instance, a piece of biscuit with a string attached to it was placed slightly out of the infant's reach. A child one year old, in general is able to secure the biscuit by using the string. Before that age, string and biscuit obviously are two different experiences for the child. One may therefore assume that the ability to synthesize and to reorganize two experiences into one novel action develops earlier in a simple sensory-motor situation than it does in a situation like the one presented by Maier, in which rather complex space relationships are involved.

In concluding this discussion, one might predict that the controversy concerning genetic stages of reasoning will be finally decided through longitudinal studies based on individual experimental analysis.

N331. The generality of the term "concreteness" should be evaluated with reference to the concept of genetic parallelism

[69] Bühler, 351; Alpert, 853; Richardson, 973.

discussed in the first chapter. The presence of concrete thought
in the young child and in the brain-injured adult should not
mislead to the identification of childlike and pathological thinking. Werner and his collaborators demonstrated basic differences between immature and abnormal forms of concrete behavior in a series of experimental studies. A test (the "picture-
object-test")[70] specifically devised to analyze thought processes,
consisted of two pictures representing a boy about to be
drowned and a building on fire. The child had to select from
a number of toy objects (animals, cars, tools, people, etc.)
those which he thought to go best with each picture; these
he had to place in front of the pictures. The performances of
brain-injured children compared with those of mentally immature children of the same chronological and mental ages
showed a number of peculiar responses. The performance of
the brain-injured children was interfered with by an exaggerated responsiveness to the perceptual stimuli. This one
characteristic of concretism—to be steered by external stimuli,
sometimes quite extraneous to the field—was rarely observed
in the non-brain-injured children. On the other hand, the
immaturity of the non-brain-injured subjects was obvious in
the definitions of semiabstract and abstract words. Here, in
strictly delimited verbal situations, the brain-injured children
were less "concrete": they defined and generalized quite adequately for their age levels.

N333. Norman Cameron, in his significant experimental
analyses of schizophrenic reasoning, found characteristics that
coincide essentially with our notions of egocentricity, globality,
syncretism, and lack of integration. "From the analyses of our
material," says Cameron, "we were able to pick out three
factors distinct enough to justify separate discussion. These
are: (1) the appearance of loose clusters of terms in place of
organically integrated concepts ('asyndetic thinking'); (2) the

[70] Werner, 995.

use of terms or phrases that approximate the meaning, striking somewhere on the periphery of the target instead of at the bull's eye; and (3) the concomitant appearance of co-ordinate themes interweaving with each other and through mutual interference producing what at first glance looks like a mere jumble of words."[71] The first factor seems closely related to lack of integration, the second factor to diffuseness, and the third to syncretism of thought.

CHAPTER XI

N343. For a modern comprehensive treatise on the taboo see the recently published book by Webster.[64]

CHAPTER XII

N414a. During the last years, attempts have been made to understand cultural patterns in terms of psychological dynamics which can be analyzed in the individual members of the group. Such a dynamic approach, forcefully initiated by Kardiner,[76] Linton,[77] a.o., presents a distinct advance beyond Ruth Benedict's phenomenological analyses. Kardiner's attempt delineates the patterns of responses and adjustments of the individual toward cultural institutions (sexual prohibitions, disciplinary measures, etc.), to which he can react, but which he cannot control. The basic constellation created in the individual by these conditions are his "basic personality structure." It is through the mirror of the basic personality structure that one can study empirically the psychodynamic nature of social patterns.

N414b. Cameron demonstrated strikingly how the autistic character of the schizophrenic world is reflected in the attempt

[71] Cameron, 1003, 14.
[64] Webster, 810.
[76] Kardiner, 772, 773.
[77] Linton, 781.

of the patients to solve test problems. One of the outstanding behavior signs of Cameron's patients is "the personal preoccupation that dominates the scene and that can not be kept outside the boundaries of the experimental problem."[78] For instance, one of the patients is greatly preoccupied with her marital and maternal responsibilities. She was profoundly disturbed when asked to separate Vigotzki's blocks into groups. "I cannot bring myself to divide them," she said. "Dividing" was not a simple operation in the objective test field but, for her, it was an act identified with marital separation in her domestic life.

CHAPTER XIII

N453. The genetic changes occurring in the attitude toward obedience are clearly indicated in an interesting study by Klein.[141] He observed a change of process patterns underlying the development of the attitude of obedience. During the first year, before a noticeable rise of resistant behavior takes place, obedience is "blind": it occurs in terms of simple stimulus-response reactions. Later on, during the second and third year, the child becomes inclined to "give in" only after deliberation; this change shows itself objectively in an increase of the frequency of hesitation and protest before obeying. During the elementary school years, the obedience pattern undergoes a new change. McGrawth questioned children of preschool and of elementary school ages and found that most of the four-year-olds, but only half of the seven-year-old children, appreciated the necessity of the act of obedience.[142]

N456. H. H. Anderson has contributed significant genetic studies to the problem of the interrelationship between indi-

[78] Cameron, 1006, 10.
[141] Klein, 931.
[142] Brooks, F. D., Cattell, Psyche, Jones, H. E., Meek, Lois, and Stoddard, G. D., 874.

viduation and socialization. He has shown that higher forms of integration appear when the individual spontaneously and flexibly responds to differences in other persons.[143] Dominant behavior, for instance, is in its pure form egocentric and rigid; domineering leadership is genetically inferior to leadership in terms of highly integrated, plastic behavior. According to Pigors' investigations, this latter form of leadership does not appear, in general, before the age of nine or ten.[144]

N458. A few remarks may be added on the development of group behavior. Much experimental evidence supports the theoretical supposition that groups and group behavior develop in terms of differentiation and hierarchic integration.

A number of studies have been concerned with the social activity and with the decrease of solitary play during early growth.[145] We may, in particular, discuss briefly the results of experiments on the development of groups with reference to complexity, articulateness, and stability of organization.

Complexity: The number of group members increases with advancing age. In general, during the first year of life direct social contacts are limited to two individuals at a time. Not before he reaches school age will the child, in general, spontaneously participate in the activity of a well-defined group composed of more than three members.[146]

Articulation: Primary relationship between group members is egocentric, the interaction between them rather loose. The homogeneous, vaguely integrated character of primordial groups has been well observed in the "parallel" play of children. A higher step has been determined by Parten and Newhall as "associative" play: here the group is united by a common activity, such as road building, but the structure is still ill-defined and division of labor lacking. Better articulated

[143] Anderson, **856.**
[144] Pigors, **965.**
[145] Bott, **872**; Hetzer, **909**; Loomis, **939.**
[146] Bühler, **350**; Wilslitzky, **998**; Parten and Newhall, **962.**

groups develop in the "co-operative" play. In co-operative play there is division of labor, group censorship, centralization of control, and subordination of the individual aspiration to that of the group. Parten and Newhall found clear evidence of a relation between age and degree of group organization.[147] One cannot, however, accept these genetic relationships as dependent on age in an absolute manner: genetic steps of this sort are apt to repeat themselves whenever the child meets with a novel, more complex situation. This is well illustrated by the development of group behavior at the elementary school level, as studied by Reininger.[148] The beginners' class as a whole displays, at first, a low form of group structure, that possesses all the characteristics of a crowd. Organization grows through the initial forming of a few isolated nuclei. The nuclei are small units, each having its leader. Further organization develops by the merging of the enlarged nuclei and by the differentiation of the rôles assumed by the group members.

Stability: Many observers in genetic social psychology have commented on the developmental trend toward stabilization, duration, and definiteness of groups and on relations within the groups. Russian psychologists have shown that during Kindergarten age, groups exist only for a short time. Only one third of the groups observed remained intact for longer than twenty minutes. During school years, groups grow in endurance; however, larger groups are less stable than smaller ones. In general, it is not before the age of eight to ten years that relatively larger groups—such as boys' gangs and girls' clubs—begin to form.[149]

Definiteness of group relations have been measured in terms of consistency of the bond between group members. Moreno, by means of his sociometric technique, demonstrated the relation that exists between age and the degree of certainty with

[147] Parten and Newhall, 962.
[148] Reininger, 969.
[149] Doroschenko, 891; Zaluzhni, 1000.

which a child chooses another child as a preferred partner.[150]

The beginnings of the development of a rank order in terms of superiority and inferiority, of relations of equality and rivalry, have been observed in children as young as eight months old. Development of stabilization of rank order relationships between members of larger groups has been studied by Reininger.[151] Here again, as in other aspects of social development, the ten-year level seems to be an age mark of important changes. Before ten, these social relationships are vague and fluid; afterwards, rank order becomes increasingly more definite and stable.

[150] Moreno, 456.
[151] Reininger, 968.

BIBLIOGRAPHY

1. General Works. Ethnopsychology

1. Allport, G. W., *Personality*. 1937.
2. Allport, G. W., and Vernon, P. E., *Studies in Expressive Movement*. 1933.
3. Ankermann, B., Kulturkreise und Kulturschichten in Afrika. *Zschr. Ethnol*. 1905. 37.
4. Baldwin, James M., *Die Entwicklung des Geistes beim Kinde und in der Rasse*. 1898.
5. Bartlett, F. C., *Psychology and Primitive Culture*. 1923.
6. Boas, Franz, *Kultur und Rasse*. 1922.
7. Boas, Franz, *The Mind of Primitive Man*. 1924.
8. Boas, Franz, *Primitive Art*. 1927.
9. Boule, Marcellin, and Anthony, Raoul, L'encéphale de l'homme fossile de La Chapelle-Aux-Saints. *L'Anthrop*. 1911. 22.
10. Brodmann, K., *Vergleichende Lokalisationslehre der Grosshirnrinde*. 1909.
11. Bücher, Karl, *Arbeit und Rhythmus*. 1919.
12. Carus, Carl Gustav, *Vorlesungen über Psychologie*. 1831.
13. Carus, Carl Gustav, *Psyche*. 1846.
14. Cassirer, Ernst, Begriffsform im Mythischen Denken. *Stud. Bibl. Warburg*. 1922.
15. Cassirer, Ernst, *Philosophie der symbolischen Formen*. 1923–29.
16. Cassirer, Ernst, Sprache und Mythus. *Stud. Bibl. Warburg*. 1925.
17. Crawley, A. E., *The Idea of the Soul*. 1908.
18. Dessoir, Max, *Outlines of the History of Psychology*. 1912.
19. Dixon, R. B., *The Building of Cultures*. 1928.
20. Duckworth, W. L. H., *Morphology and Anthropology*. 1904.
21. v. Dürckheim, Graf Karlfried, Untersuchungen zum gelebten Raum. *N. psychol. Studien*. 1932. VI, 4.
22. Durkheim, Emile, *The Elementary Forms of the Religious Life*. N. D. (French ed., 1912.)
23. Durkheim, Emile, *The Rules of Sociological Method*. Univ. of Chicago Sociol. Ser. 1938.

507

24. v. Economo, Constantin, *The Cytoarchitectonics of the Human Cerebral Cortex.* 1929.
25. v. Economo, Constantin, Probleme der Hirnforschung. *Med. Klin.* 1931.
26. Edinger, L., *Vorlesungen über den Bau der nervösen Zentralorgane des Menschen und der Tiere.* 1908.
27. Edinger, L., *Einführung in die Lehre vom Bau und den Verrichtungen des Nervensystems.* 1912.
28. Ehrenreich, Paul, *Die allgemeine Mythologie und ihre ethnologischen Grundlagen.* 1910.
29. Fauconnet, Paul, *La Responsabilité.* 1920.
30. Flügel, O., Das Ich im Leben der Völker. *Zschr. Völkerpsychol.* 1880. 11.
31. Franz, Victor, *Die Vervollkommnung in der lebenden Natur.* 1920.
32. Frazer, J. G., *Totemism and Exogamy.* 1910.
33. Frazer, J. G., *The Golden Bough. A Study in Magic and Religion.* 1911–1913.
34. Freud, Sigmund, *Totem und Tabu.* 1922.
35. Friedemann, Max, Zur Psychologie des magischen Weltbildes. "Die Dioskuren." 1921. 2.
36. Frobenius, L., *Paideuma, Umrisse einer Kultur- und Seelenlehre.* 1921.
37. v. d. Gabelentz, Georg, *Die Sprachwissenschaft.* 1891.
38. Galton, Francis, *Inquiries into Human Faculty and Its Development.* (Everyman's Library. N. D.)
39. van Gennep, Arnold, *Les rites de passage.* 1909.
40. Graebner, Fritz, Kulturkreise und Kulturschichten in Ozeanien. *Zschr. Ethnol.* 1905. 37.
41. Graebner, Fritz, *Methode der Ethnologie.* 1911.
42. Groos, Karl, *The Play of Animals.* 1898.
43. Groos, Karl, *The Play of Man.* 1919.
44. Hartmann, G. W., *Gestalt Psychology.* 1935.
45. Hauer, J. W., *Die Religionen, ihr Werden, ihr Sinn, ihre Wahrheit.* I: Das religiöse Erlebnis auf den unteren Stufen. 1923.
46. Heiler, Fritz, *Das Gebet.* 1918.
47. Hirn, Yrjö, *The Origins of Art.* 1900.
48. Hocart, A. M., The Psychological Interpretation of Language. *Brit. J. Psychol.* 1912–13. 5.
49. v. Hornbostel, Erich, Psychologie der Gehörserscheinungen. *Bethe's Hdbch. d. Normal. u. Pathol. Physiol.* 1926. XI, 1.

50. v. Hornbostel, Erich, Laut und Sinn. Festschr. C. Meinhof. 1927.
51. Hubert, H., and Mauss, M., Esquisse d'une théorie générale de la magie. *Ann. Sociol.* 1902–03. 7.
52. Hubert, H., and Mauss, M., Mélanges d'histoire des religions. *Trav. Ann. Sociol.* 1909.
53. Irwin, O. C., The Organismic Hypothesis and Differentiation of Behavior. *Psychol. Rev.* 1932. 39.
54. Jaensch, E. R., Einige allgemeinere Fragen der Psychologie und Biologie des Denkens. *Arb. Psychol. Philos.* 1920. 1.
55. Jespersen, O., *Language: Its Nature and Development.* 1922. (Germ. ed., 1925.)
56. Kafka, Gustav, (ed.), *Handbuch der vergleichenden Psychologie.* I–III. 1922.
57. Kandinsky, Wassily, "1901–1913." *Der Sturm.* 1913.
58. Kappers, Ariëns, Cornelius U., *The Evolution of the Nervous System in Invertebrates, Vertebrates and Man.* 1929.
59. Karutz-Lübeck, Der Emanismus. *Zschr. Ethn.* 1913.
60. Keith, Arthur, *The Antiquity of Man.* 1925.
61. Keith, Arthur, *New Discoveries Relating to the Antiquity of Man.* 1931.
62. Klages, Ludwig, *Ausdrucksbewegung und Gestaltungskraft.* 1913.
63. Klages, Ludwig, *Der Geist als Widersacher der Seele.* 1929–33.
64. Klineberg, Otto, *Race Differences.* 1935.
65. Klüver, Heinrich, The Study of Personality and the Method of Equivalent and Non-Equivalent Stimuli. *Charact. a. Personal.* 1936. 5.
66. Koffka, Kurt, *The Growth of the Mind.* 1925. (Germ. ed., 1921.)
67. Koffka, Kurt, *Principles of Gestalt Psychology.* 1935.
68. Krueger, Felix, Magical Factors in the First Development of Human Labor. *Am. J. Psychol.* 1913. 24.
69. Krueger, Felix. Über Entwicklungspsychologie. *Arb. z. Entw.-Psych.* 1915. 1.
70. Krueger, Felix, Über psychische Ganzheit. *N. Psychol. Stud.* 1926. I, 1.
71. Krueger, Felix, Zur Entwicklungspsychologie des Rechts. *Arb. z. Entw.-Psych.* 1926. 7.
72. Krueger, Felix, Das Problem der Ganzheit. "Ganzheit und Form" (ed. Krueger). 1932.

73. Krujt, A. C., *Het Animisme in den Indischen Archipel.* 1906.
74. Lang, Andrew, *The Making of Religion.* 1900.
75. Lang, Andrew, *Myth, Ritual and Religion.* 1909.
76. Lazarus, Moritz, and Steinthal, Heinrich, Einleitende Gedanken über Völkerpsychologie. *Zschr. Völkerpsychol.* 1860. 1.
77. Le Bon, Gustave, *Les lois psychologiques de l'évolution des peuples.* 1894.
78. Le Bon, Gustave, *The Psychology of Peoples.* 1898. (French ed., 1894.)
79. van der Leeuw, G., *Einführung in die Phänomenologie der Religion.* 1925.
80. van der Leeuw, G., *Mystiek.* 1925.
81. van der Leeuw, G., La structure de la mentalité primitive. *Rev. d'hist. et de phil. rélig.* 1928.
82. Lehmann, Alfred, *Aberglaube und Zauberei.* 1919.
83. Lehmann, Fr. Rudolf, *Mana.* Diss. Leipzig. 1915.
84. Lévy-Bruhl, Lucien, *Primitive Mentality.* 1923. (French ed., 1922.)
85. Lévy-Bruhl, Lucien, *How Natives Think.* 1925. (French ed., 1910.)
86. Lévy-Bruhl, Lucien, *The "Soul" of the Primitive.* 1928. (French ed., 1927.)
87. Lewin, Kurt, *Vorsatz, Wille und Bedürfnis.* 1926.
88. Lewin, Kurt, *A Dynamic Theory of Personality.* 1935.
89. Lowie, Robert H., *Primitive Society.* 1920.
90. Luria, A. R., *The Nature of Human Conflicts.* 1932.
91. McDougall, William, *The Group Mind.* 1927.
92. McThomas, W. J., Primitive Numbers. *Report Bur. Am. Ethnol.* 1900. 19.
93. Mabilleau, Léopold, *Victor Hugo.* 1907.
94. Maine, H. S., *Ancient Law.* 1920.
95. Makarewicz, Julius, *Einführung in die Philosophie des Strafrechts auf entwicklungsgeschichtlicher Grundlage.* 1906.
96. Malinowski, Bronislaw, The Problem of Meaning in Primitive Languages. Suppl. to Ogden, C. K., and Richards, I. A., *The Meaning of Meaning.* 1927.
97. Malinowski, Bronislaw, Culture. In: *Encyclopædia of the Social Sciences.* 1931. IV.
98. Malinowski, Bronislaw, *Culture as a Determinant of Behavior.* (Factors Determining Human Behavior. Harvard U.) 1937.
99. Marett, R. R., *The Threshold of Religion.* 1909.

100. Mayer-Gross, W., and Lipps, H., Das Problem der primitiven Denkformen. *Philos. Anz.* 1930. 4.
101. v. Monakow, Carl, Die Lokalisation der Hirnfunktionen. *Verhdl. d. Ges. dtsch. Naturforscher u. Ärzte.* 1910.
102. Murphy, Gardner, Murphy, L. B., and Newcomb, Th. M., *Experimental Social Psychology.* 1937.
103. Nieuwenhuis, A. W., Die Wurzeln des Animismus. *Intern. Arch. f. Ethnogr.* 1924, Suppl. 24.
104. Nilsson, Martin P., Primitive Time-Reckoning. Lund. 1920.
105. Otto, Rudolf, *Das Heilige.* 1922.
106. du Pasquier, L.-C., Le développement de la nation du nombre. *Mém. Univers. Neuchâtel.* 1921. I, 3.
107. Powell, J. W., On the Evolution of Language. *1st Rep. Bur. Amer. Ethnol.,* 1881.
108. Preuss, Karl Theodor, Ursprung von Religion und Kunst. *Globus,* 1904–05. 86–87.
109. Preuss, Karl Theodor, *Die geistige Kultur der Naturvölker.* 1914.
110. Radcliffe-Brown, A. R., Present Position of Anthropological Studies. *Brit. Ass. Advanc. Science.* 1931.
111. Radin, Paul, *Primitive Man as Philosopher.* 1927.
112. Radin, Paul, *Social Anthropology.* 1932.
113. Radin, Paul, *The Method and Theory of Ethnology.* 1933.
114. Rivers, W. H. R., *Social Organisation.* 1924.
115. Rivers, W. H. R., *Psychology and Ethnology.* 1926.
116. Romanes, G. John, *Die geistige Entwicklung beim Menschen.* 1893.
117. Scheerer, Martin, *Die Lehre von der Gestalt.* 1931.
118. Schurtz, Heinrich, *Altersklassen und Männerbünde.* 1902.
119. Smith, G. Elliot, *The Evolution of Man.* 1924.
120. Stern, William, Tatsachen und Ursachen der seelischen Entwicklung. *Zschr. angew. Psychol.* 1908. I.
121. Stern, William, *Person und Sache. System der philosophischen Weltanschauung.* I. Ableitung und Grundlehre. 1906.– II. Die menschliche Persönlichkeit. 1918. – III. Wertphilosophie. 1924.
122. Stern, William, *Studien zur Personwissenschaft.* 1930. I.
123. Stern, William, *General Psychology from the Personalistic Standpoint.* 1938.
124. Stumpf, Carl, *Die Anfänge der Musik.* 1911.
125. Stumpf, Carl, and v. Hornbostel, E. M., *Sammelbände f. vergleichende Musikwissenschaft.* Vol. I.: Abhandlungen zur ver-

gleichenden Musikwissenschaft von A. J. Ellis, J. P. N. Land, O. Abraham und E. M. v. Hornbostel. 1922.

126. Tarde, Gabriel, *The Laws of Imitation*. 1903. (French ed., 1921.)

127. Thomas, Cyrus, *Indian Languages of Mexico and Central America*. 1911.

128. Thurnwald, Richard, Probleme der ethnopsychologischen Forschung. *Zschr. angew. Psychol.* Beiheft 5. 1912.

129. Thurnwald, Richard, Ethnopsychologische Studien an Südseevölkern. *Zschr. angew. Psychol.* Beiheft 6, 1913.

130. Thurnwald, Richard, Die Psychologie des Totemismus. *Anthropos*, 1917–18. 12–14.

131. Thurnwald, Richard, Psychologie des primitiven Menschen. *Hdb. d. vergl. Psychol.* (ed. Kafka). 1922. I.

132. Tschulok, S., *Deszendenzlehre*. 1922.

133. Tylor, E. B., On a Method of Investigating the Development of Institutions. *J. Anthr. Inst. Gr. Brit.* 1888. 18.

134. Tylor, E. B., *Primitive Culture*. 1920.

135. Vatter, Ernst, *Religiöse Plastik der Naturvölker*. 1926.

136. Vierkandt, Alfred, Das Zeichnen der Naturvölker. *Zschr. angew. Psychol.* 1912. 6.

137. Vierkandt, Alfred, Das Heilige in den primitiven Religionen. "Die Dioskuren." 1920. I.

138. Vierkandt, Alfred, *Gesellschaftslehre*. 1922.

139. Visscher, H., *Religion und soziales Leben bei den Naturvölkern*. 1911.

140. Vorschläge zur Untersuchung primitiver Menschen. Ed.: Inst. angew. Psychol. *Zschr. angew. Psychol.* Beiheft 5, 1912.

141. Werner, Heinz, Die Ursprünge der Metapher. *Arbeit. Entwickl.-Psychol.* (ed. Krueger). 1919. 3.

142. Werner, Heinz, *Die Ursprünge der Lyrik*. 1924.

143. Werner, Heinz, Raum und Zeit in den Urformen der Künste. *Zschr. Aesthet.* 1931. Suppl. Vol. XXV.

144. Wertheimer, Max, Über das Denken der Naturvölker: Zahlen und Zahlgebilde. *Zschr. Psychol.* 1912. 60.

145. Wertheimer, Max, *Drei Abhandlungen zur Gestalttheorie*. 1925.

146. Wheeler, R. H., and Perkins, F. Th., *Principles of Mental Development*. 1932.

147. Wheeler, W. M., *Emergent Evolution and the Social*. 1927.

148. Winckler, Hugo, Babylonische Geisteskultur. *Wiss. u. Bildg.* 1919. 15.

149. Wissler, Clark, *Man and Culture*. 1923.

150. Wundt, Wilhelm, *Grundzüge der Physiologischen Psychologie.* 1903.
151. Wundt, Wilhelm, *Völkerpsychologie.* 10 vols. 1912–21.
152. Wundt, Wilhelm, *Elemente der Völkerpsychologie.* 1913.
153. Zimmer, Heinrich, *Kunstform und Yoga im indischen Kultbild.* 1926.

2. ANTHROPOLOGY

154. Anderson, Ch. J., *Reisen in Südwestafrika bis zum See Ngami.* 1858.
155. Andrews, Lorrin, *A Dictionary of the Hawaiian Language.* 1865.
156. Baldus, Herbert, Indianerstudien im nordöstlichen Chaco. *Forsch. z. Völkerpsychol.* 1931. XI.
157. Bastian, Adolf, *Zur Kenntnis Hawaiis.* 1883.
158. Belo, Jane, The Balinese Temper. *Char. Pers.* 1935. IV, 2.
159. Benedict, Ruth, The Concept of the Guardian Spirit in North America. *Mem. Anthr. Assoc.* 1923. 29.
160. Benedict, Ruth, *Patterns of Culture.* 1934.
161. Bergaigne, A., *La réligion védique.* 1878–83.
162. Bernau, E. *Missionary Labours in British Guiana.* (N. D.)
163. Best, Elsdon, *Maori Religion and Mythology.* I. Wellington, N. Z. 1924.
164. Blumentritt, Ferdinand, Versuch einer Ethnographie der Philippinen. *Petermanns Mitteil.* 1882. Suppl. 67.
165. Boas, Franz, The Central Escimo. *6th Report, Bur. Amer. Ethnol.* 1888.
166. Boas, Franz, The North-West Tribes of Canada. *Reports Brit. Assoc. Adv. of Science.* 1890–91.
167. Boas, Franz, Handbook of the American Indian Languages. *Bull. Bur. Amer. Ethnol.* 1911. 40.
168. Bridges, T., A Few Notes on the Structure of the Yahgan. *J. Anthropol. Inst.* 1894. 23.
169. Brooke, Charles, *Ten Years in Sarawak.* 1866.
170. Bugeau, Fr., La Circoncision en Kikuyu. *Anthropos.* 1911. 6.
171. Bunsen, Chr. K. J., *Egypt's Place in Universal History.* 1848–67.
172. Catlin, George, *Illustrations of the Manners, Customs and Condition of the North American Indians.* 1876.
173. Catlin, George, *The North American Indians.* 1903.
174. de Charlevoix, P. F. X., *Journal d'un voyage dans l'Amérique septentrionale.* 1744.

175. Codrington, R. H., *The Melanesian Languages.* 1885.
176. Codrington, R. H., *The Melanesians. Studies in their Anthropology and Folklore.* 1891.
177. Cope, Leona, *Calendars of the Indians North of Mexico.* Univ. Calif. Publ. Amer. Archaeol. Ethnol. 1919. XVI, 4.
178. Curr, Edward M., *The Australian Race.* 1886.
179. Cushing, Frank H., Outlines of Zuñi Creation Myths. *13th Report, Bur. Amer. Ethnology.* 1896.
180. Cushing, Frank H., *Zuñi Breadstuff.* Mus. Am. Indian, N. Y. 1920.
181. Dahl, Edmund, Nyamwesi-Wörterbuch. *Abh. Hamb. Kolonialinst.* 1915. XXV, 15.
182. Dawson, G. M., *Australian Aborigines.* 1881.
183. Dennet, R. E., *The Folklore of the Fjort.* 1898.
184. Dobrizhoffer, Martin, *An Account of the Abipones.* 1822.
185. Dorsey, G. A., Traditions of the Skidi Pawnee. *Mem. Amer. Folkl. Soc.* 1904. 8.
186. Ehrenreich, Paul, Über die Botokudos. *Zschr. Ethnol.,* 1887. 19.
187. Emerson, Nathaniel B., Unwritten Literature of Hawaii. *Bulletin Smithsonian Inst. Bur. Amer. Ethnol.* 1909.
188. Erdweg, M. J., Die Bewohner der Insel Tumleo, Berlinhafen, Deutsch Neuguinea. *Mitt. Anthrop. Ges.* Wien. 1902.
189. Erman, Adolf, *Ägypten und ägyptisches Leben im Altertum.* 1922–23.
190. Fletcher, Alice C., and Francis La Fleche, The Omaha Tribe. *27th Report, Bur. Amer. Ethnol.* 1911.
191. Flinders Petrie, W. M., *History of Egypt.* I–VI, 1894 ff.
192. Fritsch, Gustav, *Die Eingebornen Südafrikas.* 1872.
193. Gabb, W. M., On the Indian Tribes and Languages of Costa Rica. *Proc. Am. Philos. Soc.* 1876.
194. Gatschet, Albert S., *The Klamath Indians of the Southwestern Oregon.* Contributions to North American Ethnology. 1890. Vol. II, 1: The Klamath Language.
195. Gill, W. W., *Life in the Southern Isles.* 1872.
196. Goddard, Pliny Earle, *Life and Culture of the Hupa.* Univ. of California Publications. Archaeol. and Ethnol. 1903. I. 1.
197. Grey, George, *Journals of two Expeditions of Discovery in N.-W. and W.-Australia.* 1841.
198. De Groot, J. J. M., *The Religious System of China.* 1892–1912.
199. Guppy, H. B., *The Solomon Islands.* 1887.

200. Gutmann, Bruno, Amulette und Talismane bei den Dschag-ganegern. *Arb. Entwickl.-psychol* (ed. Krueger). 1923. 7.
201. Gutmann, Bruno, Ehrerbietung der Dschagga Neger gegen ihre Nutzpflanzen und Haustiere. *Arch. ges. Psychol.* 1924.
202. Gutmann, Bruno, Das Recht der Dschagga. *Arb. z. Entwick-lungsps.* 1926. 7.
203. Hagen, Berthold, *Unter den Papuas in Deutsch-Neu-Guinea.* 1899.
204. Hahn, Josaphat, Die Ovaherero. *Zschr. Gesellsch. Erdkunde Berlin.* 1869. 4. ˙
205. Hallowell, A. I., Fear and Anxiety as Cultural and Individual Variables in a Primitive Society. *J. Soc. Psychol.* 1938. 9.
206. Hambruch, Paul, *Nauru. Ergebnisse der Südsee-Expedition 1908–1910.* (ed. Thilenius). 1915, II, B, 1, 1 and 2.
207. Henri, Joseph, Les Bambara. *Anthropos-Bibl.* 1910. 1.
208. Hobley, C. W., British East Africa. Anthropological Studies in Kavirondo and Nandi. *Journ. Anthropol. Instit.,* 1903. 33.
209. Hollis, A. C., *The Masai.* 1905.
210. Hornbostel, Erich v., Wanyamwezigesänge. *Anthropos.* 1909. 4.
211. Hornbostel, Erich v., Musikalischer Exotismus. *Melos.* 1921.
212. Hose, Charles, and McDougall, William, *The Pagan Tribes of Borneo.* 1912.
213. Howitt, A. W., Further Notes on the Australian Class Sys-tem. *J. Anthrop. Inst.* 1889. 18.
214. Howitt, A. W., *The Native Tribes of S.-C. Australia.* 1904.
215. Immenroth, Wilhelm, Kultur und Umwelt der Kleinwüch-sigen. *Stud. Völkerk.* Leipzig. 1933.
216. Junod, Henry A., *The Life of a South African Tribe.* 1910.
217. Keane, A. H., *The Lapps.* 1885.
218. Keysser, Ch., Aus dem Leben der Kaileute. In: Neuhauss, R., *Deutsch-Neu-Guinea.* 1911. III.
219. Kidd, Dudley, *Savage Childhood.* 1906.
220. Koch-Grünberg, Theodor, *Anfänge der Kunst im Urwald.* 1905.
221. Koch-Grünberg, Theodor, *Südamerikanische Felszeichnungen.* 1907.
222. Koch-Grünberg, Theodor, *Zwei Jahre unter den Indianern Südamerikas.* 1909.
223. Kohl, J. G., *Kitchi-Gami.* 1860.
224. Krämer, Augustin, *Die Samoa-Inseln.* 1902.
225. Krause, Fritz, *In den Wildnissen Brasiliens.* Ber. u. Ergebn. d. Leipziger Araguay–Exped. 1908–11.

516 *Bibliography*

226. Kroeber, Alfred L., The Eskimo of Smith Sound. *Bull. Am. Mus. Nat. Hist.* 1899. 12.
227. Kroeber, Alfred L., The Arapaho. *Bull. Am. Mus. Nat. Hist.* 1902. 18.
228. Langloh-Parker, K., *The Euahlayi Tribe.* 1905.
229. Lowie, Robert H., The Assiniboine. *Anthr. Pap.* Am. Mus. Nat. Hist. 1909. 4, 1.
230. Lowie, Robert H., Plains Indians Age-Societies. *Anthropol. Pap.* Am. Mus. Nat. Hist. 1916. XI, pt. 13.
231. Lumholtz, Carl, Symbolism of the Huichol Indians. *Mem. Am. Mus. Nat. Hist.* 1900.
232. Maass, Alfred, *Durch Zentral Sumatra.* 1910.
233. Malinowski, Bronislaw, Classificatory Particles in the Language of Kiriwina. *Bull. School Orient. Stud.* II. (N.D.)
234. Malinowski, Bronislaw, *Argonauts of the Western Pacific.* 1922.
235. Malinowski, Bronislaw, *Coral Gardens and Their Magic.* 1935.
236. Man, E. H., On the Aboriginal Inhabitants of the Andaman Islanders. *J. Anthr. Inst.* 1883. 12.
237. Martin, Rudolf, *Die Inlandstämme der Malayischen Halbinsel.* 1905.
238. Matthews, Washington, The Mountain Chant: A Navaho Ceremony. *Report, Bur. Am. Ethnol.* 1883–84. 5.
239. Matthews, Washington, The Night Chant. *Mem. Am. Mus. Nat. Hist.* 1902. 7.
240. Maximilian, Prinz zu Wied, *Reise nach Brasilien.* 1821.
241. Maximilian, Prinz zu Wied, *Reise in das innere Nordamerika.* 1841.
242. Mead, Margaret, *Coming of Age in Samoa.* 1928.
243. Mead, Margaret, *Growing Up in New Guinea.* 1930.
244. Meinhof, Carl, *Grundzüge einer vergleichenden Grammatik der Bantu-Sprachen.* 1906.
245. Meinhof, Carl, *Grundriss einer Lautlehre der Bantu-Sprachen.* 1910.
246. Meinhof, Carl, Ergebnisse der afrikanischen Sprachforschung. *Arch. f. Anthrop.* 1910.
247. Meinhof, Carl, *Die Dichtung der Afrikaner.* 1911.
248. Merker, M., *Die Masai.* 1904.
249. Meyer, A. B., *Die Philippinen.* 1893.
250. Mooney, James, Sacred Formulas of the Cherokees. *Report, Bur. Am. Ethnol.* 1891. 7.
251. Moszkowsky, Max, Bericht aus Neu-Guinea. *Zschr. Ethnol.* 42.

252. Müller-Wismar, Wilhelm, Yap. *Ergebn. d. Südseexped.* (Thilenius). 1917. II, B, 2.
253. Musters, G. Ch., *Unter den Patagoniern.* 1873.
254. Neuhauss, Richard, *Deutsch-Neu-Guinea.* 1911.
255. Parkinson, R., *30 Jahre in der Südsee.* 1907.
256. Passarge, Siegfried, Die Buschmänner der Kalahari. Mitt. a. d. Deutsch. Schutzgeb. 1905. 18.
257. Pechuël-Loesche, E., *Volkskunde von Loango.* 1907.
258. Peekel, P. G., *Religion und Zauberei auf dem mittleren Neu-Mecklenburg.* 1910.
259. Polack, J. S., *Manners and Customs of the New Zealanders.* 1840.
260. Portmann, M. V., *Notes of the Languages of the South Andaman Group of Tribes.* 1898.
261. Preuss, Karl Theodor, *Die Nayarit-Expedition.* I. Die Religion der Cora-Indianer. 1912.
262. Preuss, Karl Theodor, *Religion und Mythologie der Uitoto.* 1921-23.
263. Quatrefages de Bréau, J. L. A., *Les Polynésiens et leurs migrations.* 1886.
264. Radcliffe-Brown, A. R., The Social Organization of Australian Tribes. *The Oceania Monographs.* I. (N. D.)
265. Radcliffe-Brown, A. R., *The Andaman Islanders.* 1922.
266. Read, C. H., Some Spinning Tops from Torres Straits. *J. Anthr. Inst.* 1902. 32.
267. Rehse, Herrmann, Eigentümlichkeiten in der Sprache der Bazinza in Deutsch-Ostrafrika. *Zschr. Kolonialsprachen.* 1914. IV.
268. *Reports of the Cambridge Anthropological Expedition to Torres Straits,* ed. by A. C. Haddon. 1901—35.
269. de Rienzi, Domény, *Océanie.* 1836. 1.
270. Risley, H. H., *The Tribes and Castes of Bengal.* 1892.
271. Rivers, W. H. R., Observations on the Senses of the Todas. *Br. J. Psychol.* 1905. 1.
272. Rivers, W. H. R., *The History of Melanesian Societies.* 1914.
273. Roth, H. Ling, *The Natives of Sarawak and British North Borneo.* 1896.
274. Roth, H. Ling, *The Aborigines of Tasmania.* 1899.
275. Roth, Walter E., *Ethnological Studies Among the N. W. Central Queensland Aborigines.* 1897.
276. Roth, Walter E., *N. Queensland Ethnography.* Bulletin 1—8, 1901—05.
277. Sapper, Carl, *Das nördliche Mittelamerika.* 1897.

278. Sarasin, Paul and Fritz, *Die Weddas von Ceylon*, Ergebnisse naturwissenschaftlicher Forschungen auf Ceylon. 1892—93. 3.
279. Sarasin, Paul and Fritz, *Reisen in Celebes*. 1905.
280. Sarfert, E., Kusae. *Ergebnisse der Südsee-Expedition* 1908— 10. (Thilenius.) II, B, IV. 1919—20.
281. Schadenberg, Alexander, Über die Negritos der Philippinen. *Zschr. Ethnol.* 1880. 12.
282. Schneider, Herrmann, *Kultur und Denken der alten Ägypter.* 1909.
283. Schneider, Herrmann, *Kultur und Denken der Babylonier und Juden*. 1913.
284. Schoolcraft, Henry Rowe, *Historical and Statistical Information Respecting the Indian Tribes of U.S.A.* 1851—60.
285. Schultze, Leonhard, *Aus Namaland und Kalahari*. 1907.
286. Schwanhäusser, Hans. *Das Seelenleben der Dschagganeger.* 1910.
287. Seligmann, C. G. and Brenda, Z., *The Veddas*. 1911.
288. Sherman, M., and Henry, T. R., *Hollow Folk*. 1933.
289. Shortland, Edward, *Traditions and Superstitions of the New Zealanders*. 1854.
290. Skeat, Walter William, *Malay Magic*. 1900.
291. Skeat, W. W., and Blagden, Ch. O., *Pagan Races of the Malay Peninsula*. 1906.
292. Smith, R. Brough, *The Aborigines of Victoria*. 1878.
293. Spencer, Baldwin, and Gillen, F. C., *The Native Tribes of Central Australia*. 1899.
294. Spencer, Baldwin, and Gillen, F. C., *The Northern Tribes of Central Australia*. 1904.
295. Spieth, Jacob, *Die Ewestämme*. 1906.
296. Spix, J. B., and Martius, C. F., *Reise in Brasilien*. 1823—31.
297. Steinen, Karl v. d., *Unter den Naturvölkern Zentral-Brasiliens.* 1894.
298. Stephan, Emil, *Südseekunst*. 1907.
299. Stephan, Emil, and Gräbner, Fritz, *Neu-Mecklenburg*. 1907.
300. Stevenson, S., Zuñi Indians. *22nd Report, Bur. Am. Ethnol.* 1904.
301. v. Strehlow, Carl, *Mythen, Sagen und Märchen des Aranda-stammes in Zentralaustralien*. Veröffentl. Völkermus. Frankfurt. 1907.
302. v. Strehlow, Carl, *Mythen, Sagen und Märchen des Loritjastammes*. Veröffentl. Völkermus. Frankfurt. 1908.
303. v. Strehlow, Carl, *Die totemistischen Kulte der Aranda und*

Loritjastämme in Zentralaustralien. Veröffentl. Völkermus. Frankfurt. 1910.

304. v. Strehlow, Carl, *Das soziale Leben der Aranda und Loritja.* Veröffentl. Völkermus. Frankfurt. 1913.
305. Swanton, J. R., Contributions to the Ethnology of the Haida. *Memoirs, Amer. Museum Natural History.* 1905. VIII, 1.
306. Taplin, George, The Narrinyeri. In: J. D. Woods, *The Native Tribes of S. Australia.* 1879.
307. Taylor, Richard, *Te Ika a Maui.* 1885.
308. Tessmann, Günther, *Die Pangwe.* 1913.
309. Thurnwald, Richard, *Forschungen auf den Salomoinseln und dem Bismarckarchipel.* Vol. I: Lieder und Sagen aus Buin. 1912.
310. Torday R., and Joyce, T. A., Les Bushongo. *Ann. Mus. Congo Belge. Ethnogr. Ser. III; ii.* 1911.
311. Turner, George, *Nineteen Years in Polynesia.* 1861.
312. Vedder, H., Die Bergdama. *Abhdl. d. Hamburg. Univers. a. d. Geb. d. Auslandskunde.* 1923, XI, 7–8.
313. Velten, C., *Sitten und Gebräuche der Suaheli.* 1903.
314. Waitz, Theodor, *Anthropologie der Naturvölker.* 1859–72.
315. Warneck, Johann, *Die Religion der Batak.* 1909.
316. Warner, W. L., Morphology and Function of the Australian Mungin Type of Kinship. *Am. Anthr.* 1930–32.
317. Werner, Alice, *The Natives of British Central Africa.* 1906.
318. Westermann, Diedrich, *Grammatik der Ewesprache.* 1907.
319. Westermann, Diedrich, *The Shilluk People.* 1912.
320. Westermann, Diedrich, Die Gola-Sprache in Liberia. *Hambur. Univers. Abhandl. Auslandsk.* 1921. 6. B, 4.
321. Westermann, Diedrich, Laut, Ton und Sinn in Westafrikanischen Sprachen. *Festschr. Meinhof.* 1927.
322. Weule, Karl, Ostafrikanisches Kinderleben. *Westermann's Monatsh.* 1899.
323. Weule, Karl, Wissenschaftliche Ergebnisse meiner ethnographischen Forschungsreise in den Südosten Deutsch-Ostafrikas. *Mitt. a. d. Deutschen Schutzgeb.* 1908. Suppl. 1.
324. Wilson, C. T. and Felkin, R. W., *Uganda und der ägyptische Sudan.* 1851.
325. Wirz, Paul, Die Marind-anim von Holländisch Süd-Neu Guinea. *Abhdl. Hamburg. Univ. a. d. Geb. d. Auslandsk.* 1922.
326. Wissler, Clark, Social Organisation and Ritualistic Ceremonies of the Blackfoot Indians. *Anthrop. Papers,* Amer. Mus. Nat. Hist. 1912. VII.

327. **Wissler**, Clark, Ceremonial Bundles of the Blackfoot Indians. *Anthropol. Papers.* Amer. Mus. Nat. Hist. 1912. VII.
328. **Zahn**, Heinrich, Die Jabim. In Neuhauss: *Deutsch-Neu-Guinea.* 1911. 3.

3. CHILD PSYCHOLOGY

329. **Allport**, G. W., Eidetic Imagery. *Br. J. Psychol.* 1924. 15.
330. **Ament**, Wilhelm, *Entwicklung von Sprechen und Denken beim Kinde.* 1899.
331. **Argelander**, Annelies, *Das Farbenhören und der synaesthetische Faktor der Wahrnehmung.* 1927.
332. **Baldwin**, Bird T. and Stecher, Lorle I., *The Psychology of the Preschool Child.* 1924.
333. **Barnes**, E., *A Study in Children's Interests.* Stud. Educ. Stanford Univ. 1896–7.
334. **Bean**, C. H., An Unusual Opportunity to Investigate the Psychology of Language. *J. Genet. Psychol.* 1932. 40.
335. **Beckmann**, H., Beitrag zur grammatischen Entwicklung im Schulalter. *Zschr. paed. Psychol.* 1927.
336. **Bernfeld**, Siegfried, *Psychology of the Infant.* 1929.
337. **Beyrl**, F., Die Grössenauffassung bei Kindern. *Zschr. Psychol.* 1926. 100.
338. **Bloch**, Oscar, La phrase dans le langage de l'enfant. *Jour. de Psych.* 1924. 21.
339. **Bos**, Maria C., Über echte und unechte audition colorée. *Zschr. Psychol.* 1929. 111.
340. **Brehmer**, Fritz, Melodieauffassung und melodische Begabung des Kindes. *Zschr. ang. Psychol.* 1925. Beih. 36.
341. **Brian**, Clara R., and Goodenough, Florence L., The Relative Potency of Color and Form Perception at Various Ages. *J. Exp. Psychol.* 1929. 12.
342. **Bridges**, Katharine M. B., *The Social and Emotional Development of the Preschool Child.* 1931.
343. **Brownell**, W. A., Development of Children's Number Ideas in the Primary Grades. *Suppl. Educ. Mo.* 1928. 35.
344. **Brunswik**, Egon, Zur Entwicklung der Albedowahrnehmung. *Zschr. Psychol.* 1928. 109.
345. **Brunswik**, Egon, Über Farben-, Grössen- und Formkonstanz in der Jugend. XI. *Kongr.-Ber. f. exp. Psychol.* 1930.
346. **Brunswik**, Egon (with Goldscheider and Pilek), Untersuchungen zur Entwicklung des Gedächtnisses. *Zschr. ang. Psychol.* 1932. Beih. 64.

347. Brunswik, Egon, Untersuchungen über Wahrnehmungsgegenstände. *Arch. f. ges. Psychol.* 1933 ff.

348. Bühler, Charlotte, Hetzer, Hildegard, and Tudor-Hart, Beatrix, Soziologische und psychologische Studien über das erste Lebensjahr. *Quell. Stud. Jugendk.* 1926. 5.

349. Bühler, Charlotte, *The First Year of Life.* 1930.

350. Bühler, Charlotte, *Kindheit und Jugend.* 1931.

351. Bühler, Karl, *The Mental Development of the Child.* 1930. (Germ. ed., 1922.)

352. Caille, Ruth K., Resistant Behavior of Preschool Children. Teach. Coll., Columbia Univ., *Child Devel. Mo.* 1933. 11.

353. Chase, W. P., Color Vision in Infants. *J. Exp. Psychol.* 1937. 20.

354. Claparède, Ed., *Psychologie de l'enfant.* 1916.

355. Clem, O. M., and Smith, M., Grade Differences in Attitudinal Reactions of Six-Year Secondary School Pupils. *J. Ed. Psychol.* 1934. 25.

Colby, Martha. (cf. Guernsey.)

356. Compayré, Gabriel, *Die Entwicklung der Kindesseele.* 1900.

357. Cramaussel, E., Le premier éveil intellectual de l'enfant. 1911.

358. Decroly, O., and Degand, J., Observations relatives à l'évolution des notions de quantités continues et discontinues chez l'enfant. *Arch. de Psychol.* 1912. 12.

359. Decroly, O., and Degand, J., Observations relatives au développement de la notion du temps chez une petite fille. *Arch. de Psychol.* 1913. 13.

360. Descœudres, Alice, Couleur, Forme ou Nombre. *Arch. de Psychol.* 1914.

361. Descœudres, Alice, *Le développement de l'enfant de deux à sept ans.* 1921.

362. Dix, Kurt W., *Köperliche und geistige Entwicklung eines Kindes.* 1912.

363. Egger, E., *Beobachtungen und Betrachtungen über die Entwicklung der Intelligenz und der Sprache bei den Kindern.* 1903.

364. Eliasberg, Wladimir, Psychologie und Pathologie der Abstraktion. *Zschr. angew. Psychol.* 1925. Suppl. 35.

365. Eng, Helga, Abstrakte Begriffe im Sprechen und Denken, des Kindes. *Zschr. angew. Psychol.* 1914. Suppl. 8.

366. Eng, Helga, The Psychology of Children's Drawings. 1931. (Germ. ed., *Zschr. angew. Psychol.* 1927. Suppl. 39.)

367. Erismann, Th., Das logische Schliessen der Kinder im Alter von 3–10 Jahren. *Arch. ges. Psychol.* 1930.

368. Fischer, Aloys, Moralpsychologische Untersuchungsmethoden. *Zschr. pädag. Psychol.* 1928. 6.
369. Fisher, Mary Sh., Language Patterns of Preschool Children. *J. Exper. Educ.* 1932–33. 1.
370. Fisher, Mary Sh., Language Patterns of Preschool Children. *Child Developm. Mo.* 15. Teach. Coll., Columbia U. 1934.
371. Frank, H., Untersuchung über Sehgrössen-Konstanz bei Kindern. *Psychol. Forsch.* 1925. 7.
372. Frank, Lawrence K., The Problem of Child Development. *Ch. Devel.* 1935. 6.
373. Franke, E., Die geistige Entwicklung der Negerkinder. *Beitr. Kult.- u. Univers.-Gesch.* 1915. 35.
374. Freiling, H., Die räumlichen Wahrnehmungen der Jugendlichen in der eidetischen Entwicklungsphase. *Zschr. Psychol.* Abt. II. 1923. 55.
375. Gantschewa, Sdrawka, Kinderplastik Drei-bis Sechsjähriger. *Arb. z. Entwickl.-psychol.* 1930. 8.
376. Gesell, Arnold, *The Mental Growth of the Pre-School Child.* 1925.
377. Gesell, Arnold, *Infancy and Human Growth.* 1928.
378. Gesell, Arnold, and Thompson, Helen, *Infant Behavior.* 1934.
379. Goodenough, Florence L., *Developmental Psychology.* 1934.
380. Gottschaldt, Kurt, Zur Methodik psychologischer Untersuchungen an Schwachsinnigen und Psychopathen. *Kongressber. Heilpädag.* 5. 1930.
381. Gottschaldt, Kurt, Formen der Ersatzhandlung bei schwachsinnigen und psychopathischen Kindern. *Kongr. D. Ges. Psychol.* 1932. 12.
382. Gottschaldt, Kurt, Der Aufbau des kindlichen Handelns. *Zschr. angew. Psychol.* Suppl. 1933. 68.
383. Graewe, Herbert, Überblick über die Psychologie des kindlichen Zeichnens. *Arch. ges. Psychol.* 1936. 96.
384. Green, E. H., Group Play and Quarreling Among Preschool Children. *Child Devel.* 1933. 4.
385. Green, G. H., *The Daydream. A Study in Development.* 1923.
386. Greenberg, Pearl J., Competition in Children. *Am. J. Psychol.* 1932. 44.
387. Grigsby, O., An Experimental Study of the Development of Concepts of Relationship in Pre-School Children. *J. Exp. Educ.* 1932–33. 1.
388. Groos, Karl, *Die Spiele der Menschen.* 1899.
389. **Groos, Karl, *Das Seelenleben des Kindes.* 1913.**

390. Grünbaum, A. A., Die Struktur der Kinderpsyche. *Zschr. pädag. Psychol.* 1927. 28.
391. Guernsey, Martha, Eine genetische Studie über Nachahmung. *Zschr. Psychol.* 1928. 107.
392. Guillaume, Paul, Les débuts de la phrase dans le langage de l'enfant. *J. de Psychol.* 1927. 24.
393. Hall, Stanley, *Ausgewählte Beiträge zur Kinderpsychologie und Pädagogik.* 1902.
394. Hall, G. Stanley, A Study of Fears. *Am. J. Psychol.* 1897. 8.
395. Hall, G. Stanley, The Contents of Children's Minds on Entering School. In: *Aspects of Child Life and Education.* 1907.
396. Hanfmann, Eugenie, Über das Bauen der Kinder. *Zschr. Kinderforsch.* 1930. 36.
397. Harvey, N. A., *Imaginary Playmates and Other Mental Phenomena of Children.* 1918.
398. Hazlitt, Victoria, Children's Thinking. *Brit. J. Psychol.* 1929–30. 20.
399. Hazlitt, Victoria, *The Psychology of Infancy.* 1933.
400. Heiss, Alfred, Zum Problem der isolierenden Abstraktion. *N. Psychol. Stud.* (ed. F. Krueger). 1930. 4, 2.
401. Herrmann, Imre and Alice, Zur Entwicklungspsychologie des Umgehens mit Gegenständen. *Zschr. angew. Psychol.* 1923.
402. Hetzer, Hildegard, Die symbolische Darstellung in der frühen Kindheit. *Wiener Arb. z. pädag. Psychol.* 1926. 3.
403. Hetzer-Beaumont-Wiehemeyer, Das Schauen und Greifen des Kindes. *Zschr. Psychol.* 1929. 113.
404. Hoppe, F., Versuche über Erfolgs- und Misserfolgserlebnisse psychopathischer und schwachsinniger Kinder. *Kongr. D. Ges. Psychol.* 1932. 12.
405. Huang, I., Children's Explanations of Strange Phenomena. *Psychol. Forsch.* 1930.
406. Hunter, W. S., The Delayed Reaction in a Child. *Psychol. Rev.* 1917. 24.
407. Hüpeden, Marie, Der Kinderglaube. *Pädag. Magazin.* 1910. 415.
408. Hurlock, E. B., and Burstein, M., The Imaginary Playmate. *J. Genet. Psychol.* 1932. 41.
409. Idelberger, H. A., Hauptprobleme der kindlichen Entwicklung. *Zschr. pädag. Psychol.* 1903. 5.
410. Idelberger, H. A., *Die Entwicklung der kindlichen Sprache.* 1904.
411. Irwin, O. C., The Amount and Nature of Activities of New-

born Infants Under Constant External Stimulating Conditions. *Genet. Psychol. Mo.* 1930. 8. 1.

412. Isaacs, Susan, *Social Development in Young Children.* 1933.
413. Iwai, K., and Volkelt, H., Umgang des Kindes mit verschieden geformten Körpern im 9. bis 12. Monat. *Kongr. D. Ges. Psychol.* 1932. 12.
414. Jaensch, E. R., Die Vorstellungswelt der Jugendlichen und der Aufbau des intellektuellen Lebens. *Zschr. Psychol.* 1920 ff.
415. Jaensch, E. R., *Der Aufbau der Wahrnehmungswelt und ihre Struktur im Jugendalter.* 1923. (Cf. *Zschr. Psychol.* 1920. f.)
416. Jaensch, E. R., *Eidetic Imagery.* 1930.
417. Jersild, A. T., and Holmes, F. B., Some Factors in the Development of Children's Fears. *J. Exp. Educ.* 1935. 4.
418. Jones, Mary C., and Burks, Barbara, Personality Development in Childhood. *Mo. Soc. f. Research i. Child Devel.* 1936. Vol. I, No. 4.
419. Katz, David. Ein Beitrag zur Kenntnis der Kinderzeichnungen. *Zschr. Psychol.* 1906. 41.
420. Katz, David, Studien zur Kinderpsychologie. *Wiss. Beitr Pädag. Psychol.* (ed. Deuchler and Katz). 1913.
421. Katz, David and Rosa, *Gespräche mit Kindern.* 1928.
422. Kern, Alfred, *Jugendkunde.* 1930.
423. Kerschensteiner, Georg, *Die Entwicklung der zeichnerischen Begabung.* 1905.
424. Klimpfinger, Sylvia, Die Entwicklung der Gestaltkonstanz vom Kind zum Erwachsenen. (Unters. ueb. Wahrnehmungsgegenstaende. Ed. by E. Brunswik.) *Arch. f. ges. Psychol.* 1933. 88.
425. Knoblauch, Elisabeth, Vergleichende Untersuchungen zur optischen Auffassung hochgradig schwachsinniger und normaler Kinder. *Zschr. angew. Psychol.* 1934. 47.
426. Koch, Adolf, Experimentelle Untersuchungen über die Abstraktionsfähigkeit von Volksschulkindern. *Zschr. angew. Psychol.* 1913. 7.
427. Koffka, Kurt, *The Growth of the Mind.* 1925. (Germ. ed., 1921.)
428. Koffka, Kurt, Mental Development. *Pedag. Sem.* 1925. 32.
429. Köhler, Elsa, *Die Persönlichkeit des dreijährigen Kindes.* 1926.
430. Kroh, Oswald, *Subjektive Anschauungsbilder bei Jugendlichen.* 1922.
431. Kroh, Oswald, *Die Psychologie des Grundschulkindes.* 1930.
432. Kuenburg, Gräfin M. v., Über Abstraktionsfähigkeit und die

Entstehung der Relationen beim vorschulpflichtigen Kinde. *Zschr. angew. Psychol.* 1920. 17.

433. Kurz, Isolde, *Jugendland.* 1919.
434. Lau, E., Das Greifen in der frühen Kindheit. *Kongr. D. Ges. Psychol.* 1932. 12.
435. Levinstein, Siegfried, *Kinderzeichnungen bis zum 14. Lebensjahr.* 1905.
436. Lewin, Kurt, Environmental Forces in Child Behavior and Development. *Hdb. of Child Psychology* (Murchison). Ch. IV. 1933.
437. Lewis, M. M., *Infant Speech.* 1936.
438. Lindner, Gustav, *Aus dem Naturgarten der Kindersprache.* 1898.
439. Line, W., The Growth of Visual Perception in Children. *Brit. J. Psychol.* Suppl. 1930/31. 5. No. 15.
440. Lipmann, Otto, and Bogen, Hellmuth, *Naive Physik.* 1923.
441. Lombroso, Paola, Das Leben der Kinder. *Pädag. Mon.* (ed. Meumann). 1909.
442. Loosli-Usteri, M., Conscience du hasard chez l'enfant. *Arch. de Psychol.* 1931. 23.
443. Luquet, G.-H., Les dessins d'un enfant. *Bibl. philos. contemp.* 1913.
444. Luquet, G.-H., La narration graphique chez l'enfant. *Journ. de psychol.* 1924. 21.
445. Luquet, G.-H., *Le dessin enfantin.* 1927.
446. Luria, A. R. *Matters and Facts on the Genesis of Child's Writing.* Moscow. 1929.
447. McCarthy, Dorothea, Language Development. In: *Handbook of Child Psychology* (Murchison). 1933.
448. Maier, Norman, R. F., Reasoning in Children. *J. Comp. Psychol.* 1936. 21.
449. Markey, Fr. V., *Imaginative Behavior of Preschool Children.* 1935.
450. Meili, Richard, and Tobler, Erich, Les mouvements stroboscopiques chez les enfants. *Arch. de Psychol.* 1931. 23.
451. Meissner, H., *Zur Entwicklung des musikalischen Sinns beim Kind während des schulpflichtigen Alters.* 1915.
452. Meumann, Ernst, Die Entstehung der ersten Worthedeutungen beim Kinde. *Phil. Stud.,* 1902. 20.
453. Meumann, Ernst, Die Sprache des Kindes. *Abh. d. Ges. f. deutsche Sprache in Zürich.* 1903. H. 8.
454. Meyer, Toni, *Aus einer Kinderstube.* 1914.
455. Minkowski, M., Ueber fruehzeitige Bewegungen und musku-

laere Reaktionen beim menschlichen Foetus. *Schweiz. Mediz. Woch.* 1922. 3.

456. Moreno, J. L., Who Shall Survive? *Nerv. Ment. Disease Mo.* 58. 1934.

457. Muchow, Martha, Zur Problematik der Testpsychologie im allgemeinen und einiger Ordnungstests im besondern. *Hamb. Arb. z. Begabungsforschung, Zt. ang. Psychol.* 1925. 6.

458. Muchow, Martha, Beiträge zur psychologischen Charakteristik des Kindergarten- und Grundschulalters. *A. D. L. V.* 1926.

459. Muchow, Martha, Psychologische Probleme der frühen Erziehung. *Erfurter Ak. gemm. Wiss.* 1929.

460. Muchow, Martha, Zur Frage einer lebensraum- und epochaltypologischen Entwicklungspsychologie des Kindes und Jugendlichen. *Festschrift W. Stern. Beih.* 59. *Zt. ang. Psychol.* 1931.

461. Muchow, Martha and Muchow, Hans, *Der Lebensraum des Grosstadtkindes.* 1935.

462. Murchison, C. (ed.), *Handbook of Child Psychology.* 1933.

463. Murphy, Lois Barclay, *Social Behavior and Child Personality.* 1937.

464. Nestele, Albert, Die musikalische Produktion im Kindesalter. *Zschr. ang. Psychol.* 1930. Suppl. 51.

465. Neugebauer, H., Sprachliche Eigenbildungen meines Sohnes. *Zschr. Kinderf.* 1913–14. 3 and 5.

466. Neugebauer, H., Aus der Sprachentwicklung meines Sohnes. *Zschr. ang. Psychol.* 1914. 9.

467. Neugebauer, H., Beobachtungen über Träume des kleinen Kindes. *Zschr. ang. Psychol.* 1929. 32.

468. Neugebauer, H., Spiel und Fantasie in der frühen Kindheit meines Sohnes. *Zschr. ang. Psychol.* 1932. 42.

469. Oakden, E. C., and Sturt, M., The Development of the Knowledge of Time in Children. *Brit. J. Psychol.* 1902. 12.

470. Oehl, Wilhelm, Psychologische Untersuchungen über Zahldenken und Rechnen bei Schulanfängern. *Zschr. angew. Psychol.* 1935. 49.

471. Peck, Leigh, and Hodges, Amelie, B., A Study of Racial Differences in Eidetic Imagery of Preschool Children. *J. Genet. Psychol.* 1937. 51.

472. Peiper, A., *Die Hirntätigkeit des Säuglings.* 1928.

473. Pérez, Bernard, *L'enfant de trois à sept ans.* 1901.

474. Pérez, Bernard, *L'éducation intellectuelle dès le berceau.* 1901.

475. Pérez, Bernard, *Les trois premières années de l'enfant.* 1911.

476. Peters, Wilhelm, Zur Entwicklung der Farbenwahrnehmung

nach Versuchen an abnormen Kindern. *Fortschritte der Psychologie.* 1915. 3.

477. Peters, Wilhelm, Die Entwicklung von Wahrnehmungsleistungen beim Kinde. *Zschr. Psychol.* 1927. 103.

478. Piaget, Jean, La pensée symbolique et la pensée de l'enfant. *Arch. de Psychol.* 1923. 18.

479. Piaget, Jean, Les traits principaux de la logique de l'enfant. *J. de Psychol.* 1924. 21.

480. Piaget, Jean, *Language and Thought of the Child.* 1926. (Fr. ed., 1923.)

481. Piaget, Jean, *Judgment and Reasoning in the Child.* 1928. (Fr. ed., 1924.)

482. Piaget, Jean, *The Child's Conception of the World.* 1929. (Fr. ed., 1926.)

483. Piaget, Jean, *The Child's Conception of Physical Causality.* 1930. (Fr. ed., 1927.)

484. Piaget, Jean, *The Moral Judgment of the Child.* 1932. (Fr. ed., 1932.)

485. Pohlmann, Hans, Beitrag zur Psychologie des Schulkindes. *Pädagog. Mon.* (ed. Meumann). 1912.

486. Pratt, K. C., The Neonate. In: *Handb. of Child Psychology.* (Murchison.) Ch. III. 1933.

487. Pratt, K. C., The Organization of Behavior in the Newborn Infant. *Psychol. Rev.* 1937. 44.

488. Preyer, William, *The Mind of the Child.* Intern. Educ. Ser. (ed. H. W. Brown). 1888–89. Vol. VII. (Germ. ed., 1895.)

489. Queyrat, Fr., *La logique chez l'enfant et sa culture.* 1902.

490. Queyrat, Fr., *Les jeux des enfants.* 1920.

491. Raspe, Carla, Untersuchungen über Kinderträume. *Zschr. pädag. Psychol.* 1924. 25.

492. Raspe, Carla, Kindliche Selbstbeobachtung und Theoriebildung. *Zschr. angew. Psychol.* 1924. 23.

493. Révész, Géza, Über audition colorée. *Zschr. angew. Psychol.* 1922. 21.

494. Révész, Géza, Expériences sur la mémoire topographique et sur la découverte d'un système chez les enfants et les singes inférieurs. *Arch de Psychol.* 1923. 18.

495. Reynolds, Martha M., *Negativism of Preschool Children.* Teach. Coll., Columbia Univ. Cont. to Educ. 1928. 288.

496. Roloff, Else, Vom religiösem Leben der Kinder. *Arch. Relig.-Psychol.* 1921. 2-3.

497. Rouma, Georges, *Le langage graphique de l'enfant.* 1912.

498. Rubinow, O., and Frankl L., Funktionswechsel in der Dingauffassung. *Zschr. f. Psychol.* 1934. 133.
499. Rüssel, Arnulf, Über Formauffassung zwei bis fünfjähriger Kinder. *N. Psychol. Stud.* 1931. 7, 1.
500. Scholl, Robert, Die teilinhaltliche Beachtung von Form, Farbe und Grösse im vorschulpflichtigen Kindesalter. *Zschr. Psychol.* 1928. 109.
501. Schüssler, Heinrich, Ist die Behauptung Meumann's richtig: "Kinder können vor dem 14. Lebensjahr nicht schliessen"? *Zschr. angew. Psychol.* 1916.
502. Scupin, Ernst, and Gertrud, I. *Bubis erste Kindheit.* 1907. II. *Bubi im 4.-6. Lebensjahr.* 1910. III. *Lebensbild eines deutschen Schuljungen.* 1931.
503. Sherman, M. S., and Key, C. B., The Intelligence of Isolated Mountain Children. *Child Devel.* 1932. 3.
504. Sherman, M. S., Sherman, I. C., and Flory, Ch. D., Infant Behavior. *Comp. Psychol. Mo.* 1936. 12, 4.
505. Shinn, M. W., I. *Notes on the Development of a Child.* Univ. of Calif. Public. 1893/99. II. *Development of the Senses in the First Three Years. Ibid.* 1907. (Germ. ed., 1905.)
506. Sliosberg, S., Zur Dynamik des Ersatzes in Spiel- und Ernstsituationen. *Psychol. Forsch.* 1934. 19.
507. Smith, M. E., *An Investigation of the Development of the Sentence and the Extent of Vocabulary in Young Children.* Univ. Iowa Stud. in Child Welfare. 1926. 3, 5.
508. Staples, Ruth, The Responses of Infants to Color. *J. Exp. Psychol.* 1932. 15.
509. Starbuck, E. D., *The Psychology of Religion.* 1899.
510. Stern, Clara and William, Zeichnerische Entwicklung eines Knaben vom 4. zum 7. Lebensjahr. *Zschr. angew. Psychol.* 1910.
511. Stern, Clara and William, *Die Kindersprache.* 1927.
512. Stern, Clara and William, *Erinnerung, Aussage und Lüge.* 1931.
513. Stern, William, *Psychology of Early Childhood.* 1930. (Germ. ed., 1928.)
514. Strauss, Alfred, and Werner, Heinz, Deficiency in the Finger Schema in Relation to Arithmetic Disability. *Am. J. Orthopsych.* 1938. 8.
515. Stumpf, Carl, Eigenartige sprachliche Entwicklung eines Kindes. *Zschr. pädag. Psychol.* 1900. 2.
516. Sully, James, *Studies of Childhood.* 1896. (Germ. ed. 1897.)
517. Sully, James, *Children's Ways.* 1897.

518. Szymanski, J. S., Versuche über die Entwicklung der Fähigkeit zum rationellen Handeln bei Kindern. *Zschr. f. Psychol.* 1917. 78.
519. Tobie, H., Die Entwicklung der teilinhaltlichen Beachtung von Farbe und Form im vorschulpflichtigen Alter. Beih. 38. *Zschr. ang. Psychol.* 1926.
520. Tracy, Frederick, *The Psychology of Childhood.* 1895.
521. Usnadze, D., Die Begriffsbildung im vorschulpflichtigen Alter. *Zschr. ang. Psychol.* 1929. 34.
522. Usnadze, D., Gruppenbildungsversuche bei vorschulpflichtigen Kindern. *Arch. ges. Psychol.* 1929. 73.
523. Valentine, C. W., Color Perception of an Infant. *Brit. J. Psychol.* 1913/14. 6.
524. Varendonck, J., Recherches sur les sociétés d'enfants. *Trav. Inst. Solvay.* 1914. 12.
525. Vigotsky, L. S., Thought and Speech. *Psychiatry: J. Biol. Pathol. Interpers. Rel.* 1939. 2, 1.
526. Vogel, Peter, *Untersuchungen über die Denkbeziehungen in den Urteilen des Schulkindes.* Giessener Diss. 1911.
527. Volkelt, Hans, Primitive Komplexqualitäten in Kinderzeichnungen. *Kongressbericht d. Gesellsch. f. exper. Psychol.* 1924. 8.
528. Volkelt, Hans, Fortschritte der experimentellen Kinderpsychologie. *Kongr. f. exp. Psych.* 1926. 9.
529. Volkelt, Hans, Neue Untersuchungen über die kindliche Auffassung und Wiedergabe von Formen. *Kongr. Heilpäd.* 1929. 4.
530. Vorwahl, H., *Psychologie der Vorpubertät.* 1929.
531. Weigl, Egon, Zur Psychologie sogenannter Abstraktionsprozesse. I. Untersuchungen über das Ordnen. *Zschr. Psych.* 1927. 103.
532. Werner, Heinz, Die melodische Erfindung im frühen Kindesalter. *Sitz.-Ber. d. k. Akad. d. Wiss. Wien, Mitt. d. Phonogramm-Arch.-Komm.* 1917. 43.
533. Werner, Heinz, Ordnen von Begriffsreihen. Beiheft 18. (Peter-Stern.) *Zschr. ang. Psychol.* 1919.
534. Werner, Heinz, Über magische Verhaltungsweisen beim Kinde und Jugendlichen. *Zschr. pädag. Psychol.* 1928. 29.
535. Werner, Heinz, Process and Achievement. A Basic Problem of Education and Developmental Psychology. *Harvard Educ. Rev.* 1937. 7.
536. Werner, Heinz, Perception of Spatial Relationship in Men-

tally Deficient Children. *J. Genet. Psychol.* (Will appear 1940.)

537. Werner, Heinz, and Strauss, Alfred, Functional Analysis in Mentally Deficient Children. *Am. J. Abn. Soc. Psychol.* 1939.

538. Werner, Heinz, and Strauss, Alfred, Types of Visuo-Motor Activity in Their Relation to Low and High Performance Ages. *Proc. Am. Ass. Ment. Defic.* 1939/40.

539. Zeininger, Karl, Magische Geisteshaltung im Kindesalter und ihre Bedeutung für die religiöse Entwicklung. Beih. 47. *Zschr. ang. Psychol.* 1929.

4. ABNORMAL PSYCHOLOGY

540. Baudelaire, Charles, *Les paradis artificiels. Œuvres compl.* (ed. Gautier.) Vol. III. 1921.

541. Benary, Wilhelm, Studien zur Untersuchung der Intelligenz bei einem Fall von Seelenblindheit. (Psychol. Analysen hirnpath. Fäll, hgg. v. Goldstein u. Gelb.) *Psychol. Forsch.* 1922. 2.

542. Beringer, Kurt, Beiträge zur Analyse schizophrener Denkstörungen. *Zschr. Neurol, Psych.* 1924—26. 93, 103.

543. Beringer, Kurt, Der Mescalinrausch. *Mon. a. d. G. d. Neurol. u. Psych.* 1927. 49.

544. Berze, Josef, and Gruhle, Hans, Psychologie der Schizophrenie. *Monogr. a. d. Gesamtgeb. d. Neurol. u. Psychiat.* 1929. 55.

545. Bleuler, E., Dementia praecox oder Gruppe der Schizophrenien. *Hdbch. d. Psychiatrie.* (ed. Aschaffenburg.) Spec. Pt. IV. I. 1911.

546. Bolles, Marjorie, and Goldstein, Kurt, A Study of the Impairment of "Abstract Behavior" in Schizophrenic Patients. *Psychiatr. Quart.* 1938. 12.

547. Bouman, L., and Grünbaum, A. A., Experimentell-psychologische Untersuchung zur Aphasie und Paraphasie. *Zschr. Neurol.* 1925. 96.

548. Bouman, L., and Grünbaum, A. A., Eine Störung der Chronognosie und ihre Bedeutung im betreffenden Symptomenbild. *Mtschr. Psych. Neurol.* 1929. 73.

549. Bürger, Hans, and Mayer-Gross, Willi, Über Zwangssymptome bei Encephalitis lethargica. *Zschr. Neurol. Psych.* 1928. 116.

550. Bychowski, Gustav, Metaphysik und Schizophrenie. *Abhdl. Neurol. Psychiatrie, Psychol.* (ed. Bonhoeffer.) 1923. 21.

551. Engerth, G., Sprachphysiognomische Beobachtungen im Rückbildungstadium aphasischer Störungen. *Wiener Kl. Woch.* 1937. 50. 9/10.

552. Fischer, Franz, Zeitstruktur und Schizophrenie. *Zschr. Neurol. Psych.* 1929. 121.
553. Fraenkel, F., and Joël, E., Beiträge zu einer experimentellen Psychopathologie. *Zschr. Neurol. Psych.* 1927. 11.
554. Fuchs, W., Untersuchungen über das Sehen der Hemianopiker und Hemiamblyopiker. *Zschr. Psychol.* 1920. 86.
555. Gelb, Adhémar, Über den Wegfall der Wahrnehmung von "Oberflächenfarben." *Zschr. Psychol.* 1920. 84.
556. Gelb, Adhémar, Remarques générales sur l'utilisation des données pathologiques pour la psychologie et la philosophie du langage. *J. de Psychol. Norm. et Pathol.* 1933. 30.
557. Gelb, Adhémar, and Goldstein, Kurt, Das Wesen der amnestischen Aphasie. *Verhdlg. d. Ges. dtsch. Nervenärzte.* Sept. 1924.
558. Gerstmann, J., Fingeragnosie. *Wiener Klin. Woch.* 1924. p. 1010.
559. Gerstmann, J., Fingeragnosie und isolierte Agraphie. *Zschr. ges. Neurol. Psych.* 1927. 108.
560. Goddard, Henry H., *Psychology of the Normal and Subnormal.* 1919.
561. Goldstein, Kurt, Die pathologischen Tatsachen in ihrer Bedeutung für das Problem der Sprache. *Kongr. D. Ges. Psychol.* 1932. 12.
562. Goldstein, Kurt, *The Organism.* 1939. (Germ. ed. 1934.)
563. Goldstein, Kurt, The Problem of the Meaning of Words Based upon Observation of Aphasic Patients. *J. Psychol.* 1936. 2.
564. Goldstein, Kurt, The Modifications of Behavior Consequent to Cerebral Lesions. *Psychiatr. Quart.* 1936. 10.
565. Goldstein, Kurt, and Gelb, Adhémar, Zur Psychologie des optischen Wahrnehmungs- und Erkennungsvorgangs. *Zschr. Neurol. Psych.* 1918. 41.
566. Goldstein, Kurt, and Gelb, Adhémar, Über Farbennamen-amnesie. *Psychol. Forsch.* 1924. 6.
567. Goldstein, Kurt, and Rosenthal, Olli, Zum Problem der Wirkung der Farben auf den Organismus. *Schweiz. Arch. Neurol. Psych.* 1930. 26.
568. Gruhle, Hans W., Chapter on the Psychopathology of the Schizophrenics. *Handbuch der Geisteskrankheiten* (O. Bumke). 1932. Vol. IX.
569. Hanfmann, Eugenia, Analysis of the Thinking Disorder in a Case of Schizophrenia. *Arch. Neurol. Psych.* 1939. 41.
570. Hanfmann, Eugenia, Thought Disturbances in Schizophrenia

as Revealed by Performance in a Picture Completion Test. *J. Abn. Soc. Psychol.* 1939. 34.

571. Hanfman, Eugenia, and Kasanin, Jacob, A Method for the Study of Concept Formation. *J. Psychol.* 1936. 3.
572. Head, Henry, *Aphasia and Kindred Disorders of Speech.* 1926.
573. Head, Henry, in conjunction with Rivers, W. H. R., Holmes, G., Sherren, J., Thompson, Th., and Riddoch, G., *Studies in Neurology.* 1920.
574. Hochheimer, Wolfgang, Analyse eines Seelenblinden von der Sprache aus. *Psychol. Forsch.* 1932. 16.
575. Hochheimer, Wolfgang, Zur Psychopathologie räumlicher Leistungen und ihrer "Restitution." *Zschr. Psychol.* 1932. 127.
576. Israeli, Nathan, *Abnormal Personality and Time.* 1936.
577. Jackson, Hughlings, The Croonian Lectures on Evolution and Dissolution of the Nervous System. *Brit. Med. J.* 1884.
578. Jaspers, Karl, Strindberg und van Gogh. *Arb. angew. Psychiatrie* (ed. Morgenthaler). 1922. 5.
579. Jaspers, Karl, *Allgemeine Psychopathologie.* 1923.
580. Joël, E., and Fraenkel, F., Der Haschischrausch. *Klin. Woch.* 1926. ˙
581. Kerner, Justinus, *Die Seherin von Prevorst.* Reclam Edition. N. D.
582. Klüver, Heinrich, Mescal Visions and Eidetic Vision. *Am. J. Psychol.* 1926. 37.
583. Klüver, Heinrich, *Mescal.* 1928.
584. Kraepelin, Emil, *Die Sprachstörungen im Traum.* 1906.
585. Kretschmer, Ernst, *A Textbook of Medical Psychology.* 1934. (Germ. ed., 1922.)
586. Kurz, Isolde, *Traumland.* 1919.
587. Merlos, A. M., Über Entwicklung und Störung des Zeitsinns. *Zt. Neurol. Psych.* 1935. 153.
588. Minkowski, E., Zeit- und Raumprobleme in der Psychopathologie. *Wiener Klin. Woch.* 1931. 44.
589. Morgenthaler, W., Ein Geisteskranker als Künstler. *Arb. angew. Psychiatrie* (ed. Morgenthaler). 1921. 1.
590. Pfeiffer, R. A., *Der Geisteskranke und sein Werk.* 1923.
591. Pick, Arnold, *Uber das Sprachverständnis.* 1909.
592. Poppelreuter, Walther, *Die psychischen Schädigungen durch Kopfschuss im Kriege.* 1917.
593. Pötzl, Otto, Experimentell erzeugte Traumbilder in ihren Beziehungen zum indirekten Sehen. *Zschr. Neurol. Psych.* 1917. 37.

594. Prinzhorn, Hans, *Bildnerei der Geisteskranken*. 1922.
595. Rust, Hans, Das Zungenreden. *Grenzfr. d. Nerv.- u. Seelenlebens*. 1924.
596. Schilder, Paul, Selbstbewusstsein und Persönlichkeitsbewusstsein. *Monogr. a. d. Ges.-Geb. d. Neurol. u. Psychiat.* 1914.
597. Schilder, Paul, Wahn und Erkenntnis. *Monogr. a. d. Ges.-Geb. d. Neurol. und Psychiat.* 1914.
598. Schilder, Paul, *Seele und Leben.* 1923.
599. Schilder, Paul, *Medizinische Psychologie.* 1924.
600. Schneider, Carl, *Die Psychologie der Schizophrenen.* 1930.
601. Siekmann, W., Psychologische Analyse des Falles Rat. . . . *Psychol. Forsch.* 1932. 16.
602. Sittig, Otto, Zur Psychopathologie des Zahlenverständnisses. *Zschr. Pathopsychol.,* 1919. 3.
603. Storch, Alfred, Das archaisch-primitive Erleben und Denken der Schizophrenen. *Monogr. a. d. Gesamtgebiet d. Neurol. u. Psychiatrie.* 1922. H. 32. (Engl. transl., *Nervous and Mental Disease Mo.* 36. 1924.)
604. Storch, Alfred, Bewusstseinsebenen und Wirklichkeitsbereiche in der Schizophrenie. *Zschr. f. d. ges. Neurol. u. Psychiatrie.* 1923. 82.
605. Storch, Alfred, Der Entwicklungsgedanke in der Psychiatrie. *Ergebn. d. inneren Medizin u. Kinderheilkunde.* 1924.
606. Storch, Alfred, Die Welt der beginnenden Schizophrenie und die archaische Welt. *Zschr. Neurol. Psych.* 1930. 127.
607. Storch, Alfred, Über Orientierungsfähigkeit auf niederen Organisationsstufen. *Zt. ang. Psych.* 1932. 42.
608. Straus, Erwin, Das Zeiterlebnis in der endogenen Depression und in der psychopathischen Verstimmung. *Monatschr. Psych. Neurol.* 1928. 68.
609. Tuczek, Karl, Analyse einer Katatonikersprache. *Zschr. f. d. ges. Neurol. u. Psychiatrie.* Bd. 72.
610. Urbantschitsch, V., *Über subjektive optische Anschauungsbilder.* 1907.
611. Varendonck, J., *Über das vorbewusste phantasierende Denken.* 1922.
612. Vigotsky, L. S., Thought in Schizophrenia. *Arch. Neurol. Psychiat.* 1934. 31.
613. van Woerkom, W., Über Störungen im Denken bei Aphasiekranken. *Monatschr. Psych. Neurol.* 1925. 59.

5. ANIMAL PSYCHOLOGY

614. Angulo y Gonzàlez, A. W., The Prenatal Development of Behavior in the Albino Rat. *J. Comp. Neurol.* 1932. 55.
615. Baltzer, F., Beiträge zur Sinnesphysiologie und Psychologie der Webespinnen. *Mitt. Naturf. Ges. Bern.* 1923. 1924.
616. Bierens de Haan, J. A., Über Wahrnehmungskomplexe und Wahrnehmungselemente bei einem niedern Affen. *Zool. Jbchr.* 1925. 42.
617. Bierens de Haan, J. A., Zahlbegriff und Handlungsrhythmus bei einem Affen. *Zool. Jahrb.* 1935. 54.
618. Bingham, H., Size and Form Perception in Gallus domesticus. *J. Animal Behav.* 1913. 3.
619. Buddenbrock, W. v., *Grundriss der vergleichenden Physiologie.* 1924. 1.
620. Buytendijk, F. J. J., L'instinct d'alimentation et l'expérience chez les crapauds. *Arch. Néerl. de Physiol.* 1918. 3.
621. Buytendijk, F. J. J., Über die Formwahrnehmung beim Hunde. *Pflügers Arch.* 1924. 205.
622. Buytendijk, F. J. J., Zur Untersuchung des Wesensunterschieds von Mensch und Tier. *Bl. f. Deutsch. Philos.* 1929. 3.
623. Buytendijk, F. J. J., *The Mind of the Dog.* 1936.
624. Buytendijk, F. J. J., and Fischel, W., Methoden zur psychologischen Untersuchung wirbelloser Tiere. *Abderhaldens Hdbch. d. biol. Arbeitsmeth.* 6. D.
625. Buytendijk, F. J. J., and Fischel, W., Teil und Ganzes bei der Orientierung von Ratten. *Arch. Néerl. de Physiol.* 1931.
626. Buytendijk, F. J. J., and Hage, N., Sur la valeur de reaction de quelques excitants simples dans la formation d'une habitude par les chiens. *Arch. Néerl. de Physiol.* 1923. 8.
627. Buytendijk, F. J. J., and Remmers, J., Nouvelles recherches sur la formation d'habitudes chez les poissons. *Arch. Néerl. de Physiol.* 1923. 8.
628. Carmichael, Leonard, Origin and Prenatal Growth of Behavior. In: *Handb. of Child Psychology.* (Murchison.) 1933. Chap. II.
629. Carmichael, Leonard, The Development of Behavior in Fetal Life and the Concept of the "Organism-as-a-Whole." *Proc. Soc. Res. Child Devel.* 1936. Pt. 2.
630. Child, C. M., *The Origin and Development of the Nervous System from a Physiological Standpoint.* 1921.
631. Child, C. M., *Physiological Foundations of Behavior.* 1924.

632. Coburn, Charles A., The Behavior of the Crow. *J. Anim. Behav.* 1914. 4.
633. Coghill, G. E., *Anatomy and the Problem of Behavior.* 1929.
634. Coronios, J. D., Development of Behavior in the Fetal Cat. *Genet. Psychol. Mo.* 1933. 14.
635. Demoll, R., Über die Vorstellungen der Tiere. *Zool. Jb.* 1921. 38.
636. Dexler, H., Der heutige Stand der Lehre vom tierischen Gebaren. *Lotos.* 1921.
637. Dexler, H., Das Koehler-Wertheimersche Gestaltungsprinzip und die moderne Tierpsychologie. *Lotos.* 1922.
638. Dusser de Barenne, J. G., "Corticalization" of Function and Functional Localization in the Cerebral Cortex. *Arch. of Neurol. Psych.* 1933. 30.
639. Fabre, J. H., *Souvenirs entomologiques.* 1879–1910.
640. Fields, Paul E., Studies in Concept Formation. *Comp. Psychol. Mo.* 1932. 9.
641. Fischel, Werner, Methoden zur psychologischen Untersuchung der Wirbeltiere. *Abderhaldens Hdbch. d. biol. Arbeitsmeth.* VI. D.
642. Fischel, Werner, Über die Bedeutung des Strebens bei tierischen Wahlhandlungen. *Zschr. vgl. Physiol.* 1932. 16.
643. Frisch, Karl v., Der Farben- und Formensinn der Bienen. *Zool. Jb., Abtl. Zool.* 1914. 35.
644. Frisch, Karl v., Über die "Sprache" der Bienen. *Zool. Jb., Abt. Physiol.* 1923. 40.
645. Frisch, Karl v., *Sinnesphysiologie und Sprache der Bienen.* 1924.
646. Gellermann, Louis W., Form Discrimination in Chimpanzees and Two-year-old Children. *J. Genet. Psychol.* 1933. 42.
647. Goltz, Fr., Der Hund ohne Grosshirn. *Arch. f. d. ges. Physiol.* 1892. 51.
648. Grünbaum, A. A., Über das Verhalten der Spinne (epeira diademata) besonders gegenüber vibratorischen Reizen. *Psychol. Forsch.* 1927.
649. Guillaume, P., and Meyerson, J., Recherches sur l'usage de l'instrument chez les singes. *Journ. de Psychol.* 1930-31. 27 and 28.
650. Hamilton, J. A., and Krechevsky, I., Studies in the Effect of Shock upon Behavior Plasticity in the Rat. *J. Comp. Psychol.* 1934. 17.
651. Hempelmann, Friedrich, *Tierpsychologie.* 1926.
652. Herrick, C. J., *Brains of Rats and Men.* 1927.

653. Hertz, Mathilde, Beobachtungen an gefangenen Rabenvögeln. *Psychol. Forsch.* 1926. 8.
654. Hertz, Mathilde, Weitere Versuche an der Rabenkrähe. *Psychol. Forsch.* 1928. 10.
655. Hertz, Mathilde, Die Organisation des optischen Feldes bei der Biene. *Zschr. vgl. Physiol.* 1929. 1930. 8. 11.
656. Hunter, W. S., Delayed Reactions in Animals and Children. *Behav. Mo.* 1913. 2.
657. Jacobsen, C. F., Studies of Cerebral Functions in Primates. *Comp. Psychol. Mo.* 1936. 13. 3.
658. de Jong, H., Recherches sur la formation d'idées chez le chien. *Arch. néerl. physiol.* 1919. 3.
659. Kafka, Gustav, *Einführung in die Tierpsychologie.* 1914.
660. Kafka, Gustav, Tierpsychologie. In: *Hdb. d. vgl. Psychol.* 1923. I.
661. Katz, Dav., and Révész, Géza, Experimentell-psychologische Untersuchungen an Hühnern. *Zschr. Psychol.* 1909. 50; *Zschr. angew. Psychol.* 1921. 18.
662. Klüver, Heinrich, *Behavior Mechanisms in Monkeys.* 1933.
663. Koehler, Wolfgang, Optische Untersuchungen am Schimpansen und am Haushuhn. *Abhdl. d. Preuss. Akad. Physik.-mathem. Kl.* 1915.
664. Koehler, Wolfgang, Nachweis einfacher Strukturfunktionen beim Schimpansen und beim Haushuhn. *Abhdl. d. Preuss. Akad., Phys.-Math. Kl.* 1918.
665. Koehler, Wolfgang, *The Mentality of Apes.* 1927. (Germ. ed., 1917.)
666. Krechevsky, I., Brain Mechanisms and Variability. *J. Comp. Psychol.* 1937. 23.
667. Krechevsky, I., Brain Mechanisms and Umweg Behavior. *J. Comp. Psychol.* 1938. 25.
668. Lashley, K. S., *Brain Mechanisms and Intelligence.* 1929.
669. Lashley, K. S., Integrative Functions of the Cerebral Cortex. *Physiol. Rev.* 1933. 13.
670. Lashley, K. S., The Mechanism of Vision. VII. The Projection of the Retina upon the Primary Optic Centers in the Rat. *J. Comp. Neurol.* 1934. 59.
671. Lashley, K. S., The Mechanism of Vision. VIII. The Projection of the Retina upon the Cerebral Cortex. *J. Comp. Neurol.* 1934. 60.
672. Lashley, K. S., The Mechanism of Vision. XII. Nervous Structures Concerned in the Acquisition and Retention of

Habits Based on Reactions to Light. *Comp. Psychol. Mo.* 1935. 2.

673. Lashley, K. S., The Mechanism of Vision. XV. Preliminary Studies of the Rat's Capacity for Detail Vision. *J. Gener. Psychol.* 1938. 18.

674. Layman, John D., The Avian Visual System. I. Cerebral Function of the Domestic Fowl in Pattern Vision. *Comp. Psychol. Mo.* 1938. 12, 3.

675. Maier, Norman, R. F., Reasoning and Learning. *Psychol. Rev.* 1931. 38.

676. Maier, Norman, R. F., The Effect of Cerebral Destruction on Reasoning and Learning in Rats. *J. Comp. Neurol.* 1932. 54.

677. Maier, N. R. F., and Schneirla, T. C., *Principles of Animal Psychology.* 1935.

678. Marquis, D. G., Effects of Removal of the Visual Cortex in Mammals. *Proc. Ass. Res. Nerv. Ment. Dis.* 1932. 13.

679. Marquis, D. G., Philogenetic Interpretation of the Function of the Visual Cortex. *Arch. of Neurol. Psych.* 1935. 33.

680. Owen, Sir Richard, *Lectures on Invertebrate Animals.* 1843.

681. Perkins, F. Th., Genetic Study of Brain Differentiation. *J. Comp. Psychol.* 1936. 21.

682. Rabaud, E., *How Animals Find Their Way About.* 1928.

683. Raney, E. T., and Carmichael, L., Localizing Responses to Tactual Stimuli in the Fetal Rat. *J. Genet. Psychol.* 1934. 45.

684. Révész, Géza, Tierpsychologische Untersuchungen (Vers. an Hühnern). *Zschr. Psychol.* 1921. 88.

685. Révész, Géza, Experiments of Animal Space Perception. *Brit. J. Psychol.* 1923. 14.

686. Révész, Géza, Expériences sur la mémoire topographique et sur la découverte d'un système chez des enfants et des singes inférieurs. *Arch. de Psychol.* 1923. 18.

687. Rothmann, H., Zusammenfassender Bericht über den Rothmannschen grosshirnlosen Hund nach klinischer und anatomischer Untersuchung. *Zschr. Neurol. Psych.* 1923. 87.

688. Russell, E. S., *Form and Function.* 1916.

689. Sarris, E. G., Sind wir berechtigt, vom Wortverständnis des Hundes zu sprechen? *Zschr. angew. Psychol.* 1931. Suppl. 62.

690. Sears, R., Effect of Optic Lobe Ablation on the Visuo-motor Behavior of Goldfish. *J. Comp. Psychol.* 1934. 17.

691. Szymanski, J. S., Abhandlungen zum Aufbau der Lehre von den Handlungen der Tiere. *Pflüg. Arch. ges. Physiol.* 1918. 170.

692. Thorndike, E. L., *Animal Intelligence*. 1911.
693. Tinklepaugh, O. F., Representative Factors in Monkeys. *J. Comp. Psychol.* 1928. 8.
694. Tolman, E. C., *Purposive Behavior in Animals and Men*. 1932.
695. v. Uexküll, Jacob, *Umwelt und Innenwelt der Tiere*. 1921.
696. v. Uexküll, Jacob, *Theoretische Biologie*. 1928.
697. v. Uexküll, Jacob, *Streifzüge durch die Umwelten von Tieren und Menschen*. 1934.
698. Upton, M., The Auditory Sensitivity of the Guinea Pig. *Am. J. Physiol.* 1929. 41.
699. Volkelt, Hans, Über die Vorstellungen der Tiere. *Arb. Entwickl.-Psychol.* (ed. Krueger). 1914. 2.
700. Warden, C. J., Jenkins, T. N., and Warner, L. H., *Comparative Psychology*. 1935/36.
701. Washburn, M. F., *The Animal Mind*. 1936.
702. Watson, J. B., *Behavior*. 1930.
703. Yerkes, R. M., The Mind of the Gorilla. *Comp. Psychol. Mo.* 1928. 5.
704. Yerkes, R. M. and A. W., *The Great Apes*. 1929.
705. Yerkes, R. M. and D. N., Concerning Memory in the Chimpanzee. *J. Comp. Psychol.* 1928. 8.

6. EXPERIMENTAL PSYCHOLOGY

706. Ach, Narziss, Über die Begriffsbildung. *Unters. z. Psychol. u. Philos.* (ed. Ach.) 1921. 3.
707. Akishige, Y., Experimentelle Untersuchungen über die Struktur des Wahrnehmungsraumes. *Mitt.* IV, jur.-lit. Fakult. Kyushu-Universität. 1937.
708. Bichowski, F. R., The Mechanism of Consciousness: The Pre-Sensation. *Am. J. Psychol.* 1925.
709. Börnstein, Walter, Über den Geruchsinn. *Dtsch. Zschr. Nervenheilk.* 1928. 104.
710. Börnstein, Walter, On the Functional Relations of the Sense Organs to One Another and to the Organism as a Whole. *J. Gener. Psychol.* 1936. 15.
711. Brunswik, Egon, *Wahrnehmung und Gegenstandswelt*. 1934.
712. Cattell, R. B., The Subjective Character of Cognition and the Pre-Sensational Development of Perception. *Mo. Brit. J. Psychol.* 1930. XIV.
713. Dembo, Tamara, Der Ärger als dynamisches Problem. *Psychol. Forsch.* 1931. 15.

714. Gilbert, G. M., Dynamic Psychophysics and the Phi Phenomenon. *Arch. of Psychol.* 1939. 237.
715. Heiss, Alfred, Zum Problem der isolierenden Abstraktion. *N. Psychol. Stud.* 1930. 4.
716. Henning, Hans, Psychologische Methoden zur Untersuchung des Geschmacksinnes. *Hdb. biol. Arbeits-meth.* (Abderhalden.) 1922. 6. A. 4.
717. Henning, Hans, *Der Geruch*. 1924.
718. Hoppe, Ferdinand, Erfolg und Misserfolg. *Psychol. Forsch.* 1930. 14.
719. v. Hornbostel, Erich, Über Geruchshelligkeit. Pflügers. *Arch. Physiol.* 1931. 227.
720. Karsten, A., Psychische Sättigung. (Unters. K. Lewin V.) *Psychol. Forsch.* 1928. 10.
721. Katz, David, Der Aufbau der Tastwelt. *Erg.-Bd. 11, Zschr. f. Psychol.* 1925.
722. Katz, David, *The World of Colour*. 1935. (Germ. ed., *Zschr. Psychol.* Suppl. 7. 1911.)
723. Krauss, Reinhard, Über graphischen Ausdruck. Beih. 48. *Zschr. angew. Psychol.* 1930.
724. Lagercrantz, Eliel, Über Gestaltbildung in den Dialekten der lappischen Sprache. (Werner, Stud. ü. Strukturgesetze VII.) *Zschr. Psychol.* 1927. 104.
725. Lewin, Kurt, Untersuchungen zur Handlungs- und Affektpsychologie. *Psychol. Forsch.* 1926 ff. Vol. VII ff.
726. Metzger, Wolfgang, Optische Untersuchungen am Ganzfeld: Zur Phänomenologie des homogenen Ganzfelds. *Psychol. Forsch.* 1929. 13.
727. Ovsiankina, Maria, Die Wiederaufnahme unterbrochener Handlungen. (Unters. v. K. Lewin VI.) *Psychol. Forsch.* 1928. 11.
728. Sander, Fritz, Experimentelle Ergebnisse der Gestaltpsychologie. *10. Kongr. f. exp. Psychol.* 1927.
729. v. Schiller, Paul, Das optische Verschmelzen in seiner Abhängigkeit von heteromodaler Reizung. (Werner. Unt. ü. Empfindung u. Empfinden 4.) *Zschr. Psychol.* 1932. 125.
730. v. Schiller, Paul, Die Rauhigkeit als intermodale Erscheinung. *Zschr. Psychol.* 1932. 127.
731. Werner, Heinz, Grundfragen der Intensitätspsychologie. *Zschr. f. Psychol.* 1922. Suppl. 10.
732. Werner, Heinz, Über Strukturgesetze und deren Auswirkung in den geometrisch-optischen Täuschungen. *Zschr. Psychol.* 1924. 94.

733. Werner, Heinz, Das Problem der motorischen Gestaltung. *Zschr. Psychol.* 1924. 94.
734. Werner, Heinz, Über Mikromelodik und Mikroharmonik. *Zschr. Psychol.* 1925. 98.
735. Werner, Heinz, Über die Ausprägung von Tongestalten. *Zschr. Psychol.* 1926. 101.
736. Werner, Heinz, Das Problem des Empfindens und die Methode seiner experimentellen Prüfung. *Zschr. Psychol.* 1929. 114.
737. Werner, Heinz, Die Rolle der Sprachempfindung im Prozess der Gestaltung ausdrucksmässig erlebter Worte. *Zschr. Psychol.* 1930. 117.
738. Werner, Heinz, *Grundfragen der Sprachphysiognomik.* 1932.
739. Werner, Heinz, Sprache als Ausdruck. *Kongr. Dtsch. Ges. Psychol.* 1932. 12.
740. Werner, Heinz, L'Unité des Sens. *J. de Psychol.* 1934. 31.
741. Werner, Heinz, Studies on Contour. *Am. J. Psychol.* 1935. 47.
742. Werner, Heinz, Dynamics in Binocular Depth Perception. *Psychol. Mo.* 1937. 49, 2.
743. Werner, Heinz, and Lagercrantz, Eliel, Experimentell-psychologische Studien über die Struktur des Wortes. *Zschr. Psychol.* 1924. 95.
744. Wertheimer, Max, *Über Schlussprozesse im produktiven Denken.* 1920.
745. Wertheimer, Max, Untersuchungen zur Lehre von der Gestalt. *Psychol. Forsch.* 1922/23. 1/4.
746. Willwoll, Alexander, *Begriffsbildung.* 1926.
747. Witte, Otto, Untersuchungen über die Gebärdensprache. *Zschr. Psychol.* 1930. 116.
748. Wohlfahrt, E., Der Auffassungsvorgang an kleinen Gestalten. *N. Psychol. Stud.* 1928. 4.
749. Zeigarnik, Bluma, Das Behalten erledigter und unerledigter Handlungen. (Unters. ed. K. Lewin.) *Psychol. Forsch.* 1927. 9.
750. Zietz, Karl, and Werner, Heinz, Über die dynamische Struktur der Bewegung. (Werner, Stud. Strukturgesetze 8.) *Zschr. Psychol.* 1927. 105.
751. Zietz, Karl, Gegenseitige Beeinflussung von Farb- und Tonerlebnissen. (Werner, Unters. ü. Empfindung u. Empfinden 3.) *Zschr. Psychol.* 1931. 121.

ADDENDA

ADDITIONAL REFERENCES

1. General Works. Ethnopsychology

752. Barcroft, J., *The Brain and its Environment.* 1938.
753. Barnett, H. G., Invention and Cultural Change. *Am. Anthrop.*, 1942, 44, 14-30.
754. Benedict, Ruth, Continuities and Discontinuities in Cultural Conditioning. *Psychiatry.* 1938, 1, 161-167.
755. Chapple, E. D., and Coon, C. S., *Principles of Anthropology.* 1942.
756. De Beer, G. R., *Embryos and Ancestors.* 1940.
757. De Crinis, M., Die Entwicklung der Grosshirnrinde nach der Geburt in ihrer Beziehung zur intellektuellen Ausreifung des Kindes. *Wien. Klin. Wochschr.* 1932, 45, 1161-1165.
758. Du Nouÿ, Paul Lecomte, *Biological Time.* 1937.
759. Eysenck, H. J., and Halstead, H., The Memory Function. *Am. J. Psychiat.* 1945, 102, 174-179.
760. Frank, L. K., Cultural Control and Physiological Anatomy. *A. J. Orthopsychiat.* 1938, 8, 622-626.
761. Frank, L. K., Man's Multidimensional Environment. *Scient. Monthly.* 1943, 56, 344-357.
762. Goodsell, W., *A History of Marriage and the Family.* 1934.
763. Heider, Fritz, The Description of the Psychological Environment in the Work of Marcel Proust. *Char. a. Pers.* 1941, 9, 295-314.
764. Hallowell, A. I., Temporal Orientation in Western Civilization and in a Preliterate Society. *Am. Anthrop.* 1937, 39, 646-670.
765. Hallowell, A. I., Some Psychological Aspects of Measurements among the Salteaux. *Am. Anthrop.* 1942, 44, 62-77.
766. Hallowell, A. I., Sociopsychological Aspects of Acculturation. In: *Science of Man.* (Linton.) 1945, 171-200.
767. Herskovitz, M. J., *Acculturation.* 1938.
768. Herskovitz, M. J., The Process of Cultural Change. In: *Science of Man.* (Linton.) 1945, 142-170.
769. Hilgard, E. R., and Marquis, D. G., *Conditioning and Learning.* 1940.
770. Hoeltker, George, Zeit und Zahl in Nordwestafrika. *Publ. d'Hommage P. W. Schmidt.* 1928, 282-302.

771. Hooton, E. A., *Up from the Ape*. 1946.
772. Kardiner, Abraham, *The Psychological Frontiers of Society*. 1945.
773. Kardiner, Abraham, *The Individual and His Society*. 1946.
774. Katona, George, *Organizing and Memorizing*. 1940.
775. Klineberg, Otto, *Social Psychology*. 1940.
776. Kluckhohn, C., Patterning as Exemplified in Navaho Culture. In: *Language, Culture and Personality*. (Spier a.o., ed.) 1941.
777. Kroeber, A. L., The Superorganic. *Am. Anthrop.* 1917, 19, 163-213.
778. Kroeber, A. L., and Warden, C. J., *The Emergence of Human Culture*. 1936.
779. Langworthy, O. R., Development of Behavior Patterns and Myelinization of the Nervous System in the Human Fetus and Infant. *Contr. Embryol., Carnegie Inst. Wash.* 1933, 24, No. 139.
780. Lee, D., A Primitive System of Values. *Philos. of Sci.* 1940, 7, 355-378.
781. Linton, Ralph, *The Cultural Background of Personality*. 1945.
782. Linton, Ralph (ed.), *The Science of Man in the World Crisis*. 1945.
783. Lowie, R. H., Individual Differences and Primitive Culture. *Publ. d'Hommage P. W. Schmidt*. 1928, 495-500.
784. Maier, N. R. F., Reasoning and Learning. *Psychol. Rev.* 1931, 38, 332-346.
785. Malinowski, Bronislaw, *Sex and Repression in Savage Society*. 1927.
785a. Marquis, D. G., The Criterion of Innate Behavior. *Psychol. Rev.* 1930, 37, 334-339.
786. Marrett, R. R., *Primitive Religion*. 1932.
787. Marrett, R. R., *Head, Heart and Hands in Human Evolution*. 1935.
788. McGraw, Myrtle, Maturation of Behavior. In: *Manual of Child Psychology*, (ed. Carmichael.) 1946. Ch.7.
789. Mead, Margaret, A Lapse of Animism Among a Primitive People. *Psyche*. 1928, 9, 72-79.
790. Mead, Margaret. *Cooperation and Competition Among Primitive Peoples*. 1937.
791. Miller, Neal, and Dollard, John, *Social Learning and Imitation*. 1941.
792. Murdock, G. P., *Our Primitive Contemporaries*. 1934.
793. Murphy, G., Murphy, Lois B., and Newcomb, T., *Experimental Social Psychology*. 1937.

794. Needham, J. G., *About Ourselves: A Survey of Human Nature from the Zoological Viewpoint*. 1941.
795. Novikoff, A. B., The Concept of Integrative Levels and Biology. *Science*. 1945, 101, 209-215.
796. O'Neale Lila, and Dolores, Juan, Notes on Papago Color Designations. *Am. Anthrop*. 1943, 45, 386-397.
797. Rapaport, David, *Emotions and Memory*. 1942.
798. Riese, Walther, and Réquet, André, *L'idée de l'homme dans la neurologie contemporaine*. 1938.
799. Russell, E. S., *The Interpretation of Development and Heredity*. 1930.
800. Sapir, E., *Language, an Introduction to the Study of Speech*. 1921.
801. Schneirla, T. C., Problems in the Biopsychology of Social Organization. *J. Abn. Soc. Psychol*. 1946, 41, 385-402.
802. Seligman, E. R. A., and Johnson, A. (ed.), *Encyclopedia of the Social Sciences*. 1930-34.
803. Sherif, Muzafer, A Study of Some Social Factors in Perception. *Arch. Psychol*. 1935, 187.
804. Sorokin, Paul, *Contemporary Sociological Theories*. 1928.
805. Sorokin, Paul, Social Time. *Am. J. Sociol*. 1937, 42, 615-629.
806. Thomas, N. W., Counting on the Fingers. *Publ. d'Hommage P. W. Schmidt*. 1928, 726-734.
807. Tilney, F., *The Brain from Ape to Man*. 1929.
808. Tilney, F., and Kubie, L. S., Behavior in its Relation to the Development of the Brain. *Bull. Neurol. Inst*. 1931, 1, 229-313.
809. Wallis, W. D., Individual Initiative and Social Compulsion. *Am. Anthrop*. 1915, 647-665.
810. Webster, Hutton, *Taboo*. 1942.
811. White, L. A., Energy and the Evolution of Culture. *Am. Anthrop*. 1943, 45, 335-356.
812. Whorf, B. L., The Relation of Habitual Thought and Behavior to Language. In: *Language, Culture and Personality*. (Spier a.o. ed.) 1941.
813. Wilson, D. W., *Religion in Primitive Society*. 1939.

2. ANTHROPOLOGY

814. Ashley-Montagu, M. F., *Coming into Being Among the Australian Aborigines*. 1938.
815. Bateson, Gregory, and Mead, Margaret, Balinese Character, *Spec. Pub. N.Y. Acad. Sci*. 1942, 2.

816. Beaglehole, Ernest, and Pearl, Ethnology of Pukapuka. *Bull. Bishop Mus.* 1938, 150.
817. Beckwith, Martha, *Hawaiian Mythology.* 1940.
818. Benedict, Ruth, Zuñi Mythology. *Columbia Univ., Contrib. Anthrop.* 1935, 21.
819. Bunzel, Ruth, Introduction to Zuñi Ceremonialism. *Rep. Bur. Am. Ethnol.* 1932, 47.
820. Bunzel, Ruth, Zuñi Ritual Poetry. *Rep. Bur. Am. Ethnol.* 1932, 47.
821. Dubois, Cora, *The People of Alor.* 1944.
822. Erikson, E. H., Observations on Sioux Education. *J. Psychol.* 1939, 7, 101-156.
823. Evans-Pritchard, E. E., *The Nuer.* 1940.
824. Firth, Raymond, *We, the Tikopia.* 1937.
825. Firth, Raymond, *Primitive Polynesian Economy.* 1939.
826. Firth, Raymond, The Works of the Gods in Tikopia. *Monog. Soc. Anthrop.* 1940, 1.
827. Folsom, J. K., *The Family.* 1934.
828. Fortune, R. F., *Sorcerers of Dobu.* 1932.
829. Fortune, R. F., Arapesh. *Public. Am. Ethnol. Soc.* 19. 1942.
830. Grenville, Goodwin, *The Social Organization of the Western Apache.* 1942.
831. Hambley, W. D., Source Book for African Anthropology. *Field Mus. Nat. Hist., Anthrop. Series,* 1937, 26.
832. Henry, Jules, *Jungle People. The Kaingang Tribe of the Highlands of Brazil.* 1941.
833. Herskovitz, M. J., Culture Areas in Africa. *Am. Anthrop.* 1924, 50-63.
834. Herskovitz, M. J., African Gods and Catholic Saints in New World Negro Belief. *Am. Anthrop.* 1932, 39, 635-643.
835. Hogbin, H. I., *Law and Order in Polynesia.* 1934.
836. Kroeber, A. L., Elements of Culture in Native California. *Univ. Calif. Publ. Archeol. Ethnol.* 13, 1917-23.
837. Llewellyn, K. U., and Hoebel, E. A., *The Cheyenne Way.* 1941.
838. Linton, Ralph, The Tanala, a Hill Tribe of Madagascar. *Field Mus. Nat. Hist., Anthropol. Ser.* 1933, 22.
839. Lowie, R. H., *The Crow Indians.* 1935.
840. MacGregor, Gordon, Ethnology of Tokelau Islands. *Bull. Bishop Mus.* 1937, 146.
841. Mead, Margaret, *Sex and Temperament in Three Primitive Societies.* 1935.

842. Mead, Margaret, The Mountain Arepesh. *Anthrop. Pap. Am. Mus. Nat. Hist.* 1938, 36.
843. Opler, M. E., *An Apache Life-way.* 1941.
844. Powdermaker, Hortense, *Life in Lesu.* 1933.
845. Schebesta, Paul, *Die Bambuti-Pygmäen von Ituri.* 1938.
846. Seligman, C. G., *Races of Africa.* 1930.
847. Speck, F. G., *Naskapi.* 1935.
848. Stayt, H. A., *The Bavenda.* 1931.
849. Richardson, Jane, Law and Status Among the Kiowa Indians. *Monog. Ethnol. Soc.* 1940, 1.
850. Whiting, J. W. M., *Becoming A Kwoma.* 1941.
851. Williams, F. E., *Orokaiva Magic.* 1928.

3. CHILD PSYCHOLOGY

852. Abel, T. M., Unsynthetic Modes of Thinking Among Adults. *Am. J. Psychol.* 1932, 44, 123-132.
853. Alpert, A., The Solving of Problem Situations by Preschool Children. *Teach. Coll. Contrib. Educ.* 1928, No. 323.
854. Ames, Louise, Development of the Time Sense in Young Children. *J. Genet. Psychol.* 1946, 68, 97-125.
855. Anastasi, Anne, The Influence of Specific Experience Upon Mental Organization. *Genet. Psychol. Monog.* 1936, 18.
856. Anderson, Harold H., Domination and Socially Integrative Behavior. In: *Child Behavior and Development.* (Barker-Kounin-Wright.) 1943, Ch. XXVII.
857. Anderson, J. E., Child Development and the Interpretation of Behavior. *Science.* 1936, 83, 245-252.
858. Anderson, J. E., The Development of Social Behavior. *Am. J. Sociol.* 1939, 44, 839-857.
859. Anderson, J. E., The Development of Spoken Language. *38th Yearbook Nat. Soc. Stud. Educ.* 1939, Part I, 211-224.
860. Arrington, Ruth, Time Sampling in Studies of Social Behavior. *Psychol. Bull.* 1943, 40, 81-124.
861. Asch, S. E., A Study of Change in Mental Organization. *Arch. Psychol.* 1936, No. 195.
862. Balinsky, Benjamin, An Analysis of the Mental Factors of Various Age Groups from Nine to Sixty. *Genet. Psychol. Monog.* 1941, 23.
863. Barker, Roger G., Dembo, Tamara, and Lewin, Kurt. Frustration and Regression. In: *Child Behavior and Development.* (Barker-Kounin-Wright.) 1943, Ch. XXVI.
864. Barker, R. G., Kounin, J. S., and Wright, H. B. (Eds.), *Child*

Behavior and Development. 1943.
865. Bartelmez, S. W., Man from the Point of View of His Development and Structure. In: Nature of World and Man (Newman). 1926.
866. Bayley, Nancy, and Espenschade, Anna, Motor Development from Birth to Maturity. Rev. Educ. Res. 11, 562-572.
867. Bayley, Nancy, Mental Growth During the First Three Years. In: Child Behavior and Development. (Barker-Kounin-Wright.) 1943. Ch. VI.
868. Bayley, Nancy, A Study of the Crying of the Infants During Mental and Physical Tests. J. Genet. Psychol. 1932, 40, 306-329.
869. Bender, L., and Vogel, B. C., Imaginary Companions of Children. Am. J. Orthopsych. 1941, 11, 56-65.
870. Blatz, W. E., Emotional Episodes in Nursery School Children. 9th Internat. Congr., Princeton. 1930.
871. Blatz, W. E., and Millichamp, D. A., The Development of Emotion in the Infant. Univ. Toronto Stud. Child Devel. 1935, No. 4.
872. Bott, H., Personality Development in Young Children. Univ. Toronto Stud. Child Devel. 1934, No. 2.
873. Bridges, K. M. B., Emotional Development in Early Childhood. Child Development. 1932, 3, 324-334.
874. Brooks, F. D., Cattell, Psyche, Jones, H. E., Meek, Lois, and Stoddard, G. D., Mental and Physical Development. 1936
874a. Bruner, J. S., and Goodman, C. C., Value and Need as Organizing Factors. J. Soc. Abn. Psychol. 1947, 42, 33-44.
875. Burt, Cyril, Mental and Scholastic Tests. 1921.
876. Caille, R. K., Resistant Behavior of Preschool Children. Child Develop. Monog. 1933, No. 11.
877. Carmichael, Leonard, Manual of Child Psychology. 1946.
878. Clarke, Frances M., A Developmental Study of the Bodily Reactions of Infants to an Auditory Startle Pattern. J. Genet. Psychol. 1939, 55, 415-427.
879. Collmann, R. D., The Psychogalvanic Reactions of Exceptional and Normal School Children. Teach. Coll. Contrib. Educ., N.Y. 1931, 469.
880. Cook, Willie M., Ability of Children in Color Discrimination. Child Development. 1931, 2, 303-320.
881. Courtis, S. A., Maturation as a Factor in Diagnosis. Yearbk. Nat. Soc. Stud. Educ. 1935, 34, 169-187.
882. Danzinger, D., and Frankl, E., Entwicklungspruefungen an albanischen Kindern. Zeitsch. Kinderforsch. 1934, 43.

883. Day, E. J., The Development of Language in Twins. *Child Development.* 1932, 3, 179-199, 298-316.

884. DeAngelis, F., Reflexes of the New-born. *Am. J. Diseas. Child.* 1923, 26, 211-215.

885. Dearborn, W. F., and Rothney, J. M. W., *Predicting the Child's Development.* 1941.

886. Decroly, O., Comment l'enfant arrive a parler. *Cahiers, Centrale P. E. S. Belgique.* 1934, vol. 8.

887. Dennis, W., Infant Development under Conditions of Restricted Practice and of Minimum Social Stimulation. *J. Genet. Psychol.* 1938, 53, 149-158.

888. Deshaies, E., La notion de relation chez l'enfant. *J. de Psychol.* 1937, 33, 112-133.

889. Deutsche, Jean Marquis, The Development of Children's Concepts of Causal Relations. In: *Child Behavior and Development.* (Barker-Kounin-Wright.) 1943, Ch. VIII.

890. Dewey, Evelyn, *Behavior Development in Infants.* 1935.

891. Doroschenko, O., Einfluss des Milieus auf das Verhalten und den Aufbau der Kollektive im schulpflichtigen Alter. *Zeitsch. Angew. Psychol.* 1928, 30, 150-167.

892. Emerson, L. L., The Effect of Bodily Orientation Upon the Young Child's Memory for Position of Objects. *Child Development.* 1913, 2, 125-142.

893. Fenichel, Otto, *Outline of Clinical Psychoanalysis.* 1934.

894. Frank, L. K., Research in Child Psychology: History and Prospect. In: *Child Behavior and Development.* (Barker-Kounin-Wright.) 1943, Ch. I.

895. Freeman, F. N., and Flory, C. D., Growth in Intellectual Ability as Measured by Repeated Tests. *Monog. Soc. Res. Child Development.* 1937, 2, No. 2.

896. Friedmann, P., Die taktile Raumschwelle in Kindern. *Zeitsch. Psychol.* 1927, 103, 185-202.

897. Garrett, H. E., Differentiable Mental Traits. *Psychol. Record.* 1938, 2, 259-298.

898. Garrett, H. E., Bryan, A. I., and Perl, R. E., The Age Factor in Mental Organization. *Arch. Psychol.* 1935, No. 176.

899. Gesell, Arnold, and Thompson, Helen, Learning and Maturation in Identical Infant Twins. In: *Child Behavior and Development.* (Barker-Kounin-Wright.) 1943, Ch. XIII.

900. Glaser, Edward M., An Experiment in the Development of Critical Thinking. *Contrib. Educ. Teach. Coll. Columbia Univ.* 1941, No. 843.

901. Goodenough, Florence L., *Anger in Young Children*. 1931.
902. Goodenough, Florence L., Bibliographies in Child Development. *Psychol. Bull.* 1944, 41, No. 9, 615-633.
903. Halverson, H. M., The Development of Prehension in Infants. In: *Child Behavior and Development*. (Barker-Kounin-Wright.) 1943, Ch. IV.
904. Harrower, M. R., Social Status and the Moral Development of the Child. *Brit. J. Educ. Psychol.* 19, 1937, 75-95.
905. Harter, G. L., Overt Trial and Error in the Problem Solving of Preschool Children. *J. Genet. Psychol.* 1930, 38, 361-372.
906. Heidbreder, E. F., Problem Solving in Children and Adults. *J. Genet. Psychol.* 1928, 35, 522-545.
907. Heidbreder, E. F., A Study of the Evolution of Concepts. *Psychol. Bull.* 1934, 31, 673.
908. Heider, F. K., and Heider, G. M., A Study of the Phonetic Symbolism of Deaf Children. *Psychol. Monog.* 1940, 52, No.1, 23-41.
909. Hetzer, Hildegard, *Das volkstuemliche Kinderspiel*. 1927.
910. Hildreth, G., The Success of Young Children in Number and Letter Construction. *Child Development*. 1932, 3, 1-14.
911. Hilgard, J. R., Learning and Maturation in Preschool Children. *J. Genet. Psychol.* 1932, 41, 50-65.
912. Hollingworth, L. S., *Gifted Children*. 1926.
913. Honzik, M. P., The Constancy of Mental Performance During the Preschool Period. *J. Genet. Psychol.* 1938, 52, 285-302.
914. Hooker, Davenport, Reflex Activities in the Human Fetus. In: *Child Behavior and Development*. (Barker-Kounin-Wright.) 1943, Ch. II.
915. Huang, I., Children's Conception of Physical Causality. *J. Genet. Psychol.* 1943, 63, 71-121.
916. Irwin, O. C., The Activities of Newborn Infants. In: *Child Behavior and Development*. (Barker-Kounin-Wright.) 1943, Ch. III.
917. Isaacs, Susan, *Intellectual Growth in Young Children*. 1945.
918. Jersild, Arthur T., Training and Growth in the Development of Children. *Child Development Monog.* 1932, No. 10.
919. Jersild, Arthur T., *Child Psychology*. 1939.
920. Jersild, Arthur T., Studies of Children's Fears. In: *Child Behavior and Development*. (Barker-Kounin-Wright.) 1943, Ch. XIX.
921. Jersild, Arthur T., and Holmes, F. B., Children's Fears. *Child Development Monog.* 1935, No. 20.
922. Jersild, Arthur T., and Markey, F. N., Conflicts Between

School Children. *Child Development Monog.* 1935, No. 21.

923. Jones, H. E., and Jones, M. C., Fear. *Childhood Educ.* 1928, 5, 136-143.

924. Jones, H. E., Learning in Young Children. *Calif. Parent-Teacher.* 1932, 8, 8-9.

925. Jones, H. E., The Galvanic Skin Reflex as Related to Overt Emotional Expression. *Am. J. Psychol.* 1935, 47, 240-251.

926. Jones, H. E., Bayley, Nancy, Brooks, F. D., Cattell, Psyche, and Stoddard, G. D., Mental and Physical Development. *Rev. Educ. Res.* 1938, 9, 3-139.

927. Jones, M. C., and Jones. H. E., Genetic Studies of Emotions. *Psychol. Bull.* 1930, 27, 40-64.

928. Jones, M. C., Emotional Development. In: *Handbook of Child Psychology.* (Murchison.) 1933.

929. Kelley, H. J., and Redfield, J. E., Physical Growth from Birth to Maturity. *Rev. Educ. Res.* 1941, 11, 573-591.

930. Ketterlinus, E., Learning of Children in Adaptation to Mirror Reversals. *Child Development.* 1931, 2, 200-223.

931. Klein, R., Autoritaet als eine Form der sozialen Beeinflussung. *Zeitsch. Kinderfor.* 1932, 39.

932. Kluever, H., Eidetic imagery. In: *Handbook of Child Psychology.* (Murchison.) 1933, Ch. XVII.

933. Kreezer, G., and Dallenbach, K. M., Learning the Relation of Opposites. *Am. J. Psychol.* 1929, 41, 432-441.

934. Laycock, S. R., Adaptability to New Situations. 1928.

935. Lazarsfeld, Paul, *Die koerperliche und geistige Entwicklung.* Quelle 79, 1929.

935a. Ling, B. C., Form Discrimination in Infants. *Comp. Psychol. Monog.* 1941, 86.

936. Lippman, H. S., Certain Behavior Responses in Early Infancy. *J. Genet. Psychol.* 1927, 34, 424-440.

937. Locke, N. M., Perception and Intelligence. *Psychol. Rev.* 1938, 45, 335-345.

938. Loewenfeld, Victor, *The Nature of Creative Ability.* 1939.

939. Loomis, A. M., A Technique of Observing the Social Behavior of Nursery School Children. *Child Development Monog.* 1931, No. 5.

940. Lorimer, Frank, *The Growth of Reason.* 1929.

941. McCarthy, Dorothea, Language Development in the Preschool Child. In: *Child Behavior and Development.* (Barker-Kounin-Wright.) 1943, Ch. VII.

942. McGeoch, J. A., The Influence of Sex and Age Upon the Ability to Report. *Am. J. Psychol.* 1928, 40, 458-466.

943. McGraw, M. B., A Study of Johnny and Jimmy. 1935.
944. Marbe, Karl, and Sell, Ludwig, Die Abhaengigkeit der Schulleistung vom Lebensalter. Zeitsch. Psychol. 1933, 122.
945. Markey, J. F., The Symbolic Process and its Integration in Children. 1928.
946. Meredith, Howard V., The Rhythm of Physical Growth. University of Iowa Studies. Stud. in Child Welf. 1935, XI, No. 3.
947. Meredith, H. V., Physical Growth of White Children. Monog. Soc. Res. Child Development. 1936, 1, No. 1.
948. Meyer, Edith, Comprehension of Spatial Relations in Preschool Children. J. Genet. Psychol. 1940, 57, 119-151.
949. Miles, K. A., Sustained Visual Fixation of Preschool Children to a Delayed Stimulus. Child Development. 1933, 4, 1-5.
950. Miller, N. E., The Perception of Children. A Genetic Study Employing the Critical Choice Delayed Reaction. J. Genet. Psychol. 1934, 44, 321-339.
951. Monnin, J., Quelques données sur les formes de l'intelligence. Année Psychol. 1934, 35, 118-146.
952. Monroe, W. S., Encyclopedia of Educational Research; Section on Child Development. 1941.
953. Moore, T. V., The Reasoning Ability of Children in the First Years of School Life. Stud. Psychol. Psychiat. Cathol. Univ. Amer. 1929, 2, No. 2.
954. Muller, H. T., Syllogistic Reasoning in Children. J. Hered. 1935, 16, 435-436.
955. Munn, N. L., Psychological Development: An Introduction to Genetic Psychology. 1938.
956. Murphy, Lois B., Social and Emotional Development. Rev. Educ. Res. 1941, 11, 479-501.
957. Nat. Soc. Stud. Educ., Child Development and Curriculum. Thirty-eighth Yearbook, Part I. 1939.
958. Nelson, V. L., An Analytic Study of Child Learning. Child Development. 1936, 7, 95-114.
959. Nice, M. M., The Development of a Child's Vocabulary in Relation to Environment. Ped. Sem. 1915, 22, 35-64.
960. Nice, M. M., A Child That Would Not Talk. Proc. Okla. Acad. Sci. 1922, 2, 108-111.
961. Olson, Willard C., and Hughes, Byron O., Growth of the Child as a Whole. In: Child Behavior and Development. (Barker-Kounin-Wright.) 1943, Ch. XII.
962. Parten, Mildred, and Newhall, S. M., Social Behavior of Pre-

school Children. In: *Child Behavior and Development.* (Barker-Kounin-Wright.) 1943, Ch. XXIX.

963. Patrick, J. R., Studies in Rational Behavior and Emotional Excitement. *J. Comp. Psychol.* 1934, 18, 1-22, 153-195.

964. Peckham, R. H., Visual Discrimination in Preschool Children. *Child Development.* 1933, 4, 1-5.

965. Pigors, P., Leadership and Domination Among Children. *Sociologus.* 1933, 9, 140-157.

966. Ray, J. J., The Generalizing Ability of Dull, Bright, and Superior Children. *Peabody Contrib. Educ.* 1936, No. 175.

967. Razran, G. H. S., Conditioned Responses in Children: A Behavioral and Quantitative Critical Review of Experimental Studies. *Arch. Psychol. N.Y.*, 1933, No. 148.

968. Reininger, Karl, *Ueber soziale Verhaltungsweisen in der Vorpubertaet.* 1925.

969. Reininger, Karl, Das soziale Verhalten von Schulneulingen. *Arb. z. paed. Psychol.* 1927, 7, 14. Rev. in Pigors (965).

970. Renshaw, S., Wherry, R., and Newlin, J. C., Cutaneous Localization in Congenitally Blind Versus Seeing Children and Adults. *J. Genet. Psychol.* 1930, 38, 239-248.

971. Richards, T. W., and Nelson, V. L., Studies in Mental Development. *J. Genet. Psychol.* 1938, 52, 303-331.

972. Richardson, H. M., Growth of Adaptive Behavior in Infants. *Genet. Psychol. Monog.* 1932, 12.

973. Richardson, H. M., Adaptive Behavior of Infants in the Utilization of the Lever as a Tool. *J. Genet. Psychol.* 1934, 44, 352-377.

974. Roberts, K. E., The Ability of Preschool Children to Solve Problems in which a Simple Principle of Relationship is Kept Constant. *J. Genet. Psychol.* 1932, 40, 118-135.

975. Roettger, Fritz, Phonetische Gestaltbildung bei Kindern. *Arbeit. Entwickl. Psychol.* (Krueger). 1931, 10.

976. Sanford, F. H., Speech and Personality. *Psychol. Bull.* 1942, 39, 811-845.

977. Schuler, E. A., A Study of the Consistency of Dominant and Submissive Behavior in Adolescent Boys. *J. Genet. Psychol.* 1934, 46, 403-432.

978. Scott, F., and Myers, G. C., Children's Empty and Erroneous Concepts of the Commonplace. *J. Educ. Res.* 1923, 8, 327-334.

979. Shirley, M. M., Is Development Saltatory as well as Continuous? *Psychol. Bull.* 1931, 28, 664-665.

980. Shirley, M. M., *Postural and Locomotor Development.* 1931.

981. Shirley, M. M., *The First Two Years.* Vol. II, 1933.

982. Shuttleworth, Frank, Sexual Maturation and the Physical Growth of Girls Age Six to Nineteen. *Monog. Soc. Res. Child Development.* 1937, 2, No. 5.

983. Skalet, M., The Significance of Delayed Reaction in Young Children. *Comp. Psychol. Monog.* 1931, 7, No. 4.

984. Skeels, H. M., A Study of Some Factors in Form Board Accomplishments of Preschool Children. *Univ. Iowa Stud. Child Welfare.* 1933, 7, No. 2.

985. Smith, M. E., A Study of Some Factors Influencing the Development of the Sentence in Preschool Children. *J. Genet. Psychol.* 1935, 46, 182-212.

986. Strasheim, J. J., *A New Method of Mental Testing.* 1926.

987. Terman, Lewis M., Mental and Physical Traits of a Thousand Gifted Children. In: *Child Behavior and Development,* (Barker-Kounin-Wright.) 1943, Ch. XVII.

988. Terman, L. M., and Burks, B. S., The gifted child. In: *Handbook of Child Psychol.* (Murchison.) 1933.

989. Welch, L., The Genetic Development of the Associational Structures of Abstract Thinking. *J. Genet. Psychol.* 1940, 56, 175-206.

990. Werner, Heinz, Development of Visuo-Motor Performance on the Marble Board Test in Mentally Retarded Children. *J. Genet. Psychol.* 1944, 64, 269-279.

991. Werner, Heinz, Perceptual Behavior of Brain-injured Children. *Genet. Psychol. Monog.* 1945, 31.

992. Werner, Heinz, and Bowers, Mabel, Auditory-motor Organization in Two Clinical Types of Mentally Retarded Children. *J. Genet. Psychol.* 1941, 59, 85-99.

993. Werner, Heinz, and Carrison, Doris, Measurement and Development of the Finger Schema in Mentally Retarded Children; Relation of Arithmetic Achievement to Performance on the Finger Schema Test. *J. Educ. Psychol.* 1942, April, 252-264.

994. Werner, Heinz, and Carrison, Doris, Animistic Thinking in Brain-injured Children. *Abn. Soc. Psychol.* 1944, 39, 43-62.

995. Werner, Heinz, and Strauss, Alfred, Disorders of Conceptual Thinking in the Brain-injured Child. *J. Nerv. Ment. Disease.* 1942, 96, 153-171.

996. Werner, Heinz, and Strauss, Alfred, Causal Factors in Low Performance. *Am. J. Ment. Defic.* 1940, 45, 213-218.

997. Williams, Malcolm, *The Influence of Specific Experiences on Children's Concepts of Causal Relations.* Unpublished Ph.D.

Thesis, Univ. of Michigan, 1940.

998. Wilslitzky, S., Beobachtungen ueber das soziale Verhalten in Kindergarten. *Zeitsch. Psychol.* 1928, 27.

999. Winch, W. H., *Children's Perceptions.* 1914.

1000. Zaluzhni, A. S., Collective Behavior of Children at Preschool Age. *J. Soc. Psychol.* 1930, 1, 367-378.

4. ABNORMAL PSYCHOLOGY

1001. Arieti, Silvano, Primitive Habits and Perceptual Alterations in the Terminal Stage of Schizophrenia. *Arch. Neurol. Psych.* 1945, 53, 378-384.

1002. Bolles, M. M., and Goldstein, Kurt, A Study of the Impairment of "Abstract Behavior" in Schizophrenic Patients. *Psychiat. Quart.* 1938, 12, 42-65.

1003. Cameron, Norman, Reasoning, Regression and Communication in Schizophrenics. *Psychol. Monog.* 1938, 50, No. 1.

1004. Cameron, Norman, A Study of Thinking in Senile Deterioration and Schizophrenic Disorganization. *Am. J. Psychol.* 1938, 51, 650-664.

1005. Cameron, Norman, Deterioration and Regression in Schizophrenic Thinking. *J. Abn. Soc. Psychol.* 1939, 34, 265-270.

1006. Cameron, Norman, Schizophrenic Thinking in a Problem-solving Situation. *J. Ment. Sci.* 1939, 85, 1012-1035.

1007. Goldstein, Kurt, and Scheerer, Martin, Abstract and Concrete Behavior. *Psychol. Monog.* 1941, 53.

1008. Hanfmann, Eugenia, and Kasanin, Jacob, Conceptual Thinking in Schizophrenia. *Nerv. Ment. Dis. Monog.* 1942, 67.

1009. Hanfmann, Eugenia, Rickers-Ovsiankina, Maria, and Goldstein, Kurt, Case Lanuti: Extreme Concretization of Behavior due to Damage of the Brain Cortex. *Psychol. Monog.* 1944, 57.

1010. Maclay, W. S., and Guttmann, E., Mescaline Hallucinations in Artists. *Arch. Neurol. Psychol.* 1941, 45, 130-137.

1011. Rickers-Ovsiankina, M., Studies on the Personality Structure of Schizophrenic Individuals. *J. Gen. Psychol.* 1937, 16, 153-196.

1012. Scheerer, Martin, Rothmann, Eva, and Goldstein, Kurt, A Case of Idiot Savant. *Psychol. Monog.* 1945, 58.

1013. Scheerer, Martin, Problems of Performance Analysis in the Study of Personality. *N.Y. Acad. Sci. Annals.* 1946, 46, 653-678.

1014. Wegrocki, H., Generalizing Ability in Schizophrenia. *Arch. Psychol.* 1940, 254.
1015. Weigl, Egon, On the Psychology of So-called Processes of Abstraction. *J. Abn. Soc. Psychol.* 1941, 36, 3-33.
1016. Weisenburg, Theodore, and McBride, Katherine, *Aphasia.* 1935.
1017. Werner, Heinz, Abnormal and Subnormal Rigidity. *J. Abn. Soc. Psychol.* 1946, 41, 15-24.
1018. Werner, Heinz, The Concept of Rigidity: A Critical Evaluation. *Psychol. Rev.* 1946, 53, 43-52.

5. ANIMAL PSYCHOLOGY

1019. Bierens de Haan, J. A., *Labyrinth und Umweg.* 1937.
1020. Furness, W. H., Observations on the Mentality of Chimpanzees and Orang-utans. *Proc. Am. Philos. Soc.* 1916, 55, 281-290.
1021. Harlow, H. F., Solution by Rhesus Monkeys Involving the Weigl Principle Using the Matching-from-sample Method. *J. Comp. Psychol.* 1943, 36, 217-227.
1022. Jacobsen, C. F., Marion, M., and Yoshioka, J. G., *Development of an Infant Chimpanzee During her First Year.* 1932.
1023. Jacobsen, C. F., Studies of Cerebral Function in Primates. *Comp. Psychol. Monog.* 1936, 13.
1024. Katz, David, *Animals and Men.* 1937.
1025. Kleemeier, R. W., Fixation and Regression in the Rat. *Psychol. Monog.* 1942, 246.
1026. Nissen, H. W., and Harrison, Ross, Visual and Positional Cues in the Delayed Responses of Chimpanzees. *J. Comp. Psychol.* 1941, 31, 437-446.
1027. Riesen, A. H., Delayed Reward in Discrimination Learning. *Comp. Psychol. Monog.* 1940, 15.
1028. Spragg, S. D. S., Anticipatory Responses in Serial Learning by Chimpanzees. *Comp. Psychol. Monog.* 1936, 13.
1029. Weinstein, Benjamin, Matching-from-sample by Rhesus Monkeys and by Children. *J. Comp. Psychol.* 1940, 31, 195-213.
1030. Weinstein, Benjamin, The Evolution of Intelligent Behavior in Rhesus Monkeys. *Genet. Psychol. Monog.* 1945, 31.
1031. Windle, W. F., and Orr, D. W., The Development of Behavior in Chick Embryos. *J. Comp. Neurol.* 1934, 60, 287-308.
1032. Wilson, M. O., Symbolic Behavior in the White Rat. *J. Comp. Psychol.* 1934, 18.

1033. Wolfe, J. B., Effectiveness of Token Rewards for Chimpanzees. *Comp. Psychol. Monog.* 1936, 12.
1034. Yerkes, R. M. *Chimpanzees: A laboratory colony.* 1943.
1035. Yerkes, R. M., and Learned, B. W., *Chimpanzee Intelligence and Its Vocal Expressions.* 1925.
1036. Yerkes, R. M., and Nissen, H. W., Pre-linguistic Sign Behavior in Chimpanzee. *Science.* 1939, 89, 585-587.
1037. Zuckerman, S., *Functional Affinities of Man, Monkeys and Apes.* 1933.

Trait ethnology, 12 f.
Trance language, 281
Transduction, inference from, 327
Transformation of personality, in
    child, 447 f.; in primitive man,
    420 f.; in psychotic, 464
Typology of primitive, 35

Undifferentiated, *see* Differentia-
    tion.
Universal concept, 243, 247, 269
Universal system, 311, 356
Universal thought, 299, 323

Valence, 61
Value, material, 384, 385; moral,
    426, 455
Vibration, 14, 105
Vision, development of, 46 f.;
    pathological levels of, 32
        See also Brightness; Color;
        Form perception; Visual
        acuity.

Visions, 81, 151, 157, 334, 339,
    407, 415
Visual acuity, 36
Vital sensation, 96
Vowel configuration, 222

Weaning, 453
Whole vs. element, 7 f., 21 f.
    See also Global.
Wish, and magic, 363, 371; and
    reality, 151, 390, 396, 416
Word, realism, 263; vs. sentence,
    279, 315
World, of action, 382, 403; of ani-
    mal, 379 f.; of child, 382, 385;
    of primitive man, 402; of schizo-
    phrenic, 334, 414; spheres of,
    see Reality spheres; system, 311,
    356
Writing, and drawing, 263; holo-
    phrastic, 281; physiognomic,
    263, 265